HENRY WILSON AND THE COMING OF THE CIVIL WAR

John L. Myers

University Press of America,® Inc.
Lanham · Boulder · New York · Toronto · Oxford

University Press of America,® Inc.
4501 Forbes Boulevard
Suite 200
Lanham, Maryland 20706
UPA Acquisitions Department (301) 459-3366

PO Box 317
Oxford
OX2 9RU, UK

Printed in the United States of America
British Library Cataloging in Publication Information Available

Library of Congress Control Number: 2003053364
ISBN 0-7618-2608-4 (paperback : alk. ppr.)

™ The paper used in this publication meets the minimum requirements of American National Standard for Information Sciences—Permanence of Paper for Printed Library Materials, ANSI Z39.48—1984 *for Peg*

I am ready to stand with any man, or set of men — Whig, Democrat, Abolitionist, Christian, or Infidel—who will go with me in the cause of emancipation. . . . All sorts of unworthy motives will be ascribed to me, and my judgment and discretion questioned. Sir, I have no personal motive: I see nothing to be gained, and something to be lost. At any rate, I know I shall lose the good opinion of some friends, who will doubtless regard me as a fanatic. But I have made up my mind, . . . that we must either destroy slavery, or slavery will destroy our government and our liberties; and I had far rather act according to the dictates of duty and of patriotism than to receive the approving smiles of friends. I shall go for the abolition of slavery at all times."

— Henry Wilson, in the Massachusetts House of Representatives, 1846

CONTENTS

PREFACE ix

1. Out of Poverty 1
2. The Natick Cobbler 25
3. Texas 49
4. A Conscience Whig 71
5. The Free Soil Movement 95
6. Wilson Takes Control 119
7. Successful Coalition Leader (1851) 145
8. Coalition Success, National Party Leadership 171
9. The Constitutional Convention and Voter Rejection 199
10. The Kansas-Nebraska Bill and the Know Nothings 231
11. A Know Nothing-Elected Senator 259
12. Antislavery Versus Nativism 285
13. Kansas, Sumner-Brooks and the Rise to Republican Senate Leadership 309
14. A Year Dominated by Kansas 337
15. In Power in Massachusetts, Gaining in the Nation 363
16. Consolidation and Preparation for 1860 391
17. The Election of Lincoln and Secession 419

NOTES 446

BIBLIOGRAPHY 531

INDEX 551

PREFACE

Many years ago I read the two-volume biography of Charles Sumner by David Donald. Although Sumner's life deserves such lengthy treatment and although he played a major role in mid-nineteenth century American history, I was puzzled as to why the life of his colleague Henry Wilson had not inspired an equally thorough narrative and analysis. After all, it was said that when Sumner spoke in the Senate, those favoring his point of view were fearful his support would kill the legislation he was advocating; he seldom got any legislation enacted. Furthermore, Sumner usually lacked the interest or ability as a politician to create or greatly influence the development of political parties and to play a major role in political campaigns. But Wilson was a major force in both the Free Soil and Republican parties, and in political canvasses he spoke to more Americans than any other campaigner of his generation, both in his own state of Massachusetts and in the nation.

I concluded Wilson's role had been minimized by historians. Contemporaries published a number of studies of his life, or parts of it, and two twentieth century historians a generation ago brought to press their analyses of Wilson, one concentrating more on his earlier years, the other on the Civil War and Reconstruction. But using the Donald books as a partial model, I have in this volume sought to place Wilson within the context of the movement of the nation towards Civil War. This involves dealing not only with the man, but his interaction with those around him and the "Road to Civil War."

I found Wilson helped me to understand a number of issues of the middle half of the nineteenth century. How could a boy born into such poverty rise to political leadership and the second-highest position in the nation, the vice-presidency? Other members of his family, and hundreds of other poor boys born in the United States in those years, did not overcome their birth and deficient upbringing. How could a man in aristocratic nineteenth century Massachusetts begin a political career without education, political connections, and money, and yet become the architect—as much as or more than any other man—of two political parties, the editor of a newspaper, and the author of the longest study of the causes of the Civil War? Wilson was accused of having too great ambition and he changed parties frequently, yet his goals—the abolition of slavery and protection of black rights—were clear and his political path a result of those goals. How much is political leadership the result of chance and how much planning? Wilson's career in politics was several times seemingly at an end, yet he came back strong. He became a leader in the Free Soil movement when Massachusetts Whigs disowned him, a proponent of third party action after his leadership in the state Constitutional Convention of 1853 was rejected by the voters, senator elected by a Know Nothing legislature when the nativist movement shoved aside the fledgling Republican party, and Republican leader after he helped destroy the Know Nothings.

Readers may think I have been too soft on Wilson, especially regarding his role in the breakup of parties and his becoming a Know Nothing. He was ambitious, but he also was a practical idealist. Above everything—family, political gain, money—he believed in the abolition of slavery. Few politicians, especially in Massachusetts, would subject themselves to the criticism of attending meetings of Garrisonian antislavery societies. Wilson did with regularity. Wilson was also criticized by Democrats and by some of his own associates for becoming a Know Nothing. I started out agreeing with their critical view, but I have since concluded the matter was not so simple. Colleagues such as Charles Francis Adams thought more of their integrity, as they saw it, than the condition of slaves. But Wilson's focus was clear: he wanted to end slavery as quickly as possible, and the means sometimes had to be adjusted to fit realities. Had I been a slave, I would have forgiven Wilson for joining a disreputable nativist movement if it, as Wilson believed, and I believe, speeded up my freedom. In any case, his integrity among American politicians rates high. No politician worked harder, few knew as many voters, and few were as influential in determining the nation's history.

A pitfall in writing a biography of Wilson is the lack of many papers of his own. The task is especially difficult when one compares it with that of writing about a Jefferson, with hoards of papers. To follow Wilson's career, one has to use papers of others (and many of his associates retained vast collections); concurrent newspapers, speeches, and government documents; his own published works, including speeches, articles in newspapers, and his published books; and especially monographs and articles by historians and contemporaries. Too little is known about his personal life, so I have used stories from nineteenth century biographies, newspaper articles, and remarks by Wilson's contemporaries. This provides less of Wilson the human being than I would like, but more than other biographies have been able to provide. Yet the focus of this study is the public life of Henry Wilson, his contributions to efforts to halt the expansion of slavery and to the coming of the Civil War.

John L. Myers

1

Out of Poverty

Contemporaries liked to tell over and over again the success story of Henry Wilson. Few men rose so far from such humble beginnings: vice-president of the United States, indefatigable chairman of the Senate Committee of Military Affairs during the Civil War—when that position was perhaps more important than it ever had been before or has been since, molder of the Republican party and, as one contemporary called him, "chief of all the chiefs . . . for the national political contests of 1856 and 1860."[1] Wilson was responsible for more legislation countering slavery than any other American. He was a member of the Senate "establishment," one of the most influential Republicans during Reconstruction, and author of one of the best contemporary publications about the contest between the forces of slavery and antislavery in American society. That is not all Wilson was and did but that alone is an impressive list. A sometimes critical colleague and eulogist related that when Wilson's body was carried through the streets of New York City en route to burial in Massachusetts, more than two hundred thousand people stood in the cold, in spite of the procession's being late, to witness the scene; no American's death but Lincoln's had generated a greater amassing of people.[2]

Despite his impressive record, Wilson has not fared well in history. While contemporaries were generous with vignettes about the man and a few biographers preserved facts, only two twentieth century historians, ErnestMcKay and Richard Abbott, within a year of each other, published narratives and interpretations of his life. Both emphasized Wilson's pragmatism and his realistic appraisals of the possible. They confronted his ambition with good humor. They appreciated his principles and commended his adherence to them. Apparently the rest of the generations of historians between 1880 and 1970 either did not discern Wilson's importance or, in contrast to his contemporaries, were uninterested in his life.

Students of Abraham Lincoln have poked ad nauseam into almost any possible source to discover additional information concerning his family background, birth, and early childhood. Lincoln himself, Benjamin Thomas recorded, told a campaign biographer that his boyhood could be condensed into a single sentence.[3] During Wilson's lifetime much was written concerning his family background and his early life. Some of what was said could have been myth which he wanted to create or reinforce. Some of the material was intended to advance Wilson's career. Some of it came from the pens of associates who saw Wilson through rose colored glasses. Some was authored by the man himself. Admittedly, some of the material was tendered by reporters who sought to interest others in what they wrote; yet to sell what they recorded, they did not necessarily have to praise Wilson or misrepresent the facts concerning his life and services. In fact, too many people were alive who could have refuted these accounts, had they been untrue. Since much the same information was repeated so often, one has to conclude that most of it was factual.

Henry Wilson was born into poverty. So were many of his contemporaries who also rose above their difficult beginnings. Abraham Lincoln was assisted by a stepmother who encouraged her children to overcome their lack of formal schooling and the paucity of physical comforts in their home. Horace Greeley had a father who worked hard and a mother who was interested in the rearing of her children. Thad Stevens and his family were abandoned by their father, but benefited from a hard working and foresighted mother. Wilson, on the other hand, seems to have been born into a family which had been poor, perhaps even shiftless, for several generations.[4]

Wilson's ancestors on his father's side had emigrated from Argyleshire in Scotland to Northern Ireland in the early seventeenth century; a later generation embarked for New Hampshire about 1719. The family name—Colbath, Coolbroth, Calbreath—is found on the records of Newington by 1725. Wilson's great-grandfather James worked in Portsmouth from 1750 to 1783 or 1784. With the Revolutionary War over and the country suffering from economic hard times, James and Olive Leighton Colbath removed to Rochester, now Farmington, New Hampshire, and subsequently to Middleton in the same state. The couple had eight children, including Winthrop, grandfather of the future vice-president. Winthrop married Hannah Rollins of Newington. Among their children was another Winthrop, born in Rochester on April 7, 1787. On October 14, 1811, in the First Congregational Church of Rochester, the younger Winthrop married Abigail Witham, who had been born in Kittery, Maine, and who was two years older than he.[5]

Many years after Winthrop Colbath's death, a Rochester resident characterized the man as tall, agile, and handsome, with a "quick wit and ready tongue," and "too much interested in cider."[6] Apparently Wilson's father was not the only intemperate one among his "kith and kin." Colbath worked at a sawmill near his home. Wilson in a Senate speech later depicted his father as a "hireling manual laborer."[7] The Colbaths had lived in poverty for several generations; Winthrop neither expected nor aspired to improve that state. A reporter who described himself as intimately acquainted with Wilson in his declining years claimed he heard Wilson speak of his father only once.[8]

Little is known about Abigail Witham Colbath. The Withams were as poor a family as the Colbaths. Abigail's obituary notice (1866) described her as "an exemplary woman, of sound judgment, and great force of character."[9] Wilson biographers Elias Nason and Thomas Russell, who knew the family well, described Mrs. Colbath as "handsome, fond of reading, sensible, and industrious."[10] Jonathan Mann, another contemporary biographer, who must have been well acquainted with his friend's mother, chose when he spoke of Mrs. Colbath to cite others' opinions. He spoke of her reputation for "great sense and discretion," and reported that Henry acquired his moral and mental attributes from her.[11] Wilson in the 1870s was saddened over some press accounts about his mother; he owed his best characteristics to her influence, he claimed.[12]

A number of contemporaries, usually those who did not otherwise think highly of Wilson, referred to the Colbath's alleged "gypsy" status. Charles Wright, in a Civil War attack upon the senator, quoted the *New Haven Register* as the source of his charge. The unfriendly *New York Herald* in 1866 published a similar inference. An angry and condescending Edward Everett in 1858 several times in his diary referred to Wilson as "the gypsy." Another associate, Richard Henry Dana, alluded to him in 1875 as "half-gypsy." Neither of the latter private comments sought to damage Wilson politically; one must explain them as motivated by the all-too-frequent pretentiousness of the Massachusetts gentry. An uncle shortly after Wilson's death tried to account for the often-repeated rumor and firmly denied its truth.[13] Whatever else one might infer from the use of "gypsies," the word refers to a nomadic people or to people who live like gypsies. The Colbaths were not at all nomadic, nor did they live a gypsy life-style. On the contrary, the evidence is ample that the male forefathers of Wilson lived within a short distance of the Portsmouth port where the first American Colbath landed, and moved their households infrequently. The wives, before their marriages, had usually lived in the same communities as their husbands, or not very far away.

Portsmouth and southeastern New Hampshire had been settled for generations before the birth of Wilson. Farmington was only thirty-five miles from Concord, eighteen miles northwest of Dover. Yet in 1812 the area was still "new country," incorporated as a town only fourteen years before Wilson's birth. It was a sparsely settled area, "rough, rocky, broken country," Wilson's friend and biographer, Jonathan Mann, described it.[14] One gazetteer used the words "broken and rugged" to characterize the land. Another favorably testified to the greater fertility along the banks of the Cocheco, which "meanders" through the northeastern part of the town. Timothy Dwight, who traveled through the area from Dover to Wolfboro in 1813, recorded that several miles outside Dover, the country looked "unpromising" and the soil "poor." Within twenty-eight miles of Portsmouth the road was so rocky and hilly as to be dangerous. The town had about twelve hundred inhabitants.[15]

As long as they remained in Farmington, the Colbaths lived in the same area. Their first house, containing two rooms and the loft where Henry was born, was located on the right side of the Cocheco River, on the Rochester road, a mile below the village. It must have been of little value, for it had been torn down by the early 1850s. Sometime after Wilson's birth, the family moved another mile away towards Rochester. The houses of that area differed little from pioneer cabins, "little low buildings with two rooms and four windows, an outer door at one corner, and rough shingling, unpainted, indicating . . . the absence of . . . luxuries."[16] The community did not even have a church. This was farming country, but neither the length of the growing season nor the fertility of the soil bred prosperity. The village itself contained only a dozen houses; Rochester was eight miles distant. Most purchases had to be hauled from Dover.[17]

One of Wilson's close friends recorded that Winthrop and Abigail Colbath had six children, all boys; they were Jeremiah, John, Charles, Samuel, George, and Albert. Another friend and contemporary biographer declared there were eight boys. Wilson obituary notices sometimes reported seven. The best evidence supports eight children; three of the eight died before Jeremiah was ten. The oldest of the Colbath children, born in Farmington February 16, 1812—the later Henry Wilson—was named Jeremiah Jones. Whatever the number of children, the parents could not support so many, following so rapidly one upon another. Wilson later observed to a New Hampshire audience that "want sat by my cradle. I know what it is to ask a mother for bread when she has none to give."[18] A Rochester native recorded that the boy was sent out to beg for food at other houses.[19]

Like other young children, Jerry, as his family called him, attended an unpainted district schoolhouse to learn how to read and spell. Probably his parents were grateful to have one fewer boy engaged in mischief or contending for attention. In the only story which survives concerning those school years, a biographer sought to demonstrate Wilson's early concern for others in difficulty. One cold morning when Jerry saw some older boys crowded around the schoolhouse fire, keeping the younger children away, Wilson challenged one of the larger boys to a fight, won, and extracted an assent to share the warmth. Mistress Guy, the teacher, was unimpressed with the victor's motives, for she rewarded Jerry with a flogging.[20]

Contemporary writers were fond of retelling the story of the eight-year-old boy's chance encounter which altered the course of his life. Mrs. Anstress Woodbury Eastman was the sister of Levi Woodbury—senator, governor, Andrew Jackson's secretary of the treasury, and United States Supreme Court justice—and the wife of Nehemiah Eastman, then the only lawyer of Farmington. Mrs. Eastman was riding in her carriage one day when she saw Wilson and another boy fighting along the roadside. She stopped to reprimand them. She also asked them if they knew how to read. When Jerry replied he could, she invited him to her house to test him. Impressed with his performance, she rewarded him with a New Testament which he reportedly retained the rest of his life. The boy finished reading his new book within a week. The surprised donor quizzed him to make certain he had understood what he had read. She was so pleased by his responses that she opened her husband's library thereafter to the boy's use. Wilson termed this experience the beginning of his intellectual life.

Both Eastmans took an interest in the boy and he continued to borrow their books, even when his indenture severely limited his reading time. He also obtained books from Judge George L. Whitehouse, a grocer, deputy sheriff, judge, and politician in the community. Wilson's friend Mann recorded that Plutarch's *Lives* and a memoir of Napoleon were among the books to which he was most attached. Nason cited Washington Irving, James Fenimore Cooper, and Sir Walter Scott as Wilson's favorite authors; the *North American Review,* the nation's best literary magazine, also attracted his attention. The story of Lincoln's hiking many miles to borrow or return books is a staple of Americana. Wilson would walk to the Eastman home Rochester to obtain a book, covering twenty-eight miles in all to fetch and return it. He reputedly read more than a thousand volumes during his youth, often rushing through his meals or staying up late by the fireside so that he would have enough time. He sometimes carried books under his arms to the fields. He developed a particular appetite for newspapers, which few Farmington residents obtained. Jerry persuaded his mother to borrow a neighbor's *Dover Gazette*, which he would quickly read and return. The Eastmans had volumes of *Niles Register*, one of the era's better newspapers. In the Eastman home Jerry also encountered his first political discussions.[21]

Farmington was growing just as Wilson was. It was also becoming a better community in which to live. The town increased in population between 1810 and 1820 from twelve hundred to more than seventeen hundred people. A Congregational church was established. The town had eleven schoolhouses, a tavern, four stores, four sawmills, six grain mills, four tanneries, and a clothing mill. The Colbaths, however, benefited little from this progress.[22]

The poverty of the Colbaths, the size of the family, and the customs of the area combined in August, 1822, to prompt the indenture of Jerry to William Knight, an industrious farmer who lived a mile below Farmington. This status was to last eleven years until the boy attained the legal age of twenty-one. By the terms of an agreement reached in 1828, Jerry was to work on the farm; was to be provided with his housing, food, clothing, and health care; could attend school one month every winter; and would receive at the end of his service a yoke of oxen, six sheep, and two suits of clothing, one appropriate for Sunday wear, the other suitable for every other day. He was bound not to play cards or dice or to frequent taverns, playhouses, or alehouses. He was not to "commit fornication, nor contract marriage." He could not absent himself without his master's permission. Late evenings and Sundays only were available to the boy for his own interests. He could learn more about farming, which might or might not provide him a vocation. Considering Wilson's subsequent eschewal of agriculture, he must have learned he did not like it.

The indenture was hard work. At first, of course, Jerry's duties were limited to tasks in accordance with his age and size. Since he knew the area, he could productively drive the cows. He cut wood and swung the scythe. But Knight easily found additional duties for him; the farmer was a hard worker himself and a careful economizer. Pigs had to be fed, water had to be carried, butter needed churning, fields had to be plowed, corn had to be husked, peas and beans needed to be shelled. Even in rainy weather Wilson had tools to repair and other inside tasks to perform. He never had a dollar to spend; his master only once gave him money, three cents to spend while attending a muster seven miles from home; Jerry walked to and from the event. Another oft-repeated story recounted Wilson's earning a rare copper for many days work removing a stump from his master's field.[23]

Had Wilson been able to attend school even the month provided for by the indenture agreement, his education might have been better. But Knight interpreted the contract to mean twenty-six days of instruction per year, whenever most convenient to the farmer. That meant odd days, too rainy or cold to work, often weeks apart. One usually does not learn much in small, isolated segments. One term Wilson attended the first day, then returned three weeks later, but with the entire grammar book memorized. Wilson's teachers undoubtedly were familiar with indentures, so they may have assigned tasks which could have been completed before the boy returned to school next time. Since he was interested in education and loved to read, Jerry profited from some of the assignments.[24]

While reading opened a world to Jerry, the paucity of his schooling and the absence of free time limited opportunities to make friends. He had little time to play. One acquaintance commented that he had never seen Wilson hunt or fish, nor could he sing; he avoided social activities. Another contemporary reported that when Jerry was about eighteen he persuaded a group of boys to form a debating club which met at the schoolhouse. Their first topic was "Did Columbus Discover America?" The boys, however, were too young and uneducated and the club soon failed. Neither Wilson nor his contemporaries spoke of any relationships he developed with members of the Knight family. When biographer Mann later questioned those who had attended school in Farmington during Wilson's youth, none could remember much about him. Mann reported he had never heard his friend speak of any young persons from his youth whom he held in affection. Jerry worked long and hard. He devoted late evening hours to reading. He also visited his family and the Eastmans.[25]

At the end of his apprenticeship, on February 16, 1833, Jerry received his yoke of oxen and six sheep, as promised. He sold the latter for nine dollars. Unable to dispose of the oxen on a weekend, he asked his former master to keep them. Knight assented, but charged fifty cents for the two days' care. Wilson in his lifetime had saved only fifty-seven cents and now paid out most of it. He subsequently sold the oxen for seventy-five dollars. The boy had money for the first time, but his freedom also left him unemployed. While the nation had recovered from the effects of the Panic of 1819, southeastern New Hampshire remained poor. Wilson initially hired himself out for six dollars for a month, cutting and hauling timber for twelve to fifteen hours a week. He then procured work for eight months on the Wingate farm. He had to get up before daylight and feed the stock, then drive the team into the forest for cutting wood, often working fourteen hours a day until after dark. For this he received nine dollars a month and board.[26]

His friend John Greenleaf Whittier characterized much of Wilson's early life in the beginning lines of his poem:

The lowliest born of all the land,
He wrung from Fate's reluctant hand
The gifts which happier boyhood claims;
And tasting of a thankless soil
The bitter bread of unpaid toil,
He fed his soul with noble aims.
By the low hearth-fire's fitful blaze
He read of old heroic days,
The sage's thought, the patriot's speech;
Unhelped, alone, himself he taught;
His school, the craft at which he wrought,
His lore, the book within his reach.[27]

In 1833 the New Hampshire legislature, at Jeremiah Colbath's request, legally changed his name to Henry Wilson. The petition was presented by Assemblyman Jones of Farmington on June 11 and voted on the last day of the session, July 6. Applications for name change were so common that the legislature had a Committee on Alteration of Names; approximately twenty-five persons were granted a change of name during this session.[28]

Speculation was widespread during Wilson's lifetime concerning why he changed his name and why he selected the name he did. Oddly enough, some of those contemporaries who wrote about his life, including friends Oliver Bacon and John Greenleaf Whittier, ignored the subject. Mann offered no explanation for the change. Wilson himself appears not to have responded to the uncertainties and speculations concerning the issue, nor to have provided information to biographers to account for his decision. The *Boston Herald* in 1875 contended Wilson made the change because the family name reflected no honor on him. The *New York Tribune* and the *Army and Navy Journal* obituary notices had similar explanations. One is inclined to give considerable weight to this interpretation, for the reporters for the two newspapers knew Wilson well. A Rochester, New Hampshire, resident in 1875 contended that Wilson so disliked his nickname Jed that he determined to change it; his father was so upset with that idea that he goaded his son to change his entire name.[29]

Others had different explanations. Nason and Russell, perhaps the best available source, in their biography reported the action and commented that it was "done by the advice of the family he lived with [presumably the Wingates], and with the approval of his parents."[30] Adelaide Waldron of Rochester recorded that when Wilson decided to change his name, "all thought it would be to his advantage."[31] In any case, Wilson never disassociated himself from other members of his family. Quite the contrary, during his early years in Massachusetts, he visited his New Hampshire relatives often. His parents and several brothers later moved to live alongside him in Natick. The other brothers retained the Colbath name. Wilson employed both John and Samuel in his shoe business. He also later got Samuel appointed to one of the better United States Senate positions.

No clearer explanation surfaces as to why Jerry Colbath selected the new name he did. Mrs. Waldron contended Wilson liked General James Wilson of Keene and had a fond recollection of a portrait of the Reverend Henry Wilson of England. Mann claimed his friend had read a biography of a Henry Wilson, whose character had so impressed him that he chose that name. A *New York Times* article in 1875 also alluded to the influence of General James Wilson, Democratic speaker of the New Hampshire House. Another issue of the same newspaper cited Wilson's aunt as asserting her nephew chose the name because of Elder Wilson, who frequently patted the young Jerry on his head. Nason and Russell offered no explanation for the choice.[32]

Wilson had no desire to remain forever a farmer's helper. While still employed by Wingate, he walked to nearby New Hampshire communities—Great Falls, Dover, Newmarket, and Salmon Falls—seeking work; he could find none. He was most hopeful of obtaining a job in the mills, which would have paid eight or nine dollars a month. Some other young men from Wilson's town had been learning shoemaking and had recently returned from Natick, Massachusetts, to New Durham to establish their own businesses. Wilson walked to New Durham, where he received offers of a two-year apprenticeship; having just completed eleven years indenture, he considered this too high a price to pay to learn the trade. Instead, he decided to move to Natick. On December 2, 1833, he packed his "scanty wardrobe in a bundle, tied it with a cotton handkerchief, . . . cut a straight hickory stick by the roadside," and set out.[33]

Almost twenty-two years old, Wilson had been prepared for the work ahead of him by years of hard labor, by a clear knowledge of the type of life which laziness or drunkenness might yield, by having read extensively, and by being able to exist with little but the necessities of food, drink, and a roof over his head. He was strong, healthy, and determined.

Wilson's trip of more than one hundred miles to Natick was in some respects characteristic of other aspects of his life. He had little choice but to walk. Since he reached Saugus the third night, he must have found someone with whom to ride part of the way. The fourth day was the highlight of his journey, for he had long wanted to visit the Bunker Hill battlefield and to see the office of the *North American Review* in Boston. The ravenous reader, who could recite every battle of the American Revolution and the War of 1812—the date and the numbers engaged, killed, wounded, and taken prisoner on each side—must have thrilled to view the site of one of those important engagements. From Boston, having been misdirected, he did not arrive in Natick until about midnight. His trip had cost him only one dollar and five cents.[34]

Massachusetts was a society in transition when Henry Wilson arrived. Both as a colony and as a state, it had been dominated by its agricultural and seafaring interests. The mid-1830s was a period of prosperity. Manufacturing and finance were replacing trade as dominant influences in the state's economic, political, and social life. New communities were being created. Lowell, which had not even existed in 1825, had a population of more than twenty thousand in 1840. Fall River increased in size more than 300 percent, New Bedford more than 200 percent, Springfield almost as much, Cambridge and Worcester approximately 150 percent. The state's population rose from 610,000 in 1830 to almost 1,000,000 in 1850. The smaller seaports were losing their business to Boston. But even in Boston the sources of wealth were changing. And manpower was being diverted to these new occupations. First unskilled labor was sought; later immigrant labor would be available. In 1810 the state had only thirty-four cotton factories; by 1837 the number was nearer two hundred. Joining shipbuilding, shipping, and fishing as major occupations were the manufacture of shoes, soap, candles, shovels, ploughs, and iron goods. Even the religious character of the state was being transformed, as the Congregational Church was finally disestablished and Unitarianism became as important an economic and political factor as it was a religious creed.[35]

In one sense, prosperity brought with it the dispersion of people, as newer communities away from the seacoast were established or grew. Manufacturing sites, for example, were selected in part because of the availability of waterpower. Boston had no textile mills. Transportation to bring in raw materials and take out manufactured goods was also a determining factor for industrial location, encouraging the establishment of new factories near the coast or along the Connecticut River. Labor was an insignificant ingredient in the selection of sites; workers would come. But in another sense, prosperity was centering money and power in Boston. Not only was sea transportation increasing to and from there, but as the railroad age began, construction emanated from the capital. Finance increasingly centered in Boston, too; so did warehousing, merchandizing, and selling. One recent study has concluded that Boston's influence dominated all of eastern Massachusetts—except those areas near to Providence—as far west as the region west of Worcester, and as far north as Rockingham County, New Hampshire. If a young tradesman, as Henry Wilson was to become, needed financing, he probably would have to obtain it in Boston. His marketing certainly would occur in or through that city.[36]

Natick, only sixteen miles west of Boston, and twenty-four miles east of Worcester, had been settled in the mid-seventeenth century. Notwithstanding, previous to 1790 its population was still less than 600. By 1830 that number had increased to 890, but then the coming of the railroad and the growth of the boot and shoe industry brought an increase to almost 1,300 in 1840 and to over 4,100 in 1855. The Charles River, which flows through the town (South Natick today), provided some waterpower. The locality had a Congregational church and a Masonic Lodge, both dating from the eighteenth century. When Wilson arrived, it had no high school, no library of any consequence, no lawyer. Less than eight hundred dollars was appropriated to support the public schools. While many communities of the Northeast had busily organized philanthropic and reform societies, Wilson's new home had only the Natick Benevolent Society, established just the year before. In 1830 most people made their living as farmers. There were a few skilled craftsmen such as carpenters, blacksmiths, and masons. Several mills, nail making, and paper making provided other employment.[37]

Natick, like many New England communities, contained artisans who fabricated or repaired custom-made shoes. In contrast to many other developing industries in the period from 1815 to 1845, the boot and shoe industry was not dependent upon waterpower and thus almost any locality could participate in the business; those which did were often widely scattered geographically. About 1828 Edward Walcott began the manufacture of boots and shoes in Natick on a larger scale than before. A number of people in the community were soon turning out brogans, or coarse, poorly fitting work shoes of a sole and a piece of upper leather. Weekly a team of horses would transport the brogans to Boston dealers who would subsequently dispatch them to the South or the West Indies for use by slaves. Trade was in part by barter. Boston houses would pay two-thirds of the value of the brogans in leather, the other one-third in cash.[38]

Blanche Evans Hazard, who studied the boot and shoe industry in Massachusetts, characterized four stages in its development, two of which had been reached when Wilson arrived at Natick. The business began with what Hazard termed the Handicraft Stage. The shoemakers, in their own homes, worked for specific customers; in time itinerant cobblers participated, too. The four steps of producing a shoe—cutting, fitting, lasting, and bottoming—were carried out by one person. Many communities contained bark houses and tanning pits. Apprentices and journeymen might work with the master craftsmen, but each person made a complete shoe. In some communities, by the time of the American Revolution, masters were fabricating unordered shoes for general sales. A market traffic thus had been created. As early as 1768 Lynn, Massachusetts, alone produced eighty thousand pairs; that number increased to eight hundred thousand in 1783. Primarily still a handicraft in 1810, the industry produced over one hundred thirty-five thousand boots and shoes for export alone.

Next came the Domestic Stage, in which the craftsmen were divorced from the purchasers. Entrepreneurs collected shoes from the producers and located the markets. In time less skilled and irregularly employed people, increasingly women and girls, joined the operation. Markets also broadened, particularly in the South, West Indies, and South America. Most of the leather was domestically produced; as settlement moved westward in the state, more cattle were driven east for market. Hides were also frequently imported. With demand growing and the producer divorced from the wearer, the quality of workmanship declined. Beginning around 1810, in some communities central shops were established in which cutting was done and from which leather was distributed. The businessmen bought their stock in Boston, transported it to their communities, controlled the cutting in their central shops, and "put out" the leather to be made into shoes. Binding and making shoes became separate processes. The binders, often women, stitched together parts of the upper shoe. The shoemakers fitted the upper and attached it to the sole.[39]

By 1830 the shoe industry was taking new form. Those who benefited most were the distributors and large manufacturers with access to markets. Preeminent at the manufacturing level were the boss and the cutters or clickers. The latter worked in the central shop, cut the pieces, and examined the quality of work done by the outsiders. The boss supplied only the small plant and raw materials, no tools. He obtained the leather, assumed responsibility for preparation of the shoes for market, and sold them. In contrast to textile manufacturing, little was required in money, facilities, or tools to get started in the shoe business. On the other hand, with so many people able easily to enter the occupation, competition could be intense and business failures frequent. The cutters or clickers were the best paid among the workers, often receiving an annual salary. Next on the socioeconomic scale were the shoemakers or cordwainers, who worked on materials, owned their own tools, and prepared the uppers. Lowest on the scale in this "putting out" system were those who assembled uppers and stitched linings, often women, usually working at home. They took out cases of shoes from the shop and returned them when their work was completed. This system of manufacturing shoes continued until mechanization overtook the industry at midcentury.[40]

Notwithstanding Walcott's leadership, Natick in 1833 produced so few shoes that charts showing the value of tanned leather production that year did not include the community. It would rank eighth in the state in 1850 with $838,000 worth of boot and shoe production. One authority credited the hostility between the northern and southern parts of the town and the want of adequate roads as contributing to this tardy development of the industry. Since many shoemakers in Natick still fabricated the entire shoe, the process was slow. Transporting the finished goods to Boston was also initially expensive. In 1834 and 1835, however, the Boston and

Worcester (later the Boston and Albany) Railroad reached Natick, transforming the community. There was "energy, action, new life in every direction."[41] It guaranteed cheaper transportation of shoes to Boston and hides back. The railroad would also presently bring in new laborers—Irish, Canadian, English, and German immigrants. Natick could then compete with other shoe manufacturing communities.[42]

The stories of several entrepreneurs of the mid-1830s, when Wilson arrived in town, are instructive for understanding the boot and shoe business. Asa Felch, the first Natick commercial shoemaker, manufactured brogans for the Boston market. Boston merchants went out to meet Felch at the Worcester Turnpike tollgates. When the railroad arrived, his brother gave up horse-team contracting between Boston and Lake Champlain and joined Asa's business. The life of another shoe manufacturer, Martin Luther Hayes, began similarly to Wilson's; Hayes was born in Farmington in 1812. At fifteen Hayes was bound out to a shoemaker who tanned and cured leather as well as manufactured shoes. Hayes was permitted to buy his freedom before he reached twenty-one by finishing extra work. He then departed for Natick and procured employment with Edward Walcott, bottoming shoes. He returned to Farmington in 1837 or 1838 to establish his own firm. That New Hampshire community, however, was so isolated and Panic times were so difficult that Hayes had difficulty surviving. Hayes would later purchase the land on which Wilson, his boyhood friend, had been born and deed it to Wilson.[43]

Edward Walcott was one of the earliest shoe manufacturers in Natick. Only two years older than Wilson, Walcott was born in Danvers and migrated to Natick when he was seventeen or eighteen. In 1828 Walcott began his own shoe manufacturing business. He was so successful that he eventually paid over one million dollars to his laborers and he became the largest taxpayer in the community. A man of energy and integrity, Walcott was also a civic leader. He reclaimed swampy land and laid out many of the streets of Natick. He purchased much of the land along West Central Street, from Main Street to the cemetery; this later became the thoroughfare on which the elite of the community, including Wilson, lived. Walcott built and owned twenty houses, including his own. He was credited with laying out the rows of shade trees for which the town became famous. As one might surmise, Walcott was a valuable economic and political friend for Wilson to have. An antislavery advocate, Walcott was known to have engaged in Underground Railroad activities.[44]

Wilson did not have to select Natick. Many Massachusetts towns were prospering in the mid-1830s. Natick was not the largest and certainly not the most renowned community in which to learn the shoe trade. Lynn, most famous for its shoe production, may have been overcrowded with workmen. But Haverhill, just across the New Hampshire border, ranked second in 1833 in the production of boots and shoes, while Danvers, also nearer to his home than Natick, ranked third. Perhaps Wilson chose Natick because other Farmington boys had preceded him there. In any case, when he arrived in the community, he obtained a room in the

Sherman House, a tavern on the turnpike. The next day his former schoolmate, Martin Luther Hayes, who had gone to Massachusetts in 1832, suggested that Wilson call on William P. Legro, whose shop was located in the western part of the town. The young man bound himself to Legro for five months' apprenticeship. He had been working only seven weeks when he determined to extract himself from a bad bargain. He obtained his release by paying Legro fifteen dollars. Wilson then arranged with another shoemaker to provide instruction for a month. Wilson's limited funds provided his own board; the shoemaker was rewarded by having ownership of all the shoes the two produced.[45]

Wilson was thereafter on his own. He moved into new quarters, where he often worked with his hammer into the night. He could earn a minimum of twenty dollars a month plus board. Brogans sold for about fifty to sixty-five cents a pair; the leather cost nine to twelve cents; wages ranged from fifty cents to one dollar a day. Twenty to thirty dollars a month must have seemed substantial to Wilson, for farm hands seldom received more than seven to nine dollars a month. The first day on his own Wilson made eight pairs of brogans. In the course of time, working long hours, he once made forty-seven and a half pairs in a single day. Hazard contended that Massachusetts shoes produced before 1837 were probably the worst ever made. Entrepreneurs were incapable of inspecting and overseeing work; shoemakers often did not know enough about their trade; and many of the new manufacturers were irresponsible, anxious to make money fast in a seller's market. Wilson himself was not known as a quality shoemaker. One contemporary reported that Wilson's pay was frequently cut because of the defects resulting from rushing his work. He accepted the forfeitures, for he recovered in quantity what he lost in quality.[46]

One of the stories about Wilson the cobbler during that first year was published by his friend Mann. In April of 1834 two shops were located across the street from one another. One was owned by the sons of Isaac Morse; the other was the shop of William Coolidge, where Coolidge, Mann, Matthew Griffin, and Albert Leighton worked. The men in the latter workroom were Congregational in religion and, except for one, Whig in politics. They labored at low seats, sewing women's shoes. The Morse men worked at stand-up benches on men's shoes. Most of them were Universalist in religion and Democrat in politics. Wilson, new in Natick, was acquainted with few people. He had been disturbed by President Andrew Jackson's order for the removal of national government money deposited in the Second Bank of the United States. One day after dinner Wilson went to the Morse shop to argue his position. The Morses thought Griffin would be a stronger antagonist, so they took Wilson over to the Coolidge shop. Isaac Morse, postmaster and a Democratic party leader in the town, had reared Griffin.

Mann described the young man he was meeting for the first time. Wilson was twenty-two, looking like an "over-grown boy," imperfectly filled out. His hair was black, long, and improperly groomed. His clothes were coarse and poorly cut. He was bashful. He spoke with an impediment of speech and such a range of pronunciation and poor grammar that Mann had difficulty understanding him. Mann, no sophisticate himself, viewed Wilson as a "backwoods curiosity." Stories of Wilson's initial childhood meeting with Mrs. Eastman sometimes referred to Wilson's cursing. Mann also reported his friend's "torrent of invectives" and his "use of contraband language."

Nevertheless, in his encounter with Griffin, Wilson reportedly overwhelmed his adversary with his argument, earnestness, and array of facts. When the Democrat accused the penniless Wilson of Whiggish designs against the common people, Wilson's anger provoked an even more devastating response. When the debate was over, Wilson and Mann, who was only seventeen years old at the time, talked at length. Thus began their life-long friendship. Mann contended he was the first friend Wilson made in Natick. He later would be the last man to see the vice-president alive.[47]

As a young shoemaker, Wilson was satisfied neither with his location nor his occupational prospects. His quarters and work were two miles from a post office or church, among a group of scattered shops. Having by hard labor accumulated some money, Wilson left shoemaking in the fall of 1834 to return to New Hampshire, where he invested in poultry for sale in the Boston market. The price he obtained for what he sold barely covered his outlay of cash and his expenses. He concluded he had better return to Massachusetts.[48]

When Wilson arrived in Natick the second time, he selected a new location in the center and engaged board with Deacon William Coolidge on South Main Street. Coolidge in 1825 had purchased many of the lands in the northern part of Natick. The deacon housed in his sitting room the facsimile of the town library of about fifty books, probably one reason Wilson selected the site. Because of his honored position in the community, Coolidge did not have to accept just any boarder; he must have liked the young man. The Coolidges, who boarded a few others, accepted Wilson as one of their own and opened what little society there was in Natick to him. He attended social gatherings and church with them. Coolidge's social connections were to be valuable to furthering Wilson's political career. Mann, who also resided at the Coolidge's, reported that he and Wilson often slept together so they could talk longer. He marveled at Wilson's objectives for life, but quickly learned that his friend would not aspire to anything for which he did not prepare himself.[49]

One of the more amusing stories about the young Wilson concerns these years. Wilson carried his stock to and from the manufacturer's shop, as most Natick shoemakers did, with a borrowed wheelbarrow. One evening he left his shoes in front of Walcott's while he went across the street to a store to obtain additional materials. Prankster Walcott deposited a large rock in the barrow and then covered it so Wilson would not know it was there. When Wilson left for Coolidge's barn, he had a case of wet shoe leather and the uppers on top. He expected a heavy grind.

The weight was so great, however, he had to stop frequently to rest. Walcott and his friends watched and enjoyed the predicament. Wilson staggered slowly down the street until the wheelbarrow overturned, disclosing the rock.[50]

The young Jeremiah Colbath had seldom traveled far from his birthplace. Reading had been almost the only thing to broaden his vision and challenge his parochial conceptions and prejudices. But to the transplanted Henry Wilson, travel, a new environment, and particularly his proximity to Boston opened new vistas. He trekked to Boston to listen to Edward Everett, who would become one of the nation's most renowned orators and would deliver the main address at the 1863 dedication of the Gettysburg Cemetery. Wilson also heard Daniel Webster speak. Russell and Nason claimed these experiences awakened in Wilson a new determination for more education.[51]

Wilson developed a close relationship with the Congregational pastors of Natick. His contemporary biographers never mentioned Wilson's attending church as a boy in Farmington. In fact, he did not join any church until after the Civil War. Nevertheless, he quickly became a friend of Erasmus D. Moore, the minister of the only Natick church. Nason and Russell termed him Wilson's "earnest friend and counsellor."[52] Wilson himself characterized Moore as a man of influence and power, a friend when Wilson had no other.

Erasmus Moore had arrived in Natick for his first pastorate shortly before Wilson. Born in Connecticut in 1802, educated at Amherst and Yale Colleges and at Yale Theological Seminary, ordained November 6, 1833, Moore was a scholar and writer as well as a minister. His fate was to lead the most important institution in the community at just the time Natick was growing so rapidly. A new meeting-house was erected in 1835 at a cost of eight thousand dollars. Thirty-three members were added to the congregation during Moore's short ministry. One commentator characterized the man's pastorate as the "Seven Years Revival." In 1838 Moore left Natick to accept another call. He subsequently edited several newspapers and helped prepare the Old Colony and Bay State records for publication. Wilson in July of 1855 obtained a position for Moore in the Massachusetts secretary of state's office. In 1861 Moore accepted appointment to the Boston Custom House, undoubtedly also secured for him by Senator Wilson. He stayed until 1877. Moore was an early member of the Natick Anti-Slavery Society. This abolitionist position must have had an effect upon the maturing mind of Wilson.[53]

Wilson was one of the founders of the Natick Debating Society. Alexander W. Thayer, another founder, wrote in 1876 that in the winter of 1834 to 1835, or the following spring, a friend told him about a young man who had just arrived from New Hampshire and whose passion for American history was similar to Thayer's. Shortly thereafter the two men met. Thayer, who had attended Andover, began to go to Deacon Coolidge's shop to discuss history and politics with his new acquaintance. The uneducated Wilson must have developed intellectually to have interested a man like Thayer. Several of his associates credited Wilson with organizing the debating society. Thayer and John Bacon wanted rules which required writing and declamations, but Wilson opposed "rote." They compromised by making writing voluntary; Wilson never wrote. The Natick schoolhouse, near Deacon Coolidge's residence, was opened for their meetings. On June 30, 1835, thirteen or fourteen young men launched their new society; four or five others later joined. Meetings were weekly, sometimes twice a week. Obviously little factual preparation could occur prior to the debates. These were mostly laboring men who had to steal time away from money-earning activities. The society held more than one hundred sessions before it merged into the lyceum in 1840.[54]

The debating society, prominent in Natick folklore, was an influential cultural force at a pivotal moment in the village's history. Harriet Bacon recorded that the society "had great influence among the young men." Many of its members, then between the ages of sixteen and twenty-one, later became national, state, or community leaders. Four subsequently edited newspapers, two became lawyers, one was a doctor, and three were graduated from college. They served in the legislatures of Connecticut, New Hampshire, and Massachusetts. They were active in churches, benevolent societies, and business affairs. At a reunion in 1860 the men credited the debating society for their influential standing in society. Many debating society members became Wilson's lifelong friends, men to whom he turned for counsel, men who assisted him in political campaigns.[55]

The society examined a wide variety of topics. It began with "Can the works of fiction collectively be considered as beneficial to society in general?" The boys also debated the government's treatment of Indians, whether the Roman Catholic Church was dangerous to the political institutions of the country, what rights labor had, whether capital punishment should be abolished, whether women were mentally inferior to men, whether Washington or Lafayette was the greater man, and slavery and abolition.

Who were these friends and associates of the young Wilson? They were a healthy lot for that time and taking into account how hard they worked. By the Civil War only three had died. Among the debaters was George M. Herring, who in 1843 moved to Wilson's home community of Farmington. He remained one of Wilson's close friends and an effective advocate for the ambitious Massachusetts politician in his native state. Herring served as New Hampshire representative and state senator and as collector of internal revenue. An obituary notice credited him with being more responsible than any other man for establishing and building up Farmington's shoe business. Another debater, Alexander Thayer, a native of Natick, attended Phillips Academy at Andover and was graduated from Harvard in 1843. Thayer was a scholar, the author of an outstanding nineteenth century biography of Beethoven, a correspondent for the *New York Tribune,* and the American counsel at Trieste for almost twenty years.[56]

Many more of the debating society members remained in Natick or the surrounding area. John W. Bacon, another Harvard graduate, was a lawyer, overseer of the college, state senator, associate judge of the superior court, and an author. Austin Bacon became a scientific buff, a civil engineer, farmer, and occasional schoolteacher. Oliver Bacon authored a history of Natick. Jonathan B. Mann, one of those closest to Wilson, wrote one of his friend's biographies and served as deputy auditor of the United States Treasury Department. Edwin C. Morse, a shoemaker, served as assistant paymaster in the army, edited a Natick newspaper, and was a Middlesex County trial justice. Willard A. Wight, first president of the society, taught school and served as deacon of his church.[57]

Most of these young men were better educated and more experienced in what passed for learning than Wilson. Thayer many years later recorded that Wilson had not distinguished himself by his reasoning. If the topic being debated dealt with American history or politics and if facts about and opinions of great men were useful to the argument, then Wilson sparkled. At first he trembled when he had to speak. His language, pronunciation, and sentence structure and grammar were all deficient, but then one object in belonging to the society was to better oneself. Mann remarked how rapidly Wilson improved. Thayer described him as passionate, tenacious, and courageous. Wilson did not want his statements doubted. Since he had difficulty arguing a position in which he did not believe, Wilson would sometimes obtain a substitute. Mann remembered his friend's intensity and earnestness. The debating experience was not only to improve the participants' minds, but it was also to train them in the correct use of parliamentary procedure. Thayer contended that within two years after formation of the society, half a dozen of them could have presided over the legislature. In his later career, Wilson often was called to presiding duties, including over the Massachusetts Senate, as alternate presiding officer in the 1853 state Constitutional Convention, and as vice-president of the United States. The debating society was Wilson's training ground.[58]

Fiske, the Methodist ministerial candidate, was at first the only debating society member opposed to slavery. Most of the men, however, would later become antislavery Whigs, then Republicans. At their 1860 reunion, fourteen of them called themselves Republicans, only one would vote for the Constitutional Unionist presidential candidate John Bell, none were Democrats, one's views were unknown. The mid-1830s was not a good time to debate questions concerning slavery; abolitionists were being mobbed in a number of communities and were being prevented from speaking in others. Many people in Natick were opposed to the society's considering the subject.[59]

When Wilson became an opponent of slavery is difficult to determine. Biographer Mann declared that his friend was converted to abolition by Lydia Maria Child, the author and antislavery leader. Child's father was a resident of Natick; she did develop an interest in Wilson and of course wanted to persuade him and the other young men of the correctness of abolition principles. When he departed for Washington in the spring of 1836, Mann asserted, Wilson viewed slavery in a new light. Thayer—who lived near Child's father, knew the family well, and was himself converted to abolition by the famous writer—doubted Mann's story and suggested another version of the Child-Wilson conversations. Child's correspondence includes no claim of credit for the famous senator's antislavery stance. Wilson himself stated that he had expressed no public disapproval of slavery until his trip south in June, 1836. Biographer Charles Phelps asserted Wilson had been affected by the visit of George Thompson, the English abolitionist and agent of the American and New England Anti-Slavery societies, who toured Massachusetts from September of 1834 to the fall of 1835. Natick's antislavery society of ninety members was established in December of 1836 while Wilson was again living in New Hampshire. Pastor Moore was its representative to the meeting of the American Anti-Slavery Society in New York City in May of 1837. By the spring of the following year membership had increased to 163, a large number for a community as small as Natick. Yet no claims have been made that Wilson was a society member.[60]

Mann also emphasized the role of the debating society in standing up against the Natick economic and political establishment. Since shoemakers were paid by the piece, hours were not a labor issue for workmen; strikes were not contemplated. The community did, however, have a political and social class structure based on landholdings and family name. This worked against men such as Wilson. He and his friends challenged the elite and gained a broader entry into community decisions. They sought to improve education, to raise methods of conducting business, and to improve roads.[61]

Among the books to be found in the collection of Wilson memorabilia in the museum in South Natick is *The Young Man's Aid to Knowledge, Virtue, and Happiness* by Hubbard Winslow. There is no way of knowing for certain if Wilson purchased it. Writing in the front is that of Charles Colbath, Wilson's brother. Its 1837 date of publication establishes that Wilson had reached adulthood before this book could have been purchased or read. Yet many of the principles which governed Wilson's life are so similar to those encouraged by the author of the book that one is tempted to conclude that Wilson approved of the book's contents and might have purchased it shortly after its publication. It therefore might have influenced the young man's personal development. The object of the book, the author stated in its preface, was to awaken character in young men so that they would "forego the allurements of idleness and dissipation, and seek intellectual and moral improvement which will render their future lives honorable and happy to themselves and to the world."[62]

Chapter one fits well into the nationalism and optimism of the age of Jackson. The country's commanding physical characteristics and the character of its people enjoined the United States to serve as an example for the rest of the world, the author asserted. The nation's values and institutions would spread over the globe. Young men who would meet the high demands of the age had to possess thorough and extensive knowledge, sound principles, well-formed habits, piety, and benevolence towards their fellow men. Knowledge included both facts and a value system to enable one properly to use the facts. Knowledge should be acquired early in life, when it was easier to gain and when it could help the young person to escape the perils of temptation and sin. Practical knowledge to assist with one's occupation was critical, but understanding of arithmetic, English grammar, composition, geography, and history were almost as essential. History should be systemically pursued, one book at a time in some order. The sciences, a foreign language, and intellectual and moral philosophy were of lesser importance.[63]

A young man also needed to develop moral principles. The lowest level of motivation, according to the book, was sensuality, next vanity. Honor was third; ambition of wealth, intellectual eminence, conquest and glory, rank and office, dignity and power followed. All of those should be rejected. Instead, a young man should be accountable to and motivated by his love for a Supreme Being. The principles embedded in the Ten Commandments were discussed in nineteenth century language. Winslow also advised adoption of good habits early in life. These included proper subordination and respect towards all superiors in age and rank, including parents; temperance in all things: "moderate use of whatever nourishes, and total abstinence from whatever injures"; fixed attention to the subject or business at hand; industry, frugality, and benevolence; prudence; discipline; and shaping one's conduct in light of the certainty of an eternity.[64]

What good could the moral power of a young man achieve? One could give oneself to God; one could do for one's parents; one could exert influence upon siblings and females in society; one could render service to one's pastor; one could support benevolent societies; one could be a faithful citizen, acquainted with the nation's institutions. As far as business was concerned, Winslow advised getting settled and permanent as soon as possible. Preparation involved discipline, probably five to seven years for learning. Men were told to begin cautiously and advance slowly. They should depend upon their own resources rather than upon relatives and friends. Marital advice was also given. The author opposed the idea that a man should have his fortune before marrying. It was evil to wait too long and then marry a woman twenty years younger. What qualities should be looked for in a wife? A good disposition, domestic virtues (knowing how to keep house), good sense and intelligence, an agreeable personality and good health, neatness, sympathy with the husband's calling, and conviction in her religion.[65]

Wilson had thrown himself too much into his work. He set targets to meet, an established number of shoes each week. He could work sixteen hours a day, even nineteen. His lights often burned until midnight. On occasion he labored two continuous days, including the intervening night. His landlady complained the one fault she found in him was that his hammer went long after others were in bed. By the end of two years and five months he had made and sold six thousand pairs of shoes and saved seven hundred dollars. Wilson later declared he had worked "fourteen and fifteen hours a day, month after month to earn forty dollars a month."[66] He had so overworked himself that friends advised him to rest. "He had raised blood."[67] A doctor told him to take off two months. Since his experience in the debating society had made him aware that he needed more formal education, he resolved to return to New Hampshire for study.[68]

But first, in May of 1836, Wilson departed for Washington. He stayed for four weeks. What a thrill it must have been for the young nationalist to visit the capital city and to listen to debates in Congress! He later recorded that while passing through Maryland, he first encountered slavery. He was particularly disgusted to see slave women working in the fields. When he remarked to a man seated next to him that slavery was an evil, he was told sharply that he could not express such a view in Maryland. Upon arrival in Washington, he found Congress discussing the Pinckney Resolutions, which were intended to restrict debate over petitions dealing with slavery. Massachusetts politicians were unanimous in their opposition to the resolutions. Congress was also dealing with issues concerning Texas. Wilson saw slavery every day in the District of Columbia or in Maryland or Virginia. Over and over again he later told of his repulsion when he confronted Williams's notorious slave pen. When he openly expressed his disgust towards slavery one day while he was eating with Senator Thomas Morris of Ohio, the only avowed antislavery advocate in the Senate, Wilson was told to be careful what he said. Morris was shielded by being a senator; Wilson had no such protection. He left the capital, he later asserted, with a determination thereafter to oppose slavery openly.[69]

When he returned to New Hampshire in July 1836, Wilson began his studies at the academy at Strafford. The community was selected both because it was near his home and because a Farmington friend, W. W. Roberts, was also a student there. In the fall Wilson moved to Wolfeboro's academy for one term under Miss Eastman, the daughter of his former benefactors. He, and those who employed him, apparently thought he was then qualified enough to teach that winter at the district school in Wolfeboro. He devoted his leisure time to continuing his studies. Wolfeboro was described in an 1823 gazetteer as even less prosperous than Wilson's native Farmington; two nineteenth century gazetteers concurred that soil in that area was hard to cultivate. Wolfeboro was the largest community in Carroll County, located on the southern shore of Lake Winnipesaukee. Timothy Dwight, in his travels in 1813, described the village as consisting then of only twenty houses, but with a beautiful location. He maintained the soil was rich and grains, flax, vegetables, and fruit—except peaches—all flourished. He also complained of the early fall frosts and the cold and "backward" spring. The population in the whole town was then under fifteen hundred and was primarily affiliated with Free Will Baptist congregations.[70]

For the spring and summer terms of 1837 Wilson transferred to Concord Academy, directed by the Reverend T. P. D. Stone. While he studied rhetoric, "intellectual philosophy," geometry, astronomy, and religion, his special interest was extemporaneous speaking and debate. In Concord he developed another important friendship, with classmate John R. French. French later would be a framer of the Reconstruction constitution of North Carolina, a candidate for Congress from that state, and sergeant-at-arms of the United States Senate.[71]

In the meantime the Panic of 1837 had devastated the nation's economy and thrown many people out of work. This was the most serious and long lasting depression in the nation's history until 1929. Wilson had loaned to a friend much of the seven hundred dollars he had saved from his Natick shoemaking. The man's bankruptcy left Wilson almost penniless. Upon learning of the financial loss, Wilson asked French to walk with him to talk. When they reached a woods, Wilson broke down and cried. He was certain his life had been ruined. Fortunately, Samuel Avery of Wolfeboro offered Wilson board on credit to continue another term in school. When that was complete, Wilson in November of 1837 returned to Natick to teach the winter term at the school in the town center. He was so impoverished he had to secure credit to buy a new suit of clothes.[72]

The message of abolition was reaching New Hampshire communities with increasing frequency and force during Wilson's months there. It was beginning to influence his life. With the publication of William Lloyd Garrison's *The Liberator,* the establishment of the New England Anti-Slavery Society in Boston, and the founding of the American Anti-Slavery Society in New York City, all in the early 1830s, the antislavery movement had moved into a new, militant stage characterized by a demand for the immediate and uncompensated emancipation of slaves. At first few people were willing to listen to what the abolitionists were saying. The message was too radical. A few Northerners still had slaves; many more could remember when they or their relatives had. Most people believed blacks were inherently inferior. In any case, agitation against an institution which was increasingly intrinsic to the values, institutions, and way of life of a major part of the country could be dangerous to the very existence of the nation, could contaminate personal relations between those who held slaves and those who did not, could interfere with the functioning of national institutions such as church bodies and benevolent and humanitarian societies, and could endanger good business relations.

The task of arousing the conscience of the nation against slavery was more difficult than the abolitionists had anticipated. They had begun their crusade with the expectation that they could use the same tactics which other benevolent and reform societies employed to produce change. They would employ both the printed word and lecturing agents to proclaim the evils of slavery and the practicality and necessity of taking steps to end the institution. Southern leaders and state legislatures, alert to the dangers it foreshadowed, had quickly protested against the attack on their "peculiar institution." Antislavery speakers were not permitted to lecture in the slave states and abolition publications were excluded from the mails and prevented from being individually distributed.

Northern state and local governments initially were also tempted to limit the abolitionists' rights to be heard, but soon turned to inaction. Of course, many Northerners in the abstract were opposed to slavery. But agitation was not the way to respond to the situation, it was argued. Patience, understanding of the problems of Southern whites, temperate discussion of the issues were all permissible. The Northern elite would turn over to majority or influential opinion in each community the decision of how to respond to (meaning control of) the activities of the abolitionists. Making unavailable the buildings where abolition meetings might be held, refusing to publish any information about antislavery meetings, condemning abolition agitation in the press, socially ostracizing those who joined antislavery societies, permitting or even encouraging mob action—these were some of the responses in Northern communities to the growing demands for action against slavery. In the latter half of 1835 opposition to the abolitionists was particularly strong. Garrison's office in Boston was attacked and the editor was threatened by a mob. Agents encountered rioters in Haverhill and Worcester, Massachusetts; Montpelier, Vermont; Concord, New Hampshire; Newport, Rhode Island; and in a number of communities in New York and Ohio. Mobs attacked the black sections of Philadelphia and Pittsburgh. English abolitionist George Thompson was harassed until he left the country.

New Hampshire had been hearing the militant abolition message since 1832. A state antislavery society had been created in November 1834 and about a dozen communities had auxiliaries affiliated with it by May of 1835. But work in the state had been too often an offshoot of activities in Massachusetts or Maine. In the summer of 1835 George Storrs, a Methodist clergyman, began an agency which lasted through August of 1836. He almost single-handedly carried the abolitionist message over the state. By the time he left, shortly after Wilson returned to the state, the number of antislavery societies had increased from sixteen to fifty-one, with over thirty-one hundred members, and the New Hampshire organization supported its own newspaper. During 1836 and 1837 the American Anti-Slavery Society dispatched two paid lecturers to reach even more of the state with "the word" of abolition.[73]

Wilson's antipathy to slavery deepened during his sojourn in New Hampshire. While at the academy at Strafford in the turbulent summer of 1836, he participated in a debate, "Ought slavery be abolished in the District of Columbia?" His Concord friend French was one of the most ardent abolitionists; sources differ as to how actively Wilson participated in antislavery societies. In March of 1846 he asserted he had been a member of an antislavery society for "nearly ten years."[74]

John French, without consulting his friend, nominated Wilson as one of twelve delegates from Concord to the 1837 Young Men's Anti-Slavery Convention, held on August 22. Two hundred men attended. Many years later one of Wilson's Washington newspaper correspondent friends reported that when the convention considered censure of John Quincy Adams for not taking a strong enough antislavery position in congressional debates, Wilson spoke in opposition. Wendell Phillips, soon to become one of the leaders among Boston abolitionists, entered during the speech and subsequently defended Wilson's position. The convention passed a strong statement in support of Adams. Among the many other resolutions adopted was one commending those who belonged to political parties, but calling upon them to prevent their parties from participating in the political sin of slavery. Resolutions were also passed emphasizing the duty of churches and ministers to work to end slavery, opposing the annexation of Texas, calling on young men to speak out on the issue of slavery, and condemning the New Hampshire Congressional delegation for its failure to speak and act against slavery. The convention decided against creating a new society, preferring that young men participate in the activities of the already existing state organization.[75]

2

THE NATICK COBBLER

In the fall of 1837 Wilson returned to Natick, where he would now make his permanent residence. By teaching in the winter he was able to repay his Wolfeboro board debt. With twelve dollars in his pocket in April of 1838 he reentered the shoe industry, this time in the more prominent position of manufacturer. A manufacturer purchased the leather, contracted for the making of the shoes, prepared the finished products for market, and sold them. Wilson initially used David Whitney's shop but soon moved to several locations of his own near the town center.[1]

The low point of the Panic of 1837 was an unpropitious moment to begin a business. Yet Natick weathered the Panic years better than many communities. If nothing else, bankruptcy opened opportunities for new men to enter the field. Communities like Natick whose manufacturers did not have large capital investments were the least injured. People needed boots and shoes, even in a depression; furthermore, footwear was comparatively inexpensive. Shoe production was therefore an industry which recovered more quickly than some others. Only a limited capital was needed; a manufacturer sold at his own risk. Ease of transportation and nearness to the financial and distribution facilities of Boston were increasingly important factors in the industry. The railroad had arrived in Natick just in time. Furthermore, new ways of cutting, finishing, and packing shoes reduced expenses or attracted sales. Natick in 1837 produced 250,000 shoes valued at more than $213,000. The business employed 263 males and 189 females. The community was becoming a shoe town, although admittedly in a small way compared with Lynn's $1,690,000 or Haverhill's more than $1,000,000 worth of production that year.[2]

Paul Faler, in discussing the Lynn shoe manufacturers of the late 1830s and early 1840s, concluded they were increasingly like the merchants of Salem in terms of wealth and style of life. Most of the more successful entrepreneurs had the right family connections. Property was desirable as security for credit with which to purchase materials. Even in Lynn, which was particularly buffeted by the Panic, the number of shoe manufacturers increased from 68 in 1832 to 110 in 1841. There, also, businessmen had to work hard and travel extensively to survive. As shoe prices declined, both workers and entrepreneurs had to put forth additional effort.[3]

Wilson had none of the advantages of the Lynn manufacturers. He had to begin small and gradually expand. He benefited from his willingness to work and good reputation; also, except for the Walcott and Felch firms, Natick was still in what Hazard characterized as the first phase of the domestic system of shoe manufacturing, and Wilson could compete. Since he supplied neither tools nor physical facilities, the boss needed little capital to get started. Wilson began by obtaining leather enough to fabricate a single case of brogans and sold the case in Boston for more leather and cash. He employed a helper and returned to Boston with two cases. On the next trip he had three. Wilson had a renowned capacity for work and great powers of endurance. The business must have expanded rapidly to turn out eighteen thousand pairs of shoes—three hundred cases—that year, for he did not even begin until the school term was over. He learned how to turn over capital rapidly and he apparently obtained small loans and bank discounts. He rather soon bought some land and built his own shop.[4]

Wilson's account book for 1846, available for Hazard's research, tells much about his life for more than a decade as a shoe manufacturer. On January 1, 1846, Wilson had 12,300 pairs of firsthand stock brogans with consignees. Shoes were distributed to jobbers in the community and payments were later made based on the number of brogans produced. Wilson recorded the number of pairs, sizes, selling price per pair, and total value. He had 3,200 pairs on hand unsold, almost 1,000 pairs in the hands of workmen. Among his liabilities were $9,780 in notes, $9,780 in stock, $4,300 notes in market, $3,362 in bills, and $265 in borrowed cash. He was getting his lasts at reduced wholesale prices. His shoes sold at thirty to eighty cents a pair. His success in business depended in great part upon the accuracy of his opinions concerning the financial reliability of his customers. By 1846 the young businessman had accumulated real property worth approximately $5,000, including houses, lots, and shops; his total property, real and personal, exceeded his liabilities by more than $5,000.[5]

As early as 1838 Wilson employed eighteen hands and engaged in $17,000 worth of business, a remarkable record for his first year of operation. His output increased from 18,000 pairs of brogans in 1838 to 58,000 pairs in 1845. In 1839 he was already selling 31,000 pairs. His workforce grew from eighteen to fifty-two people. For some reason in 1847 he employed 190 people and turned out 122,000 pairs of shoes, 2,000 cases. But that was an anomaly, for in 1848 he had returned to 63,000 pairs production with only sixty-eight employees. In all he manufactured 664,000 pairs. Mann claimed that Wilson's political activities made his name better known so that new people sought to buy shoes from him. His widening social and economic connections also brought information and advice on how to conduct business.[6]

One can better understand Wilson's manufacturing career by comparing his business with those of others. Oliver Bacon in his *History of Natick* estimated that from the mid-1830s to the mid-1850s the average number of shoes manufactured in the town was 600,000; during several of those years over 1,000,000 pairs were turned out. Edward Walcott employed about one hundred people, manufacturing about 150,000 pairs annually, a total of 3,000,000 between his start in 1828 and 1855. Isaac Felch, who began business in 1836, employed about seventy-seven people, turning out an average of 31,200 pairs in his first five years. Thereafter, he manufactured 50,000 pairs a year. E. & F. Hanchett & Company, which began business in 1843, produced between 30,000 and 40,000 pairs per year, employing between forty and fifty people. John B. Walcott, who began business in 1835, in twenty years sold over 1,000,000 shoes. Interestingly, in spite of John Walcott's three-year head start over Wilson, Walcott turned out only 28,000 pairs in the period from 1838 to 1840, during which Wilson produced 87,000 pairs. Only in 1846 and 1848 did John Walcott surpass Wilson's production. Wilson clearly was one of the largest manufacturers and employers in Natick, a fact often not sufficiently considered in accounting for his political success and his standing in the community.[7]

Because Wilson, the Walcotts, and others were successful, one might conclude that success was common among those with industry and ability. Alan Dawley and Paul Faler in their studies of the Lynn shoe industry contended otherwise. A large majority of the Lynn journeymen owned no real property, in contrast to what is often assumed about most Americans of that age. Furthermore, the rise of the manufacturing system in shoes produced a class of entrepreneurs and another of laborers. Few shoemakers rose from the bench to become manufacturers. Of one hundred Lynn shoemakers of 1832, none had become a manufacturer by 1839, only three by 1851. Wilson, of course, was lucky he entered the business when and where he did. But Natick had other enterprising young men who did not succeed. Wilson's hard work and business and social connections were obvious advantages. He also must have been a wise entrepreneur, with the right personality characteristics for his supervisory and ownership status.[8]

We know something about Wilson's product. His brogans were cheap, intended for Southern plantation slaves, requiring only the closing of short seams on the uppers and lasting. Mann revealed that Wilson never questioned whether he wanted the slaves' feet covered. Once a bankrupt customer offered to pay 50 percent of his bill by selling slaves. Wilson cancelled the debt. The 1846 records listed six men bottoming or lasting the brogans, eight women closing or sewing the short seams. When work was done by young boys and girls, payment went to the fathers. Agents often came to Wilson's shop, picked up materials, and distributed them over the surrounding area. Later the agents would return with more materials, pick up the finished brogans, deliver them to Wilson, and receive payment. At one time 1,830 brogans were brought in; this could have represented a winter's work of several people or a week's work of many.[9]

Wilson became known as a friend of labor. His own early work experiences contributed to that reputation. When he participated in the political campaign of 1840, he was heralded as the "Natick Cobbler." Both the Mann and Nason and Russell biographies present Wilson as a genial boss. Harriet Beecher Stowe had the same view. These writers asserted he paid good wages, was known as generous and fair in his settlements, and participated in few lawsuits and quarrels. Among his employees were three of his brothers and two of his wife's relatives. In his ten and a half years as an employer (1838 to 1848) he paid $130,000 in wages. In his famous 1858 answer to Senator James Hammond's attack on the Northern labor system, Wilson revealed much concerning his perceptions of himself. While a worker, he never felt degraded, he told the Senate, but he saw himself as the "peer" of his employer. Subsequently, when he hired others, some of whom would later acquire more property than he, he was not conscious that they were his inferiors. Taking into account this attitude in many ways is indispensable for understanding basic differences between Wilson and many of his Massachusetts political antagonists in the late 1840s and early 1850s and between Wilson and the "Slave Power" which controlled the South and dominated the nation in the 1850s.[10]

One of the anecdotes about Wilson-the-employer disclosed that he once hired a boy whose drunken father did not adequately provide for his family's support. When the day arrived to pay the boy, the father demanded the money and Wilson had to surrender it to him. The boy, who had worked so hard, felt miserable. The concerned Wilson made an effort to praise the boy's work and paid him money equal to what the father had taken.[11]

Shortly after Wilson returned from school in New Hampshire, Moore was replaced as pastor of the Natick church by Samuel Hunt. The new minister quickly became a friend of Wilson's, and was influential at a formative moment in Wilson's political career, in his antislavery development, and in his family affairs. In their later lives the two men would work closely, Hunt as clerk to the Senate Military Affairs Committee, chaired by Wilson, as secretary of the vice-president, and as a collaborator in writing Wilson's three volume history of the rise and fall of the Slave-Power in America. Hunt, approximately the same age as Wilson, had studied theology at Andover and Princeton and was called to the Natick Congregational Church in 1839. He would stay until May of 1850. Hunt later reminisced that Wilson had been among the first to take him by the hand when Hunt arrived in Natick and was among the last to bid him goodbye.[12] Hunt served in Franklin, Massachusetts, from 1850 to 1864 and then found himself a "superannuated minister" at the age of fifty. He subsequently tried and failed at various activities, including farming. In late 1868 Wilson rescued Hunt from poverty with the first of the two secretarial appointments. Hunt, early in his career, perhaps even before Wilson, became an outspoken advocate of the abolition of slavery.[13]

On October 28 or November 3, 1840 (sources differ), Wilson married Harriet Malvina Howe, who had been born in Natick and was the daughter of Amasa and Mary Toombs Howe. Amasa Howe had come from Medway. His wife Mary, born in 1786, was the daughter of Joseph and Mary Toombs of Hopkinton. Mrs. Howe resided with the Wilsons from almost the beginning of their marriage. She survived both, living until 1881, the oldest citizen of Natick when she died. The wedding ceremony took place at the residence of Mrs. Lucius H. (Mary Ann) Munroe, Harriet Howe's sister. The Munroes and Wilsons remained on intimate terms and lived close to one another. Wilson would later be executor of Lucius Munroe's estate. One of Harriet's sisters subsequently married Timothy Coolidge, son of the deacon. The Munroes' son William was Wilson's financial advisor in the vice-president's declining years and was executor of the Wilson estate. The marriage, in other words, brought to Henry Wilson a new circle of intimates and a support group important for a successful family life and political career.[14]

Harriet Howe had been a student of Wilson's that winter term of 1837 to 1838; she was only sixteen when they were married. Mann characterized her as "a young lady of excellent mind, intelligent, amiable, and beautiful, but whose early loss of health and vigor prevented her taking the active part in society she was fitted for."[15] Harriet Wilson often was in ill health, even when a young woman. Frequent poor health was not uncommon. Blanche Glassman Hersh, in a study of women of this era, records that "chronic illness and frailty were widespread . . . at least among middle-class women who left records of their nervous disorders, frequent dyspepsia, headaches and general indisposition."[16] Nason and Russell spoke of Harriet as a woman of "good education, refined in sentiment, gentle in manner."[17] A number of commentators, including the sophisticated Mary C. Ames, praised her intelligence. Wild Bill Hickok, who guided the Wilsons and others on a western trip, characterized Harriet as a "woman of superior wit, and jolly under almost any circumstances."[18] Others noted she was "retiring by nature"[19] and "modest."[20] She was "earnest in purpose," loyal to her family and friends, and benevolent.[21] Although she lived in a hotbed of political intrigue, Washington, off and on for sixteen years, she made few enemies. When she died, the Boston press was united in its praise of her. Clearly she was devoted to her church and its activities.

The Nason and Russell biography used words which cause one to conclude that Wilson placed Harriet on a pedestal. "In her he held a pattern of true womanhood. . . . His ideal of womanly virtue and devotion was realized in her pure and lovely life of trust and duty." Later, "he revered her excellences. To him her word and her wishes were sacred." Wilson characterized Harriet as "a lady of unusual mental and personal attractions, blending grace with dignity in manner, and ornamenting . . . the doctrines of her Lord and Master."[22] Keith Melder, in his description of what a good woman in the antebellum North should be—"pious, pure, selfless, delicate, domestic," a person devoted to working in the church and being religious—described Harriet Wilson. So might the qualities of piety, purity, submissiveness, and domesticity, which Barbara Welter concluded were the prized characteristics of the "Cult of True Womanhood," although we have no evidence one way or the other whether Harriet was submissive. The woman's place was in the home, yet her inherent moral capacity also called for her to be working to improve society.[23] The sparse surviving correspondence between Henry and Harriet, the comments which Wilson made to others about his wife, and the observations of contemporaries corroborate that Wilson loved his wife and had a deep appreciation of her as a person.

Besides fulfilling the duties expected of her as a wife and mother, Harriet Wilson was supportive of her husband's political career. Mary C. Ames reported Harriet was "conversant with public questions and interested in all those movements of the day in which her husband takes so prominent a part."[24] In 1860 she was an occasional writer to the *Natick Observer* under the signature "Melina." During the difficult days of the Civil War she was active in aiding soldiers stationed in the Washington region. While she had to conduct affairs and supervise the household when her husband was attending to legislative responsibilities in Boston or, in those sessions when she did not accompany him, in Washington, she was sustained by a supportive family and a small community whose values approved of her comportment.[25]

After their marriage, the couple for a few months resided at the Munroe home. In 1841 or 1842 the Wilsons contracted to have a house built on West Central Street. Charles Francis Adams, speaking in Natick in 1843 at Wilson's invitation, had tea with the couple before the lecture and spent the night with them afterwards; he characterized the house as "a small, new building in the center of a new looking part of the town." Two to four years later a second house was constructed further out on the same street. There on November 11, 1846, the Wilsons's only child, Henry Hamilton, was born. A third house at 33 West Central, was erected in 1853. The land was purchased from Wilson's brother George Colbath in 1849; the Colbath house was across the street. To be finished like that of the Munroe's, it was thirty feet by twenty-five feet, its roof projecting by four and one-half feet at the north and supported by columns; it had two chimneys and five fireplaces.[26]

The manufacture of shoes gave Wilson more time for family and personal and political activities than work in the shop had permitted. Between his return to Natick in 1838 and its absorption into the lyceum in 1840, Wilson again participated in the activities of the debating society. He was thereafter a sponsor of the lyceum, which he described as "composed of a few mechanics," but with the payment of ten dollars and travel expenses able to obtain some good speakers.[27] Harriet is credited by a number of contemporaries with attracting her husband to regular church activities. Hunt's influence also brought the young shoe manufacturer to a greater consideration of religion. Wilson taught a Bible class for several years.[28]

The young Wilson early became an advocate of temperance. Studies have documented the magnitude of alcohol consumption and of drunkenness in the 1830s and 1840s. Wilson had learned his lesson while yet a boy at home; he had taken the temperance pledge and kept it. He told an audience in 1867 that although he had recognized the evils of intemperance while a small child, he was grateful that he had no desire or taste for intoxicants. Wilson was careful in his speeches not to insist upon a particular approach to temperance—moderation or abstinence—but he preferred total abstinence. He regarded liquor as the greatest cause, next to slavery, of human wretchedness. One of his most difficult temptations, he reported, occurred in 1845 when John Greenleaf Whittier and Wilson carried antislavery petitions to Washington. John Quincy Adams hosted a dinner for them. With so many eminent men present, Wilson had difficulty in refusing a glass of wine. But once he did, he was never again embarrassed refusing liquor. For a man who enjoyed the company of others and whose political success was in part sustained by his congenial and sociable nature, Wilson's abstinence is remarkable. Communities in which he lived contained temperance societies; Wilson joined and supported them. As early as 1831 he was a member of the society in Farmington. Natick contained both a Young Men's Temperance Society, founded in 1845, and a Sons of Temperance, founded in 1848.[29]

Robert L. Hampel, in his study of *Temperance and Prohibition in Massachusetts, 1813–1852,* concluded that the temperance movement, especially until the 1840s, was composed of people from diverse classes of society, including a considerable number of men of property and position. There was a religious difference; the more evangelical the denomination to which people belonged, the more its members were likely to be temperance advocates. More Congregationalists were temperance supporters than Unitarians. The American Temperance Society, organized in Boston in 1825, was controlled by its Massachusetts leadership. The state society was founded in 1825; until 1853 its president was always the governor of the state. In the early 1830s Massachusetts temperance adherents advocated moral suasion; by the end of the decade they were increasingly calling for prohibition.

Those determined to control liquor consumption legally first tried to harass drinkers by stiffening licensing standards and raising operating fees; most of these actions were at the local level. In 1837 the state legislature prohibited Sunday sales of liquor and provided for temperance inns. In the late 1830s the temperance movement split. The new Massachusetts Temperance Union supported passage of the fifteen-gallon law, which Hampel counted as a moderate approach. Passed in 1838, this law banned the sale of distilled spirits in quantities of less than fifteen gallons. It also removed the state from the licensing of liquor businesses. Strong sentiments by both the advocates and opponents of this law shook the political parties, just as they would on many other occasions during Wilson's lifetime. The electorate responded in 1839 by awarding an unaccustomed victory to the Democratic candidate for governor. The fifteen-gallon law was consequently repealed.[30]

Wilson began his political career running on a temperance platform in the fall of 1839. He lost by a few votes in a year when temperance advocates and Whigs generally did not do well. This decision to run, however, opened a new life to Wilson. By the next year he was a candidate again and this time he won. He continued for most of the next decade to be a part-time politician as his shoe business grew. After 1848 he abandoned manufacturing and became as much a professional politician as the antebellum era produced.[31]

Wilson had been brought up a Democrat, according to reports published during his lifetime.[32] One of his childhood benefactors, Judge Whitehouse in Farmington, was a Democrat; so, as the story goes, was Wilson's father. Mann contended that at the age of fifteen Wilson read in the *Dover Gazette* a sharp criticism of John Marshall's biography of George Washington, which had convinced the writer that Democratic doctrines were wrong. The perplexed boy walked many miles and lost two nights' sleep to obtain the book to judge for himself. He arrived at the same conclusion the other man had and became a Whig, Mann asserted. Wilson was fortunate to have escaped from the Democratic party, which would control New Hampshire almost until the Civil War. Had he become a Democrat, he either would have been subservient to the Slave Power or he would have had no, or a very different, political career. Marshall's book may have influenced Wilson's thinking; it could hardly have determined his political affiliation, even when he was twenty-one. The second party system of Democrats and Whigs was only beginning its development in the years between the election of John Quincy Adams to the presidency in 1825 and the reelection of Andrew Jackson in 1832. Furthermore, Mann himself offers other explanations. His 1884 report of Wilson's argument with fellow cobblers over the removal of the bank deposits by Jackson portrayed that issue as being of greater importance. Mann's 1904 article suggested the young Wilson's inability to obtain a job when his indenture was completed caused him to question an administration, and a party, whose policies had failed to create better national economic conditions.[33] Wilson himself asserted that he had "shouted" for Jackson in the campaign of 1828—he hadn't been old enough to vote—and that he cast aside his Democratic affiliations only when he became an abolitionist, because of the impossibility of being a Democrat and an antislavery advocate at the same time.[34]

Other sources assert the trip to Washington in 1836 or the strong support given by Massachusetts Whigs to the freedoms of press and petition made Wilson a Whig. Bacon, who ought to have known, credited the Southern trip, with its exposure to slavery. Nason and Russell, in equally informed positions, considered the ruinous financial policies of the Martin Van Buren administration in response to the Panic of 1837 as propelling Wilson to Whiggery. If the latter were true, Wilson's political conversion would be late. He had been old enough to vote since 1833. No contemporary disclosed for whom he voted prior to support of the Whig ticket in 1838. Probably his frequent changes of residence left him ineligible at least for several of the elections and 1838 was his first vote cast. In any case, being a Whig in Natick offered the best opportunity for political success. The Whig candidate for governor in 1838, Edward Everett, received 136 votes in Natick; his Democratic opponent, Marcus Morton, garnered only 52.[35]

In the first fifty years of American independence, only four states furnished presidents: Virginia, Massachusetts, Tennessee, and New York. Massachusetts had played and would continue to play a primary role in national political affairs. Too much tied to the Federalist party in the early nineteenth century, the state declined in influence after the War of 1812. The election of John Quincy Adams to the presidency in 1825, the return of a two party system in the late 1820s and early 1830s, and the leadership of Massachusetts in the emerging industrial revolution restored the state's influence. Between 1820 and the end of the Civil War Massachusetts furnished the secretary of state for four presidents and the secretary of the treasury for two. Its senators—Webster, Everett, Davis, Winthrop, Sumner, and Wilson—would be among the most influential of those serving in Congress.

One of the new parties which came into existence was the Democratic, united behind Andrew Jackson from the mid-1820s to the late-1830s. Former seacoast Federalists and more radical elements among the Jeffersonian Republicans became the nucleus for the Democratic party in Massachusetts. Among the founders were David Henshaw, wire puller of the urban wing of the party, who became its strategist and press spokesman, and Marcus Morton, leader of the rural element. Between 1828 and 1833 the Anti-Masonic party also garnered support, gathering the second highest number of votes in the state elections of 1831. Its press spokesman was Benjamin F. Hallett, who subsequently became a Democratic leader. In the early 1830s as well a Workingman's movement and party temporarily competed for influence. Democrats, especially George Bancroft, the historian and diplomat, wooed many of its members and attached them to the emerging Jacksonian party. Morton and Bancroft sought to make the Democrats the party of reform, but the Boston clique was more concerned with protecting property rights. In any case, Henshaw, Hallett, Morton, and Bancroft dominated Massachusetts Democratic politics for more than two decades.

This was a strange political party, not expecting and seldom attaining statewide political victory. Its primary source of strength derived from patronage awarded from Washington. After eleven attempts, Morton won the governorship by a few votes in 1839, primarily because of the Whig position on the fifteen-gallon law. He lasted only a year. In 1842 Morton was returned principally because of issues extraneous to Massachusetts and elected not by a majority of the popular vote, but by the legislature in a three-cornered contest including the Liberty party candidate. By then the Democrats were dividing into Morton-Bancroft and Henshaw-Hallett wings.[36]

The Whig party both in Massachusetts and the nation has sometimes been characterized as the organization of the rich. Was a shoe manufacturer, a Henry Wilson, an unusual adherent? If so, then charges which opponents sometimes raised that Wilson was primarily motivated by ambition and became a Whig because that party controlled the state, might have been true. However, the evidence supports the opposite view. First, Wilson's best chances for a political career lay within the majority Whig party, which he left in 1848. Second, while most Northern rich men were Whigs, most Whigs were not Northern rich men. William R. Brock insightfully has pointed out that Horace Greeley, more than any other man the editorial spokesman of Whiggery, supported the protective tariff, just as Wilson did. Greeley believed the tariff secured higher living standards for American working people while at the same time contributing to industrial development, which he regarded as essential for promoting the general welfare. As a further example, two other New York Whigs and later Wilson friends, William H. Seward and Thurlow Weed, did not see themselves in the 1830s as emissaries of the rich, but as representatives of the anti-elitist, anti-monopoly, anti-Masonic people of the small towns and farming areas of western New York. The Whigs of 1840, Brock wrote, were the party of "moral, social, and political regeneration." They were the party of "character," and included not only the rich, but hard-working, respectable, and thrifty workingmen.[37]

The merchant class as Federalists had dominated Massachusetts politics until the 1820s. For the first fifty years of the commonwealth's history, according to a study by Edward Pessen, Boston's richest 10 percent owned slightly more than 50 percent of the city's wealth. Through the Suffolk Bank, through railroads, through marketing and manufacturing, one group dominated the state economically. Having captured economic control of the state, manufacturing became politically dominant, too. The Lawrences, Lowells, and Appletons were assured and dynamic. As Massachusetts developed, the distance between the elite and others became greater—in Boston as in other large American cities. The wealthiest men were commonly not self-made. Boston's social structure possessed little fluidity. Seldom did anyone fall from high to low class; while the population of the city rose 70 percent between 1833 and 1848, 74 percent of those men in the richest group of the earlier date were still there fifteen years later; 21 percent had disappeared, died, or moved. This was a social nobility, as well as economic. Leaders of the pre–Civil War generation had names familiar to colonial society: Winthrop, Saltonstall, Sedgwick, Lyman. Clergy families, many politicians, professors at Harvard, and lawyers intermarried with the new manufacturing class to "forge an aristocracy," as Ronald Story labeled it. Essex County and the new Lowell-Lawrence gentry intermarried with the Boston leaders.

In the 1820s the merchants declined in economic strength and were gradually replaced by a group which would command Massachusetts politics until the 1850s, first as National Republicans, later as Whigs. Between 1824 and 1830 John Quincy Adams, Daniel Webster, and Levi Lincoln created the party. They put forth impressive candidates for office in the 1830s: "Honest John" Davis and Daniel Webster as United States senators, Edward Everett as congressman and governor. While power resided in Boston and its environs, this was an age of emerging democracy, when increasingly large numbers of men could and did vote. State elections could not be won, nor enough legislators persuaded to vote "right," unless agricultural and some other economic interests of the state were willing to support what the Boston industrial and financial leadership wanted. That support came.[38]

Third party movements confused the emerging political system. The Anti-Masons were second in the gubernatorial contest in 1831, garnering more votes than the Democrat Morton; but they declined rapidly after 1833. The Liberty party, organized in 1840 as an antislavery alternative to the two major parties, was also opposed by the William Lloyd Garrison faction of the abolitionists, who objected to political action. As a result, one of the most antislavery states in the nation contributed only a little over 1,000 votes to James G. Birney, the 1840 Liberty party presidential nominee. Yet in 1841 the party received almost 3,500 votes and it continued to grow until 1846. By 1843 its 6,000 votes prevented major party candidates for state office from attaining a majority, bringing about the selection of Morton as governor by the state legislature.[39]

With the Democrats divided into factions, Henshaw and Hallett quarreling over banking, Henshaw antagonistic to the Morton-Bancroft faction over patronage, and President Martin Van Buren, a Democrat, blamed for the consequences of the Panic of 1837, Whigs rather easily elected Everett governor in 1837 and 1838. The controversy over the fifteen-gallon law resulted in a Democratic victory in 1839, but Morton did not last long. The political campaign of 1840 brought out voters in numbers few campaigns ever have. John Davis became governor more on national than on state issues. Massachusetts Whigs won the governorship every election but two between 1834 and 1848. They controlled both houses of the legislature every year but one. Every United States senatorship and all but four congressional elections went to Whigs during those years. The party knew how to win. It commanded excellent leadership, able political speakers, an effective press, good organization, plenty of money, principles a majority of the voters supported, and, in an age of viva voce voting, the ability to use economic pressure to help assure the right outcome when the votes were counted.[40]

Shortly after Wilson lost his first bid for political office, a fortuitous debate invigorated his political prospects. A new Natick resident, Charles Herring, a Democrat, engaged Wilson in a lively discussion at the country-store post office. Soon the two decided to argue the merits of their respective political parties at the lyceum. They later agreed to a public debate near the end of February or the beginning of March, 1840. Attendance was large; this was the opening volley in what was to become one of the nation's most exciting political campaigns. Herring was badly beaten. He blamed his loss on his inexperience as a debater. Mann declared the Democrat lacked the facts to match Wilson.[41]

What began as a personal encounter turned into a prominent event. Wilson generated in writing eighteen or twenty charges against the Democratic party and the administration of Van Buren. The defeated Herring proposed that the currency controversy alone be debated further at an additional meeting on March 21. Joseph Fuller of nearby Framingham, the party's "big gun" in that part of the state, would be substituted as Democratic spokesman. Wilson hastened to Westford to persuade Mann to return to Natick to help him prepare. The honor of Natick, the reputation of the Whig party, the esteem held for the debating society were all at stake, Wilson contended. Mann was needed for a week to help gather evidence. Later in Deacon Coolidge's parlor they worked. Mann assumed Fuller's role. They both attacked the Democratic currency stance; then they took Whig positions and perfected them. In a few days they had so much ammunition that the rest of the week could be spent separating the most usable from the remainder.[42]

The Democrats expected victory. The Methodist church was filled. Fuller and his friends were late. When they arrived, they were taken back by the mass of evidence assembled by Mann and Wilson and laying on the desk. Fuller claimed he had misunderstood: he thought he was to discuss only the Van Buren subtreasury system; Wilson had come to treat the broader currency question. But provisions for the debate had been put in writing so Herring had to confirm Wilson's interpretation. While he had prepared to respond to Fuller's initial defenses of Democratic currency positions and while the narrowed topic would render the first part of his speech useless, the angry Wilson was so eager to debate that he consented to speak first. He sought to demonstrate that the national government had the power to furnish the country with a sound and uniform currency and that every American president had acknowledged that power. Even Andrew Jackson, in ending the Second United States Bank, had promised a better currency system. Jackson's had the government's funds deposited in "pet banks," state-chartered banks which had the right political connections. This had kindled inflation and helped cause the Panic, Wilson asserted. In addition to Jackson, Wilson attacked John C. Calhoun, James Buchanan, and Robert Walker. Interestingly enough, in the 1850s and 1860s Wilson would blame the latter two more than many others for their role in producing the Civil War. When Wilson finished speaking, the audience cheered. The flustered Fuller had not anticipated a presentation so skilled and elaborate. He made a few allusions to the subtreasury system, mentioned the late hour, and sat down. Wilson claimed the remainder of his adversary's time and used it. Mann reported the debate yielded twenty-eight new Whigs. He also believed Wilson's performance assured his entry into the 1840 campaign.[43]

The Democrats were unwilling to admit defeat. Herring secured another meeting for April 3. The Democrats brought in Amasa Walker, even better known and a more effective speaker than Fuller. Walker, forty years old, had been a merchant in Boston, beginning in the boot and shoe business in 1825. He had retired in 1840 in a sound financial condition. He had participated in the antislavery movement since the early 1830s and was prominently connected with the Massachusetts Anti-Slavery Society. He was also active in both the temperance and peace crusades. A National Republican until 1829 or 1830, then an Anti-Mason, Walker was a Democrat at the end of the 1830s, both because he was an advocate of free trade and because he regarded the National Bank as dangerous to the nation. Walker was not the typical Democrat. In the previous two debates, Wilson's opponents had supported Jackson's policy of placing government funds in pet banks. Walker, in contrast, was allied with the Thomas Hart Benton wing of the party, which objected to banking in principle, whether national or state. Walker was a formidable adversary to debate on economic issues.[44]

After his previous experience with Fuller, Wilson must not have been surprised when Walker ignored the Jackson position on financial matters. Wilson charged that the Democrats had agreed on a topic, "Is the financial policy of the past and present administrations beneficial to the country?" Walker had not defended that policy. The chairman of the debate agreed. In fact, Walker was not prepared to meet the question, as defined. Wilson's argument was not against paper money, but against the Democratic abuse of it; he also contended that specie did not deserve the importance which Walker bestowed upon it. By the conclusion of the evening, Wilson had made a new friend. He also had begun a new career.[45]

The Whigs needed a different approach if ever they were to win on the national level. The party had tried nominating nationally recognized leaders like John Quincy Adams, in 1828, and Henry Clay, in 1832, and had lost. It had employed another tactic in 1836—putting forth different men in different sections of the country—and had again been defeated. In 1840, with the nation still suffering from the Panic of 1837 and with an unpopular Martin Van Buren as president, Whigs scented victory; yet they needed another type of candidate and another kind of campaign. Charged by their opponents as being antagonistic to the rise of the common man and as being a party controlled by aristocrats and industrialists, the Whigs determined they would win only by out-demagoguing the Democrats. They would utilize tactics similar to those Van Buren himself had employed to secure the election of Jackson in 1828. Adopting no platform, they nominated for the presidency William Henry Harrison, victor over the Indians at the Battle of Tippecanoe and over the British at the Battle of the Thames, and for the vice-presidency John Tyler, a conservative states-power advocate from Virginia. They would present their patrician candidates as men of the people and herald "Tippecanoe and Tyler, too." Before long a Democratic editor had attacked Harrison as content to retire to a log cabin with hard cider and thus supplied the

Whigs with another opportunity to set forth their community with the common people.

What the Whigs needed for this campaign were speakers "of humble origin with the vocabulary and accent of the workingmen."[46] Among this new breed of campaigners were John W. Bear, "the Buckeye Blacksmith," who delivered 331 speeches in eight states; teamster Tom Corwin, the later Ohio Whig leader who in 1840 in four months stumped for one hundred speeches; Elihu Burritt, "the learned blacksmith"; and Abraham Lincoln. These men would convince the voters "that the Whig party was the party of the blacksmiths, cobblers, wagon drivers, and railsplitters of America."[47] No political campaign until then had aroused so much enthusiasm. Mass meetings were held; log cabins were erected, sometimes hauled from town to town; immense processions were formed, including many by torchlight. Even the usually sedate Massachusetts Whig state convention had a log cabin, hard cider atmosphere.[48]

Massachusetts was one state in which the Whigs desperately needed to project a new image. It is surprising how many of the politicians who would work closely with Wilson during the next three decades began their rise to political prominence about this time. Some, like E. R. Hoar, would have blossomed in the old aristocratic setting. Young Democrats active in this campaign, like Nathaniel P. Banks, George S. Boutwell, and Benjamin P. Butler, would also have carried their party's standard if campaigns had continued in the style of the 1830s. But Wilson, Charles R. Train, William S. Robinson, and others emerged in this new setting. Wilson was nicknamed "the Natick Cobbler," a title effectively utilized by the Whig press to attract the votes of the workingmen.[49]

Wilson was discovered by party leaders when he attended an East Needham meeting featuring John C. Park and some other Boston Whigs. When the speakers had finished, the crowd began to call for an additional address from Wilson. The embarrassed country boy hesitated to try and, at first, he did poorly. But as he continued, Wilson's speaking became more effective. Audiences of the time expected either humorous stories or an array of facts; Wilson gave them the latter. Park and his friends concluded this would be an effective representative to be sent into the agricultural and industrial communities of the state. Wilson subsequently delivered more than sixty speeches in the campaign, an amazing demand on his time, considering his dependence upon income from his shoe business and the fact that this was the summer of his marriage. Among the localities in which he spoke were Cambridge, Charlestown, Roxbury, Lowell, Lynn, and Taunton.[50]

A few comments and accounts survive about this period in Wilson's life. William P. Kelley, subsequently Republican congressman from Pennsylvania, later spoke of Wilson's "earnestness, simplicity, directness of character, his knowledge of facts, his clearness of statement" in the campaign.[51] N. A. Richardson, a Democratic opponent, charged at Woburn that if the Whigs were elected, they would assume state debts by using the proceeds from the sale of public lands or the surplus in the treasury, favorite proposals of Henry Clay. Wilson a few nights later denied the charge and retorted that Richardson must have "brass enough in his face to make a skillet and sap enough in his head to fill it."[52] The *Boston Post,* one of the most partisan of the Democratic newspapers, began to speak favorably about the new politician. Reporting on a large meeting in Charlestown, a writer characterized Wilson's address as "far superior" to most Whig speeches. Wilson's main theme was that merchants, manufacturers, and farmers were all in distress and that Jackson, who had promised reform, had engendered only a spoils system. Wilson denounced Democratic activities in the customs houses and post offices. He defended both the Second National Bank and state banks.[53]

The hard cider nature of the campaign must have troubled the advocate of temperance. Furthermore, the vice-presidential nominee was a defender of slavery, while Harrison opposed abolition agitation. Years later Wilson would write of the candidates, "While anti-slavery men had little to hope from" Harrison, "they had everything to fear from" Tyler.[54] If he thought much the same in 1840, then were Wilson's own business ambitions causing him to join forces with the wealthy and influential Boston Whigs to wage the campaign on the economic issues which had become so important in the 1830s? Or was Wilson politically ambitious and flattered by the attention he was getting? A case can be made for either contention. A better judgment would be that Wilson had seen Whig political opposition to slaveholders from the galleries of Congress and that he was satisfied with his party as the best channel through which to achieve his ends of temperance and abolition. Furthermore, he agreed with many of the economic positions of his party.

Wilson's work paid off. Harrison won Massachusetts by more than twenty thousand votes and carried the Electoral College easily. Wilson himself was elected as a Whig member of the legislature from Natick.[55]

By 1841 a junto had emerged which would control Natick politics for a generation. Wilson was its leader. Edward Walcott seldom occupied political office, but was active in counsel and one of the most influential men of the community. Pastor Hunt characterized him as imperturbable, sagacious, a "wonderful executive." George Herring was another leader; his counting room was the usual site for junto meetings. Hunt recalled Herring as being young, genial, enthusiastic, fond of books and society. Then there was Mann, intelligent, cool headed, clear thinking, and deliberate in thought and speech. His education was better than Wilson's and his services became substantial to his friend's political career. Another associate was Benjamin F. Ham, also a native of Farmington, who, after his migration to Natick, developed a lasting friendship with Wilson. A schoolmaster, Ham taught until 1853, then became a lawyer and clerk of the court. Hunt, as previously mentioned, was another important political influence.[56]

In January of 1841 Wilson began his career as a legislator. The session of the Massachusetts General Court lasted from January 6 to March 18, not too serious a drain of time from shoe manufacturing. The Massachusetts House in which

Wilson served was composed of 350 members, but only sixty were needed for a quorum. The Whigs always controlled Boston; its forty representatives were selected by a city committee dominated by an in-group. At least in part because of that unity, the city's influence in the House was out of proportion to its population or its number of representatives. Members of the House sat on long seats which did not have cushions. A drawer underneath the seat provided storage for documents. Four wood fires, one in each corner of the hall, supplied the heat for the winter sessions. Members wore their overcoats and hats; when a man arose to speak, he was to remove his hat. At the time Wilson must have regarded his new position as a happy but incidental event, without perceiving that politics would eventually become his primary interest and source of income.[57]

Wilson was not particularly active his first term. Few new House members were. He was in constant attendance and did serve on the Joint Committee on Manufacturers. While limited to observing the activities of others, Wilson nevertheless was intent on learning. He paid an old farmer who had drawn a front row seat three dollars for his place. Wilson's maiden speech, on January 25, 1841, was against a bill to exempt laborers' wages from attachment in certain cases of bankruptcy. He claimed the number of lazy men was increasing and that honest poor men wanted to pay their debts. While he sympathized with all workingmen, he said, he did not think the proposed law was what they needed. He moved to strike out the enacting clause of the bill. Biographers Nason and Russell later assessed this vote as "in favor of the working man."[58]

Mann asserted that the election of able and forceful workingmen like Wilson was the beginning of a new era in Massachusetts politics. The legislature had contained mechanics and farmers before, but these men had been expected to play little role in legislative activities. Wilson, in contrast, intended to participate actively in state affairs. His new House associate, newspaper editor William L. Schouler, was gratified by Wilson's election, characterizing him as a "young man of good talents" whose choice had been a reward for his political energy.[59]

Wilson's friendship with fellow legislator William Schouler was important at this moment in his life. Younger than Wilson, Schouler was born in Scotland in 1814 and as a boy immigrated to the United States. First living on Staten Island, the family moved to West Cambridge, Massachusetts, where Schouler worked with his father in bleaching and printing cloth. He also developed a zeal for writing. In 1839 he attended a Whig county convention, held that year in his town, and was chosen for the county committee. The next year he was active in the Whig political campaign. In 1842 he purchased the *Boston Courier,* which he and his assistant William P. Robinson turned into one of the most influential newspapers in the state, espousing the Whig cause with ability and vigor. Schouler continued to publish in Lowell until 1847, when he was offered the editorship of the influential *Boston Atlas.* He was notably instrumental in making Middlesex County Whig.[60]

In spite of his more than a year of secondary school studies, his wealth of reading, his participation in the debating society, and his associations with many of the better educated people of Farmington and Natick, Wilson had much to learn about delivering an address and writing. His speaking style was still in its infancy. On the one hand, he carefully prepared, often memorizing parts of what he would say. He sometimes rehearsed in Deacon Coolidge's oak grove. His debating experiences had also taught him extempore skills. He became renowned for speeches loaded with facts; his first campaign was no exception. Nason and Russell reported that "he usually bent ever the desk in speaking, as if to come as closely in contact with his audience as he could."[61]

Conversely, Wilson had problems that prevented greater success. E. R. Hoar recorded that during the 1840 campaign Wilson sought out a friend in Hoar's community to put into proper English a resolution which Wilson wanted to offer to a convention; Wilson could not do it himself. His long-time associate George Boutwell, who first met the young cobbler in 1842, asserted that he saw Wilson papers in which capital letters were not used to start sentences. "His style of speaking was heavy and unattractive," Boutwell also remembered.[62] In 1843 Wilson wrote to invite historian George Bancroft to speak at the Natick lyceum. One would suppose the writer would be careful in composition. The letter is legible, but is filled with run-on sentences. Pastor Hunt recorded that, considering the legislator's literary limitations and his terrible spelling, his frequent efforts to write for newspapers were bold. Wilson would jot down his ideas on paper and then take them to Hunt to prepare for the press. When Schouler asked Wilson to contribute letters about the tariff, Wilson replied he didn't write much; he did not like to. Still, he promised to send an article the next week. One of the abler journalists of his generation, William Robinson, the famous "Warrington," wrote that Wilson in 1840 was "not so much incapable of writing grammatically as of spelling and *dividing* correctly." "Warrington," however, was not distressed; he contended "the man who thinks correctly will learn to speak and write with tolerable accuracy." Wilson's rhetoric, Robinson added, was often better than that of his renowned colleague, Charles Sumner.[63]

Wilson's voting record as a House legislator is difficult to ascertain both because of the limited number of recorded votes and the sketchy nature of newspaper reports. What is clear, however, is that he was almost always voting with the majority (his party) and that he was participating in the general political and social reform movement which was still transforming the nation even after the departure of Jackson from the White House. Of course, bills which the Whig leadership did not want to reach the House floor usually did not, so Wilson could not express his views on those issues. The Whig leadership was able most of the time to restrict reforms to those with which it agreed. Twice Wilson voted with the majority to accept a report on the expediency of amending the state constitution to end a tax on voting. He also supported a bill to abolish imprisonment for debt. One committee took what was regarded as a liberal stand by seeking the abolition of capital punishment in the commonwealth, except for the crimes of murder and arson at night, if death resulted. Wilson voted with the majority for the proposal. The Natick Whig was also a supporter of internal improvements and of the national government's distributing proceeds from the sale of public lands to the states. Curiously, this legislature was the only one for years which passed no resolution which abolitionists characterized as favorable to their cause.[64]

Voters in the autumn of 1841 reelected Wilson. He again was placed on the House's Committee on Manufacturers. With the Panic continuing to affect the economy of the state, the committee was directed to inquire into the subject of the tariff and that part of the governor's annual message which dealt with the protection of labor. Wilson wrote the elaborate report, including proposed resolutions. His stance was that the gradually lower rates provided for in the Compromise Tariff of 1833 had been a failure. Those levels would become even lower in July of 1842. The revenue needs of the nation were not being met and the national debt was increasing, he pointed out. Neither was the government responding to the nation's needs for national defense. The report advocated discriminating duties. It objected to a duty on tea, which taxed the poorer people for a commodity the United States could not itself produce. Wilson argued for a duty on goods which would both obtain revenue and protect the worker. This position was one he would hold to for the rest of his life.

The report sought a commonality of interests. The "real contest" was between domestic and foreign labor, Wilson argued; if protection were not provided, American workers would have to compete with the "half-starved laborer of Europe." He admitted that consumer and producer interests clashed, but he emphasized that the two were dependent upon one another. His argument was that the more employment there was, the more wages; the more wages, the more purchasing; the more purchasing, the more business. Everyone would gain. He even asserted that the cotton-growing states would benefit as New England manufacturers and consumers bought more of their production. On recommendation of its committee the House resolved in favor of "radical revision of the revenue laws" to encourage domestic industry by the assessment of specific and discriminating duties. Massachusetts congressmen were asked to carry forth the opinions expressed in the resolutions.[65]

Wilson's other major assignment was the chairmanship of a special committee on whether and for what sum the West Boston and Canal Bridges could be purchased by the state and whether tolls should be charged to pay for the purchase. The bridges' charters had thirty-six years yet to run. If the state treated these bridges as it had the Warren and Charles River Bridges, the cost of purchase could be paid before the charters expired. The committee met with the directors of the companies that owned the bridges, and each company established a sum it expected to be paid. The West Boston Bridge directors were unable to fix a fair price, but were willing to accept an amount set by disinterested persons. The committee favored state action.[66]

Wilson had hardly begun his political life when he was accused by the *Concord* (Massachusetts) *Freeman* of seeking appointment to office. At this early stage of his career he was not used to this type of attack and he responded defensively. Wilson asserted to Schouler that he sought no office, had not applied for one, and expected to support himself by his shoe business. He asked Schouler to reply to the charges and was grateful when the editor did.[67]

Wilson had become a Whig in part because of what he perceived to be the party's position in reference to slavery. In the 1830s he had participated, admittedly perfunctorily, in the blossoming militant antislavery crusade. He read William Lloyd Garrison's *Liberator* regularly. But the still small antislavery movement itself divided in 1839–1840, primarily over two issues. One was the role which women should play in the movement. The other was caused by the conviction of some of the leaders—among them Elizur Wright Jr., James G. Birney, and Henry B. Stanton—that the religious-moral crusade could not attain its ends by the means being used and that it would dissipate over internal controversy about tactics. Abolition to succeed required political action. One result of the division was the capture of the American Anti-Slavery Society by those opposed to political action, Garrison and his associates. They continued to control it until slavery was abolished. Some of their opponents founded the weak American and Foreign Anti-Slavery Society to agitate using traditional reform methods. In Massachusetts by the 1840s the Garrisonians dominated the antislavery scene and young men like Wilson were often reluctant to get entangled in the arguments. Other abolitionists turned to politics. Those who supported the new, abolition Liberty party hoped it could secure increasing numbers of votes on both the state and national levels. Most authorities agree that the militant antislavery movement in its first decade attracted far more support from those who had been Whigs than from those who had been Democrats. Wilson as early as the summer of 1841 was disappointed with the first Whig administration in Washington under Tyler. Yet he believed the Whig party was the best political means through which to attack slavery.[68]

Wilson's trust in the antislavery position of the Whig party was based on both personal hope and past party performance. The Massachusetts delegation in Congress in 1836 been unanimous in its opposition to the "gag rule," by which the House automatically tabled memorials and petitions on the subject of slavery. It had continued that stand in 1837. In April of 1837 the Whig-dominated Massachusetts legislature passed resolutions condemning the rule. When the House of Representatives would not permit the resolutions to be presented, the Massachusetts congressmen officially informed the legislature, which responded in 1838 with more resolutions vindicating the right of petition and registering a moderate antislavery stance. The same legislature only several years before had threatened to place its prestige behind actions of its own committees which would have supported limitations upon the freedoms of speech, press, and assembly of abolitionists. By the late 1830s, however, the Whigs of the state appeared to be united in their opposition to the slave trade, expansion of slavery into the territories, and curtailments of the civil rights of those publicly working to end the institution. When Congress responded to the question of recognizing the new slave republic of Texas, Massachusetts Senators Webster and Davis voted affirmatively; the Senate passed the resolution unanimously. The Massachusetts House delegation, however, split. Conservative leaders Abbott Lawrence and Levi Lincoln both voted against recognition; so did later Conscience Whig Stephen C. Phillips. The step was hardly an endorsement of slavery. Many reasons could prompt congressmen to support recognition. More revealing of the party position, all but one of the Massachusetts delegation in Washington in 1836 voted against the annexation of Texas to the United States.[69]

Members of the militant abolition societies of the 1830s and 1840s quickly became disreputable in the judgment of the Massachusetts Whig leaders. Those otherwise acceptable to society who joined the movement, like Wendell Phillips, Edmund Quincy, and William Jackson, were ostracized. The controversy over slavery, even if legally permissible, even if morally understandable, endangered the tranquility of the nation, the good business relations between North and South, and the many social, religious, economic, and political associations among the gentry of the nation. Massachusetts manufacturing and shipping magnates had much in common with cotton planters and both knew it. Furthermore, leaders of the two sections frequently attended the same colleges, their families vacationed at the same locations, and the young men and women sometimes found their spouses among the aristocracy in the other section. The eastern Massachusetts elite believed the Founding Fathers had accepted slavery as a part of the national compact and their descendents might have to live with it. Only Southern states themselves could take action to eradicate it. Yet the eastern Massachusetts elite also believed in the late 1830s and early 1840s that they did not have to agree to the expansion of slavery, nor did they have to permit the demands of the slaveholders to interfere with the institutions and values of New England.[70]

Among the laws of Massachusetts was one which prohibited marriage between a black and a white. Garrison and his supporters agitated for repeal of that law almost from the beginning of their movement. By 1837 frequent petitions were reaching the legislature praying for an end of discrimination, meaning an end of the marriage restriction. When a house of the legislature would debate the issue, it would quarrel over the qualifications of the petitioners rather than consider the merits of the appeal. In early 1839 Garrison, Birney, Stanton, and Wendell Phillips at a public mass meeting in Boston's Marlboro Chapel attacked legislators who had opposed the petitions. The legislature was then in session; some of it members heard the speeches. By the end of 1839 support was growing; nine thousand signatures were obtained for repeal. The House in 1840 responded with the requested bill, but the Senate amended it and the House would not agree to the amended form. The following year the Senate, by a majority of only one vote, agreed to a similar bill, which lost in the House by a large 140-to-204 margin. Wilson favored passage. Again in 1842 the Senate voted for a bill by a wide margin of 24 to 9. Wilson, again supportive, on February 15 argued that the marriage statute was based upon wrong principles. He emphasized that no other New England state had such a law. After long debate, however, the proposal was again rejected. The 1843 legislature, controlled by the Democrats and without Wilson, passed the reform.[71]

Wilson's other support for the abolitionists manifested more leadership. On January 15, 1842, he presented a petition from the Massachusetts Anti-Slavery Society requesting permission to use the hall of the House on Thursday, January 27, for its annual meeting. Why Wilson, of all the many House members, was asked to present the petition cannot be explained. Furthermore, if the young politician was as ambitious as he sometimes was accused of being, then why he took an action to which the Whig gentry clearly would be averse is also unfathomable. The petition was referred to the Committee on Public Buildings, whose response on January 19 was negative. The next day Wilson moved to recommit the proposal with instructions to report in its favor. An alternate proposal to grant use of the hall, with the House at the same time disclaiming any approval of the doctrines or acts of the society, was lost by better than a two-to-one majority. The Wilson motion was adopted and the society used the room.[72]

The defeat in 1841 of the bill to end the prohibition of mixed marriages demonstrated to Wilson and others who thought like him that they needed to be better organized if the legislature were to be persuaded to take a correct antislavery stance. Wilson and his associates from the debating society began to meet in the shoeshop of George Herring to discuss what they should do. They decided that thereafter no delegate from Natick should be selected to Whig conventions unless he supported their antislavery positions. They sought to obtain a similar attitude in neighboring towns. They would promote appropriate actions from church bodies; that task was assigned to Hunt. They would obtain control of the Norfolk *Country American,* then for sale; it became the first Whig newspaper in the state devoted to their cause. Wilson became the organizer who was to persuade the press and local, county, and state Whig conventions to take appropriate positions against slavery. This took not brilliance, Mann later reminisced, but simple hard work.[73]

Many legislative districts commonly did not elect the same man more than once or twice. Only about 30 percent of House members were returned. In the age of Jacksonian democracy, unless one was particularly qualified for office by outstanding past service or by family position, the officeholder was expected to step aside and let someone else contribute. Perhaps that is the reason Wilson did not seek a third term in the House. He knew as early as June he would not be nominated, but he was willing to run for one of the five Middlesex County Senate seats. Unfortunately for Wilson, 1842 was one of the rare Democratic years. The county in any case had been Democratic.[74]

In 1843 the Whigs of Middlesex County again selected Wilson as their senatorial candidate. He was becoming so well connected that he could persuade Charles Francis Adams to come from Boston to deliver an address in Wilson's behalf. The people at the polls gave neither Wilson nor his Democratic opponent a majority. According to the state constitution, the lower House, Whig controlled, would choose. Wilson was naturally selected. His party in the Senate appointed their new colleague as chairman of the Joint Committee on the Militia.[75]

Wilson had long been interested in the military. As a youth he read extensively about the exploits of Wolfe, Wellington, Washington, Napoleon, and other generals. During his indenture on the Knight farm in New Hampshire, he enlisted in the local militia. He also joined the Massachusetts volunteer organization and served for nine years. Natick in 1841 enrolled 205 soldiers; by 1845 that number had increased to 403. In 1843, without his knowledge or consent, Wilson was elected major in the Middlesex artillery regiment. His friend and legislative colleague, William Schouler, became colonel and Nathaniel Banks, later a close political associate, was quartermaster. When Schouler moved to Boston, Wilson was elected colonel, later brigadier general for the Third Brigade, in charge of 800 men. He exercised that command for five years. He worked diligently to revive the military organizations, secure enlistments, and train the troops. Thereafter he was often referred to as General Wilson. Militia service enhanced the fame and standing of an individual in the community. Conversely, Wilson's election to positions of military rank demonstrates how highly he was regarded and how much a community leader he had become.[76]

The militia was an important institution in American folklore. Those who won the American Revolution had been militiamen willing to serve in the struggle against the mother country. The organization was provided for in the Massachusetts constitution of 1780. The American constitution also recognized the usefulness of a militia by including a provision for its organizing, arming, disciplining, and calling out to enforce the laws of the nation, suppress insurrection, and repel invasion. The states had the responsibility to appoint officers and train the men. In practice in Massachusetts the men elected their own officers and the governor could only commission those elected, no matter how unfitted they might be. As memories of the Revolution and the War of 1812 faded, and as a new war appeared unlikely, legislators, taxpayers, and eligible men had come by 1840 to neglect their militia. The 1840 legislature admitted the system wasn't working and that men regarded the service as burdensome. Volunteer companies, on the other hand, often flourished. The legislature consequently established two services. One included all able-bodied men between the ages of eighteen and forty-five; it was an inactive militia, limited to enrollment. The other service was active and voluntary and authorized to muster ten thousand men. Blacks were excluded. Men in its units did not enlist for specific terms, but participated as they chose.[77]

When Wilson assumed the chairmanship of the Joint Committee he knew much needed to be done. Arsenals were in poor condition, the militia lacked arms, the expense of obtaining uniforms and attending drill often deterred men from volunteering. The legislature had received many petitions asking for modifications of the militia laws or reorganization of the system. Wilson's committee drew up a report rejecting a return to the older scheme, which it labeled "useless and inefficient." The existing system provided for enrollment and engendered enough enlistments, Wilson concluded. The levels of discipline and compensation for service, however, were inadequate. Wilson's committee proposed the payment of one dollar for inspection duty, one dollar and a half for two company drills, and two dollars for the annual inspection and review. Payment would be made by the cities and towns, but they would subsequently be reimbursed by the state. Whig leader Levi Lincoln attacked Wilson so vituperatively that Charles Francis Adams, for one, reconsidered his own opposition to the bill. The Senate passed the proposal. This legislative experience of Wilson's was valuable for one who later would be more responsible than any other man for Civil War laws dealing with the calling out of state troops.[78]

While Wilson was obtaining experience which he could draw upon during the Civil War, he was also developing convictions about the need for a military force, peace movements, duties of citizens, and the necessity for a nation to protect itself. One of the humanitarian and reform crusades which had emerged in western Europe and the United States after the carnage of the Napoleonic Wars was a peace movement. Wilson opposed the Mexican War and, in contrast to later Senate colleagues such as Benjamin Wade and Zachariah Chandler, was troubled by the possibility of military action at the beginning of the Civil War. He was forgiving by nature, as his attitude after the Civil War towards former Confederates demonstrates. His choice of words in speeches was less belligerent than that of many of his associates, particularly than that of his longtime colleague Sumner. Yet Wilson was realistic. As he observed what was happening in Europe in the 1830s and 1840s, he concluded that the armies of Russia, Austria, and France had been able to suppress the legitimate rights of the Hungarians, Italians, and others, even their own citizens, in part because the peace movement had helped disarm peoples. He declared in 1853, "When tyranny is overthrown, and freedom established; when standing armies are disbanded, and the people armed for their own protection against arbitrary power,—then I would write 'Peace' on the banners of the people. . . . My motto is, 'LIBERTY first, PEACE afterwards!'"[79]

Wilson in the early 1840s also became a supporter of Horace Mann and his efforts to change the state's educational system. Opponents of 1830s school reform attempted in 1840 to abolish the state Board of Education, labeling it undemocratic. While the Education Committee narrowly agreed, the legislature, with the Whigs supporting Mann's reforms, refused to change. Several years later, in attempts to improve reading and control corporal punishment, Mann got into a controversy with Boston schoolmasters. Mann had published a report comparing Massachusetts schools with those of the Prussian system, which had better trained teachers and a more tempered control of its students. When some of the Boston schoolmasters ably replied, Mann's unwise response was antagonistic. His position was secured, however, when some of the schoolteachers answered in an equally poor manner. Mann emerged the victor when Everett, Sumner, Whittier, Wilson, and others came to his support.[80]

3

TEXAS

Wilson's primary interest was neither in military affairs nor schools but in slavery, and events were propelling that institution into national prominence. During the early 1830s more and more Southern farmers migrated to Texas. Many took along their slaves. The Mexican government, which at first welcomed settlement in its distant province, became increasingly concerned that Texas would be controlled by former Americans who likely would feel little loyalty to their new nation. It consequently enacted new policies which prohibited further immigration, placed additional duties on goods imported from the United States, and forbade the importation of more slaves. In the meantime friction arose between the government and the new Texas settlers over religion, land claims, and slavery. When the new Mexican chief of state, Antonio Lopez de Santa Anna, also decided to centralize the Mexican federal system, many of the former Americans rose in revolt, defeated a major Mexican army, and established their own independent nation. The Texas government sought annexation to the United States. The mid-1830s, however, was an unpropitious moment for adding new slave lands. The antislaveryites, including Wilson, detected a Southern conspiracy to obtain more slave territory, further Southern-oriented territory. Many people also opposed taking action which might provoke a war with Mexico.

Annexation of Texas became a political issue. President Martin Van Buren, seeking to avoid greater controversy over slavery, shunned annexation. In the meantime Texas's population soared from 30,000 to 142,000. Furthermore, a rebuffed Texas could not exist long without outside support, especially since the Mexican government repudiated Santa Anna's recognition of Texan independence and threatened military action. The British and French offered their support to the new republic. A nation which might provide an independent source of raw cotton and a counterweight to the growing United States was an attractive potentiality to the Europeans. Few Americans wanted on their borders either a growing and vibrant new economic or political competitor, or a nation beholden to the British or French.

The people of Massachusetts held strong opinions about Texas. The state legislature ignored the annexation issue in 1837, but in 1838 Governor Everett included the subject in his inaugural address. A joint legislative committee considered the issue and presented a report strongly opposed to annexation. In addition to practical reasons, including contentions that adding Texas to the union would lead to war with Mexico and would oblige Americans to help pay the heavy Texas debt, the committee questioned the constitutionality of annexing a foreign country. This constitutional argument was a position which the more conservative Whigs would continue to take in the 1840s. In any case, Texas in 1838 withdrew its application for annexation and the issue was set aside in the Massachusetts legislature for a number of years.[1]

John Tyler was the first vice-president to succeed to the presidency on the death of a predecessor. He had not been president long before he had alienated many of the other party leaders. He vetoed both National Bank and tariff bills devised by the Whig-controlled Congress. All members of his cabinet except Secretary of State Webster resigned. Wilson later wrote that Tyler "was an ultra slaveholder, and in feeling, sentiment, and opinion, he was narrow, bigoted, and sectional."[2] As long as Webster remained in the cabinet, Tyler did little to promote annexation. When Webster completed his important negotiations with the British and resigned, his successors eagerly sought an annexation treaty.

The United States of the second quarter of the nineteenth century was bewitched by Manifest Destiny. This concept set forth that the nation, because of the superiority of its people and institutions, was preordained to expand over most of North America and the Caribbean. The idea was not totally selfish, for Manifest Destiny would allegedly benefit other peoples who lived in the areas which might be appropriated. Citizens in all sections of the United States shared this concept. This political climate helped inspire the acquisition of Texas, the Southwest, and the Pacific coast. Until 1844, expansion was not a campaign issue dividing the two major political parties. Some leading Whigs, however,—Webster was an example—would limit their nation's ambitions by requiring that new lands be appended only through peaceful means. Some other Whigs—Henry Clay was an example—feared that a controversy over acquisition of new territory would intensify arguments over slavery and, in the process, threaten disruption of the nation. Others, of both political parties, sought to balance Northern and Southern acquisitions, presuming that people in both slave and free states would thereby be satisfied.

Tyler hoped the annexation of Texas would win for him another term as president. His own political failures prevented that. The Whigs would not nominate another unsound candidate, as they had in 1840. Rather, they sought a leader whose views accorded with those of a majority in the party. Clay was favored. The Democrats were expected to run Van Buren a third time. Willing to wage the campaign on the economic differences which had divided the parties in the 1830s, the two probable candidates agreed that each would propagate a statement at an appropriate moment by which they could disconnect the issues of slavery and Texas from the campaign.

Massachusetts Whig dissatisfaction with Tyler was early and widespread. Until the president began urging the annexation of Texas, the unhappiness was over his opposition to economic policies which the state's Whigs favored. As early as June, 1842, Wilson reported to Schouler that there wasn't a Tyler man in Natick and few in the Bay State. On the other hand, with a leader of the Massachusetts Whigs still in the cabinet, political criticism was muted. Abbott Lawrence, more than any other man the head of the Boston economic and social elite, was emphatically anti-Tyler and was angry that Webster remained in the government. The conservative Lawrence group included fellow businessman Nathan Appleton, former governors Everett, Lincoln, and John Davis, and Congressmen Robert Winthrop and Leverett Saltonstall. In the autumn of 1842 Lawrence presided over the state Whig convention in Boston, which endorsed a break between Tyler and the Whig party and precipitately nominated Clay for the presidency and John Davis for the vice-presidency.[3]

The attitudes and the convention action created a schism in the Whig party in the state. Webster, with presidential ambitions of his own, regarded the Clay nomination as rebuff. The *Boston Atlas*, Whig spokespaper in the city, had previously advocated a Clay nomination. The conservative *Boston Advertiser* now gave its endorsement. The Whig party was so divided that no candidate for governor received a majority in 1842 and the divided legislature selected Democrat Morton. Unable to get the degree of Whig support to which he thought he was entitled, Webster resigned from the Tyler cabinet in mid-1843, and Whigs in Massachusetts began to unite again. Nevertheless, Webster supporters forced Davis to decline renomination for governor in 1843 and prevented Lawrence from being chosen as Davis's successor. Fortunately for the party, George Briggs was their candidate for governor. While he failed to obtain a majority from the electorate, Briggs won four thousand more votes than Morton. The Whigs controlled the House by fifty votes and ultimately the Senate by twenty and were able to select their man. Reelected in each of the next seven years, Briggs was kind, sincere, honest, dignified, a harmonizer, and not from Suffolk County; too many Whig leaders had come from there. He was the perfect man to unify the party.[4]

The division of the Whigs into Webster and Lawrence factions conferred unusual new political influence on many men who otherwise might have been shunted aside. This included a group of young Whigs who had a common concern about slavery and a determination to keep pressure on their political institutions to act on the subject. By 1843 and 1844 these men had discovered their common interests and were working together, now formally known as the Young Whigs. Among them were Charles Francis Adams, Stephen C. Phillips of Salem, Samuel Hoar and his son E. R. Hoar of Concord, Charles Allen of Worcester, and John G. Palfrey of Cambridge. Some historians have included Charles Sumner, Richard Henry Dana Jr., and Linus Child among the group. These men had little economic connection with slaveholders. They would be some of Wilson's closest associates for the next decade.

For the first time since 1838, in early 1843, the Massachusetts legislature considered resolutions dealing with the annexation of Texas. It determined that such a step was perilous for the nation and asked the state's delegation in Congress to work to prevent annexation from occurring. In Congress twenty-one Whigs, led by John Quincy Adams, but including only five of the nine Congressmen from Massachusetts, presented an appeal to the American people opposing expansion.[5]

With the presidential election year soon to begin and with the state legislature about to meet, the Lawrence faction of the Whigs in December, 1843, sought to unite the party as much as possible behind Clay. They particularly sought to get Charles Francis Adams to commit himself. Instead, Adams agreed to lead the Young Men's Whig organization, which emphasized the Whig program rather than a particular candidate. This position had been urged by Wilson as early as June, 1842. In any case, the Lawrence faction dominated the convention and made certain few Webster supporters were sent to the national meeting. Webster was too influential to be ignored and too unmanageable to be left alone. Lawrence himself became both a delegate and a state elector. The anti-annexation position was included among the convention's resolutions.[6]

The 1844 state Senate session, as usual, had proposals dealing with slavery. Wilson himself early introduced a resolution instructing the Committee on the Militia to consider altering or amending as much of the militia law as related to distinctions on account of color. His proposal never got out of committee. He also hoped that a stronger position would be taken to counter proslavery aspirations. He proposed a resolution to declare the state's "uncompromising opposition to the further extension and longer existence of American slavery" and the state's "purpose to use every lawful and constitutional measure for its overthrow and entire extinction."[7]

The preamble Wilson proposed was even stronger. It declared that "three millions of men" were held as slaves, "deprived of their inalienable rights—robbed of their humanity, and degraded to the condition of mere property." It attacked the political and economic power slavery gave to the Southern states. Even this early in his career, Wilson, who would later entitle his great history of the slavery controversy *The Rise and Fall of the Slave Power in America*, spoke forcefully of that Slave Power, accusing it of "a long series of aggressions upon the rights and interests of the freemen of the Union," disturbing Northerners' business affairs, involving them in wars with the Indians, and restricting "by unlawful and violent measures, the freedom of speech and the liberty of the press." The resolutions assailed the efforts to add Texas to the union and accused the Slave Power of coercing Texas into legislating for slavery. The continuation of slavery had caused the nation to lose its claim on God's protection and had placed fundamental American civil liberties in jeopardy, the preamble declared. The issue was clear-cut: "unconditional and pusillanimous submission or a determined constitutional resistance."[8]

Since slavery issues were so much on the minds of so many, the legislature established a joint special committee to deal with the subject. Adams was selected as chairman. He brought forth a sixteen-page report challenging the constitutional power of Congress to admit a foreign nation to statehood and expressing fear that annexation would lead to dissolution of the union. Slavery as a moral evil was not considered. Kinley Brauer, in his study of Massachusetts Whig politics in the 1840s, contended these views were conservative in tone both to unite the party in a presidential election year and to win votes. Wilson was not satisfied. He proposed to add an amendment which would ask Massachusetts senators to use their utmost efforts to prevent annexation. He was not trying to instruct the senators, but his proposal was clearly a rebuke to them for their timidity and their "want of spirit." He insisted the senators needed to know how the people of Massachusetts regarded slavery. He was angry that the senators had not effectively presented previous resolutions of the legislature on the subject and had not demanded that they and their state be treated with more respect.[9]

Wilson understood the difficulty he would have in getting his amendment adopted. He was exposing himself to criticism for introducing it, but he insisted in his defense that the legislature owed it to itself and to the people of the state to condemn the action of the United States Senate. He acknowledged he had a larger program. He would stand by the constitution and the union, but the national government should take certain antislavery actions it had the constitutional power to take. He would have it abolish slavery in the District of Columbia and the territories, end the interstate slave trade, forbid federal officers from participating in the arrest of alleged fugitive slaves, and amend the Constitution to eliminate the three-fifths provision which was providing the slave states with extra representation. In one of the earliest statements enduring of Wilson's views about the relationship of the national government to slavery, the future founder and leader of the Republican party thus advocated actions which that party would prescribe in the 1850s. Wilson's proposal passed and the Senate then almost unanimously accepted the amended Adams resolutions. Friends of the Massachusetts senators, particularly Suffolk County Whigs, rallied to their defense in the House and tabled the matter.[10]

On March 8 Adams revived his resolutions and asked others on the committee what to do. Many of them appeared to be embarrassed by the subject. At the meeting on the following day not one other member appeared. When a quorum did assemble on March 13, one day before scheduled legislative adjournment, the members disagreed so much they voted to request the committee be discharged. The House the next day insisted it wanted Texas resolutions and appointed three men to a new joint committee. The Senate concurred and selected Adams and Wilson. Wilson did not insist upon his amendment. On March 15, just before adjournment, the joint committee reported resolutions similar to Adams's proposals. These were passed unanimously by voice votes in each house.[11]

Rumors from Washington had altered the situation and assured conservative support for an anti-Texas resolution. In late February Robert Winthrop, the most influential Massachusetts conservative Whig in the national capital, urged that the North respond. Tyler and Secretary of State Abel Upshur were quietly negotiating with Texas. Congressman Charles Hudson on March 13 wrote that he could prove nothing, but his fears were that an annexation treaty would soon be proposed. Six days later he was more certain; he anticipated a treaty proposal to the Senate within days. Webster, in Washington at about that time, was equally convinced and he became one of those most actively promoting opposition to the president's plans. At Webster's urging Robert Winthrop on March 15 tried to persuade the House to pass an anti-annexation resolution. Winthrop failed by a large vote. The conservative Whig press of Boston then joined the chorus of concern.[12]

When Calhoun was nominated for secretary of state, manifestly to assure the completion of the Texas project, Abbott Lawrence assembled at his home a number of conservative Whig leaders to discuss what should be done. The legislature was not in session and could not respond. Perhaps it was not to be trusted in any case. Lawrence was concerned not only about the problems which annexation might engender, but that the Liberty party in the developing anti-Texas climate might attract Whig voters. Adams, probably because of his having headed the joint committee shortly before, because of his family name and his standing in the state, and because of his association with those party members who favored strong action to prevent annexation, was included among those invited. Others suggested he take the lead in whatever action they might all agree upon. The businessmen didn't want to be connected publicly with what might ensue. Both for fear that the abolitionists might capture control of the movement and that too outspoken a stance might embarrass Southern Whig congressmen whose votes against annexation were needed, the Lawrence group drew back. They hoped New York might take the lead.[13]

Opposition among the different factions of Massachusetts Whigs varied. The Lawrence group worked primarily through the press, which assailed the annexation scheme. Adams contended that otherwise the wealthy were inactive. He also reported that Webster wanted the matter settled. Adams himself attempted to marshal opposition with newspaper articles which subsequently were published in pamphlet form. Only the *Boston Courier,* however, would print the articles. Adams recorded in his diary that only his relatives seemed aware of their publication. Wilson also sent a long letter to the *Courier's* editor on April 24. The press of the

North, he maintained, was not adequately reflecting the people's opposition to annexation. It was "too tame and confident." Predicting that the Democrats would support annexation and that opponents were relying too much on Senate Whigs, Wilson argued for the need to arouse the North. He had just returned from Washington, where everyone was discussing the subject. Later Wilson was to become known as the nation's most accurate prognosticator of congressional and political campaign votes. He now forecast defeat of the Texas treaty along party lines, with only one Whig voting for it.[14]

The treaty was defeated but that was more a result of mistakes by its advocates than the effectiveness of its opponents. When Calhoun in a diplomatic message to Great Britain indiscreetly coupled the treaty with a defense of slavery, many different segments of public opinion were able to unite. In Massachusetts the conservative Boston Whig press, to isolate the abolitionists, continued to downplay the question of slavery. The strategy of the Lawrence faction temporarily worked. John Quincy Adams assured his son on April 12 that the Massachusetts delegation was more determined to prevent annexation than Charles Francis gave them credit for. Wilson reported that Democrats in Washington were predicting that if Southern Whigs voted against annexation, they would lose every Southern state in the next elections. They were wrong. The Whig party presidential candidate, now selected, was in opposition to annexation, under the conditions being proposed, and the Calhoun diplomatic message and the Polk presidential nomination made the issue so political that Southern Whigs could safely vote with their Northern brethren. On June 8 all Whigs but one, as Wilson had predicted, were joined by seven Democrats and defeated the treaty of annexation. Tyler's plan had failed.[15]

Wilson long was undecided as to whom his party should nominate for the presidency in 1844. In mid-1842 he was hoping Massachusetts Whigs would not soon commit themselves to anyone. By December of 1843, in spite of the state convention nomination of Clay, Wilson was advocating Supreme Court Associate Justice John McLean, who would persist as a Wilson favorite for years. Whether he viewed the nomination as inevitable, or had become convinced that it was the best, by April of 1844 Wilson supported Clay. He predicted the Whigs would win, unless injured in the South by the Texas question. In April, for two weeks, he visited Washington, where the Massachusetts congressional delegation gave him a good deal of attention. He dined with Adams and Winthrop, among others, and was invited onto the floor of the House. He was assured that Clay would oppose Texas annexation. Within two weeks Washington newspapers published the "Raleigh letter," in which Clay declared annexation at that time inexpedient and dangerous for the nation. The consent of Mexico was necessary to avoid war, Clay maintained, knowing that agreement could not be obtained. Robert Walker, Democratic congressman from Alabama, predicted Clay would be defeated if he took an anti-annexation position. Wilson was convinced that Southern and western

Democrats favored annexation as much to put down Northern manufacturers as to spread slavery. In any case, during the first week of May Clay was nominated.[16]

Clay's Raleigh letter did not prevent his selection, but a similar letter by Van Buren cost him the Democratic candidacy. If they united, Southern delegates to the party's convention could prevent any man from being nominated, for rules required a two-thirds majority vote. After a number of ballots, the Democrats selected James K. Polk, a former Speaker of the House of Representatives, former governor of Tennessee, and Jackson's protégé. Both Polk and majority sentiment in the convention favored expansion. The party called for "fifty-four forty or fight"—American ownership of all of the Oregon Territory, disputed with Great Britain, or war. It also sought the "reannexation" of Texas coupled with the "reoccupation" of Oregon.

Manifest Destiny dominated the campaign. A worried Clay began to backtrack from his opposition to the annexation of Texas, not enough to win many votes, but enough to lose some antislavery support in crucial New York to the Liberty party candidate, James G. Birney. Polk squeaked through to victory.

Wilson did not play a major role in the campaign. His participation in 1840 had been frequent and influential. Contemporaries and biographers often referred to it. Presumably the young man was now a more effective speaker and better known in his state, so that his 1844 contributions should have been even more important. Yet little has been discovered in correspondence or newspapers about his speeches, and his contemporary biographers practically ignored the campaign. Perhaps Wilson was too busy with his business. He did participate with Adams, Stevenson, Hudson, and others in the June 19 mass meeting in Boston. On August 17 he wrote that he had received Schouler's orders and would report at the place and time designated; that could have been in reference to a military assignment or to a political address. Pastor Hunt remembered that the two men "breakfasted, dined, supped and lunched on politics" from April to November. Hunt, who was supporting Birney, viewed the election differently from his friend. The minister maintained that a Christian and an abolitionist could not vote for Clay, a duelist and a slaveholder. Wilson dissented, even this early in life demonstrating his pragmatism and his willingness to modify his principles if he could advance his objectives. The Whigs were not as proslavery as the Democrats, he asserted; a Democratic victory was tantamount to annexation of Texas. While he conceded that both parties were unsound, he would choose the lesser of the two evils.[17]

The reaction of other antislavery Whigs helps in understanding Wilson's attitude. Charles Francis Adams, who, like his father, diligently wrote in his diary, recorded that he was unhappy with the Clay nomination and position on annexation. Both the conservative and Webster factions of the Whig party in Massachusetts were laboring in the late spring to downplay the issue of Texas. The substitution of Polk for Van Buren and the expansionist character of the Democratic platform influenced Adams, among others, to reconsider his position.

Webster and Rufus Choate convinced him that Clay's opinions about Texas were nearer his own than Clay's statements had led him to believe. Webster himself had objected to Clay's nomination more because of his own ambitions than because of Clay's position on Texas or Webster's aversion to slavery. In mid-June a state convention assembled in Worcester to rally support for the party's national ticket. The mass meeting in Boston followed. Adams had never before participated in as large an assemblage. Wilson was among the speakers. All three factions of the party were uniting. The Whig Young Men's Club met weekly during the fall with Wilson one of its speakers. Adams commented upon their zeal. But Adams and Wilson weren't the only antislavery Whigs who sustained slaveholding Clay. Even David Lee Child, an associate of Garrison and editor of the American Anti-Slavery Society's *National Anti-Slavery Standard*, espoused the cause of the Kentuckian.[18]

Polk may have pulled off a close triumph nationally, but in Massachusetts the Whigs were victorious, a tribute to Briggs, to their unity, and to the division within the Democratic party, caused in part by one faction's support of Tyler. Outwardly the Henshaw-Hallett group sustained Polk and annexation; they would have preferred Tyler or Calhoun. The Morton wing stumped for Polk and Texas also, although it had wanted Van Buren and professed to be opposed to the spread of slavery. In the three-way race for the presidency, Clay garnered more than 51 percent of the votes cast in Massachusetts; in the three-way contention for the governorship, Briggs defeated Bancroft and Sewell with 52 percent. Some Whigs had unquestionably voted for Birney. The one-issue candidate had done surprisingly well in Massachusetts, with 8 percent of the vote, a significant increase since 1840. That strength would soon decline, but at the time, the Liberty upsurge appeared fraught with danger to the Whigs. The majority party nevertheless won in every county except Berkshire, Hampden, and Bristol. Its victory was by only a plurality in Worcester and in Wilson's Middlesex, where Liberty strength was significant.[19]

Tyler construed the election as a national mandate for the annexation of Texas, war or not. The closeness of both the Electoral College and popular votes hardly justified that conclusion; a majority of Americans had voted against the president. Tyler still could not muster the necessary two-thirds affirmative vote for Senate approval of a treaty. On the other hand, annexation by joint resolution of both houses of Congress would require only a simple majority. The proposal even then evoked a long debate in the lame duck Congress. The House agreed by January 25. Just before adjournment in March, 1844, the Senate passed its own resolution by only a one-vote margin. The House hurriedly concurred. When Polk took office several days later, he naturally carried forward what his predecessor had initiated; Texas accepted the proffered terms and in December, 1845, became a new state.

Most of the Whig leaders in Massachusetts had opposed the annexation of Texas during the 1844 fall campaign. There were, nevertheless, other matters which concerned some of them, including their own political careers, their business success, and the unity and welfare of the nation. Much could be endangered by a continued, too provocative, and useless battle against annexation. At first disagreements within the party were unnecessary. Winthrop in the House and Rufus Choate in the Senate attacked the Tyler plan for Texas. Winthrop emphasized the constitutional-legal disadvantages of annexation, which the conservative faction had spoken about for so long, and the dangers to the permanence of the union which annexation might provoke. He was careful not to alienate Southern Whigs. He did, however, assert his opposition to the extension of slavery. The Massachusetts Whig press throughout the winter of 1844–1845 continued to resist annexation. Yet Lawrence, Appleton, Everett, Choate, and Winthrop were cautious.[20]

When the legislature assembled in January, 1845, Briggs called attention to the expected annexation. The governor was concerned about the possibility of war with Mexico, the spread of slavery, the cost of annexation and war, and the greater power Texas would give to the slaveholding class. Adams characterized the message as containing little about state affairs and much about Texas. He was gratified such a strong stand had been taken.[21]

The legislature was also confronted with the necessity to respond to a related concern, the expulsion of Samuel Hoar. South Carolina had a law which provided for the removal of blacks from vessels which docked in state harbors and the confinement of the men in jail until their ships were ready to sail. Naturally both the blacks and the shippers objected to the practice. The issue simmered for years. The 1844 Massachusetts legislature had commissioned Hoar to resolve the problem. When Judge Hoar arrived in Charleston, however, he was bullied by a mob and warned by a committee of citizens that he would be expelled if he did not leave the city voluntarily. Even worse, Massachusetts was humiliated when the South Carolina legislature directed the governor to deport the official representative of the state. Hoar returned to Boston in November, 1844, with his mission unaccomplished, but having conducted himself in as honorable a manner as possible.[22]

The Massachusetts legislature established a special committee to consider the two problems. Since Adams had chaired the special committee the previous session and since he was a leading antislavery Whig, he had to be included. But the legislature's leaders selected Linus Child to chair the group. Adams concluded the committee was to be managed as Webster wanted. Adams was asked to write the report concerning the Hoar expulsion, about which legislators would have greater agreement and in which legal and constitutional issues would predominate. Some of the language he used was strong. In the lengthy address and accompanying resolutions Congress and the other states were asked to take actions which would help protect citizens of Massachusetts. The proposal passed in March, twenty-seven to zero. Nothing resulted.[23]

The Texas question produced greater argument. Joseph Bell, whom Wilson many years later characterized as "a lawyer of eminence and a gentleman of conservative opinions," formulated the proposals. Webster confided that Whigs in the legislature were determined to be moderate and, while they had to consider public opinion, they would not embarrass their Southern colleagues, whose votes they needed to prevent annexation. Adams was so dissatisfied that he threatened to present a minority report. Bell then decided to revise his draft to add to the constitutional protests an assertion that Massachusetts would not consent to the admission of a state while slavery was part of its claims. The resolutions denied the constitutional power of Congress to annex a nation by legislation, declaring such an action would have no binding effect on the people of Massachusetts and proclaiming that the state would not consent to the further extension of slavery.[24]

The fall campaign had encouraged factions within the Massachusetts Whig party to pull together. Yet personal and ideological differences had not died. Webster in 1844 sought to replace Choate, who wanted to retire, in the United States Senate, but he concluded he could not be elected. So Choate agreed to continue in office until the end of his term in March, 1845. Webster during 1844 sought to reestablish his Whig credentials and to gain support among the Young Whig element of the party. He therefore agreed to write the address for the January public meeting which was called to protest the annexation of Texas. His strategy worked and on January 17, 1845, he was elected to the Senate, with votes from the Lawrence faction as well. Lawrence, however, was conspicuous in his refusal to participate in the subscription of $100,000 to assist Webster in remaining in public service. Furthermore, a few weeks after Webster's election, Senator Isaac Bates died. The legislature selected John Davis, a favorite of Lawrence with whom Webster had not spoken for two years, as the state's second senator. The action was at least in part a result of the conservatives' aversion to the prominent role Webster played in planning the anti-Texas meeting.[25]

Those who wanted a strong position taken recognized their need to organize. At a Whig caucus on January 8 someone advocated a state convention of those who opposed annexation. The committee to which the proposal was referred recommended that Whig members of the legislature not call the meeting; individuals could. The establishment was opposed to party sponsorship of a meeting, but was divided about the seriousness of the situation and what should be done. J. Thomas Stevenson, John H. Clifford, and Leverett Saltonstall, usually in alliance with Lawrence, subscribed to the convention call. The Webster faction was also divided. Child told Adams on January 11 that the aspiring senator preferred that all discussion about Texas be postponed until after Congress adjourned in March; yet Webster would soon be writing the address opposing annexation. The next day, following afternoon consultations, a poorly attended evening meeting of subscribers to the call rejected Adams's advice to delay and referred various suggestions to a committee to be selected by a nominating group of five, including Allan,

Adams, Phillips, Wilson, and Senator Asahel Foot from Berkshire County. The five men consulted twice and agreed upon the names of those to be nominated. The meeting that evening, including some Democrats, ratified the committee's suggestions, selected January 29 as the convention date, and established a four-man group to organize the convention. Phillips drafted the call and on January 14 the others, including Adams and Allen, altered and accepted it and cast the committee. Phillips was to call the conclave to order. Adams would propose the appointment of a nominating committee which would present the names already agreed upon. Allen led the resolutions committee.[26]

The call, signed by a thirty-two-man Committee of Arrangements, including Wilson, requested that all those who opposed the annexation of Texas, without distinction to party, meet and select delegates from their towns for a two-day convention in Faneuil Hall. The people of Massachusetts had a duty, the call declared, to protest and take action against annexation. The Founding Fathers had consented to recognize slavery as a temporary institution. Those who attended the meeting were to cooperate for the good of the nation to halt the expansion of slavery. George Hillard, later a leader of the conservatives, wrote in the *Advertiser* two days before the conclave that annexation was intended "to give support, permanence and a wider extension to the system of slavery" and attacked it as both unconstitutional and immoral. Response to the call among the newspapers of the state was favorable.[27]

When the Boston establishment shifted from nonaffiliation with the convention to opposition is not clear. Former Governor Lincoln pointedly refused to add his name to the call. Kinley Brauer, in his study of the split between the Cotton and Conscience Whigs, contended that the conservatives did not alter their anti-Texas stance until after the convention. They were initially concerned that the abolitionists had almost gained control of the proceedings. Their attitude also increasingly was determined by their hope that Southerners and Northerners in Congress might cooperate enough to lower the tariff. Webster, whose selection as senator did not occur until January 17, was cooperating with the anti-annexation faction. Adams wrote on January 24 that, because Webster favored the project, Lawrence, Davis, and Lincoln stood aloof. Still, he characterized the attitude in Boston as one of indifference toward the convention, not hostility. Wilson, on the other hand, later dated the division between the Conscience and Cotton Whigs from this month.[28]

Webster's position was a peculiar one. He did not want to play a visible role. He urged the nomination of Phillips for convention president. He did work with Allen, Adams, and Phillips to compose the address, Webster forging the constitutional section, Allen the strong antislavery position. George Hoar, more than a half-century later, recorded that Webster left the meeting after completing one portion of the address with the promise to return the next day. Instead, he departed for New York and did not attend the convention three days later. Wilson later described the address as possessing "great vigor and force."[29]

Faneuil Hall was filled for the two-day protest meeting with over six hundred delegates from 141 towns; a new atmosphere of cooperation among those of antislavery sentiment in Massachusetts was evident. Adams, for example, had never seen Garrison before. The address was adopted in spite of Garrisonian objection; the abolitionists had sought to expand the issues beyond Texas. It reminded those who would read or hear about it that Massachusetts had opposed the annexation of Texas at every stage. Phillips, Adams, Hillard, Caleb Stetson, and Child, antislavery Whigs; Garrison and Samuel J. May, abolitionists; and Henry B. Stanton, Liberty party leader, were among the speakers. Edmund Quincy, the Garrisonian, Joshua Leavitt and Samuel Sewell, Liberty party leaders, and Palfrey, the Young Whig, were also there. Wilson played no major role.[30]

While the Young Whigs dominated the organization for the convention, the participants included many others who opposed the annexation of slaveholding Texas and who believed they had to do what they could to prevent it: Garrisonian abolitionists, anti-Garrisonian abolitionists, Liberty party men, and Democrats. *The Emancipator*, spokespaper for the Liberty party and for many non-Garrisonian abolitionists, declared the convention was the best ever held in the state in dignity and weight of character of the people who attended. It remarked on the courtesy Whig speakers extended towards Liberty men and hoped for future cooperation among those opposed to slavery. The Garrisonians spoke of the "great freedom and ability" of the discussions and labeled the address as an antislavery argument. Wilson later characterized the meeting as "large in numbers and strong in talent and character." Some of his fellow Whigs, however, at the time were concerned that the abolitionists might capture control of the proceedings. Garrison proposed a resolution asking for dissolution of the union; Adams worried that they were being associated with another Hartford Convention. Garrison's resolution failed by a ten- or fifteen-to-one majority. Nevertheless, some of the more conservative Whig sponsors decided not to attend the second day. At times the uninitiated Young Whigs feared that the two groups of abolitionists in disagreeing with one another might destroy the convention. At the end the Garrisonians had been contained and Adams would rate the meeting as the most important event of his public life.[31]

The convention, the Massachusetts Anti-Slavery Society declared, presented effectively the position against annexation of Texas, but did not state what Massachusetts could or would do. It did establish a Committee of Correspondence, advocated by S. C. Phillips in his opening address. Since this and the adoption of Adams's address were all the organizers sought formally from the convention, one has to assume the committee was important to them. Wilson characterized the committee's discussions as marked with "freedom, earnestness, solemnity, and determination." While some historians have recorded that the committee didn't function during its first six months, Adams's diary establishes at least three meetings in its initial six weeks of existence. As early as February 13 some of the Boston supporters were withdrawing their affiliation.[32]

While those in Massachusetts opposed to annexation were attempting to prevent or delay action, the United States House of Representatives, on January 25, by a twenty-two-vote majority, passed a joint resolution of annexation and admission of Texas as a state as soon as the usual constitution acceptable to Congress had been formulated and ratified by the people. Wilson asserted twenty-five years later that the proposal was expected to fail by thirty votes, but passed by twenty. In the debates which preceded this vote, Robert Winthrop, generally recognized as one of the ablest men in Congress, had argued at length against the step, primarily for constitutional and legal reasons, but also because he opposed the extension of slavery. In the Senate Choate also enunciated the state's position, but limited his opposition to constitutional reasons and the inexpediency of annexation. With the death of Bates, Massachusetts was not as effectively represented in the upper house.[33]

The General Court of Massachusetts was acting much too tardily to affect events in Washington. The Bell resolutions were accepted by the committee on February 1 and sent to the House; they passed with 80 percent of those voting in favor. When they reached the Senate, Wilson, on February 15, attempted to add another resolution: if Texas should be admitted by majority action of both houses of Congress, that decision should be repealed as soon thereafter as possible. He termed annexation by majority vote an "act of violence." The Senate rejected the proposal by a vote of twenty-four to eight—Adams and Child among those supporting Wilson—and then unanimously on February 18 adopted the House resolutions. The Massachusetts Anti-Slavery Society later singled out Wilson, Adams, and Senator Nathaniel Borden for the "courage and consistency with which they opposed this act of treason [Texas annexation] to freedom and humanity."[34]

The United States Senate did not listen to the Massachusetts General Court. On February 27 the Senate amended the House resolution and passed it with two votes to spare; five Democratic senators had been won over. The House agreed to the amendment the next day and President Tyler signed the resolution on March 1.

As the weeks had passed in Massachusetts, the Lawrence faction of the Whigs had grown progressively more convinced that the Texas issue had been decided by the election. With the vote in Congress, they were now willing to accept defeat and spend their energies on issues about which they believed they could exercise more influence, such as the tariff. Wilson did not agree. He introduced into the Senate a resolution that any slave entering Massachusetts from Texas would be free and that any individual claiming or molesting the slave would be punished by imprisonment. The legislature, he argued, in its joint resolution had declared the admission of Texas would have no effect on Massachusetts. It should do more than resolve; it should act. On March 3 Phillips proposed that the Committee of Correspondence decide how to respond to the Congress's annexation resolution. Fortunately, the legislature was still in session. Phillips declared that slavery had to be regarded as the most important issue before the nation. He predicted the Whig party would not take a stand, that it might therefore disappear, and that the Democrats would be opposed by a new antislavery party. Adams introduced a proposal the committee had approved, that the Senate inquire whether further action should be taken.[35]

The legislature was being forced to react. Bell, Child, and Adams conferred on March 7 about how the special legislative committee should respond. They sought the support of Briggs, who was "staggered" with the suggestion that he on his own take action. He apparently agreed with the Lawrence faction. Winthrop informed Adams several days later that he would do no more in Congress to halt Texas annexation. Still, the Young Whigs did not give up. On March 14 Adams got resolutions out of the Senate committee over the opposition of Bell. They declared that the state did not acknowledge the annexation of Texas as legal, would try to reverse the decision, and remained opposed to the extension of slavery. When they were debated ten days later, just before the legislature was to adjourn, John H. Clifford moved to table the resolutions, but he was supported by only four other voters. In the debate Wilson declared his agreement with the report, but he would go further, asserting again that the national government did not possess the power to admit a foreign nation into the union. The majority in favor of annexation in the House, he charged in a strong statement, had been obtained by treachery. If Texas were aware that the congressional resolution might yet be repealed, it would not agree to annexation. He particularly attacked Massachusetts Democrats for abandoning their previous opposition to Texas. Adams's resolutions passed, with only Clifford willing publicly to vote against them, and the next day the House added its concurrence by a five-to-one majority. Briggs gave his signature.[36]

Wilson was less successful with his resolution. The Judiciary Committee reported on March 18 that it was inexpedient to legislate about slaves coming into Massachusetts from Texas. The chairman of the committee maintained that whenever slaves came into Massachusetts, they were free. Wilson countered that under the fugitive slave provisions of the Constitution, slaves escaping from one state to another had to be returned to their masters, but Massachusetts could legislate to free slaves entering from foreign nations. Wilson moved that the proposal be recommitted to committee with instructions to report on the bill as originally proposed. He lost. Trying to save something, he then moved for indefinite postponement, but again lost. The committee's report was then accepted.[37] The Garrisonians called Wilson's effort, "though well meant, absurd, either as a practicable mode of opposition or as *quid pro quo,* even supposing the whole North to have taken this stand along with Massachusetts."[38]

In the meantime Wilson had also strongly advocated passage of a bill which would have provided any child refused admission to the public schools the right to sue for damages and costs in court. The bill had been reported by the Education Committee as a result of a petition signed by Nantucket blacks and whites. They had shown that the Nantucket school committee had deprived black children of equal benefits in the school system. Elementary grades were segregated and blacks were then prevented from enrolling in the high school because of their lack of preparation. The Senate on February 19 refused to send the bill to its third reading. Wilson would not be denied. Calling for reconsideration, he contended the state's common schools system was the cause of its greatness and that system was based upon equality of opportunity. He agreed that segregation was illegal, but it sometimes occurred; the bill was intended to provide redress. He won support and the bill by a large majority was reactivated and sent to the Judicial Committee. That committee reported a bill, which soon became law.[39]

Adams called the 1845 legislative session quiet. The Democrats were in such a minority that they seldom were able to halt Whig legislation. The state had recovered from the Panic, so that the people were asking little of their legislature. Wilson had only one regular committee assignment, Militia. It was assigned a number of unimportant and routine tasks. The Senate journal is full of social issues; Wilson and Adams, for example, frequently cast opposing votes.[40]

Many Whig leaders must have been relieved when the legislature adjourned. The conservative faction must have been fearful the Young Whigs would steer the party and the state into a radical position. With the governor unwilling to do more about Texas, the legislature in adjournment, and without a national political campaign in 1845, time might heal divisions in the party and allow the congressional representatives, who could be trusted more on the slavery issue, to speak for the state. Perhaps they could repair some of the political damage the presidential campaign, the debates over annexation, and the resolutions of the General Court had engendered. Adams deceived himself in concluding he had in his five years in the legislature placed his party and the state in resistance to the proslavery directions of the general government. Wilson, whose business was flourishing in the mid-1840s and who had been away for the better part of three months, now turned his energies to the work he needed to do to support his family.[41]

Adams characterized Massachusetts in May as in a state of "profound quiet." This continued until midsummer. In June the Texas committee created by the January convention issued a circular letter; the only hope it held out was that if the people could be aroused against the consummation of annexation, their representatives might yet be forced to prevent it. On July 4, 1845, however, a convention at San Felipe de Austin formally accepted the American proposal for annexation. The same evening in Boston, Winthrop delivered an address understood by all factions as the conservative Whig pronouncement that opposition to annexation was over and agitation should cease. To close ranks in August, Nathan Appleton mediated between Lawrence and Webster. Harmony would both assist the passage of Whig economic policies in Congress and assure conservative control of the party in the state.[42]

At the September party convention the united conservatives were in complete control. They sought John Quincy Adams as chairman and, when he would not agree, selected another antislavery member of the party. Many Young Whigs simply stayed home. Winthrop delivered the main address, reemphasizing his July position of the inevitability of annexation. The platform, written by Bell, in nationalistic tones, prevented the Whig party's nullification, but again included resolutions condemning the annexation of Texas. The leaders made certain, however, the fall campaign was waged on state issues.[43]

A circular letter was sent by the Texas Committee in June to people all over the nation, asking for suggestions as to what might yet be done about annexation. Some respondents, including Horace Greeley, prescribed some practical measures. Even as confirmed an antislavery activist as William Robinson, however, concluded annexation was assured. He suggested that Massachusetts representatives in Congress withdraw as a symbolic act, but admitted the people of the state would not support that. He hoped opponents of annexation would speak in protest. In his reply in July, Wilson disclosed he was discouraged and disappointed. The people did not appear to realize what was happening. Clearly those who wanted annexation controlled the national government. But Wilson emphasized duty. Texas might be a closed issue, but the North still must be aroused against slavery. Opponents should try to touch the public conscience by holding public meetings and persuading the press. The committee did nothing.[44]

The abolitionists were less discouraged. For years on August 1 they had celebrated the British emancipation of slaves in the West Indies. In 1845 they scheduled at least seven public meetings in eastern Massachusetts, which they intended to use as forums to continue their attacks against slavery. They hoped more of the antislavery politicians of the two major parties would join them. Adams declined his invitation, but Wilson agreed to speak at Waltham, where Suffolk and Middlesex County people were to gather. Special train arrangements were made and between five and six hundred people attended. Wilson's speech was characterized as "thorough anti-slavery and anti-Texas." He repeated his accusations that Texas annexation had been agreed to as a result of "treachery of Northern men." But he differed from many other speakers concerning what now should be done. Congress's action, he contended, had no binding force; the slave states had violated the Constitution. Massachusetts, however, was obligated to remain in the union and keep other states, even South Carolina, in the union as well. Wilson would contest every step of Texas annexation and participation. If the state were admitted, he would later cast it out. He called for meetings in "every district, town, and county of the State." Wilson was almost alone among Whig politicians in his determination to continue the battle against annexation. A committee of seven, including Wilson, was appointed to plan for a meeting the third week of August to protest against the admission of Texas. The meeting was never held.[45]

When the committee did nothing, Wilson decided to act on his own, at least for Middlesex County. He was evincing a leadership and independence that he had not previously shown on a state or county level. His initiative would subsequently arouse other Young Whigs to action. Wilson prepared a call to meeting and procured forty-seven supporting signatures, including Hunt, Edward Walcutt, Caleb Stetson, Ralph Waldo Emerson, E. R. Hoar, William Jackson, and Child. They spawned a meeting at Concord on September 22 to consider "the encroachments of the slave power, and to recommend such action as justice and patriotism shall dictate." Wilson called the conclave to order and then turned over presiding responsibilities to Elisha Huntington, mayor of Lowell. Wilson was included on the five-man Business Committee and reported a preamble and series of resolutions which had been prepared by Hunt. While many of the more "respectable" among those devoted to opposing slavery, including Adams and Whittier, only sent letters of support, the abolitionists, including Garrison, Wendell Phillips, and William Henry Channing, were out in force. S. C. Phillips and E. R. Hoar appeared to help Wilson. One unfriendly newspaper commentator contended the Whigs had to struggle to keep the Garrisonian disunionists from taking control. Whittier did not see what could be gained by dissolving the union; what was needed, he asserted in a letter, was a "life-long consecration of tongue and pen" against slavery and a refusal ever to vote for a slaveholder. The Garrisonians, nevertheless, attempted to commit the meeting to a disunion resolution; they failed. The *Boston Post* was especially irritated that Channing had traveled from New York City to attack Winthrop in his own state and that Wilson and Hoar had not defended their congressman.[46]

Given Wilson and Hunt's important roles, one can surmise that these resolutions contained what they especially thought vital. The preamble accused the Slave Power for half a century of trampling upon the rights and interests of freemen, disturbing commercial and business relations, interfering with the right of petition, restricting by force freedom of speech and the press, arresting and selling into slavery free people of color, driving from their soil by violence Massachusetts's legally appointed agents, and forcing a foreign nation into the union. Resolutions were passed which asserted that the right to hold people in bondage was limited to states; that the national government had the power to abolish slavery in the District of Columbia and the territories, and to abolish the interstate slave trade; that the annexation of Texas was a violation of the Constitution and Massachusetts should hold to its declaration not to recognize the act; and that annexation would absolve the North of its constitutional obligations.[47]

Finally, aroused by Wilson, some of those opposed to annexation were responding. In addition to the resolutions, the Concord gathering established a committee of nine to organize statewide resistance with the Faneuil Hall committee and with opponents of slavery in other counties. The committee adjourned to meet again at Cambridge in two weeks. Among the nine designated for the committee were E. R. Hoar, Huntington, Jackson, Boutwell, and Wilson. In the meantime, Liberty party leaders had thrown their resources into a convention for people from throughout the New England and middle states in Boston's Tremont Temple on October 1; the eastern leadership of the party came en masse. The convention asserted that, since representatives from Northern states outnumbered those from Southern, annexation of Texas was not concluded and they could yet prevent it. They appointed committees of action for all free states. Because those in charge did not send out notices, the Cambridge conclave on October 7 was less successful, termed "a failure" by *The Liberator*. Among those who did attend were most of the leaders of the previous meeting, including Wilson, who called for freeing of the slaves. *The Liberator* claimed Massachusetts Democrats, conscious of the position of Polk, were abandoning their opposition to Texas, leaving the battle to Whig and Liberty partisans. Unable to agree what should or could be done, the Cambridge conclave speakers contended something had to happen.[48]

Wilson and the abolitionists had revived anti-annexation enthusiasm and determination. Samuel Sewell, Liberty party candidate for governor, took over the chairmanship of the committee. He invited Adams to join the group, arguing that with the Whig leaders accepting annexation, Adams could no longer depend upon his party. The Texas Committee, however, was too much dominated by abolitionists. Adams set out to add Whigs, and E. R. Hoar, Allen, Palfrey, and Phillips, among others, joined. But few Democrats or other Whigs would affiliate themselves with the abolitionists. At the second Cambridge meeting, on October 21, Wilson presided and his friend Schouler served as secretary. Wilson demanded action from their Northern representatives. Garrison would have the state legislature declare the resolution of annexation null and void. A number of the speakers attacked the Whigs as derelict in principle. That was too much for Adams, who reminded the abolitionists that united action required agreement on methods. Yet Garrison's resolution was accepted. The conclave also decided to gather petitions against the admission of Texas as a slave state. By the end of October Sewell had stepped aside as chairman and Adams replaced him. One of the conclave's projects was to issue on November 3 an appeal to the clergy of the state, prepared by Palfrey and William Henry Channing, explaining the stance of the Texas Committee and asking them to devote one Sunday with their congregation to examining the annexation issue. Wilson was one of the signers. Another project was to send an address against the admission of Texas as a slave state throughout Massachusetts and even to those in other communities who might support the conclave's position. It included a helpful guide with practical suggestions on "How to Settle the Texas Question." A newspaper, *The Free State Rally and Texas Chain-Breaker*, edited by Elizur Wright, was also established.[49]

A protest meeting on November 4 at Faneuil Hall was to be the pinnacle of the campaign. Wilson had now been superseded in the leadership. Sewell, Adams, and Charles Sumner were the committee to prepare resolutions, with Sewell's first draft too radical, Sumner's second better, and Adams formulating the final set. Wright and Sewell fancied Briggs could be persuaded to preside; if not, Adams would have to. Poor weather, "rain pouring down violently, thunder roaring, lightening blazing,"[50] limited attendance to what Adams termed a "respectable" number. Liberty party men, Young Whigs, and Garrisonian abolitionists all cooperated. In presenting the resolutions, Palfrey insisted annexation was not yet "consummated." While Adams, Sumner, George Hillard, Channing, Wendell Phillips, Garrison, and Stanton delivered addresses, Wilson's presence was unreported. Garrison's sons later claimed their father cooperated to prove the "futility of attacking the slave power in 'incidents and details.'" Adams was relieved the union had proceeded in good faith. *The Liberator* reported the meeting established a new state committee to engender congressional action against annexation, but other sources ignored the supposed step, and the names listed by *The Liberator* appear to be the same as those on the old committee, including Wilson's. Two days after the convention, following another meeting of the Texas Committee, Adams feared they were wasting their time and money.[51]

Still the effort continued. In November the adjourned Cambridge meeting reassembled at Lowell City Hall, called to order by the mayor. Wilson apparently was not in attendance. S. C. Phillips, an able lecturer, delivered addresses in Boston's Tremont Temple twice within a week, but a friendly newspaper confessed the hall was "far from being crowded." Meetings were also convened in Brookline, Dedham, Higham, Roxbury, and other communities. Adams now sought the support of the state's establishment. He tactfully reminded Lawrence of his views expressed at the September Whig convention and hoped Whigs would not be outnumbered by those of other parties in opposing annexation. Lawrence and Appleton, however, pointedly refused even to give their names to one of the petitions, Lawrence terming further action useless. The committee decided to publish the two letters from Lawrence and Appleton, with responses written by Adams and Sumner. The *Boston Advertiser,* spokespaper for the conservatives, praised the men's stance. Wright's *Free State Rally* embarrassed many of the Young Whigs with an attack both on the two industrialists and the *Advertiser*.[52]

As the petitions poured in from throughout the state, the Texas Committee was confronted with the problem of what to do with them. The original suggestion was for a committee of three to take them to Washington, but no one would go. Adams, Sumner, and Wendell Phillips on November 25 were designated a subcommittee to solve the problem. Several days later Wilson was reported to be the only man willing to undertake the trip. Whittier initially declined, but was somehow persuaded to reconsider. Adams wondered where the money could be found to support the trip. If any good were to come of the effort, the petitions had to be presented before Congress took final action in accepting the admission of Texas. The two men left with documents containing 50,000 signatures and with letters to John Quincy Adams and the Massachusetts delegation. In Philadelphia Whittier tarried to convince some influential Quakers they should also journey to the capital. Wilson and Whittier stayed in Washington a week, trying to understand the political climate and provide support for those who might vote against Texas statehood. Whittier concentrated upon the Democrats and was surprised to discover that they had no understanding with one another on the issue. Wilson spoke primarily with Whigs but was disappointed in the response he received. He characterized the temper of the Southern Whigs as "utterly desperate." Whittier was convinced that if the other free states had done as much as Massachusetts they might have prevented annexation.[53]

After conferring with Joshua Giddings and some of the Massachusetts House members, Wilson and Whittier distributed the petitions among the state's delegation. John Quincy Adams presented many of the remonstrances on December 11 and 12 and tried to get them referred to a select committee. Instead, they were laid on the table by a 115-to-72 vote. A few petitions, by accident, got referred to the Committee on Territories, which had sponsored annexation and would not report favorably on them. If there had been 400,000 signatures instead of 50,000, Wilson reported, the reception would have been the same. When Stephen A. Douglas, chairman of the Committee on Territories, proposed his joint resolution for the admission of Texas, it was opposed, especially by Massachusetts Congressman Julius Rockwell, but Douglas had the votes to end debate. Admission was voted in the House by a majority of 85. Webster strongly opposed the resolution in the Senate, but again the vote was not close, 31 to 14. No Northern Whig supported the proposal. Whittier wrote: "Slave-Power rules Congress, completely, absolutely."[54]

In Massachusetts the conservative Whigs, at first taken aback by the vigor of the anti-Texas campaign, regrouped, changed their tactics of almost ignoring the Texas Committee and applied enough pressure to cause many of the Young Whigs to reconsider their position, or lack of it. Some quietly disassociated themselves from committee proceedings. Among those who remained, Adams, S. C. Phillips, and Palfrey resolved, even before the House on December 16 passed its admission resolution, to dissolve the committee. Funds were exhausted and the narrow purpose of opposition to annexation no longer had much meaning. Furthermore, Adams recorded, the committee was "growing very wild." The abolitionists had hoped the committee was the first step in a permanent organization which would oppose slavery. Adams resisted that. But even he admitted the country newspapers were not following the Lawrence-Appleton leadership as Boston area journals were. Stanton concluded the Young Whigs were afraid to break away from their "proslavery party." Neither the Garrisonians nor the Young Whigs were as committed to lasting cooperation as the Liberty party adherents were. A final address to the members of the Texas Committee, penned by Adams, blamed the conservatives for the annexation. The contest over Texas, he said, had been fought and lost, but much needed to be done in the future. Because the address included praise for the speeches of Webster and Rockwell, the abolitionists wanted to change it. Adams agreed to some verbal alterations, but he and his supporters were then even more eager to end the committee. Wilson, who had not been involved in many of the December decisions, regretted the termination of cooperation among those opposed to slavery, hoping it might continue in some new form. With acceptance of the report—Wilson was one of the forty-five signatories—the committee dissolved.[55]

Congressman William Slade of Vermont asserted the country was indebted to Massachusetts for its stand against annexation; without it, there would have been little demonstration of opposition. While the effort had failed, he was confident it would help in the long run.[56]

4

A Conscience Whig

The election of 1845 had turned out more favorably for the Whigs than their leaders could have anticipated. With the Liberty and Native American parties both attracting votes, Briggs again did not obtain the majority necessary to be elected governor by the people, but he was easily selected by the General Court. Many of the Young Whigs, including Wilson, did not contribute very much to the campaign. The Democratic party, however, was becoming increasingly weak, split between the Morton and Henshaw factions. The number of voters in Massachusetts, including in the peak year of 1840, often was lower than in most states; that number fell to 40 percent in 1845. In any case, the Whigs garnered every Senate seat and won two-thirds of the House elections. Wilson declined running again for the Senate, but he did seek and win his town's House seat.[1]

Many of the other Young Whigs were not in the legislature and thus were unable to provide leadership. Wilson could. Adams, Sumner, Palfrey, and Wilson consulted with one another during January, but could devise no program. Wilson thought the legislature would do little and he had no confidence in Briggs. He worried that the Young Whigs' former allies might take too radical a position at the annual meeting of the Massachusetts Anti-Slavery Society. Palfrey favored making an issue of the reelection of Davis to the Senate. Adams agreed they had to act, or their influence would subside. But what could they do? Phillips seemed unable to give attention to the dilemma. The illness and then death of his son removed Adams from leadership.[2]

Wilson was the only important Young Whig to participate in the annual meeting of the Garrisonian abolitionists at Boston's Tremont Temple from January 28 through 30. Wilson, reporting on the meetings for the *Lowell Journal* at Schouler's request, praised the caliber of speaking and characterized Wendell

Phillips as one of the greatest orators of the country. The Whig leadership's view of Wilson as a dangerous abolitionist must have been reenforced when Wilson declared Phillips should be sent to Congress. Wilson feared, however, that the convention resolution urging the legislature to declare the union dissolved would prejudice antislavery actions in that body. Garrison, on the other hand, professed Wilson would yet see the futility of efforts against slavery within the Whig party and the efficacy of the rational and consistent position of the Massachusetts Anti-Slavery Society.[3]

The very day the abolition meeting adjourned, Governor Briggs gave Wilson his opportunity to get the new legislature on record with a strong antislavery statement. Briggs presented resolutions of the Georgia legislature concerning slavery and the action of the Massachusetts legislature asking for protection of its colored citizens in the slaveholding states. Wilson moved the resolutions be referred to a special joint committee of two senators and five representatives. He included a direction that the committee report contain a preamble expressing the hostility of the state to the institution of slavery. Wilson declared that "We must destroy slavery, or slavery will destroy liberty." He would work with any person or party—Whig, Democrat, abolitionist, Christian, or infidel—for the cause of emancipation. The directive to the committee created so much opposition among members of both major parties that Wilson agreed to leave the committee without instructions. Wilson was the only committee member, however, who favored taking very strong action.[4]

On February 3 Wilson continued his offensive with an additional resolution for the special committee to consider. It noted three million people were held as slaves, "deprived of their inalienable rights—robbed of their humanity and degraded to the condition of mere property." It attacked the slaveholding states for their undue influence over the national government, because of the three-fifths provision in the constitution; for their restrictions on freedom of speech and press; and for their violation of the rights of the Indians. And the resolution condemned the annexation of Texas for the purpose of perpetuating and extending slavery. It resolved that Massachusetts announce to the nation its opposition to the further extension and even the continued existence of slavery, pledging itself to use every lawful and constitutional power to assure abolition. In his defense of his resolution Wilson demonstrated he had matured as a legislator and as an antislavery advocate. *The Liberator* pronounced it to be "unquestionably the best Anti-Slavery speech that had ever been delivered in any legislative assembly in this country, more direct, more comprehensive, and more important." This was a remarkable tribute. The *Boston Courier* also praised the effort.[5]

In his speech Wilson acknowledged that unworthy motives would be ascribed to him. He pointed out he could derive no personal benefit from his stance, while he could lose much, including the support of friends. He emphasized he had given considerable thought to his responsibility. Both duty and patriotism required that he speak out. "I loathe, detest, and abhor [slavery]." He professed not to be a political abolitionist, a Liberty-party man. But he was an abolitionist and had been a member of an abolitionist society for nearly ten years. While he doubted he had received many votes from Liberty supporters, he was willing to act with anyone to arrest the extension and to overthrow the institution of slavery. He reviewed some of the actions against slavery of the Massachusetts legislature since 1838, attacked the corruption which helped attain the votes of some Northerners for Texas annexation, and called for Massachusetts and its legislature to continue their opposition to slavery. Massachusetts should remain in the union and there fight for freedom, exercising all just powers it had.

Wilson maintained the Slave Power had its eyes on California, Cuba, Haiti, and parts of Mexico. He compared the prosperity and civilization of Massachusetts with that of slave states. Insisting slavery and freedom were in a fight with one another, he knew what needed to be done: send men to Congress who would sustain the principles of the people; prevent the expansion of slavery; abolish the institution in the District of Columbia; disassociate the national government from any role in hunting down and returning fugitive slaves and instead have it defend liberty. His speech minimized the likelihood that agitation over slavery would lead to dissolution of the union. Nor could he see terrible dangers resulting from abolition: neither the North nor the British West Indies had experienced any. Nor would agitation endanger good commercial relations between the North and South: the North was economically healthy; the slave states were not paying their share in any case. Wilson called upon Massachusetts to provide the leadership for the remainder of the nation.[6]

The Liberator reported members of the House did not want to hear about the subject; some left their seats, others were indifferent, some sneered at the speaker. Accusing Wilson of providing a great deal of wind which amounted to nothing, Representative Bryant moved to postpone the resolution indefinitely. Instead, it was temporarily laid on the table, ninety-seven to seventy-one. Wilson obtained reconsideration later that month. After a series of parliamentary maneuvers, the special committee to which the Georgia resolutions had been referred was instructed to consider whether further action concerning Texas was desirable. The committee returned with a short report sustained by its other six members, characterizing the annexation of Texas as an evil, but one that Massachusetts had to accept. The Senate on April 7 agreed to that proposal. The House initially accepted the Senate report. Two days later Wilson by a twenty-six-vote majority obtained reconsideration and by a three-to-one majority got his minority report substituted for the Senate's. The latter body, however, postponed the whole matter by a twenty-to-sixteen vote. During the course of the debates, E. R. Hoar asserted that the state had as much "duty to pass resolutions in favor of the rights of man as in the interests of cotton." A fellow legislator called him a "Conscience Whig," and new titles, "Cotton Whig" and "Conscience Whig," were created.[7]

In these months following Texas annexation, a malaise had begun to settle over the state. The Polk administration was effectively silencing Democrats, not just the cooperative Henshaw faction but also the more liberal, formerly abolition-minded Morton group. The Whig conservatives had had a year to regain control of their party. Many of the Young Whigs were out of the legislature, in no position to make themselves heard. Adams had family problems, Phillips was strangely silent, Sumner was only beginning to join the others in their crusade. Except for the continued agitation outside the political arena by the Garrisonians and the weakening efforts of the Liberty party men, most of those who were opposed to slavery in Massachusetts were lifeless and quiet. Not the representative from Natick. Adams told his associate he had sustained himself "admirably well" that session. Mann later wrote that Wilson's minority report had created a sensation in the state. The support for his proposal in the House and the close vote in the Senate is a testament to Wilson's tenacity and political astuteness and to the strength of antislavery sentiment in Massachusetts.[8]

Wilson's major address had emphasized his love of union, although he had pugnaciously asserted that if made to choose between liberty and union, he would support liberty. In late February he courageously presented a petition from abolitionists, asking for the recall of the state's congressmen. At the same time he affirmed that he made the presentation only because he believed in the right of petition, and that he had no sympathy with the objective.[9]

Annexation of Texas may have concluded a national controversy, but it only produced increased problems with Mexico. A series of American administrations had experienced difficulties with their southern neighbor, including over financial claims of American merchants and court proceedings and prison conditions for Americans accused of violating Mexican laws. Mexican governments in the 1830s and 1840s were often unable or unwilling to pay merchants' claims. Added to those festering disputes now were the refusal of Mexico to recognize, first, the independence of Texas and, later, the right of its alleged province and the United States to negotiate annexation. After warning the Americans it would not consent to annexation, in March, 1845, Mexico had broken off diplomatic relations. Even if the two nations had otherwise agreed, the boundary between Texas and Mexico would have been in dispute. Polk in the summer of 1845 ordered an American force under the command of General Zachary Taylor to the Texas border. Taylor at first encamped near the Neuces River, a considerable distance from any Mexican army. In January, 1846, the administration sought to apply more pressure by sending Taylor's forces to the Rio Grande and dispatching American warships to Vera Cruz. By late April skirmishes were occurring along the border. On May 11 Polk announced to Congress that American blood had been shed on American territory, and on May 13, 1846, Congress authorized a call for volunteers for a war already existing.

Between Taylor's two battles in northern Mexico in early May and the end of 1846, much of the northeastern part of the country was occupied, California and the southwest were wrestled from Mexican control, and Tampico was captured by the American navy. By October, what Polk wanted, his military forces had taken. The Mexicans, however, still would not recognize the change which had occurred. The war was not going to be as quickly ended as the Polk administration had hoped.

With the adjournment of the 1846 legislature, the Conscience Whigs lacked a forum through which to press their views. In early May a proposal was made to Adams to purchase the *Boston Whig,* a newspaper about six months old which lacked readers and financial support. News from Washington about war with Mexico was troubling those opposed to slavery. On May 19 Adams and Wilson spoke about the newspaper and its possibilities; Wilson was inclined "to take it up." Adams, Wilson, Sumner, Palfrey, and S. C. Phillips consulted on the project on May 23; Adams had already proposed terms, which the *Whig* owners had accepted. Sumner and Wilson could not aid the newspaper with money, so Adams and Phillips each bought 40 percent of the shares, and Palfrey the remainder. Adams almost immediately left for Washington to coordinate Massachusetts Conscience Whig efforts with the work of other political groups. When he returned, he discovered most of the editorial labor for the *Whig* would fall on his shoulders. Phillips and Allen seemed uninterested; they didn't even subscribe for copies. Palfrey, whose employment was as Massachusetts secretary of state, soon began a series of twenty articles, "Papers on the Slave Power," which irritated the State Street leadership.[10]

Wilson took his connection with the newspaper seriously. He visited the editorial offices frequently, regarding his role as one of providing moral support and helping obtain subscribers. On June 26 and 27, for example, he brought in fourteen more names. Adams needed the encouragement, for he feared the paper could not survive more than three months. Wilson suggested they sign and send a circular promoting the paper, but Adams viewed that as a last resort. In mid-July Adams and Wilson discussed the publication's condition; its subscription list still amounted to only eighty-six. Wilson maintained that not enough exertion had been expended to procure support. At Wilson's request he, Adams, Sumner, Palfrey, and Phillips, joined by R. C. Spooner, discussed the problem on July 22 and determined to continue publication. Phillips agreed to assume a greater burden.[11]

A war requested and directed by Polk, a Southerner and a Democrat, started over the ownership of Texas would certainly not be popular among Massachusetts Whigs. Yet the party divided on how to respond. The *Boston Whig,* under its new ownership, left no doubt where it stood. Its June 5 editorial declared it would not counsel factious opposition, which the Federalists had given in the War of 1812; nor should Americans undertake unconstitutional actions. But annexation had been promoted for the benefit of slavery, and the responsibility for conducting the war should be left to those who had generated it. Webster was in Massachusetts when the Senate voted for war; he tactfully remained silent in August while Congress debated David Wilmot's amendment to prohibit slavery in territory which might be acquired from Mexico. Yet he opposed the volunteer system, some bills which provided means for the prosecution of the conflict, and the acquisition of territory; he called the conflict "Polk's war." John Quincy Adams and four other Massachusetts representatives were among fourteen voters in the House against the war bill and its authorization of the employment of volunteers; Davis was one of only two senators to oppose it. The *Boston Advertiser* attacked the president and his war.[12]

Others were more supportive of the war effort. Winthrop voted in favor of the original bill. He insisted he had to swallow the preamble, which declared war had been begun by Mexican action, to provide aid to the army. And Briggs issued a proclamation for volunteers. Although Garrison took the offensive against the governor, the *Boston Whig* continued to support Briggs and instead concentrated its fire upon the industrial leadership and Winthrop. Sumner, who had enjoyed friendly relations with the congressman, not only assailed him in the *Whig,* but signed the articles. Winthrop was hurt and broke off their social relations. Palfrey also got the paper involved in a controversy, this time with Appleton. The *Boston Advertiser* both defended Winthrop and attacked Adams; the *Courier*, previously open to the Conscience Whigs, began to close its columns to their use. By August both Adams and Sumner recognized that they had been ostracized by Boston society. Wilson, who had never been accepted, experienced little change in status.[13]

The backers of the *Boston Whig* had made a firm commitment to remain Whigs. The Garrisonians thought they were foolish not to recognize their untenable position. On May 16 Adams had rebuffed a proposal from Jackson to join again with those who had worked together during the fall in a protest meeting against the war. On July 9 the editor of the *Whig* reemphasized his paper's party allegiance. If on a few issues, he declared, the paper's backers went beyond most Whigs, "is that any reason why, in a fit of impatience because they would not take our dictation, we should fly off to a less eligible post to act with others, with whom, in the long run, we are likely to agree even less?" He recalled the Birney candidacy in 1844, with typical Whig logic blaming it for Clay's defeat and the subsequent annexation of Texas and war. Clearly, Adams believed the party system dealt with other important issues besides slavery. The same month Joshua Giddings visited New England, informing Adams that New Hampshire and Maine antislavery Whigs were looking to him for leadership. But Giddings told Wilson that he, on behalf of several Whig members in Congress, was sounding out others about their reactions to a third party. The *Whig,* however, asserted that if Briggs won renomination at the fall convention, it would support him; the real issue, Adams declared, was the party's platform.[14]

Kinley Brauer, the historian of the Cotton-Conscience controversy, has recorded that an anonymous letter in the *Whig* at the end of July, which he attributed to Wilson, was the "manifesto" of Conscience Whig belief and strategy. The writer of the letter condemned New England's subservience to the manufacturing interest of profits. He protested against the union of Whiggery with manufacturing. "It has no right to the party. . . . Our object is to elevate our party to its true position, to give it nobler views and a nobler aim."[15]

Whatever new relationship was developing between the members of the elite of the two wings of Whigs, neither was prepared to fracture the party. Abbott Lawrence confided to Davis that he expected resolutions to be introduced which he could sustain in the abstract, but which it would be wise to leave untouched. The Conscience Whigs had agreed to accept the nominations of the convention. So Adams, Sumner, and Hillard were selected as delegates. Adams believed the efforts of the previous four months, primarily by his newspaper, had borne fruit. The convention was going to be reasonably divided between the two factions. Congressman Charles Hudson, who belonged to neither, was selected as chairman. Samuel Hoar and S. C. Phillips balanced Nathan Appleton and Amos Lawrence among the vice-presidents.[16]

Adams, Phillips, Palfrey, Sumner, and Spooner on September 4 consulted concerning tactics. They agreed Phillips would prepare resolutions dealing with slavery and Allen would introduce them. On September 19 Sumner, Phillips, Palfrey, and Adams gathered to revise what had been prepared and to plan their strategy. John P. Hale, the maverick antislavery politician from New Hampshire, was brought in for advice. Wilson arrived for consultation on September 21 and Allen the next day.[17]

Sumner and Winthrop delivered two of the major speeches of the convention, each about an hour long. Sumner's address, urging a party stance against the expansion of slavery, particularly praised the role of Webster in relation to the war. Winthrop was more concerned about the traditional economic issues, although he also defended his own course and expressed his opposition to the admission of more slave states or the creation of more slave territories. The session had scarcely been organized when a motion was introduced to nominate Briggs by voice, a violation of an agreement Adams had obtained before the meeting. When the Committee on Resolutions rejected the proposals of the Conscience Whigs, Phillips introduced them on the floor. Fifteen in number, these antislavery proposals were lengthy and sometimes duplicated those of the committee. Child asserted that they embraced the same ideas. A primary difference between the two was a lack of call for action in the committee's resolutions. The conservative leadership would compromise enough to save the party and no more, according to Whittier. Adams believed he and his friends might have won, had not Allen delivered a speech so severe that it produced a negative reaction among the delegates. The Cotton Whigs were so apprehensive they sent for Webster to calm the deliberations. The antislavery proposals then lost 91 to 137; more than half of the delegates had not voted. Many of the country Whigs had left the capital city for home. Boston, authorized 105 representatives, could determine the outcome. Webster then delivered a short closing speech to quiet and unite the party.[18]

The Conscience Whigs were perplexed as to what they should do next. The day after the party convention Allen, Phillips, Wilson, and Adams, now joined by Theodore Parker, *Boston Courier* editor Joseph Buckingham, and a new convert, Francis W. Bird, gathered to talk it over. That night a public meeting at Faneuil Hall, presided over by John Quincy Adams, convened to consider what steps could be taken to guard human rights and to prevent abductions of free citizens. Whether Wilson was present one cannot know. Within a day or so the Young Whigs realized how strong objections were to their efforts at the state convention. The *Advertiser* launched a campaign against them, characterizing their convention resolutions as "suicidal" and denying the country was threatened by "the political power of slavery." Appleton asked Sumner who in the *Whig* had distorted his ideas so much. The conservatives were determined to crush them, Adams recorded. In fact, the absence of a national election and the growing weakness of the Democrats in the state combined to induce the Cotton faction to take the offensive.[19]

The Conscience Whigs soon learned they could not prevent the nomination of Winthrop. The Liberty party offered to nominate Sumner, but he and his associates would not leave their party. Wilson was now heavily involved in strategy planning, in contact with Adams sometimes three times a week. By late October the Suffolk County Conscience Whigs decided they had to oppose Winthrop publicly. Adams, Samuel Gridley Howe, and John Andrew managed a nomination of Sumner as an independent Whig while their associate was absent on a speaking tour of Maine. When Sumner returned, he rejected the designation; Adams also refused to be the candidate, and Howe's name was finally substituted. The *Boston Atlas* attacked Sumner and Adams for their participation in the nominating process, suggesting they had left the Whig party. Winthrop was hardly taught a lesson by the independent Whigs; he won with 64 percent of the vote.[20]

The Conscience Whigs of Middlesex County were more successful. At the regular Whig convention in Concord, on October 6, E. R. Hoar was chairman and Wilson guided the Resolutions Committee. The Mexican War was called an invasion, a conquest, "an enormous crime." The proslavery position of the national government endangered the union, the platform declared. The Whigs of the North must be "uncompromising opponents of slavery." The resolutions opposed slavery's extension and "its continuation where it already exists." The meeting also selected Palfrey as nominee for Congress, but in November he failed to get the majority needed for the election. Wilson did not run again for the legislature. In general, the turnout in the state was light and the Whigs won state offices, congressional seats, and good majorities in the legislature. Briggs obtained a majority this time, carrying every county.[21]

The Cotton Whigs had been challenged and had won. Given their usual control over the party and the already-existing plans of leading Whigs to push Zachary

Taylor for their 1848 nomination, they could afford to be more conciliatory. The *Advertiser* and the *Atlas* suspended their fire. Support was given Palfrey in his contest to win the needed majority in the second election for Congress. The Conscience Whigs, on the other hand, were depressed. Giddings arrived in December for consultations and to renew their energies. But the war continued and the two factions did not agree on what to do about it. The strategy for 1847 devised by the conservatives, and supported by even some Southern Whigs, was to oppose all addition of territory. Adams, like his father, wanted more land, especially Oregon, and even the southwest, if slavery were excluded from it by Congress.[22]

Nor did Massachusetts Whigs agree about their choice for presidential nomination in 1848. The Conscience Whigs didn't want Taylor and opposed Clay again. In February 1847 Senator Tom Corwin of Ohio—who, in his many years in the House and Senate, customarily spoke only about once a year—delivered a strong anti–Mexican War speech, announcing his intention of voting to withhold money to supply American troops, and temporarily made himself the favorite of the antislavery Whigs. In the summer of 1848 he voted for the Wilmot Proviso, to exclude slavery from territory which might be acquired from Mexico. Giddings reported that Ohio Young Whigs hoped to block nomination of either Taylor or Clay with Corwin; Corwin, however, wanted a nomination to come from Massachusetts. Another presidential possibility was Supreme Court Associate Justice John McLean, who in 1845 had opposed the annexation of Texas. *New York Tribune* editor Horace Greeley was advocating either Corwin or William H. Seward.[23]

Wilson was discouraged in early February, 1847. He had hoped Northern Democrats would resist extension and had been disappointed. He certainly had hoped for more from Webster and Davis. He suggested those who opposed slavery would have to hold their own convention and "run good and true men." Free-state Whigs should either control the party's strategy or break it up. After Corwin's speech, however, Wilson had new enthusiasm. He spoke of Corwin's "boldness and high moral tone," and hoped the senator would come out in favor of the Wilmot Proviso. Wilson was disgusted with Whig compromisers like John J. Crittenden of Kentucky, John Clayton of Delaware, and Webster. He would advocate Seward for vice-president.[24]

Wilson, who had led the Conscience Whig efforts in the legislature in 1846, who had been a candidate for the General Court seven times in succession, now had to trust to others to lead the battle against slavery. His shoe business was being affected by his absences and by competition from the growing number of firms. Furthermore, Harriet, not in good health for several years, was quite sick. This may have been connected in part with the birth of their son in early November 1846, but Harriet was still confined to her bed in the summer of 1847. Fortunately, Hamilton was "fat and hearty," at two weeks weighing nine and a half pounds.[25]

Wilson by the second half of the 1840s had moved to the foremost position politically in his community, a remarkable achievement in only seven years. Part of this was a product of his important social connections, part his effective political ability, part that he and his friends were well organized and able to preserve a Whig vote from their community. Wilson was a man of plain dress and manners, gentle, unassuming. In addition to his business Wilson had real estate in 1846 which he recorded as a house worth $1,800, a shop worth $800, another house and shop worth $1,300, two house lots worth $300 and $200, and "a half house," $500. He estimated the value of his furniture at $600 and his horse and wagon at $86. In the 1840s most of the Colbath family had left New Hampshire; brothers George, Samuel, and John had all joined Henry in Natick. All three men at one time or another worked for their brother.[26]

The community of Natick was changing in the 1840s. Its population more than doubled during that decade. Irish laborers were moving in. The Congregational, Unitarian, and Methodist denominations were joined by the Catholic and the Baptist, and in the early 1850s by the Universalist. The first lawyer to stay any length in town arrived in 1846. The fire department was organized in 1844. Land was purchased from Walcott for Dell Park Cemetery in 1849 with Wilson in charge of the ceremonies and Hunt delivering the address for the occasion. On West Central Street, where the Wilsons lived, the double row of stately trees begun in 1830 was set planted. Harriet Wilson in 1845 was secretary-treasurer of the twenty-eight member Circle of Industry, formed three years before; it attracted about fifteen women to its meetings. In 1847 a citizens' library was created which became the nucleus for the later town library and the Morse Institute. Wilson was deeply interested in the enterprise and was one of its original proprietors. In nearby South Natick stood the Eliot monument, dedicated in 1846 by Wilson, Moore, Hunt, and Walcott, among others, to honor the early missionary to the Indians.[27]

In the meantime the war with Mexico was moving into its second year. When the successes of Taylor in Mexico's northeastern provinces and the victories of other small American armies in the Southwest and California did not induce the Mexican government to seek peace, both the American military and political leadership agreed they then had to bring the war to the heartland of the enemy, with the capture of Vera Cruz and, if no request came for peace, a movement on Mexico City itself. The attack on Vera Cruz began on March 9, 1847; within less than three weeks the port city fell. Striking inland deliberately and skillfully, General Winfield Scott's small force by August 20 had advanced to Mexico City and obtained an armistice. Fighting subsequently resumed but by mid-September the capitol had fallen. The difficulty of negotiating with the Mexican governments prevented a treaty of peace from being signed until February 2, 1848.

Opposition to the government's prosecution of the war increased as the months went by. The Congress, which declared war in May, 1846, got into a major controversy in August when Representative David Wilmot, a Democrat from

Pennsylvania, attempted to attach an amendment to a bill to provide the government two million dollars to "facilitate negotiations" with Mexico. Wilmot would prohibit slavery in any territory which might be obtained from Mexico. This provision was agreed to by the House but the Senate adjourned without taking action. For the next fifteen years whenever bills dealing with territories were before a house of Congress someone would attempt to attach an amendment similar to the Wilmot Proviso.

The short second session of the Twenty-ninth Congress, beginning in December, 1846, was more contentious and difficult for the Polk administration to work with. The Whigs, having won the fall elections, were looking forward to control of the House in the next session and a victory in the 1848 presidential race, possibly with General Taylor as candidate; they had good reasons to harass the administration. Some Northern Democrats were angry at the government's acceptance of a compromise with Great Britain over the Oregon Territory; others were displeased with Southern dominance of the Polk administration. Westerners were dissatisfied with the government's curtailment of funding for internal improvements. Many were unhappy with a war that was not the easy victory they had been promised. Others were vocal in their opposition to the likelihood of large additions of possible slave territory. Even appropriations bills were difficult to get passed. While all of this pleased national Whigs, in Massachusetts the party leadership recognized two divergent needs: one, to keep the party and state as quiet as possible on issues which might antagonize Southerners and lose 1848 votes in the slave states; and two, to persuade voters in the North that the Whigs truly represented their interests, including opposition to the expansion of slavery.

The Whig-controlled legislature in 1847 easily adopted resolutions, urged by Governor Briggs in his inaugural address, in opposition to the further extension of slavery. Edward Keyes, editor of the *Dedham Gazette,* subsequently introduced other resolutions, framed by Sumner, and similar to the Phillips proposals to the 1846 convention. Their language was much stronger in condemning the objectives of the war and demanding the end of slavery in the nation. In spite of a desire that the resolutions not be adopted, the Cotton Whigs in the end had to agree to them; they passed 27 to 1 in the Senate and 153 to 33 in the House. In the meantime, the party division between the Webster and Lawrence factions reappeared. Webster, anxious for the 1848 presidential nomination and an 1847 state convention endorsement, visited the South and courted Conscience Whig support. While still a minority, temporarily at least, the Conscience faction again had power.[28]

Wilson continued to be discouraged during the spring. Corwin had not reenforced his antislavery stance by a second speech. Perhaps Wilson's own lack of participation in the legislature left him frustrated. In a mid-March he was unhappy about the New Hampshire election results. Adams commented that Wilson worried too much about events he could not control. A month later Wilson was convinced Taylor would be nominated; most Cotton Whigs favored him. He wrote

Giddings he could not accept the slaveholding general, no matter what. He advocated antislavery Whig cooperation in Congress and division of the party before submitting to Southern dictation. One of his suggestions involved working with Barnburner Democrats, who were supporting New York's Silas Wright. In his willingness to advocate a third party movement he clearly was more radical than some of his Conscience Whig associates. According to Wilson, Adams wrote, Giddings thought they were too cautious; but Adams was convinced they were as far advanced as their supporters would permit and that only moderation had enabled them to carry the antislavery resolutions in the legislature. *The Emancipator,* Boston newspaper of the Liberty party, whose editor declared that he and his newspaper had no more bitter enemy than the founders and supporters of the *Boston Whig,* taunted the Conscience Whigs for their lack of a program in the likely event Taylor were nominated.[29]

In June the *Boston Whig* editorially attacked the Whig party as positioning itself in favor of compromise and tried to establish the Wilmot Proviso as a mark of party conviction. Several days later a correspondent, who signed his letter "W"—probably Wilson—asserted that many Whigs would be "brought under the yoke, provided Gen. Taylor orders the march." However, truth was beginning to dawn within the minds of the best men of both the Whig and Democratic parties, the correspondent declared. They now had to unite to halt the designs of the South. Tariff was no longer the issue it had been; the need for foodstuffs abroad and prosperity at home had changed the situation. The bank issue was dead. Old controversies which had divided the Whigs and Democrats could now be replaced. Giddings arrived a week later and met with Adams and Wilson. Wilson soon thereafter left for an Independence Day trip to New Hampshire and Maine, returning with the conviction that Maine Whigs would join the Cotton element of Massachusetts in a Taylor nomination.[30]

All three Whig factions planned for the 1847 fall convention, particularly focusing on the stance they would take concerning the 1848 presidential nomination. On August 3 Wilson and Adams consulted and Wilson volunteered to write for the paper. Wilson did not return with his article until August 12. This must have been a letter, dated July 14 and printed on August 18. Wilson claimed the course pursued by some members of the party had forced the question of the presidential nomination on others. Taylor, however, was precluding his own nomination by refusing to provide any insight into his principles or policies. His selection therefore was out of the question. If he were the candidate, he would divide the party. The nominee, in any case, should come from the free states and he "should be in favor of rescuing the general government from the grasp of the slave power." Corwin should be the man. After recounting his background and talents, Wilson termed Corwin's political life "straight forward and brilliant." Independent Democrats and Liberty men would support him. He would carry every free state but Illinois. Wilson called upon the *Whig* to hoist Corwin's name to the head of its columns. The *Whig* and the *Roxbury Gazette* were soon pushing hard for Corwin. On August 19 Wilson and Adams conferred again, this time about a local convention to select two delegates to the state meeting. Wilson convinced Adams they would have to take some position, and then Adams's policy of conciliation would be unworkable. Palfrey was equally certain the paper had to oppose Webster's nomination.[31]

Unfortunately Corwin himself was complicating the Conscience Whig position. The Ohio senator confided to Giddings in mid-August that Taylor would be nominated and elected by some party. If the Whigs were to divide, the Southern segment would nominate and elect Taylor, and the Democrats would win. Corwin, unwilling to permit his name to be used to that result, soon was pleading financial and family concerns required more of his time. He consistently asserted Whigs must sustain whomever the national convention nominated. He did, however, advocate no state nominations until after the next congressional session adjourned. Clearly Corwin was not closing the door to his own nomination, but he suspected no matter what others did, Taylor would be selected. The *Cincinnati Atlas* and the *Louisville Journal* both reported Corwin was supporting the general. In any case, as the *National Era* pointed out, regardless of Corwin's "good impulses," he was without antislavery principles or an Ohio antislavery record.[32]

On August 25 and again on September 22 Wilson and other leaders of the Conscience faction consulted. The others overcame the conservatism of Adams. When the Democrats nominated Caleb Cushing as their candidate for governor, the Conscience Whigs were encouraged their influence within their own party would increase. Adams believed the Lawrence faction was permitting election of his associates as delegates to the convention in order to use them to forestall Webster's nomination. In the days before the convention the Whig press argued over the desirability of a Webster nomination, unnecessary as a compliment to the man, the *Lowell Courier* asserted, injudicious and useless as a tactic, the *Salem Register* maintained.[33]

The Conscience faction overestimated its strength, however. Its first defeat was expected. Sumner tried to commit the Boston local convention to resolutions condemning the war as "aggression" and "robbery"; they were laid on the table. Wilson was present at the state Springfield convention, but does not appear to have spoken. Adams, Sumner, Palfrey, Phillips, Buckingham, and Keyes decided upon the immediate tactics and the first four, Allen, and William Dwight carried the debate. The planners agreed first to exploit the divisions between the Lawrence and Webtser factions by promoting a resolution of inexpediency to make nominations for president and vice-president. They failed 242 to 232; Webster was subsequently selected. They were not dissatisfied with the platform, but sought to add a declaration, introduced by Palfrey, that the Whigs of the state would sustain as candidates for president or vice-president only men who by their acts or declared opinions were opposed to the extension of slavery. While only Winthrop, "with a good deal of warmth," opposed them in debate, this effort also failed.[34]

The Webster faction also emerged a loser. The numbers against nominating a candidate were so large Webster could not be presented to the party as sustained by his own state; the antislavery speech he had made to obtain Conscience Whig support, including a pledge he would not vote for annexation of more slave territory, would injure even further his chances at the national convention. Soon Webster would recognize he had little need for further Conscience Whig support. The Conscience Whigs, on the other hand, had to recognize that their success with the Keyes resolutions in the legislature was of less significance than they had thought and that they might soon have to confront the likelihood of an 1848 Taylor presidential nomination. Both Sumner and Adams recorded they probably would not attend another Whig state convention. They were now joining Wilson, who had already often expressed interest in a third party.[35] The campaign and the election further weakened the Conscience Whigs' political strength. After the state convention, the Lawrence faction moved to consolidate its position; Conscience Whigs were ignored whenever possible for state offices. Few attended the Boston party conclave on eve of the election. Concurrently, the Henshaw group had taken control of the Democratic party. Their 1847 nominee, Caleb Cushing, a formidable campaigner, was unacceptable to many antislavery independents and Democrats. Still, Cushing got more votes than the 1846 Democratic nominee. Briggs was again elected governor with a majority support, indicating that the Liberty party and the Conscience Whigs no longer had to be appeased. On the other hand, Keyes, whom *The Liberator* called the most effective legislator of the previous term, was defeated.[36]

The remaining energies of the Conscience Whigs were directed against their old antagonist Winthrop, who emerged from the congressional party caucus as the nominee for Speaker of the House. A November controversy between Adams and Schouler—since May the editor of the *Boston Atlas*—over alleged plans of the Conscience Whigs to prevent a Winthrop election preceded the selection. Schouler, who within the year had been a confidant of those planning Conscience Whig strategy, now called Winthrop one of Massachusetts's "most gifted sons." Wilson visited the *Whig* offices frequently in November and must have supported the campaign against the congressman. The division between the two parties in the House was so close, however, that if a few Southern Whigs, who resented Winthrop's anti-expansion speeches, or if a few Northern Whigs, who agreed with Sumner's attacks against Winthrop's moderation, voted against him, either no man could be elected Speaker or the minority Democrats might get their man chosen. For three ballots, no candidate was chosen, as three Southern Whigs and Giddings, Amos Tuck of New Hampshire, and Palfrey voted against Winthrop. Election came on the fourth ballot when one of the Southern Whigs voted for Winthrop, the other two abstained, and one Southern Democrat left the hall. When leading Conscience

Whigs defended Palfrey's vote, the Cotton Whigs were strengthened in their conviction that they no longer should modify their positions to retain occasional Conscience support. Their news organs for the next several months directed a steady attack particularly against Palfrey and Giddings.[37]

Massachusetts was not the only state in which members of the two leading parties were increasingly unhappy with their party's position on the expansion of slavery, or found the presidential nominees unacceptable. Giddings, formerly an independent Whig, declared he would not support any man who was not opposed to the extension of slavery. Those in Ohio who thought similarly could promote candidacies for Corwin or McLean, who were both Ohioans and Whigs. Some Democrats, particularly in New York, seemed determined to strive for a less Southern-oriented administration and nominee than they had obtained with Polk. A long controversy between Hunker and Barnburner Democrats in the state had weakened their party and given the 1847 election to the Whigs.[38]

Whether aristocratic Conscience Whigs like Adams, Phillips, and Palfrey could join with Democrats, especially if they were led by Martin Van Buren, was questionable. Furthermore, any new third party or even coalition also required cooperation with the Liberty party, and many Conscience Whigs had long refused to see much difference between Liberty party abolitionists and associates of Garrison. The spokespaper for that party in the state, *The Emancipator,* had sneered at Conscience Whig "sacrifices" and assailed what its editor regarded as the impracticality of their tactics. Adams believed the paper did its best to defeat Palfrey. Difficulties within the Democratic party in nearby New Hampshire that propelled John Hale to antislavery political leadership, the increasing differences in voting among the Massachusetts Whig congressional delegation, and the now obvious determination of the Cotton Whigs to rule the party in the state forced the elite Conscience Whigs to rethink their continued professions of loyalty to party. Relations with the Liberty party leadership began to improve. Joshua Leavitt in January invited Adams and his associates to attend the state meeting of the party, but the Conscience Whigs decided once more to decline. Sumner and Chase agreed party lines should be arranged so that Liberty men would have influence. Adams was more confident they could work with the Liberty men than with radical Democrats.[39]

In the meantime war with Mexico had come to an end. The Treaty of Guadelupe Hidalgo was signed on February 2, reached Washington on February 19, was forwarded by a reluctant president to the Senate for its consideration, and was ratified by that body on March 10. For all practical purposes the issue of war with Mexico was over. But because the treaty included not only Mexican recognition of American possession of Texas, but the cession of thousands of acres of the West, national arguments were no more ended than they had been with the annexation of Texas. Would these new lands be slave or free? The issues raised several years before by the Wilmot Proviso now became more real and more demanding of attention of those who were determined to and not to extend slavery. Fifteen states adopted resolutions favoring the Proviso.

The energy and hope of the Conscience Whigs were gradually restored. In January the legislature, against the plans of the Cotton faction, elected Keyes to the Governor's Council; a month later he was also placed on the party's State Central Committee. Correspondence of the Conscience faction throughout the first four months of 1848 is full of speculation about the chances of Corwin, McLean, and Clay for the nomination; all were preferable to Taylor. Whether the Conscience Whigs were naive or just grasping at straws, one cannot know, for the likelihood of anyone defeating Taylor was not very great. Wilson, visiting New York City the first week in January, reported that Whig leader Thurlow Weed claimed Taylor's nomination would cost the party 40,000 votes and that Democrat David Dudley Field assured Wilson the Democrats would be true to their Wilmot Proviso principles. Webster, of course, remained the candidate of the party in the state, by virtue of the 1847 convention decision. Greeley requested that Wilson inform *Tribune* readers what the political climate was in Massachusetts and on March 25 Wilson complied. Most Whigs of Boston, he reported, did not know what to do; they were watching events. Webster's chances were slim, Clay's nomination was inexpedient. He doubted Taylor had one thousand supporters in the state; he did not know half a dozen out of Suffolk County, not one in Natick or even in Middlesex County. Lawrence had thrown his support for the general in a letter to a Taylor dinner in Philadelphia, but he spoke for few Massachusetts Whigs, Wilson asserted. Wilson believed assurances had been given, however, that Massachusetts would vote for Taylor and in return the state would be awarded the vice-presidential nomination. If Taylor were nominated, Wilson predicted, perhaps a third of the Whigs in Massachusetts would not vote for him. He insisted the free states should be given the nomination, thus excluding Clay as well. He favored McLean. If Seward or John M. Clayton of Delaware were nominated with McLean, New England would be carried.[40]

In February 1848 John Quincy Adams died. Wilson was among those mentioned as a potential successor. The *New York Tribune,* with its good Whig credentials, cited Wilson, Keyes, Solomon Lincoln, and Liberty party stalwart William Jackson as possibilities. It knew only Wilson, "who is an upright, conscientious, clear-headed Whig, who will honor any seat which may be assigned him from a shoe bench down to one of the Congressional easy chairs." Palfrey characterized Wilson as a "man of great courage" and "of superior mind and uncommon powers of speech and action," but he preferred Adams. Wilson, according to Adams, wanted the nomination and attempted to convince Adams that the voters would not agree to a candidate (Adams) who had not hitherto been regarded as a resident of the district. Of course, the Cotton Whigs would not agree to Wilson. Rather, the party leaders promoted and elected Horace Mann, acceptable to the Conscience faction. Twenty years older than Wilson, Mann had been trained for the law, had served as president of the state Senate, but had won fame primarily as secretary since 1837 of the state's Board of Education. On the third ballot, Wilson withdrew his candidacy. Whittier declared the Boston managers were pleased, but soon doubted the wisdom of their choice; Wilson urged Mann to proclaim his views about slavery and in his acceptance letter Mann ignored usual Whig planks to emphasize his support of freedom.[41]

Conventions in the congressional districts clearly were willing to select delegates to the national convention who were not Taylor supporters. In spite of his pronouncements, Wilson was selected in the Eight Congressional District; *The Emancipator* speculated that the selection had been in exchange for Conscience Whig agreement to Mann's candidacy for Congress. The meeting of the Eight Congressional District passed strong resolutions opposing slavery. The Sixth Congressional District convention selected the mildly anti-extension George Ashmun, but then designated Daniel Alvord as his alternate. Alvord declared he was opposed to Taylor and would not vote for him either at the convention or at the polls. The Fifth Congressional District convention not only selected Allen as delegate, but passed resolutions declaring their "uncompromising opposition to any further extension of slavery over the territory of the United States" and resolving that no presidential candidate could receive the electoral vote of Massachusetts who was not known as opposed to the extension of slavery over territory then free.[42]

As the national convention approached, the factions organized. Lawrence sought the vice-presidency; if the state delegation voted too long for Webster, the convention might turn elsewhere for Taylor's running mate. Men devoted both to the senator and to antislavery established a Webster's Young Men's Club. Webster assured them he opposed the election of "an ignorant, swearing frontier colonel."[43] Charles Train and E. R. Hoar became important participants in the movement and even Wilson joined the club. Wilson, Adams, Phillips, and Sumner agreed the Webster efforts were only weakening their stance. Giddings still thought Taylor would not be nominated. Adams's diary shows that Wilson called on May 18 to discuss pending events and advocate holding a meeting prior to the convention to plan what the Conscience Whigs should do. Both Allen and Wilson called on May 23 and Adams agreed to extend invitations. In the meantime the national Democratic convention nominated Lewis Cass of Michigan as its candidate for the presidency. This would likely either result in factionalism within that party, and thus victory for the Whigs, or a withdrawal of the Van Buren Democrats and their willingness to work with others who opposed the nominees of the two major parties and favored the Wilmot Proviso.[44]

On May 27 Adams, Wilson, Phillips, E. R. Hoar, Keyes, Sumner, Bird, and Edward Walcutt gathered in Adams's office. They first agreed they should oppose a Taylor, or any other unacceptable, nomination. More difficult was deciding what they should do. Phillips was to return with the solution on June 1. Keyes, however, soon expressed his reservations. He asserted they should not go to Whig conventions if they were not Whigs. He described himself as in a particularly awkward position since he was on the state Central Committee and edited a Whig newspaper. On June 1 Phillips read a proposed call for convention, lengthy and unfinished. Keyes dissented, convinced Taylor's nomination was acceptable to most Whigs in Massachusetts. Wilson replied "warmly and earnestly." Keyes pleaded another engagement and left. The others could not agree what to do next. Two days later (June 3) they convened again, but Phillips was absent. Again on Monday Phillips did not join the group or send materials. Adams claimed he published the call for the state convention which he himself wrote, probably based upon Phillips's original draft. Wilson, Edward L. Pierce, Sumner, and Hoar, on the other hand, related that the initial meeting had assigned to Hoar the responsibility of drawing up a call for a state convention at Worcester, which would be signed in case Taylor were nominated.[45]

In spite of the invective they later received from their former Whig associates, Wilson and Allen consistently voted for the candidate of the fall state convention, Webster. Admittedly, unless the national convention were to deadlock and they could vote for someone more agreeable to them, Webster was preferable to Taylor, Clay, or Scott. A Webster supporter contended if any Northern man were nominated, he would have to be supported. If Scott were the candidate, they would consider what to do. *The Emancipator* wondered, given the disfavor Taylor was in among Wilmot Proviso advocates such as Wilson and Giddings, how might they respond to the nomination of Clay? Lawrence and Winthrop, in contrast, were known to be Taylor supporters and the *Atlas,* recognized spokespaper of the Lawrence faction, abandoned Webster's candidacy even before the convention met. On the day Wilson was to leave for Philadelphia, a friend of Webster's asked him to go to the senator's office. There Wilson found Webster supporters, including Webster's son Fletcher, Anson Burlingame, and others, angry at the activities of the Cotton leadership in its advocacy of Taylor and efforts to obtain the vice-presidential nomination for Lawrence. They asked Wilson what he intended to do. He answered that if the convention adopted the Wilmot Proviso, or if Taylor advocated it, he and other Conscience Whigs would support the party and its nominee. On the other hand, if the national convention did not agree with the often-stated principles of the state of Massachusetts, Wilson would return home and help unite those who agreed with him. The others present supported Wilson's position. Wilson further affirmed that he could not vote for Webster if the senator used his influence to secure Taylor's nomination. The Webster supporters insisted the senator would not support Taylor. When he reached Philadelphia, Wilson found a letter from Webster giving him "ample assurances." Burlingame told Adams his associates would resist a Taylor nomination and would "fraternize" with the Adams group.[46]

Wilson wrote en route to Philadelphia from New York City, somewhat inspirited by the amount of opposition he found to Taylor. He held out some hope that if those who favored other candidates united they might yet obtain another man. Holman Hamilton, one of Taylor's biographers, has characterized the convention as composed of a rather mediocre caliber of delegates, with Massachusetts one of the strongest represented states, including Ashmun and Rufus Choate in addition to Wilson and Allen. Those who supported nominees other than Taylor met to ascertain whether they could find ways to cooperate. Wilson openly avowed his views, but emphasized he also was opposed to any nominee who would not advocate the Wilmot Proviso. He threatened to go home and unite with others whose opinions were similar to his own. When the presidential balloting began on June 7, Webster was weaker than even the Conscience Whigs had supposed, obtaining only twenty-two votes on the first ballot, twelve of them from Massachusetts, nine from nearby Maine and New Hampshire. On the third ballot, he garnered only seventeen votes, losing one in Maine and three in Massachusetts. One of the Massachusetts delegation voted for Taylor, the other two for Scott. Clay ran very well, obtaining ninety-seven votes on the first ballot to 111 for Taylor. Scott garnered forty-three. Taylor's support was primarily from the South and from states unlikely to be carried by the Whigs in the election. As Ashmun later wrote, most Northerners voted for slave state men; Massachusetts was the only state whose representatives wanted to select a Northerner. By the third ballot, Clay was losing support, Taylor and Scott were gaining. On the fourth ballot the Taylor campaign succeeded; Webster obtained fourteen votes, nine of them from Massachusetts, including Wilson's and Allen's.[47]

After the presidential nomination, party leaders lacked a plan. Clay supporters were apparently willing to accept the results, select a vice-presidential candidate, and go home. Several of those who had opposed Taylor sought and obtained the floor to voice their support for the party nominee. Allen, always soft-spoken, was then able to gain recognition and, although not permitted to read a speech he had prepared, announced he would not support the proceedings. He pointed out that of all the able Northern Whigs, not one had received a Southern vote. The Whig party was dissolved. He contended the free states would no longer submit to slave state domination. This produced considerable excitement and many hisses. Since a Southerner could not as appropriately repel Allen's charges, Choate was called for, but he had already left the convention hall. John Bingham of Ohio then announced he would accept the Taylor selection, but he offered a resolution opposing the extension of slave territory and the future addition of foreign lands by conquest. He was ruled out of order. The convention, as a matter of fact, did not adopt a single resolution on any important issue.[48]

The delegates then turned to selection of a vice-president. Both Lawrence and Winthrop of Massachusetts were nominated. In withdrawing Winthrop's name, Ashmun attempted to improve Lawrence's chances and recover some of his state's reputation in the party by announcing Allen had not expressed his or Massachusetts Whigs' views in his response to the presidential nomination. Wilson asked Ashmun if he concurred in the convention's actions. Ashmun replied he had opposed Taylor's nomination, he sympathized with Wilson in support of Webster, but he would not offer "factious opposition." Wilson declared he would not be bound by the proceedings. An uproar threatened to silence the speaker, but Ashmun and delegate Stanley of North Carolina asked that he be heard. Wilson asserted he had come to the convention as a Whig, but Taylor had declared he would not be bound by the principles or measures of any party and he would not withdraw his third party candidacy, even if the Whigs nominated Clay. Taylor was no Whig and Wilson would not support him. "So help me God, I will do all I can to defeat him." Alexander McClure later remembered the speech as "earnest and somewhat impassioned. It was delivered in faultless style, and certainly made a profound impression." The tumult was so great, the reporter could not hear what was said. Lunt followed, condemning Wilson's position, avowing his and Massachusetts Whig support for Taylor, and asking for a continuation of the vice-presidential selection.[49]

The convention on a second ballot selected Milliard Fillmore of New York as its vice-presidential nominee. On the first ballot the New Yorker had been ahead only 115 to 109. Two of the Massachusetts delegates, presumably Wilson and Allen, withheld their votes from Lawrence. Oliver Dyer, who was official reporter of the convention, and claimed he was much involved in its backstage maneuvers, declared the Taylor supporters wanted Lawrence and his possible $100,000 contribution to the campaign, but he was not enough of an antislavery man to satisfy those who were unhappy with the presidential nomination. While Massachusetts Whig papers could blame Wilson and Allen for Lawrence's defeat, and Wilson himself later contended Lawrence lost because of his and Allen's positions, some modern historians think that with both Clay and Webster opposed to him, Lawrence's chances were not very good.[50]

The evening of the nominations Wilson called for a gathering of those opposed to what had transpired. Considering the number who had voted against Taylor, Wilson was disappointed to attract only fifteen delegates. Three (including Alvord) were from Massachusetts, three from New York, six from Ohio. In his opening remarks Wilson characterized the nomination of Taylor as a triumph of the Slave Power, objected to the convention's rejection of the Wilmot Proviso, and asked for the calling of a third party national convention. He wanted a committee of three appointed to undertake this. John Campbell and Joseph Galloway of Ohio preferred to consult their constituents before taking action. Allen and Isaac Platt of New York supported Wilson. The group finally selected a committee of Allen, Giddings, and John C. Vaughan of Ohio, set Buffalo in early August as the time and place for the conclave, and asked Vaughan to get the already-scheduled Ohio People's Convention to endorse the Buffalo meeting.[51]

In the meantime prominent party officials were taking the steps preliminary to creation of a third party. New Hampshire already had a coalition under Hale. Gamaliel Bailey wrote to Stanton, who had moved from Massachusetts to New York, and thus had important political connections in both states, to take the lead in uniting New York's Van Buren–Barnburners and Massachusetts's Conscience Whigs. Chase in Ohio was already preparing for coalition. Adams needed little urging. On June 8 he replied to Stanton that he and his associates would not try to make Barnburners into Whigs, but the Barnburners must not attempt to make them Democrats. He urged the West to take the lead in planning for a national convention. He reacted to a false report of Taylor's nomination a day early with an article in the *Whig* and he was soon busy dispatching circulars over the state. E.R. Hoar, Erastus Hopkins, Keyes, Phillips, Sumner, Walcutt, and Wilson denounced the nomination of Taylor for many of the same reasons Wilson had proclaimed in Philadelphia.[52]

The Massachusetts Whig leadership, whether of the Lawrence or Webster factions, generally accepted the results of the convention. The Lawrence faction, of course, was delighted. Lawrence himself would eventually decline an offer of secretary of navy in the Taylor cabinet but would accept the ministry to Great Britain. Sumner and Adams reported the Lawrence and Webster factions were quarreling. The results, however, would not affect the fall elections on either the national or state level. Webster was hurt, humiliated, and angry. Within a week, however, he confided to his son Fletcher that he had no choice but "acquiescence" in the results. Taylor would be elected and Fletcher's own political future could be endangered by opposition. Yet the senator remained silent publicly and permitted his son to attend the Worcester convention; Jonathan Mann claimed it was organized with his "concurrence." At Webster's request, Wilson called upon him and the senator expressed his agreement with the principles enunciated by the Worcester meeting. Antislavery supporters like Hoar all summer deceived themselves that the great man would yet join them. But Webster could not accept his old antagonist Van Buren as presidential nominee of the new party and in September, at his out-of-the-way Marshfield home, he gave Taylor what one biographer has called a "cold endorsement." His socioeconomic principles and his nationalism combined to produce this decision.[53]

Few state newspapers followed the *Boston Whig* in opposition to Taylor, although most took more time than usual to endorse the candidates of their party. Allen and Wilson were bitterly attacked by some Whig papers. Robinson was forced out of the editorship of the *Lowell Courier*, hitherto open to Conscience Whig ideas, for refusing to tone down his articles against Taylor. Neither did the other Whig factions bemoan the loss of some of their troublesome Conscience brethren. Cooperation was becoming difficult. J. N. Brewer, confident Taylor could defeat Cass, would be sorry to see Wilson "float through the gates," but he declared a general separation might rid the party of "cumbersome material."[54]

On June 12 a large group assembled at Sumner's office to hear Wilson's description of what had happened in Philadelphia. They were excited now that the break had occurred. Keyes had regained his perspective and cast his lot with the others. Burlingame and other former Webster supporters were also present. The next several weeks were busy for those who had to prepare for a convention, coordinate with politicians in other states who had different backgrounds and often different views, and take careful steps to create a new political movement. Adams characterized the feeling in the state as stronger than he had expected. Their planning brought out "more action and more courage than usual." Allen recorded sympathy in his county exceeded "his most exaggerated hopes." Sumner, Allen, and Wilson were the committee for invitations. Adams and Sumner were to persuade Giddings to speak to the convention, Sumner and Wilson sought Mann's presence or communication, Wilson tried to get Webster to commit himself, and Phillips was to pen the resolutions for Worcester.[55]

When Allen returned to Worcester he was asked to address his constituents on June 21. He believed few would be interested, so a small hall was engaged. The meeting had to be shifted to the largest room in town, and even then it was crowded beyond capacity. Wilson declared few speeches had produced a more "marked and immediate effect." At the close of Allen's address, Wilson also delivered a few remarks. Worcester County had been a Whig stronghold, albeit also strongly antislavery. Webster was popular there and it was the home of former governor Lincoln and governor and senator Davis. Its aristocracy in 1848 allied itself with Taylor's candidacy. Allen and his associates would now change the political climate. He was nominated for Congress and his new party would win forty-eight out of the county's fifty-two towns.[56]

Wilson chose to issue an address, dated June 14, to the Whigs of his district. It was a powerful letter, well written. In it he noted the resolutions passed by the convention which had elected him. He had been known for years as opposed to slavery. He then chronicled the proceedings of the national convention. His party had hitherto represented the "intelligence, morality, and decency of the nation." Taylor had no Whig principles. All that was claimed for Taylor was his military abilities. His votes on the first ballot came overwhelmingly from the slave states; he was the candidate of the Southwest. For years Whigs had denounced Democrats for their servility to the South and now they themselves were servile. The convention furthermore rejected the Wilmot Proviso. Wilson had acted, he asserted, on "mature reflection." He already was being denounced throughout the state, even by men with whom he formerly had worked closely. Yet he knew that to agree to the selection of Taylor after the specific proviso rejection would be to ignore his own convictions as well as those of his constituents. He had not abandoned his Whiggery; the convention had abandoned its. He had little choice, he wrote, but to repudiate the party's abrogation of its principles. The next night he also addressed "a large meeting" in Chelsea. However, when he attempted to speak in Lynn, Wilson encountered a mob. A correspondent of Mann's wrote Wilson's cause "would not be sustained." He predicted those opposing Taylor would have "sober second thoughts" and support the ticket.[57]

Until this time, the more elite among the Conscience Whigs had been the leaders of the movement. But Phillips and Allen had always been unwilling or unable to devote the time which organizing and leading a political movement would take. Palfrey, respected for his mind and courage, was more a scholar than an effective politician. Adams in many ways had been the true leader; others appear to have done their planning in his office. But the death of his father and his separation from his newspaper duties now were interfering with his central role, a fact Adams never seemed to understand. He came to resent the assumption of leadership by others. Sumner—who had the same "right" connections as Phillips, Palfrey, or Adams, but, in contrast to them, whose interest in the antislavery cause was consuming—was already rising to new influence. New, energetic men like Bird and Burlingame were joining the movement. But, more than any other man, Henry Wilson was taking the helm of organizing Massachusetts's political opposition to the expansion of slavery and to the Slave Power.

5

THE FREE SOIL MOVEMENT

The Free Soil party in Massachusetts began with the Worcester convention, June 28, 1848. Historian Frank Gattel termed the meeting the "high point" of the Conscience Whig movement in the state. Because so few Democrats were present and because Whigs controlled its organization, the conclave may have been as much a part of Conscience Whig history as it was the inception of the Free Soil party. Five thousand persons assembled, so many that the convention had to adjourn from the City Hall to the Commons and in the afternoon to a grove. Nevertheless, southeastern and western Massachusetts were sparsely represented. In the early morning a large crowd gathered in front of Temperance House, where Wilson and Amasa Walker spoke.[1]

Soon after it assembled, the convention approved a resolution praising the "fidelity, consistency, decision, and boldness" of Wilson and Allen at Philadelphia; in response, both men gave short speeches. George Stearns, just beginning his public life, characterized the Wilson speech as "memorable"; *The Emancipator* called it "thrilling." Wilson attacked Taylor as belonging to that class of Whigs which had voted to expel Giddings from Congress and who had supported the Mexican War and slavery. To broaden the proceedings Democrat Walker and Liberty party leader Joshua Leavitt also addressed the assembly. Walker complained that no Liberty party men were on the Resolutions Committee. In fact, a large number of members of that party were present. S. C. Phillips, committee chairman, apologized, noting he did not know whether Liberty party men would attend; Leavitt was added. Giddings in his address called the Whig party dissolved and favored Van Buren for the presidential nomination. The committee resolutions endorsed the calling of a national convention to nominate candidates opposed to the extension of slavery.[2]

The Conscience men finally had separated from their party. Adams had declared at Worcester that the Whigs were so corrupt that they could not be believed under oath. Historian Gattel termed Sumner's speech there "intemperate"; the future senator labeled the Whig nomination "a conspiracy" engaged in by Taylor advocates and Massachusetts men, "the cotton-spinners and traffickers of New England—between the lords of the lash and the lords of the loom." Angered by the remarks, Nathan Appleton demanded to know what Sumner had meant by the accusation. The *Lowell Journal* charged the Conscience Whigs had set out to "dissever" their party. The *Boston Atlas* recorded Adams, Wilson, and their associates had joined the Liberty party. For their refusal to endorse Taylor, Robinson lost his editorship of the *Lowell Courier* and Buckingham his of the *Boston Courier*.[3]

It was a talented and influential group of men that went to Worcester, although no one at the time could have predicted their success. Wilson, of course, would later become senator and vice-president. Sumner would also be sent to the Senate for four terms. Two others—John Andrew and William H. Claflin—would become governors of the state. Marcus Morton Jr., Allen, and E. R. Hoar would hold high judicial positions. Adams, Burlingame, John Kasson, and Richard H. Dana would be selected for important diplomatic posts; sixteen of those in attendance would later be elected to the House of Representatives.[4]

Only the first steps had been taken at Worcester. The leadership of the new party next had to persuade the Liberty party to abandon its separate existence, encourage Democrats and Whigs to join the new movement, and organize and propagandize their cause in the state and elsewhere in the North. They had only six weeks until a national convention would assemble at Buffalo, and four months until the national election. The Worcester convention established a State Committee of fourteen, headed by Adams and including Wilson. Giddings tarried in the state for speeches. Sumner also spoke briefly in Boston; Wilson, in attendance, was called for by the audience, but promised to return the next week. On July 7 E. R. Hoar and Wilson were the featured speakers at a meeting presided over by Richard Henry Dana Jr., a new addition to the cause. The editor of *The Liberator* reported Wilson's address was "not one of his best efforts, though it was earnest and forcible."[5]

In the meantime a similar convention had been held in Ohio and the Barnburner Democrats had gathered in Utica, New York. The latter conclave had nominated Van Buren for the presidency. The Ohio Liberty party, the same day as the state's unity convention, nominated John P. Hale. While *The Emancipator* said Liberty party men would never support Van Buren, the *Springfield Republican* correctly predicted the former president would be the new movement's nominee. As the summer moved on, large Free Soil meetings were held in Ohio. Indiana, which historian Joseph Rayback points out had never before seemed concerned about the expansion of slavery, now began to respond. So did a number of men in Democratic nominee Cass's home state of Michigan.[6]

Could the unhappy party leaders in Massachusetts now be persuaded to cooperate? If Daniel Webster would sustain the new movement, many others would also. Fletcher Webster and some of his father's friends had attended the Worcester convention as observers. E. R. Hoar had publicly stated the senator was with them. Webster invited Allen and Wilson to meet with him after the convention. He endorsed the plan of adhering to the Wilmot Proviso and the Northwest Ordinance and agreed with the resolutions passed by the convention. He declared the North had never been united and was thus unable to resist Southern plans. Wilson, Sumner, and Phillips all wrote Horace Mann to seek his endorsement. Wilson asserted that the anti-Taylor forces were steadily gaining adherents, and the right words from Mann would influence many voters. Former Democratic Governor Marcus Morton avoided Worcester, but his son Nathaniel was a participant. The elder Morton had long been such a staunch advocate of Van Buren that he might back a movement which would nominate the former president.[7]

Many historians believe the Barnburner Democrats were more motivated by the neglect and indignities they perceived Polk and his supporters had directed toward them and the nomination of Lewis Cass by the national convention than by the refusal of their party to endorse the Wilmot Proviso. In any case, the Barnburners were determined that Van Buren would be the nominee at Buffalo. It was evident by the beginning of July that former Whigs would be wasting their time promoting either Corwin or Webster. A little longer was required for McLean's candidacy to appear equally senseless. Without a candidate of national stature, the Massachusetts Conscience Whigs would either have to agree to the distasteful Van Buren or to former Democrat, Liberty-party-promoted John P. Hale. Most Liberty party men would have to accept the nominee at Buffalo, if they expected any future influence in the new party or many votes in the 1848 canvas. A Hale nomination would thus procure little additional support. But a Van Buren nomination would assure national attention, offer a good chance of wooing Northern Democrats away from Cass, and show the Whigs how unacceptable the nomination of a slaveholder was.[8]

Work was intense, with Wilson devoting as much time or more than anyone else. The State Committee first met at Adams's office July 8 with only eight in attendance, including Wilson. They decided when to hold the county conventions to elect delegates and designated a Finance Committee. Adams's diary reveals that Wilson was also in for consultations on July 10 and 25 and that he was one of only five to attend a State Committee meeting on August 4. Demands were enormous for speeches by the few available men not only throughout Massachusetts but elsewhere in New England and in New York as well. Adams recorded by July 24 that the new movement was exceeding their expectations; the problem was in controlling it. The *Whig's* circulation had doubled in June. Wilson attempted to encourage unity by delivering an address, as did Democrat Amasa Walker, at the Liberty party convention in Hopkinton on July 4. Two days later Wilson and Abraham Payne of Providence spoke in a crowded Salem Town Hall. Wilson told about the events at the Philadelphia convention. One impressed listener concluded the speaker "must have convinced every unprejudiced hearer that General Taylor . . . is the candidate of slavery propagandists of the South and their Northern abettors, and that *they know their man*." In addition to his July 7 speech in Boston, Wilson is known to have delivered a late July address in Roxbury and to have been invited to the July 26 Free Soil conclave in Maine.[9]

The convention to create a new national party assembled in Buffalo on August 9. As many as twenty thousand people may have participated. For some reason, Wilson, whose actions and efforts had done so much to lead to the meeting, was not a delegate and apparently did not attend. In addition to Phillips, Daniel Alvord, and William Jackson, among the delegates at large, were Adams, Dana, John Alley, Leavitt, David Lee Child, and Chauncey Knapp, all of whom were to play major roles in the emerging Free Soil party in Massachusetts. Adams was chairman of the mass convention, Salmon P. Chase of the smaller committee of conferees. Many of the participants both then and years later remarked about the goodwill evident among most of those in attendance. The Democrats at the Buffalo convention nominated Van Buren and many of the Liberty party men supported Hale. When the Massachusetts delegates' votes were called for, Phillips and the former Democrats announced for Van Buren. Massachusetts Liberty party delegates voted for Hale. Adams and three other Whigs cast their votes for Giddings. Van Buren, however, received a majority on the trial ballot, with the Democrats and a majority of the Whigs supporting him. Leavitt, in behalf of the Liberty party, moved to make the decision unanimous. Liberty party leaders had agreed to accede to Van Buren if the platform were acceptable to them. The vice-presidential nomination was expected to go to a former Whig from the West, with Ohio having the greatest influence. Both Ohio and Pennsylvania delegates, however, wanted Adams. Dana contended this was partly a tribute to John Quincy Adams, partly a rebuke to the Cotton Whigs.[10]

Salmon P. Chase was instrumental in writing the resolutions, with Phillips and Leavitt the important Massachusetts contributors. The platform agreed to no national interference with slavery in states but asserted the purpose of the Ordinances of 1784 and 1787 was to limit the expansion of slavery and that Congress should relieve itself of responsibility for the institution wherever it possessed the constitutional right to do so. The Liberty party's traditional positions on the fugitive slave law and black rights were ignored. Expanding on the antislavery stance of the Liberty party, the platform also called for cheap postage, advocated national monies for improvements of rivers and harbors, supported free land, and favored a revenue tariff. The slogan was "free soil, free speech, free labor, and free men."[11]

Many years later, when Wilson wrote his study of *The Rise and Fall of the Slave Power in America,* he commended the leaders of the Buffalo convention, from whatever faction they came, including many with whom he subsequently had parted politically. He was convinced the Barnburners were sincere, not out simply to hurt Hunkers and Cass supporters. He also affirmed that those of other parties who backed the former president were not simply being expedient, but thought Van Buren agreed with them in their opposition to the expansion of slavery; "they were prepared to forgive and forget the past, and hope much for the future."[12]

Abolitionists had been prominent at Buffalo. Samuel J. May had opened one of the meetings with prayer. Frederick Douglass, the great black speaker, had given a short address. Even Garrison, who would not vote or participate in the political process, had been present as an observer. Garrison had long opposed the Liberty party, but, while not happy with the limited opposition to slavery expansion of the Free Soilers, he was willing to give credit where it was due. Members of the anti-Garrison faction of abolitionists and leaders of the Liberty party also accepted the platform and the ticket. Boston's *The Emancipator*, which had been opposed to broadening the political antislavery movement even as late as July, admitted in early August that a majority of Liberty party newspapers favored the new movement. Liberty party men returning from Buffalo insisted they were reasonably satisfied with the new directions they were taking. Finally, on August 30 the paper hauled down Hale's name and accepted the new party. Richard Sewell, in his study of political abolition, has concluded that joining the Free Soil movement was not an abandonment of opposition to slavery, but tactically a reasonable stance, the result of a conviction that if slavery were curtailed, it would die a natural death. A few political abolitionists retained their independence, nominating Gerrit Smith for president, but most had affiliated themselves permanently with the broader Free Soil party.[13]

Free Soilers in Massachusetts had now to give even more direction to their efforts. They knew they would lose some former Whig supporters with the nomination of Van Buren. Webster was not long in giving his reluctant endorsement of Taylor. On August 22 a large and enthusiastic Free Soil ratification conclave convened in Boston's Faneuil Hall, with Sumner in the chair and Andrew, Dana, and Leavitt major participants. A similar assembly in Salem was reported as the largest political meeting ever held in the community. The party had next to nominate state candidates. On September 6, with John Mills, former Democrat of Springfield, as president, Free Soilers officially organized. Sumner headed the Resolutions Committee and Wilson the State Central Selection Committee. Phillips was designated as gubernatorial nominee. The next day the State Central Committee was organized in Boston, with Sumner selected to be chairman for the campaign and former Liberty party adherent Leavitt and former Democrat Marcus Morton Jr. as vice-chairmen. Wilson was not a member.[14]

An editorial in the *Boston Transcript* revealed the change in political position which was occurring. Its writer spoke of the ferment in parties' "commingling of discordant elements and re-arrangement of opposing forces." He noted politicians who had been battling each other all their lives were now in the "same basket": Marcus Morton and Joseph Buckingham, Martin Van Buren and Charles Francis Adams. "The political kaleidoscope has been well shaken."[15] Morton, as an example, supported the election of Van Buren, but would not sustain Adams for the vice-presidency and never really became a Free Soiler. The *National Era* recorded fifteen Massachusetts newspapers, most of them formerly Democratic, advocating the Free Soil ticket. The congressional nominees of the Free Soilers are an impressive group, in light of their later accomplishments. They included Sumner, Allen, Palfrey, Horace Mann, Stetson, Knapp, Alvord, and Charles Sedgwick. These candidacies would be particularly damaging when they defeated men like Congressman Charles Hudson, who had once been supportive of Conscience Whig goals.[16]

In the meantime Wilson was committing himself financially and directing his life and energies in a new way. The *Boston Whig* had gone through several changes in ownership and management since Adams had given up its leadership. Its financial condition in April was so precarious that some of its workers, in arrears on their wages, threatened to quit. Adams simply could no longer devote the time it required. Seth Webb Jr. proposed to buy the paper, but could not obtain the money. In June the growing opposition to Taylor's nomination increased sales and Adams was talking about Robinson, who had just left his position with the *Lowell Courier,* as new editor; Robinson took over the next month. The paper obviously required a new name. When Adams got back from Buffalo he noted Wilson had opened negotiations for purchase. Adams recorded that Wilson was experiencing difficulties in business, which he presumed was caused by his political activities. He was going to leave shoe manufacturing and hoped to turn the newspaper into one of large circulation and influence. Adams thought with enough effort that could be done. More surprisingly, given charges only a few years before of the cobbler's inability to write, Adams viewed Wilson as just the man to revitalize the publication. Wilson hoped to conclude the sale by the last week of August, but negotiations stretched out until mid-September. Adams, of course, sought repayment to himself and other original investors.[17]

The newspaper, renamed the *Daily Republican,* was owned primarily by Wilson, William S. Damrell, and Curtis C. Nichols. In November they established a partnership known as Wilson, Damrell, and Co. Like many papers of the era, this one had four pages. Clearly the Free Soil organ, it concentrated upon political news, with an emphasis on reporting stories about slavery and antislavery. The political position was "No extension of slavery over the Territories; no more slave territory to be added to the Union; no more slave states to be admitted to the Union; no compromise with slavery must be made."[18] It continued as a daily for the next year. A semiweekly was also published Wednesday and Saturday mornings. In the meantime the long-lived *Emancipator,* for many years edited by Leavitt, had been taken over by Nichols and, after the Buffalo convention, committed to the Free Soil party and renamed the *Emancipator and Free Soil Press.* In mid-November it was combined with Wilson's operation to produce a weekly newspaper, *The Emancipator and Republican.* Its subtitle reveals much about Wilson's ambitions for it: *Liberty the Right of All—the Ballot Box Its Defense.* The primary interest of the paper was political; as in other political weeklies, the president's annual message was printed in full and congressional and legislative news often occupied several columns. More economic news was promised, and given. While *The Emancipator and Republican* claimed to be the Free Soil newspaper of the state, the marriage and death lists principally included people from Boston and its neighboring communities. Two of his contemporary biographers report that Wilson wrote most of the original articles, including book notices. The weekly usually had from five to seven columns of advertisements.[19]

By January Wilson was dissatisfied with the operating arrangements. Adams recorded that Damrell had turned out to be a "knave." Wilson intimated he was trying to persuade Phillips's son to become proprietor and editor. Burlingame promoted an effort to change the ownership. Unhappy about the arrangements agreed to in the summer and fall, Adams was reluctant to put any more money into the enterprise. The paper had a circulation of between eight and nine thousand copies, but lacked advertising income. Burlingame could persuade only Adams, Phillips, and John Alley to consider the problem. Although these Free Soilers were all men of substance, whether they offered any financial support cannot be ascertained. In any case, on January 26 the partnership was dissolved and Wilson became sole proprietor of the *Republican.* Its editorial office was now moved from 15 State Street to the corner of Devonshire and State.[20]

In the beginning Robinson was editor. But Wilson and Robinson were very different in temperament and soon the publishers were altering editorials, especially Robinson's attacks on the Democratic *Post* and the Whig *Atlas*. Wilson considered a change in December, shortly after the election. By February the new owner was determined his associate had to leave or be better controlled. When he proposed to cut Robinson's salary to five dollars a week, Robinson quit and moved to Lowell to inaugurate a paper of his own. The wise and generous Wilson commended the new paper and praised its editor, although the two publications would be competing for many of the same readers. Wilson later tried to persuade Robinson to return, according to the latter's wife, but the editor refused. Estes Howe admitted Robinson's writing was too harsh, but asserted his successors lacked clarity and life. Adams and Wilson considered Palfrey for editorship when his congressional duties were over. However, Lucius Smith, former editor of the *Hartford Free Soil Advocate*, assumed Robinson's duties; the March 22 issue listed for the first time Wilson and Smith as editors. To attract more family reading the *Emancipator and*

Republican now devoted more space to nonpolitical topics. Unfortunately, it also included more columns of summaries from other papers. In 1873 Robinson remarked that Wilson eventually might have become a good editor, but at the time the job he did brought him little "applause."[21]

Just when in 1848 and why Wilson gave up his shoe business is impossible to ascertain. Friend and biographer Nason says Wilson left "without regret." He had employed more than one hundred hands in 1847 and had been responsible for the manufacture of almost double the number of pairs of shoes he had before turned out. There was no sudden national Panic or even a recession in the shoe business which would have affected him. By 1844–1845 the boot and shoe industry was recovering from the effects of the Panic of 1837. Mechanization was not yet altering the business the way it would in the 1850s. If Wilson cut back in production in 1848 because he was devoting too much time to politics—especially after May—he nevertheless produced more shoes (63,000) than in any year except 1847 and employed more hands than at any time except 1846 and 1847. To reach that production figure, he would have had to be still manufacturing a good part of the year, especially with half the workers of the previous year. One can only speculate whether he was gradually phasing out and was still engaged in the work all summer or into the fall, and whether relatives or friends, especially by summer, had taken over much of the management. By September, even with Robinson as the primary writer, Wilson must have had to devote considerable energy to the writing and financial supervision of the newspaper.[22]

Wilson's political activities in the three months prior to the 1848 election are difficult to ascertain. His energy and influence were enabling him to assure Free Soil support in Natick. A townsman many years later wrote that the young men met often during the campaign and discussed every voter. "Wilson was always present." Doubtful voters would be invited to one of the meetings and their aid solicited to convince their friends to vote Free Soil. Within the district Mann's supporters feared Wilson would be brought forth as the congressional candidate, with the argument that Wilson was a more open advocate of the Free Soil movement and Mann wouldn't speak. Mann soon delivered an antislavery address and was asked to send a large number of his speeches for the aid of the Whig party.[23]

But what did Wilson do in the campaign in terms of lecturing and organizing? Sumner and Hoar correspondence demonstrate how many hours each of those men spent speaking. Schouler in the mid-1850s, in a not very favorable review of the new senator's political life, claimed Wilson had been a "prominent speaker" in the 1848 campaign. An 1853 biographical sketch asserted he spoke fifty times in the summer and fall. On the other hand, neither *The Emancipator* nor the *Northampton Courier*, which generously reported Free Soil activities, tells of rallies in which Wilson participated. Wilson was a member of the Middlesex County Free Soil Committee. David Donald, Sumner's biographer, wrote that Phillips and Dana might have been good speakers, but Wilson was the organizer. He and state chairman Sumner worked well together from the beginning. Sumner, however, who emerged from the campaign as one of the party's best speakers, was not the man to head the State Committee.[24]

Whatever Wilson's role was, the campaign did not result in a Free Soil victory. In July, fresh from the enthusiasm of the state meeting, Adams recorded that a great commotion was taking place among the public which might destroy the existing parties; he was full of enthusiasm. By September 18 he was expressing surprise the Whig party had been so able to rally. Adams conceded it had plenty of money and had so much involved in the election results that it was unlikely to give in without a fight. A week later he wrote the election was not going as he had expected; the old party organizations were strong. While by the end of the month he hoped for a political revolution—at least in Massachusetts, New York, and Ohio—on October 4, after a conference with Phillips, Wilson, Robinson, and Adams, the diarist recorded the Whigs were resolved to sustain themselves no matter what; Palfrey had been denied Whig congressional renomination. Results of state elections in early October in Pennsylvania and Ohio were also depressing. The Whigs gained two seats from Pennsylvania and won control of the state legislature, assuring election of a Whig senator. Adams had to conclude the people were not sufficiently disturbed to break with their former parties. On the other hand, in Vermont, where the Whig party had consistently nominated antislavery candidates, while a Whig was elected governor, the Free Soil nominee obtained only seven thousand less votes, and exceeded the Democratic poll.[25]

Oliver Dyer, the mid-nineteenth century writer; Henry Lee, a Free Soiler; and Frederick Blue, Joseph Rayback, and Kinley Brauer, modern historians, all comment on the bitterness of the national campaign. Van Buren was a traitor to most Southern and many Northern Democrats. Adams was called "a political huckster" and Wilson a "Jesuit" and a "jackal." Schouler and other writers for the *Atlas* were particularly personal in their attacks. First term Congressman Abraham Lincoln of Illinois, campaigning in Massachusetts, charged the new party had fewer principles than any of the others. The lack of enthusiasm of Clay and Webster supporters might have modified the ill will; it did not.[26]

Taylor won the presidential contest with 163 electoral and over 1,360,000 popular votes, 47 percent of the total cast. He collected 45 1/2 percent of the Northern vote and 51 1/2 percent of the Southern votes. He carried states which, like Massachusetts, usually voted Whig, and picked up several traditionally Democratic states. In the Mid-Atlantic area he especially fared better than Clay had in 1844. How many men were voting for Taylor because he was the Whig candidate and how many were voting for him because he was a military hero one cannot know. Results, in any case, were often determined by factors unique to a certain state. In New York, as an example, the Whig leader Seward was avowedly pro–Wilmot Proviso, while Van Buren was a native son and former leader of the Democratic party. These factors would discourage Whigs from voting and encourage Democrats to vote Free Soil. Cass got somewhat less support in the slave states than Democrats usually had, but did particularly well in his own Northwest, even carrying usually Whig Ohio. He received 127 electoral and more than 1,220,000 popular votes, 42 1/2 percent of the total. Van Buren did not secure any electoral votes, but did attract more than 291,000 popular votes, 10 percent of the total. He received 29 percent of the Vermont vote, 28 percent of Massachusetts's, 26 percent of New York's and ran ahead of Cass in all three. On the Western Reserve of Ohio, in parts of Vermont and Massachusetts, in upstate New York, and in southeastern Wisconsin, Van Buren did particularly well. He received five times the number of votes Liberty party nominee Birney had secured in 1844. The party had seven of its nominees elected to Congress. Others, like Mann, who had been endorsed by two parties, were also selected.[27]

In Massachusetts the Whigs in the national and statewide contests carried every county except one; on the other hand, they were in a majority in only four. Taylor had failed to win a majority in one of the most traditional Whig states in the union; more promising for the new party, Van Buren attracted 3 percent more of the voters than Cass. In the election for governor, Briggs matched Taylor's popular vote, more than 4 percent higher, almost a majority. Phillips received two thousand fewer votes than Van Buren, but a percent more. Cushing, the widely known Democratic nominee for governor, attracted only about 20 percent of the vote, 16 percent less than the 1847 Democratic tally. Wilson listed fifty-five Free Soil representatives in the state legislature, including nineteen from Worcester, eight from Plymouth, and five from Middlesex Counties. Recent historians who have studied the national campaign have often emphasized that Free Soil tended to attract many more former Democrats than former Whigs, not surprising with Van Buren as their nominee. In Massachusetts, however, the Conscience Whigs had dominated the new party and had naturally attracted some Whig votes. Yet even in Massachusetts Free Soilers drew from the Democrats in Berkshire, Bristol, Plymouth, and perhaps Middlesex Counties. William Bean's study of the transformation in Massachusetts politics emphasized that the Liberty party nominee had attracted 9 percent of the vote for governor in 1847, and thus the party's adherents probably contributed a significant proportion of Van Buren's total. Bean decided the Democrats were responsible for 45 percent of the Free Soil vote; more recently Martin Duberman has agreed with that estimate. Kevin Sweeney has calculated the percent as nearer 30. On the other hand, Bean and Arthur Darling both noted that only Amasa Walker, John Mills, and Marcus Morton Jr., among leading Democrats, had gone over to the new party. Most liberal Democrats who opposed the Hallett-Greene control of the party—men who later would be coworkers with Wilson—adhered to the Cass nomination.[28]

Writing from a vantage point of thirty years for reflection, E. L. Pierce declared 1848 had shown the uselessness of a separate party action. That was not the conclusion at the time. The *Northampton Courier* rejoiced that so much progress could be made by a new party in ninety days. Sumner emphasized the unprecedented "virulence," energy, and money the Whigs of the state threw against the Free Soilers. His party had not achieved what the most optimistic had hoped for, but had already become the second largest party. It elected Allen congressman from Worcester County and prevented, for lack of a majority, the election of Whigs in several other districts. Whittier wrote that with all the money power mobilized against them, the Free Soilers had still prevented Taylor from winning a majority of the state's votes and had proved the expediency of taking a "right stand." Robinson noted that antislavery parties, before the advent of the Republicans in 1856, never got a larger vote than they attracted in 1848. Wilson himself, in his newspaper, concluded his Free Soil movement had accomplished more in a few months than any other American political organization. It had made slavery the primary issue of the day.[29]

What can one conclude about the courage and energy of Wilson and his fellow Free Soilers of 1848? To the abolitionists, Free Soil was, as Garrison phrased it, "a cheering sign of the times," proof of the progress of the cause. Its adherents were tardy but welcome additions who deserved commendation.[30] To others, members of the new party were idealistic and politically foolish. Some who opposed the expansion of slavery, like Morton, Bancroft, and Webster, would never take a political stand which stood much chance of implementing their beliefs. Others, like Francis Blair, Seward, Greeley, Lincoln, Boutwell, Benjamin F. Wade, and William P. Fessenden, had yet to show the courage, strength of commitment, or understanding of the situation to leave old political affiliations and advocate actions which might affect the existence or spread of slavery. Many former Massachusetts Conscience Whigs had burned their political bridges behind them and a few, like Wilson, would now dedicate their lives to attacking the institution of slavery.

Political movements make visual progress when results on election day or the activities of politicians in government can be observed and reported. Adams emerged from the fall campaign exhausted, anxious to turn to literary pursuits. Adams's son later wrote that Wilson could now devote himself entirely to politics—organizing the new party, in the process obtaining his livelihood from it—but that he did not have Adams's political advancement as an objective.[31] The statement is unfair. To support himself and his family, Wilson had to devote his efforts primarily to his newspaper and only secondarily to politics. Of course, the editorship of the party's principal newspaper in itself provided Wilson with important political possibilities. Adams had had the same opportunities with the *Whig*. Nor should Adams's political future have been an important concern for Wilson. In many ways, the party's first vice-presidential nominee, the son of John Quincy Adams, and the able, sophisticated, and a well-known leader in the state was in an unusual position to direct the new party in Massachusetts. But Adams's future lay primarily with Adams, who chose to divorce himself from active editorial and political affairs and devote his time to editing his grandfather's papers. Phillips, the party's gubernatorial candidate, an honored and experienced politician, could also have taken over the reins of leadership. He did not. Rather, Sumner, as state party chairman, and Wilson undertook the demanding and difficult task of transforming what might have been a one-campaign movement into a viable political party. The dramas of annexation, war, peace, and a presidential election were over by 1849; nor had the passionate debates culminating in the Compromise of 1850 begun. On the one hand, that meant Free Soilers now had an opportunity to build. On the other hand, the lack of immediate issues and the absence of the former Conscience Whig leadership from the state legislature would limit what could be accomplished.

The political scene was quiet during much of 1849. The country settled down to accept its second elected Whig president. Lawrence did not receive the cabinet position to which he and his associates thought he was entitled, but he was appointed minister to Great Britain. The new Congress would not meet until December; its lame duck predecessor made few waves. The Free Soil movement confronted different circumstances in different states. In Ohio Free Soilers worked with Democrats to get Chase elected to the Senate. In Connecticut and Vermont they also cooperated with the Democrats. Yet in New York, former Liberty party stalwart Stanton believed from early 1849 that the Free Soil party had little future and worked to unite Hunker and Barnburner Democrats on a platform which would include the Wilmot Proviso. With the Whigs in control of the government in Massachusetts, opportunities for the Free Soilers were limited. The Hallett-Greene faction of the Democratic party, without any demands from a Democratic national administration in Washington, was able to pacify the younger members of their party who were concerned about the expansion of slavery. The Whigs in control of the legislature had neither need nor inclination to cooperate with the Free Soilers. The *Emancipator and Republican* during most of the first half of 1849 gave little attention to the political future for Free Soil in the state.[32]

If the Free Soil party was not growing in most states, if no immediate issue was drawing together those who opposed slavery or its expansion, what could be done? Cooperation had sent Chase to the Senate from Ohio, Hale from New Hampshire, and antislavery congressmen from Connecticut. Adams predicted that, in states where Free Soilers held the balance of power, they would adopt that tactic more often. As early as February Walker was agitating to expand the Free Soil plank, a step which Adams, Allen, and J. A. Bolles resisted. The *Emancipator and Republican* began to prescribe an alliance with the Democrats. By May use of the word "coalition" was becoming frequent in the paper. In mid-May the paper was enthusiastic about a successful coalition between Democrats and Free Soilers in Wisconsin, a month later in Vermont. The cooperation in Vermont, the paper reported, was also an attack on the money power. Wilson himself visited Vermont in the late spring and dispatched back a glowing report of the union of the

Democrat and Free Soil parties and their nomination of antislavery candidates for state offices. By early summer the emphasis was also on the necessity of destroying the older parties.[33]

The 1848 alliance between former Whigs and former Democrats was still not a comfortable one. Adams was frightened about the kind of address Walker might pen on behalf of the Free Soil members of the legislature and feared a "tendency towards radicalism" among some of the party legislators. Former Liberty party leader Elizur Wright, now editor of the Boston *Chronotype*, was afraid the cancellation of a Free Soil festival in Boston meant the former Conscience Whigs leadership was returning to its old party. A correspondent of *The Liberator* questioned Wilson's fidelity when the *Republican* did not take Clay to task for his letter supporting colonization. The character of the Taylor administration's appointments of Massachusetts men generated dissatisfaction among the more moderate Whigs and prompted a strong editorial attack from Wilson. William Hayden, editor of the *Boston Atlas*, selected to be Boston postmaster, was called by Wilson the "worst of Hunkers," with the additional culpability of opposition to temperance. Equally reprehensible was the appointment of Charles Lunt as District Attorney. Lunt had made himself infamous among abolitionists a decade before when, as chairman of a legislative committee, he denied the fair hearing of basic citizen rights.[34]

On June 28 the *Republican* noted that Massachusetts Whig papers were full of denunciations of Democrat–Free Soil cooperation. Wilson advised the Whig editors to be less apprehensive, at least during the summer; let the fall political campaign be nearer before getting too concerned. They were at the mercy of their opponents in any case, he asserted; they could do nothing to prevent whatever the other parties decided to do. Conscience Whigs had tried to work with their fellow Whigs for four years; they would not now retreat from the position taken in the Buffalo platform. If the Democrats would agree to a similar stand, then cooperation was likely. The *Lowell Courier* reported that, with Cushing no longer a possible candidate, the Democrats would nominate a man who sustained the Wilmot Proviso, and the Free Soilers would abandon Phillips and accept the Democrat. Wilson disagreed. The *Lowell Advertiser* soon charged that the *Republican*, among other papers, was blocking a union because Wilson was still a Whig. Wilson, in reply, reflected upon his conscious break with his former party and the pain and sacrifices his action had engendered. He had no hope for the Whigs, but he was optimistic about the Democrats. He declared that union between the parties could occur only on a platform of no extension of slavery. He was equally enthusiastic about coalitions in Wisconsin and Vermont. While Whig papers denounced them as "disgraceful" and "reckless and unprincipled," the *Courier* editor termed coalitions opposing slavery in New Mexico and California, and the slave trade in the District of Columbia, as promoting "honorable" ends.[35]

The repeated failures to elect Palfrey to Congress from Wilson's district had affected different Free Soil leaders in different ways. Sumner professed to be "mortified" as a result of the June 1849 election, in which the local party chairman had expected a Palfrey victory by 1,500 to 2,000 votes. Two months later he predicted another failure, but reported Wilson was more optimistic. Palfrey himself was becoming exhausted by the emotional turmoil of the continuing elections. While he and some of his supporters were critical of the *Republican* for not sustaining him strongly enough, a review of the 1849 issues shows the elections were frequently reported and Palfrey praised. Since Allen had won his congressional seat only at a second election, hope was that continued presentation of Palfrey's name could attract either former Whig supporters or Democrats who might prefer Palfrey to the leader, a Whig. Yet none of the three candidates received a majority and nothing indicated any significant change of votes could be obtained. While the election of a Whig or a Democrat would have psychological advantages for the two major parties, both in Washington and in Massachusetts, the selection of a Free Soiler, particularly Palfrey, would add a proportionally significant voice in Congress.[36]

By late May Wilson was experiencing new financial problems with the *Republican.* He notified the Free Soil leadership he did not know how he could continue; if he could not sell, he would have to step aside. The paper had already lost many of its subscribers. Adams declared it needed more vigor and energy. The proposed publication by Gamaliel Bailey of a national antislavery newspaper in Washington could only weaken the *Republican* more. Two meetings at Sumner's office produced no money, only a willingness by Phillips to see what could be done in negotiation. Phillips had developed strong feelings about Wilson's character, Adams feared. A loan of $5,000 was eventually arranged, with Adams agreeing to put up some money if Phillips would also. Somehow Wilson was able to continue all three—daily, semi-weekly, and weekly—of his publications. In mid-August John Bent joined Wilson in a copartnership. In mid-September Smith left as coeditor.[37]

During the course of the summer, the likelihood of cooperation between the Democrats and the Free Soilers advanced. The latter were being renamed the Free Democracy. Wilson did not want union, only cooperation; there could be many different kinds and degrees of that. One member of the State Committee, who apparently thought similarly to Wilson, in July contended the time was not ripe for unification; the Democrats would have to lose more elections and overthrow their old leaders before union could occur. Leaders within both parties apparently resisted the efforts throughout the summer. Within the Free Soil movement, Adams, Phillips, Palfrey, and Dana were all opposed to what they perceived as the eventual destruction of their party and its objectives. Neither Adams nor Palfrey had Sumner's confidence that Democratic instincts were on their side. Bird, Alley, Keyes, Allen, and eventually Sumner agreed with Wilson's approach.[38]

The Democrats probably expected opposition from the Hallett-Greene faction. Instead, Morton became their problem. The former governor in May was attacking the past direction of his party. Its "discomfort" had two primary causes. First, there had been too great "fraternity with Slavery." But equally a problem, he declared, had been the selection of officers and leaders who neither possessed nor deserved the confidence of the people. The ex-governor's son was still serving on the Executive Committee of the Free Soil party. Morton himself accepted Sumner's invitation to attend a planning meeting of the Free Soil State Committee, and concurred with what transpired, but regarded himself as a spectator. He apparently was willing to support reunion of the two wings of the Democratic party, but was even more enthusiastic about union with the Free Democrats on the basis of the Buffalo platform and traditional Democratic principles.[39]

As the time for the fall conventions approached, Wilson declared that the principles of Buffalo now needed to be expanded to deal with problems on the state level. He suggested the party promote a secret ballot, a changed method for selection of senators, and a modification of Massachusetts's corporation policy. During the previous twelve years, he pointed out, $140,000,000 worth of business had been incorporated, about one-quarter of the wealth of the state. Too few men had been given too much power. The state should be controlled by the intellectual power and moral worth of its people, not by money. These were principles to which Democrats could also adhere. How much these proposals were motivated by Wilson's personal convictions, how much by his desire to expand the platform of the Free Democratic party, how much by his awareness that the current situation was aiding the Whig party, particularly its leadership, and how much by his recognition of a need to adopt some of the platform of the state Democratic party with which he wanted to work cannot be known. All of these factors undoubtedly influenced him.[40]

But coalition at the state level did not occur. Rather, the hope was that conventions and people in separate electoral districts could agree to single nominations. Three weeks before the Free Soil state meeting, Sumner organized a massive rally in Boston in part to choose delegates. Chase was imported from Ohio as the featured speaker. Soon thereafter Wilson was selected as one of the three delegates from Natick. Chase advocated the party take new ground. Adams was especially opposed to a statement about corporations which Sumner and Wilson wanted to include in the platform. About twelve hundred Free Soilers gathered at Worcester on September 12. Sumner served as chairman of the Resolutions Committee; Wilson chaired the Committee on Organization and managed the proceedings on the assembly floor. One newspaper reported the convention was the largest ever held in the state. Rather than quickly accept Sumner's proposed platform, the delegates engaged in lengthy debates. Adams's increasing detachment from the majority of the party was demonstrated when he had to admit that he had never understood the seriousness of the corporations' control of the state. Phillips was again selected as candidate for governor. Sumner refused to continue on the State Committee and Adams would not accept election to it. The new committee consisted of five delegates at large, including William Jackson, Alvord, Burlingame, and Keyes, and one from each of the ten districts, including William Spooner, Alley, Whittier, Estes Howe, James M. Earle, and Swan. Burlingame soon resigned his position and on September 27 the State Central Committee first elected Wilson to the vacancy and then selected him as state chairman. Keyes became full-time secretary.[41]

The Democrats, meeting a week later in Springfield, nominated George Boutwell for governor. Their spokespaper, the *Boston Post*, had cited a need for revival of the "spirit" of the party and asked for a united convention. Wilson attended in his capacity as a newspaper editor. En route by train he met Hallett and Charles C. Hazewell of the *Boston Times*. Hallett, to be chairman of the Resolutions Committee, shared the proposals he had formulated. He later presented them, defended them, and got them passed. They expressed opposition to slavery, which they termed a "municipal institution." They favored free soil and the restriction of slavery to where it then existed, and they declared the non-extension of slavery was so universally opposed in the North "as to belong to no party." Yet the institution was opposed in the South and therefore the subject could not be a test in a national party. Hazewell was concerned over how Southern Democrats would respond. Hallett, however, was angry with Southerners who had not adequately supported Cass and therefore did not deserve the consideration they had formerly received. The *Boston Post* endorsed Hallett's stance and supported cooperation between the two minority parties wherever desirable. Wilson's paper, while praising Boutwell as a "gentleman of good talents and irreproachable character," reported that never had Hallett so ruled the party and that his resolutions rejected an antislavery stand.[42]

Cooperation in Massachusetts was not as promising as in Wisconsin and Vermont. On the other hand, the action of the Free Soilers in New York was becoming an increasing concern to their brethren elsewhere. There the Barnburners rejoined the Hunker Democrats for joint nominations. Wilson in the *Republican* attacked the alliance and contended the Barnburners had abandoned the Buffalo platform, provoking Stanton to charge Wilson was still a free soil Whig who mistakenly believed he could still attract Whig support. S. A. Maynard was even more critical. While he regarded the New Yorkers as engaged in a "hazardous experiment," he held out hope for its success. What business did Wilson have interfering in New York affairs, he asked? People were saying Wilson had "gone off at half cock," and that he entirely misrepresented "the principles and motives of the Barnburners." Free Soilers as different as Leavitt and Adams supported the New York effort. Abolitionist Leavitt wrote from New York City to his former Massachusetts associates defending Barnburner strategy and contending they would continue to stand with the Free Soil movement. Boston abolitionist William

Jackson was equally condemnatory of Wilson. Adams, Allen, Palfrey, and Phillips all asserted Wilson had been unwise in his stance. Even the usually supportive Sumner, who was not happy with the Barnburner action, declared the *Republican* had been "unfortunate in its course." Wilson had ignored the counsels of his friends, he reported. Sumner had talked directly with Barnburners in New York and was "satisfied with their sincerity & earnestness." The *Republican* had embarrassed Free Soilers in Massachusetts.[43]

Wilson was not as isolated in his views as the attacks upon him might lead one to suspect. The *Northampton Courier* also expressed disappointment at the way the two New York factions united, leaving the Hunkers free to continue their pro-Southern position. The *Cleveland True Democrat* also condemned the Barnburners. The timing of these remarks was unfortunate. On the other hand, Wilson's analysis of the limited devotion to the Buffalo platform and the future course of the New York Democrats was to be more accurate than that of his critics.[44]

Cooperation in Massachusetts was incomplete. At first Wilson could not even pull it off in his own Middlesex County. On October 10 at Concord the Free Soil and Democratic parties met separately. The latter voted for a committee of thirteen to meet with the Free Soilers to agree to a joint Senate ticket, three candidates from each party. When the proposal was presented to the Free Soil convention, with Wilson to be chairman of their committee, an animated discussion followed. William Jackson, Estes Howe, and James Stone favored the proposition. Howe asserted the question was only whether the county would be represented by six Whigs, or by three Free Soilers and three Democrats. But the opponents of the idea favored their independent position and attacked Boutwell, the Democratic nominee for governor. Wilson said that, with so many opposed, the effort should be abandoned; the motion was laid on the table and six Free Soil senators were chosen. But Wilson knew what he was doing. Within three days he was ready for another attempt at coalition. Even Adams, believing cooperation was the only way to procure Palfrey's congressional election, supported the effort. In the next two weeks conventions in other counties found ways for the parties to agree. As a result, on October 24, with the election practically upon them, the two parties in Middlesex County reassembled in "large and spirited" conventions. Both were informed that three of their previous nominees had declined, and committees of conference were appointed to produce the joint ticket. Wilson asserted in his newspaper that the two weeks between the conventions permitted a fuller discussion of the issue and that the large attendance at the second assemblies argued well for the decision. Adams received a coalition nomination in Norfolk County.[45]

Wilson was chairman of the resolutions committee of the October 10 Concord convention, a position he obviously wanted since he declined serving as convention chairman. The resolutions were undoubtedly written by him and tell what he believed and what he thought most wise to assert. The antislavery statements condemned slavery as a wrong both to the bondsmen and to humanity and as a sin in the sight of God. They accepted the position of the 1830s abolitionists, declaring for "immediate emancipation." The national government, they contended, had not been established to protect slavery, but to further freedom. Slavery was limited to states; furthermore, no more slave states should be admitted to the union. The national government had the power, which it should exercise, to end the interstate slave trade and slavery in the District of Columbia and in territories. The platform also took a stance on other issues, including some which had been enunciated at the 1848 Buffalo convention and others which a broadening appeal in Massachusetts made desirable. These included calls for cheap postage, curtailment of patronage, election of more officials—especially postmasters—and river and harbor improvements. There were generalized statements about labor and the extension of lien laws. Finally, Wilson included advocacy of single Senate districts and a reform of the House districts. Some of the non-slavery planks were obviously an appeal to common interests to the Democrats.[46]

Whig newspapers naturally had a field day attacking the Free Soil–Democratic cooperation. The *New Bedford Mercury* accused Free Soil leaders of being disgruntled Whigs who had used the excuse of Taylor's nomination to leave their party when, in fact, they were motivated by disappointment they had not been rewarded with sufficient nominations and offices. Wilson in the *Emancipator and Republican* demolished that argument, showing how often the men had been rewarded by their former party and how much they had to lose in appointments to office and prestige and popularity in their communities by joining the Free Soil movement. He himself had "no wrongs or disappointments to avenge." He had been supported seven times by the Whig party for House and Senate seats, had been placed on county, district, and state committees, and had been chosen a delegate to the national convention. Neither had the Free Soilers acted in haste in their opposition to Taylor. The more moderate Whig *Boston Transcript* asserted the Free Soilers had lost their "moral prestige." The *Northampton Courier* mocked Whig outrage, noting the Whigs had worked in coalition with Free Soilers in Iowa and Michigan. When the *Boston Journal* charged Free Soil coalition leaders were conspiring against the wishes of Whig party members, the *Chronotype* replied that the leaders opposed coalition, but the voters told them to find ways to unite.[47]

Wilson himself was nominated to the House from Natick. At the first town meeting for the election, the Whig candidate received 176 votes, Wilson 175, and the Democratic candidate 96, and other votes were scattered. The meeting dissolved without a choice. When the selectmen refused to honor a petition calling for a new meeting on the fourth Monday, the justice of the peace had to issue the warrant. A dispute ensued over the number of signatures needed and attached to the petition. At the second election on November 26, initially, again, no one received the required majority. The Whigs then tried to dissolve the meeting. When that failed, because the law stated the polls had to close by sunset, they tried to stall to prevent a decision. Just a few minutes before the required time, Wilson obtained enough votes to be elected.[48]

While Sumner hoped the Free Soilers and Democrats could win control of the state Senate, the tardy and incomplete coalition was only partially successful. The union tickets for senators won elections in Middlesex, Worcester, and Plymouth, and failed in Norfolk and Essex Counties. The total state vote declined from 1848, as one might expect in a year when neither a president nor Congressmen were being selected and when union of party candidates at the last minute confused the scene. Briggs failed to obtain a majority for governor, with seven thousand fewers votes than in 1848. Boutwell was the big winner, picking up seven thousand more votes than Cushing had received in 1848. Phillips suffered an eleven-thousand-vote fall-off. The Whigs, however, would safely control both houses of the legislature and in January selected Briggs as governor. Wilson was enthused that the minority voice in the Senate would be strong enough to be heard and that the Whigs had lost some of their large majority in the House. Palfrey not only did not benefit from the Free Soil–Democratic cooperation but received fewer votes than before. Adams, who lost by only one hundred votes, was surprised at the amount of Democratic support he had secured.[49]

The contest soon thereafter shifted to Washington for the House to select a Speaker. Winthrop was again supported by the Whigs, while the Georgian Howell Cobb was the candidate of the Democrats. The House balloted for days, with Allen one of those refusing to support his fellow Massachusetts congressman. The business of the nation was being held up. Eventually the House decided to accept a plurality choice and Cobb emerged as victor. Editor Wilson called Winthrop the Free Democracy's chief enemy in Massachusetts and denounced Horace Mann for voting for him.[50]

Wilson had retained the three editions of his newspaper until the fall campaign was over. He undoubtedly received some outside support which would not continue after November. His criticisms of the New York Barnburners and his leadership for coalition had each alienated some components among the Free Soilers. So in mid-November 1849 he abandoned the daily *Republican*. It had never paid. Its circulation, at one time as high as 2,100, had declined to 1,300. Wilson's editorial office, formerly at 2 Devonshire Street, changed in December to upstairs 5 Water Street. Two decades later a reporter described the quarters as a "small room in a very shabby old building at the junction of Water and Devonshire streets and Spring lane. It was both his editorial quarters and dormitory."[51] The kind of coverage changed, with more reprints, more long articles, and less emphasis on political affairs. Elizur Wright, in his *Chronotype*, noted no party had ever supported a daily. A paper might serve a party, but it had to exist because of its own readable news. He praised Wilson as a "generous and self-sacrificing proprietor." The *Northampton Courier* declared Wilson had managed the

Republican "with much ability." It bemoaned the fact that, with the *Republican's* demise, only the *Worcester Spy* remained as a Free Democracy daily.[52]

As his acquaintance and influence in Massachusetts broadened, Wilson continued his contacts in New Hampshire and manifested a pride in his native state. During the summer of 1849 he joined other newsmen on an excursion via two railroads and a water voyage to Center Harbor on Lake Winnipesaukee. Wilson and about seventy others, including future president Franklin Pierce, continued twenty miles on the lake to his former teaching community at Wolfboro. Wilson spent the evening with old friends reminiscing about associates of thirteen years before. Of his two to three hundred acquaintances of that time, few remained in the area. After a night in Wolfboro, the party returned to Center Harbor and then back on the railroad. What a great change in transportation during the young man's life! Wilson detrained at Concord for a political visit and also stopped in Lowell to converse with Free Soil editors. He returned glorying in the beauty of New Hampshire and immensely satisfied with the experience. On October 16 Wilson joined many others in preliminary steps towards a reunion for New Hampshire natives then living in the Boston area. A thirty-person committee was established, three from each town, to help with invitations and advertisements. Wilson was one of three Strafford natives. Daniel Webster was soon selected as president of the group. The dinner celebration took place on November 7, but records do not reveal that Wilson played any part. In any case, this was the beginning of an annual event in which Wilson would regularly participate.[53]

Wilson reentered the Massachusetts House as a member of the minority, but apparently prepared to play a more conspicuous role. In the first few days of the session he was selected as one of the three tellers to count the votes for governor, one of five appointed to the ceremonial duty to wait on the governor to tell him the legislature was in session. He was nominated by his party as its candidate for Speaker, receiving 66 votes; the Whig victor received 161 votes, the Democratic nominee 59. His committee assignments included Mercantile Affairs and Insurance and a second to expedite business and shorten the session. In contrast to most members of the Middlesex County delegation, Wilson stayed in Boston, at the Marlboro Hotel. He was not absent a day the whole session. Governor Briggs's annual message noted the differences between the people of the slave and free states over what Congress could and should do about slavery in the territories. He recalled that five slave states had supported the prohibition of slavery in the Northwest Territory. He also pointed out that Congress had passed, and a Southern-born president had agreed to, the Missouri Compromise, annexation of Texas with prohibition of slavery north of 36" 30', and creation of a government for Oregon with slavery prohibited. He had no doubt Congress could and should exclude slavery from the territories.[54]

Wilson's agenda included much more than opposition to slavery. Some of the legislation he sought could weaken his Whig opponents, some would show his empathy with the Democrats, but most of it was simply a product of his own values and beliefs. Yet he terrified associates such as Samuel Hoar, Dana, and Adams. He introduced or supported efforts to end the plurality rule for election of congressmen and state officers and to elect state senators by single member districts. He wanted to control business better using a series of proposals regulating incorporation and corporation capacity for acquiring debt. He sought to put pressure on the state's congressional representation to work to end the liquor ration and the practice of flogging in the navy.[55]

One of the first subjects asked to be treated was altering election requirements for the General Court. Wilson in his newspaper of March, 1849, had declared himself a supporter of majority elections. But even then he had added that if a district were threatened with no representation, then minority selection was acceptable. The Senate, he had noted, often had a majority of its members selected by the House and was therefore no more than a reflection of the lower assembly. Senators should be selected by plurality, not by the other house. He soon was refuting part of his own argument when in April he chastised the Senate for its refusal to pass legislation well studied and adopted by the House. But the issue was not simply plurality versus majority, but general tickets versus representative districts. Both minority parties were hurt by Suffolk County's forty-four representatives elected by a general ticket, all of them Whig.[56]

On January 14 Wilson introduced a resolution to have the Judiciary Committee consider the expediency that election of representatives, in case of no majority at the regular election, be by plurality at second trial. Whitney Griswold subsequently sought to get appointed a select committee to propose an amendment to the law to provide that representatives to the General Court from cities and towns be chosen by single districts or wards. The Whigs wanted to refer the issue to their controlled Judiciary Committee and prevailed at first, with Wilson among those arguing for the Griswold proposal. But the Free Soilers and Democrats asserted the vote had been misreported and won on a recount, 127 to 122. Within a week Wilson also proposed the special committee consider an amendment to the constitution to provide for single Senate representative districts.[57]

A constitutional amendment to provide for districts for senators and representatives was reported by Hoar late in the session with recommendation it be rejected. Griswold had a minority report. One provision, supported by Wilson, would require single senatorial districts. Another would direct the governor and council to apportion every ten years the number of representatives each city and town would have. The third would create a district system for election of representatives. After three hours of debate, all were beaten.[58]

On the other hand the Whig leader Schouler sought to obtain a plurality law at second elections for members of Congress and presidential electors. The frequent elections in Palfrey's district and the consequent vacant seat in Washington had widened dissatisfaction with the current practice. The House committee, however, recommended no change. The problem was temporary, Whigs maintained, and would be solved when the state returned to a two-party system. Wilson contended that as the population of Massachusetts declined relative to the nation's total, the state needed even more its full representation. Whenever plurality candidates finally got their majority, he declared, they did it by wearing out their opposition. He dealt one by one with various arguments favoring the majority system and disposed of each. He noted no other state except Massachusetts held to the majority principle. Sentiment alone seemed to support retention of the current system. Schouler's bill passed, 146 to 114. But a month later the Senate, also after lengthy debate, killed the proposal.[59]

The efforts to regulate business were hardly a populist attack. Rather, they were to be legal restraints, which today may appear naive, but at the time were understandable as a reaction to beginning industrialization and developments towards the big business and monopolies of the late nineteenth and the twentieth centuries. Among Wilson's proposals was one to prohibit a corporation from issuing stock for less than par value, another providing the capital stock of manufacturing corporations be divided into shares of one hundred dollars each, and a third insisting that when a railroad had a debt exceeding 5 percent of the value of the stock, no dividend could be declared. When the committee reported unfavorably on the proposal to sell stock at par, Wilson attempted to substitute his ideas. Hoar opposed him. Yet Wilson barely was beaten, 111 to 102, and the committee's proposal was accepted only 107 to 102. All was not lost, for the next day Wilson got added to an incorporation bill of the Bay State Iron Company a provision that its stock could not be issued under par. He also sought to implement on an individual basis his 5 percent debt cutoff for dividends. He initially got it attached to a law to increase the capital stock of the Boston and Worcester Railroad, but the 94-to-45 vote indicates the business leadership had been caught off guard. A week later Hoar persuaded the House to reverse itself, 89 to 74. Wilson tried again the next week on a proposal to increase the capital stock of the Lowell Manufacturing Company. With Hoar and Schouler, among others, opposing him, he lost by a larger vote, 47 to 109.[60]

Limiting the hours of work of laboring people, particularly in large manufacturing establishments, was another thrust of the Democrats and some of the Free Soilers, although Wilson did not appear to take a leadership role in the effort. The former cobbler was sympathetic to the state of the working people and identified with them. But he also had been an entrepreneur. During the strikes and labor unrest, particularly in the Boston area, in the fall of 1849, Wright's *Chronotype* followed the events and asserted labor had real grievances. Wilson's *Republican*, on the other hand, was comparatively uninterested in the subject. Both papers, and the Free Soil platform, saw closer connections between the rights of laborers and slavery than many of the workers themselves saw. In any case, a special committee which was assigned the responsibility to examine the subject reported negatively.

A lengthy minority report disagreed. The latter would have limited workers in manufacturing establishments in the state after September 1, 1850, to eleven hours a day, and a year later to ten hours. A violating company could be fined fifty dollars. The House defeated the minority report, 54 to 134, Wilson voting with the losers.[61]

Harvard College also came under attack. Boutwell proposed that a committee consider how it might be rendered more beneficial to the people of the Commonwealth. Boutwell's plan would have abolished the corporation and substituted a board of fifteen men, thirteen to be chosen for six-year terms in three classes by joint ballot of the General Court. Wilson characterized the bill as the most important of the session. Harvard was controlled by Whigs and Unitarians, he charged. In a second speech the following week Wilson insisted Harvard did not graduate enough students, was geographically oriented so that it serviced only eastern Massachusetts, and was unresponsive to the needs of the people. But Samuel Hoar led the defense and got the proposal postponed.[62]

At the end of February Wilson got the House to consider abolition of capital punishment, except for in cases of murder. While many states had been lowering the number of crimes for which capital punishment was possible, Wilson was going beyond the general movement to that date. During the debate, Wilson asserted the existence of the death penalty had not deterred murder. Certainty of punishment, not severity, was what discouraged crime. He reported that when Michigan abolished the death penalty, crime had decreased. But his proposal was rejected.[63]

Wilson took leadership, in part at least, in an area in which his previous legislative career and writings had demonstrated little interest. He introduced a resolve instructing delegates in Congress to work for repeal of the liquor rations and the law permitting flogging in the navy. A week later Hoar, in behalf of the Judiciary Committee, presented a new draft which dealt only with the distribution of grog. The majority insisted naval officers needed the right of flogging. The minority, including Wilson, characterized flogging as a brutal and barbarous practice. Wilson spoke about the history of flogging and reported the navy had given fifty-seven thousand lashes in one year; he blamed the large number on Southern commanders. Schouler contended that congressmen knew more about the subject than state legislators; the General Assembly should leave the subject alone. After debate and many failed amendments, the committee proposal was defeated. The Wilson resolve then passed by a 217-to-35 vote, but the Senate subsequently rejected it.[64]

Wilson was more successful in a less partisan area. A bill was proposed which would have abolished the six dollar payment to members of the militia. Schouler and Wilson led the attack against the proposal. Wilson declared that if legislators wanted to abolish the militia, they should do it directly, not by the means proposed. The six dollars was well deserved. The proposal was voted down. Only the day before the House had been asked to consider the appointment of a major-general for the Second and Third Divisions of the militia. Wilson declined being a candidate.[65]

For all of his long interest, Wilson did not seem to be giving much energy to the temperance movement. Surprisingly little is found in the *Emancipator and Republican* on the subject. The Legislative Temperance Society was organized on January 16, a large meeting with addresses by some of the General Court's better speakers. Briggs was president and other officers included Samuel Hoar, Boutwell, Walker, and Banks, but Wilson did not appear to be present or to play any role in the society's activities. Extensive debates in the House on a bill regulating the sale of intoxicating liquors also reveal no important involvement by Wilson.[66]

6

WILSON TAKES CONTROL

The national controversy over the expansion of slavery peaked again during the congressional session of 1849–1850. Taylor may have brought the Whigs their second national victory, but his patronage policies and the necessity for his making decisions which affected the slavery-antislavery controversy alienated important elements within his party. Furthermore, while the Treaty of Guadelupe-Hidalgo terminated the bitter arguments over war in Mexico, the acquisition of western territory reinvigorated the controversies over the expansion of slavery. The politicians might have postponed decisions longer had not gold been discovered in California in 1848. During 1849 thousands, from all over the world, migrated to the Pacific coast. Most did not make their fortune, but most stayed. California was still under control of the army, awaiting congressional action to establish a territory. In his December 1849 message to Congress the president supported plans already underway for California's bypassing territorial status and seeking admission as a state. In addition, Taylor suggested the people of New Mexico might also soon apply for statehood. To complicate the situation further, a controversy between Texas and the national government over the boundaries of that new state was beginning to grow to serious dimensions.

The 1849–1850 session of Congress was not like that of its predecessor, limited to three months in which necessary business had to be transacted and difficult subjects could be—perhaps had to be—postponed. Some of the more determined, political, or ideological of the politicians quickly heated the atmosphere with their speeches. State legislatures added to the fuel with resolutions which their congressmen presented, defending or attacking slavery. In January in a special message Taylor again spoke about the future of California, New Mexico, and the Texas boundary, engendering further sectional and partisan replies.

On January 29 Clay sought to assume the leadership which many had expected of him, with eight resolutions intending to win support in both sections and to settle a number of problems confronting the nation, including the status of California, New Mexico, and Texas, but also treating the slave trade in the District of Columbia, the restitution of fugitive slaves, and the control of Congress over the interstate slave trade. This was the Great Compromiser's effort to give both slave and free state people some of what they sought. The North was to surrender more, Clay declared, because it was larger and more powerful and therefore could afford to be more magnanimous and because it, unlike the South, was asked to make no sacrifice to its way of life. In the months which followed only two Northern and perhaps five Southern Whig senators followed his leadership. Democrats would be the primary sustainers of these proposals. The Senate debate continued for a month until, on March 4, the dying Calhoun had read for him his analysis of the issues before the country. Brilliant, humorless, the intellectual leader of part of the South, Calhoun demanded as a price of continuing union a Southern share of the new territories, Northern cooperation in the return of fugitive slaves, a halt to the agitation on the slavery question, and constitutional guarantees for the South. The moderate Whig *Boston Transcript* noted Calhoun's inability to accept the change of sectional equilibrium produced by Northern growth and asserted the North could not concede additional territory to slavery, could not stop agitation of the issue, and would not disturb the constitution by providing additional guarantees to the South.[1]

Free Soilers in Massachusetts were aware that important issues dealing with slavery and its expansion needed to be settled by Congress during the year. The legislative session had scarcely begun when, on January 11, Wilson introduced a series of resolutions dealing with slavery. The first stated slavery was a wrong to the bondsman, a crime against humanity, and a sin in the sight of God, and it was the duty of every government under which it existed to abolish it. The second declared slavery to be a local institution in states which permitted its existence, for which neither the national government nor the people of the free states had any responsibility. The third asserted the national government had the powers to suppress the slave trade, regulate interstate commerce, govern the territories and the District of Columbia, and admit free states—and should use those powers to enhance freedom. Finally, senators would be instructed and representatives requested to oppose the admission of any state or the establishment of any territory which permitted slavery, and to support measures to divorce the national government from all connection with the "peculiar institution." The resolutions were temporarily laid on the table. The same day, however, the state Senate proposed a joint committee on the subject of slavery, to which the House concurred. Hillard was made chairman. The next day the parts of the governor's message dealing with the exclusion of slavery from the newly acquired territories were referred to the committee, as were resolves forwarded by the governor from the legislatures of Ohio, Maryland, and Virginia. Wilson on January 21 got his proposals also dispatched there.[2]

Nothing happened. The session of the General Court had scarcely begun and the situation in Washington was ticklish, but not critical. After all, the president was supporting statehood for a free California. A meeting of the Free Soil members of the legislature and the county chairmen on January 21 was primarily devoted to questions of corporations and financial issues, much to Adams's disgust. A week later Adams, Hoar, and Park persuaded the others to focus their efforts on slavery. The annual meetings of the Massachusetts Anti-Slavery Society, January 23 to 25, with Wilson in attendance the latter two days, gave over too much of their time, Wilson lamented, to attacks on Free Soilers, when those opposed to slavery needed to unite. Adams was increasingly convinced that many of his associates were being absorbed by other issues. While he recognized Congress would not be persuaded to attach the Wilmot Proviso to bills organizing the territory acquired from Mexico, Adams had no fears of disunion. He and those in Massachusetts who were cautious or opposed to working with the Democrats were getting support from Giddings, the recognized Free Soil leader in Washington, who was advising his party in Ohio to maintain its own organization and predicting independence in both Massachusetts and New York in the fall elections.[3]

By the first of February Wilson was concerned; he saw a likelihood that the Whigs were going to support Clay's proposals. Adams was asked if he thought it wise to propose resolutions of instructions to congressmen to work for the Wilmot Proviso. Adams was surprised at the attitude of the Whigs, but counseled delay until the Free Soilers could ascertain what was going to occur. On February 4 the Free Soil legislative members and county chairmen gathered again, with a lot of talking and a decision to call a state convention to respond to what by now was seen as an "alarming crisis" in Washington. Adams was made chairman of an arrangements committee. Dana drafted the resolutions, Wilson as state chairman called the meeting to order, Palfrey was president. The first session, on February 27, was poorly attended; the afternoon went better. The *Dedham Gazette* confessed that neither Whigs nor Democrats attended. Congressman Joseph M. Root of Ohio was to be the featured speaker, but did not show up. Sumner was ill. Palfrey, Dana, Phillips, Hopkins, Park, Adams, Seth Webb Jr., and Wilson all spoke. Wilson declared that every day brought fresh reports of Southern threats to dissolve the union or provoke civil war if slavery were not extended to new territories. He had heard Northern congressmen were intimidated by threats or frightened for the nation. But, he asserted, "union or no union, peace or no peace, compromises or no compromises, let us march boldly up to the extreme verge of our constitutional rights in resistance to the extension of human bondage."[4] In addition to the convention, Adams, Dana, and others reentered the lecture circuit in an effort to arouse the state.[5]

In the meantime, on February 4, perhaps as a result of the caucus, perhaps on his own, Wilson submitted an order instructing the Judiciary Committee to report a resolve relating to slavery, declaring Massachusetts was opposed to compromise with slavery and instructing the state's senators to oppose Clay's compromise resolutions before Congress. During the debate, Wilson contended an emergency had arisen and prompt action was needed. He characterized Clay's compromise as "derogatory to the American name and American character." Schouler got that resolve also referred to the special committee. Eventually all the proposals were taken up by the committee and presented on February 12 with a minority report by Representative Hopkins. The committee's resolutions called for "firmness, temperance, and discretion." They maintained Congress's power to deal with slavery in the territories, regretted the existence of the institution, contended Congress had the authority to end slavery or the slave trade in the District of Columbia, and asserted the slave trade in the District should be ended immediately and slavery abolished there gradually. Wilson termed the majority's statements as strong, but "not sufficiently explicit and adapted to the exigencies of the crisis." Hopkins's report would pledge to resist the extension of slavery or the admission of new slave states and sought to use every constitutional power to end the institution in the slave states. It dissented from the view of Taylor in his annual message. But Hillard secured the endorsement of the Whig caucus for his report, calling for "wisdom, discretion and forbearance," lamenting the existence of slavery, and declaring Congress had the duty of excluding it from the territories. Two weeks later, when the resolves were presented for consideration, Hopkins moved to amend with the minority proposals; the Hillard resolutions were abandoned and the matter was recommitted to committee. One Wilson biographer claimed the Whigs stole the Free Soil program and embarrassed Wilson with their plan. The refusal of the House to pass the Hillard resolutions, however, affirms that a majority agreed with Wilson that the proposals of Hillard's joint committee on the subject of slavery were inadequate.[6]

Resolutions from a Convention of the People to Devise Measures for Peaceable Secession of Massachusetts from the Union were presented to the House. Many representatives were angered by the suggestions and proceeded by an overwhelming majority to lay them on the table. Boutwell subsequently asserted that the House by its action had denied the right of petition. He obtained a vote of reconsideration and got the petitions referred to the Judiciary Committee. *The Liberator* complained the committee provided no opportunity for the petitioners to be heard or for others to present their petitions. Forty-eight hours after being assigned the petitions, the committee reported back negatively. By rules of the House the report should have laid over for a day, but Wilson moved that those rules be suspended and the vote taken immediately, so that the country would know how Massachusetts stood on the issue of disunion. Every voter but one agreed with Wilson. Garrison's newspaper was furious with Wilson and also attacked Boutwell for refusing to present additional petitions on the same subject. Wilson shortly thereafter somewhat redeemed himself with the abolitionists by declaring he was not aware the petitioners wanted a hearing, and voted with the minority in trying to get a subsequent petition sent to a special committee. So many House members were angry at these petitions that Schouler introduced a proposal providing that any member of the General Court who presented a petition for dissolution of the union would be expelled from his seat. The resolution was laid on the table.[7]

By the beginning of March the House had passed only two reform laws—Schouler's allowance of a plurality for second elections for members of Congress, and the resolution concerning flogging and the spirit ration in the navy—and acceptable antislavery resolutions were still not forthcoming. Wilson was angry and frustrated and complained in the *Emancipator and Republican* on Saturday, March 2: "The Senate of Massachusetts has rejected the resolves against the spirit ration and flogging in the Navy, which passed the House after a long debate by a 220-36 vote. The Senate is a great body; stupidity and gross ignorance are its chief characteristics. Few subjects are fully examined or discussed in that body, or decided according to facts and arguments."[8] Hillard, who chaired the committee to which the House proposal had been referred, the following Tuesday called the article to the attention of the Senate, certainly not without consultation. The Senate voted to complain to the House about Wilson's "libel" of the Senate. Upon its receipt, the House moved to refer the complaint to the Judiciary Committee. Wilson said he did not care what happened on the matter. He was the representative from Natick and not responsible to the Senate. The Senate had to protect its own character. If, as editor of the *Emancipator and Republican*, he had offended members of the Senate, their remedy was clear. He admitted he had written the paragraph with undue haste and he was sorry if it had offended. He asserted he had served in the legislature for six years and had never been called to order for words spoken in debate or had had personal controversy with any member. He declared the press was free, which meant free to attack the Senate.[9]

Within two days, on March 7, the House committee reported. It noted the two branches of the legislature were coordinate, each the judge of its own privileges. If the alleged breach were to be punished, it could only be done by the Senate; the House would not act. The House debated the matter for the better part of a week, recommitted it to committee, and finally disposed of the case only on April 5. Representative Frothingham of Charlestown objected to the committee report, which he charged virtually turned the matter over to the Senate. He knew of no such crime as a public libel. The *Boston Post* had already noted that only individuals could be "libeled," not a body of men. Furthermore, the Senate had made no specific charges, Frothingham asserted. Frothingham's amendments included a statement: "the House declines to take further action on the message." The editor of the *Worcester Spy*, a member of the House, reported the vote was almost unanimous in its support of Frothingham's proposal; the building fairly rang with the legislators' response. Frothingham in person delivered the resolution to the Senate.[10]

Wilson was not done with the issue. For a time during the crucial weeks following the Seventh of March address, the *Emancipator and Republican* was quiet. But on April 11 Wilson called attention to the Massachusetts constitution's provision prohibiting a person holding at the same time a United States government office and one of a number of state offices. He attacked Hillard for filling both Senate and United States commissioner positions. He said Hillard had been the butt of community jokes for six weeks, so much so that he might want to leave the Senate. A week later a sharp article, in which Wilson's antagonist was continually referred to as "the young man of the best hopes," reported that Hillard, conscious he was the subject of public ridicule, was "stalking about the State House with a nervous, agitated, sneaking look." About thirty editors in the state, four-fifths of them members of his own party, had denounced Hillard's efforts against Wilson. Finally, in the April 25 issue of the Republican, Wilson gave a lengthy and impressive description of the controversy.[11]

Wilson was experiencing increasing troubles with the *Emancipator and Republican*. Adams had been angry the previous fall when Wilson, promising to show it to him first, printed one of Adams's speeches "with all its imperfections." Nevertheless, Adams continued to write for the paper. He commented that Wilson was "rapidly developing his want of qualification for the post which he occupies."[12] But Adams did not know how to get out of the difficulty; he would not again become an editor himself. The following January he recorded Sumner had visited him to bemoan the tone of the *Republican*. Adams called the paper sometimes "treacherous."[13] In early March Adams forwarded complaints to Wilson which Adams had heard while at a Northboro speech. He suggested the two talk about the problem. He now indicated a willingness to take over the editorship for six months. But the changed political situation must have induced Wilson to struggle on. By spring the number of columns of advertisement had declined, with consequent less income. In mid-March Phillips, William Jackson, Spooner, Adams, and others again gathered to discuss the paper's condition. W. A. White laid before them its bad financial state. Adams insisted a businessman had to be placed in charge. But little was done. Bent had left the paper by May. In June the semiweekly ceased publication. In mid-May Adams, White, Jackson, and others talked with Damrell about beginning another paper. Thomas Wentworth Higginson volunteered to be editor. Adams was more optimistic than usual, but nothing happened. In August Higginson was still striving for a new paper and sought Palfrey as editor. The Free Soil party was so divided over strategy for the fall campaign, however, that no one was foolish enough to risk his money on a losing venture.[14]

Rumors began to circulate that Webster, from whom most Free Soilers expected more support than from Winthrop, Davis, or many other Massachusetts congressmen, was going to vote for Clay's compromise proposals. Palfrey warned that no man had a reputation so great that he would not suffer if he took the wrong side. Davis, on the other hand, on March 3 wrote Briggs that he had tried to "feel solemn and recognize the union was in danger."[15] But while the noise was loud, Congress had not forgotten the Wilmot Proviso or the Ordinance of 1787. Briggs belittled the Faneuil Hall meeting and insisted the union was safe. Winthrop believed his colleague would sustain Taylor's proposals, not Clay's compromise, with its strict fugitive slave law. Wilson reported Webster was expected to take a Northern stand, and had conferred with Giddings, Thaddeus Stevens, and other antislavery leaders.[16]

The rumors, not Davis, were correct. Webster had known of Clay's compromise proposals before they were introduced. While Webster said nothing in public, he had promised Clay to support the plan. On March 7 he rose before a packed Senate visitor's gallery with a speech emphasizing his love of the union and the necessity for the North to make sacrifices. He spoke of the legitimate grievances each section had, he discounted the likelihood of slavery being extended into western territories, and he spoke of slavery as more an unfortunate historical accident than a moral evil. He would support a strong fugitive slave law. He criticized his state's personal liberty law, on the books for seven years, although he had never paid attention to it before nor used his considerable influence to get it altered. He attacked abolitionists, whom he had hitherto generally ignored. Webster's speech won few adherents. Most Northern Whigs were supporting Taylor, not Clay. On the other hand, Southern extremists were not going to have a free California.[17]

The Seventh of March address only divided Whigs in Washington more; Webster's stance also badly divided his party in Massachusetts. Some of the most conservative Whigs condemned the speech or the man. Winthrop said the address would have politically killed anyone but Webster. Everett refused to sign a public letter supporting the senator. Those who did sign often would not in private defend their support. Webster admitted to Everett that he had not read Mason's proposed Fugitive Slave Bill before endorsing it. Amos Lawrence was disgusted. The Whig *New Bedford Mercury* attacked new laws for recapturing fugitive slaves. The Whig *Hartford Courant* also repudiated the Webster position, declaring the constitution did not guarantee the extension of slavery into the territories, or assure admission of an equal number of slave and free states, or provide for the carving up of Texas to accommodate the South. Out in Ohio a future American president, Rutherford B. Hayes, who had attended Harvard Law School for three terms, recorded in his diary his valuation of Webster's genius and his lack of integrity; Hayes regretted Webster was pursuing a course so different from what he had formerly advocated.[18]

Only in Boston did Webster receive much Whig newspaper support. The *Advertiser* took four days before commenting, and then sustained Webster. The *Boston Courier*, which had opposed the Compromise, now endorsed the address. The *Transcript* gave unenthusiastic support. But the *Boston Atlas*, usually

Webster's strongest adherent, declared not a single member of the Massachusetts delegation sustained their senator. It maintained that only six Whig journals in New England concurred with Webster, while seventy, itself among them, opposed his position. Later, when Webster entered the cabinet, he got his revenge by withdrawing government patronage from the paper, forcing Schouler to give up the editorship.[19] The *Boston Post*, of course, as spokespaper of a national Democratic viewpoint, complimented Webster and characterized his views as "frank, honest and fearless, . . . in [a] spirit of compromise."[20]

It is surprising, particularly in light of the four-year-old Webster-Lawrence divisions, how rapidly the conservative Massachusetts business leadership came to the senator's support. By April, Ashmun, long considered a moderate voice for opposition to slavery among western Massachusetts Whigs, sustained Webster. More than eight hundred prominent Bostonians in May signed a public letter. But many more simply kept quiet. Wilson laughingly recorded his surprise that no more names could be obtained. Never were greater efforts used to obtain signatures, he contended. The Merchants' newsroom was "perverted . . . for partisan purposes." Both the *Advertiser* and the *Courier* strongly advised their readers to sign.[21]

Horace Mann, who had balanced his Whig and Free Soil connections so well for so long, now could no longer stomach the Whig stance, if Webster was to be spokesman for it. Jackson, who had left the Whigs in 1840, in a private letter on March 22, summarized the Massachusetts party's new position. Mann's organizational voting had achieved nothing, he contended. Mann must have agreed, for in letters in the *Boston Traveller* and *Journal* in early April he publicly took issue with Webster. Wilson believed Mann's independence was creating trepidation among the Whig leadership. The Whigs proved their strength when they denied him renomination in the fall. The Free Soilers selected him again and, with independent Whig support, Mann won.[22]

Wilson in his *Emancipator and Republican* reported that he had heard of Webster's speech "with deepest regret." The address was one of "great ability," he admitted, but was counter to what New Englanders believed. Webster had characterized Taylor's nomination as one "not fit to be made"; Webster's speech was the same. The senator, Wilson asserted, had "been seduced by the blandishment of power."[23] Wilson's angry response of the moment can be accounted for by remembering his Whig background and his expectations for Webster, whom he had supported for a presidential nomination less than two years before. Until this speech, Wilson had always hoped for the best. After March 7, Wilson regarded Webster as a traitor to the people of Massachusetts. More than twenty years later, when he wrote his history of the causes of the Civil War, in which he tended to smooth over many differences among public figures, Wilson still attributed self-seeking motives to Webster's 1850 position. While Webster reconciled himself to his change by declaring the country was in danger and the South had to be pacified, the real reasons for the Seventh of March address, Wilson wrote, were that Southerners had flattered him and Webster still dreamed of the presidency.[24]

Webster's support for compromise propelled Wilson to take new steps. The hesitancy of Adams, Hoar, Palfrey, and the conservatives was thwarting actions which might halt the series of slavery victories. As chairman of the state Free Soil committee, as editor of the Boston Free Soil newspaper, as spokesman of the Free Soilers in the House, Wilson was in a position to direct strategy as he never before had been able. The leaders among his former Conscience Whig associates could still block Wilson's tactics, but they had no strategy of their own and would not devote the time to organization that the moment demanded. On the day after Webster's Seventh of March speech, Wilson walked through the Boston Commons with Boutwell and Banks. Wilson denounced Webster. If the Whigs did not denounce him, too, he asserted, coalition was necessary. Banks did not believe the Whigs would break with Webster. Boutwell was "rather reticent."[25]

Contemporaries agreed that during the next few months Wilson captured the leadership of efforts which would lead to coalition of the Free Soil and Democratic parties. His friend and biographer, Jonathan Mann, admitting his cobbler friend's ambition, went on:

> to the organizing brain, the settled purpose, the sagacious counsel, the strong faith, the unyielding tenacity, and constant fidelity of Henry Wilson, more, I think, was due than to any single person in shaping the course of the Free-soil party. . . . He performed a work no other man of our time was qualified to perform. Other men contributed eloquence, thought, inspiration, counsel, labor, faith, and gave their time and wealth, and voice and brain, to push along the work. But Wilson gave himself. He lost all thought or care for money, and business, and ease, and convenience, and sleep, and bodily health, and social enjoyment, and went in, with all he had and all he hoped for, to aid the cause.[26]

Others also commented on Wilson's leadership. Edward L. Pierce, crediting him with organizing the coalition, also characterized Wilson as the "most indefatigable of all Free Soilers, [who] made more addresses, wrote more articles, and knew more men in the party than any other leader."[27] George Hoar, a youth at the time, later recalled that Wilson, "who, as he gathered and inspired the sentiment of the people, seemed often to be in ten places at once, used to think it worth his while to visit me to find out what the boys were thinking of."[28] Archibald H. Grimke, one of Sumner's nineteenth century biographers, declared Wilson surpassed Sumner in "party management."[29] Another, George H. Haynes, noting the leadership taken by Wilson at this time, claimed he had "probably never been excelled in Massachusetts in his power of getting close to the great masses of the people and in understanding their thought and will."[30] Jonathan Mann characterized

Wilson as "alive with energy and boiling over with enthusiasm." He was everywhere working and urging others on: at conventions, consultations, mass meetings, and school district gatherings.[31]

Others agreed that Wilson was a masterful politician. Charles Francis Adams in 1875, after the arguments of the early 1850s had been moderated, spoke of Wilson's innate aptitude for politics. Wilson's greatest strength was his flexibility, Adams asserted. Perhaps enviously, Adams noted Wilson could associate with "all sorts of men." And his former colleague's disposition was so kind that he could move easily through conflict.[32] A Natick commentator remembered his fellow townsman as a tireless worker. A twentieth century Wilson biographer has concluded Wilson was well suited to his state committee chairmanship, because he enjoyed power, but did not need glory. He was good at organization and could use office as a means to an end.[33] That may be a good definition of a politician.

How frustrating it must have been to those who opposed the compromise measures that the potential for action by the Massachusetts legislature lay in the Hillard committee. Free Soilers gathered on March 11 to discuss tactics. Webster himself returned to Boston to quiet the objections to his speech. Wilson in his newspaper declared Hillard had intentionally kept the matter in committee too long, when events in Washington had cried for prompt action. The resolutions were reported out again and the House considered them on March 19. The events in the capital had much altered the situation. Hopkins got a report, against the desire of a majority of the committee, with the understanding that there would be no debate. In the House, Schouler, joined by Hopkins, Hoar, and Wilson, supported the plan, but Representative Branning sought to amend the plan to instruct the state's senators and request the representatives to follow the resolves. The debate lasted through the week. Wilson asserted that Webster on March 7 had presented the Northern position and then had advocated the Southern side. The senator, because of his intellect, name, and experience, could have rallied the people, but instead had failed them. Wilson defended the abolitionists whom Webster had attacked. "The truths which they have nursed and breathed into the people will live," he declared; "the work of their hands will endure after his [Webster's] petty compromises have passed away from the remembrance of mankind."[34]

While Wilson originally sustained the Hopkins resolution, and planned to follow that with a separate instruction to Webster to vote for the Wilmot Proviso and against the Fugitive Slave Act, when the decision came on the Branning proposal, Wilson voted for it. The Suffolk County delegation was unanimous in opposition. The amendments having failed, the committee's report then passed to a third reading.[35]

On March 23 when the resolves came for a final consideration, Boutwell sought to substitute proposals of his own. One of these asserted Congress had the power and duty to make all needful rules and regulations dealing with slavery in the territories and one needful rule was the prohibition of slavery. Another called for the admission of California as a free state. National senators and representatives were requested to sustain the principles of the resolutions. Boutwell's proposals failed 86 to 146, with Wilson opposed. Wilson must have believed strategy called for supporting the committee's work in order to assure passage of something. Hopkins, however, was able to add to the resolutions Boutwell's proposals on California and on asking the governor to transmit the action to senators and representatives. The resolves then were enacted, 207 to 6. In the Senate an amendment condemning Webster's course, offered by Amasa Walker, failed. Henry L. Dawes secured an amendment asking for trial by jury for alleged fugitive slaves. Buckingham added another, employing the same strong words which Webster earlier had uttered against the extension of slavery. But the differences between the two houses caused the resolutions to be referred to committee, where the jury trial amendment was modified and Buckingham's change omitted. The proposals as reported by committee were then passed by the Senate with four dissenting votes, concurred on by the House, and signed by the governor.[36]

Out of the Free Soil leadership meetings in mid-March emerged a decision for a Faneuil Hall conclave on March 25 to muster support against the Clay proposals and increasing acceptance of the Webster position by the Boston gentry. Wilson was among the signers of the call, which included surprisingly few important Free Soilers. The *Boston Transcript* reported the meeting was "largely and respectably attended." With Francis Jackson, Wendell Phillips, and Samuel G. Howe securing the speakers, Samuel Sewell presiding, and Theodore Parker and Wendell Phillips both delivering addresses, the abolitionists unquestionably made their presence known more than at usual assemblies of this sort in Massachusetts. The meeting decided to send petitions to the legislature, asking for instructions to Webster to vote for the Wilmot Proviso and against the proposed Fugitive Slave Act.[37]

On April 30 the House began consideration of an adverse committee report on the resolutions instigated by the Faneuil Hall meeting and by others who wanted the legislature to instruct Webster. Wilson responded, hoping to salvage something, by substituting "respectfully but earnestly request" for "instruct." He said he presumed every member would vote for the proposals, since they were worded respectfully and only furthered principles already agreed to by the House. The state needed to tell its senator what it wanted him to do. But the majority of Whigs, including even Schouler, would not agree; their tactic was to claim the resolutions were unnecessary. Wilson's efforts were defeated 47 to 122. A few days later, on May 3, the legislature adjourned. During the debates an angry Wilson denounced the "Doughfaces with their ears and eyes filled with cotton."[38] More important, he issued a declaration which would become a guide for his conduct during the next four years. He asserted that when he left the hall, he would unite with any party or body of men to drive the Whigs from power, rebuke Webster, and elect a senator in agreement with the principles of the state. Wilson later maintained that the refusal of the legislature to send Webster any message gave the senator and his supporters the liberty to ignore popular sentiment. Still, the length and ferocity of the fight and the resolutions passed by the legislature, Webster biographer Claude M. Fuess affirmed, had delivered a message, even if unwanted and ignored, to the senator.[39]

The failure of Palfrey to garner Democratic support and his continual inability to win congressional election somewhat weakened Wilson's efforts to produce a coalition of Free Soilers and Democrats. After all, Adams's willingness to cooperate—in a limited way—with the Democrats in the 1849 elections had been motivated in great part by his hope this would help his friend. Adams and his followers were not the only individuals to see the congressional election in this light: Democrat John Bigelow of New York wrote Sumner in mid-May that his party's support of Palfrey was the test of Free Soil–Democratic cooperation. Wilson was later blamed by the Adams-Palfrey faction for not doing enough to get Palfrey elected. On April 20, however, Wilson praised Palfrey's recent speech and asked for a copy to place in the *Republican*. Several meetings were held that month to plan for the next election. Wilson sought to persuade the Democrats to withdraw their candidate; Banks in return wanted an understanding that Palfrey would serve only one term. Adams and Palfrey were unwilling to bargain for office in that way. Wilson was not discouraged. He assured Adams the Democrats would "act better." In the end Wilson accomplished about all a politician could. Just before election day, the Democrats of the district met and agreed to make no nomination of their own; the close majority of four votes in the convention, however, indicated individual Democrats might vote for the Whig nominee, might write in a name of their own choice, or might stay home. That is what happened. Palfrey defeated the Whig Thompson by more than three hundred ballots, but more than eight hundred people scattered their votes, preventing anyone from receiving a majority.[40]

Meanwhile, in Washington, Congress had continued its debates about the issues which Clay had attempted to compromise. Seward's "higher law" contention was perhaps the most memorable of the speeches. It permitted the compromisers to take the offensive against the alleged radicalism of Seward and Calhoun. In mid-April a special Senate committee, headed by Clay and including Webster, was established to formulate the appropriate legislation. The *Republican* charged Webster and Clay were determined to destroy the Taylor administration. Clay would "rule or ruin." Webster "veers, shifts, hesitates."[41] On May 8 Clay reported three bills: one dealt with the status of California, New Mexico, Utah, and the Texas boundary; a second dealt with fugitive slaves; and the third would end the slave trade in the District of Columbia. That formed the focus for the late-spring debates. By late May Clay and Taylor had openly broken in their determinations that each had the best solution to the developing crisis. But the compromisers did not have the votes, and as the weeks went by, a few Democrats changed their views to support Benton and Taylor more than their Douglas-Cass leadership.

Events in the nation were complicating the Washington decision process. A flare-up occurred in the controversy between Texas and New Mexico authorities as each took actions to implement their beliefs. New Mexico held a constitutional convention in late May and petitioned Congress for statehood. The Texas governor countered with a call for a special session of the legislature in August to provide for military forces sufficient to guarantee Santa Fe for Texas. Congressman Alexander Stephens asserted the whole South would sustain Texas. Taylor correctly saw the solution as a legislative function of Congress, which should establish the boundary and decide whether to admit New Mexico as a state. Meanwhile, in June the Nashville Convention, called by Mississippi, met to consider the alleged interference with Southern rights and what the South's response should be. It was marked with fiery speeches, resolutions demanding the extension of the Missouri Compromise border line between slave and free territory further west as necessary for Southern security, and threats of resistance to be taken, if necessary, by a November assembly.

Wilson's summer activities are difficult to ascertain. He no longer had the responsibility of publishing his paper twice a week, somewhat lessening his need to be in the office as often. Yet he remained living primarily in Boston. Harriet joined him for four weeks about the time the legislature adjourned. Harriet's mother then went to Boston to help maintain the quarters while Harriet's sister arrived in Natick for the summer. For three days in late June Henry attended with many others, including Schouler, a railroad celebration in Burlington, Vermont. He looked forward to the line's continuing on to Montreal, which, he predicted, would help promote the American annexation of Quebec. In July the three Wilsons vacationed in New Hampshire, Henry and his son going for a little over a weekend to Farmington and Harriet staying nearly two weeks at the Eastmans, visiting with Freeman Colbath, Luther Hayes, and George Herring, among others. She also went by stage to Wolfboro and stayed in the lake area about a week. Her health improved on the trip.[42]

Henry continued his active service with the militia. In the late summer of 1849 he reported in the *Emancipator and Republican* about the encampment of his Third Brigade at Concord for two days in drenching rain. There were three bands and about eight hundred men. They engaged in a dress parade and military drills and listened to speeches from Wilson and other leaders. A month later he was attending another encampment at Northampton. The next summer the paper announced Wilson's appointments to officer positions of the Fifth Infantry at Cambridge on August 29 and the Third Infantry at Charlestown on September 3. The annual encampment took place at Groton Junction on September 12 and 13. The paper quoted from the *Nashua Telegraph* and *Boston Atlas* in praise of the behavior and activities of the troops. Wilson himself commended Boutwell and other town authorities for their assistance in preserving order.[43]

The *Emancipator and Republican* continued its harsh attacks on Webster. It termed him "the great apostate," untrue both to his own principles and those of his state. No one should be chosen for the General Court who would vote for him again as senator. In reporting on the Garrisonian's June New England Convention, which he attended, Wilson praised Parker Pillsbury's broadside against Webster as "an admirable speech." In the meantime the Boston establishment had been able to muster its social and economic forces so as to withdraw business from and isolate socially those with whom it formerly had had contact, such as Palfrey, Sumner, and Dana. Still, Webster himself lamented in mid-June that he did not have a single Massachusetts congressional supporter.[44]

In Washington one of those unexpected events occurred to alter both the nation's history and political circumstances in Massachusetts. On July 4 President Taylor took sick. By the ninth he was dead. After his harsh criticism of Taylor in the 1848 campaign, Wilson's response to the death is interesting. He first noted how many newspapers which had attacked the president were publishing indiscriminate eulogies of him. Wilson characterized Taylor as "honest, sincere, kind-hearted," and loved by his countrymen. But he had been unfit for the presidency, Wilson added. Taylor had administered the government better than his countrymen could have anticipated. His defense of the New Mexico boundary claims and his opposition to the Clay compromise were two of his achievements. Wilson predicted the new president, Millard Fillmore, would support the Clay compromise. He characterized Fillmore as a man of respectable abilities, considerable experience, and large acquaintance. He praised his pure and unsullied private reputation.[45]

Fillmore was known to favor compromise. A Clay-Webster-Fillmore coalition was expected. The new president soon reorganized the cabinet, with Webster as secretary of state. To preserve an expression of Whig unity and continuance of the previous administration, Taylor supporters Corwin and Crittenden were included in the cabinet. The compromisers were now in control, with a determined and dominant Webster directing political affairs. Many Northern Whigs shifted to support the administration. Clay was so optimistic he brought his omnibus bill to vote on July 31. It failed and an exhausted Clay left Washington. The long effort at compromise had united the small band of Free Soilers in Congress, who were happy yet apprehensive with their success. Stephen A. Douglas, who had always insisted he could obtain passage of the compromise measures one at a time, now confidentially took over the leadership. Skillful use of patronage by Fillmore helped. By August 9 Webster was writing that the Rhode Island senators had "waked up." The next day he reported Winthrop and Davis had finally succumbed.[46] On August 9 the Senate approved an enlarged Texas boundary bill; California statehood and New Mexico territorial status followed. By August 26 even the Fugitive Slave Act was passed. Finally, the Senate agreed to end the slave trade in the District of Columbia. The House made some changes in the Texas and

New Mexico bills, requiring Senate reconsideration, but that was secured. Only Mann and Orin Fowler among the Massachusetts representatives voted against the Texas bill. By the end of September Congress adjourned its longest session.

When Webster resigned his Senate seat, Briggs angered the Free Soilers by selecting Winthrop as the replacement. Wilson expressed surprise that a governor who claimed to support the Wilmot Proviso would make that appointment. It was the most unworthy nomination that could be made. Since Winthrop would likely become the candidate for the permanent position, Wilson argued, the legislature had to be captured from the Whigs. Soon thereafter Samuel Eliot was nominated for Winthrop's congressional seat. Wilson termed Eliot a man of respectable talents and considerable experience. A man of great wealth, he was "extremely conservative, bigoted, and intolerant." Worse, of 348 councilors, senators, and representatives, Eliot was one of only seven to endorse Webster's Seventh of March speech. The Free Soilers had little hope of defeating a Whig candidate in Boston, but they nevertheless nominated Sumner for the position. Eliot won by a large majority. He arrived in Washington in time to vote for the Compromise. On the same day Eliot was chosen, voters in the Fourth Congressional District again failed to elect Palfrey or any other candidate. By August even Adams had concluded Palfrey might be wise to withdraw.[47]

Winthrop had not gone as far as Webster in support of Douglas's proposals. Both Winthrop and Davis, for example, voted for the Texas boundary bills. Winthrop, however, tried to amend the Fugitive Slave Act to guarantee some rights of due process to the alleged slave. He failed and so voted against the law. Webster was willing to accept that much opposition. He was more concerned with resolutions of the September state Whig convention. They were carefully worded so as not to embarrass the secretary, but they showed Massachusetts Whigs were opposed to the Fugitive Slave Act and they refused to make acceptance of the Compromise as a mark of Whiggery. Some of the Whig district conventions propounded even stronger resolutions. One from the Middlesex County convention called the Fugitive Slave Act "odious" and asked for its unconditional repeal. The renomination of antislavery Briggs for governor helped unite the party and promote loyalty from some Whigs who were unhappy with the Compromise.[48]

Wilson was convinced by August that without some better plan of action the Whigs would again elect their state candidates, control the legislature, and select Winthrop as senator. He was right. All too often historians have excused the natural antipathy of Hoar, Adams, Palfrey, and others to the economic and social consequences of working with the Democrats. Apparently their determination to halt the expansion of the Slave Power was not important enough in their hierarchy of values to overcome their economic and social concerns. In fairness, too, they had little confidence in the constancy and dependability of the Democrats and they feared combination would end Free Soil independence; their principles would be swallowed up by a party whose real commitment to the containment of slavery was suspect. Adams, who went to Washington in the summer before the Compromise votes, to persuade men like Seward and Preston King to stand firm, asserted Webster would be working with the Democrats in another year.[49]

But conservative Free Soilers were not just opposed to amalgamation; they also objected to coalition. What they were unable to see, and some historians since have chosen to ignore or minimize, was that they had no viable alternative. Through the remainder of their lives men such as Adams, Palfrey, and Dana criticized Wilson for his work to produce coalition, often accusing him of lack of principles. Yet it was his very principle of opposition to the extension of slavery which caused him to adopt tactics that offered some chance of achieving his objectives. After the amazing endorsement of the Seventh of March speech by the Massachusetts Whig party, the continual refusal of the 1850 legislature to instruct or even ask its senators to vote against a stricter Fugitive Slave Act and for the Wilmot Proviso, and the death of Taylor and the ascension of Fillmore and Webster to power, the conservative Conscience Whig group offered no plan at all for success. The three district elections in late August all had gone badly for the Free Soilers. Wilson and his supporters who were advocating cooperation with the Democrats were not being impulsive. A decade of struggle against the increasingly militant Slave Power had not improved the situation. Nor had the suggested response of those who hoped for an end of slavery, or at least of its extension, promise much for the future. But tardy 1849 election cooperation with the Democrats had produced some favorable results. A better-organized and timely alliance was at least an alternative to accepting long-term domination of the nation by the slaveholders and their allies.

Then, too, the Free Soil coalitionists were not operating in a vacuum. They could see the decline of the party in other states. The agreement by former New York party leaders, like Stanton and John Van Buren, to a Democratic platform which did not even include the Wilmot Proviso showed how weak Free Soil had become nationally. The support for coalition wherever feasible by Free Soilers in other states, and its endorsement by Gamaliel Bailey, editor of Washington's *National Era*, establishes that Wilson's strategy was not an aberration.

Of course, Wilson and many of his associates had found more in common with some of the Democrats than their opposition to slavery and its expansion. Members of the two parties had cooperated extensively in the 1850 legislative session and had been consistently blocked by the Whigs, who seemed especially responsive to the desires of their Boston constituents. A majority of Democrats and the coalition Free Soilers were especially eager to end general tickets in Senate and House elections, adjust apportionment, provide for the secret ballot, and control the excesses of business better.

Where were additional votes to come from either in 1850 or the future? Kevin Sweeney has estimated approximately 98 percent of 1847 voting Liberty party men cast Free Soil ballots in 1848; they probably continued to do so, making them an important, but not dominant, element in the party. Many of them would support a strategy in 1850, however, which would promise to produce results. Sweeney also concluded that 17 percent of the Democrats who voted in 1847 cast their ballots for the Free Soilers in 1848. Many of them returned to their former party in the 1849 and 1850 elections, when Van Buren was not a presidential candidate and Boutwell headed the state ticket. They would not be likely in 1850 to vote for Phillips, nor were they likely to become Free Soilers in the future, as long as the Democratic party was wise enough to nominate men of respectable antislavery convictions and the Free Soilers selected former Conscience Whigs. Finally, 19 percent of the 1847 Whig vote went Free Soil in 1848, according to Sweeney. The absence in 1849 of a Van Buren candidacy to repel ex-Whigs had not helped Free Soilers, as Phillips, an ex–Whig leader, had received twelve thousand fewer votes. Adams, Palfrey, and Hoar were justified in hoping to attract additional Whigs to vote Free Soil in 1850, in the climate of the Compromise debates. But Phillips would not attract a majority on election day; nor would Whigs in the legislature, accustomed to governing the state and now steered by Webster, support a turncoat, ex–Conscience Whig. Furthermore, the party would be even less likely to produce a winner in 1851 or 1852 after the Compromise became "old hat." Nor, with apportionment as it was and a general ticket in Suffolk County, and with two other organized and well-financed parties, would the Free Soilers control the General Court anytime in the foreseeable future. Clearly then those who advocated coalition held some prospect for success; those who opposed them did not.[50]

The Free Soil state committee on July 23 decided to call the annual convention for Boston on September 17. Although the time was fairly typical for Massachusetts political parties, Sumner and Adams opposed the date as too early. State politics were at the moment too uncertain, Sumner wrote Chase. Keyes, Bird, and Buckingham led the fight for an early date. On August 10 the advocates of cooperation sought at a Free Soil state meeting to obtain endorsement for a committee to work with the Democrats. Wilson many years later asserted he had opposed fusion, except on the basis of the Buffalo platform, which he knew he could not obtain from the Democrats. He instead advocated coalition. While a majority favored the proposal, with Adams and some other important leaders opposed, the Wilson group agreed to Whittier's motion to lay the matter on the table rather than divide the party. On August 22 a long letter, signed "Anti-Slavery," appeared in the *Republican* urging fall campaign cooperation with the Democrats. The objective was to get Phillips, Adams, or Sumner into the Senate. Each party would run its own candidates but the end would be cooperation. That strategy had sent Hale to the Senate from New Hampshire. Wilson himself endorsed the idea in the lead editorial on August 29. In a number of states, he advocated, Free Soilers should work with the other minority party, whatever it might be, to secure control from the dominant party. Massachusetts needed the right man in the Senate.[51]

Adams claimed the fusionists tried to bypass him and did not invite him to the next session of the state committee later that month. His disagreement with the direction of the party had reached the stage that Adams was calling those opposed to him "traitors." Burlingame reported Wilson had personally and too sharply attacked Adams, Palfrey, and several others. This brought a reaction within the party leadership and defeated a proposal calling for Democratic–Free Soil union. As a result of the second meeting, Wilson as state party chairman and Keyes as secretary postponed the state convention until October 3. In the meantime Wilson had also gone to Salem to ascertain Phillips's sentiments about withdrawing as Free Soil candidate for governor.[52]

On September 10 a third meeting was called; two large parlors were full. Dana wrote that its purpose was to authorize mixed tickets for senators and representatives who might give the Democrats the governorship and the Free Soilers a senator. Wilson conducted the meeting and invited anyone present to speak. Hoar wanted an explanation about the purpose of the meeting. Adams recorded the reply indicated Wilson wanted to leave everyone uninformed. But the *Emancipator*, Wilson's history of the period, and even his own diary reveal Adams and others were well informed about what was taking place. About twenty or thirty persons, including Morton, Jackson, Swan, and Alley, spoke in favor of cooperation with the Democrats. Edward L. Pierce, who was not present, later recorded that the supporters had been Democrats or Liberty party men and that Wilson was the only ex-Whig to advocate cooperation, but Pierce was wrong. Palfrey, Adams, Phillips, Samuel Hoar, and Dana led the opposition. Discussion lasted most of the day. At the end a plan was agreed to which forbade the central committee from working officially with the Democrats, but allowed individuals to act as they saw fit. Adams contended some conservatives were unwilling to accept even that step of cooperation. The Adams forces believed they had won. A twentieth century Wilson biographer, J. Daniel Loubert, agrees. He contends Wilson was denied party authorization and had thereafter to work less openly, in smoke-filled rooms. But Wilson had not sought union. He must have known for a month that coalition at the state level would alienate an important segment of the leadership, particularly financial, of both parties. As unrealistic as he believed the conservative Free Soilers to be, he had not isolated them and he could not work without them.[53]

Sumner was out of the state when the September 10 meeting was held. He wrote to Wilson for reading at the September caucus a letter opposed to departing from past strategy, if the new course did not have the support of all elements of the party. He sought to continue acting with the Democrats in town and senatorial elections. He was maintaining his close relationships with both factions of the Free Soil party. Many historians believe he saw that as the path to the senatorship. Many Democrats were willing to accept Sumner, not only as a price for the important state offices, but because he was regarded as an impractical visionary who would do little harm in Washington.[54]

Wilson had a plan. The Free Soil party was being taken over by Sumner, Bird, Keyes, Alley, Stone, Webb, and Wilson. A new campaign newspaper, the Free-Soiler, advocating cooperation and edited by Bird, Alley, and Horace E. Smith, was started. All of the state's Free Soil newspapers—Wilson's *Emancipator and Republican*, the *Dedham Gazette*, the *Worcester Spy*, the *Lowell American*, and the *Northampton Courier*—sustained the coalition program, not that of the conservatives. When the *Northampton Courier* endorsed coalition on September 24, it claimed the idea came from the Democratic *Greenfield Republic*, which had suggested coalition in town elections. Its emphasis was on the current representative system and its effects on the country towns. Not one Whig had supported the reform of that system in the last legislature, the newspaper declared. The *Courier* also noted the successful cooperation in 1849 between the two minority parties for Senate candidates. Adams and Palfrey believed they were to be left out of the state convention. Wilson and his supporters clearly understood that if the two minority parties could together control the General Court, the election of a Free Soiler to the Senate was to be achieved. On the eve of the state convention, the *Emancipator and Republican* published a new, strong editorial urging cooperation with the Democrats.[55]

One forum for the developing new power structure was the Bird Club. It began during the 1848 campaign, when Bird, Andrew, Henry L. Pierce, Stone, and Robinson began dining together on Saturdays at 30 School Street, later moving to Young's Hotel. Editors Wilson and Elizur Wright next joined the group. Howe, Webb, and Sumner soon were invited. Then Edward Pierce, J. M. S. Williams, Charles Slack, Harvey Jewell, William Claflin, Daniel Gooch and others joined. Never formerly organized, it had no officers, no agenda; it was held together by common political interests and social affinities. The lunch offered an opportunity to talk with others of similar mind and increasingly to plan political strategy. Discussions were frank and open. Often participants would criticize one another. Some would sign petitions which others would refuse to sign. Robinson would use information imparted for his newspaper columns. The Know Nothing movement would cause some participants to leave, others to join. In the mid-1850s the site was changed to the Parker House. Anyone could bring a guest. When out-of-towners like Dawes or Joseph Hawley of Connecticut or Anthony of Rhode Island came to Boston, they might join in. George L. Stearns and Franklin Sanborn, famous for their interest in Kansas and John Brown, were added. The group, however, did not include the Adams conservative faction or Democrats.[56]

Wilson must have felt confident to absent himself from the state at this crucial moment. On September 25 twenty-one railroad cars containing approximately 1,350 people, the largest excursion ever to leave Boston, departed for Burlington, Vermont, on the first leg of a trip to St. John, Montreal, and Quebec City. At Burlington Wilson boarded a boat for St. John, his first trip on Lake Champlain. His party received an enthusiastic reception in Montreal. About three hundred visitors continued downstream to Quebec to another "rousing welcome." Wilson, the history enthusiast, had since boyhood dreamed of standing on the Plains of Abraham. In his short stay he walked through the citadel and visited the Falls of Montmorency. He returned for two more days of sight-seeing in Montreal. Then he traveled back by boat to Burlington and by rail to Boston. Among his conclusions were that the French Canadians demonstrated too little enterprise and intelligence and that Quebec should be annexed to the United States.[57]

On October 3 in Boston Wilson called the state convention to order. The theme of the meeting was a denunciation of the Compromise and of Webster. Palfrey was a vice-president, Adams headed the Resolutions Committee, and Burlingame was one of the speakers, but the coalitionists controlled the convention. Adams recorded Whittier had not prepared the resolutions and at the last minute Wilson asked him if he had any; Sumner had intimated that might occur and he was ready. One cannot believe, however, that Wilson was so careless with plans when so much else at the time was being skillfully handled. Sumner, Alley, and Robinson served on Adams's committee. Still, the decision on official coalition had been made a month before and Wilson and his associates did not need to challenge the conservatives. Their alternative plan was already being implemented. Phillips had dispatched a letter declining to run again for governor, unwilling to be involved in an arrangement with the Democrats. Adams and Sumner agreed the letter should be ignored. Wilson, chairman of the Candidate Committee, reported a Phillips nomination and the convention concurred. While Adams and Burlingame were included on the new state committee, Wilson would again be chairman and it was dominated by coalitionists. Among its sixteen members were Alley, Whittier, James M. Earle, Daniel Alvord, Bird, Swan, Sumner, and Jackson.[58]

Two parties had, of course, to work together to create unified nominations at House and Senate levels. Some Democrats approved of the Compromise of 1850; others were willing to acquiesce to it to promote peace and union; the party leadership, now under the control of Hallett, to maintain its position and obtain patronage once the Democrats returned to the White House, needed a record which Southerners would accept. So Hallett, Greene, Cushing, and others either attacked coalition efforts or, more frequently, separated themselves from the arrangements. While the Democratic state convention endorsed coalition, it avoided both the slavery issue and, with the exception of approving of the admission of California, the Compromise. Banks and Boutwell were joined by Robert Rantoul Jr., Benjamin Butler, and Griswold in providing the drive for cooperation. Butler saw coalition as a way to promote labor reform, especially the ten-hour day. Banks was particularly concerned for education. Banks roamed the state setting up coalition tickets.[59]

The September 26 and October 3 and 10 issues of the *Emancipator and Republican* were full of announcements of county conventions; the party machinery was working well. It didn't take Wilson and his fellow coalitionists long to set the example in Middlesex County. On October 7 in separate conventions the Free Soil and Democratic parties united on a Senate ticket of six, including Buckingham, Banks, and Wilson. The vote at the Free Soil assembly was 69 to 6, with Burlingame leading the opposition. Speakers clearly stated their purpose: "the condemnation of the administration, and the election of a Senator."[60] The *Chronotype* reported neither party had surrendered its principles, but they had made an arrangement on state issues, out of which was expected to emerge also the selection of an antislavery United States senator. Adams, on the other hand, recorded the Free Soil movement had been debased by the action. He was astonished at the "procivility" of Wilson, of whom he had formerly thought well. Wilson had been corrupted by politics, he asserted. Yet Adams seemed more willing to accept the combination in Norfolk County.[61]

The refusal of many of the former Conscience Whigs to see that the Whigs had burned their bridges behind them with the acceptance of Webster's leadership on the Compromise of 1850 further complicated political life for Wilson and his associates. Samuel Hoar, declaring the coalitionists had abandoned Free Soil principles, was unwilling to accept the results of the Middlesex County Free Soil convention and led a call for a new meeting, October 14. He was supported by Dana and Burlingame. Wilson and another coalition senatorial nominee in Middlesex County then declined their nominations. Thirty Free Soilers met in Concord the same day as the Whig County and District Conventions. The Whigs nominated their senatorial ticket, including Hoar. What transpired is unclear, and varies depending on the source. One report was that the Free Soilers, by a close vote, endorsed the Whig ticket on the condition the Whigs not nominate a candidate against Palfrey for the current term, only three months of which remained. The Whig district convention then adjourned until October 21 to await the results of the Free Soil County Convention on October 18. Hoar contended the Whigs would accept Palfrey, but the Whig spokesman reported the Free Soilers had agreed to withdraw Palfrey's name. The Whig convention took no action. Wilson's paper reported the Free Soilers agreed to sacrifice Palfrey in the next Congress to get Whig support for his election for the remaining months of the current term. After condemning the cooperation between county Free Soilers and Democrats by a close 16-to-15 vote, the convention nominated its own candidates. Wilson examined the nominees one by one, showing most were not even against slavery. He also pointed out how often Hoar had aided the Whigs in the last session of the legislature. The *Boston Traveller* courageously commented that Whigs, having attacked the coalition with the Democrats, now were willing to accept coalition with the Hoar Free Soilers.[62]

The day after the Hoar-sponsored convention Wilson made his only visit to Palfrey's home with a request from the Democrats to accept a Senate nomination, apparently in place of Wilson himself. Palfrey might then have the Senate presidency. But he would have to abandon the congressional race. The same day

Sumner in writing emphasized the importance of securing an antislavery senator. He attacked Hoar's tactics as sure to produce a Whig majority in the state Senate. The alternative was to give the Free Soilers the balance of power; that could be obtained only by coalition. Palfrey may have objected in theory to combination or may have simply misunderstood what could be accomplished, but he rejected Wilson's suggestion.[63]

The Democratic and Free Soil conventions in Concord on October 18 were "united and harmonious." Wilson, who delivered the major speech for the Free Soilers, spoke of the need to unite to secure the balance of power. He favored most of the state reforms proposed by the Democrats and noted how frequently in the last legislature members of the two parties had worked together. He propounded that one-third of the Whigs agreed with them. He wanted, above all else, to determine the senator for Washington. Free Soilers, he later was to point out, had been willing to work with Whigs in their nomination of Mann and Fowler; they also had to be open to cooperate with Democrats. A joint ticket including Wilson was again nominated. Middlesex County was then safe for the coalition. The Hoar seceders were embarrassed when the Whig District Convention renominated Thompson and ignored Palfrey.[64]

At the Eighth Congressional District Free Soil convention at Dedham two groups vied for control. One unrealistically sought resolutions and nominations which would avoid offending the Whigs; thus they nominated Mann. The other, led by Keyes, had abandoned any hope for Whig cooperation. Adams, as convention chairman, appointed the Resolutions Committee based upon former party affiliations, producing a platform including both points of view. Mann was unanimously nominated. The *Boston Advertiser* and the *Boston Courier* immediately denounced the selection. When the Whigs assembled, Mann came within three votes of nomination on the first ballot. After an hour's adjournment, the opposition united on Samuel Walley. The opponents of Palfrey had usually centered on his refusal to vote for Winthrop for Speaker. The same accusation could not be levied against Mann; rather, he was being rejected for his attack on Webster's Compromise position. The resolutions presented the Compromise as a compact necessary for national peace and unalterable. The Whig rebuff prompted Adams to volunteer to speak anywhere in the district. He recorded Wilson and Keyes were cool to him and his offer. No wonder, given that the election was only two weeks away and help had been needed all month. Dana refused to participate at all, either by speaking or attending Free Soil meetings.[65]

Wilson immediately moved to make certain the public saw Mann as a Free Soil candidate. Writing from the *Republican* office on October 31 he asked Mann to go to Boston the next morning to plan their short campaign. If Mann would address people in all parts of the district, Wilson predicted, the congressman would win. They had to announce a series of meetings at once. Mann, however, also obtained

Whig support. George Russell instigated a second Whig convention, which nominated the educator.[66]

The two factions of the Free Soil party could unite better on their opposition to the Fugitive Slave Act. Wilson, among others, was a signer of a call for a Faneuil Hall conclave on October 14. An effort was made, he reported, to make the meeting nonpolitical. The Whigs, who claimed in their platform to be opposed to the Fugitive Slave Act, were offered the management of the proceedings, if they would participate. They refused. Nevertheless, the crowd was so large that many people had to be turned away. Adams presided and pronounced his duties as second in importance only to those at the 1848 Buffalo assembly. Speakers included Dana, Frederick Douglass, Theodore Parker, Wendell Phillips, and Charles Redmond. On October 4, when Congressman George Julian of Indiana didn't show up, Wilson substituted as the featured speaker at a similar meeting in Lowell. He bemoaned the flight of colored men of Massachusetts to refuge in Canada. He warned that slave-catchers were invading the state. Blacks had a right to defend themselves from these attackers, Wilson declared. He held Webster responsible for the Fugitive Slave Act; his support had obtained the votes it needed. Massachusetts had a responsibility to get the act repealed and to end the political careers of those who voted for it. Similar protest meetings were held in Hingham, Lynn, New Bedford, Worcester, and Springfield.[67]

When the county and district nominations were made, Wilson in the *Emancipator* enunciated clearly the objectives of the campaign. Free Soilers had tried to achieve their ends within the two major parties and could not. Some had left in 1840, others in 1844, others in 1848, he noted. The party did not expect to win a majority. Rather, it sought only to hold the balance of power. Cooperation had elected Mann and Fowler. The only way the Free Soilers could get congressmen, a state Senate, and a United States senator favorable to their point of view was coalition. Otherwise the Whigs would carry a few counties, the House would elect Whigs in others, and Winthrop would become senator. If the plan did not work, how could they be worse off? The plan would no more weaken the party than Free Soil was being weakened by coalition in Ohio. Free Soilers had no obligation to vote for a single Boutwell measure.[68]

While Free Soilers in 1848 had the comfort of knowing about and receiving support from the movement in other states, the workers in Massachusetts in 1850 wisely concentrated upon state issues, knowing the national movement was tottering. In Michigan the 1849 cooperation with the Whigs had fizzled in 1850 to support for three antislavery Whigs for Congress; the Free Soil party itself was little larger than the Liberty party had been. In Wisconsin Free Soilers were joining the Democratic party. In Indiana the party practically ceased to exist. In Vermont ex-Democratic Free Soilers returned to their former party and the Whigs controlled the state. In New York the Hunker and Barnburner Democrats were cooperating again by 1849, and by 1850 reunification was almost complete. Even Stanton did not campaign against the Compromise. With Seward the acknowledged Whig Senate leader against the Compromise, antislavery Whigs were comfortable with their own party. Thus, the Free Soil party was about dead in New York. Perhaps only on Ohio's Western Reserve was the Free Soil movement still as strong as in Massachusetts. Frederick Blue in his history of the Free Soil movement credits the minority Adams faction for retaining the party's identity in Massachusetts. But the Wilson faction had not been united in seeking unification with the Democrats. The choice had been threefold: independence, coalition, or unity. More important, what distinguished the party in Massachusetts from that in most of the rest of the nation was that it stayed alive because it won elections. The conservative faction played little role in that. Wilson directed the campaign and his associates provided the press support, finances, and energy to produce the victories.[69]

In many towns and in all counties but Suffolk and perhaps Barnstable the Free Soilers and Democrats united. The state committee made certain Free Soil speakers covered most of the state. The long list of speeches for the last ten days of the campaign carried in the October 31 issue of the *Emancipator* attests to the thoroughness and organization of the effort in the eastern counties. Wilson himself was scheduled for Franklin on October 29, Milford October 30, Marlboro October 31, Plymouth November 1, Natick November 2, Gloucester November 4, Andover November 5, South Walpole November 6, Haverhill November 7, and Framingham November 9. Other heavy campaigners included Adams, S. P. Adams, Palfrey, Webb, Thomas Russell, Park, Keyes, and White. Wilson, who was to become one of the country's most accurate political prognosticators, was convinced by late October that if the coalition could carry Essex County, it would win. He declared in the October 31 issue of the *Emancipator* that the Senate was safe and the major effort had to be made for the House.[70]

The climax of the campaign was a Faneuil Hall meeting on November 6. Sumner was assigned the main speech, and an able performance could help get him the Senate seat if the coalition won. He strongly condemned the Fugitive Slave Act. He emphasized the most important issue facing the nation was freedom; therefore, Free Soilers would work with Whigs to send two antislavery congressmen to Washington and with Democrats for controlling influence in the Massachusetts legislature.[71]

The Whigs were in a confused position. Webster had simply demanded too much of them. They had tried to strike a position acceptable to voters with the state convention's call for revision of the Fugitive Slave Act. Winthrop would contend to the end of his life that Wilson and Sumner "drew away from us; not we from them."[72] But as Wilson demonstrated in his 1852 state Senate speech and as the chronology in this book proves, the Massachusetts Whig party had steadily become more conservative in its pronouncements and, after Webster demanded endorsement of the Compromise, had taken a radically different stance. Webster, the party's political leader more than at any other time, was so determined to enforce party regularity that he preferred election of a "respectable Democrat" for Congress to a Whig who was "stained" with Free Soilism. He characterized the campaign months as a state of confusion, with many Whigs refusing to act for fear of losing abolition votes. And when the Whigs lost, he attributed the results to the conduct of some of the state's congressmen and the stance of some of the Whig newspapers in opposing the Compromise. The *Boston Atlas's* tactics to woo ex-Whig Free Soilers back to the Whig party failed.[73]

On election day the Whigs captured a plurality for governor. Briggs had more than 57,000 votes (47 percent), Boutwell more than 36,000 (32 percent), and Phillips near 28,000 (21 percent). Many more voters turned out; Briggs and Phillips both increased their totals by 3,000, Boutwell his by 4,000. Briggs had a plurality in every county except Worcester. The two coalition candidates garnered only 1 percent more of the vote than they had obtained a year before. Only three congressmen were elected: Mann, Fowler, and Appleton. Palfrey's vote fell to 35 percent. The coalition clearly won the Senate initially, with 11 Free Soilers, 10 Democrats, and 11 Whigs—eventually 27 coalition, 13 Whigs. Wilson was selected in Middlesex County. The first news about the House was also favorable to the coalition, and the subsequent election produced 113 Free Soilers, 107 Democrats, and 176 Whigs.[74]

Whigs were shocked at election results. They seldom lost. The defeats by Morton (Chapter I) had been at least by a gentleman, not by a cobbler and his "common" Democratic associates. Furthermore, a two-party system produced occasional victories for the minority. No one had expected the Democrats to reelect Morton. The *Emancipator* reported nothing seemed to disturb the *Atlas* as much as the election of Wilson and Keyes. The *Advertiser* claimed the Whigs were the party of union and the voters were not supporting union. But Whigs of Massachusetts had to "open their eyes" to the need for "cordial cooperation" with Southern Whigs. The *Atlas* and *New Bedford Mercury* asserted the Whigs lost because of Webster; Winthrop agreed. A political defeat had not, however, convinced the Boston elite their views were wrong. Some of those who were eager to end the national controversy over the Fugitive Slave Act assembled at Faneuil Hall at the end of November. Two Whig and two Democratic leaders—Benjamin Curtis, Choate, Hallett, and Samuel Bradford—gave the addresses. Henshaw and Appleton attended. Curtis maintained the Compromise had passed and people of Massachusetts had to abide by it. Hallett denounced opposition as treason.[75]

Free Soil response was jubilant. "The Cause of Man Triumphant . . . Massachusetts Redeemed" heralded the *Chronotype*. The *Northampton Courier* termed the election the "most severely contested" in the state's history. It was a "real, complete, and brilliant victory." The paper was especially pleased that not one bolting Democrat had been elected to either house. Whittier wrote Wilson the union ticket had "exceeded beyond his expectations." In a *National Era* article Whittier characterized the results as a repudiation of Webster. If Briggs, "one of the most popular men in the Commonwealth," could not obtain a majority for his party, who could? Henry Adams, writing many years later, praised his father's position, but rejoiced in the election's results. Webb told Sumner they had carried "everything" in the state. Wilson's *Emancipator* reported the Whigs had suffered a crushing defeat. Those who doubted the expediency of coalition had now been answered. Wilson credited the daily labors of Keyes, Bird, Alley, and Horace Smith and the speeches of S. P. Adams, Webb, White, and Russell as most important to Free Soil victories. He noted he had devoted himself for sixty days entirely to the campaign. The Whig Central Committee had spent money and had been effective, he concluded, and was not to blame for the loss, as the *Courier* and the *Advertiser* contended. Rather *Boston Whig* newspapers themselves had aided the Free Soil campaign.[76]

Victory was the product of the work of many men, but Wilson received and deserved more praise than any other Free Soiler. He had advocated and stuck to a strategy of coalition; he had been the organizer and energizer. Swan wrote the Fugitive Slave Act and Websterism "prepared the mind," but organization won the election.[77] It was to Wilson that Whittier wrote in congratulations on the outcome.[78]

7

Successful Coalition Leader (1851)

Wilson was now entering a new period in his life, in which politics would be his only professional activity. He had relinquished the shoe manufacturing business; now he also abandoned journalism. One can only guess, as busy as he was with the fall campaign, how much time he devoted to the weekly *Emancipator*. The party had to have a newspaper for the campaign, so in the absence of willingness by others, Wilson had continued his publication. Burlingame, who was both working with the Free Soilers and maintaining his Whig connections, in September characterized the *Emancipator* as "a sickly paper which pretends or tries to speak for the Free Soil Party." Wilson, he believed, was beyond his depth in editing. During the late spring of 1850 continuing efforts had been made by others to establish a new paper. At the September 10 meeting which decided against statewide coalition, a committee was appointed to investigate what might be done. The next day the members met and created subcommittees to do the work. Five thousand dollars were readily available for the project. Adams offered the editorship to Palfrey, who agreed to accept it, but with many conditions. This paper may have been the *Free Soiler*, but subsequent events indicate this *Free Soiler* was to have been a more long-range project. By October a committee of Bird, Alley, Smith, and Light asked Adams take over the campaign newspaper; he refused but suggested Palfrey again.[1]

After the November election Wilson, among others, reopened the newspaper question. Another committee was established, with Adams as chairman. Damrell was recommended again, but Adams had never thought highly of him. Wilson, who had differed with his partner while they were running the *Emancipator*, probably agreed. Howe next took over the leadership. Wilson was trying to sell out for whatever he could get. The December 5 issue included a notice seeking settlement of all bills by January 1. Eventually three papers, including the *Emancipator and Republican* and Wright's *Chronotype,* were combined, and a new daily, the *Commonwealth* was created. It was to be the Free Soil organ. Trustees were Howe, Bird, Jackson, and John P. Jewett. Palfrey was to be the primary editor, but his strong letter opposing cooperation with the Democrats angered many coalitionists, including Wilson. The first issue of the new paper recorded no editors. Two days later, Palfrey, Richard Hildreth, and Wright were all listed. Wright was termed the "working editor." Within several weeks, Palfrey withdrew and Adams at about the same time took his money out. The paper did little better under Wright and Bird than it had under Wilson, so in the spring Joseph Lyman became publisher and Palfrey was engaged, over the objections of the coalitionists, as a contributing editor.[2]

In the last issue of the *Emancipator* Wilson was nostalgic about his experiences. He particularly noted how the editorship had enabled him to make acquaintances all over the state. What Wilson received for his *Emancipator* interests we cannot know. The new owners did make a purchase, took over the subscription list, and were entitled to receive the outstanding bills. But Wilson had lost seven thousand dollars in his more than two years' publishing experience. That was a very large amount for someone at his income level.[3]

Wilson, Keyes, Bird, Alley, and their fellow coalitionists had about six weeks between the elections and the assembly of the General Court to determine in what ways the Democrats and Free Soilers would cooperate. Individuals in all three parties at the time and historians since have occasionally asserted that no prior agreements had been reached. One has only to review the clear declarations of the press and to study the papers of the important figures of the coalition to recognize the extent of the informal agreement. Those who were not party to it, like Palfrey, Dana, or Hallett, might refuse to cooperate in carrying out the understandings, but most Free Soilers and Democrats knew what they were to do. Bird and Pierce many years later asserted that the Democrats were to receive the entire state government and they would then be accountable for what transpired, but that they would not take it and forced the Free Soilers to share responsibility. That interpretation is open to debate. What is clear is that Boutwell was to become governor and the Free Soilers could select the senator. Whittier wrote Wilson he would yield all state offices to the Democrats; he wanted only the senatorship. Swan would give most of state offices to Democrats; there was no compromise of principles in that, he asserted. But the Free Soilers had to have the senator, "sink or swim." Adams, who opposed agreement, admitted 90 percent of Free Soilers would vote for Democrats for state office in exchange for the senatorship.[4]

Sumner was the favorite candidate for senator among those Free Soilers most able to make the decision, but that choice was not universally recognized. The Whig *Boston Atlas* and *Lowell Journal and Courier* in mid-October reported a deal had been reached selecting Phillips. The *Emancipator and Republican* on the eve of the election reported Phillips, Sumner, or Palfrey would be selected. Realistic Whigs recognized after the election that Winthrop could not be chosen; some had hopes Briggs might attract enough Conscience Whig–Free Soil support. The Whigs did not abandon hope they might yet achieve something. Within days after the November election Morey, a member of party's state committee, visited Burlingame to bargain however he could. Apparently Adams was more acceptable to them than Sumner, and Adams in November agreed to be considered. By late December, however, he was unwilling to compete against Sumner and would not personally participate in negotiations with the Whigs. The *New York Tribune,* the most influential Whig newspaper in the country, was offering hope to its readers that a Whig–Free Soil deal could be worked out. On the other hand, an ex-Democratic Free Soiler, former party nominee for lieutenant governor John Mills, declared he and other Democrats favored Sumner over Adams, Palfrey, or Phillips.[5]

Divisions in the Massachusetts House were so close that a few dissatisfied members of either coalition party could affect the outcome. Wilson's political skills were proved as he organized the Free Soilers before the legislative session began and then kept them in line throughout months of voting. And this had to be done in the face of opposition from many of the former leaders of the party. Banks, Rantoul, and their associates were not as successful. They not only had to work around the opposition of Hallett and the organizational leadership, but now confronted the active opposition of two of the most influential and well-known members of the party, Morton and Cushing. Morton declared the coalition leaders of both parties were guilty of "selfishness, greediness, and intrigue," and "downright corruption." He objected to Free Soil selection of the senator, but was willing for Democrats to support the candidate if he were an ex-Democrat. A majority of Free Soilers were former Democrats, he contended, yet the ex-Whigs dominated affairs.[6]

The election was hardly over before Adams was reporting Cushing was trying to break up the alliance. Wilson's newspaper at about the same time commented that Cushing's Essex County had always been considered the deciding region of the campaign and therefore every effort had been made to conciliate Democrats there. Yet some of them refused to cooperate, not voting for Free Soilers on the coalition ticket and producing vacancies from which Whigs were subsequently chosen. A Democrat in Whittier's district openly announced he preferred a Whig to a Free Soiler. Cushing had begun political life as a Whig, but had supported Tyler when most of his party had broken with the president. During the 1840s he became a Democrat and was the nominee of his party for governor in 1848. Boutwell termed Cushing as destitute of convictions, blaming it upon his residence as minister in China, where Cushing lost faith in Christianity, western civilization, and the American political system. Boutwell also contended his fellow Democrat had strong prejudices against shoemakers, which alienated him from any movement in which Wilson, Alley, and Amasa Walker played prominent roles. Never really popular nor trusted, but intensely ambitious, Cushing was regarded as so able, had read so widely, was so charming, and had such a political ability that he had unusual influence. After all he did against Wilson and the cause of opposition to slavery in the early 1850s, for example, Wilson was willing to recommend Cushing for a general's appointment in 1861.[7]

Wilson was worried. He told Adams in late November that the leaders of the Democrats would not concede the senatorship, but he had confidence in the rank and file. He praised the trustworthiness of Rantoul and Griswold. A month later Wilson expressed his concern about the "treachery" of some Democrats. He believed Free Soilers needed some positive agreements or they could not achieve what they had sought. Leavitt hoped the country Democrats would not be dictated to by Hallett. They wanted to change the representation system and that could be accomplished only if they united with the Free Soilers.[8]

The *Emancipator and Republican* was forthright about the future. On December 12 it announced Boutwell would be the next governor. A week later it explained that the two parties had gone into the elections without a bargain or arrangement, but an understanding that Boutwell would become governor, certain reforms advocated by the Democrats would be enacted, and a Free Soiler would be elected senator. Another article quoted from several Democratic newspapers confirming the agreement. The *Dedham Gazette* and *Northampton Courier,* among Free Soil papers, and a number of Democratic papers also recognized the validity of the understanding. The *Courier* noted there could be no alternative to some agreement by some party since the houses otherwise could not organize.[9]

To complicate Wilson's position further, Palfrey, against the recommendations of Adams and Dana, decided publicly to advise coalition members of the legislature. In his circular he reviewed the formation of the party, evaluated its prospects, and asked it to be faithful to its principles. He contended Phillips had a chance to be governor and Free Soilers could not in good faith support Boutwell. The *Dedham Gazette* characterized Palfrey's effort as ill-timed; if proper at all, those views should have been stated before the election. The circular went so far that within a week Adams published a letter designed to separate himself from Palfrey's position, emphasizing the need for the political end of Webster and supporting the election of Sumner as senator. Phillips publicly commended Palfrey's purity of purpose and devotion to the cause, but begged off supporting his colleague's circular from "considerations of propriety."[10]

The legislature that Wilson was to help lead had changed during the 1840s. In 1850 farmers were less numerous than in former decades and there were fewer professional men. Artisans were still few. But businessmen and industrialists were increasing in number. Twenty-six members were characterized as boot and shoe manufacturers. While only eleven in number, editors and printers were particularly influential; they were selected to three of the four leadership positions. Only 85 out of 395 members of the House had served prior to 1850; 241 were in their first term. The turnover in personnel still hampered effectiveness. Of course, few coalition members had hitherto served in leadership roles, as presiding officers or committee chairmen. Wilson stayed in Boston, at the Marlboro Hotel, rather than return to Natick. Chauncey Knapp, a veteran abolitionist and now a Free Soiler, was secretary of the Senate and also a resident at the Marlboro.[11]

As the time for the legislature to convene approached, negotiations intensified. Before the opening of the session, each of the coalition parties caucused and appointed committees to confer about how the offices would be divided. At the first caucus they agreed to divide control of the two houses; subsequently, Wilson was elected president of the Senate and Banks Speaker of the House. Wilson, in assuming his chair, acknowledged his want of experience and asked for the senators' patience. He promised to give to the position "an earnest determination to perform its duties with fidelity and impartiality." Massachusetts was beginning a revolution. The former apprenticed farm laborer and Natick cobbler and the Essex County "bobbin boy" were to occupy the leadership positions formerly held by representatives of some of the most eminent families of the state. Many of the Boston-area aristocracy could not accept this.[12]

The Democrats on January 1 first sought to consult just about state offices, but were soon authorized by their caucus to discuss all elections by the legislature. At the January 2 conference the Free Soilers unanimously agreed to Boutwell, with no pledges requested from the Democrats about his policies nor any pledges offered that the Free Soilers would support them. In return, the Free Soilers could name the senator and he would be free to vote according to Free Soil principles in Washington. Dana charged that Wilson's control of party machinery had prevented election of Free Soilers who might have opposed such an arrangement. The charge is nonsense; Wilson had no such thorough control. Too many of the conservative faction had refused to be legislative candidates. Cushing submitted resolutions to the Democratic caucus opposing the arrangement agreed to by their conference committee; the resolutions were rejected. In spite of all the December maneuvering the two parties took another week to reach agreement, with the two caucuses differing on which offices each preferred for its share. A Whig paper complained that the taxpayers were paying one thousand dollars a day while the legislature did nothing and the coalition leadership argued. At one time Wilson offered to step down from his Senate presidency in return for a Free Soiler as short-term senator. Finally the division was agreed to. The Democrats received five of nine state offices, and Rantoul was to complete Webster's six-year Senate term. That gave the Free Soilers the secretary of state, auditor, sergeant-at-arms, four councilors, president of the state Senate, and the six-year United States senatorship. The Free Soilers generously selected the incumbent Whig as their candidate for sergeant-at-arms. Sumner was unanimously selected by the Free Soil caucus for the Senate. The Democratic caucus, at Cushing's insistence, agreed to abide by a two-thirds vote. After a fierce debate and Free Soil concession of another councilor position, the Democrats at the second ballot accepted Sumner with only six opposing votes. Twenty-one of the twenty-seven who had rejected Sumner at an earlier election were silent.[13]

Massachusetts law provided that the House would nominate two candidates for governor, from which the Senate would select one. The coalition took until January 11 to initiate this. The Whigs used all their accumulated skills at parliamentary procedure and it took all Banks's political agility to keep his members under control. To be safe, the House majority selected Boutwell and Phillips. This, however, placed the Free Soilers in the Senate in the awkward position of abandoning their candidate; Phillips was "embarrassed," "mortified and disgusted." The Senate Whigs misjudged coalition strategy and helped promote a gubernatorial election first. They recovered in time, with the help of a few Democrats, to force selection of state officers before the senatorship. In any case, half of January was gone before the state officers were chosen and the House organized.[14]

In the meantime the Hallett-Greene group of Democrats had launched an offensive against the coalition. The *Boston Post* was willing to a division of state offices, but opposed any bargain over the senatorship. It contended Massachusetts men had the right to make decisions affecting themselves, but who they sent to Washington influenced the party nationally. Henshaw called the Free Soil a "disunion party." Free Soil and Whig papers were full of rumors about prominent Democrats from other states opposing an agreement for election of a Free Soil senator. While only a few Democrats had voted against accepting Sumner, twenty or thirty had not participated in many of the caucuses. On January 13, with Boutwell safely elected, the bolting Democrats met and resolved not to nominate a candidate of their own, but for each man to vote as he pleased.[15]

The *Commonwealth*, the new Free Soil daily, characterized the new governor as "self-reliant, inquisitive, ambitious," a party man, not indebted to the wirepullers in Washington.[16] Boutwell, probably to reemphasize his Democratic affiliations and certainly to establish that he had not "sold out" to get Free Soil votes, in his inaugural address chose not only to argue for typical Democratic principles, but urged acquiescence to the Compromise of 1850 and attacked those who would repudiate the Fugitive Slave Act. Whittier, characterizing the message as "insulting and monstrous," was so disgusted he wanted those Free Soilers who had accepted important positions in state government to resign and Sumner to withdraw his name for senator. Alley was equally "indignant." But officially, while they characterized Boutwell's statement on slavery as more conservative than that of any Whig governor in ten years, and asserted that he was wrong in his views, the Free Soilers acknowledged the governor's right to his statement and did not complain.[17]

On January 15 the House, after defeating a Whig effort to postpone, finally turned to the six-year-term Senate election. With 194 votes needed for a majority, Sumner received only 186. That was the entire Free Soil vote plus 76 from

Democrats. Winthrop received several Democratic votes, while the others were scattered. By the end of the week five ballots had been taken with little change. Cushing then by a 189-to-178 vote obtained a postponement for a week. With their majority so large and perhaps to influence the House, the coalitionists decided that the Senate should proceed to elect the senator and on January 23 by voice vote, with only one Democrat against, it selected Sumner. The Whig *Springfield Republican* admired the "commendable pluck" the Senate demonstrated by the vote.[18]

Some of the Free Soil leaders were quickly discouraged. After the first two days of House voting Whittier would have Free Soilers abandon the whole effort, resign the state offices they had obtained, perhaps even vote for Briggs for the senatorship. Dana thought the cause was lost. Sumner himself wrote on January 21 that had the senator election been held the same week as the governorship, he would have been selected, but his chances were now ruined "beyond recovery." Pressures from Washington, especially from Webster and Cass, had worked.[19]

The opposition mobilized. National Democrats launched an attack against Sumner and the bargain. The *Boston Post* declared Democrats had fulfilled their pledges for Sumner and could now vote as they chose. Morton urged Sumner be abandoned: "a bad promise is better broken than kept."[20] On the other hand, the Democratic *Lowell Advertiser,* which had opposed the nomination of Sumner, concluded both sides had made a bargain in good faith and that if Sumner were not elected, Briggs might be. The alternative would be no senator election; the Whigs would win in the fall, and then choose Winthrop. In either case, Boutwell would be without a majority in the legislature and unable to govern. The Whig press also kept up a steady assault against the coalition and Sumner. Everett declared a deal for offices was as corrupt as giving money. Lawrence is reported for three months to have conducted subscription drives for money to be used in the effort.[21]

The *Boston Courier* reported, "groanings are issuing from Free Soil ranks." A Free Soiler said the Democrats made a bargain, reaped the advantages, and then refused to deliver the goods. The *Springfield Republican* reported Wilson and Keyes were the angriest among the coalitionists. Wilson was threatening to resign. Many were unhappy with Earle's withdrawing his motion for the senatorship election to proceed at the same time as the governorship election.[22]

But the party leadership was not giving up. The *Northampton Courier* reported the House's failure to elect Sumner was not unexpected. Outside influences on the Democrats could yet be overcome by the nonbolters standing firm and Democrats at home putting pressure on their representatives. The *Commonwealth* declared the names of all of the bolters were known. Free Soilers expected Democrats to fulfill their party's agreement. The *Worcester Spy* predicted a Sumner choice the next week. The Washington *National Era* congratulated Free Soilers for sticking to their part of the bargain. If they erred at all, it stated, they had been too trusting. The week before the next vote was one of intensive organization by the Free Soil leadership. Free Soilers were called to Boston for the January 23 vote to see if they could influence events. Oddly enough, the Whig *New York Tribune* supported Sumner's election, criticizing Massachusetts Whigs for not reaching an agreement which would have placed Phillips in the governor's chair and sent Briggs to the Senate.[23]

Matters did not improve for the coalition. Congressional elections were repeated in mid-January in seven districts in which no candidate had received a majority in November. The coalition did poorly. Palfrey's vote fell to only about one-third. Whigs won in three districts. The *Commonwealth* blamed the Cushing Democrats for the result. Then on January 23 and 24 the House balloted five more times, with Sumner attracting as many as 188 votes. Further voting was postponed for two weeks. A Whig paper characterized Wilson as an "unhappy man."[24]

Wilson did have one ace in the hole, which he subsequently decided not to use: the short-term senatorship. The *Springfield Republican* contended that, unable to coerce the Democratic bolters, they would shame them. On January 28 the Senate elected Rantoul, as the coalition had agreed, to the remaining months of the Webster term; two Free Soilers, however, voted for Phillips. The House followed two days later, but only with the exact minimum votes necessary. The *Commonwealth* interpreted the Rantoul election as a signal to national Democratic leadership that the Hallett-Greene faction no longer controlled the state.[25]

On January 30, in an attempt to counter Whig and national Democratic attacks on the coalition, Wilson published in the *Commonwealth* a long explanation of what had happened primarily in January between the coalition parties. The Free Soilers, he declared, had fulfilled their part of the bargain, acting with "frankness, truth, honor, and fidelity." The Democrats had yet to redeem their pledge. In private, Wilson informed a Vermont supporter that they had been "most shamefully treated by the old Hunkers." He did not appear to be discouraged. When the *Springfield Republican* reprinted the Wilson article, it titled it "Confessions of a Criminal." There could not be a better Whig electioneering document, it declared. While admitting the article revealed nothing not already known, the *Republican* expressed surprise that Wilson would be so open about the bargaining. When Benjamin R. Curtis, in behalf of the Whigs, later wrote about the senatorial contest, he also called the division of offices "a misdemeanor, punishable by indictment."[26]

Frederick Robinson of Essex County, chairman of the Democratic joint committee that met with the Free Soilers during the first week of January, in a letter to his constituents, sought to explain why he continued to vote for Sumner. He reemphasized the distinction between a preelection bargain and an understanding about the governorship and the senatorship. There was an understanding before the election, he claimed. They tried long and hard to get the Free Soilers to give up the senatorship or name a Democratic antislavery man as the nominee, but the Free Soilers would not. His history of the negotiations agreed with that of Wilson. Cushing attacked Robinson in print and demanded the party support its principles.

Griswold also published his confirmation of the essentials in Wilson's explanation. He emphasized that most Democrats expected the five or six who voted against accepting Sumner to refuse to support him in the House. But not until the state officers were selected did the legislative Democratic leadership believe so many Democrats would refuse to fulfill the party's agreement.[27]

In the meantime, the Free Soilers did possess one important power which they might utilize to their advantage: the possibility of working with the Whigs to prevent enactment, even consideration, of the many reforms that both coalition parties had favorably discussed during the campaign. The *Commonwealth* noted on January 27 that prospects of reform, which had looked so good a few weeks before, could only be restored through cooperation. The next day, responding to a *Salem Gazette* article that suggested reform delay was a conscious Free Soil policy, the *Commonwealth* asserted it was all a matter of timing. Free Soilers would vote for many reform measures, *after* the Democrats proved their willingness to work with their associate party. A review of Senate activities for January reveals that with the exception of committee appointments and the consideration of rather unimportant bills, almost no business was transacted.[28]

On January 24 about three hundred and fifty people assembled in Cochituate Hall in Boston for a dinner celebration of the twenty-fifth anniversary of the beginning of Garrison's *Liberator*. The chairman of the evening, Edmund Quincy, remarked how much progress against slavery had been made when the third officer of the Commonwealth, the president of the Senate, would attend. Wilson was asked to speak. No previous high official of the state would ever have been present and spoken at a Garrisonian abolitionist meeting. Wilson said he had attended to convey his love for the cause of freedom and his respect for Garrison's sacrifices. He had read *The Liberator* for twelve years and his own hatred of slavery was at least partly engendered by Garrison. He also congratulated the English abolitionist George Thompson, who had been driven out of Faneuil Hall in the 1830s for daring to speak against slavery. Wilson expressed his feeling of shame at that treatment. How this speech must have confirmed Whig and Democratic antagonisms of Wilson and the coalition which had elevated him to the leadership of the Senate! His speech was not as courageous as it was important for what it said about the man: he was willing to endanger his own political fortunes by affiliating himself with the Garrisonians. It additionally gave a new respectability to abolitionism. Wilson also joined and attended meetings of the Massachusetts Legislative Temperance Society.[29]

Wilson's absorption in his legislative duties was hard on his family. About Christmas his son Hamilton had fallen against the stairs in their home, cut his face badly, and was laid up for weeks. Harriet was lonesome for Henry. She spent the third week of January with her husband in Boston and she, Hamilton, and her mother decided to join him for two weeks in early February.[30]

When the House resumed its voting for the senatorship in early February, Sumner came within two votes of being selected. The matter was then postponed for another two weeks. The Free Soilers have performed their part of "the engagement to the letter," the *Commonwealth* commented. Democrats must elect Sumner or "disgrace" Boutwell and ruin his party. Sumner himself was sufficiently discouraged to notify Wilson that his name might be withdrawn, if that were desirable. That brought some of the Conservative Whigs like Adams and Phillips to Sumner's support, for fear the alternative would be a former Whig less agreeable to them or a former Democrat like Walker or Mills.[31]

Howe was critical of Wilson's leadership. He admitted Democrat and Free Soil constituents were exercising insufficient pressure on their representatives, but he seemed to think all Wilson had to do was put pressure on Boutwell and threaten that Free Soilers would resign their state offices, and Sumner could be elected. Boutwell would not use his influence unless Wilson forced him, Howe contended, and "Wilson will not force him unless he is forced by outside pressure."[32] But Boutwell had limited influence with Cushing, the Hallett leadership, or Morton, and they could promise more in the long run for those Democrats who were voting against Sumner than the governor could. After the mid-February failure, however, Wilson dug in for a long haul, creating a committee of coalition legislators, with himself as chairman, to organize even more systematically to keep loyalists voting right and to find ways to obtain a few more supporters. A Free Soil caucus on February 17 unanimously reemphasized its belief in Sumner. In the meantime, while major legislation was on hold, Wilson carefully kept the coalition together on minor issues before the legislature. On February 14, as an example, the legislature replaced two Whigs with a Democrat and a Free Soiler as directors of the Western Railroad.[33]

Wilson composed his second explanation of coalition maneuvering for the *Commonwealth's* February 18 issue. His argument was effective. He proved that by participating in the caucuses which reached agreements with the Free Soilers, the bolters had obligated themselves to cooperate. At no point could they have doubted what the Free Soilers wanted. Wilson termed the bolters' actions "deliberate fraud." Wilson would later become known as an unusually patient political leader. He certainly was developing this quality during this fight.[34]

On February 28 the House tried twice again to elect a senator, with the largest number of legislators yet participating. Sumner on both ballots came within two votes of selection. The matter was again postponed for two weeks. That helped little; on March 13 the House conducted its seventeenth and eighteenth ballots and was again unable to choose, with Sumner now seven votes short. Cushing launched a severe attack on the coalitionists, declaring they were embarrassing public business. Adams considered that the end; the only question was who the coalitionists would select instead of Sumner. Boutwell suggested Phillips. The Free Soilers caucused before the next trial and resolved they would present no other name "under any circumstances whatsoever."[35] A week later Sumner was nine votes short. But Cushing was also feeling pressure. Whether because of that or to destroy the coalition by getting its participants quarreling among themselves, the bolting Democrats offered to Wilson to vote for any other man, including Wilson himself. When Wilson turned down the proposal, Cushing made a personal appeal, especially advocating Wilson. Wilson later told Pierce he had informed Cushing he might some day go to the House, but he thought the Senate was absurd for him. In fact, he had much more legislative and political experience than Sumner. With Sumner and many of his supporters discouraged, Wilson could have accepted the offer and been elected. The Adams-Palfrey faction could not have prevented it. He had become the party's leader. If, in retrospect, coalitionists had objected, they would have six years to forget before the senator would be up for reelection. But Wilson stood firm.[36]

As the stalemate continued, rancor grew. On March 18 Wilson wrote an extensive expose of the "intrigue" in which he believed Morton was engaged. Wilson was angry with Morton's "disreputable course." He referred to a strong letter authored by Morton to Free Soil and Democratic members of the legislature. While filled with the "loftiest of disinterestedness and devotion to principle," it was characteristic of Morton's "cowardly and false insinuations" against Sumner. Wilson insisted Morton began soon after the election to work to assure the senatorial nominee would be an ex-Democrat. He tried to secure pledges from Democrats not to vote for Phillips or Sumner, the only men seriously considered by Free Soilers. The article cited case after case of Morton's trying to influence various Democrats in person or by letter. It told of meetings in December of Morton with Wilson and Alley. When Boutwell was safely chosen, Morton arrived again in Boston to aid those Democrats refusing to vote for Sumner. Again Wilson was careful to cite dates and people with whom Morton consulted. Yet at visits to the *Commonwealth* office and to Wilson in the Senate Morton expressed the expectation Sumner would be elected. Wilson said Morton had been a strenuous advocate of coalition in the early fall of 1850. The *Burlington Courier* proclaimed Wilson had "laid out Gov. Morton cold." The Democratic *Worcester Palladium* declared Wilson had "cut deep" and had shown the governor "to have practiced duplicity." The Whig *Springfield Republican* called Wilson's letter "sharp, bitter and intensely personal." It believed the public would find little credit to either man in what was revealed and written.[37]

Morton denied to Sumner that he had gone to Boston to lobby against Sumner's election. He refused in a letter to the *Commonwealth* to comment on Wilson's charges, except to say that nearly every fact relating to him was untrue or perverted. But at about the same time Morton wrote a series of letters to various men, whose names had been used in Wilson's letter, requesting information or corrections he could use to refute Wilson. To Alley, Morton declared their conversation had been much different from what Wilson had written. He attacked

Wilson for being partial to the election of Whig Free Soilers. Since Alley was one of Wilson's closest associates, the effort could hardly have improved Morton's position. The replies available indicate Morton did not get the answers he wanted.[38]

Before the next senatorial election, the *Commonwealth* tried a new tactic. Its editorial sought to attract Whig votes by emphasizing Sumner's conservatism and his agreement with past legislative positions against slavery. On the other hand, the writer included a calm evaluation of Winthrop, his vote for the Mexican War, his unfortunate committee chairmen appointments while Speaker, and his absence in the last Congress when a vote on the Wilmot Proviso was taken. It did not help. The next day a motion to postpone the senatorial vote for four weeks failed, but when Sumner was twelve votes short of election on the ballot, the House by a 175-to-133 majority postponed the succeeding vote for three weeks. The *Dedham Gazette* reported sixteen House members had been absent, fourteen of them Free Soilers. The *New York Tribune* declared no man could now be selected. The private papers of leading Free Soilers evince a general agreement that if Sumner could not be elected, no other man could.[39]

As much as citizens of Massachusetts might have supported or objected to the Fugitive Slave Act in principle, the presence of alleged fugitives within the state forced a more personal reaction out of people, especially if those opposed to either the bill or slavery itself chose to make an issue of the efforts to return the slaves to the South. Not only had radical abolitionists like Garrison declared they would not obey the law, but so had Ralph Waldo Emerson. During early 1851 Boston twice was confronted with the reality of a fugitive slave, and the challenges to implementing the new law created new political antagonisms within and among the parties. The controversies further deepened Whig and Democratic opposition to Sumner. The first case was in February, when Shadrach got away. In that case Elizur Wright, long an antislavery leader and an editor of the *Commonwealth*, was brought to trial before Hallett for assisting in Shadrach's escape. Some of those who opposed the law sought to call a protest meeting. But Wilson persuaded the planners to postpone their efforts so as not to endanger Sumner's chances of election.[40]

The second case occurred in April and Thomas Sims was sent back into slavery. On the day after the arrest two public meetings assembled on the Boston Common. But the more important protest took place at Tremont Temple five days later, April 8, in a crowded hall, with many more turned away. The meeting, whose intent had no relation to the Sims affair, had originally been scheduled two weeks earlier but was postponed when Faneuil Hall was denied for the assembly's use. While abolitionists, conservative Free Soilers, Wilson supporters, and even a Democrat George Bancroft signed the call, for this gathering, Wilson's name was surprisingly not included. In the end Adams found a reason not to attend, fearful the activities would be too radical. Palfrey was temporary and Horace Mann permanent chairman of the meeting; Mann delivered the primary address. Others who spoke included Wilson, Palfrey, S. C. Phillips, Burlingame, Higginson, and Remond. Wilson termed the Fugitive Slave Act "barbarous, inhuman and unconstitutional." He emphasized the right of Americans to discuss it and work for its repeal. He deplored the state of the community, in which the Court House had been converted to a Bastille, Faneuil Hall was garrisoned by soldiers, and Boston merchants applauded all this. The hope was the people, to whom the meeting must appeal.[41]

But Wilson was not done. On Friday evening after the convention adjourned, he participated in a second assembly at Washington Hall under the control of the Garrisonians. Considering his already important contribution to the earlier meeting this was hardly a necessary appearance. The speeches would likely be far more radical. Wilson was choosing to make this association at this moment. Remond, Parker Pillsbury, and Garrison also spoke. The Boston press was virtually unanimous in its relief that the Sims crisis was over and the law maintained. Since Sims was being returned to slavery and the rights of trial by jury and habeas corpus of Sims were being trampled upon, a Senate committee was established to look into enforcement of the Fugitive Slave Act and determine whether state legislation was expedient. The trustees of Faneuil Hall were so criticized for denying use of their facilities for the Fugitive Slave Act meetings that they determined that an assemblage to honor Webster would also at that time be inappropriate.[42]

Early in the term the General Court had established a joint special committee on slavery to which were sent the governor's remarks on the subject and various proposals from legislators. On March 28 Committee Chairman Buckingham presented a report by which the state would reaffirm its hostility to slavery and a bill to extend the writ of habeas corpus and further protect personal liberties. He followed, the next day, with two resolutions, one protesting against the Fugitive Slave Act as destructive of rights and hostile to the spirit of Christianity and the other asking for the overthrow of slavery however and wherever it could constitutionally be done. The *Springfield Republican* termed the proposal a "violently abolition report." Keyes on April 5 got the subject placed on the Senate docket. Some reason for this timing must have existed, but the proposals were not called up until May. In the meantime Rantoul complicated the Democratic position by an anti–Fugitive Slave Act speech in Cushing's Essex County.[43]

Whether as conscious strategy, or to respond to Whig newspaper attacks that the coalition-dominated General Court could not or would not consider legislation, Wilson decided the log jam of inactivity should break in late March. The Senate debated public school bills, passed a homestead exemption tax bill, dealt with railroad legislation, and debated proposals for the Hoosac Tunnel. More important, however, was a secret ballot bill, agreed to by the Senate 21 to 16 on March 14. It was similar to what Walker had proposed the year before, requiring voters to seal their ballots in an envelope furnished by the state. Ballots had usually been printed by the parties and election officials receiving ballots could tell for whom a vote had been cast. Some Whigs, of course, feared employers would thereafter have too little control over the voting decisions of their employees. They argued a voter would degrade himself with secrecy. They also charged that the use of envelopes would be too costly. The next day the Senate considered a plurality bill for Congressional elections at second trial. This had carried in the House by a 219-to-42 majority with members of all three parties in favor. After amendment, which the House readily accepted, it was passed with only three votes in opposition.[44]

Another effort of the coalitionists, however, was clearly intended to diminish traditional Whig strength in the General Court. Griswold, in charge of a joint special committee on the legislature, proposed major constitutional changes. The Senate would be left the same size, but senators would be chosen by districts, established after the census every ten years, rather than county-wide. The House would be cut to approximately 380 members, a representative permitted to each town of 1,000 inhabitants or more, and a second representative for every 5,000 inhabitants thereafter, with no town or city having more than 30 representatives. Towns with fewer than 1,000 inhabitants would have representation as often in ten years as their percentage would permit. Smaller towns would benefit by the proposal—Boston could lose as many as seventeen seats, Lowell three. When the vote came in the Senate, a few Whigs supported the coalitionists for the change in Senate districts, but Whigs were unanimous in opposition to the proposals for the House. When the House considered the two amendments in May, it did not obtain the necessary two-thirds majority.[45]

Wilson as presiding officer of the state Senate by law was a member of the Board of Overseers of Harvard College. The aristocracy which controlled Massachusetts, mostly Whig and Unitarian, in part did so through its influence over the important institutions of the Boston area, including the Athenaeum, the Massachusetts Historical Society, the Massachusetts General Hospital, and Harvard. Most Unitarian congregations were in eastern Massachusetts. Edward L. Pierce declared the Boston area had but one society, "and every one in it knew every one else in it. It was close and hard, consolidated, with a uniform stamp on all, and opinion running in grooves—in politics, Whig; in faith, Unitarian and Episcopalian." Harvard was nearby to control the academic spirit. The elite was accustomed to having its own way and resented interference by outsiders. Harvard, with a charter from the state government, after 1825 was supervised by a Board of Overseers composed of fifteen Congregational ministers, fifteen laymen from nearby towns, and the current occupants of designated political offices. Many non-Congregationalists objected to Harvard's church affiliation, many Trinitarians disliked its Unitarianism, many westerners charged it was biased towards the east, and many nonelite believed it was kept small and expensive so as to exclude their children. Democratic leaders had regularly criticized the institution.[46]

It was one thing for the able and cultured George Bancroft to attack Harvard. For the unlettered Wilson to take the leadership would not only be unusual but would deepen the dislike of the Boston elite for the new Free Soil leader. Wilson must have been very aware of that, yet decided that his bridges were burned and he would move ahead. He complained of both Harvard's political and sectarian connections. Of the thirty-one permanent members of the Board of Overseers, he charged in an autumn speech, all but five or six were Whigs and Unitarians. His opportunity to make his views known came soon after his joining the Board. The Harvard corporation had recommended Francis Bowen, former editor of the *North American Review,* an instructor of history, to a permanent professorship. The *Commonwealth* a month before had noted the impending decision and suggested public opinion had to be brought to bear on the college. It made a distinction between appointment of a professor of Greek, Latin, or math and one in history. It questioned whether Bowen was "imbued with American principles," was a friend of American institutions. It believed he had made "dishonest evasions" and had "no reverence for truth." In a subsequent article, the same newspaper contended Bowen's influence would be bad; he seldom mastered subjects about which he wrote, and it called him incompetent in his writings about Eastern Europe. Wilson then had support in the position he took.[47]

Wilson, in a speech which he and his biographers Nason and Russell regarded as one of the more important of his life, agreed with the *Commonwealth* article: Bowen entertained opinions which unfitted him to be a teacher of history to youth. He also was rejected for the misquotations and perversions in his analysis of Hungarian affairs. His temperament had constantly interfered with impartiality. Wilson went to some length to attack both the quality of the *North American Review* under Bowen and the "narrow, intolerant, bigoted organ of conservatism" into which Bowen had turned it, slandering and libeling the great republican leaders of Europe. Wilson was especially disturbed that the *Review* had given comfort to opponents of Kossuth and the Italian patriots. The Bowen appointment was rejected, with almost all of the permanent members of the Board supporting the man and almost all political members opposed.[48]

A few weeks later the coalition members sought to revise Harvard's rules and bylaws to limit election to the board, nomination to the corporation, or appointment to permanent professor except at a meeting of the board held during a session of the legislature. The argument was that too few board members were present in the summer, sometimes only ten or twelve. Wilson again was a leading spokesman. He denied he and others were questioning the purity of motives of those who advocated the status quo. He noted that every time anyone proposed change, those who saw themselves as guardians of the college talked about prejudice and jealousy. He sometimes wished his official position did not require him to participate in the governance of Harvard, he declared. But he had a responsibility and the Board should be so constituted that he and others could perform their responsibilities. Official members were as interested in the college as permanent members. For a quarter of a century after 1823 the board had rules limiting certain actions unless the legislature was in session. That had worked. No one was showing how a return to those rules of operation would inconvenience the college.[49]

In early April the people in most districts of Massachusetts tried again to select congressmen, the last time under the majority rules. Allen won by about two hundred votes. Palfrey's position improved, although he remained behind his opponent.[50]

The antagonism over the Fugitive Slave Act was keeping the state in turmoil. Webster, denied use of Faneuil Hall, delivered his speech at the Revere House. The Senate was asked, but refused, to adjourn for the address. Wilson, Burlingame, and Thomas Russell the same day spoke at Lowell. Sumner, breaking his long silence, issued a statement against the law. In the meantime the Senate committee to investigate whether state laws had been violated with the arrest and detention of Sims was examining witnesses, including Hallett, whose appearance and replies were characterized by some papers of all three parties as "insulting insolence." The report of the special committee concluded Boston authorities had been hostile to the laws of the state and the police had countered state laws with armed resistance; it recommended limiting the powers of city authorities. The legislature, however, took no action.[51]

As the time for the next House vote on senators approached, Wilson was reported to be discouraged. Howe expected defeat: the anticoalitionists wouldn't work; Alley was "paralyzed and discouraged"; Keyes was too much bluster; Wilson couldn't do much though he tried to do more than the others. The House held four ballots and stayed in session until after eight in the evening. So complicated was the procedure and so many men were there to vote, it commonly took an hour and a half to count the ballots. After the first vote announcement was made Sumner had been selected by the exact number needed, but a disputed ballot was subsequently thrown out. On the next count, Sumner was again one vote short. The *New York Tribune* was impressed at what a fight the coalitionists could put up for so many months. Why the coalitionists had now decided to oppose postponement and force the issue, no one has explained. The next day Sumner was two votes short on the first trial. Twice it appeared someone had cast two ballots. To prevent that, Mills asked for viva voce. But a Boston Whig proposed instead that each member get an envelope giving the procedures for tabulating results. This in essence permitted a secret ballot and on the next (twenty-sixth) vote, Sumner received the exact minimum number to win. Wilson many years later reported that Nathaniel Borden, an antislavery Whig, and probably Israel Haynes, a Sudbury Democrat, switched their votes. Butler thought the changes were by Hunker Democrats.[52]

The Free Soilers were jubilant. In Salem the Free Soil newsroom was brilliantly lighted. They celebrated their victory in Boston with rockets and lights before approximately ten thousand people near the *Commonwealth* offices. A crowd later assembled in front of Old City Hall, where Wilson made the congratulatory speech, characterizing the choice as one for the constitution and union, for law and order. He contended the victory was the result of the Seventh of March address, which had gone against the principles of the people of Massachusetts. Sumner had not sought the office, so he would go to Washington "untrammeled by party ties or personal pledges." Wilson looked toward the future by advocating also the congressional elections of Palfrey and Rantoul. One-hundred-gun salutes were fired in a number of Massachusetts communities. Even Hartford, Connecticut, and Burlington, Vermont, celebrated Sumner's selection.[53]

Coalitionists of New Bedford had also scheduled a celebration, and when the speakers did not arrive, Wilson, Amasa Walker, Frederick Robinson, Thomas Russell, and E. L. Stansbury of Vermont hurried to the community for a meeting the next evening. In his address Wilson congratulated the people of Massachusetts on their new senator and eulogized Sumner's abilities. He directed an attack against Webster. Wilson emphasized his Free Soil party had not sought power and had even left two of its appointments to able Whigs. He urged free soil men of all parties to put aside their differences and work for liberty.[54]

Shortly thereafter at Holliston about two hundred Free Soilers and Democrats attended a supper in honor of Sumner's election. One of the toasts was to Wilson, "an uncompromising foe to oppression; a firm friend of The Union, 'including the North.'" In his response Wilson praised the Democrats who had remained true in spite of the press and some politicians. The coalition had saved the state from domination "by Webster and his retainers." The Free Soil party, he asserted, had maintained its principles and its party organization. Boutwell was not pledged to free soilism, Sumner was not pledged to the Democratic party. Twenty-eight of the thirty-one states were now free of Fillmore-Webster domination.[55]

Among the Whig papers the *Springfield Republican* declared the election in no way harmed the Whigs, who had been "consistent and honest." It helped the Free Soilers and probably would damage the Democrats. The moderate *Boston Transcript* also played down the results, predicting Sumner would vote with Whigs on issues other than slavery. But the *Advertiser* saw the election as "the grossest outrage" of minorities combining against a majority. It was relieved, however, that the contest was over. The *Courier* blamed the results on the new way of voting. "A band of political hucksters have trafficked away the honor and good name of the Commonwealth," it declared. Both papers thought two Democrats had shifted their votes to Sumner and two Whigs had cast blank ballots. The *Atlas* ascribed the results to patronage. Edward Everett, writing in his diary, called the coalition "the most discreditable character." On the day after the election the Boston elite wore bands of crape on their arms. The Democratic *Post,* responding to the *Transcript's* remarks, insisted Sumner was just another Whig, but also an abolitionist and an agitator who could endanger the union.[56]

Sumner, those Free Soilers working for the election, and historians since have correctly credited Wilson as the man primarily responsible for the victory. The *Commonwealth* devoted an article to Wilson's contributions, attesting to his energy, skill, "untiring perseverance, and to his unwavering faith." It was impressed with his knowledge of human nature and ability to win the confidence of others. He had been violently and unjustly attacked, but had ignored the abuse. At the time Sumner wrote

> To your ability, energy, determination, and fidelity our cause owes its present success. For weal or woe, you must take the responsibility of having placed me in the Senate of the United States. I am prompted to add that while you have done all this I have never heard from you a single suggestion of a selfish character, looking in any way to any good to yourself; your labors have been as disinterested as they have been effective.[57]

His friend and biographer Mann spoke of Wilson's "indomitable perseverance in the leadership, and absolute integrity of the leaders of the Free-soil party." His other contemporary biographers, Nason and Russell, declared the victory "was largely due to the sagacity, the organizing power, and the unremitting activity, of Mr. Wilson." Sumner's contemporary and biographer, Edward Pierce, recorded no one had contributed as much to the election as Wilson. Wilson insisted on adherence to Sumner and turned aside offers for his own election. He was conciliatory when that was desirable, aggressive when needed. He conducted almost daily meetings. Others might have particular assignments, but Wilson led. Templeton, Boston reporter for the *Connecticut Courant*, in 1869 remembered how bold and enterprising Wilson had been. A leader of ordinary shrewdness would never have allowed his followers to vote for Boutwell until Sumner was elected, he declared, but Wilson kept his Free Soil forces in line and then demanded the Democrats fulfill their part of the bargain. Another contemporary, Carl Schurz, termed Wilson the "engineer of the coalition," who was an "upright, brave, and generous character, and in the better sense a politician of great activity and skill."[58]

Later historians have agreed. Sumner's 1910 biographer Walter Shotwell marveled that Wilson never despaired. He exercised good judgment, was never willing to punish the Democrats, but kept his vision towards Sumner's election. David Donald in 1960 concluded Wilson had done more than any other man to procure the election.[59]

One Whig response was the "Address to the People of Massachusetts," penned by Robert B. Curtis and signed by 167 prominent party members. Charges were strong against the coalition, which Curtis declared should better be termed a conspiracy, and especially against Wilson. While Wilson had been open for the past six months in explaining what was being agreed to, Curtis presented him as naive. He charged Wilson would yet personally profit by the coalition. At no point would Curtis accept that a commonness of interest between the two parties had motivated the coalition. But twentieth century historians have accepted the wisdom of the cooperation, and the electorate in the fall endorsed it by returning the coalition to power.[60]

The General Court would now take a month to enact the reform legislation which coalitionists, particularly the Democrats, had wanted. Since much of it would not be endorsed by the politically astute and able Whigs, leadership and organization would be required. Fortunately for the coalition, Cushing was cooperative. On Monday, April 28, Wilson appointed a committee to work out business between the two houses. Within a week Buckingham, as chairman, reported, providing no more new business could be sent from committees after May 10. Several of the bills, in addition to the constitutional amendments to change representative units for the two houses of the legislature, passed the Senate but failed in the House, which Wilson later accused of being unrepresentative. The bills included one proposal to move the seat of government from Boston and another for single unit representative districts, both directed against the Whigs and the special strength of Suffolk County. Bills also failed to change the time for holding annual state elections to correspond with the date of the presidential election and to lend state credit up to two million dollars to the Greenfield and Troy Railroad for construction of the Hoosac Tunnel.[61]

Other important legislation was passed. A second hospital for the insane was authorized. Many railroad bills were enacted. In 1850 the legislature would have nothing to do with a homestead exemption law. With Wilson in strong support, it now enacted a protection for the poor, exempting a homestead up to a five hundred dollars value from attachment. Mechanics for years had sought a lien law; one now passed. For years too the Whigs had been able to control the incorporation of new industrial and banking concerns, requiring separate legislative action for each. Under new general laws, at least five individuals could establish banks and at least three could incorporate manufacturing enterprises by meeting established, minimum, and equal guidelines. There were also reforms in legal procedures and court structure. To alter some characteristics embedded in the social and political fabric by the constitution, the legislature—again with Wilson an open supporter—voted to submit to the people whether they wanted to call a constitutional convention.[62]

Changes in the control of Harvard were more difficult to produce. An act was passed to reorganize the Board of Overseers, providing its members be elected for a specific number of years by joint ballot of the two houses of the legislature and replacing those overseers selected for life. Wilson was active in pushing the bill; as presiding officer, he did not have to be recorded, but did vote. Another reform, to increase the membership of the corporation to fifteen men elected by the legislature, failed.[63]

Some of the Democrats were not less willing to cooperate with antislavery actions, nor were they required to by terms of their consultations. The Free Soilers attempted to push for antislavery resolutions soon after Sumner's election, perhaps to place additional pressure on the Democrats before the other legislation was enacted. Whig support, which might have been counted on in earlier years, was unlikely. The *Advertiser*, *Courier*, and *Journal* sustained the Fugitive Slave Act, while the *Atlas*, *Springfield Republican*, *New Bedford Mercury*, and most other Whig newspapers opposed it, but wanted it enforced. When the Buckingham report on personal liberty came up for debate, Russell of Boston sought to amend, disclaiming the power of nullification and denying the right of citizens to annul or prevent execution of the constitution. Only Keyes voted against the amendment, contending the legislature would "compliment" those who had forced the Fugitive Slave Act on the nation. The first of the resolutions, affirming the state's hostility to slavery and devotion to and longing for harmony in the union, passed 34 to 4, but Buckingham's illness and other business delayed further consideration.[64]

The next week the Senate returned to the resolves. The second protested against the Fugitive Slave Act as alien to the spirit of the constitution, destructive of rights, hostile to the feelings of Christianity, and abhorrent to the sentiments of the people of the state. The Whigs tied up action for two days, seeking elimination—over the objections of Wilson, Buckingham, and Keyes—of the phrases, "destructive of rights secured by that instrument, hostile to their sentiments of Christianity." During the debates an angry Wilson left the chair for a lengthy response to what he termed the "political malignity and the unreasoning fanaticism of State Street." He denied Whig senators' claims that the resolutions were comparable to South Carolina's nullification. For fifteen years the state had expressed its abhorrence to slavery, Wilson contended. The resolutions were "mild, temperate, guarded." He looked back to 1850 to pin the responsibility for the Fugitive Slave Act on Webster and then attempted to connect Webster and his supporters with the Toryism of the 1763–1780 era and disloyalty in 1814. He claimed these men, partyless after the collapse of the Federalists, worked their way into the Republican party, where they had opposed progress, including the French and Hungarian revolts of 1848. In spite of Wilson's efforts, the amenders succeeded, 21-15. Then with Whig cooperation the three remaining resolves were passed 33-5, 35-2, and 28-5. Wilson chose to vote each opportunity. The rules were suspended by a very large majority to dispense with a third reading to enable the resolutions to get quickly to the House. But there, by a 167-to-165 vote, with every Boston member but one with the majority, the resolutions were laid on the table.[65]

The Senate, even after amending it, rejected 13 to 16 Buckingham's other bill to protect personal liberty. Only one Whig voted for it. The *Commonwealth* lamented the loss of this bill more than the resolves. The Massachusetts Anti-Slavery Society's *Annual Report* wondered if the election of Sumner was worth the lack of legislative accomplishment in other areas, especially that of personal liberty.[66]

The Senate adjourned on Saturday, May 24. The legislature had passed and the governor approved 439 bills and 93 resolves. While Whig papers long had been blaming coalitionists for the lengthy session, the electorate understood who and what had held up the selection of a senator. Furthermore, the Whigs had the more experienced speakers, who had done more than their share of talking. At the final meeting Whig Senator Seaver moved thanks to Wilson for the "able, impartial and satisfactory manner in which he discharged the duties of the Chair." Senator Wilkinson also decided to speak to the motion. Wilson replied at some length. He seemed truly pleased. He noted veteran senators had offered their support when he assumed the leadership and he appreciated it. Admitting his lack of experience, he had been convinced if he worked at the job, he could succeed. He had found appointment of committees, especially the chairmen of joint committees, difficult. He had attempted to give the three parties equal shares of responsibilities and duties.[67]

The excitement of the legislative session had scarcely passed before attention had to be turned to the congressional elections, for the first time to be determined by plurality. In the previous contests the Whigs had already elected five congressmen, including Fowler, who also had been supported by the Free Soilers. The Free Soilers had elected Mann and Allen. Palfrey's modern biographer incorrectly reports that Sumner and Wilson gave Palfrey little support. Sumner, who regarded himself as a friend and who understood his own controversial reputation that spring, did not want to endanger Palfrey's position. Wilson had certainly done his share. He cheered Palfrey on by letter. He organized an effort in which he sent himself, Hale, Mann, Burlingame, Rantoul, S. C. Phillips, Dana, Park, Emerson, and Charles Slack into the second and fourth districts. Sewell, the Free Soil candidate, agreed to withdraw in Rantoul's district, assuring a coalition selection. Coalitionists, of course, could not so easily endorse Palfrey. Wilson informed the candidate that his letter to the legislature had damaged his chances. Not only were many Democrats repelled, but so were some Free Soilers.[68]

The results were more antislavery than procoalition. In District Seven the Whig John Z. Goodrich was chosen over the Democrat-coalitionist Bishop, but Goodrich was recognized for his opposition to slavery and would subsequently become a leader in the Republican party. In District Two Rantoul, coalition candidate, won by more than one thousand votes. But while Palfrey carried most of his district, the Whig votes in Cambridge and Charlestown—bedroom communities for some of Boston's elite—carried Thompson to a plurality of fewer than one hundred votes. One of his strongest supporters reminded Palfrey that he had received more votes than had ever before been given to a candidate in his district and nothing more could have been done to secure his election. The *Dedham Gazette* correctly blamed Palfrey's legislative letter for the results.[69]

Wilson was now the dominant figure within the state's Free Soil party. Sumner chose to retire from everyday political activities. Palfrey had lost both his election and his rapport with many of his former colleagues. Adams was dissatisfied with the coalition and willingly involved in personal rather than political life. Dana's biographer noted how obnoxious leaders like Wilson and Boutwell, who had come from obscure families and had been laborers in their younger days, were to the well-educated Boston lawyer. Dana withdrew from political affairs controlled by that breed of men.[70]

Wilson's public activities continued during the summer. Although not a speaker, on June 16 he again associated himself with the Garrisonians, one of more than one thousand participants in Worcester to honor George Thompson just before his return to England. Unable to persuade Sumner or Rantoul to attend, on May 29 en route to Albany on business Wilson visited Montpelier, Vermont, where he and John Van Buren helped launch a coalition between Democrats and Free Soilers in that state's election. Wilson spoke for nearly two hours about the current state of political affairs and the necessity of union among parties to prevent Slave Power domination. As a member of its Board of Overseers, Wilson in July sat on the platform along with ex–college president Everett, Chief Justice Shaw, Palfrey, and Winthrop at Harvard's annual commencement exercises.[71]

The principal political effort of the Free Soilers during the summer was called for Worcester on July 4. Over two thousand people sat down to a dinner under a big tent. Hale was imported to deliver the primary address; Congressman Allen presided. Palfrey, Stansbury, Burlingame, and Wilson also spoke. Wilson's flowery address was widely reprinted. It was partly an attack on Webster. Wilson asserted Webster had helped induce the young men of Massachusetts to declare for freedom, and then had abandoned them. The senator's supporters in the summer of 1848 had begged the emerging Free Soil party to treat their favorite with kindness and the state convention had. Webster had personally told Wilson he approved of the Worcester resolutions. The senator had bemoaned the lack of spirit among Northern leaders who would not defend their own section's interests. Now he was stalking over the land, denouncing those he had previously praised. What motivated Webster then and now was not protecting Northern interests, but hankering for the presidency. Wilson scoffed at that likelihood. Southern politicians would not support him. Not one newspaper west of the mountains had declared for him. Even the nearby middle states ignored him. Wilson predicted Webster could not get thirty votes at a Whig convention. In a recent speech in Virginia the secretary had attacked the Free Soilers as abolitionists. Wilson said they would accept that characterization as one of "honor," not "one of reproach."[72]

Webster was angry that the Whig state leadership was not sufficiently interested in what he termed "national concerns." The great Whig leader predicted an end of the party and advocated the creation of a union replacement. In the meantime he was supporting Walley over Winthrop for the gubernatorial nomination. But Webster was prescribing a position too pro-Southern for his party. The *Commonwealth* devoted extensive space during the summer to trying to separate Webster and Winthrop supporters. If Briggs could not win, it declared, certainly no other Whig governor candidate could. Even the *Boston Courier* admitted that without the senatorial issue and with no national election, the coalition would be stronger in 1851.[73]

Cushing and the Hallett faction of Democrats were not ready to accept a continuance of coalition or a secondary position in their party. The state committee in June took the unusual step of issuing an Address, setting forth its views on slavery and the Compromise. It insisted the Fugitive Slave Act had to be enforced to avoid disunion. Somewhat surprising to the Free Soilers, Robinson signed the paper. Rumors said Banks and Boutwell had assented to its issuance. The Free Soil *Dedham Gazette* declared most Democrats did not agree with the *Boston Post* clique: "To repudiate the coalition is equivalent to voting for the Whig party." When the Democratic state convention met in late August, the Hallett Hunkers had worked hard and had elected a disproportionately larger number of delegates. There was sharp sparring between the two factions. Some of the speeches were an attack upon Hallett and Greene. The other faction denounced coalition. "The wildest disorder prevailed." Hallett, chairman of the Resolutions Committee, altered the propositions without the knowledge of his committee. Although vigorously opposed, they were passed. They reaffirmed the principles of the 1848 national platform and advocated enforcement of and acquiescence in the Compromise of 1850.[74]

The Whigs followed with a peaceful convention, the state committee working to engender harmony. While Winthrop was chosen as gubernatorial candidate, three Webster supporters were elected as delegates to the 1852 national convention. The platform, other than denouncing coalition, was so structured that it produced almost no press comment.[75]

With their leaders who had opposed coalition now playing little role in party affairs, the Free Soilers could look forward to more unity than the Democrats. As early as June the *Lowell American* and *Northampton Courier* advocated continued coalition in the fall campaigns. The *Courier* cautioned, however, that more care had to be taken choosing the nominees; Free Soilers should not again be asked to support Democratic Hunkers. Wilson called the state committee to meet July 23 and made a particular effort to invite Adams to participate. Adams would not. He presumed Wilson was intriguing for the governor's nomination. Wilson tried again, urging Adams to attend and deliver an address at the state convention. He praised Adams's past achievements and was humble concerning his own contributions. He admitted the two men had differences about how the party should proceed, but emphasized Free Soil included men of many shades of opinion. Wilson hoped for convention unanimity on national issues and town and county conclaves again deciding state strategy. Adams eventually accepted election, but used the excuse of his son's ill health not to attend.[76]

Wilson, along with Park and David L. Elder, the editor of a Kentucky emancipation newspaper, were featured speakers at the meeting August 28 to select Boston's delegates to the state convention. Noting the recent Whig meeting in the city which had endorsed Webster for president and Winthrop for governor, Wilson predicted the Whig party in the state was dying, its nomination of Webster would hasten that, and it would be beaten in November by twelve thousand votes. Whigs could not recover until they disowned Webster, he declared.[77]

The Free Soil gubernatorial nomination was a major contention. Phillips refused to stand for election again. Mann, Palfrey, Adams, and Wilson were mentioned as possibilities. Adams would not be a candidate. The conservative faction was convinced Wilson was attempting to secure the nomination for himself. But the *Adams Sentinel* and *Northampton Courier* both declared Wilson was so important to organizing the campaign, he could not be spared for the nomination. "To him more than any other single individual was the coalition indebted for its success last year," the *Courier* contended. "The General is wise and sagacious, doing every thing right, and at the right time, and in the right place." According to conservative sources (Adams, Dana, and Palfrey), Palfrey was to be convention chairman, then nominated, but that Wilson first got Mann substituted as chairman, then sought to produce so much confusion in the convention that Palfrey would be rejected and Wilson would be chosen. Palfrey, however, made an effective speech and was selected on the first ballot. In fact, while William Jackson, Mann, and Walker received votes, Wilson was not considered. While anyone might be pleased with the honor of a nomination for governor, Wilson knew the designation would be meaningless, for Boutwell would be elected. He would be much wiser to run for the Senate and again be a candidate for its presidency. Furthermore, he had every reason as state chairman to oppose the selection of Palfrey, who, after his letter to the Free Soil legislators, would alienate Democratic and attract few new Free Soil voters.[78]

Other than the gubernatorial nomination, Wilson was in full control of what was described as a "large and enthusiastic convention." Mann's selection as permanent chairman took the assembly by surprise. Palfrey, Allen, Wilson, Burlingame, and Buckingham delivered addresses. Wilson himself chaired the Resolutions Committee. The party denied the right of Congress to establish slavery and condemned the Fugitive Slave Act as inhumane and unconstitutional. It declared its adherence to and love for the union. Resolutions also favored election of state senators from single districts, advocated the secret ballot, and commended the legislature for passing the constitutional convention call. The conclave elected nine delegates-at-large to the 1852 national convention, including Wilson. The central committee would again be dominated by coalitionists, including Wilson, Keyes, Allen, Alvord, Hopkins, Bird, Claflin, Swan, and Rodney French.[79]

Wilson must have been exhausted even before the campaign began. His brigade held its annual encampment at Lowell on September 11 and 12. He had held a commission in the unit for nine years and had served as commander for five. The two days included a review by Governor Boutwell, a visit from the Nashua, New Hampshire, militia leaders, and a dinner Wilson hosted in Lowell. He resigned from his command a few days after the encampment.[80]

A month later, on a beautiful autumn day, Natick celebrated its bicentennial. The First Congregational Church was crowded; the Reverend Calvin Stowe, a town native, delivered the address. Dinner was served under a large tent with the town's now most illustrious citizen, Henry Wilson, presiding. What an astonishing change in a community and a young man in a little over a decade! After dinner the celebrators marched to South Natick for more speeches, including one by Wilson.[81]

Wilson's other diplomatic duty was much more important. He had had to leave the Free Soil state convention on September 17 for Fall River where, as chairman of the reception committee, he delivered the welcoming speech to President Millard Fillmore, who was visiting the state for three days of a railroad jubilee to celebrate the opening of connections to Canada and the West. The activities had been planned at a meeting presided over by Wilson in Boston on the fifteenth. Banks, Schouler, and Keyes were dispatched to Newport, Rhode Island, to accompany the president to Massachusetts. A railroad trip to Boston with many stops en route and a parade and receptions in the capital followed. The weather was beautiful, spirits excellent. Lord Elgin and a Canadian delegation were present. Wilson officially presented Fillmore first to the mayor, later to the governor. At an evening dinner at the Revere House Wilson was among those to make an impromptu speech. Finally, the Senate president accompanied the guests to the state border. Wilson's friend Jonathan Mann recorded that the able way Wilson conducted himself "was a surprise to many who looked upon him as a mere political manager, unable to sustain the dignity of the State on occasions of such imposing character." In addition, with so many of the activities in the hands of those who politically opposed the president, the conduct of the Massachusetts officials and their handling of courtesies due the president undermined the charges of treason the Whig press had been casting at the coalition.[82]

The evening following Fillmore's departure Wilson addressed the people of Webster. He admitted he was exhausted by the activities of the previous ten days—encampment, preparations for the state convention, and the receptions for the president. But before a large audience he vindicated the actions of his party and defended the achievements of the past legislature. He was about to embark on what would be his most exhausting campaign but an effort in which he would prove both his organizing skills and his improving capabilities as a stump speaker.[83]

8

Coalition Success
National Party Leadership

As he began the 1851 fall campaign, Wilson recognized his own Middlesex County could take the lead towards coalition with senatorial nominations. The Democratic and Free Soil parties convened in Concord on the same day. There was little opposition to coalition within either meeting. John A. Bolles, who had opposed coalition for two years, now endorsed it and presided over the Free Soil assembly. Wilson delivered the main speech, which Free Soil newspapers reprinted. He defended the legislature from Whig attacks, emphasized the determination of his party to get the senatorship, and reviewed the various reform measures passed. He noted the two parties did not agree on "national issues" but credited the Democrats with being on the side of reform. Wilson received the most votes as a Free Soil candidate. The parties selected six senate nominees, including Free Soilers Wilson, Burlingame, and Samuel Sewell and C. C. Hazewell, editor of the *Boston Times,* among the three Democrats. The Free Soil leadership was unwilling to reject anyone whom the Democrats selected. The *Commonwealth* noted in reporting the Wilson nomination that he was as widely known as any man in the party. "In talent, in zeal, in energy, and in devotion to the cause he has few equals in our ranks; his political sagacity, his plain, manly and effective eloquence, and his frank, straight-forward character have been of essential service to the Free Soil Party."[1]

The Boston Whig papers launched an attack against the county coalition, especially Wilson's nomination as leader of an opposition party. The *Atlas* charged the nominations were dominated by men from the city, but each had a residence in the county. The *Commonwealth* replied that Democrats liked Wilson "because no man has done so much as he has towards breaking down the Whig dynasty." The

Atlas also assaulted Wilson's Concord speech, characterizing it as "a melancholy spectacle of envenomed wrath against a party which warmed him in its bosom, only that he might sting it." After an attack on Wilson in the *Boston Bee*, its editor had to admit Wilson was honest and honorable, a sociable fellow who probably did not have an enemy in the world.[2]

The new state central committee assembled in Boston on September 27. Thereafter, working out of an office in the same building occupied by the *Commonwealth*, Wilson mapped out an extensive personal campaign. On the evening of September 30 he participated in the nonpolitical annual meeting of the Bromfield lyceum. By mid-October he had sent Burlingame, Allen, Keyes, and Russell out on the stump. Sumner predicted in September that Winthrop could not secure a majority from the electorate. The *Northampton Courier* in mid-October was equally certain the Senate was safe for the coalition. After getting the schedule organized, Wilson headed into the western counties, virtually for the first time since he had assumed the state chairmanship. He began at the Berkshire County convention at Lenox on October 10, encouraging the two parties to nominate a joint ticket, and speaking to the Free Soil assembly. That evening he lectured at Pittsfield and on October 11 at Adams. He left the county convinced the coalition ticket would win. After resting on Sunday, he spoke at Northampton, attacking the Whig party for its proslavery stance, defending the coalition and praising the last legislature's reforms, and expressing confidence the coalition would carry the election. Wilson next addressed the Franklin County Free Soil convention at Greenfield, able to assist in the nomination of his close coalition associate Griswold. That same evening he spoke at Springfield. Addresses in the next nine days followed in five more communities.[3]

Cooperation was not easy everywhere. In Norfolk and Hampden Counties the Democratic Hunkers, unable to prevent coalition, withdrew from their conventions and nominated their own tickets. The Norfolk County agreement produced a controversy for Wilson. Whig newspapers reported on a conversation between N. R. Childs and Wilson in which the former asked what would happen if a vacancy occurred in either national senatorship. Wilson allegedly replied Sumner wouldn't die, but when pressed by Childs, declared another trade would be made by the coalition partners. The meeting apparently was a chance encounter on the street, not a call by the Free Soil state chairman on a Democrat whose votes at the state convention he was seeking, as reported by Whig papers. What Wilson said in reply, Wilson, Childs, and a second Democrat who heard the conversation remembered differently. Childs was embarrassed by the controversy and apologized to Wilson. The state chairman was more concerned that the reports would suggest he was interfering in Norfolk County affairs than that he had been misquoted by the press.[4]

Wilson continued his almost daily speaking efforts during the last two weeks of the campaign. Hopkins and Horace Mann were now also in the field. Wilson begged George Hoar "in our hour of distress" to join the efforts. Wilson himself between October 24 and November 7 spoke in thirteen different communities. He concluded the campaign at Natick November 8. In all, he made thirty-two addresses. For the last week Congressmen Giddings and Root were imported from Ohio. An analysis of issues of the *Commonwealth* in October and early November indicates a well-organized and effective campaign.[5]

A report on Wilson's speech at East Boston may exemplify what he was saying. He presented the objectives of the Free Soil party and demonstrated where they did and did not agree with the Democrats. The two parties differed most about slavery. Wilson contended they were alike on matters of state reform. The Whigs, in contrast, he argued, had no principles except dealing with banking and railroad power. The secret ballot was necessary. He pointed with pride to the laws enacted by the last legislature, calling them the best in six or seven years. The Free Soilers were not endorsing Democratic principles or the Democrats advocating Free Soil by their coalition.[6]

The status of the *Commonwealth*, upon which the Free Soil caused so depended, must have concerned the former editor. In its first six months of life the paper had gone through a series of owners, editors, and associate editors. In the summer of 1851 Bird withdrew, Lyman took over, and Palfrey was reinstated as a contributing writer. Adams renewed his financial support. But by September the capital of twenty thousand dollars was gone and the paper's debts equaled its assets. On October 4 Lyman and Palfrey retired from their positions. Unfortunately for the Free Soil movement, the conservative Adams faction had the money, but the coalitionists controlled party machinery. Howe tried to keep the paper afloat, for it was essential during the campaign. In late November the publication was sold to Samuel E. Sewell and Elizur Wright returned as editor.[7]

The conservative faction was equally unhelpful in waging the campaign. While agreeing the defeat of Winthrop was important, Phillips and Adams decided to stand aside. Having already given between six and seven thousand dollars in five years, Adams also declined to contribute further to the campaign war chest. In an enthusiastic and optimistic letter on October 16, Wilson pleaded with Adams to speak. Calls were arriving for his services from all over the state, Wilson reported; they needed Adams's assistance in this "emergency." Adams carefully replied, not totally declining, but limiting where and when he would participate. Bird and G. F. Williams added their appeals for support to little avail.[8]

Hearing that Wilson was to speak at Quincy, Adams the day before tardily wrote to invite his former colleague to tea. Wilson went. Adams recorded both men were ill at ease. Adams resented the ex-cobbler and his rise to power, which Adams called "curious." Wilson had begun well with high principles, but his work in politics had "corroded his heart," the diarist had written in September. Although Adams's own papers reveal he knew most of what the Free Soil party was doing under Wilson's leadership, Adams spoke of Wilson's "duplicity." He now was attracted by Wilson's "natural good temperament," but recognized how tired his visitor was from the lengthy canvass. Adams accompanied Wilson to the town hall, which was crowded, including with many Democrats. Wilson spoke for less than two hours, "very easily and fluently." To obtain that kind of compliment in the privacy of Adams's diary, Wilson's speaking abilities must have greatly improved. Adams concluded Wilson spoke too little about slavery and too much about the activities of the last legislature. The visit may also have encouraged Adams to accept four speaking assignments, including the Faneuil Hall conclusion to the campaign.[9]

The coalition united in virtually all counties. Their best expectations were for senatorships in all except Suffolk, Barnstable, and Dukes and no choice in Hampden. They recognized Essex, Plymouth, and Bristol Counties were very close. They were less optimistic about the House. Winthrop himself did not expect to obtain a majority from the electorate. The *Atlas* was the only Whig paper which asserted Winthrop could win. Wilson predicted the Whig candidate would lose by more than the eight thousand votes by which Briggs had been defeated. Morey and Schouler organized an effective Whig campaign, with Schouler concentrating his verbal attacks on the unholiness of the coalition and the secret ballot, as well as on general banking laws. The *Boston Pilot*, a Roman Catholic publication, hysterical in its attack, declared the state would be safe with either a Democratic or Whig victory. Free Soilers were sustaining radicals in Europe and counseling resistance to authority at home, it charged. They also were socialists.[10]

Election day decided several issues. More people voted than ever before at a state election. While the *Northampton Courier* declared Winthrop could not possibly secure more than 62,000 votes, the Whig obtained nearer 65,000. He attracted eight thousand more votes than Briggs had the year before, a plurality of eight thousand statewide, and a plurality in every county, yet was beaten. He himself characterized it as a good fight. He would never again be willing to run for office. Adams believed it was the largest vote any Whig candidate could have obtained. The coalition increased its votes for governor by more than seven thousand, most of those for Boutwell. The Democrat was especially stronger in Boston. Palfrey secured 2 percent less support than Phillips had in 1850. The constitutional revision proposal, however, was beaten, receiving 11,600 fewer votes than the Boutwell-Palfrey totals. The Senate would be coalition dominated, initially 17 to 11, eventually by a 28 to 19 majority. The *Atlas* was particularly interested in Wilson, whom it at first insisted had been defeated. He won with only a 173-vote majority. The House showed a Whig lead, one-quarter of which came from Suffolk County, but more than one hundred seats were undecided. A number of Democrats who had fought the election of Sumner were beaten. Ben Butler believed the coalition's success was made possible by the secret ballot law.[11]

The next day Wilson called the Free Soil state committee into session to organize for the November 24 second House election. Lowell's Whig city officials disallowed the results of the first election, in which coalitionists had been selected, and insisted on a second. In the city a coalition committee called upon Linus Child, agent of a local mill, to verify reports that he had tried to coerce his workmen into voting Whig. Child replied that if any man employed by his corporation voted for coalition candidates, he would be fired. A member of the committee said in that case the legislature might take away the corporation's charter. Child was unimpressed. Elsewhere other towns nominated coalition candidates. The results of the second election are difficult to assess, but the coalition was approximately six votes ahead, with forty-one vacancies.[12]

Reactions to the election results varied. The Whigs were not willing to retreat. On November 25 at Faneuil Hall, they assembled to advocate Webster for the presidency. On the other hand, the Democratic *Worcester Palladium* and *Lynn Bay State* looked forward to another year of coalition cooperation. They saw their party as indebted to the Free Soilers's "superior activity and indefatigable perseverance." They had spoken for reform as earnestly as the Democrats had. The Free Soilers were not burdened as their partners had been by disagreement on national issues—meaning slavery. Boutwell was trying to placate Cushing by again, offering him the attorney general appointment. Conservative Free Soilers continued to rejoice at Whig losses, but were less enthusiastic about the coalition victory. Howe declared they would have to fight the Democrats soon. The masses lacked the intelligence to overcome their prejudices about color, he declared. Ignoring the unity the Whig leaders had displayed on major issues, he dreamed that when Webster had gone, Free Soilers could again work with the Whigs. Adams feared amalgamation of the coalition parties and wished the Free Soilers and Whigs could combine on a national level, with the joint nomination of someone like McLean. The Wilson faction was living in the real world; the conservative Free Soilers continued to dream and hope.[13]

For all the criticism the conservative faction aimed at coalition, the Free Soil party was still alive in Massachusetts. In the absence of a national election and as most Americans came to accept the Compromise of 1850 as the law of the land, the party had been gradually dying elsewhere. Admittedly, the political situation in many states was still in flux. While Massachusetts in the spring of 1851 had been having trouble selecting a senator, New York and New Jersey had also experienced difficulty and Thomas Hart Benton, an associate of Andrew Jackson and the recognized spokesman of the West, had been retired from the Senate by the Missouri legislature. There were also areas of encouragement. Free Soilers and Whigs in New Hampshire in March had turned an 1850 Democratic majority into a 1851 plurality of only four thousand. In Ohio Chase was working to unite Free Soilers, now called the Free Democracy, with the Democrats. The Barnburners of New York may have rejoined their former party, but they refused to endorse the Compromise measures. But overall the Free Soil movement was winning few elections. While the new United States Senate might now have more antislavery voices than ever before, including Sumner's, the Thirty-Second House would count only five Free Soilers; its predecessor had contained twelve.[14]

Previous cooperation between Democrats and Free Soilers and the absence of a senatorial election meant Wilson would have less to do between the November election and the assembly of the legislature. Whig papers sought to create problems by charging Wilson was threatening Boutwell to assure certain elections and Wilson was traveling over the state to obtain votes for his reelection as president of the Senate. Neither charge was true, for both actions were unnecessary. Leaders of the two parties knew each other and what was expected of each. Somewhat more serious were suggestions of the Whigs that they might vote for Palfrey for governor if Erastus Hopkins were selected as Speaker. The coalition majority in the House was so small and Democratic leadership so weak that Alley was concerned; so was Wilson at first, but by January 5 he confided to Sumner matters were under control. The legislature convened on January 7 and Wilson was immediately reelected as president and Banks as Speaker. Wilson addressed the Senate briefly, expressing his desire to preside "with faithfulness and impartiality." The coalition did not repeat its mistake of 1851 in sending from the House the names of Democratic and Free Soil candidates, but rather dispatched the names of the Democratic and Whig nominees. Boutwell was then chosen as governor and vacancies in the Senate were in all cases but one filled within coalition men.[15]

The session began with promise. Boutwell's short message, ignoring national issues, drew praise from the Free Soil *Northampton Courier*. His speech advocated fundamental changes in the government, including single election districts in cities and large towns, which meant submission again to the people of a proposal for a constitutional convention. He indicated he would not stand again for election as governor. All three parties then worked together to select Harvard Overseers, hardly the radical group the Whig debaters of the previous year had forecast. They included Palfrey, Winthrop, Briggs, and Cushing. The flimsy coalition control in the House soon broke down on the lesser offices, with their candidates for sergeant-at-arms, auditor, and one senator beaten. Wilson again elected not to commute from Natick, but to stay at the Marlboro Hotel in Boston. It is fortunate he did, for the winter of 1851–1852 was a remarkable one; heavy snowfall covered much of New England and the temperature was unusually cold. Frosts occurred as far south as New Orleans, rivers in Washington were frozen, and even Long Island Sound was closed for a time.[16]

The session had hardly begun when Schouler submitted a resolution in the House to have a special committee consider amendment of the constitution to get plurality elections for all state officers, a Senate of forty members chosen by single districts, a House of from two hundred to three hundred members representing equal districts, and election of officers appointed by the governor and council. The Whigs had taken the offensive to divide the coalition. The proposal was laid on the table.[17]

Wilson had begun his political life as an advocate of temperance. As a young politician in 1844 he was already appearing at Faneuil Hall among renowned state figures speaking for the cause. His career from 1852 on was marked by his consistent and frequent advocacy of the movement. Yet, strangely, during much of the later 1840s he had not devoted much public effort to temperance. While Wright's *Chronotype* reported frequently about alcohol issues, the *Emancipator and Republican* devoted little space to the subject. When Father Matthew, the renowned Irish temperance advocate, visited Massachusetts in 1849, the *Emancipator* comparatively ignored the man. Many of Wilson's political colleagues had been much more active. Governor Briggs was not only president of the state Legislative Temperance Society but participated in its affairs. Boutwell and Amasa Walker were vice-presidents of the society and Banks and Goodrich were members of its executive committee. When the society held its 1851 initial meeting with Boutwell now president, Wilson, Banks, and Walker were, because of their important state offices, designated as vice-presidents, but the Senate president appears not to have delivered any addresses to the organization during the year. Nor was he active in the state temperance convention, whose president was Banks and whose other officers included Emory Washburn, Stone, and Goodrich.[18]

After 1845 Massachusetts experienced a resurgence of legal suasionists. Prohibition and other legislation to limit the consumption of alcohol by 1852 had resulted in Maine going dry and the end of liquor sales in a number of Massachusetts counties and towns. More than 2,000 voters petitioned the legislature in the fall of 1851 to prohibit liquor sales. An 1852 petition included more than 133,000 signatures. Although liquor had not been a major issue in the fall campaign, clearly a portion of the electorate was interested in the subject. When the Legislative Temperance Society was organized in 1852, Wilson presided and again was made a vice-president. The legislature in January established a special joint committee on the subject of prohibition and the *Northampton Courier* predicted the Maine law or something similar would pass; Wilson agreed. The committee held hearings at which Neal Dow, the father of the law in Maine, and Lyman Beecher and John Pierpont, leaders of the temperance movement among the clergy, testified.[19]

By February 14 the committee reported a long and "stringent" bill. It outlawed property in intoxicating drink but authorized possession for medical, sacramental, and chemical purposes. Enforcement was to be the responsibility of city marshals and constables. The *Commonwealth* pronounced temperance to be the primary issue of the session. To provide additional fuel for the fire, a Boston temperance auxiliary sponsored a meeting with addresses by Wilson, Boutwell, Banks, Russell, and others. When the Democrats proposed to amend the bill to send it to the people for their decision, Wilson made a long speech in support. It was the only way the people could respond, he asserted. Because so many legislators insisted the people did not want prohibition, they should be consulted. He predicted the people would sustain the law by a fifty thousand majority. He then defended the bill itself, maintaining prohibition had succeeded in Maine, where pauperism and crime had declined by 75 percent. The Whigs firmly objected to a referendum, but lost. On the important vote for passage of the bill to a third reading, only nine senators opposed the motion, six of them Whigs from Suffolk County. Although its advocates could not get the bill through the Senate until March 18, approval was by a rather large 20-to-11 majority. While most Whigs opposed it, coalitionists divided.[20]

In celebration after the House passage, the Legislative Temperance Society convened at the State House on April 14. In his speech Wilson claimed he had never doubted the prohibition bill would be passed, but he predicted the problem would be in its enforcement. Massachusetts would present more difficulty than any other New England state. After legislative agreement, the bill went to the governor, who kept it on his desk the maximum number of days and then vetoed it on the grounds that the people's vote did not guarantee secret ballot. Boutwell was a temperance man, although never known as an advocate of stringent legislation. He had, however, long argued against referring laws to the people in open ballot. The Senate, with Wilson in the affirmative, failed to override the veto. In the debates Wilson carefully tried not to alienate Democrats who were supporting prohibition or Boutwell, but termed the governor's position "indefensible." The legislature then accepted a bill with no referendum, which the governor signed, indicating he preferred submission to the people.[21]

For all the beliefs which Wilson, in the fall campaign, had claimed the Democrats and Free Soilers had in common, they disagreed on prohibition. Howe was distressed that his party legislators were acting like "mere officeholders," ignoring Free Soil and slavery. The law finally passed was not a party measure, although most Free Soilers endorsed it. The vote was more geographical than partisan. Whig leaders tended to be opposed and the bulk of the country Whigs in the House in favor. The Democrats divided, those from the city especially opposed. To some of them prohibition was as objectionable as the slavery position of their coalition partners. In any case, the emergence of this issue seriously injured the coalition. The Whigs anticipated a Boutwell veto of the revised bill and were surprised when he signed it. The governor must have known another veto would have destroyed the coalition.[22]

The Massachusetts Anti-Slavery Society, later evaluating the performance of the 1852 session, concluded it had achieved little. One cannot help but be impressed with the number of issues considered. But bills would be introduced, proposals amended or voted down, passed in one House and defeated in another. Both houses established committees to investigate the interference with voting by Lowell corporations, but little was accomplished except an improvement of the 1851 secret ballot act to compel election officials to accept only sealed envelopes. The Senate also set up committees to consider what action might be taken to procure the freedom of four Massachusetts black citizens sold into slavery in

Galveston and to consider the abolition of capital punishment. The more liberal Senate passed a more liberal divorce bill, as well as legislation guaranteeing personal liberty, protecting married women's property, and recognizing of the right of a jury to determine law as well as facts in criminal cases, but the House would not concur. Surprisingly, given the political divisions, the legislature agreed rather easily on congressional redistricting, necessary after the 1850 census. The Senate passed the bill unanimously, Wilson choosing to be recorded. It was based upon Whig expectations for an end of the coalition, thus acceptance of districts with likely Whig pluralities; Democrats and Free Soilers, on the other hand, could support a proposal which offered the hope of a coalition majority.[23]

The two coalition legislatures produced no record in guaranteeing black civil rights, but this was a product of Whig and Democratic views and policies, not Free Soil. The battle in the state for intermarriage and equality of travel on the railroads had been won in the 1840s. Wilson wanted more. For his generation he was advanced on race issues. In the *Emancipator and Republican* he praised Frederick Douglass's intellectual powers, his polish, courtesy, and "manly bearing" at the 1849 anniversary of the New England Anti-Slavery Society. He attacked Secretary of State Clayton for denying a passport to a black, pointing out blacks were recognized as citizens in several states, including Massachusetts where they voted, testified in courts, and were taxed. His 1852 Free Soil platform called for protection of Massachusetts blacks in the South. At the 1853 convention Wilson would advocate legislation authorizing black participation in the militia.[24]

Wilson's attitude towards the Indian is more difficult to characterize. Editor Wilson in 1849 complimented Bird's report to the legislature on the condition of Indians in the state, a report which Sumner characterized as teaching "the reader to hate oppression wherever it showed itself, whether in the condition of the poor Indian, the African slave or the free colored." Wilson's newspaper remarks demonstrated an awareness of the connections between the white response to the blacks and to the Indians and a sympathy for the plight of both. In his three-volume study of the slavery controversy, he devoted a chapter to the Seminole War, propounding the needs of slavery and the Slave Power as its cause. On the other hand, he told David Lee Child in 1858 that "The Indians must perish—for we *Christians* want their places and their lands. They can go no further westward."[25]

The coalitionists were determined again to have a constitutional convention. Their report called for a large number of changes, including a new system of representation, single senatorial districts, election of many more state officers by the people, provision for general rather than special laws, the plurality system in more elections, rescheduling state and national elections to coincide, and appropriating income from the sale of Maine lands to education. The Whigs wanted some of the changes, but chose to oppose the resolution primarily on the grounds that many of the reforms were within the legislature's jurisdiction; others should occur by amendment. The Senate passed the bill 22 to 12. The legislature divided along party lines.[26]

The Kossuth mania seemed to occupy the attention of many of the coalition Free Soilers, including Wilson, and helped further to divide the party. Louis Kossuth was a leader in the Hungarian revolt which the Austrian Hapsburgs had put down. Wilson's *Emancipator and Republican* in the summer of 1849 had been full of references to the revolution. Cass perhaps more than any other leading American politician was a strong sympathizer for Kossuth and his objectives. In a society with a sense of mission, an intense nationalism of its own, and a belief in progress, Americans naturally responded favorably to the desire of Hungarians to rule themselves. When the Hungarian effort collapsed, many Americans were shocked. The American government eventually invited Kossuth to visit, but President Fillmore was uninterested in the man and his future; while Secretary of State Webster was willing to use Kossuth for whatever personal advantages the Hungarian might bring, he was unwilling for the United States to intervene in Austria's internal affairs. On the other hand, Seward and some other Whigs were energetic in supporting Hungary. Kossuth landed in December in New York City to a great reception. Kossuth proceeded in triumph via Harrisburg, Pittsburgh, and Baltimore to Washington, where he was endorsed by Cass and Douglas, among others. Sumner's first congressional speech was in support of the Hungarian.[27]

Wilson knew where he stood. Every nation, he told Sumner, should be allowed to adopt its own form of government without outside interference. If the United States and Great Britain would enunciate these principles and back them up, even at the cost of war, Russia would not then violate them. The first action of the 1852 Massachusetts legislature was a motion to invite Kossuth to visit the state. Introduced one day, it was passed the next. Governor Boutwell's address to the legislature supported the offer. Only once before had the state extended a similar invitation to anyone other than an American president.[28]

Unable to secure tangible support in Washington, Kossuth undertook a six-week western tour, obtaining the endorsement, among others, of Chase in Ohio. When Congress debated, but did not authorize anything, the Hungarian turned to the South. Most communities there officially ignored his presence; audiences were small and seldom friendly. In early April Kossuth dispatched a telegraphic message from Mobile, announcing he was accepting Massachusetts's invitation to visit. A legislative committee of eight senators and fifteen members of the House, including Wilson, Keyes, and Burlingame, but not including Speaker Banks, were appointed to receive him. First there was a triumphal tour through Connecticut and then a welcoming to Springfield by the committee, a visit to Northampton, and a return to Springfield for greater celebrations on April 26. Wilson delivered the main address, a patriotic speech about Massachusetts, a declaration that the people of the state believed Kossuth's armies had been fighting the battles for everyone, and condemnation of the czar who "had outraged the law of nations and the sentiment of the civilized world." Sumner and Seward were both complimentary of the Wilson speech. Five thousand people turned out to see the visitor. The welcoming officials and Kossuth had dinner, and then left for a rail procession to Boston.[29]

The Hungarian's entry into Worcester was also triumphant. Artillery thundered and city bells were rung. Kossuth delivered a speech on the Common and later a second at City Hall. En route to Boston, his train stopped in three communities, including Natick. In the capital the parade required two and a half hours to move through six miles of shouting people. Wilson introduced the Hungarian to Boutwell on the capitol steps. There were dinners, speeches, reviews, fireworks. On Wednesday Kossuth spoke in the crowded Senate chamber, where Wilson again gave a welcoming address, expressing "profound sympathy for your country in her misfortunes and for you." The next day Faneuil Hall was opened for a Kossuth speech; one had to buy a Hungarian bond to get admitted. Boutwell spoke; Wilson was a vice-president of the evening's festivities. The next night the legislature hosted a banquet of nine hundred people. Wilson was chairman of the meeting and spoke again, calling his guest the "rightful Governor of Hungary."[30]

Wilson returned to his legislative duties the next week, but others, often Banks, escorted the Hungarian. For the next month Kossuth moved over the state, talking about freedom and encouraging American assistance for revolution abroad. On May 10 and 11 Wilson accompanied the guest to Roxbury, West Cambridge, Lexington, and Concord. On May 14 the Hungarian delivered his final address in Faneuil Hall, with Wilson calling the meeting to order. Several days later a Boston committee of twelve, including Wilson, was created to raise funds for the Hungarian cause. Kossuth collected thousands of dollars, but not the support of the government, whose patronage counted. His remaining hope rested with the party nominating conventions. Northern Democrats had been warm toward him in the winter, but their convention's platform ignored Kossuth and his country. The Whigs were more negative, declaring their sympathy for the doctrines of Washington's Farewell Address, meaning opposition to foreign intervention. And while the Free Soil platform, with Wilson's endorsement, declared its opposition to kings preventing the emergence of republican governments, that statement by a weak third party could be of little help. Kossuth sailed in mid-July for England.[31]

A *New York Tribune* reporter complimented the Massachusetts Legislative Committee for the manner in which it had managed Kossuth's activities. In no other state, he declared, had the Hungarian clan and the official group got along so well. Wilson reported the reception had been all he could have hoped for. All who met Kossuth loved him; he was "a great and honest man." Sumner contrasted the state government's reception with the opposition of the Boston leadership. Over fifteen thousand dollars had been collected in the state for the cause. But it had been a costly reception. Wilson left the chair to answer questions about bills to the state. Calling out the military had cost $6,200, the Revere House housing more than $1,400, decorations between $450 and $500, advertising $300.[32]

One can speculate about why Wilson was so captivated by the Hungarian and expended so much energy in his behalf. The Garrisonians had supported the Hungarian revolution and welcomed its leader to the country, but Kossuth's ignoring slavery had condemned him in abolitionists' eyes. He had hardly arrived when a delegation of blacks had provoked a public statement from Kossuth that he was determined to keep out of American controversies. His trip to the South had not won back Garrisonian endorsement. So Wilson's enthusiasm for the Hungarian cause could not bring him abolition endearment. Neither could it help repair relations with the Massachusetts aristocracy, who opposed the favorable references to revolution and were conspicuously absent from the state's receptions for the guest. Nor were Catholic Democrats pro-Kossuth, for the Hungarian was reported to have insulted Catholics in Great Britain and had been deposed by Catholic rulers. *Brownson's Quarterly* would soon report Kossuth had been received as a "champion of Protestantism," and declare his movement was directed against the Catholic Church. The more conservative Free Soilers were equivocal. Howe was entranced with the visitor while Adams, responding to requests from Seward, Sumner, and Kossuth himself, unenthusiastically agreed to meet the man. Wilson's ardor was sincere, a result of his personal beliefs, not cunning for political gain. Strangely, Wilson's biographers Nason and Russell reported that Wilson had been pleased with his "brief" interviews with Kossuth.[33]

Wilson's Massachusetts legislative career was over. At the time he would have no way of knowing that, for, even if he did not seek reelection, he was a young man who might have expected to return to the state house some year in the future. Wilson had missed, to attend the funeral of a friend, but one day's session in his two years in the Senate. Before the Senate adjourned Wilson was presented a gold watch and chain, valued at $120, as "a memorial of the regard which they entertain for you as a man, and our high appreciation of the faithful and impartial manner in which you have discharged the duties of your office." The president seemed overwhelmed by the honor extended to him. Wilson noted how courteously he had been treated; he appreciated that the House had complimented him upon his fairness and impartiality. He had tried to be fair to all three parties in committee assignments, including appointing chairmen with whom he disagreed. He begged forgiveness if he had injured anyone by remarks he might have made. Only once had a question been raised concerning his ruling and the Senate had sustained its president with only five opposing votes.[34]

Immediately after the legislature adjourned, Boutwell, who had already angered Free Soilers by his veto of the prohibition bill, appointed Cushing to the state Supreme Court. No man was so objectionable to the Free Soil party. *The Liberator* and the *Northampton Courier* were angry. But Cushing worked for his own nomination, getting Rantoul to write in his behalf, interviewing many Free Soilers, and suggesting his appointment would strengthen the coalition. A Free Soil–controlled council confirmed the nomination. Several weeks later Cushing retired as commander of his militia artillery corps. He was honored by Boutwell and the council, and Wilson, president of the Senate and former militia commander, attended and delivered one of the evening's toasts.[35]

The Free Soil leadership in 1851 had given up much to get their man elected to the United States Senate. By midway through the 1852 state legislative session some were beginning to question whether their efforts had been worth it. Hoping to make himself acceptable to his new colleagues, Sumner in Washington had refrained from speaking about slavery. But the capital was an inhospitable environment. Only Chase and Hale were also Free Soil. Whigs Benjamin Wade of Ohio and Seward were friendly. Sumner's Massachusetts associate Davis was civil. Corwin told Sumner Southerners thought of him as an ogre and advised him to move around socially and make a favorable speech. He soon found a pleasant social circle and became acquainted within the diplomatic corps. Sumner delivered his first address about Kossuth, welcoming the visitor, but advocating a continuation of American policy of nonintervention in European affairs. Dana, Stone, and Webb congratulated the senator. Wilson was naturally unhappy. So were Burlingame, Bird, and Alley. Massachusetts Whig newspapers either ignored the senator or reported about him poorly.[36]

The congressional session was about two months along before Sumner spoke again, carefully choosing a debate concerning land policy and taking a position that would win him western concurrence. Wilson was glad the speech was made. The coalition was soon embarrassed, however, when Free Soil leader Keyes introduced into the Massachusetts Senate resolutions objecting to federal land grants to new states when older states did not also receive them. On the first day of debates, Wilson left the chair to speak against the Keyes resolutions and defend Sumner's speech. Keyes replied heatedly. But Wilson was on firm ground. Ease of getting land and inexpensive price were a part of Free Soil principles, even though they had not been emphasized in Massachusetts to the degree that opposition to the expansion of slavery had. When the Senate debate resumed the second day, Wilson attacked the resolutions as placing the state in a false position. The growth of the West, he declared, benefited Massachusetts. In any case, public lands were not "plunder" for the states, but benefits for American citizens to receive. Massachusetts should concur in the liberal distribution of lands. Later Wilson offered resolutions of his own, which would designate public lands as "a sacred trust" held by the national government for the future use of millions who would later move West, to be disposed of in a way to promote settlement. Massachusetts would also endorse granting portions of the public domain to states for purposes of furthering education and internal improvements. His proposal lost by a large vote.[37]

The debate continued. The Whigs were eager to embarrass Sumner. Griswold sought to protect the coalition by getting the subject recommitted but lost, 16 to 18. A subsequent effort to postpone was defeated 15 to 19. Keyes then revised his resolutions, but they were beaten 13 to 22, with most Whigs in favor. The Wilson proposals were then brought up again, voted on one by one, and passed. They included an endorsement of Sumner's speech. The coalition had organized in the meantime and, with the exception of Keyes, voted together. Wilson was angry with what he termed Keyes's "insolence." Three weeks later, however, the Whigs in the House used the resolves as an opportunity again to attack Sumner. With almost 130 representatives absent, especially coalitionists from nearby counties, they almost succeeded in passing new resolutions which sought to embarrass Sumner.[38]

While the coalitionists were defending their senator, the abolitionists had lost patience. At the April annual meeting of the Norfolk County Anti-Slavery Society, Garrison, who had never met him personally, attacked Sumner for his failure to discuss slavery. While Wendell Phillips and others opposed the proffered resolution, clearly the antislavery community was dissatisfied. In March Wilson was counseling Sumner that he needed to speak about slavery, but was adding that the timing was up to the senator. In May Wilson still was patient, discounting the attacks of *The Liberator* and repeating that Sumner had a duty to address the issue but could decide when the time would be appropriate. Adams was less tolerant; in a Washington visit in late May he found Sumner insufficiently aware of the harsh criticism he was receiving and told him he must say something soon. The senator did at least then present a petition from the Society of Friends in New England, asking for the repeal of the Fugitive Slave Act. By the end of June Wilson was more pressing. "You must not let the session close without speaking," he wrote. If Sumner did, he would be denounced by nine-tenths of the people. Whigs all over the state were tormenting coalitionists about their senator's silence.[39]

Sumner was waiting too long. Giddings was critical. Even former Free Soilers, like Preston King and Rantoul, who had endorsed the Democrat Pierce for the presidency had spoken. Sumner himself wrote of his diligence with regard to his duties and the impatience of his friends. He was "biding his time." The Free Soil *Commonwealth* was not critical, but practically ignored Sumner for months. Although the Senate customarily permitted a newcomer to make a major address at his request, when Sumner chose July 27, submitting a resolution requesting the Committee on the Judiciary to consider the expediency of reporting a bill for immediate repeal of the Fugitive Save Law, he was denied the hearing. The *Commonwealth* now took the offensive, attacking the Senate for its lack of courtesy and predicting Sumner would yet find a way to be heard.[40]

But Sumner was neither a coward nor stupid. In the lengthy session he had learned about Senate rules. He proposed on August 26 a germane amendment to the Civil and Diplomatic Appropriations bill which enabled him to deliver his attack on slavery. Howe characterized the speech as having been all that Sumner's friends could desire. Wilson called the address "glorious" and spoke of his own pride in having helped place Sumner in the Senate.[41]

The coalition in Massachusetts in the end was beaten neither by divisions within the legislature nor over discouragement about Sumner's activities but because of the events of the 1852 election. The tactics of the Free Soil party in both the state and nation, of course, would be determined by the nominees and the actions of the two major party conventions and, unfortunately for them, Free Soilers could have little control over that. The Adams conservatives lacked a candidate for presidential nomination. Amazingly, Adams himself in December, 1851, was again considering McLean, but an interview with the judge ended that inclination. While Adams could not imagine whom the two major parties might nominate, Wilson could. He had decided as early as mid-1850 that Scott would be the Whig candidate and from time to time he found that choice palatable. He preferred Scott be president rather than a "Hunker Democrat." Alley and Sumner predicted the same nomination. As long as Cass was a Kossuth supporter, Wilson spoke well of him, too, if the country had to have a Democrat.[42]

Free Soil leaders continued their speculations about the political picture during the late winter and spring. In mid-February Wilson was enthusiastic about the condition of the coalition, claiming in a nonpresidential election year they could select another Free Soil senator and elect seven of the state's eleven congressmen. He was equally optimistic about the coalition's status in May. But Wilson knew the presidential race could determine the results. He was no supporter of Scott, whom he characterized as a friend of the compromisers. He wondered if Free Soil newspapers should begin an attack on the general. Amasa Walker and William Spooner favored union with Democrats in selecting electors from the state; Banks was agreeable. But Wilson opposed the proposal, fearing such a course would drive Free Soilers back into one of the major parties. By April Wilson was publicly advocating Free Soilers remain uncommitted until the major party nominations. Gamaliel Bailey predicted just before the conventions that if the Democrats nominated a new man, Free Soil Democrats nationally would acquiesce and if Whigs selected Scott, Free Soil Whigs would also accede. He and Adams agreed then no worthy Free Soil nomination was possible and their party should simply meet in convention and decline to nominate.[43]

The Free Soil leadership assembled in Boston in early June, after the Democratic convention, to discuss tactics. Bird, Earle, and G. F. Williams were unalterably opposed to supporting Scott. Wilson was publicly unwilling to commit himself, but he could not accept combination with or endorsement of the Whigs if Webster or Fillmore were nominated. If Webster's failure of nomination would somehow divide the party in Massachusetts, then a remote possibility of agreeing to Scott existed. Adams, unduly influenced by his opposition to continuing coalition, was favorable to supporting Scott if the Whig platform were agreeable to him, but he opposed alliance with the Democrats under any conditions. Phillips agreed. Park, Webb, and Stone believed Scott as president might further Free Soil principles. While the conservatives had long been accusing him of wanting to unite the party with the Democrats, at this meeting Wilson was the strongest proponent of maintaining an independent organization.[44]

Both major parties convened in Baltimore in June. A few of the Massachusetts Whigs were backing Webster for their presidential nomination, but the secretary of state was widely opposed even in his own state and he attained only twenty-nine votes on the first ballot. Scott was nominated, getting his votes primarily from Northern delegations. The decision, however, required fifty-three ballots. Webster and Fillmore hoped the party would commit itself to the Compromise of 1850. While most Northern Whigs sought to avoid the issue, Southerners would not be denied. The Fugitive Slave Law was "acquiesced in." The Democratic convention endorsed the Compromise more enthusiastically. The nominee was more of a surprise. New York Democrats had reunited and the Free Soil movement appeared virtually dead in the state. In Ohio Chase had also maneuvered the party toward the Democrats. But the national convention could not choose among Cass, Douglas, William L. Marcy, and James Buchanan, and turned to Franklin Pierce, party regular from New Hampshire whose record and views were known and acceptable to Southerners. With Cushing one of those most prominent in promoting Pierce, the meaning of the convention's result was clear to Massachusetts coalitionists. The nomination and platform should have made Barnburner support impossible. Yet former party leaders like Stanton, John Van Buren, and John A. Dix remained Democrats.[45]

Wilson and Alley went to Baltimore to observe the proceedings of the Whig convention. Some historians have suggested Wilson was hoping to make whatever contribution he could to the defeat of Webster. His presence was telegraphed all over the country. Whig newspapers reported that if Scott were elected, Wilson would be appointed secretary of war. He was quoted as shouting after Scott was nominated, "We have dirked him! We have dirked him!"[46] That is absurd. Wilson would have no influence among Massachusetts Whigs who would vote for Webster or among those who had long preferred Scott. Nor did he have connections, especially after the 1848 national convention, within the national Whig party, which could alter delegate votes. Furthermore, he had long known Webster could not be nominated. Wilson was simply an interested spectator. He might have been influenced in subsequent Free Soil tactics by what he saw happening on the convention floor. After Baltimore Wilson went on to Washington. He returned with reports that some Free Soilers wanted to nominate a Barnburner Democrat to take away votes from Pierce.[47]

The Free Soilers knew they could not win the presidency. The nomination of Pierce and his endorsement by so many Barnburners threw them into disarray. Formerly pro-Whig, Adams could see no difference between the two major parties after their conventions. R. M. Devens worded their predicament well: Pierce was so proslavery, Democrats would find difficulty abandoning the coalition. Scott might have been alluring to many Free Soilers, but the Whig platform's acceptance of the Compromise of 1850 had prevented former Whigs from deserting the Free Soil movement. All Free Soilers could now do was nominate their own presidential candidate; if the people did not vote for him, the fault would be theirs, Devens wrote Sumner. On June 23 Wilson hoped, and believed, Scott would be elected. Free Soilers must nominate their own candidate and he preferred someone who could attract votes, suggesting David Wilmot of Pennsylvania, Benjamin Butler of New York, or Chase. Wilson still expected coalition with the Democrats on state issues. Yet six days later Wilson's views had changed and he was predicting a Pierce victory.[48]

At a June 5 meeting the Free Soil leadership prepared for the fall campaign by trying to solve the problem of providing adequate press support. Carter was selected to be political editor of the *Commonwealth*, which would at the same time propel him into a more influential role in party decisions. Howe, Claflin, and Alley, the latter two among Wilson's closest associates, became the supervising committee of the paper.[49]

The Free Soil leadership called their state convention for July 6. To make final plans the State Committee convened on June 26. Adams was proposed for chairmanship of the Resolutions Committee, but he declined. In the end, Wilson would be elected. An address to the Friends of Freedom in Massachusetts was published, setting forth the party's views of the political situation in the nation and state. Pierce had been nominated, it affirmed, primarily because of his unwavering support of the South, Scott because he was a military chieftain. By their platforms the two parties had contended the Fugitive Slave Law was permanent, the Compromise not to be changed. Getting agreement among Free Soilers on their platform was difficult. Adams reported arguments at the June 26 meeting with Richard Hildreth and Carter and at the Dedham district convention with Keyes. On July 3 Wilson, Hildreth, Palfrey, Stone, and Carter prepared the resolutions. Palfrey and Stone particularly objected to endorsement of intervention in European affairs. Of the early leadership of the party, only Wilson and Palfrey remained to serve on this influential committee during the important presidential election year.[50]

Wilson was otherwise actively engaged in the state convention plans. The Free Soilers of Natick selected him one of their three delegates to the district convention at Dedham on June 30 and as a representative to the state convention. On July 2 Wilson and Walker spoke at the Boston party conclave. Wilson there reported on the activities of the Whig convention in Baltimore, especially the conduct of Massachusetts delegates, and then examined what the responsibilities of Free Soilers were at this moment.[51]

The state convention was thoroughly and richly reported by the Free Soil press, national papers favorable to Free Soil principles, and even Massachusetts Whig publications. July heat was so intense, the afternoon session adjourned to the Worcester Common. While some leaders had wondered whether their party could or should continue, the turnout was one of the largest antislavery meetings ever held in New England. Nearly five thousand people assembled. Wilson entered the hall to "rapturous applause."[52] As state chairman, he called the meeting to order.

Phillips was made permanent chairman. Hale, Palfrey, Walker, Hopkins, Keyes, Swift, and Wilson all spoke. The *Commonwealth* characterized Wilson's speech as one of "great feeling, and, at times of thrilling eloquence, portray[ing] the utter abandonment of the Whig party to the demand of the slave power."[53] Wilson was savage in his attack on the Massachusetts delegates to the Baltimore convention, who, under the lead of Ashmun and Choate, he reported, surrendered their principles. Ashmun was "one of the boldest, most adroit, and unscrupulous politicians that ever trod the soil of Massachusetts."[54] Wilson asserted Whigs were determined to carry the state. To regain the cooperation of the Webster adherents, the party had promised them their share of state offices, including the senatorship for Webster or Ashmun. The speech was undoubtedly crafted to deal with those who might want to promote Scott's candidacy. Many of the delegates favored cooperation with the Democrats on their national ticket; others wanted to work with the Whigs. Most sought to maintain their movement's independence. Wilson gave less attention to the Democrats, asserting he would not waste his time over the "treachery" of the New York Barnburners, who had abandoned their promise to work forever for the principles of the 1848 Buffalo convention.[55]

The platform presented by Wilson emphasized that Free Soil was the party of union and the Constitution; it was opposed to secession, sectionalism, and disunion. Its main thrust, however, was against slavery, terming the institution a sin against God and a crime against man. The platform demanded the federal government exercise its powers to halt the African slave trade, abolish slavery in the District of Columbia, prohibit slavery in the territories, and refuse to admit more slave states. Congress, it declared, was limited in its powers and thus could not legislate concerning fugitive slaves. The Fillmore administration was denounced and Webster especially assaulted. Kossuth's doctrines of intervention were endorsed. The platform commended the call for the national convention and promised to support Hale, Chase, or other possible nominees if they were true to party doctrines. To win additional backing, the platform also favored internal improvements for rivers and harbors, called for making western lands available to people free of charge, and advocated lower postal rates.[56]

Wilson was delighted. The convention had been "glorious," he told Sumner. Everything had gone well. He had never seen a better feeling among members of the party. They had demonstrated a determination to produce a good vote and defeat the Whigs. July was marked by an unusual number of Free Soil meetings in the state. The Webster Whigs, in the meantime, were not yet ready to accept Scott, but as Wilson pointed out, they by the fall would have little other choice.[57]

Wilson got himself into a newspaper argument with Bell over the history and consistency of Whig and Conscience Whig support of antislavery principles. Wilson and Allen, who had broken from the majority of the delegation at the national convention in 1848, he demonstrated, had continued to represent the Whig sentiments of the early and middle 1840s. From 1837 to 1848, he declared,

Massachusetts Whigs had time and time again committed themselves and their state "in favor of all constitutional measures for the extinction of slavery," but now had bowed to the Slave Power. "History can furnish no other case of such utter, shameless abandonment of principles, of such outrageous folly and madness," Wilson concluded. The *Commonwealth* termed Wilson's letter a "complete and most masterly vindication." The *Worcester Spy* noted Wilson had written with "usual clearness, terseness, and directness." The Democratic *Boston Times* emphasized how useful the article was for the facts it revealed; it was "written with eminent ability." Plymouth's Democratic paper thought Wilson was performing invaluable service in breaking down the Whig party and in explaining its lack of principles. The *Greylock Sentinel* of North Adams called the "indictment" "overwhelming and masterly." Whigs were particularly attacking Wilson, the *Commonwealth's* editorial asserted, because as a prominent member of their party for so many years, he was a special danger to them.[58]

Wilson's attention also turned to the national meeting. In the spring Wilson, Adams, Allen, and Phillips were among nine men selected to be statewide delegates to the Pittsburgh Free Soil convention. District conventions selected Alley, Walker, Bird, Sewell, Stone, Estes Howe, William Jackson, and French, among others. After the Pierce nomination had alienated Chase and assured his fidelity to the Free Soil party, Wilson appears to have favored the Ohioan's nomination. In early July he unrealistically hoped Free Soil might carry Maine, New York, Pennsylvania, Ohio, Indiana, Wisconsin, Michigan, and perhaps Iowa. By the end of the month Wilson regained his perspective, but was not yet ready to concede to Pierce, although he admitted the Democrat would carry most of New England. Massachusetts would vote for Scott by about a fifteen-thousand-vote plurality, he predicted. Stone favored a western Democrat for the Free Soil nomination, perhaps Benton, but wondered how a Chase-Phillips ticket would attract votes. Adams, by the end of July, was inclined towards selection of Hale.[59]

The national convention convened in Pittsburgh on August 11. About two thousand people were present. Mass meetings were called for other parts of the city to supplement convention activities and one of those, on the evening before the convention opened, was addressed by Wilson. The North Adams *Greylock Sentinel*, praising his achievements for the party and his impartiality as a presiding officer, in its July 26 issue had suggested Wilson for the presidency of the assembly. Adams recorded in his diary that Wilson was seeking the position. The Massachusetts delegation was strong. Adams was placed on the Resolutions, Alley on the Financial, and Bird on the Organization Committees; the latter was responsible for nominating the permanent chairman. With sixteen votes in committee, Wilson received six on the first ballot, seven on the second, and ten on the third. Wilson was then proposed to the convention and elected. In his speech the new chairman emphasized the agreements on major issues among those present, called for unity, and pledged the party to attempt to relieve the national government from any responsibility it had for slavery. Reports about the convention and the resolution of praise at the end attest to Wilson's able performance of his duties.[60]

After looking at the list of those who spoke and held important positions, one can conclude that old-time abolitionists played a far more influential role than they had at Buffalo in 1848. Longtime antislavery advocates Gerrit Smith and Julius LeMoyne contended with Adams and Austin Willey of Maine, the former trying to commit the party platform to denying that slavery had any legal base in the nation. Adams easily won. Yet the platform was more radical than that of 1848. The most significant change was to the position that slavery was a "sin against God and a crime against man." A party which could have been discouraged by its loss of the Barnburner faction and the acceptance of the Compromise of 1850 by the nation showed surprising vitality. Adams commented on the convention's faithfulness to principles. On the second day Wilson was selected as Massachusetts's representative on the national committee. With his friend Fogg appointed from New Hampshire and E. D. Barber from Vermont, Wilson had support for his views and ambitions. He was chosen as national chairman.[61]

Determination of candidates was difficult. Before the convention assembled Hale asked not to be considered for the presidential nomination. Chase was favored by Wilson, although by convention time Wilson believed the nomination unlikely. The Ohio delegation was divided and, without support from his own state, Chase was unacceptable to most other delegations. Massachusetts gave Hale eight votes, Chase two, Phillips one, and Adams one. On the first ballot Hale was nominated but the convention adjourned uncertain about whether its candidate would accept. The *Commonwealth* asserted the Hale candidacy had been inevitable; no other man could so unite the party. The *New York Times* considered Hale a worthy nominee, respected by many people for the consistency of his position, but it correctly predicted his party would not attract many votes. Most Americans viewed the issue of slavery in the territories settled and they would not support the Free Soil insistence upon resistance to the Fugitive Slave Act, the *Times* contended. In a September 6 letter to Chairman Wilson, Hale accepted his nomination.[62]

Most delegates believed the northwest was entitled to the vice-presidency. George W. Julian of Indiana was the surprise selection; the Indiana delegation and Julian himself had favored Samuel Lewis. Adams recorded Wilson had schemed to persuade the Massachusetts representatives to support Julian because Ohio's delegation was so divided, when, in fact, Ohio Free Soilers expected the nominee to be chosen from their state and had agreed on Lewis. The Ohio delegation was bitter toward Wilson, Adams asserted. Chase certainly was not supporting Lewis. Furthermore, if Adams was correct, Wilson was a political genius, for Julian received 104 votes on the first ballot, almost a majority. Lewis then withdrew. What organizational and communication skills would have been required in several days to attain that election while performing all the responsibilities of the presiding officer! Lewis himself recognized that he had a number of factors working against him, including his age, the fact that his voice was "used up" from too much speaking, rumors Hale did not want him as a running mate, and Chase's opposition.[63]

Movements within the Democratic party were altering the political scene in Massachusetts. Wilson's hopes for success had been diminished by the Pierce nomination, by the return of some Democrats to their party, and by the reluctance of others to cooperate with Free Soilers in a presidential election year. Hallett tried to reestablish his position by attacking Rantoul as leader of his opposition who, Hallett claimed, did not represent the true Democracy of the state. Rantoul nevertheless defeated Lord to be delegate to the Democratic national convention. The Baltimore assembly, however, refused to accept the Rantoul's credentials, because of his antislavery views. After the convention, Rantoul was undecided about what coalition Democrats should do. He considered war against the Hallett faction. "As to slavery," he wrote Ben Butler, "there must be a mutual toleration of opinions, & no more attempts to nauseate four fifths of the people of New England with things which they cannot swallow."[64] Even though Hallett anticipated all the patronage a Pierce administration after March would provide him, Boutwell in the summer and fall of 1852 was governor and the Rantoul-Boutwell-Banks faction was supported by a majority of Massachusetts Democrats. The political climate altered, however, in August with Rantoul's sudden death. At approximately the same time, the state Democratic committee, with the chairman breaking a tie vote, adopted as the call for the state convention an address intended to keep the party convention small and break up the coalition.[65]

Wilson's active political life continued throughout August. In contrast, Dana, admitting he would not stand against the threats of the Boston elite, would play no role in the political campaign, Adams was initially willing only occasionally to speak or help with organization, Sumner would be heavily criticized for his lack of activity, and Phillips would even arrive late for his presiding duties at the Free Democracy fall convention. On the first of August Wilson was willing openly to subject himself to criticism by Democrats, Whigs, and conservative Free Soilers by again joining the abolitionists at Framingham in their annual celebration of the end of slavery in the British Empire. Following the Pittsburgh convention the new national party chairman went to Philadelphia to help organize Free Soil activities in Pennsylvania. Soon after his return to Massachusetts, Wilson delivered a speech at Worcester on August 23. He also initiated a broad and demanding correspondence with party supporters.[66]

As fall approached, Wilson's schedule became absorbing. The Free Democracy, as the former Free Soil party wanted to be called, sought attention by a ratification meeting in Faneuil Hall on August 27. Wilson, Hopkins, Lewis Tappan, Walker, and Swift were speakers. Wilson's assignment was to report on the Pittsburgh convention. He emphasized the orderly, harmonious, and sober nature of the assembly. He warned the Whigs were organizing to regain control of the state. Most of the speakers emphasized the better qualities of Hale over their 1848 nominee, Van Buren. Wilson then left for a trip to Syracuse, Utica, Troy, and Albany. When he returned, he participated in the party meeting in Lynn on September 3, his speech along the lines of his July controversy with Bell. He gave a brief history of legislation in Massachusetts on the subject of slavery and demonstrated the slavery doctrines of the Free Democracy were those formerly supported by the Whigs. He was scheduled to participate in the convention of the Connecticut Free Soil party in Hartford on September 8. He also spoke in Fall River on September 10.[67]

Wilson's speech which received the most coverage in the Free Soil press, obviously intended to be his main address of the campaign, was delivered at the Worcester City Hall on September 11. The *Worcester Spy* characterized him as "an eloquent and faithful advocate of the cause." The *Northampton Courier* was so impressed it printed an extra two thousand copies of the speech for campaign distribution. The address was an answer to the platform and remarks of the Whig convention. It was primarily a defense of two years of coalition, particularly responding to Whig charges of inefficiency and lack of economy. Wilson listed and reviewed the accomplishments of the legislature during the past two years. Praising the stance of the Democrats on state policies, he defended working with them while remaining free to differ with them on national issues. He contrasted coalition control over the various executive departments with the corruption, inefficiency, and questionable practices of the previous Whig leaders, especially in the adjutant general and warden of state prison departments. He defended the call for a constitutional convention as the only way to produce change when Whigs in the House in 1851 defeated proposed amendments. In answer to Whig charges of "incapacity" of coalition politicians at the national level, Wilson demonstrated the ability of Sumner, Mann, Rantoul, and Allen. No sacrifice of principle occurred in getting these men elected, he contended. Slavery was a primary concern of the Free Soil party, he asserted, but he also emphasized the breadth of the party platform.[68]

The major parties met and organized. The Whigs attempted to unite, with the nomination of John Clifford for governor. The *Commonwealth* conceded this was about the strongest selection the Whigs could make. It reported the *Advertiser* was "very much pleased," the *Atlas* "jubilant," while the *Bee* and *Courier*, Webster papers, "caved in." For the first convention in thirty years, Webster was not cheered. He was politically dead in the state. The Democrats endorsed their national candidate and platform, but the antislavery element prevented any allusion to the Compromise of 1850. That so angered the Hunkers, they withdrew. They found themselves more outnumbered than they had been the year before. Hunker Democrats established a state committee of their own. The absent Hallett chose to interpret the endorsement of the national platform as the dissolution of the coalition. His supporters attacked both coalition and the proposed Maine liquor law.[69]

Speculation about Free Soil gubernatorial candidates had included Allen, Mann, Palfrey, Phillips, Walker, and Wilson. To some, the nomination had greater importance than ever before; Adams and Dana, among others, fancied the coalition this year should be obligated to support the Free Soil candidate. They also believed Palfrey was entitled to receive the nomination; Palfrey wanted it. Carter, who claimed he would have to take a position in the *Commonwealth,* became the emissary to Adams, Palfrey, Dana, and perhaps others in an attempt to prevent too much alienation. Palfrey's letter had antagonized those who sustained the coalition. If elected governor, he was unlikely to cooperate in plans for divisions of offices. To those who advocated a Maine liquor law—perhaps 90 percent of the convention—Palfrey was also unacceptable. The diaries and journals of Adams, Dana, and Palfrey are revealing, as the scribes contended for the rights of Palfrey—as if the nomination had any worth without the coalition's first preventing a Whig majority and second, uniting on one man for the legislature. Palfrey's nomination could have engendered neither a Free Soil nor a coalition victory.[70]

If Palfrey were not nominated, then who? Carter told the Adams faction that Phillips was an acceptable candidate, but the former nominee was unwilling to run. He declined publicly on September 10. Three days later Allen's letter asking that he also not be considered was published. Adams feared either Walker or Wilson might be selected. Adams's diary had become shrill in its views about Wilson. On September 11 Adams discussed the position of Wilson in the party, avowed the "crafty" manner in which the chairman had "undermined" them for his own purposes, and declared his adversary would sacrifice the party to "this insane thirst for official distinction of a third rate man with the art of a first rate demagogue."[71] In the end, the Adams-Palfrey faction threw its support to Mann, who could obtain prohibition votes and who in January might be acceptable to coalition Democrats.[72]

Wilson, in the same issue of the *Commonwealth* as Allen, also declined the nomination. He wrote that he was being requested from all over the state to run, but that he could not allow his name to be used. Adams recorded that Phillips had obtained the declination in exchange for Palfrey's withdrawal. But the papers of the Adams faction are full of convictions Wilson wanted the position. On September 13 George White disclosed to Adams that Wilson had asked for his support. A correspondent for a Whig newspaper reported Wilson was popular with the people and his friends wanted him to run. Adams recorded that when he reached the convention city he found Wilson advocates, including Rodney French, were circulating petitions for their candidate. On the day following the publication of his declination, Wilson's name was presented to the convention, surely with the candidate's agreement. The *Commonwealth* reported Wilson had not sought the nomination and many of his closest friends had opposed the action. The paper hoped Wilson would be selected for Congress.[73]

The Free Soilers convened in Lowell on September 15. The Central Committee had called both a mass meeting and a delegate assembly. Wilson, as state chairman, called the conclave to order and in his short speech spoke about the opportunity to place another antislavery senator alongside Sumner. The convention nominated Horace Mann for governor with 401 votes to 259 for Wilson, 59 for Allen, and 31 for Walker. Adams headed the Resolutions Committee, which endorsed the accomplishments of two years of a coalition-led legislature. Wilson was again selected for the state central committee. The convention skillfully avoided the divisive issue of prohibition in its platform, but nominated candidates known for their temperance views.[74]

Wilson delivered one of the principal addresses of the convention. It was styled so as to promote interruptions of applause and support. He praised the Massachusetts Free Democracy for their firm and unyielding stance. Thirty thousand of them were exercising important influence, Wilson contended. They had prostrated Webster and saved the reputation and honor of the state. He thanked those who had voted for his nomination for governor, but denied he had intimated to anyone he sought the position. Noting Mann's six years' service in Congress, Wilson characterized the nominee as one of the nation's ablest men. No one could tell Free Soilers to "trim their sails for national" reasons, Wilson declared. They could and would be true to their principles. Even Adams characterized the speech as "earnest and liberal," but it "was well but not enthusiastically received."[75]

Adams recorded that shortly after the nomination he encountered Wilson, who bore a look telling "of the stormy nature of the passions boiling within him." The Wilson supporters blamed Adams's management for their leader's defeat, the diarist asserted, and would hold his actions against him. Burlingame allegedly told Adams that Wilson was so shaken, he thereafter would have to be more humble. Adams believed Wilson left for a western speaking tour because of his bitterness. One could better conclude that Wilson, as national chairman, ought to confer with leaders in other states and, as a recognized able speaker, should contribute to the campaign nationally. The Adams faction had not really won even if Wilson had lost; Mann was a compromise. Furthermore, the coalitionists still controlled the Central Committee and the machinery in many of the districts. Wilson was reelected state chairman. Soon Bird was encouraging Adams to run for Congress; he was easily nominated over Keyes. Adams was not particularly popular, nor did he or his friends usually organize well. One has to conclude the Wilson faction was willing for that selection to occur. On the other hand, the conservatives expected Palfrey to win the congressional nomination in his district to replace Thompson, who had died. Palfrey's biographer, Frank Gatell, blames the Wilson faction for preventing this. Bolles, a former Democrat and a coalitionist, was selected. The same writer, however, admits the convention was sparsely attended, indicating a lack of organization. Palfrey, furthermore, had been given plenty of chances to win the congressional seat; with his additional alienation of Democrats his chances were so poor, his nomination would have been equivalent to awarding the position to the Whigs.[76]

Wilson's severe charges in Worcester against former Whig adjutant general George H. Devereaux aroused a hornet's nest of opposition. He accused the general of "gross negligence" in his supervision of public property. Wilson also had a paper showing that on June 11, sixteen months after Devereaux left office, the adjutant general paid the state treasury $171,000 for a shed and other public property he had sold, pocketing the money in the meantime. Wilson charged that the general appropriated two saddles for his own use, making no record, and much later paying the state forty-five dollars. Devereaux also sold without authority two pieces of brass ordinance, made no record of the sale, received $225, and pocketed the money; they were returned only after threats of legal action. The *Transcript* reprinted that part of the address; the *Atlas* demanded a further explanation of Wilson. The *Commonwealth* advised the general and his supporters to ignore the issue, rather than provoke Wilson to offer more information.[77]

Devereaux, however, replied in the *Salem Gazette*, denying public property under his charge had been left in a state of decay and neglect and offering an explanation of how he got the saddles belonging to the government. The impression in Salem was that the general was "floundering in the sea of official neglects, forgettings, omissions, unauthorized commissions. . . ." The *Commonwealth* maintained the government had known the information for months, but had avoided exposing the general until the Whig decided to charge the coalition with maladministration and corruption. The *Courier* had to admit that Devereaux denied only part of the charges. After the Devereaux reply, the Whig press generally ignored the controversy.[78]

Wilson replied at length to each of his seven previous charges. He insisted he had not been vague or indefinite, but his language had been carefully chosen. Devereaux had admitted several of the charges were true, but had pled loss of memory or repayment of what he'd taken after the matter had been called to his attention. Wilson's temperament was such that he had not tried to leave the impression his opponent wanted to defraud the state, only that the general had been an ineffective administrator. The *Boston Transcript* suggested Wilson's charges had so "pointedly contradicted" Devereaux and had been so fortified by evidence that the general should prove himself by suing Wilson for libel.[79]

Chairmen of national political parties could fulfill their responsibilities by staying at a party headquarters in a central city, could travel widely while spending much of their time in private consultations, or, if their speaking abilities were thought highly of, might themselves deliver important political addresses. Of course, the Free Soil movement had neither the state organizations nor financial resources which Democrats and Whigs had available. Still, with the state convention in Massachusetts over and a state organization in existence for several years, Wilson could devote part of his attention to his national responsibilities. By the November elections he had visited fourteen states and traveled more than five thousand miles. Wilson was perhaps the most hard working party chairman

American politics had ever seen. And he made contacts which would help make him thereafter an influential figure in American politics. Wilson claimed he spent nearly three weeks in New York during the campaign; if Free Soil candidates could garner between forty-five and fifty thousand votes and elect Gerrit Smith to Congress, Wilson told Smith, he would be pleased.[80]

Wilson must have been in the West about three weeks, returning around October 10. He visited Ohio, Indiana, Illinois, Michigan, Wisconsin, and New York and addressed meetings in the latter four. Wilson reported the New York Free Democratic convention in Syracuse on September 29 was "united and enthusiastic" and had nominated about the best candidate possible for governor. Wilson addressed the conclave, providing a history of the movement in Massachusetts and offering suggestions on how to organize in New York.[81] The *Milwaukee Free Democrat* reported his October 4 much-applauded lecture was an "eloquent review of the positions and principles of the three parties, and a clear expose of the apostasy of Daniel Webster and Millard Fillmore from the faith of LIBERTY." Wilson also spoke in Chicago and joined Hale for addresses in Detroit and at the Michigan state convention in Ypsilanti. He seemed most encouraged by the situation in Wisconsin, where, he reported, the people were imbued with Free Soil principles. The party had a greater chance of carrying that state than any other. He pronounced Indiana and Illinois Free Soilers as giving a "good account of themselves." The party in Michigan had done little, but was beginning to work, he reported. In New York, from forty-five to sixty thousand votes were anticipated for Free Soil.[82]

Wilson returned just in time to attend the Eighth Congressional District Free Soil convention. Perhaps he had organized to assure his nomination for senator before he departed for the West; perhaps his friends were able in his absence to get votes to bring about his selection. More likely, Wilson had become so strong among Free Soilers in his district that he could relax and let the designation take place. The nomination resolution spoke of Wilson's "faithfulness to principle, and fearless and untiring devotion to Freedom." The convention also asked him to take to the stump and address the voters. The Free Soilers nominated men in each congressional district, a strong slate which included—in addition to Bolles, Adams, and Wilson—Burlingame, Alley, Alexander DeWitt, French, and James T. Robinson.[83]

In his acceptance letter Wilson avowed he had not solicited the nomination. The Free Democracy, he declared, had not been created to elevate men to office, but to achieve principles. Free Soilers were obligated to accept their party's nominations, he maintained; how else could it achieve its ends? This point of view must have made men like Dana additionally irritated at Wilson. If, during the canvass, Wilson continued, the withdrawal of his name would advance the ends of the party, he would consent. While he would like to engage Whig and Democratic nominees in debates, as the convention had requested, he cautioned that, because he was both national and state chairman, he could devote little time to his district.[84]

Wilson had no opportunity to rest. Not only was he responsible for a national correspondence, but he had to supervise the campaign in the state. Wilson and Burlingame appear to have been the primary organizers. Both also spoke extensively. Adams was persuaded to appear more often than in any other campaign for years, but Sumner's refusal to undertake a political tour was widely resented. Wilson's speaking schedule, beginning October 13, was to carry him to western Massachusetts, including Northampton, Hinsdale, Springfield, and Fitchburg, but was to concentrate on Essex and Middlesex Counties. Some of these communities were near enough to the Boston office that Wilson could supervise campaign activities during the day and speak during the evening. He closed in Natick November 6.[85]

Wilson's speech in Northampton on October 13 was fully reported and may have been representative of others. He spoke rather highly of the personal qualifications of Scott and Pierce, but denounced the principles upon which their national parties stood. He attacked the Whig resolutions, supported by the Massachusetts delegation, as subservient to the South. Whig administrations had been vigorous in their efforts to put down antislavery agitation, Wilson contended. He reviewed Webster's course from his cooperation in 1845 in drawing up the antislavery resolutions to his support in 1850 of the passage of the Fugitive Slave Act. The Free Soil party, Wilson emphasized, included a broad spectrum of principles in addition to its opposition to the spread of slavery. It sought to free the nation's capital from slavery and to repeal the Fugitive Slave Law. It favored the improvement of rivers and harbors, asked for intervention to aid the struggling peoples of Europe, and advocated peaceful arbitration of international disputes. Wilson praised Hale for both his public and personal life. He reported on the advances Free Soil was making in the West. Finally he turned to state issues, praising both Mann and the achievements of the coalition.[86]

During the course of the campaign Daniel Webster died. The secretary of state had returned to his farm in Marshfield on September 12. He would neither support Scott nor respond to any attempt to gather votes for himself for the presidency. He died early on October 24 and services were held there in New Hampshire. A special train was arranged for in Boston to carry city and state officials, including Wilson, Boutwell, and Banks, and many of Webster's friends, such as Abbott Lawrence, Winthrop, and Everett, to New Hampshire. "Warrington" later reported President of the Senate Wilson and Speaker of the House Banks had to walk from the funeral, while the Boston aristocracy rode in their carriages. Unwanted or not, the President of the Senate and Speaker also attended the obsequies in Boston, November 30; they had to listen to Hillard's defense of the Great Man.[87]

Wilson and his associates again attempted to find electoral districts in which they could unite with the Democrats. In Middlesex and Essex Counties, for example, coalition was reached on state senators. The Democrats would not agree to a joint senatorial ticket in Berkshire until November 3. In Hampden, Hunkers controlled the Democratic convention and refused to join with Free Soilers in nominations. The results depended on the area; opposition between the national Democratic party and the state central committee often prevented cooperation. Against Wilson the Democrats nominated Ben Butler, the Whigs Tappan Wentworth. Frequent consultations and extensive efforts to enable Wilson to defeat Wentworth without committing Butler and the Democrats too far did not produce the hoped–for victory.[88]-

The future of political antislavery in the nation and the political career of Wilson were both uncertain as election day approached. On the one hand one objective of the Free Soilers was being achieved: the Whig party was so weakened the election would later come to be seen as its demise. On the other hand, the Democratic party was more united than it had been since 1844. It would sweep the nation, taking all but four states in the Electoral College. Wilson's career might also have been at a crossroads. He, as chairman of both the Free Soil national convention and of its Central Committee, had gained political stature outside his state. But he had surrendered his prominent role in the state legislature to run for Congress. His chances of election, especially in the absence of coalition with the Democrats, were not good. The more conservative faction of his own party could use Free Soil defeats in the state to gain control of party policy. His allies within the Democratic party might be so weakened that cooperation in the coming years would be impossible. Did he have a future in politics? If not, did he even have an income to support his family?

9

The Constitutional Convention and Voter Rejection

Much was decided on election day in 1852. The Whigs had been too optimistic; the October voting in Pennsylvania, Indiana, and Ohio was a disaster, a portent of what would soon happen elsewhere. In November Pierce swept the nation; when the Electoral College met, only four states, including Massachusetts and Vermont, supported Scott. Still, the Democratic nominees obtained only 51 percent of the ballots cast. The Free Soil vote fell from 293,000 in 1848 to 155,000. About 100,000 of the votes lost were those of Barnburners in New York. Scott received a plurality in Massachusetts, about 41 percent of the total. Hale attracted about 28,000 voters. Approximately 11 percent fewer men went to the polls in Massachusetts than in 1848. The Free Soil vote fell 10,000, the Whig almost 9,000, while Pierce received 9,000 more votes than Cass had attracted in 1848. The Whigs carried all but three counties, which went to the Democrats. The latter won both Middlesex and Suffolk. In only two counties, however, did the Whigs procure a majority. As overwhelming as the defeat was, the Free Soil presidential vote was a larger percentage in Massachusetts (22) than in any other state. Wilson's tactics had worked; more men remained loyal to Hale than deserted to Scott. Democrats had come out in force, however, carrying Boston for the first time and attracting Democratic Free Soilers back to the party. Worcester County, which had voted Free Soil in 1848, narrowly went Whig. In Wilson's Middlesex County the major parties together garnered more than 17,600 votes to 4,200 for the Free Soilers.[1]

In the elections for governor, Clifford polled better than Scott had. A few commentators have speculated that some Webster Whigs had been willing to vote for Clifford, but not for Scott; perhaps some Hunker Democrats preferred Clifford over H. W. Bishop, or feared a deal between Bishop and Mann supporters. Opponents of the state's temperance law often voted Whig. Kevin Sweeney concluded one-quarter of those Democrats who voted for Pierce, changed their party support at the state election because of the liquor question. Mann also did better, with six thousand more votes than Hale received. The *Boston Transcript* forecast Clifford would be chosen by the legislature, but so many parties had nominated so many different candidates, other offices might go to almost anyone. Among the congressional districts, the Whigs carried two. All others, including Wilson's district, required a second vote. In the next election a plurality would be all that was required and the Whig candidates had attained that in all districts but one. The proposed constitutional convention carried. Voting for the legislature was inconclusive, with the Whigs and coalition obtaining approximately equal numbers in the House, most candidates in the Senate lacking majorities.[2]

Newspaper evaluation of the election was surprisingly in agreement. The *Commonwealth* was optimistic; the national election had sealed "the doom of the great Whig party." The Free Soil *Northampton Courier* declared the state results were all it could hope for. Among the Whig papers, the *Boston Journal* admitted its party had been "put to rout." The *Atlas* was surprised and disappointed. Wilson, writing almost two decades later, characterized the elections as "decisive and signal," an endorsement of the finality of the Compromise. He lamented that after a quarter of a century of antislavery agitation, only 150,000 men would vote for a Free Soil candidate.[3]

In the nation the election had been somewhat quiet. The agitation of the 1840s had calmed with a gradual acceptance of the Compromise of 1850. Many Barnburners had returned to their party. Many Southern Whigs had been suspicious of Scott. Free Soilers won fewer congressional seats than before, limited to Giddings and Benjamin Wade in Ohio and Gerrit Smith in New York. While Morton and his followers in Massachusetts were now reunited with their former party, the exodus from Free Soil had been much greater in other states, especially in New York and Pennsylvania.

The Democrats and Free Soilers of Massachusetts had another opportunity to join forces before the next election. The *Northampton Courier* noted two-thirds of the towns had had a coalition majority in the first election. The possibility of spoils from the national administration and the encouragement the election had given to the Hunkers, however, interfered with cooperation plans. The results of the presidential election were hardly reported before the chairman of a large meeting of Salem Democrats made "a decided and energetic speech" against coalition. He was followed by another who devoted an hour and a half to explaining what a disaster working with Free Soilers had been to New Hampshire Democrats. The Catholic *Boston Pilot* declared the coalition had resulted in giving Democrats no party to vote for in state elections. The Free Soilers dominated the coalition, it charged; that party was hostile to the American constitution, supported the Maine temperance law, and was determined to shift political power to the smaller communities.[4] Hampden and Bristol County Democrats thwarted cooperation strategies. Strong opposition in Berkshire County, on the other had, was overcome.[5]

Immediately after the election Wilson went on the offensive. In a speech at Marlboro on November 5 he pronounced the Whig party as fallen, never to rise again. He noted even Webster from his dying couch had seen that vision of the future. Allen in 1848, Wilson declared, had correctly prophesied the national convention had killed the party. Whigs there had repudiated their long-held principles. After a lengthy review of the Whig adherence to an antislavery position, Wilson condemned the 1850 abandonment by Clay and Webster. Scott in 1852 had been required to run on a platform on which he could not win. The work the Whigs had begun in 1845 had destroyed them, he concluded. The Fillmore administration was so unpopular the party now controlled only three state legislatures. The Free Soil Central Committee on November 11 congratulated the party for its "success." Mann had attracted the most votes a Free Soil candidate ever had obtained, the General Court would have more party members than before, and the constitutional convention proposal, defeated a year earlier, had won voter approval. The committee enthusiastically called Free Soilers to battle for the fourth Monday elections.[6]

In fact the election results were more complex than Wilson and the Central Committee were predicating. In many states, Massachusetts included, temperance had been a major issue. The Democrats had won in Connecticut in April with liquor the focus. Even Neal Dow in Maine had been beaten by a larger turnout in the spring Portland election. The *Commonwealth* asserted the Massachusetts election turned on that subject; Clifford's large vote in Boston was part of the proof. While temperance may have cost Mann a few votes, it did not divide the Free Soil party. It did injure the Whigs and Democrats. Edward L. Pierce saw temperance as defeating coalition in the larger towns.[7]

Perhaps the year—1852—better explains the results. Both William G. Bean in his study of the antislavery party in Massachusetts and J. Daniel Loubert in his dissertation biography of Wilson concluded the presidential election was the primary factor in accounting for the results in the state. This was true. What is not true is the assertion of Frederick Blue in his study of the Free Soilers that bickering—he cites Sumner, Wilson, Adams, and Palfrey—prevented the election of more Free Democrats to Congress. Sumner played little role in the campaign, but not because of differences with its organization. Adams spoke more frequently than usual. Palfrey had so isolated himself politically, his support would be of little help. Wilson could not have worked harder; more specific aid to conservative Free Soilers—Adams in his congressional district, for example—would have changed nothing. Some Free Soilers undoubtedly opposed certain candidates of their own party; that is true in any election. Nevertheless, the Democrats, not the Free Soilers, determined the results.[8]

While the House appears to have been about equally divided as a result of the first election, clearly the Whigs won on November 22. Even Natick voted Whig. Yet the party obtained fewer votes than in 1851; its victory, although real, was a product of the end of the coalition. The division in the House was close, but between fifteen and twenty Hunker Democrats, pledged to oppose coalition, assured Whig control. Since only eighteen senators had been chosen, the Whigs would fill the vacancies in the upper house. Coalition had simply not taken place in many districts; Democrats had stayed home or voted Whig. Splinter tickets had been additionally damaging. The *Commonwealth* asserted the coalition should have been able to control the Senate 30 to 17. The Central Committee, the paper declared, had done all it could. Between five and six hundred speeches had been delivered by Free Soilers. The state had been flooded with documents. "Hunkers, Whigs, and rum" had been too much.[9]

The third election, for members of Congress in those districts in which no majority was received in early November, also brought Whig triumphs. Two Democratic organs of Boston, the *Post* and Catholic *Pilot,* both denounced coalition attempts, especially when the results—sending a congressman to Washington—would have national ramifications. Their attacks helped prevent broad cooperation. Banks was the only Democrat selected, this in a district in which the Free Soil candidate withdrew. DeWitt was the only Free Soiler elected. Alley withdrew in the Sixth District, but his action didn't help. Fewer than six hundred votes determined Adams's failure; more than seven hundred had been scattered among noncontenders. An arrangement was finally agreed to in Wilson's district, although Butler never officially withdrew. The Democrats and Free Soilers would together have had a majority at the first election, although Whig Wentworth had a plurality of fourteen hundred over Wilson. Not enough Democrats, however, would vote for Wilson in December. Still, he failed by fewer than one hundred votes; he had attracted thirteen hundred supporters since the previous election. More than eight hundred votes were thrown away on other candidates. Even the Massachusetts Anti-Slavery Society was sorry to see Wilson and Adams defeated.[10]

What was the result of the congressional elections? The *Commonwealth* and *National Era* continued to profess enthusiasm. But the coalition was one casualty. Not only were men like Palfrey and Adams pleased by that result, but so were Whittier and *The Liberator*.[11]

Many, including Wilson and Adams, were openly critical of Sumner's lack of participation in the crucial campaign. An attack against the senator in the *Commonwealth*, however, was counterproductive. Wilson quickly regretted what he said, at least its public nature. Neither Sumner's personal characteristics nor the political climate would promote an estrangement between the two men. Wilson assured Pierce the party leadership would stand by their senator. Nor could Free Soilers be comforted by Sumner's performance in the short congressional session of 1852–1853. The two major parties excluded Free Soilers Hale, Chase, and

Sumner from all committee assignments and Sumner found no opportunity to speak. Resolutions introduced in the Whig-dominated Massachusetts General Assembly, deploring the snub of the state's senator, were allowed to die. Even Palfrey concluded Sumner's personality precluded effective senatorial service.[12]

What now for Wilson and the Free Democrats? One wonders what was to be the source of Wilson's income. What also were the feelings of this man who had given so much to the campaign? Unfortunately, little evidence remains to help us arrive at answers. Robinson many years later did report that the existence of the convention gave both Wilson and Banks support during much of 1853. That Wilson expected to continue as a Free Democratic leader is demonstrated by his appearance as the featured speaker at the Maine state convention of the party at Augusta on February 10. He also continued his prominent role in his county, presiding over the March Middlesex County Free Democratic convention.[13]

In many ways the victories at the second two elections were unfortunate for the Whigs. Their optimism was unwarranted. Scott, a candidate acceptable to most Massachusetts Whigs, had been badly beaten outside the state. The party had waged its last national campaign. Even Clifford, who would restore the state House to his party, had received fewer votes than Winthrop had attracted the year before. The Whigs's primary victory was the destruction of the coalition, a result of the national campaign and the confusion over state issues. That opponent, however, could be revived by the constitutional convention and the absence of a presidential campaign for four more years. The Free Democratic *Dedham Gazette* noted that the governor's speech and the choice of officers for the General Court manifested how little the Whigs had learned; they might be able men, but they represented the "Old School," the ideas of State and Beacon Streets. The historian of the *Lords of the Loom* believed Whig leaders were unaware their state's political structure was disappearing. Even control of the legislature was a mixed blessing. The Whigs could select their man for senator. The *New York Post* asserted that Davis was so unpopular he had to decline. Only Everett and Clifford had the prestige to keep the party from dividing, the *Post* declared. Clifford was needed as governor, Winthrop declined being considered, Ashmun was passed over, and Everett was selected. While the new senator was popular, the choice of a second man from the Boston area antagonized western Whigs. Furthermore, whatever they did, the Whigs would be held responsible for a temperance policy.[14]

In his initial address to the legislature Governor Clifford questioned the constitutionality of the convention and attacked what he termed the tendency of the General Court in the previous two years to over-legislate. Although several Whig newspapers asked for the repeal of the convention call, the party was wise enough not to pursue that. After criticizing the coalition for having held too lengthy sessions, the Whigs, in a rather unproductive term, did not adjourn until May 25, not even in time to turn the facilities over to the convention. Free Soil papers charged the majority party did not want to alienate the voters before the election of convention delegates in March. But even thereafter, little was done. February was devoted to changing the secret ballot law; that needed to be and was done barely four days before the convention vote. Since the call for the convention had electorate approval and stated voting could be done by the new ballot laws of 1851 and 1852, even this Whig change was limited to giving voters a choice between open and secret ballot.[15]

Division within the Whig party made action to alter the prohibition law even more difficult. Nothing was done. The *New York Post* reported the legislature in three months had not passed a single measure of importance. Two weeks later the *Commonwealth* compared the joy in the Whig camp in November with the "inefficiency, incompetency, and impotent fossilism" since. The *Northampton Courier* characterized the legislature as "more corrupt, unprofitable, and infamous" than any of its predecessors.[16]

The political pot was kept in more turmoil by the advent of the constitutional convention than by the futility of the Whig-dominated legislature. Democrats and Free Soilers together had received a majority of votes in the autumn elections. They just had been unwilling or unable to form coalitions. Members of both parties, even the Hallett Hunkers, recognized they yet had an opportunity to achieve some of their aims if they could obtain control of the convention. The state constitution had been drawn up in 1780. It had been infrequently altered since, primarily in 1820 when Maine separated from Massachusetts; nine of fourteen proposed amendments were then accepted by the voters. On March 7, 422 delegates were to be elected. Each town, no matter how small, was entitled to one representative. Otherwise, the number was determined by the size of the delegation to the General Court. Delegates did not have to reside in the districts from which they were selected.[17]

The Whig campaign was poorly planned. Some of the leadership erred by opposing the meeting, although it had already been sanctioned by the voters. One can understand their antagonism. Western Whigs feared a loss of political influence if distribution of House seats were altered. Eastern Whigs feared what might emanate from a convention with a large number, perhaps a majority, of Free Soilers and Democrats. The party had trouble reversing its anticonvention position. Every Whig senator and representative in both 1851 and 1852 had opposed the call. Every 1852 fall Whig convention which acknowledged the proposal also objected to it. By mid-February the Whig Central Committee finally abandoned the opposition. Between fighting the principle of a convention and enjoying the afterglow of the fall elections, the Whigs did not adequately organize for the delegate choice.[18]

Wilson, as chairman of the Free Democratic state committee, in a January 25 letter pointed out how important the convention was. After noting the Whigs' opposition to the idea, he urged Democrats and Free Democrats to cooperate in the election of delegates. He declared that, since neither national concerns nor prohibition were issues, the two coalition partners could again work together. He enunciated what his party considered were the primary issues, including (1) the unequal and unjust system of representation in the lower house, (2) the creation of forty single senatorial districts, (3) the election of councilors by the people and the division of the state into councilor districts, (4) the election of more state officers, including the secretary of state, treasurer, auditor, adjutant general, and sheriffs, (5) a limit on the length of legislative sessions to ninety or one hundred days, (6) improvement of the method of organizing government at the start of the year, (7) change of the day for state elections to correspond with national voting, and (8) freedom of the ballot. The method for determining representation in the House was certain to divide the coalition; so would majority versus plurality requirements for elections. Both issues were left vague or avoided by Wilson and other coalition commentators. The *Commonwealth* declared the "best" men had to be selected; the destiny of the state for the next half century was being determined.[19]

Some of the leaders of the two coalition parties recognized they could not be selected from their own communities, either because they in their political lives had antagonized too many adherents of the other coalition party, or because the Whigs would carry that town. Many of the Adams faction of the Free Democrats were convinced Wilson and his supporters were working against their election. While one can find declarations of this in the papers of Adams, Dana, and Sumner, one can discover no evidence. On the contrary, when Sumner, Burlingame, and Dana could not be elected from their own communities, Wilson and his supporters found other districts for them. Carter toured the state seeking communities which would accept coalition leaders. Naturally most towns did not want to be represented by an outsider and in the end only nine elected one. When Carter proposed to Dana that he discuss his views with a Manchester Democrat whom Dana did not know and Dana refused, Wilson and Alley approved of his action. Victory often was only possible if the Free Democrat was acceptable enough to the Democrats to bring about a unified nomination. Clearly the enlarging Catholic and working-class element in Quincy was difficult to persuade to support Adams. When he refused to run in any other community, he lost by forty votes. Wilson tried to get Marshfield to take Mann, for he thought several communities might be willing to elect Sumner, but that town insisted on the senator. Phillips declined to run in Abington, so Keyes was nominated. Several days before the election Wilson was still trying to find a town nomination for Mann and Palfrey. He "spared no pains" to achieve that, Robinson subsequently reported. Wilson told Sumner more labor was expended in the three weeks before the election than he had ever seen before. He himself lectured in Lowell on February 19 in behalf of the convention. Wilson predicted a sweeping coalition victory.[20]

While the conservative faction blamed Wilson for the absence of some among their number, what is most significant is that Mann, Howe, and Adams could not get elected; their failure was their responsibility more than that of the state committee. Most convincing in arriving at some conclusion about Wilson's attitude towards the Adams faction is an 1871 reflection by Robinson, published in the

Springfield Republican—meaning that participants in 1853 events could have challenged him had he been wrong. Robinson, in 1853 in a position to know, noted one of Adams's "fancies" was that Free Soil leaders had tried to keep him out of the convention; it was not true, Robinson declared. Howe was convinced Wilson wanted to be elected governor in the fall and through the inaction of others, might be. Palfrey wanted Adams to lead an attack on Wilson, but Adams believed, with no national election in 1853, the time was not right. Adams contended of all those who founded the party in 1848, Wilson had the "lowest level of mind," yet by his demagoguery, he had assumed party leadership. Indicative of how little he understood the man he had come so to dislike, Adams predicted Wilson would drift into the "Boston Hunker house." After the election Howe spoke of Wilson as coveting the convention presidency, shunning former friends, and spending most of his time with Democrats. Interestingly enough it was the election losers—Adams, Palfrey, and Howe—who at this time were so bitter in their denunciations and characterizations of Wilson. Those elected, who must have been representative of the party, supported him. In addition, Free Democrats were not the only men who failed election. Ex-governor Boutwell, because of his position on prohibition, was defeated in his home community. Hallett also lost.[21]

Wilson wanted election to the convention so badly, he agreed to run in two towns, including his home community. His friend Mann reported Natick was so divided, victory could not be assured. As a matter of fact, Wilson won in both, in Berlin 107 to 6, in Natick 246 to 232. Peculiarly, Wilson had never been in Berlin until he went to decline its designation. He urged Boutwell in his place.[22]

The coalitionists had clearly won control of the convention. The Whig *New York Tribune* reported the results as 149 Whigs, 135 Democrats, 90 Free Democrats, 34 coalitionists, and 18 no choice. The Free Democratic *Northampton Courier* knew only that the coalition had a hundred-vote majority. Every part of the state had voted for reform, it declared. Bristol County hadn't elected a single Whig. Middlesex County had gone 44 to 15 against the Whigs. A "most disastrous result," the Whig *Boston Advertiser* conceded.[23]

Whatever Adams and Palfrey thought, the list of those elected is an impressive one. Boutwell, with years to reflect, in his 1902 autobiography characterized the convention as the ablest body of men who ever sat in Massachusetts. Among those chosen were two members of the state Supreme Court; Schouler of the *Boston Atlas*; Nathan Hale of the *Boston Advertiser*; other Whigs Choate, Dawes, Otis Lord, Samuel Eliot, Stevenson, Hillard, and Luther Bell; several ex-governors including Morton, Briggs, and Boutwell; Free Soilers Walker, Alley, Sumner, Burlingame, Dana, Allen, Bird, DeWitt, and Keyes; and Democrats Banks, Butler, Rantoul, and Griswold. When Boutwell and Hallett were beaten, Wilson procured their elections in other, safe towns. Abbott Lawrence, Winthrop, and Everett declined their nominations. Their names weren't needed; Boston returned forty-four Whigs. The *Commonwealth* charged these Whigs were the most conservative men within the party; thirty-nine of them lived in three wards in the Beacon Street neighborhood.[24]

This convention was dominated by native sons, a characteristic few states would likely have provided in the early 1850s. One newspaper reported that 366 of the representatives were Massachusetts natives; 31, including Wilson, had been born in New Hampshire; 45 had been born elsewhere in the United States; 7 in foreign nations. Farmers were the largest occupational group with 128, followed by 73 lawyers, 65 merchants and traders, 24 clergymen, 24 manufacturers, 18 boot and shoe manufacturers, 18 physicians, and 14 editors and printers.[25]

Before the convention opened, Wilson was heavily involved in planning for an important dinner at Boston's Fitchburg Railroad station on May 5 honoring 1852 Free Soil presidential candidate John P. Hale, now retired from the Senate. Fourteen hundred people attended. This was an impressive assemblage of men. When he wrote his history of the abolition movement, Willey credited this gathering with helping revive the cause after the debility produced by the Compromise of 1850 and the disaster of the elections of 1852. Wilson, still strangely holding on to an issue now dead, in his remarks to the meeting compared Hale to Kossuth, each man important for the principles he represented. Adams, ever critical, instead of commending Wilson for his organizational work and his willingness to have others to play an important role, decided the state chairman did and said little because he didn't want to alienate Democrats on the eve of the convention.[26]

As convention time approached the more moderate Whig papers began to hope for positive results. The *Boston Transcript* approved of equal senatorial districts, a plurality law to prevent recurrent elections, reduction of the number of House members to about two hundred, a change of basis for House representation, and abolition of the Executive Council.[27]

Shortly before the May 4 scheduled opening for the convention, delegate leaders gathered to organize. Hallett, the leader against coalition, made the motion in the Democratic caucus to unite with the Free Democrats. The Democrats had won more seats and were entitled to the chairmanship. Banks, a former Speaker of the House and a renowned presiding officer, was selected to be nominated. His election the next day, 250 to 137 votes for Briggs, discloses the approximate strength of the coalition and the Whigs. Most participants subsequently agreed Banks did a superb job. The Free Soilers were to receive the next two most important positions. Robinson, editor of the *Lowell American* and a legislative veteran, was nominated as secretary and Wilson was appointed as chairman of the Ways and Means Committee, the floor organizer and replacement for the presiding officer should Banks be absent. Wilson also chaired the Committee on the State Senate.[28]

Wilson was responsible for organizational motions. He submitted the resolution that committees be composed of one man from each county and got that accepted over Hooper's proposal for one from each Congressional district. Because the legislature had not yet adjourned, an argument ensued over whether the convention should recess. Wilson contended for immediate beginning of work, which was agreed to—not along party lines. The House, which remained in session until May 25, had use of the facilities until midafternoon, the convention thereafter. Free Democrats Sumner, Allen, and Walker, in addition to Wilson, were selected for several of the important committee chairmanships. The convention itself spent the better part of a week arguing over its authority in, or the desirability of calling elections in, towns unrepresented.[29]

During the course of the debates over the right of the convention to ask unrepresented towns to hold new elections and to specify the use of a secret ballot, Clifford and Choate, each of whom had served as the state's attorney general, maintained the legislature was sovereign. It had called the convention; the constitution could only be amended, not replaced. Benjamin Butler, on the other hand, asserted the convention was a revolutionary body, above the state government and constitution. The controversy also included what the term "people" embraced. Wilson's philosophy of government in part may be found in his answer to these issues. While in his address he disagreed with Butler that they were part of a revolutionary body, he insisted the people had the right "to institute government, and to reform, alter, or totally change the same." That had been the precedent in the two previous conventions. He referred to the right of revolution found in the Declaration of Independence and to the definition of "people" found in that document, national and state constitutions, and court decisions. When the people went to the polls to vote on whether to have the convention or not, he contended, they did not create a right, but were simply exercising their right and were accepting a proposal from the legislature concerning the mechanics of the convention. Once the people had spoken, the legislature possessed no power to undo their will. It could not amend or alter the call once the people had agreed to it. By the time Wilson spoke the majority of convention members were weary of the topic; the question was insisted upon 220 to 117. The Whigs had been beaten on a secondary issue, leaving the impression of opposition to democracy.[30]

Wilson's Committee on the State Senate quickly reported back. It advocated forty senatorial districts, established on the basis of population. Elections would be held at the same time as national ballots. Wilson's speech revealed much concerning his opinions about the rights of women and of aliens. Apparently he was unwilling to endanger defeat of a proposed constitution by advocating that women should vote, but, he insisted, no valid argument could be advanced against their possession of that privilege. He confined himself to contending that they had influence in the community and were entitled to representation. In light of Wilson's later participation in the anti-foreign Know Nothing movement, his insistence on counting foreigners for representation is also revealing. Aliens participated in business affairs, in schools, churches, and social life and influenced the views of their neighbors, he argued. Thus, they should be represented. Of course, his coalition partners—the Democrats—could benefit from this opportunity for increased numbers in the urban east, into which immigrants were moving in growing numbers. The committee proposal was accepted. Later the same month, when the convention considered qualifications for governor, Wilson opposed including American citizenship as one of them. He saw nothing in the existing constitution that could prevent election of an alien and he did not want that changed. He also feared that American citizenship might be defined, as the Supreme Court later did, on the basis of race and he would not deny public office to blacks. After a long debate, at the suggestion of Morton, Massachusetts citizenship became a qualification for governor. The proposal would also wipe out the property qualification for governor.[31]

Another early committee action was for a plurality requirement for elections. Wilson, in what the *Commonwealth* characterized as one of his best speeches, was opposed. He derided the idea that plurality election would destroy the Free Democratic party. He advocated majority elections because he believed in the principle and because plurality tended to degrade politics by awarding the business of nominations and elections to politicians. Briggs had made the debate more political by observing that farmers had for years swapped oxen at town meetings but of late the practice of "swapping oxen" had been carried into the state House. Wilson retorted that "if people were satisfied with the trade, it did not become the oxen to complain."[32] Keyes disagreed with his fellow Free Democrats concerning majority requirements. In the past fifteen years, he asserted, he had seen too many caucuses and conventions. Let plurality decide the matter at a second election. Keyes declared the coalitionists and Whigs were shifting their positions on the issue. Many of the latter believed they could carry many elections by plurality. They could at least make coalition impractical; the other two parties could never unite for a general election for statewide offices. Democrats were seriously divided on the question. Many believed a plurality rule would kill the Free Democratic party and the Democrats would be the winners. Others feared just the opposite. The debates reveal divisions within all three parties, accounting for the inability of the convention to arrive at an early decision on the issue. The *Commonwealth* predicted the compromise would be to provide for plurality in some elections, majority in others.[33]

Wilson's dislike of pretension and aristocracy revealed itself in his opposition to the titles of "his Excellency" for the governor and "his Honor" for the lieutenant governor. The convention quickly supported him for the latter office. In the same debates, Wilson argued successfully against a change which would make the lieutenant governor presiding officer of the Senate. He contended the Senate needed to have confidence in its own leadership and that a role for the lieutenant governor in the legislature violated the principle of separation of powers. Furthermore, a man selected by the Senate should appoint its committees. Wilson also believed the people wanted the Governor's Council abolished. Hallett and Butler attacked the body, but Wilson was distressed that the conservatives were winning support for retention. If the Council were continued, he declared, its members should be elected by the people, it should be reduced in size from nine to five, and its duties should be limited to examining accounts against the state and reviewing pardon requests. Boutwell, who favored continuing the Council, obtained amendment to the committee's proposal to provide for a smaller body. Its membership would be elected by people of a district, rather than by the legislature.[34]

An argument over oaths threatened to divide coalition partners further. Hallett sought to require elected officials to swear an oath to the American constitution as well as to the state. Since the national government sought to define resistance to the Fugitive Slave Act as treason, this was an important concern. The proposal was defeated.[35]

The majority of delegates were clear on what they wanted to do about the secret ballot. Wilson claimed the people of Massachusetts had enjoyed secrecy until 1839, when, on the grounds that purity of the ballot box required openness, the privilege was changed. When the legislature in 1853 reversed the 1851 secret ballot law, it demonstrated that the voter could be protected only by constitutional guarantees. Wilson saw no inconsistency in the people's voting secretly and the legislative members openly. The latter, as agents, should be held accountable. The people, on the other hand, were sovereign and could do as they chose. He recited a long list of examples in which the people's free vote had been curtailed by intimidation. Before it was over the controversy became personal between Lord and Wilson, with the latter keeping a moderate tone, but knowing when he had a political advantage. After days of debate, the Committee of the Whole on June 10 passed the proposal, 233 to 91. Even Schouler had abandoned his opposition. Shortly thereafter, by a similar majority, the convention forbade payment of taxes as a requirement for suffrage.[36]

By the end of its first month, considering that the General Court had been occupying needed quarters for three weeks and that much organizational time was necessary, the convention had accomplished a great deal. But some of the most difficult issues, including representation in the House and plurality or majority vote for elections, had not been settled. By June 4 the correspondent of the *New York Herald* was reporting the thermometer was above ninety degrees outside and five hundred delegates were packed into a room fit for half that number. Henry L. Dawes wrote on June 19 that the weather was so hot that the convention would be recessed before the week was over. A motion on June 25 to adjourn until September was opposed by Wilson. He complimented the convention for how much it had accomplished in fifty-two days. It had spent more time in deliberations within the same period than any body he could remember. He hoped if it persevered, it could finish in another three weeks.[37]

Progress did not continue as rapidly as before. Both a lengthy argument over House representation and an attention to less fundamental, but controversial, issues bogged down the sessions. In mid-June for most of four weeks the convention turned to representation. The current system permitted Boston, with its forty-four representatives, to elect on a general ticket, assuring that all those chosen would be Whigs. Elsewhere in constituencies in which a candidate did not receive a majority, the town might be unrepresented. The committee proposal, which would have provided for a House of approximately four hundred members, could not obtain enough votes while the minority report, favoring districts, was beaten by a 3-to-1 margin. Eventually Butler formulated a plan more acceptable. As modified by Hallett and Wilson, it stated that all towns with fewer than 1,000 inhabitants would receive six representatives every ten years; those with populations from 1,000 to 4,000 would be allowed one representative; those with more than 4,000 inhabitants would have an additional representative for each additional 4,000 people. Towns could unite and obtain representation every year. Cities would be divided into districts. The coalition remained surprisingly united, with the two Mortons joining the Whigs in opposition. Many of the rural Whigs voted with the coalition. Even after final passage, Morton reopened the question by suggesting several alternatives be sent to the voters.[38]

Wilson's primary speech on the subject was delivered on June 30. Wilson declared his personal preference was for a House of 300 members, based on legal voters, with districts of contiguous territory. The Senate would be based on population, the House on legal voters. He wished Griswold, Boutwell, Dana, and others had favored his plan. He had not pressed his views, however; those who had been assigned the responsibility for presenting this issue should be supported. Since the constitution was going to provide for a mixed system, it should be as fair as possible. If the convention would lower the ratio from 5,000, as Butler wanted, to 4,000, only eight more representatives would be added, with Boston getting six of the eight. If people want a smaller House, they would have to abandon the town representation system. Hallett, Walker, and Stetson supported Wilson, and Hallett got the 4,000 number substituted.[39]

Wilson had strong opinions about the role of the militia. Bird even opposed having one. Wilson was, of course, an advocate. He asserted the constitution framers had been especially careful to differentiate between state and national functions and duties. Providing for a militia was a state responsibility. Van Buren had lost the presidential election in 1840, at least in part, Wilson asserted, because he attempted to centralize federal control over militias. The governor, who had duties at home, would cease to be commander-in-chief when and if the militia were called into federal service. Wilson's states' power position was useful also in making possible a provision which would forbid discrimination on the basis of race in the militia. Whatever United States law provided, Wilson insisted, Massachusetts's volunteer system differed in terms of age and responsibilities of its members, and could also differ on race. Wilson's official biographers valued this stance so highly that they quoted extensively from this speech, while ignoring most others. The controversy provoked three days of spirited debate. Not only Hallett, but Boutwell and Choate also opposed Wilson's position.[40]

Wilson also spoke for limitations on the length of the legislative session. If the constitution required a short time, he argued, the legislature would have to work faster. The committee reported a provision limiting the number of days for which the state would pay legislators. Wilson believed they should instead limit the number of days work. The majority, however, voted for pay for no more than one hundred days.[41]

Inevitably the convention would find difficulty resolving economic issues. Wilson's Whiggery now reemerged. The committee proposed a general incorporation provision in the constitution. Wilson favored this. Special acts often occupied one-third of the time of the legislature, he reported. Once he had seen nine men, all representing the same corporation, seeking privileges at the same time. Wilson would exempt railroads, however. Since railroads had eminent domain, Wilson believed the convention would be unwise to permit any group of men, no matter what their previous activities had been, to have this power. But railroad influence was so strong in the legislature, he had fears about its capacity to react fairly. His solution was exempting railroads from the constitutional provision, and hoping the legislature would itself provide for general incorporation under special legislative guidelines. Wilson won Whig support and got his idea accepted.[42]

Another proposal dealt with limiting the power of the state to grant credit to private corporations. Wilson declared that when Jackson had become president, the likelihood of internal improvements at federal expense had ended and states had been forced to undertake whatever needed being done. In the process Pennsylvania had lost forty million dollars, Illinois and Mississippi had suspended specie payments. This had prompted some states to include provisions in their constitutions forbidding loans. Massachusetts was different, Wilson argued. Its loan of four million dollars to the Western Railroad had generated major benefits to the state. This had cost the taxpayer nothing, for all that had been done was to loan the state's credit. The decisions of other states were therefore irrelevant for Massachusetts. The constitution should not be changed in this area.[43]

Debates during June had become sharper, but in July the length of the session, the heat, and the constant disagreements over principles fostered debates of new intensity and quarrelsomeness. Wilson seldom got involved, but since he had the primary responsibility for moving business along, he often was called upon as a moderator. He did, on occasion, lose his composure. After one lengthy debate on whether to permit American army and navy men and students to vote in Massachusetts, Wilson could not suppress his feelings that the debate had wandered too long. He spoke about differences among "the able and learned gentlemen of the legal profession—I call them learned, because that is the custom in this Convention." He noted how infrequently the lawyers concurred with one another, adding, "nobody expects to find lawyers agreeing unless they are paid for it." During another debate Hillard suggested to Dana that he be mindful of the "hand that fed him." Dana had done little to provoke an attack and his reply earned broad admiration from others present. After one lengthy speech by Hillard, Wilson expressed his amazement at the "exhibition of harsh language, ill-temper, and ill-manners." Called to order by the chair, Wilson continued his address, still highly critical of Hillard, and seeking to defend Alley, Butler, and Dana. Wilson especially attacked Hillard's "lofty airs." He wondered why Hillard attempted to inject so much partisanship into the convention. The other parties had treated Whigs as equals and as gentlemen, Wilson declared; he questioned whether Hillard and some of his associates had been as courteous.[44]

Wilson continued his efforts of his General Court days to democratize Harvard College. Hillard had accused coalition members of rejecting for political reasons Francis Bowen's appointment to the faculty. Wilson avowed he had played a role, characterizing Bowen's article in the *North American Review* as "dishonorable and disgraceful." A month later Wilson launched an effort to make the college responsible to the legislature. The appointment of Bowen after he was rejected by the Board of Overseers demonstrated the convention needed to change the relationship between the college and the state, Wilson contended. He would have the legislature choose corporators for seven-year terms. He could not discover one corporator among the thirty-three appointed during the nineteenth century who had not been Unitarian and either Federalist or Whig. The corporators filled their own vacancies and were unresponsive to the state. The 1852 legislature, with Wilson presiding, under the new law had selected three Whigs, three Free Soilers, and four Democrats to be overseers, a proof of the coalition's fairness. But the legislature in 1853, he noted, first took no action; then the Whigs in caucus nominated ten men, eight of them Whig, none Free Soil. He charged the Boston delegation with a "spirit of partisan and sectarian bigotry, intolerance, and exclusiveness" in their defense of Harvard. He launched another attack against Bowen and the *North American Review*. In the convention were three of the seven corporators, two members of the law faculty, and a number of members of the Board of Overseers. Undaunted, Wilson accused Bowen of plagiarism, misquotations, and falsifications. He got his motion passed, 121 to 28, with 276 delegates not voting. [45]

Throughout June and July Wilson was the master strategist. Even when Adams and his faction growled about him, they were admitting how important Wilson was. Dana credited Wilson as being a successful manager and knowledgeable about voter opinion. He was good natured and had few personal enemies. His opponents trusted his honesty, Dana admitted. In the debates over whether convention members should be paid two dollars a day, as legislators were, or three dollars, Wilson pushed for three and won. Leading Democrats Boutwell, Butler, and Griswold, along with former Democrats Walker and the younger Morton, opposed him. Wilson wanted to pay convention members only for those days they had been in attendance. Briggs argued that to do so would penalize those who came from a distance, for they frequently went home on Saturday and returned on Monday. Wilson took what must have been an unpopular stand, noting the legislature paid members for almost every day, even when not in attendance; he termed that "plunder." In the last five legislatures, he charged, one hundred thousand dollars had been drawn which had not been earned. He had not been home while the convention had been in session and had not been absent a single hour, he announced. During a long debate, Wilson stood his ground, but his proposal was laid on the table, 137 to 44. On July 15, most subjects having been thoroughly discussed, the convention agreed to limit further debate to thirty minutes per speech. By the fifty-ninth day, July 16, a committee was established, including Wilson, to report what time the sessions should be brought to a close. Soon thereafter Banks became ill, and Wilson also assumed the duties of president pro tempore.[46]

The judiciary, which had not even been an issue before the convention, emerged as a major stumbling block to completing work and, as it turned out, to obtaining ratification of the proposed constitution. One controversy occurred over mandatory retirement of judges at age seventy. This was first accepted, later rejected. The Whigs did manage to get the Council, rather than the Senate, as the ratifying body for judicial appointments. A long debate also ensued over the right of juries to interpret the law; this was connected to enforcement of the Fugitive Slave Act. Lawyers Burlingame and Allen were the strongest advocates. This proposal passed, 192 to 45, with most Free Soilers, including Wilson, and Democrats in favor and the Whigs and Dana in opposition. Later the convention by a closer 182-to-153 vote reaffirmed its position. Whether judges would be appointed, and for how long, was the primary controversy. The committee, with former governor Morton as chairman, reported it did not want changes. The convention first voted down a judiciary elected by the people for seven years. That was rejected by a large majority, with Wilson, Allen, Alley, Boutwell, Dana, Hallett, and the Mortons joining the Whigs in the majority. The convention then turned its attention to a middle-ground proposal by Wilson to limit the appointment of future Supreme Court judges to ten years and Court of Pleas judges to seven years. This initially failed by several votes but later was revived and passed.[47]

Wilson's primary speech on the judiciary contended the convention lacked a consensus. Some delegates wanted no change, some wanted election with removal on grounds, others sought election for life, others election for terms. Some wanted appointment with removal for grounds, others appointment for life, others appointment for terms. Wilson was unwilling to imperil the whole constitution by asking for more than what the people would accept. Since the question of an elective judiciary had not been widely discussed during the winter canvass, it should not now be pushed. Five hundred speeches under the auspices of the Free

Democracy had been delivered; the speakers had been cautioned not to urge an elective judiciary. He subsequently was consistent and voted against an elective judiciary. On the other hand, he argued in his address, many people, including judges and lawyers, favored limited terms for judges. The average term of those on the Supreme Court was thirteen years; on lesser courts, six years. He concluded many men did not intend to serve for life, but to make a name for themselves to obtain a more lucrative law practice. With specific terms, he hoped judges would feel more responsible to complete their appointments.[48]

Basic rights were another concern. Dana and other Free Democrats sought to include in the constitution a guarantee of habeas corpus. Hallett saw that as an attempt to circumvent the Fugitive Slave Law. Wilson's reply was simple and effective. Habeas corpus was a basic Anglo-Saxon right, derived from the Magna Charta, he reminded his listeners. He saw no danger to the union in this guarantee. With widespread Whig support, the advocates won their point. The Committee on the Bill of Rights had not reported anything about imprisonment for debt. With the support of Wilson and most Free Democrats and Democrats, as well as many Whigs, this was added, 120 to 45. Oddly, both Bird and Boutwell opposed the proposal.[49]

A proposition to allow women to vote was rejected, 108 to 44. The proposal did elicit lengthy debate. Wilson, who had already spoken on the subject, neither participated in the discussion nor voted. In fairness, he knew the convention would not widen the suffrage in that way and he was one of twenty delegates to attend that day the funeral of Francis R. Gourgas, a convention delegate and personal friend.[50]

Two major subjects remained to be decided. One was plurality or majority vote for election. This was settled, as anticipated in June, by compromise. Governor, lieutenant governor, secretary, treasurer, adjutant general, and auditor would require majority vote at elections. If none of the candidates received that vote, the House would elect two from among those three receiving the most votes, and the Senate would choose one. Senators, councilors, and county offices would be selected by plurality vote. Representative election would require a majority at the first ballot, plurality at the second. City and town offices would also be by plurality. On the convention's final day Wilson introduced a new representation proposal, to be submitted to the people in 1856. It would require the legislature to divide the state into single member senatorial districts and single or double member House districts in 1856 and every ten years thereafter. It passed, 209 to 138.[51]

A revising committee was established, headed by Boutwell, with Dana the principal representative for the Free Democrats. Boutwell termed this the hardest work of his life. They had to take the constitution of 1780, its amendments, and approximately thirty-five changes agreed to by the convention, and weave them into a final form. The convention majority decided to submit the constitution as a whole to the people, with seven separate sections which the voters could individually accept or reject. Then on August 3 the assembly adjourned, after three months of hard work and sometimes bitter debate.[52]

One has little difficulty deciding who was most influential at the convention. Commentators generally agreed that Banks presided effectively, yet he apparently played little role in forging decisions. Among the Whigs, who had so many well-educated and professionally competent men, an absence of leadership appears to have existed. Contemporaries agreed that Choate delivered able speeches. Briggs, the recognized leader, often failed either to forestall coalition plans or to furnish real alternatives to what the majority proposed. Schouler, seeing need for reform, sometimes voted with the coalitionists. Hallett appears to have played an important role during the first month, and then diminished in influence. Griswold was the floor leader of the Democrats and therefore must be credited for the frequency with which the coalition united. Boutwell emerged more favorably in the eyes of commentators than any other man, both for the quality of his work and for his skill in debate. Butler also rose in influence. Morton had prestige but voted too often with the Whigs. Among the Free Democrats, Dana had surprising influence, considering his isolation from the leadership. Sumner made some effective speeches, but apparently was not a leader. Allen was a poor speaker and often absent. Bird and Keyes were among the inner circle, but their usual independence limited their influence.[53]

Wilson was the man who had done more than any other to promote the convention. He had organized to get a coalition majority and was clearly the Free Democrat strategist. Edward Pierce recorded Wilson "had a larger following than any one,—a leadership which was due to his acquaintance with all the Free Soil and Democratic members. . . . He was the one to rally and inspire with a common purpose the allied forces; and a hundred delegates looked to him for the signal to move in any given direction."[54] The *Springfield Republican* contended Wilson was "more powerful in effecting a political purpose than any other man in Massachusetts." The *New Bedford Standard* agreed, characterizing Wilson as "the Napoleon of Massachusetts politics."[55] A *National Era* correspondent that year termed Wilson "wise and conciliatory." No man had contributed more to the convention's activities.[56] Boutwell half a century later remembered Wilson's judgment of popular feeling as "unequalled," but added that Wilson was incapable of preparing specific provisions. Several contemporaries criticized Wilson's effectiveness in debate. The *Commonwealth*, however, reported Wilson, as the usual chairman of the Committee of the Whole, did not often speak, so his participation had to be during the less frequent convention debates. Biographer Jonathan Mann concluded the work of the convention was "more the result of his energetic labor and thought than that of any single mind." He praised his friend's speeches as characterized by "strong common sense, liberal views, force of statement, devotion to popular rights. . . ."[57]

A century later Jean Kenney, in a detailed study of the 1853 convention, concluded that Wilson had "shaped the proceedings." "Most of his influence was exerted in the unrecorded portions of the Convention's proceedings." He analyzed voter response and skillfully framed compromises.[58]

One has to doubt, however, several of David Donald's assertions in his esteemed biography of Sumner about the motivation of the two leaders. For one, Donald claimed Boutwell used the convention to take over the state's Democratic machine. This cannot be true. Morton had lost control permanently and Boutwell knew the Hallett-Greene faction, backed by the new administration in Washington, was in control at least for the next four years. Donald is also incorrect in asserting Wilson was using the convention to force old Conscience Whigs out of the Free Soil party. Wilson's leadership of the party was based on similarity of views with the large majority. The lack of cooperation from the Adams-Palfrey faction weakened the party and harassed Wilson, but did not challenge his leadership.[59]

One also can dispute Frederick Blue's contention in his history of the Free Soil movement that the Democrats and Free Democrats wanted to use the convention, not to reform, but to destroy the Whigs. A coalitionist, undoubtedly a Free Soiler, writing to the *New York Tribune* in January 1853, objecting to that newspaper's charge that convention advocates sought political gains, enumerated four reforms the minority party partners sought. They included changing the system of representation for both the House and the Senate with no at-large districts, reducing the patronage of the governor, substituting general incorporation laws for special grants by the legislature, and requiring secret ballot. The *Commonwealth* ran a series of articles between April 5 and May 13 dealing with the changes it hoped could be produced by the convention. These changes included single districts with election by plurality for the Senate, choice of most statewide officers by the people, alteration of the Council, and reform of the method of selecting judges for life, including election of at least some lower court judges. The most difficult task would be to determine how to apportion seats in the lower house, the newspaper asserted, but a general ticket was unacceptable and changes in the method of determining House representation were necessary. Wilson's official report on what needed to be changed has been noted.[60]

These were not radical or unreasonable suggestions or positions taken simply to weaken the Whig party. Even the most controversial of these goals, election or term appointment for judges, was utilized in other states then and is used today; nor, since judges then in office were exempt from the new provisions, was this an attempt to attack the Whigs. Jacksonian Democracy had already altered government and constitutions elsewhere. For one example, most states by 1853 had general incorporation laws. For another, the trend was nationwide to abandon property qualifications for voting and office holding. Members of all three parties quickly agreed to changes needed for election to the Senate. The secret ballot was needed to protect voters from retribution by their employers and the Whig legislature had just demonstrated the weaknesses of trying to provide protection by law. The plurality-majority requirements for elections were producing chaos and needed revision. The result was a compromise. All parties agreed with senatorial plurality; statewide office requirements remained similar to what they had been, an advantage to Democrats and Free Soilers only in the unlikely event that the coalition could be restored; the decision on House elections was an improvement. One can argue that the compromise arrived at for town representation in the House was political, but few people who today look at the situation then would dispute the need for some reform. The House had too many members and the at-large system in Suffolk County and elsewhere had produced an unrepresentative and undemocratic system. In other words, provisions concerning House representation and the judiciary, among other objections, alienated certain groups and endangered ratification, but except for the method of apportioning the House, these were not aimed primarily at weakening the Whig party.[61]

Dana, who was not happy with the constitution he had helped prepare, predicted the people would ratify it. Leading coalition newspapers—the *Northampton Courier,* the *Commonwealth*, the *Worcester Palladium*, the *Worcester Spy*, the *Salem Freeman*, and the *Springfield Post*—endorsed its actions. The *Courier* looked forward to its adoption by at least a 25,000-vote majority, the *Commonwealth* by 20,000. The Whig *Boston Transcript* charged the convention was an "experiment" which "failed." It compared the assemblage to that of 1777–1778, whose work was rejected by the people. It had met three times too long and cost three times too much. The *Commonwealth* countered that the Whigs had purposely prolonged the meetings. Knowing the people were opposed, they had converted to the district system for representation, to defeat the document. Wilson's final representation proposal had confused them and allowed the people to make their own decision.[62]

Wilson labored in August on a speech, which he delivered to his Natick constituents, advocating ratification of the new constitution. He and Carter then perfected the address for pamphlet publication. It was endorsed by the Free Democratic State Committee and given wide circulation in Free Soil newspapers. The *Courier* called it "an admirable speech." The *Boston Times* reported it had "never read a production entitled to more praise," calling the work "a complete and reliable history" of the convention. The *Commonwealth* said if people truly wanted to understand the constitution, this was the document to read. By September 10 it reported the second edition of the pamphlet was nearly exhausted; 10,000 copies had been requested within the past two days. Even Everett, the new Whig senator, was impressed. He recorded he read the Wilson speech and discovered the convention proposals were less radical than he had been led to believe; the Whigs would be unwise to reject them, Everett concluded.[63]

Much of the sixteen-page pamphlet was an explanation of what the convention had done. Wilson praised the participants' abilities, courtesy, and good temper.

They had worked with great industry in the heat of summer, often meeting eight or nine hours a day. He defended the convention's length, pointing out the limitations placed on speakers and the frequent use of the previous question to move business along. The convention lasted fifteen days more than he had expected, but it had exceeded anticipated costs by only a few dollars. The new limits on payments to the legislature would recover that money in five years. One by one, he discussed the major changes in the proposed document. Naturally, the most consideration was given to House representation. The evils of the present system, he declared, had contributed more to the call for a convention than any other factor. Now 138 towns were unrepresented, large towns were gaining power. Yet people were wedded to the town system. About twenty propositions had been suggested. A district system was easily voted down. The proposal accepted passed by an almost two-to-one majority. His last-minute suggestion permitted those who yet favored a district system to vote for that and anticipate legislative action.[64]

The State Committee chairman was occupied with more than writing his pamphlet. On August 24 he returned to Wolfboro, New Hampshire, where he had formerly taught school, to participate in the state Free Soil convention. He also began to line up speakers for the fall campaign. He was anxious to have better newspaper support. He wanted Carter to take over the editorship of the *Commonwealth*, which he characterized as too respectable and unwilling to fight.[65]

Whig newspapers in August launched an attack against Wilson personally. They had concluded he would be the Free Soil nominee for governor. The Boston correspondent of the Whig *New York Tribune* reported Wilson had extensive government experience, had risen to brigadier general in the militia, and had been the leading tactician of the majority in the convention. Governor Clifford was increasingly unpopular, the correspondent wrote, and if the Whigs wanted to defeat Wilson, they would have to nominate a candidate hostile to the Maine liquor law. Both the *Northampton Courier* and the *Greenfield Republic* were pushing Wilson's nomination.[66]

Opposition to the constitution seemed muted at first. Adams sought to distance himself from general Free Soil activities. On August 6 he resigned from the State Committee, citing the press of business affairs, but anticipating he could return in another year. He must have changed his mind, for a month later Carter was seeking his endorsement, along with that of other committee members, to Wilson's pamphlet. Adams recorded in his diary on September 12 that neither he nor Palfrey had examined the proposals much and he had not yet made up his mind whether he favored them or not. On September 7 Adams was elected a delegate to the Free Democratic state convention, but he was determined not to participate. He would not help make Wilson governor, he wrote. When he learned he was expected to speak at the state convention, he angrily refused. Adams's and Palfrey's names were then removed from the call.[67]

The Whigs seemed to lack the energy or will to organize against the constitution. The *Atlas* attacked Wilson's speech for its "inconsistency" on the abolition of property qualifications for voting in state and national elections, but not on local issues. This was simply a misrepresentation. The *Boston Transcript* charged the constitution contained inconsistencies, citing secret ballot requirements for some elections, not for others, and provisions for majority support for election to some offices, plurality for others. This type of attack was unlikely to endanger ratification. What they needed to fight ratification, Choate was reported to have said with a smile during the convention, was $500,000.[68]

The Free Democrats assembled in Fitchburg on September 15. Wilson called the assembly to order and was subsequently one of the featured speakers. About seven hundred delegates attended. The *New York Tribune* reporter wrote he had expected to see an "unhealthy organization," for that is how Democrats and Whigs had been characterizing the Free Soilers. Instead, he was impressed with the enthusiasm; "they look as if they can't be stopped." Wilson, whom Edward Pierce characterized as "the acknowledged leader of his party in the State," was nominated for governor, receiving 610 out of the 615 ballots cast. Walker was selected for lieutenant governor. The *Northampton Courier* reported the reception of Wilson's nomination "was a perfect whirl of enthusiasm." Mann was about to leave for Ohio to become president of Antioch College and thus harbored no ill will about being replaced. In his departing speech, the educator paid a warm compliment to the new candidate. The Free Soil platform, presented by Bird, attacked the Fugitive Slave Law, dedicated the party to ending the influence of the Slave Power in the national government, and protested against efforts of Southerners to secure a transcontinental railroad built from the South. The platform's state components included reforms primarily found within the proposed constitution.[69]

The alcoholic's son, the indentured, poorly educated, New Hampshire backcountry teenager, the Natick cobbler, the rebel against proper Whig leadership, was nominated for his state's highest office. Historians have so frequently quoted from the papers of Adams and Palfrey, one can get a wrong impression of the response to Wilson's selection. It had not been obtained by some clever tactics against the wishes of the majority of the party. Not only was the choice almost unanimous, but the state committee was dominated by men affiliated with the Wilson wing of the party, including Keyes, Spooner, Carter, Swan, Stone, Alley, Walker, Alvord, and Claflin. One would expect the Free Democratic press to praise the party's nominee; they were working for votes. Yet what the press said still reveals much concerning contemporaries' opinions about Wilson. The *Greylock Sentinel* emphasized the nomination was a testimony to Wilson's character; no management had been needed to secure it. It contrasted 1848 with 1853, noting elections of Free Soilers and men acceptable to Free Soil principles at the state and national level, and credited Wilson, more than any other man, as responsible for this. The *Commonwealth* editorialized no other man had done so much for the party. It praised Wilson's work as state party chairman, his "unswerving devotion to the cause of human rights," and his "integrity, ability, and force of character." The *Dedham Gazette* mentioned the "universal respect and admiration for the man." Garrison's *Liberator* contended "no more popular nominations could have been made."[70]

Other party presses joined the praise, sometimes obliquely. The editor of the Whig *Newburyport Herald* praised Wilson's service during the convention. He was "honorable and high-minded," a man of "foresight, shrewdness and energy." The Democratic *Newburyport Union* noted how Wilson had "slowly won his way into the affections and confidence of the community." He ranked high for "general information, for oratory, for statesmanship, and for political ability." The editor of the Democratic *Haverhill Banner*, claiming he had known Wilson since 1840, praised the Free Democrat's consistency in his opposition to slavery and his honesty. The independent *Boston Sunday News* predicted a Wilson victory. The Democratic *Boston Times* said Free Soilers owed so much to Wilson for his zeal and labors, they would have to repay him by bringing out the votes.[71]

In a tribute to one of his party's leading politicians, Gamaliel Bailey in the Washington *National Era* presented a history of Wilson's career. Bailey concluded that few men were better known in Massachusetts. He commented on the constant abuse the Whigs directed towards Wilson, despising him both because he was a shoemaker who had attained high honors and because he had overthrown Whig control of Massachusetts. Wilson was "one of the most honest, energetic, and industrious men in the State," Bailey reported. His speeches were increasingly exhibiting ability, with his Natick address on the constitution, his speech on Harvard at the convention, and his defense of the coalition in 1852 generating special praise. Wilson this early in his career had probably delivered more political addresses than any man in the state. His speaking was characterized as "direct and forcible, oftentimes very effective." He excelled as a debater.[72]

The Democrats met in Worcester and as expected, with little opposition, nominated Judge Bishop of Lenox, a man likely to unite the party. A few bolting Hunker Democrats would not go along. The Whigs had more trouble finding a candidate. For once, Wilson's prediction was wrong. He thought Lawrence would be selected. He shuddered at the money that nomination would guarantee to the Whig campaign, but he nevertheless regarded Lawrence as more beatable than someone less well known and he knew how objectionable Lawrence was to Democrats. By custom the Whigs were obligated to renominate Clifford. The man's unpopularity, however, was widely discussed in the press and he rather ingloriously withdrew from consideration. When some of the more obvious leaders refused to run, the convention turned to Emory Washburn of Worcester, a temperance advocate, but opposed to the liquor law. Traveling in Europe until just before the election, he could make no unwise remarks on the alcohol question. Washburn had sustained Scott in 1852. He had denounced the convention. He was a more formidable opponent for Wilson than Clifford would have been. The Whig platform called for defeat of the proposed constitution and instead advocated amendments, to be proposed by the legislature, for plurality elections, single member Senate districts, reduction in the size of the House, and a district system for House representation.[73]

The nominee for governor traditionally did not participate in the political campaign. He could not even address audiences in other states, Wilson wrote E. A. Stansbury, the Vermont Free Soil leader. He did agree to visit Vermont for a week and work behind the scenes; Massachusetts Free Democrats would send young John L. Swift as speaker. Wilson, however, could help organize the campaign in Massachusetts. Even before the end of September Sumner had been engaged for twelve addresses, Burlingame for thirty. Democrats Banks and Boutwell were scheduled for every night, except Sunday, between October 1 and the election.[74]

Wilson could devise some opportunities for public appearances. On October 13 in Boston's Tremont Temple primarily Free Democrats commemorated Hale's labors to promote the abolition of the lash in the navy. Dana was the principal speaker, but Wilson was made president of the meeting and delivered a short address, confining himself to the subject of the lash and the navy. A week later, however, he was not present at the Faneuil Hall Free Democratic rally. In fact, throughout October the party paper included surprisingly little election news, with Wilson's name barely mentioned. Wilson also participated on November 2 in the festival of the Sons of New Hampshire with other residents of Boston and the vicinity. A procession of fifteen hundred to two thousand men marched to the Grand Hall of the Fitchburg Railroad depot for a dinner, with Wilson one of those responding to toasts. On October 31 Wilson also contributed a long letter to Bird, as chairman of the State Committee, with another history of constitutional reform.[75]

With four candidates for governor in the field and with a confusing variety of issues, analysts generally agreed Wilson might receive a plurality of votes. Free Democrats were entitled to their turn at the governorship. Bolting Democrats, primarily anxious to obtain spoils from Washington, were expected to attract only several thousand voters. The influence of prohibition was difficult to measure. Clearly both Democratic candidates opposed the law, Wilson favored it, and the Whigs were obscuring their position. The proposed Hoosac Tunnel, the money for which was to be loaned by the state, wanted by many living in the northern—particularly the northwestern—part of Massachusetts, might also affect election results. Wilson in 1851 in the Senate had voted in favor of a two million dollar loan. Furthermore, during the convention he had opposed efforts to limit the credit of the state, supporting Hoosac Tunnel advocates.[76]

The Whig *Advertiser* and Free Democratic *Commonwealth* agreed in the beginning of October that the important issue was the constitution, not the governorship. "If Wilson would be elected Governor, he could be turned out at a subsequent election," the *Advertiser* asserted, "but the Constitution would affect the state for years." Acceptance of the constitution would also give the coalition renewed life, the *Advertiser* declared. George T. Curtis published a series of articles in the *Boston Courier* to counterbalance the pamphlet of Wilson. Abbott Lawrence vigorously opposed the document. "Essex," the *New York Post* correspondent, reported even the amendments everyone thought a good idea were being condemned by the Whig press. But most newspapers concluded in September that the public simply was not excited about the issue.[77]

The Free Democratic speakers list was considerably different from those of previous campaigns. Burlingame spoke more often than anyone else and Sumner played a major role. Because of his prominence at the convention, Dana was also an important contributor. Younger Free Soilers, like Swift and Webb, were now taking over. But S. C. Phillips went to Montreal during the fall and Adams and Palfrey declined speaking. Campaigns themselves had changed, as the patrician Everett bemoaned in his diary. Earlier in his political life each party met in caucus, usually in Boston, shortly before the election. But state conventions now were held, followed by ratification conclaves, then by countless meetings addressed by "itinerant speakers throughout the state." This had thrown political power more and more into the hands of the young and able-bodied, and, he might have added, those interested enough to devote their time and energy to the campaign.[78]

What were the expected results of the election? Writing in the 1880s, Sumner's biographer and friend, E. L. Pierce, provided an accurate analysis of the 1853 campaign. He termed it a "vigorous canvass." Until just before the vote, Pierce claimed, most supporters expected the constitution to be adopted. Most analysts also anticipated the coalition would carry the legislature and assure Wilson's selection as governor. The Whigs had reconciled themselves to the constitution when the attacks upon it by Palfrey and Adams renewed their spirits. Adams, in early October 1853, agreed. Free Soilers were full of energy and expecting victory, he recorded. Whigs were divided. Robinson, the *New York Post's* Boston correspondent, on October 24 reported how energetic those who favored the constitution were. The *Times* and *Commonwealth* were giving notices of more than one hundred meetings while the *Atlas* listed only three for the Whigs. Free Soil and Democratic audiences had been larger than ever, Robinson declared. He did note that Whig money was at work.[79]

As the date of the election approached coalition was evoked in some of the counties. At meetings on October 31 Free Soilers and Democrats agreed to three Senate candidates from each party in Wilson's home of Middlesex County. The Free Soil *Northampton Courier* went out of its way to praise Hallett's defense of the proposed constitution. The *Commonwealth* predicted adoption of the document by between 5,000 and 20,000 votes. Coalitionists would remain loyal and liberal Whigs would support them. Wilson would obtain 40,000 votes for governor, Bishop an equal number, Washburn 50,000, and Hunker Democrat E. L. Wales 5,000. That would be a 20,000 coalition majority. The Democratic *New York Post's*

Boston correspondent predicted a 15,000- to 20,000-vote majority for the constitution, with the coalition carrying the legislature and selecting a Democratic governor.[80]

The political scene altered, however, with surprising speed. An embittered Palfrey resolved to break publicly with those with whom he had so long fought against slavery, and to attack the constitution in print. By October 8 Palfrey had a pamphlet written. The *Commonwealth* on October 18 denied the truth of Whig newspaper reports that Palfrey and others were against the constitution, a strange position for the paper to take if its editors expected soon to be proved wrong. A week later the publication was out, signed "A Free Soiler from the Start." The *Commonwealth* derided Whig reports that it was Palfrey's work. Palfrey, it maintained, would "be ashamed" to write an essay of so "poor logic and misrepresented fact." It must have been authored by a Whig in disguise. A day later the paper insisted, after close examination, that a Free Soiler could not have made these arguments. The writer was just rehashing Whig views, was illogical and inconclusive, and without sympathy for the people. Palfrey would not publish anonymously, the *Commonwealth* declared. Neither would Palfrey attack his friends. Wilson, for example, had worked diligently for Palfrey when the Whigs had discarded him. The pamphlet was Palfrey's, however. Biographer Frank Gatell labels Palfrey a conservative Whig in all except his antislavery views.[81]

Gatell has concluded that Palfrey's primary objective in writing was to injure Wilson. Palfrey had been unable or unwilling to compromise and to adjust to the world of 1853. Unable to understand political and social reality, Palfrey sought a scapegoat. Wilson had no acceptable family background by the standards of Palfrey's circle. He was welcome as an ally as long as he followed others. But Palfrey had lost reelection to Congress, the governorship, a convention seat, and an influential role in the inner circle of the party. Rather than recognize these failures might have resulted from his own insufficiencies, Palfrey decided that Wilson had been out to block him. In fact, Gatell concluded, Palfrey's problem was his own lack of political skills.[82] Wilson's abortive efforts to get Dana into the convention might be viewed as cunning. Wilson, however, understood politics far better than Palfrey or Adams. His cooperation with Dana demonstrated that he could employ the abilities of an able conservative to produce a better constitution and could then persuade Dana to speak for the proposed document. Wilson was wise enough to understand that getting a constitution framed and ratified was more likely with Palfrey's support.

Not published until the last week of October, Palfrey's pamphlet might have appeared too late to influence the voters. Yet it became a determining factor in the defeat of the constitution. Whigs boasted they circulated between eighteen and twenty thousand copies. When the second edition identified Palfrey as the author, the *Commonwealth* professed it had been sincere in its doubts; it thought it knew Palfrey better. "Essex" in the *New York Post* asserted Palfrey, who had expressed little unhappiness with constitutional proposals while they were being drawn up, was only attacking the document because he wanted to harm Wilson.[83]

Adams, in contrast, vacillated in his opinion concerning the merits of the constitution. Nevertheless, he had developed an intense antipathy to Wilson which affected his judgment concerning ratification. By the end of October Adams was getting invitations to speak on the issue which he invariably declined, unwilling to set himself against his friends, he recorded. The *Commonwealth* on October 20 insisted there was "not the slightest authority" for Whig statements that Adams would come out against the constitution. But on November 5 Adams broke his resolution and spoke to more than four hundred of his Quincy townspeople. He argued the constitution had neither coherence nor consistency. None of the proposed changes were well carried out. Adams recorded the papers gave more "fire" to his speech than he had employed. One address was all the Whigs needed. It was widely circulated.[84]

The Democratic contribution to the coalition was also in jeopardy. Former governor Morton early announced his opposition and denounced the document in a series of speeches. The *Boston Pilot* urged all Catholics to oppose the constitution. The objective of the document was to bring Free Soil rule to Massachusetts, it declared. The crowning blow came when President Pierce's Attorney General Cushing on October 31 dispatched a letter to Massachusetts Democrats, threatening to destroy, through use of national patronage, all those who cooperated with the Free Democrats. Cushing noted coalition had been agreed to in several counties and accused the participants of committing "a fatal error." They had "abandoned principle." The president was immovable on the point, Cushing wrote. Abolitionism had to be "crushed out." No other policy was acceptable for the welfare of the country, the integrity of the constitution, and the permanency of the union. Happy Whigs recognized the difficulties the Cushing letter had created for Massachusetts Democrats. Charles C. Hazewell, editor of the Democratic *Boston Times,* was a coalition candidate for senator in Middlesex County; Knowlton, editor of the *Palladium,* had recently been appointed postmaster of Worcester. The *New York Post* declared 90 percent of Democratic appointees in the state were coalitionists.[85]

The coalitionists would not capitulate. Carter was dispatched to visit towns in Middlesex County to persuade Democratic friends of the constitution to join in coalition efforts. Democrats and Free Soilers agreed to joint senatorial nominations for Berkshire, Essex, Franklin, and Worcester Counties and expected them in others. The *Commonwealth* compared Cushing's letter to czarism. Coalition Democrats denounced Cushing's interference in their state affairs. One predicted the letter would hurt Bishop, alienating so many that Wilson would attract fifty to sixty thousand voters. The Essex County Democratic Committee, of Cushing's home region, charged the Attorney General with committing a "fatal error," and urged Democrats to support the constitution and the coalition ticket. At the last minute Hallett, with Cushing's permission, placed a notice in the newspapers, stating the national administration's opposition to the coalition had no reference to the constitution. Robinson contended the Free Soil organization had been "almost perfect." No party in the state had ever had an organization equal to this one.[86]

But the political contest had been invigorated. Samuel Lawrence, brother of Abbott, ran the Whig campaign and money poured in. Hillard was redeeming himself, the hardest Whig worker. The *Advertiser* claimed Dana and Allen were both opposed to the constitution, although both were speaking in its favor. Only E. R. Hoar, among Free Soil leaders, joined Adams and Palfrey in open opposition. During the final week the Whigs scheduled more meetings than either the Democrats or Free Soilers. The Cushing letter did win some votes for Wales. But the analysis of the Boston correspondent of the *New York Post* on the eve of the election was that the constitution would still be carried by between an eight- and twelve-thousand-vote majority. The *Commonwealth* pronounced the constitution "secure beyond every contingency."[87]

The results on the constitution on November 15 were close, but definitive. It was rejected by five thousand votes. All of the seven separate amendments also failed, the one prohibiting use of the school fund for sectarian schools going down by only 150 votes. Suffolk County was two to one in opposition; 22 percent more voters turned out than had in the spring election for delegates. As expected, the constitution was heavily supported in Worcester and by lesser majorities in some of the western counties, but it lost in seven of the state's fourteen counties, including Middlesex. Kevin Sweeney has estimated 93 percent of Free Soilers supported the constitution, demonstrating how little influence Palfrey, Adams, and Hoar had had. But four percent of coalition Democrats and 71 percent of Hunker Democrats opposed ratification. Dale Baum, in his study of Massachusetts voting, has a similar Whig figure. He also asserted 5 percent of the Democrats who supported Pierce in 1852 stayed home in this election. Large Whig opposition was the most important influence.[88]

Those writing editorials for the *New York Post* and the *Commonwealth* were mystified as to why a majority of the participants had voted against their own best interests. The constitution was not a perfect document, but, with such guarantees as the secret ballot, Senate districts, and the ten-hour law, it was an improvement, these advocates believed. Rejection left Massachusetts where it had been: to be run by a minority for the benefit of the wealthy in Boston. Sumner's explanation to Adams for his support of the document makes sense: it was an improvement over the current system and it would break the back of the Boston oligarchy.[89]

Contemporaries had different opinions concerning the relative influence of factors affecting the results. Sumner believed three actions brought about defeat: the defection of Adams and Palfrey, encouraging the Whigs and neutralizing some coalitionists; Cushing's letter, paralyzing Democratic workers; and the "positive intervention of the Catholic church." Without any one of those, the constitution would have been accepted, he concluded. The *New York Post* and the *Dedham*

Gazette agreed. Some other commentators would add the wide use of Whig money. Everett belittled the importance of the Cushing letter, except in that it incited the Free Democrats. Adams, in contrast, thought it was a major factor. He also thought he himself had played an important role. The Boston correspondent of the *New York Tribune* estimated Cushing's letter had cost five thousand votes for the constitution. The *Northampton Courier* contended that, if not for the appearance of Palfrey's letter, the constitution would have been accepted by a ten-thousand-vote majority. The *Commonwealth* declared the constitution would have been ratified had the vote been held on November 1, before the Whigs organized and before the effects of the Cushing letter and Palfrey pamphlet were felt.[90]

Certainly the Catholic vote played a role. The Boston correspondent of the *New York Tribune* said Orestes Brownson and the publishers of the *Boston Pilot* wanted the city to retain its at-large district, for they expected the Catholics would soon dominate the election rolls. The *Commonwealth* agreed. It later denied Whig and Catholic leaders had reached a bargain. But it did insist the two consulted and sought the same end, defeat of the document. This was the first time in Massachusetts history the Catholic Church had actively entered politics, the *Commonwealth* reported. The *Dedham Gazette* said, take away the Catholic vote and the constitution would have been adopted. *The Liberator* drew a similar conclusion. Butler emphasized the Catholic objection to the provision forbidding use of state funds for religious schools.[91]

From an issue point of view, Joshua Leavitt blamed representational inequality among towns. Theodore Parker agreed. James Schouler, writing in 1903, discounted the judiciary as an issue and also emphasized representation. Others have insisted the provisions dealing with the judiciary brought out the opposition.[92]

Wilson in an unsigned letter to the *National Era* agreed with his Free Soil contemporaries. Interestingly, editor Gamaliel Bailey noted he omitted several personal allusions from Wilson's letter; he would use "proper reserve" toward "differing friends." The Whigs were the largest group to oppose the constitution, Wilson declared. He estimated only 5,000 out of 60,000 Whigs voted for its ratification. Even reform Whigs convinced themselves they could bring about needed changes by acts of the legislature or amendment. Money and organization were used with effect. Hunker Democrats were the next group to join in opposition, Wilson continued. They contributed another 5,000 votes. Liquor interests also "took out" after the document. They wanted to maintain the solid bloc of representatives from Suffolk County. The Catholics and their spokespaper *The Pilot* assailed the proposal. Like Butler, Wilson pointed out that the section dealing with sectarian schools particularly offended them. The strength of this resistance surprised constitution proponents. All of this, Wilson claimed, could not have defeated the document. Then Palfrey came to their aid and Whigs printed and distributed his pamphlet widely. Next Adams joined, an opposition not "unexpected." Finally came the Cushing letter, which "paralyzed" a portion of the

Democratic party. Active Democrats stopped their labors, Democratic presses refused to print coalition tickets.[93]

In the succeeding half decade a number of the issues dealt with in the constitution were subsequently enacted, after the Whigs had been driven from power. Amendments provided for plurality election for state officers; fixed the state election day to be the same as the national; provided for election of secretary of state, treasurer, auditor, and attorney general by the people; forbade spending of public money on sectarian schools; gave the people the responsibility of electing sheriffs, probate registers, clerks of courts, and district attorneys; changed the Senate representation basis from the amount of taxes paid to the number of voters; established the maximum size of House at 240 members and the Senate at 40; and designated the legislature to apportion representation among the counties according to their number of legal voters.[94]

Not all Free Democrats were unhappy. Palfrey confided he had rarely felt better than when he heard of the election results. Adams also was pleased; the coalition was dead. He was relieved the *Commonwealth* treated him "gently" for his stand against the constitution. On the other hand, he withdrew his subscription to the *Lowell American*, provoked that Robinson had attacked him and claiming the newspaper no longer took an antislavery stand. Whittier was willing to see the coalition end so that the Free Democratic party could again turn its full attention to slavery.[95]

Adams characterized the Whigs as arrogant in their enjoyment of the defeat of the constitution. Pierce wrote that the victors spit most of their "venom" on Wilson. Accustomed to hard looks, he now encountered more than he could take and for some weeks he went by "unfrequented streets." The *Boston Advertiser* had gleefully reported election results, "Henry Wilson is no where"; he had received fewer votes than Bishop. A correspondent of Sumner's expressed his pity. "The Whigs are taunting, sneering, and leveling all their envenomed shafts at him. . . . It seems to me as if all the honors he has received would not compensate this one defeat and humiliation." By mid-December the *Commonwealth* could ignore the attacks no longer. It spoke of the "spite" Whig leaders were manifesting towards Wilson. Since the November 14 election they had shown "more ill-manners, more intolerance, more insolence, and more meanness toward their opponents than any party has ever manifested at any election in our country." The largest share of "their vile abuse" had been directed towards Wilson.[96]

The coalition, according to a *New York Tribune* reporter, was now prostrate, its leaders and presses stunned. Robinson told *New York Post* readers that the Free Soil party was disheartened and the Democratic party now "good for nothing." This was not an accurate analysis of the Democratic position. The Cushing letter and election results had combined to weaken the Banks-Boutwell wing of the party and throw control to the Boston clique. While the latter was dependent upon the Catholic vote to stay in power, its purpose for being was to protect not Catholic interests, but patronage. The *Commonwealth* at least was trying to sound optimistic, admitting the Whigs had been returned to power and the coalition was "vanquished." But reform was not over, it insisted.[97]

The election defeat was more decisive than the numbers should have produced. Pierce wrote that the party was disheartened and its adherents began to desert. Wilson was the saddest of all; he "enjoyed political position for its excitement." He was "far from being a self-seeker, loving his party as few have loved it, and ready to make sacrifices for it." He was angry at Palfrey and Adams. The party was not dead, however. When the State Committee assembled on December 1, with Wilson among those present, discussion was "lively." The *Commonwealth* tried to convince its readers that the leaders were "unanimous and enthusiastic" in carrying on the antislavery work for which the party had been formed. It promised they were already planning for the 1854 campaign.[98]

10

The Kansas-Nebraska Bill and the Know Nothings

Whatever the defeat of the constitution, the collapse of the coalition, and the Whig electoral victory meant for the future of the Free Democratic party and the antislavery political movement in Massachusetts, the results of the 1853 fall elections meant that Wilson no longer had a means of support. He would have to evaluate his own life and his role in the party. Wilson had obtained his livelihood, often poorly, as publisher and politician since he had abandoned his shoe business. He could not and did not want again to depend upon a newspaper. He was one of the most well known men in the state and still had a political future, but at the moment he could not sustain himself and his family with income from party or office. So Wilson returned to the shoe business. The boot and shoe industry by the 1850s had become the most important manufacturing enterprise in the state, exceeding cotton textiles in value by eight million dollars and only somewhat behind the combined cotton and woolen industries. Natick had come to specialize in brogans; except for binding and stitching done by women at home, most work was now accomplished in the central shop. Wilson began his new venture in January of 1854 and continued for more than a year, until April of 1855, when politics again occupied too much of his time. He employed twenty-eight workers who produced 23,000 pairs of shoes in 1854. That was half of what he was fabricating in the mid-1840s. Before he gave up the business in 1855, he produced 8,000 pairs.[1]

For some reason the Wilsons in 1852 decided their home of ten years was inadequate. In 1852 they purchased for $1,000 a lot, approximately 120 feet by 62 feet, almost across West Central Street from where they lived. This was sold almost immediately to Walcott, and then repurchased a few months later for $500. This time a home was built, still standing, where the Wilsons would live the remainder of their lives. It was a two-story structure with bay windows and no entrance on the street side. A porch faced east, providing the main entrance from a walk or a yard carriage stop. It had two chimneys, wooden brackets supporting the roof, and shutters for all of the windows. The 1855 state census establishes that Henry's parents sometime during the previous five years had joined their four sons as Natick residents.[2]

Natick in the mid-1850s was developing into a modern community. During the decade its population doubled to 5,500. Natick Center, along the railroad, in 1856 consisted of 275 homes, 65 shops, 4 churches, 6 stores, 2 markets, 2 drug stores, and even a hotel. Felchville, a mile away, had 55 homes and 20 shops. South Natick included 65 homes, 2 stores, and a meetinghouse. By 1855 the town had seven school districts, the buildings constructed at a cost of $40,000, and had had a high school for three years. Property values in 1857 exceeded two million dollars. The Congregational Church, which Wilson attended, erected a new building in 1853–1854. The Universalists took over the old meetinghouse; Baptists also joined the community in 1852, which, with Methodists and Unitarians, brought the total number of church denominations to five.[3]

Wilson continued to be a close friend of the town's Congregational pastors. During Samuel Hunt's tenure Wilson for several years taught sabbath school. Hunt left Natick in 1850. At his departure party Wilson, although not a member of the congregation, was chosen to deliver the speech and present a watch as a token of remembrance. Hunt was succeeded in 1852 by Elias Nason, who would stay until 1858 and who would later become one of Wilson's biographers. Nason was born the same year as Wilson. A native of Massachusetts, he had lived four years in Georgia, where he had become well acquainted with slavery. He had been an editor, a lecturer, and, for ten years, a schoolteacher. Natick was his first parish. Nason not only presided over the construction of the new church structure, he also added 120 new members to the congregation. Among them, shortly after his arrival, was Harriet Wilson. Able to read twelve languages and a skilled musician, Nason would publish thirty-nine books and pamphlets and would serve as editor of the *New England Historical and Genealogical Register.* Like Hunt he would have an important influence on Wilson.[4]

The Whigs had hardly begun to enjoy their November victory when they were beaten in the Boston municipal election by the Citizens party, controlled by Free Democrats, and in Lawrence by a coalition majority. The Boston vote was the largest ever cast in a mayoral election. That may have tempered the Whigs' legislative plans. Whig newspapers in December were calling on Sumner to resign, contending, as a result of the defeat of the coalition, he lacked a constituency. Some papers also advocated the legislature instruct its senator and when he failed to vote as instructed, to demand his resignation. Wilson declared the legislature would not he so foolish. He wondered what it could instruct Sumner about that would not hurt the Whig party. With the retirement of Hale, only Chase and Sumner remained as Free Democratic senators in Washington. Embarrassed by the publicity given to the failure to appoint Free Soilers to committees in the 1852–1853 session, the two major parties considered each designating committee appointments assigned to them for Chase and Sumner. Chase received two minor assignments from the Democrats, but Everett prevented the Whigs from selecting Sumner for anything. Wilson called Everett's conduct "mean and pitiful." In Massachusetts the Whigs proceeded more cautiously. The legislature met from January 4 until the end of April, passed 454 acts and 86 resolves, few of them, except for an initial appropriation for the Hoosac Tunnel, of consequence. They did attempt to fulfill their fall campaign rhetoric by beginning the process of constitutional reform. They passed amendments to fix a Senate of forty members selected in districts; provide for annual election of secretary of state, treasurer, receiver general, auditor, and attorney general; and establish plurality election for town, city, and county officers.[5]

The Free Democratic cause was in better shape in some other states than it was in Massachusetts. After the 1852 Hale loss, the party, particularly in the West, rebounded quickly. The Whigs in that section of the country had been so badly beaten, the party collapsed. In 1853 in Ohio the Free Soil candidate for governor attracted 50,000 more voters than Hale had in 1850, while the Whig nominee received the smallest vote since the party had been organized in the state. In both Michigan and Wisconsin, Free Democrats made major gains. In Wisconsin and Ohio, with cooperation with the Democrats impossible and with the Whigs in a weakened condition, coalition with the Whigs or party reorganization was more likely in 1854. Temperance, for which Free Soil candidates generally stood, was helping break down the old party system.[6]

National events revitalized the Free Democratic movement in both Massachusetts and the nation. Stephen A. Douglas, chairman of the Senate Committee on the Territories and machinator of the Compromise of 1850, was already dissatisfied with the Pierce administration when Congress met for the first time under the new president in December of 1853. As one of Congress's acknowledged advocates of rapid western development and as a champion of the Northwest, Douglas decided to take greater leadership, particularly on the intermingled issues of organizing all or part of the Unorganized Territory (most of the Louisiana Purchase, which had not yet been admitted to statehood) and of getting a transcontinental railroad built through a northerly route. These were concerns important to the future development of the nation and especially vital to the growth of Douglas's own Illinois.

For years many members of Congress had sought to get the unorganized territory west of Iowa, Missouri, and the Minnesota Territory opened for settlement. Missouri had come into the union more than thirty years before; western farmers, who for a quarter of a century had been occupying the lands along the Mississippi River, were itching to move on to the good soil just across the Missouri and Iowa borders. Many other Americans were also eager to get the area organized in hopes that territorial status would be followed by construction of a railroad. Douglas himself had invested heavily in real estate in Chicago and Superior City, Michigan, two possible termini of western railroads.

Efforts to secure passage of a railroad bill had floundered in preceding Congresses over disagreements as to where the road should be built. If Douglas were to get a bill passed to organize the area, he would have to attract votes from previous opponents in the South and East, while at the same time not alienating westerners who had long advocated opening up the territory. He needed the support of the Senate establishment, dominated by Southerners, and at least the neutrality of the Pierce administration. What could induce Southerners to vote for an organization bill if it both weakened their arguments for a Southern-built railroad and guaranteed, as the Missouri Compromise had affirmed, the territories would exclude slavery? Douglas, to get the votes he needed, introduced legislation in January of 1854 to organize the whole area north of the Indian Territory (Oklahoma) and with language taken from the Compromise of 1850 about slavery and statehood. The bill evaded the issue of slavery in the territory. When Southerners responded negatively, Douglas reframed his proposal to divide the territory into two parts and specifically repeal those provisions of the Missouri Compromise which forbade slavery in territories of the Louisiana Purchase north of 36' 30".

Those who opposed opening up these territories to local decisions about slavery had known about Douglas's plans. Senators Sumner and Chase and four antislavery House members, as six "Independent Democrats," published in late January in Washington's *National Era* a potent attack on the proposal. Douglas was an effective and able battler, dominating Senate debate for the next two months and turning himself into perhaps the most well-known politician in the nation. By early March he had driven through the bill over some of the strongest opposition ever displayed in the nation's capital. The House proved even more difficult for advocates of the proposal, but it agreed also, by a 113-to-100 vote, on May 21.

Historians have disagreed whether those opposed to the expansion of slavery into the territories were alert to the ramifications of the Douglas proposals or not. Many were. The bill was reported out of committee on January 4; by Monday, January 9 the *Commonwealth* was calling attention to the dangers of the proposal, declaring it provided for the virtual repeal of the Missouri Compromise. The *New York Tribune* and the *New York Evening Post* throughout January were also concerned. On the other hand, the more conservative Boston Whig papers initially disregarded the subject, as did more tempered publications such as the *Boston Transcript* and the *New York Times*. Howe recorded at midmonth that only the Garrisonians were doing very much. Belatedly on January 24 the *Times* attacked both the bill and Douglas's personal motives. Two days before, the six "Independent Democrats," including Massachusetts's Sumner and DeWitt, had signed their appeal to alert the nation. Before the end of the month, three thousand people, in response to a call signed by some of New York City's most respected and conservative businessmen, met to protest the Nebraska bill.[7]

Wilson lacked his usual resiliency after the defeat of the constitution and his loss of the governorship to the Whigs. Recovery of energy took time. Furthermore, getting a business started meant a man who once had given his full attention to politics and opposition to slavery had less time available for public affairs. Howe reported that Wilson lacked "much heart for a fight," but he would soon call a convention to plan the party's future. The coalition was shattered. The public was shelving the slavery issue, even undisturbed about fugitive slaves. Whig self-assurance and legislative inaction and rising controversy over temperance and immigration contributed to the lack of concern about slavery. As Douglas's territorial plans became more ominous, Wilson comforted himself with the thought that Sumner's position in the Senate was even more important. By mid-January he was encouraging Sumner to meet Douglas's proposals headlong but was still bemoaning that Whig control of the legislature was preventing Massachusetts from responding effectively.[8]

The hope among the Free Democratic leadership was that the state's antagonism to the Nebraska proposals could be nonpartisan, or at least that many Whigs would join in opposition. The *Boston Atlas* reported favorably that all Massachusetts House members were hostile to Douglas's scheme, but both it and the *Advertiser* were reluctant to recognize the importance of the territorial issue. Howe consulted some of the leading Whigs, but was convinced they would not cooperate. A reluctant Wilson was persuaded the Free Democrats would have to call their own convention. They also began a petition campaign to prod the legislature to action.[9]

Wilson was determined those Free Democrats who had opposed the constitution would not be invited to the convention. He contended their presence would engender a row. The opening part of the State Central Committee's call tied it to the rejected constitution. It spoke of the defeat of efforts in the state to reform policy and amend the constitution which had been "stricken down by a political combination too strange and unnatural to have been foreseen," with the Slave Power preeminent in that amalgamation.[10] Howe tried to heal the breach by persuading the Committee on Arrangements that Adams and Palfrey should be invited. Adams was eventually asked to speak, but declined. Palfrey was defeated as delegate from Cambridge, so he also would not attend. Furthermore, Dana, Phillips, and Allen stayed away. Adams did agree to participate in an anti-Nebraska meeting at Dedham the day after the Faneuil Hall convention, but so few others were there that he viewed his appearance as a waste of time.[11]

The difference of response at this crisis in antislavery history between Wilson on the one hand and Adams and Palfrey on the other is telling. Wilson, who had far greater reason to be sensitive—he had given an important part of his life to a rejected constitution and his own political career was in ruins—was less so than Adams or Palfrey. Albert G. Browne, soon to become a major figure in the state's history, condemned the two for letting personal feelings interfere. Browne had lost respect for Palfrey and saw no hope of "resurrecting Adams." On the other hand, either Wilson's forgiving nature, or his sense of needing whatever support he or his cause could obtain, altered his attitude. Howe, who could be highly critical of Wilson, reported that the latter's "evil mood" lasted only a few days and he "behaved well thereafter." Browne believed Wilson lacked "polish and dignity," but he deserved kinder treatment than he had received from the Adams-Palfrey clique. Free Democrats were fortunate Wilson had the temperament he had.[12]

February was characterized by a rising chorus of opposition to the Nebraska bill. The *Commonwealth* launched an able attack. The *Dedham Gazette* declared only a united voice of the North would crush the proposal. Most Massachusetts Democratic journals condemned the Douglas bill. The *Boston Post*, the organ of the Hunker Democrats, tried to associate the New York City anti-Nebraska meeting with the Free Democrats by omitting the names of prominent Whigs and Democrats who had written letters. The proadministration *Worcester Palladium* contended the president and his cabinet were not supporting the bill. By midmonth the Whig *Boston Transcript* was reversing its previous position that the bill's enactment into law was inevitable and advocating increased political activity to halt its passage. The Whig leadership in the legislature, however, seemed unable to decide how to proceed. It finally acted on February 18, after Everett delivered his speech. The vote was unanimous in the Senate, nearly so in the House.[13]

The position of the new senator, Everett, was embarrassing both for those who opposed the Nebraska bill and for the man himself. A member of the Committee on Territories, he offered no opposition to the proposal when Douglas first presented it on the Senate floor. Replying to Everett's request for advice, Winthrop on February 6 maintained Douglas had been laying a trap. He was working in behalf of the South. Former President Fillmore, who had helped push through the Compromise of 1850, in a letter to Everett, took a confidential but unqualified stand against the repeal of the Missouri Compromise. When he spoke on February 8, Everett was as concerned not to antagonize the South as he was to oppose the bill. The Boston Whig press praised the address. The Whig *New York Tribune* tried to put a good face on it, calling Everett's effort "gentle as a sucking dove, . . . but audibl[e] and intelligibl[e]." The *Commonwealth* reported it had not been "what it should have been"; Everett had better kept quiet. Adams termed it "a miserable effort." As the weeks went by, more and more Whigs decided their senator had failed them.[14]

Shortly before the Free Democratic convention was to meet, Democratic and Whig leaders of the legislature persuaded its organizers to change the call to open it to members of all parties. But when the call was presented to leading Whigs of the legislature, not one would sign.[15]

Vocal opposition in Massachusetts to the expansion of slavery in the territories had been resurrected by Douglas and Nebraska. On February 16 about four thousand delegates from all over the state assembled in Faneuil Hall. Bird, who opened the proceedings, spoke of the "betrayal" of the North. By midafternoon snow was falling rapidly, but attendance was even larger. Even Palfrey sent a letter to be read. The resolutions, presented by Wilson, the committee's chairman, emphasized the right of Congress to make all needful rules and regulations dealing with the territories, and, in doing that, its obligation was to establish justice, insure domestic tranquility, provide for the common defense, and protect liberty. It could not fulfill those responsibilities by permitting slavery to be established. The Missouri Compromise was an agreement which had to be discharged. Any attempt to place slavery in the heart of the continent was just another example of the aggrandizement of the Slave Power. Garrison's *Liberator* praised the resolutions for being much stronger than it had anticipated.[16]

In the evening Wilson was one of the main speakers. He told of the passage of the Missouri Compromise, pushed through by Clay in opposition to "almost unanimous sentiment of the freeman of the North" and supported by Southern leaders such as Calhoun, Lowndes, and Monroe. Many were now in despair that its repeal would permit slavery to continue into the vast Western territory. Wilson was usually more accurate in his history than in the part of his speech that followed. Slavery, he maintained, had been forced on America by England. But Americans since 1789 had limited it; sixteen states had forbidden its existence. Supporters of the Nebraska bill thought they could sneak it through, but instead they had aroused the North. Zeal of office was attracting some Democrats, but others were revolting; two-thirds of the party adherents in Massachusetts supported freedom for the West. Wilson thought he would not live long enough to see the end of slavery in America. The institution would govern the nation another twenty or thirty years. But it would end. He feared the Nebraska bill would pass. But he insisted every Massachusetts delegate in Congress would oppose the bill. The voice of the state in the Senate had not yet been heard, Wilson continued. When Sumner did speak, nineteen out of every twenty Massachusetts voters would support his position.[17]

Clearly Wilson's attitude and political position had changed in six weeks. First, his energy and determination to continue his battle against slavery had been restored. Second, his position of leadership in the party was again recognized. He now lacked legislative office, control of a newspaper, and party title, all of which had helped him attain and continue in Free Soil leadership. Furthermore, he was limited in time by the necessity to conduct his reopened shoe business. Yet his influence was so great with the mass of Free Democrats and the state's executive committee, that he was once again its primary spokesman, planning for the convention, drawing up the resolutions, delivering a major address.

A week after the Free Democratic conclave the Whigs held their own meeting to oppose the Nebraska proposals. Three thousand people, headed by Abbott Lawrence, Winthrop, and Samuel Eliot, attended. The mayors of Boston, Roxbury, Cambridge, Charleston, Lynn, Salem, and Lowell permitted their names to be presented as convention vice-presidents. And a week later even the Boston Democrats assembled to adopt some weak resolutions against the Kansas-Nebraska proposal.[18]

The United States Senate, in the meantime, occupied itself primarily with the Douglas bill. Sumner, who had demonstrated a firmness of position and, with the January address, a greater recognition of the leadership role he would have to play, delivered his primary speech against the bill on February 21. Wilson, in two February letters, had told the senator that his friends were not impatient and fully expected the speech to give voice to the state's sentiments. Sumner was more generally commended than after any of his previous Senate attacks on slavery. The *New York Tribune* termed his speech the "most comprehensive, complete, and convincing review of the policy of the early Republic towards Slavery that has ever been presented to Congress within our recollection." Like Wilson in his Faneuil Hall speech, Sumner characterized the Missouri Compromise as the invention of Southern statesmen.[19] Wilson called the address the best Sumner had ever made. Even Child and Hillard praised the effort. But neither the speeches of senatorial opponents nor the resolutions of Northern legislatures or meetings halted the progress of the Kansas-Nebraska bill in the Senate. It was ordered to a third reading, 20 to 14, and then passed, 37 to 14. Southerners John Bell and Sam Houston opposed it. Everett, who was ill, and five others did not vote on either roll call.[20]

Everett became more unpopular in mid-March when he presented a petition in opposition to the Kansas-Nebraska bill signed by more than three thousand Protestant clergymen of New England. An angry Douglas initiated a stormy debate. Many believed Everett was too moderate and conciliatory in defending the clergymen. His diary reveals the senator was having difficulty confronting the intensity of opinion and feeling both in the Senate and among the people. He called the differences "irreconcilable," and asserted there could be "no amicable solution." While he had been a leader much of his life, he had no plan to respond to the crisis. Shortly after the the debate over the clergy petition, Everett returned to Boston and discovered just how many people were angry or disappointed with him and that even many conservative Boston Whigs, including the press, would not defend him. As early as March 9 Everett had confided in his diary that he might resign. He was lonely in Washington when neither his wife nor other members of his family accompanied him. Wilson was hoping for a resignation as early as mid-March. But Everett's friends counseled delay. During the ensuing month his health deteriorated and his family difficulties worsened. In early May he returned to Boston, determined to resign, only holding up the announcement to give the governor time to consider a replacement. This vacancy would eventually provide the opportunity for Wilson to enter the Senate.[21]

In each state those who had long opposed the expansion of slavery wondered how best to respond to the immediate issues which the Kansas-Nebraska bill presented. They also discussed the more long-term challenge of how to organize so as to attract more supporters to the Free Democratic party, or to convert their Whig or Democratic parties to respond effectively. Because Pierce and Douglas were Democrats, the Democratic party in the North was unlikely to become an agency for halting slavery expansion. Van Buren and other 1848 Barnburner New Yorkers remained loyal. Future leaders among the Republicans, such as Gideon Welles, Hannibal Hamlin, and Lyman Trumball, still professed to be Democrats. In Massachusetts, at least, the Whigs—in the majority of the legislature and persuaded their views had been endorsed by the electorate in the fall—had no intention of abandoning their party, no matter how weak it had appeared in the 1852 national elections or in an increasing number of other states. The Free Democrats in Massachusetts had new purpose and renewed vigor. Soon after the February convention the party leaders, including Wilson, determined to raise a million dollars and obtained pledges of $70,000 on the spot.[22]

One way to demonstrate to members of Congress what the people thought was to win the spring elections. On March 1 Wilson left for a two-week stumping tour of his native New Hampshire. Both sides recognized the importance of the elections to the Pierce administration and the Nebraska proposal; all Democratic newspapers in the state, except two, supported the bill. Wilson traveled more than a thousand miles, a demanding undertaking in 1854. He reported he encountered only one man who would speak in favor of the Douglas bill. But he was unable to bring about political fusion among those opposed to Nebraska. A popular Democratic candidate won the governorship by a reduced majority and the Democrats retained the state Senate. The lower house, however, would be narrowly controlled by a Whig-Free Democratic coalition. Free Soilers could not elect their own man as senator, but they did prevent the Democratic candidate from being chosen. Shortly thereafter, the Whigs and Free Democrats cooperated to defeat the Democrats in Connecticut and Rhode Island. A month later the Connecticut legislature elected Francis Gillette, a Free Democrat, and Lafayette Foster, then an antislavery Whig, later a Republican, to the Senate. Closer to home, the town of Natick on April 3 adopted resolutions opposing the Kansas-Nebraska bill.[23]

In Massachusetts, however, Wilson remembered too well his years of cooperation with the Democrats. So during April he devoted much of his energy trying to persuade the Democrats in convention to voice their opposition to Kansas and Nebraska. He also understood that the Whigs controlled the state government. Bird contended that Wilson's work with the Democrats was aimed at obtaining the governorship for himself in the fall. The state party chairman believed that coalition was supposed to have been temporary; Democrats had not been indoctrinated with

Free Soil ideas, as had been anticipated. The Free Soilers had to disentangle themselves from coalition. Several weeks later Bird was begging Adams to attend the meeting of the state committee to help return the party to the principles of 1850. He must have been fairly desperate to want to use Adams as an additional counterweight to Wilson and a majority of the committee.[24]

Agitation in Massachusetts continued during the spring. Town meetings passed resolutions opposing the Senate Nebraska bill. Wilson was scheduled to speak in Hanover, Lawrence, and Ashburnham in late March. His emphasis was on union of opponents of Douglas's bill. E. L. Pierce, writing more than thirty years later, remembered the Free Soilers became heroes during the Nebraska debates. And Wilson, who more than any other man, Pierce declared, had been attacked in the cause, was everywhere greeted by a grateful public with applause for his "tireless" agitation and organization. Yet while only a handful out of 400 members of the General Court had opposed the anti-Nebraska resolution, the two Washington leaders of the major parties in the state, Everett and Cushing, had different agendas. Sustaining opposition when nothing was happening in Washington was difficult. The *New York Tribune* was almost silent on the issue throughout April.[25]

During the course of the debates Eli Thayer, Worcester representative to the General Court, had decided the North needed to be prepared in case the Nebraska bill were passed. He determined to create a company, which the legislature chartered before it adjourned, whose purpose was to help with transportation costs and provide information, supplies, and facilities to emigrants to the new territories. Among the other incorporators of the Massachusetts Emigrant Aid Company were Wilson, Allen, S. C. Phillips, Bullock, Samuel Sewell, Bird, and Burlingame. Wilson did not play a major role in the company's activities. But surprisingly, some of the Cotton Whigs, radicalized by the Kansas-Nebraska debates, did. Amos A. Lawrence eventually became the company's treasurer and most prominent spokesman. Even Everett subscribed for stock.[26]

Thayer traveled over the North and made hundreds of addresses. He obtained $100,000 in New York City alone. By July 300 settlers were ready to leave, sixty-seven from Boston. During the year five companies, 750 people, departed. The next year a hundred fewer left.[27]

On May 8 the Democratic leadership, confident that it had won over enough Northern votes, revived the Nebraska bill in the House. Forty-one representatives from free states, more than half of them from Pennsylvania, New York, and Indiana, voted to take up consideration. Wilson went to Washington for about two weeks to help with the fight and to ascertain how to unite politically those who opposed the further extension of slavery. After a week of debate, the opponents, who thought they had the bill beaten a month before, recognized they could not prevent its passage. All of the effort of four months, aimed to influence the Northern majority in the House, had not achieved its objective. On May 22 the House passed the bill and the Senate and the president, who had made support of the bill a test of party orthodoxy, willingly accepted the House substitute. Democrats in the House were two to one in support, Whigs more than three to one opposed. Only in the last hours did Free Soil, Whig, and Democratic opponents work together.[28]

The *Commonwealth* termed the Nebraska proposal an "atrocious" bill. The *New York Times* said the repeal of the Missouri Compromise had done more than any event in ten years to strengthen antislavery opinion in the free states.[29] Wilson, in writing in the 1870s his lengthy history of the era, concluded "no single act of the Slave Power ever spread greater consternation, produced more lasting results upon the popular mind, or did so much to arouse the North and convince the people of its desperate character."[30]

Public feelings in Massachusetts were further agitated by the rendition of fugitive slave Anthony Burns. Wilson, incidentally, was not in Boston during the affair. On the same day the House of Representatives was passing the Kansas-Nebraska Act, Charles F. Suttle, a Virginia slave owner, applied to Commissioner Edward G. Loring for a warrant to seize his slave. The next day it was granted and Burns was arrested and taken to the courthouse. Loring began hearings the following day. On the afternoon of May 26 a hastily called public meeting decided that action must be taken, although it did not endorse Albert Browne's proposal to seize Burns if the marshal would not release him. That evening more than three thousand people assembled. The meeting broke up when reports came back that an attack was already underway to free Burns. Higginson, Swift, Webb, and others had gone against an afternoon agreement not to take action on their own. In the ensuing scuffle, one of Burns's guards was killed. As expected, Loring decreed the black man should be returned to slavery. Burns was led through the crowded streets of Boston to embark on a revenue cutter especially made available by the Pierce administration.[31]

Most of the Boston-area community was shocked. It was the greatest excitement the city had ever seen, Alley reported. The Compromise supporters of 1850 now saw the "folly" of their position, a *New York Post* correspondent wrote. Many former supporters of the fugitive law now signed petitions for its repeal. Burns would be the last fugitive to be seized on Massachusetts soil. Furthermore, antislavery leaders thereafter had a much easier task in stimulating opposition to slavery. More than one hundred men joined a secret Boston Anti-man-hunting League. Loring himself was widely condemned. The *Commonwealth* advocated impeachment or petition for removal by the two houses of the legislature. Massachusetts had a law forbidding any judge or other officer holding commission from the state to take part in the rendition of any individual claimed to be a fugitive slave. Yet Loring was both a judge of probate and United States commissioner. The *Atlas* attacked the mayor for calling out the citizen soldiery to enforce the decision. Indictments were issued against Parker, Phillips, Browne, Higginson, and others, but the suit was dismissed.[32]

When news reached Natick that Loring had turned over Burns, church bells were tolled for half an hour. Churches on Sunday gave notice of a protest meeting the next day. People of all parties attended. Speeches were delivered by John W. Bacon, Wilson, four community ministers, a Whig lawyer, a Whig businessman, and a Hunker Democrat, among others. On motion of Wilson, a committee of five men and five women, to which the eight clergymen of the town were added, were appointed to canvass the area for signatures to petitions for the repeal of the Fugitive Slave Act.[33]

The Free Soil party leadership, long before the Anthony Burns episode occurred, had planned a convention in Boston at midday on May 31. The purpose of the meeting, Bird declared when he called it to order, was to find ways to organize antislavery sentiment, either in support of an existing party or in creation of a new one. With Hale and Giddings appearing from out of state, about two thousand people attended. Local speakers included Wilson, Bird, Andrew, Walker, and Swift. Wilson declared in his address that those there had no new principles to avow; they had only to sustain the old. Their first duty was to exterminate the forty-four Northern "traitors" who had voted for the Kansas-Nebraska bill. Second, they should support those who would pledge themselves to repeal the bill. And third, they needed to revoke the Fugitive Slave Act. It was time for the Whig party to die, Wilson declared; a Northern party was needed. He would vote for no more Whigs. Free Soilers would play whatever role others wanted, as long as they could attain their principles. On his return from Washington, he had spent two days in New York City, where he had encountered no one who would defend the Nebraska bill, he reported. His speech was one of the more radical delivered. He attacked Samuel E. Eliot, the Boston representative who had voted for the fugitive bill. Wilson mourned for Anthony Burns. The time had come to place the country on the side of liberty. Alley reported to Sumner that Wilson had made "a capital speech."[34]

That evening Wilson, among other Free Soilers, attended the meeting of the New England Anti-Slavery Convention. After the planned addresses by Phillips and Quincy, Wilson was called upon. He spoke of his admiration for the antislavery pioneers. "Differing with them in policy," he emphasized, "I am proud to acknowledge their unswerving fidelity." The abolitionists and the Free Soilers needed to work together for common ends. Reacting to the Anthony Burns excitement, Wilson attacked Massachusetts for its role in getting the Fugitive Slave Acts of 1793 and 1850 passed. But the Nebraska debates, he declared, were moving the nation through a revolution. Wilson believed in the overthrow of slavery peacefully, by the ballot box. Northern public opinion had to be changed. Henry C. Wright asked him what should be done. Wilson's answer was the strategy from which he never deviated: appeal to the people through press and voice, maintain clear constitutional principles, and ask governments to constrict slavery in every way they possibly could. Abolitionist Abby Kelly wondered how a vote for the Free Soil party would help; it would only again make Boutwell governor and place Cushing on the bench, she asserted.[35]

The turmoil which four months of national debate over Nebraska had produced in the North might have led to party reorganization. Whig Benjamin Wade of Ohio and Democrat Preston King of New York did abandon their parties. In Washington immediately after the passage of the bill, at the call of Israel Washburn Jr. of Maine, thirty members of the House met to consider what kind of unity they could establish, but men beholden to parties which had helped elect them could not easily guide reorganization of a political system. Wilson asked Seward to assume the leadership in the creation of a new fusion party. But while he regarded Seward as the wisest statesman in the nation and hoped he would attain the presidency, he wrote the New York senator, Wilson would sooner vote for the hated Douglas than for a candidate of the Whig party. The time had come to dissolve the connections between Whigs North and South, Wilson contended. If Whigs would join with Free Soilers and unhappy Democrats, they could carry all of New England and most of the North. Seward could do more than any other man to unite the North. The same day, in a letter to Israel Washburn, he emphasized the absolute necessity of Whig division. However, the New York senator and his close associate, the journalist Thurlow Weed, would not abandon the Whig party of their state to the rival Silver Grey faction, nor risk Seward's political future on a movement which might collapse within a year.[36]

In every Northern state, angry citizens viewed the South differently and concluded their hope for ending slavery or its expansion through the regular political process was either more difficult than they had expected or impossible. Meetings in February and March began the process which would lead to the creation of the Republican party in Wisconsin. Both the *Chicago Tribune* and the *New York Tribune,* the latter heretofore the spokespaper of eastern Wiggery, called for a political reorganization. The *Commonwealth* proclaimed on April 27 that the old system must be broken up and the only question was which party would collapse first. By June other New England newspapers were agreeing. The *Chicopee Journal* declared old issues were dead and the Whig party broken; agreeing, the *Lowell Courier* favored a state mass convention. The *Portland Advertiser* maintained the Whigs were willing to join a new organization which would sweep Maine by a ten- to fifteen-thousand-vote majority, but it urged no action until states with more Whig influence, like New York, Massachusetts, and Vermont, responded. In Ohio Wade and Chase were among the leaders in creation of a new freedom party. By the end of June Whigs of Vermont had dissolved their connections with Southern members of their party and were willing to join Free Soilers in convention for joint nominations.[37]

Wilson emerged from the meetings in late May and early June enthusiastic, sanguine, and determined. Alley spoke of Wilson's joy after the successful May 31 meeting. "Now is the time for action, bold, and decisive," Wilson wrote Israel

Washburn, about the same time. Several weeks were occupied with meetings between Free Soilers and a few Whig and Democratic leaders.[38]

Political reorganization, however, was not in the program of most of the managers of the two major parties or even of the minority faction among the Free Soilers. The Whigs controlled state government and their leaders remained angry with their opponents who in coalition had superseded them for two years. As the *Atlas* pointed out, the Whigs had taken the correct position on Nebraska and they had received more than double the votes of the Free Soilers at the last election; those who opposed the Pierce administration and Democratic territorial schemes could become Whig. By mid-June much of the Whig press was retreating from its earlier suggestion of fusion or cooperation. One of Sumner's correspondents reported the Whig Central Committee was at work to quiet the people. On the other hand, leaving the Democratic party at this moment meant giving up influence and spoils not only for the remainder of the Pierce years, but probably for years to come. At the same time negotiations were occurring with leaders of the other two parties, party chairman Bird was again telling Adams that "Free Soilers needed to return to the original principles of the party." But Adams was also unenthusiastic. Adams, Palfrey, and their associates had refused to participate in the May 31 meeting. Adams asserted the people had to be convinced before party reorganization could occur.[39]

In the midst of all the controversy over Nebraska and Anthony Burns, Governor Washburn made a wise choice to replace Everett in the Senate. He first offered the post to several leading Boston-area Whigs, who fortunately declined. He then appointed Julius Rockwell of Pittsfield, another Whig, but who had been opposed to the Kansas-Nebraska bill and who was from a section of the state which had been offended that both senators had been from the Boston area. Whittier publicly praised the appointment, remembering how Rockwell had led the fight against Texas annexation while Whittier and Wilson had been in Washington in 1845.[40]

By mid-June Wilson had taken to the stump. He spoke to a crowded town hall in Milford, New Hampshire, on June 15, and he and Keyes addressed a large and widely reported anti-Nebraska meeting at New Bedford on June 16. Their objective was to create interest in a new political party. For July 4 Wilson ventured to an anti-Nebraska meeting at North Weare, New Hampshire. Returning to Massachusetts after six months away, Stone marveled at the antislavery enthusiasm he found.[41]

The negotiations with the other parties must have discouraged Wilson and the State Committee. When a state convention eventually met to attempt reorganization, its call emerged out of a meeting in Concord, not as a result of the Free Soil leaders' efforts. Some historians have accepted Adams's view that Wilson and his associates sought fusion to save their own political lives. This ignores the party reorganization which was occurring in many Northern states and would take place within two years in all states. Furthermore, Wilson, while wanting reorganization, as Adams did, was not precipitating it in late June and early July. He either had to participate in the process a majority of his party seemed to want, or be thrust aside, as Adams and his associates so often had been, when they did not concur with the majority. Wilson had agreed to lecture in Onondaga County, New York, on July 4, but the importance of events in Massachusetts was probably the primary factor in his decision to accept an engagement closer to home.[42]

On July 7, in response to the Concord initiative, members of the three parties gathered at the American House in Boston for about two hours to plan for a state convention. The *Courier* reported twenty-six men participated, only five of them Whigs, two Democrats. Among the Free Soilers present were Wilson, Adams, George F. and Samuel Hoar, Phillips, Marcus Morton Jr., Bird, and William Jackson. Among the Whigs were William Aspinwall, Charles T. Russell, George Morey, and Congressman Goodrich. Arguments ensued over whether to have a delegate or mass assembly. Since a call already was in existence for a meeting in Worcester on July 20, that time and site were adopted. The call was broad enough that it could attract all those opposed to Nebraska; it included no commitment to radical action.[43]

One can debate whether the American House leaders were wise in continuing their efforts, without support from very many leaders of either of the major parties. Perhaps they had little choice. The Boston correspondent of the *New York Evening Post* reported on July 5 that prospects for forming a new party were poorer than even a week before. The Whig *Springfield Republican* contended that, even though the Whigs were being shortsighted, the convention advocates were "hasty" and premature in meeting this early and trying to create a new political party. The *New York Tribune* reporter approved the tone of the call, but asserted it came from the wrong source and was for the wrong time of year. Seth Webb, whose views at this time generally were close to Wilson's, also believed the convention was assembling too early.[44]

In the meantime organization efforts in some other states continued to bear fruit. On July 6 the new Republican party came officially into being at a convention in Jackson, Michigan. Both Wisconsin and Vermont the same month took action to formalize their Republican parties.

When the state convention assembled in Massachusetts, its participants were primarily Free Soilers. Yet members of that party spoke only when others would not. Pierpont reluctantly delivered an address after repeated calls. Parker, Allen, and Burlingame kept aloof. Wilson spoke only near the close, against his wishes and intentions, and primarily to counter some of the remarks of Keyes, who had denounced Whigs and Democrats and opposed unity. The "most moderate and best speeches" were those of Wilson and Walker, the Whig *Springfield Republican* reported. The *Northampton Courier* characterized Wilson's speech as one of the two best, "firm, conciliatory, and eloquent"; he had rebuked Keyes "with great effect." Wilson emphasized the need to forget past differences to unite to overthrow the slaveholding oligarchy. He favored fusion, although he would accept whatever coalition became necessary. Few prominent leaders of the three major parties were included either on the planning committee or among the speakers. The chairman, secretaries, and other permanent officers were mostly unknowns outside their own communities. The Committee on Resolutions included Webb, Carter, and Lucius B. Comins—later a congressman—two Whigs, and two Democrats.[45]

The *Springfield Republican* accused Wilson of being the master strategist, but Wilson replied quickly, maintaining he played no role in selecting the Resolutions Committee or in drawing up the resolutions. The *Republican* countered that Free Soil leaders had gathered in Worcester the day before the meeting, and that the resolutions had been written by a Free Soil friend of Wilson's (Carter), who was subsequently placed on the Resolutions Committee. No man had more power and influence in Worcester than Wilson, the *Republican* contended. That he played little role openly was "politic." Carter, whose draft served as the basis for the resolutions, demonstrated how much in agreement committee members were and how open they were to suggestions.[46]

The resolutions, criticized by the moderate *Springfield Republican* as too radical, were, to the contrary, framed to attract broad support. They called for political union to counter the Slave Power's attempt to convert the nation into a "slaveholding despotism." They sought the repeal of the Fugitive Slave Act, restoration of the prohibition of slavery in Kansas and Nebraska, prohibition of slavery in any territory, refusal to admit more slave states, and abolition of slavery in the District of Columbia. They maintained Massachusetts had a constitutional duty to protect its own citizens. They advocated a national convention to take action—and thus form a new political party—to halt slave expansion and called for a convention to nominate candidates for state offices. In spite of intense heat and the unseasonable time of year for a statewide meeting, attendance was large. Sources varied in their estimates between twelve and twenty-five hundred people. The new party took the name Republican. At the conclusion of the convention a provisional state committee was selected, led by Andrew, later wartime governor of Massachusetts. The committee was authorized to call a state delegate convention August 10, an unpropitious date, Wilson publicly wrote. The committee agreed, for within a week it postponed the meeting until September 7.[47]

The Boston Whig press and leadership intensified its opposition to a new party. The Whig State Committee issued what the *Commonwealth* termed an "edict" against Whigs attending the Worcester meeting. The *Boston Journal* maintained the new party would only interfere with cooperative efforts so widely participated in since midspring. The Free Soil *Dedham Gazette* was angry at the attacks by the *Courier* and *Journal* and characterized Massachusetts Whig leaders as "bitter, timid, selfish," in comparison with those in Vermont, Ohio, and Michigan. As usual, E. L. Pierce wrote, the Boston Whig press saved "most of its abuse for Wilson." Samuel Bowles, editor of western Massachusetts's most influential Whig journal and participant in the Worcester convention, attacked Free Soil control. He withdrew from the movement, declaring he was pledged to fusion, but not necessarily to this party.[48]

One cannot know when Wilson concluded that fusion would not be productive, at least in 1854. More than twenty years later, when he published his history of the battle against slavery, he emphasized how "the formation of a national and successful party from the materials afforded by the disintegration of hitherto hostile organizations was the work of great delicacy and difficulty." More important, he briefly concluded that the failure of the fusion movement induced many antislavery advocates to see that their most propitious course of action was to destroy the two main parties by producing "political chaos." That meant uniting or cooperating with the Know Nothing movement. The three Wilson friends who wrote biographies about him while he was still alive also attributed his Know Nothing participation to the failure of fusion.[49]

Wilson's support of Know Nothingism was to many of his contemporaries the most odious and unpalatable action of his political career. It is regarded just as negatively by many people today. But the fact that his action was self-serving—procuring a United States senatorship and a new source of income—does not mean it was also not a rational and deliberative way of achieving the ends he sought for the slave. Coalition was impossible; fusion was impossible. The militant antislavery movement was more than twenty years old. Clearly those whom the Know Nothings disparaged, especially the Roman Catholics of Massachusetts, were helping to prevent Wilson and those who thought like him about slavery from achieving their ends. Should the slaves remain in hopelessness while Wilson carefully sustained the civil rights and personal dignities of more privileged whites?

In the 1830s, 1840s, and 1850s the number of immigrants to the United States grew dramatically. There were more than 100,000 in 1845, more than 400,000 in 1853. Still, the foreign-born were only 7 percent of the population in the 1840s, less than 10 percent in the 1850s. The problem was the newcomers did not distribute themselves widely over the country but tended to congregate in certain areas, especially in or near the cities of the Northeast. In Rhode Island and Wisconsin immigrants were approximately half of the population; so were they in St. Louis and Cincinnati. That meant that objections to them might not produce a pervasive national response, but would engender hostility in certain geographical areas. The traditions, lifestyles, and values of the immigrants were sometimes different from those of native Americans. Especially objectionable to some was the large number of Roman Catholics, primarily from Ireland.[50]

In Massachusetts the population increased in the 1840s by more than 50 percent in Suffolk, Middlesex, and Norfolk Counties, more than 40 percent in Essex, Hampden, and Worcester. This continued in the 1850s. Sixty percent of the state's increase came from migration, much of it from abroad. By 1855 Boston had a larger foreign-born than native-born population. The immigrants often lived in squalor. Immigration was accompanied by an increase of crime and pauperism. Some said lunacy and idiocy were also higher among immigrants. Illiteracy among immigrants was widespread. Taxes had to be increased to respond to some of these problems. Many native-born workers objected to the additional competition for jobs. Many Americans insisted Irish and German immigrants were intemperate; the latter two groups did commonly oppose efforts to limit and regulate liquor consumption. Newcomers did not observe the sabbath in ways older Americans thought appropriate.[51]

Massachusetts as early as the 1830s had enacted laws to deal with the introduction of paupers, idiots, and other undesirables, and as the years went by these became more stringent. Efforts among nativists of the East to get Congress to lengthen the naturalization period and force ship captains to post bonds to pay for costs of those who might end up being public charges failed. Many congressional districts were unconcerned and votes of naturalized citizens could be lost by taking action. Because of the increasing need for labor as Massachusetts industrialized, no efforts were made, even once Know Nothings obtained power, to restrict immigration.

If one looks only at the mercurial growth of the Know Nothings in 1854 one could wrongly conclude the political objection to foreigners suddenly burst upon the American scene. Quite the contrary; roots of dissatisfaction can be discerned as early as the 1830s. The Democratic party not only refused to act against the immigrants, but often nominated candidates who would attract the new Americans's votes. The Whig party usually avoided the issue or supported state laws likely to control only limited aspects of the problem. The antiforeign movement turned to separate political action, and a national convention met for the first time in 1845. Because of improving economic conditions, the controversy over the Mexican War, and the movement's sanction of bloodshed and mob rule, the political crusade faltered, but secret societies supporting nativism continued, some indifferent to politics, some secretly supporting selected candidates. But immigration vastly increased in the early 1850s, reinvigorating antiforeignism. The new political movement grew at different rates, to different degrees, and at different times in different states. State councils were organized in seven states in 1853 but efforts in that year to establish a new American party in New York failed. On May 11, 1854, a convention of New York's Know Nothing bodies assembled and a few days later representatives from thirteen states or other governmental units, including Massachusetts, convened. In mid-June the Grand Council, with James W. Barker as president, was established. The members had begun to be called the Know Nothings.

The organization was similar in most states and was in many ways like other social or lodge operations of the day. The Order was secret and oath bound. Members received passwords, signs, grips, and phrases of recognition. But the party gave no public notices of its meetings. To be inducted one had to be native born, a Protestant with Protestant parents, and not married to a Roman Catholic. One had to agree to vote only for native-born Americans. Members had to abide by party decisions in their public voting. A candidate for membership, after examination, could be kept out with five blackballs cast against him. A Grand Council for the state ruled through quarterly meetings and granted charters to local councils. When making political nominations, the entire membership could participate, but once agreement was reached, everyone was obligated to follow the decision of the majority. That worked well at least through 1854.

The Know Nothing movement was anti-Catholic as well as anti-immigrant. Most historians who have studied the party in Massachusetts have concluded its anti-Catholic impetus was stronger than its nativist.[52] One can trace these religious prejudices back to before the first English settlements and follow their reenforcement during the colonial period. But increased Catholic immigration, celebration of the Papal Jubilee in 1827, and the religious crusades of the 1820s and 1830s, among other factors, spawned new anti-Catholicism. There were increasing arguments over Bible versions. The 1830s was characterized by a growing violence against church buildings and the homes of Catholics. [53]

At the same time numbers of immigrants were dramatically increasing in the 1850s—with all the problems that would produce—the circumstances of Catholicism changed, too. With more adherents, the church became more visible. Pierce, acknowledging the increasing numbers of voters of that faith, appointed a Catholic as his Postmaster General. Some priests encouraged clannishness. Some made bold and antagonistic statements. Most outspoken was Archbishop John J. Hughes of New York City, who in an 1850 sermon attacked Protestantism and who after riots in Philadelphia advocated his parishioners arm themselves. There were increasing arguments over control of church property. In an age in which thousands of Americans were exulting in their triumph of securing free public schools, Catholic education might be tolerated, but separation was still regarded as undesirable. How could society assure that children outside the public schools were adequately tutored in American democracy? Nativists also believed the church, a European-dominated institution, heavily involved there in politics, should divorce itself from elections.

For what did the Know Nothing organization profess to stand? According to its June, 1855, national convention statement, it sought (1) a radical revision of laws regulating immigration, keeping out felons and paupers; (2) an end of state laws authorizing foreigners to vote and of Congressional legislation permitting noncitizen participation in elections in the territories, and an end to alien eligibility for land grants; (3) resistance to the "aggressive policy & corrupting tendencies of the Roman Catholic Church in our country"; (4) opposition to excluding the Bible from the schools. By 1856 the party platform had added a twenty-one-year residence requirement for naturalization.[54]

But opposition to immigrants and to Roman Catholics does not alone account for the strength of the movement nationally. The party disintegration of the early 1850s, as already discussed for Massachusetts, was an additional factor. The Whigs were destroyed on the national level. Lincoln and Seward, Illinois and New York Whigs, might still support their party, but in many states little was left to sustain. Most Whigs could not become Democrats. Know Nothingism was an alternative. Furthermore, additional confusions in society were disturbing the political scene. Temperance was a—sometimes the—major issue, with many voters. Workingmen's parties were strong in some communities. In this political chaos, those who did not want to vote Democratic might either vote Know Nothing or stay home and leave the decision to their fellow citizens. Many of this variety of people not only voted, but joined the movement and, with such irreconcilable objectives, would find dwelling together difficult.

In Massachusetts additional reasons existed to be anti-Catholic. Catholics had voted overwhelmingly against the 1853 constitution. Catholic clergy for the first time had openly counseled voters how to cast their ballots. Catholics tended to vote primarily Democratic, the block voting antagonizing members of the other two parties, but also angering some Democrats who resented Catholic opposition to antislavery and support of the *Boston Post* clique. Catholics were generally opposed to the new liquor licensing laws. *Brownson's Quarterly Review* was regarded as an expounder of Archbishop John B. Fitzpatrick. Brownson was a Calhoun Democrat who accepted slavery, denounced abolition agitation, praised the Fugitive Slave Act, and opposed the Maine liquor law. The Catholic newspaper *The Pilot* had criticized the three thousand Protestant clergymen who had petitioned against passage of the Kansas-Nebraska bill and had not joined others in voicing the state's distress at the time of the Anthony Burns rendition. Irishmen had been prominent among those helping with Burns's return to slavery.

The existence of the Know Nothings as a political force dawned slowly on the leadership of Massachusetts. The Know Nothing and temperance tickets won the Lynn elections in mid-March. They triumphed in Whig Salem. Stone, who was not a member of the Order, wrote Sumner in the spring that the movement was a political force in a number of eastern Massachusetts communities, including Lynn and Salem. He understood the Know Nothings had played a major role in defeating the Whigs in the Boston mayoral race. They had about five thousand members already in the city and were adding more each meeting, he advised. Burlingame had already joined and hoped to win a congressional seat in Boston. In the city, Stone recorded, the movement was controlled by Free Soilers who were angry at the defeat of the constitution by the Catholics. Banks asked Boutwell if he intended to join; Boutwell many years later wrote significantly that he had left politics and "did not have to join." Banks did. [55]

Who joined the movement in Massachusetts, and when, is not always easy to ascertain. Adams wrote about the society in his diary for the first time on July 2, when a friend told him of Know Nothing strength, opinions, and objectives. Three days later two men whom Adams did not know, but likely Know Nothings, spoke to him about the senatorship. He was invited to join the Order in late August. He would not, in part because he had always agreed with his father's public stance, during the Anti-Masonic era, against secret societies. A few days later a delegation proposed to Winthrop that if he joined the Order he could obtain the governorship in the fall and the senatorship later. Wilson joined rather early, in March 1854. Frank Bird, who refused to affiliate with the movement himself and was always highly critical of Wilson for his participation, writing before his colleague died, claimed Wilson was blackballed for membership in Natick. This is probably because his townspeople knew that Wilson was neither antialien nor opposed to equality in social, economic, or political life for Catholics. Burlingame, Slack, and others then proposed his name to a Boston lodge. Even there objections were made, but he was accepted.[56]

Know Nothing strength developed rapidly in Massachusetts. On July 2, before the call for establishment of the Republican party, Wilson told Sumner the Know Nothings would win the fall elections. His associate, Seth Webb, two weeks later, predicted the nativist party would be the controlling element in the state. Both men spoke of the political disorder; Wilson told of the many Whigs and Democrats who would vote Know Nothing. Webb wondered into whose hands a Know Nothing victory would put the state. The Boston correspondent of the *New York Herald* reported that, except for Free Soilers and Americans, little political excitement existed in July. The number of local Know Nothing lodges had reached 250, he also confided. A day later the *Springfield Republican* announced the new party was better organized in Massachusetts than in any other state and suggested it might win in November.[57]

At the beginning of August the Order convened in Boston for business. In contrast to former Know Nothing activities, the press was aware a meeting was held, but still knew little about what took place. The conclave was "spirited and harmonious," and plans for the fall campaign were made, the *Boston Herald* stated. The *Newburyport Herald* predicted the Know Nothings would carry the November elections. The Order controlled the large cities already, and was gaining in the country towns. A Worcester correspondent of the *New York Tribune* forecast 50,000 Know Nothing votes. By the end of the month the Free Soil *Northampton Courier* claimed the new party would obtain between 30,000 and 50,000 votes and win control of both the House and Senate. Banks and Burlingame were already perceived to be Know Nothing candidates for Congress.[58]

The Whig state convention met on August 17. The Central Committee in June had decided an early convention might help keep the party together and might persuade others opposed to the Kansas-Nebraska bill that joining the Whig party would be necessary to rebuke the Democrats. Some out-of-Boston Whig papers advocated nomination of Rockwell, Palfrey, Samuel Hoar, or Morey to attract Free

Soil votes. But the party remained in the hands of those who had controlled it for a decade, even though many of those lived in Boston, which the party no longer controlled and which many commentators openly predicted would be carried by the Know Nothings. Washburn was renominated. The moderate platform called for restoration of the Missouri Compromise and the nonextension of slavery into free territories.[59]

The important roles of Douglas, Southern Democrats, and the Pierce administration in getting the Kansas-Nebraska Act enacted weakened what had been the second largest party in Massachusetts. The longtime support the party had given to immigrants and the association of the Irish in the state with the party alienated many Democrats who might have nativist sentiments. The Boston clique on the State Central Committee in August tried to obtain an endorsement of the administration and the Nebraska bill, but was prevented. But the country Democrats and the Banks-Boutwell wing had lost control. Most people knew the Democrats would not for years win again in Massachusetts.[60]

Speculation about a Republican nomination for governor included Phillips, Wilson, and even Banks, as candidate of both Know Nothings and Republicans. The temporary leadership continued summer-long efforts to get Adams, Palfrey, and their associates again to be active in the party. They failed. Those who assembled were mostly the same men who a year earlier had been Free Soilers. The Whigs sought to get the convention cancelled, but their own platform was too weak to attract Free Soilers. The convention assembled on September 7 and listened to an able speech by Sumner. The platform called for the repeal of the Fugitive Slave Law, abolition of slavery in the District of Columbia, and encouragement of western migration. The party opposed the addition of more slave states or territories and the annexation of Cuba unless slavery were prohibited. The platform emphasized the party stood for union, the constitution, and law and order. Wilson was selected for governor on the first ballot with 316 out of 489 votes. Phillips, his nearest competitor, received 68. Wilson's nomination was balanced with that of Increase Sumner, a former Democrat from the Berkshires, for lieutenant governor. The politically acute Wilson knew he could not win either as a Republican or subsequently in coalition.[61]

The reactions to Wilson's choice varied. The Boston correspondent of the *New York Herald* remembered that, except for during presidential years, Wilson had been the strongest vote getter of the party; he would be attractive to the prohibitionists. Bird declared the nomination was against the unanimous judgment of the party leaders and would be disastrous for both the party and Wilson. With Wilson, nativism would destroy them. Both the *Northampton Courier* and the *Springfield Republican* were surprised by the selection. The *Republican* called it "distasteful" to many members of the party and contended it was brought about by the energy of Wilson's friends and the lack of a real alternative. The *Northampton Courier* declared party members wanted nominated a new convert, a member of one of the other parties. The paper liked Wilson, thought he deserved support, but concluded his selection had been unwise. He had been too involved in the battles of the previous five years and he could not attract Whig votes. Perhaps, the *Courier* editor speculated, Wilson might also secure the Know Nothing nomination and thereby win. Otherwise, his designation was "most unfortunate." To the Whig *Boston Advertiser*, the selection was final proof the new Republican party was little more than the old Free Soil.[62]

But why would Wilson lend his name to what would be an embarrassing result? Adams wondered if a deal had been made that would provide Wilson some important position. Palfrey speculated an arrangement existed with Banks, who would be the Know Nothing candidate for governor. Wilson had joined the Order in March, six months before the Republican state nominating convention. Under the canons of the Order, he was obligated to support the choices of the Know Nothing party. Furthermore, he already not only recognized that the Republican candidate would not receive a majority vote in November, but that, in case no one secured a majority, his name would not be one of the two forwarded by the House to the Senate. The nomination was worthless to him; it would anger even more those who would oppose him and the Know Nothings. Having run for the same office in 1853, he was receiving no new honor. One has to conclude either he had made some deal with non–Free Soil components in the Know Nothing movement or he expected the Know Nothings also to nominate him for governor.[63]

Perhaps Wilson reconsidered the wisdom of being the Republican candidate. His acceptance letter, although dated September 18, was not published until nearly four weeks after the convention. In it, he noted how the aggressions of the Slave Power had produced a political reorganization in so many states. He deplored the failure of cooperation in Massachusetts, but he anticipated an end of the existing political system and he expected the Republican party to survive. The letter supported the Worcester resolutions and favored passage of state personal liberty laws. If he became governor, Wilson promised, those laws would be enforced. He hoped temperance would not be a party question. Recalling that as a legislator he had voted for the current liquor law, he pledged to support whatever modifications were necessary to secure the objectives for which it had been passed.[64]

Was Wilson's Know Nothing adherence known before the Republicans nominated him? The Boston newspaper of the party in September 1854 doubted Wilson was a member. The *New York Herald*, a good source of Know Nothing information, on August 24 correctly claimed membership for Wilson and Banks, but incorrectly for S. C. Phillips. The *Springfield Republican* on September 9 suggested Wilson was a member. Winthrop, the same month, upon hearing Wilson had joined the Order, credited him with being too shrewd to allow himself to get involved in a movement from which he could not benefit. The *Advertiser*, perhaps trying to make trouble for the Republicans, predicted on September 8 that Wilson would be the Know Nothing candidate for governor. The *New York Tribune* seconded that. Throughout late September the Boston Whig press continued its attack on him.[65]

A few Free Soilers were reluctant to accept the end of their party and the birth of the Republican. Even before Wilson was nominated, these men talked of an October meeting of their own. But only about fifty delegates attended. Walker presided and Hale was brought in from New Hampshire to provide legitimacy for the assemblage. In the end the meeting accepted the Republican nominations. Alvord may have been typical of those who attended. He was willing to accept Wilson as the nominee, but he refused to endorse the new Republican party or serve on its Central Committee. He was suspicious of what it was or would become; in Iowa, Vermont, and New York, he asserted, it was simply the Whigs with a new name.[66]

In the political confusion of the summer and fall of 1854, many Free Soilers, witnessing the growth of the nativist movement and realizing they could not win that year as Republicans, joined the Know Nothing party. Fusion was working in Michigan and Wisconsin, but had failed in Massachusetts. Cooperation with Whigs was possible in Vermont, but was rejected by the Whigs in the Bay State. How else in Massachusetts could one react with any effect to the abuses of the Pierce administration and the Democratic-controlled Congress than by joining with the only other viable party? As a further inducement, both in Massachusetts and elsewhere in the North, the new party often ran on a temperance plank. Wilson, in his history of the era, declared the Free Soilers sought to use Know Nothing "machinery" to disrupt the major parties. He also claimed the tactics in part worked, the Know Nothings shaping the nominations and cooperating with Whigs, anti-Nebraska Democrats, and Free Soilers in Pennsylvania and New Jersey and joining with Whigs in New York to elect congressmen opposed to the expansion of slavery in the territories. The Democrats, he asserted, were beaten in almost every Northern state, and the Whig party was further disrupted. Seventy-five Know Nothings were sent to Congress, most antislavery and most later Republican.[67]

Many of those who worked with Wilson, but did not become Know Nothings, agreed with this explanation. His long-time associate Robinson characterized Wilson's participation in the Know Nothing movement as the most "disrespectable part of his career," but added that Wilson did not organize the movement, but "fell into it" as the only way to destroy the Whigs. His greater offense, Robinson believed, was being a Know Nothing and at the same time Republican candidate for governor. George Hoar in 1896 wrote how consistent Wilson had been: he espoused the unpopular antislavery cause early in life and stuck to it. Schouler agreed with that. In 1872, explaining why he was not supporting the Grant-Wilson presidential ticket, Schouler credited his associate with having been "true" from the beginning on the question of slavery and human rights. Hoar declared Wilson went into the Know Nothing movement to break up the major parties, and when he had accomplished that, he left it. He did not justify Wilson's association with nativism, adding that Wilson himself never did. Hoar said Wilson did evil that good might come. When the evil was done, and good came, Wilson repented. His brother, E. R. Hoar, also credited those Free Soilers who joined the Know Nothings as being out to destroy the other parties.[68]

Wilson was consistent. As far back as 1846 he defended himself, in an address in the Massachusetts House of Representatives, from accusations that he, a Whig, was trying to court the political abolitionists by declaring he would act with any group of men who would work to overthrow the system of slavery. He had repeated those sentiments often in speeches in the summer of 1854. By 1854 many Free Soilers had come to regard parties as a means toward an end, not an organization to which one owed deep-rooted loyalty.[69]

Those who knew Wilson well contended he was not anti-foreign or anti-Catholic. He had "not a drop of bigotry or intolerance" in his blood, George Hoar maintained.[70] "Warrington" asserted Wilson had no prejudice against either foreigners or Catholics. His faith "by education and circumstances" was orthodox Congregationalist, but not with "a welding heat." But he was anti–Catholic Church, both because of personal experiences and perceptions and because of the role the church had been playing in Massachusetts politics.[71]

Wilson's concern about other issues, of course, might make him appear to be antiforeign. While he was serving in the state Senate in 1845, for example, he submitted a resolution asking Massachusetts senators and representatives to get federal naturalization laws altered. It spoke for a liberal policy towards foreigners, but claimed statutes were deficient. The resolution's limited objective was to halt alien voting. Hardly a malicious proposal, it was unamended by the Judicial Committee and won on the key Senate vote by a 22-to-5 margin. While an editor in 1849 Wilson defended the legislature's refusal to charter Holy Cross as a Catholic college. Wilson maintained other colleges were not limited by their charter to accepting one denomination; charters should be given for the public benefit. Holy Cross was therefore being treated equally. Theological seminaries Wilson accepted as different; they could be discriminatory.[72]

Two statements at the time, when he supposedly was courting Know Nothing legitimacy, suggest the limits of his support of nativism. In an address at Brattleboro, Vermont, Wilson declared he had no sympathy with the bigoted spirits who would reject those who sought admittance to the United States. He opposed laws to abolish naturalization or deny the right of suffrage to those who were naturalized. When he was seeking votes for the senatorship and had to be careful not to alienate nativists, Wilson took a moderate stance with which most Americans would have agreed. Believing in the creed that all men are created equal, he asserted this had to apply to those born abroad as much as it did to blacks. The American movement, Wilson declared, had grown out of unhappiness with the evils resulting from massive immigration of peoples whose social, religious, and political institutions were different from those of the United States. The American movement sought to revise (a weak word, since he did not say in what way) naturalization laws, reject foreign paupers and criminals, and destroy the political influence of aliens. He was also opposed to organization of military companies composed of men of foreign birth. This was not a harsh or uncharitable position. In disagreeing with a position of Secretary of State Cass in 1859, Wilson characterized citizenship as being reciprocal. When immigrants renounced their former citizenship and became naturalized Americans, they were to give "no partial or divided allegiance" to the United States. In return, they possessed the same rights as native-born Americans, including the right to travel anywhere and receive the fullest protection of their government.[73]

Free Soilers, of course, would have been foolish to join the Know Nothing party in such numbers and not either capture control of the movement, or at least make the best bargain possible to achieve their own ends. The evidence appears overwhelming that, although many men joined the Order in Massachusetts because of their nativist sympathies, that element seldom controlled policy. Rather the Free Soilers and the opportunists like Henry Gardner made the decisions. So those Free Soilers who joined could defend their action as a marriage of convenience, which, at least in the short run, worked.[74]

In other states, the movement might be quite different. In Virginia, for example, the Whigs, as proslavery as the Democrats, controlled the Know Nothing party. That was typical of the South. But a nativist movement was strange in Virginia in any case, for 91 percent of the whites had been born in the state, another 6 percent born elsewhere in the United States. Rather, in the South the movement was (1) an alternative to the Democrats, the only other party with chances of winning, and (2) a result of anxiety over what massive immigration was doing to the sectional balance and settlement of the West.[75]

Of course, many Free Soilers in Massachusetts and elsewhere did not join the Know Nothing movement. They included Adams, Palfrey, Dana, and E. R. Hoar among the conservative Free Soilers, men who had already shown themselves willing to accept frequent defeat, rather than compromise their principles on issues other than slavery. Likewise, Sumner, Bird, Allen, and Stearns, among those who had worked with Wilson, were repelled by the ideas of the Know Nothings. Bird never fully respected Wilson again. On the other hand, Bird spent much of his life in the minority because he would not bend. In other states where the Whig party still might win, men like Seward and Lincoln could more easily maintain their friendship with and concern for aliens by rejecting nativism. Hale would work with the party, but would not join it. In the West Julian, Giddings, and Wade rejected Know Nothingism; so did Chase, although he tried to soften the differences. The *National Era* was stinging in its condemnation of the party. Among the Free Soilers of Massachusetts who did become Know Nothings were Burlingame, Keyes, Swift, and Stone.[76]

The Republicans were so weakened that in September, in the midst of a major political campaign, they lost their primary newspaper support. The *Commonwealth* could not be continued. Adams claimed it had taken $30,000 from its backers during its three-and-a-half-year life. Its successor, the *Evening Telegraph*, had other concerns in addition to slavery. It would be devoted to "temperance, human freedom, and Protestantism."[77]

The political caldron bubbled throughout much of the North in the late summer and fall of 1854. Slavery and antislavery, fugitive slaves, expansion westward and outside American borders, liquor, religious reform and spiritualism, labor issues, feminism—all concerned some of the people. The first elections were held in Iowa in mid-August. This was a state whose legislature in the late 1840s had refused to pass antislavery resolves. Even in the spring of 1854 the Democrats had elected the superintendent of public instruction. But in August James W. Grimes, soon to become Republican leader in the state, running as a Whig with Free Soil and temperance support, opposed by some conservatives of his own party, won a victory which pleased both the members of his own party and Republicans. A month later the Whig fusionists of Vermont replaced the Democratic governor with one of their own and captured the House by a majority of over one hundred. Anson Morrill, the candidate of the anti-Nebraska, temperance men of Maine, surprised the Democrats and Whigs; his legislature would be overwhelmingly fusion.[78]

A pattern of voter behavior is more difficult to ascertain in the October elections. Clearly the Democrats were the losers. In Pennsylvania the Know Nothings often cast their ballots for selected members of the other parties, producing strange results. The Democratic governor William Bigler failed reelection while anti-Nebraska candidates, Whig and Know Nothing, captured eighteen of twenty-five congressional seats; four of the seven Democrats were anti-Nebraska. Ohio had given Pierce a large majority in 1852 and the Democratic gubernatorial candidate an even larger one in 1853. The results were now devastating for the administration. The entire Ohio House delegation would be anti-Nebraska. While the Whig *National Intelligencer* called the election a Whig victory, the *National Era* termed the victors anti-Democratic, rather than Whig. In Indiana the antiadministration forces took nine congressional seats, the Democrats two. The state legislature would be controlled by an anti-Nebraska majority. While the newspapers differed in their analysis of who won, clearly the Know Nothings—often anti-Nebraska and temperance advocates as well—controlled the results.[79]

Wilson had committed himself to a new, secret movement as the only way to have any effect on the election in 1854. The Kansas-Nebraska controversy had first surprised, then angered the North. By midspring it had galvanized most of the North into a cooperation and similarity of thought few could have hoped for when the year began. But this had not engendered unity of action. The confusing political scene permitted temperance and nativism to become greater issues than they otherwise might have been and dampened possibilities of political fusion among those who opposed the new "aggressions of the Slave Power." Furthermore, the Whigs were still numerous in many states. Their leaders would neither surrender their positions of power nor plunge themselves into the unknown of party reorganization. The promise of June to create a new party dedicated to opposing the expansion of slavery in the territories was not fulfilled, except in several of the less-populated states. By the time the Massachusetts Know Nothing convention met in mid-October Wilson and his associates could only hope they still had the numbers and ability to turn the November election to their benefit.

11

A Know Nothing Elected Senator

The Know Nothing nominating convention for state offices was scheduled for Boston on October 18. Under party principles, delegates were free to support whomever they wanted, but once the convention had decided, members of the Order were obligated to vote in the public election for those selected. Already local, county, and congressional conventions had spawned extensive controversy between those who were primarily nativist and others who were as or more interested in temperance or slavery.

Many people at the time and in the years which followed professed to be virtually unaware of the existence of the Know Nothing party, but those who read the newspapers or participated very actively in the political process had to have known how important this new movement had become. Most commentators expected Know Nothing state candidates to obtain at least 30,000 votes; many expected majorities. Party decisions were no longer totally secret. The new *Boston Telegraph* on October 5 published the list of the party's candidates for Suffolk, Middlesex, and Norfolk Counties and some names for three other counties. The *Northampton Courier* two weeks later provided congressional nominations, many correct, for most districts. The *Boston Transcript* throughout October was full of information about Know Nothing activities.[1]

Because of the influence of Wilson and his antislavery associates, historians have sometimes ignored the importance of Whig Know Nothings. A Boston correspondent of the *New York Tribune,* in early September, claimed that since their own candidates could not win, many Whigs were joining the new party. The plan of the Whigs, he maintained, was to establish as many new lodges as possible and dominate the October nominating convention. The *New York Herald* reporter had a similar view. Six of the Know Nothing candidates for Congress were ex-Whigs. The press suggested a number of candidates for governor. These included Nahum F. Bryant of Barre, a lawyer and sometimes editor, described as a Whig of Free Soil tendencies; Ephraim M. Wright, Massachusetts secretary of state, former legislator and customs officer; Simeon Brown of Concord, an editor of an agricultural newspaper and a former Democrat; Marshall Wilder of Dorchester; and Wilson. The *Herald's* Boston reporter suggested eventual winner Henry J. Gardner's name. The week before the convention was to assemble, the *Atlas* declared a majority of delegates supported Wilson. This prompted a public denial from Wilson. He claimed he had not sought a single delegate. Given the depressed condition of his business and the responsibilities he had to forty people in his employ, he stated he had neither the time nor money to "pack conventions."[2]

Approximately fifteen hundred Know Nothings assembled in Boston's Tremont Temple on October 18. Henry J. Gardner was made presiding officer. The story commonly told after the convention was that Wilson and Burlingame had made a deal with Gardner to assure the gubernatorial nomination for Gardner in exchange for the United States Senate seat for Wilson. Why Gardner might have had that much influence at the convention or before has never been made clear. On the first ballot Wilder received 343 votes, Wright 180, Bryant 80, Wilson 66, and Brown 66. Wilder, who had joined the Order only a week before, was the candidate of the Boston Whigs. The convention was in an uproar, with recriminations leveled indiscriminately. Wilson was present, spoke, and withdrew his name. Peculiarly, contemporary sources do not reveal what he said. His biographer Mann twenty years later claimed that Wilson emphasized his long association with political antislavery, the need to break up the two larger national parties, the wisdom of selecting the Know Nothing nominees from among ex-Whigs and ex-Democrats, and his personal duty to support the decisions of the Republican convention. On the second ballot Bryant attained 323 votes, Wright 222, Eli Thayer 113, and Wilder fell to 109. On the third ballot Gardner suddenly was first with 396; Bryant had 254, Wright 108, Thayer 67, and Wilder 43. Gardener won with 623 votes on the fourth ballot. Brown was nominated for lieutenant governor to attract Democratic support.[3]

Gardner was thirty-five, a graduate of Bowdoin College, and a Boston dry goods merchant. He had been a life-long Whig. Although not a leader of the party, he had held several political offices, including two or three years in the state legislature and president of the Boston Common Council. Schouler characterized him as "a young man of fair abilities." The same month he received the Know Nothing nomination Gardner was continuing his Whig activities. He served as president of the Suffolk County Whig convention on October 5 and as chairman of the county ratification meeting a week later. A Webster follower, he had been a defender of the Fugitive Slave Law and an opponent of the liquor law. Almost alone among the members of the Boston Council, Gardner had supported President

Fillmore's actions in the Sims case. He had no past history of nativism. Gardner had served in the constitutional convention and had been an outspoken opponent of its ratification. Most of those who knew of him and his October actions regarded him as an opportunist. Within the next three years, that judgment would be confirmed. But Gardner was, or became, what George Hoar termed "a very skillful political organizer."[4]

What kind of person became a Know Nothing? Clearly the party included a large labor component, which tended to be more supportive of Wilson and Banks than of Gardner. The 1855 legislature contained fewer farmers, more men from the building trades and shops industries. Clergymen, physicians, teachers, and clerks were also more numerous. A large number of coalitionists, Democrat and Free Soil, voted Know Nothing. So did a large majority of the Whigs.[5]

Neither newspapers nor private correspondence reveals much about the fall campaign of the Republicans. The leaders knew that many of their supporters were becoming Know Nothing. Adams asked Bird in mid-October what the party was when 80 percent of its members had joined the Order. Sumner, anxious to campaign, was warned off, so that his reputation would not be damaged. In the crucial last weeks Republican leaders Alley and Claflin went to Cincinnati. Adams was invited to take a Whig nomination. Republican unhappiness with developments reached a climax at the Central Committee meeting on October 24. Many of those who attended were angry with their gubernatorial nominee, his participation in the Know Nothing convention, and his alleged deal with Gardner. Was he trying to prove that a man could not serve two masters, Allen asked? A *New York Post* writer reported Wilson, on being questioned by Allen, would not deny he and Gardner had an understanding.[6]

Allen was angry. The next day, at a Republican meeting in Worcester, he attacked. Acknowledging the good motives of some of those who had joined the Know Nothings, Allen nevertheless called their efforts a mistake. He condemned the Order's secrecy. More strongly, he went after Gardner for his support of the Fugitive Slave Law, including his being one of the marshal's bodyguards in the Sims rendition, and his record against temperance. Allen avoided direct criticism of Wilson, but in praising Increase Sumner and ignoring the primary Republican candidate, Allen was letting the world know what he thought.[7]

Gardner immediately issued a denial. He had headed the movement for the anti-Nebraska meeting the last winter, he contended, had spoken before it, and was an opponent of slavery. He had attempted to persuade the Whig State Central Committee to encourage fusion, but had been rebuffed. He repented his legislative votes against temperance. The *Springfield Republican* thought Gardner had bested Allen, at least on the slavery issue. The Boston correspondent of the *New York Herald* believed the public was satisfied, not so much because of the letter's contents but because of the boldness of Gardner's effort. In the meantime, the candidates for governor and lieutenant governor had been asked to define their position on the liquor law. Washburn and Wilson both expressed themselves in favor, but Washburn would not commit himself to approve the details of a particular prohibition statute. The temperance group endorsed Wilson for governor. In his letter to the state temperance society Gardner claimed he had been a member of the Total Abstinence Society for fourteen years and in that time he had never permitted a glass of wine or spirituous liquor to be served in his house. He explained his vote against the prohibition law as prompted by his conviction that the proposal was unconstitutional.[8]

Not everyone was persuaded. The editor of the moderate Whig *Boston Transcript,* in a lengthy editorial, attacked Gardner. He reported the candidate, while a member of the Committee on the Railroad Jubilee, had ordered liquor on board the excursion vessel. In addition, at the time of the Shadrach fugitive case, Gardner had insisted the Common Council pass a resolution pledging the city to enforce the laws. The editor concluded hardly a man in Boston had been so little attached to antislavery principles as Gardner. Schouler wrote from Cincinnati, astonished at Gardner's claims for Free Soil and temperance. Nor was Allen placated, although election day was so close, his efforts could have little effect.[9]

The private criticism by his Republican associates, the difficult position in which he had placed himself by attending the Know Nothing convention and working for the nomination of Gardner, and Allen's backhanded criticism prompted Wilson on November 1 to withdraw from the race. He claimed others felt compromised by his candidacy and that self-respect demanded he act. He emphasized he was not a candidate for any other office. No matter how hurt or angry his associates were, the party could not at that late moment select an alternate. The next day the Central Committee refused to accept the withdrawal. Nevertheless, several local conventions nominated Allen as their replacement for Wilson. His friend and biographer, Jonathan Mann, reported that Wilson voted for the Republican ticket.[10]

If one recalls that no governor had been elected by popular vote since the rise of the Free Soilers, then the 1854 election results become even more astounding than otherwise. Rain fell rapidly for forty-eight hours but the Know Nothing voters were not to be denied. Gardner received more than 81,000 votes (63 percent), the largest number any candidate for governor had ever attracted. Washburn collected more than 27,000, Bishop, the Democratic nominee, fewer than 14,000, and Wilson approximately 6,500. Wilson's vote had fallen by almost 80 percent. The Know Nothings captured every state Senate election and 376 out of 379 for the House. All eleven congressional seats went to Know Nothing–supported candidates; only Banks, also nominated by the Democrats, and DeWitt, also candidate of the Republicans, were reelected. Analysts estimate that between 74 and 78 percent of the Free Soilers voted Know Nothing. Historian William Gienapp concluded the Know Nothings won a large proportion of the Whig and a majority of both Free Soil and Democratic votes.[11]

The Massachusetts press was surprised. The *Boston Courier* spoke of the "most thorough and effectual organization," whose "discipline was perfect everywhere." Everett pronounced the "revolution complete." The Whig party was dead. Newspapers also used the word "revolution." The Republican *Boston Telegraph,* the Democratic *Boston Post,* and Catholic *Pilot* were as staggered at the Know Nothing sweep as Whig papers were. The editor of the *Northampton Courier* declared the old parties had been broken, the power of State Street ended. He didn't care that the Free Soil party was also destroyed, for he was confident its principles would yet be adopted. Outside of Boston the press in general, if surprised at the overwhelming nature of the vote, was pleased. Howe was correct also that the prestige of family and standing, which the Boston elite had been able to maintain in the face of thirty years of rising democracy, was also wounded.[12]

The Know Nothings had won, but what did that mean? The Massachusetts Democrats, who had ceased to be concerned about state victory, and the Pierce administration had been repudiated. The Whigs had been turned out of office permanently. Most commentators at the time and many historians since have seen in the vote a dissatisfaction with the existing parties and a support for not always defined reforms. Could the Know Nothing alliance of dissatisfied voters and leaders with conflicting objectives accomplish anything? The *Boston Advertiser* consoled itself that only 55 percent of the Whigs had deserted their party, compared to 62 percent of Democrats and 77 percent of Free Soilers. The antislaveryites, then, were the big losers. S. C. Phillips correctly commented the Free Soil movement was dead and was not replaced.[13]

Had Wilson and his associates attained their goals by abandoning the Republican party and joining the Know Nothings? They had destroyed Whig power. Perhaps that would have been done by the Know Nothings whether Wilson joined or not. Second, had the Free Soilers gained significant influence in Know Nothing councils? Yes, perhaps more than they deserved as a result of their contributions at the polls; they had cast only about 28 percent of the votes. They would not have one of their own as governor; Gardner was Whig and nativist. But he also could be antislavery. They would win the senatorship. The legislature would pass a personal liberty bill and an address to remove Judge Loring. And they could boast that seven of the eleven Congressmen were Free Soil. These were not lukewarm abolitionists: Robert Hall had been a founder of the New England Anti-Slavery Society; Mark Trafton and Chauncey Knapp were old Liberty party men; Burlingame, Comins, and Damrell had been leaders of the Free Soil movement; DeWitt and Banks had already voted their opposition to slavery in Congress. Furthermore, the Know Nothing-controlled General Court never passed any legislation which restricted the influence of immigrants.[14]

Elsewhere in the North the November election results were more confusing than they were in Massachusetts. The Democrats did not carry a single Northern state. Only seven Northern Democrats who had voted for the Kansas-Nebraska bill were reelected. The Democratic House majority of 75 was turned into a minority. In Wisconsin and Michigan, the only states in which it was effectively organized, the new Republican party won. In New York the Whig candidate for governor was elected by about 300 votes over the Democrat, each with only 33 percent of the total cast. The Know Nothing nominee was only 35,000 votes behind. Temperance and nativism were more important than Nebraska as issues. The Whigs swept the New Jersey races. In Illinois the Whigs and Republicans elected a majority of the nine congressmen and obtained enough control of the state legislature to prevent election of a Douglas supporter to the Senate. While the spring elections had injured the Democrats, the voters in the fall had spoken even more clearly. Only in Massachusetts among Northern states did the Know Nothings win, but they dominated the anti-Democratic movement in Indiana and played major roles in Maine, Ohio, Pennsylvania, and New York.

Wilson had clearly cast his lot with the Know Nothings. Know Nothings marched through the streets of Boston election night; both Swift and Gardner spoke. Wilson went to Gardner's residence to congratulate him, an act which pleased neither Howe nor *The Liberator*. The following evening three thousand Know Nothings were out and Wilson spoke to them from the balcony of the Marlboro Hotel. He praised the new governor as a "young, able and competent man" who would bring honor to the state. A new phenomenon in politics, *The Liberator* sarcastically commented, for a defeated candidate to be so joyous over his opponent's victory.[15]

Although holding no office, Wilson was a major Know Nothing speaker. On November 24 Wilson, Gardner, and Brown attended a festival at Waltham to honor the newly elected Congressman Banks. Wilson, in his address, expressed his pleasure at being together with men with whom he had previously differed politically. He cautioned fellow Know Nothings about what majorities the Democrats had enjoyed in 1853 and how quickly they fell. He emphasized his antislavery commitment. While deploring the efforts of other political parties to attract Irish and German voters, Wilson emphasized he was not against foreigners just because they had been born abroad. Four nights later fifteen hundred Know Nothings celebrated their election victories at the Fitchburg Railroad Station in Boston. The governor-elect, lieutenant governor-elect, Wilson, Banks, and three new members of Congress spoke; when the chairman had to leave early, Wilson presided. The new congressmen all emphasized the importance to them of antislavery, with Comins repudiating the platform Senator Clayton of Delaware had recently offered for the Know Nothings.[16]

Inspired by their victories, delegates from state Know Nothing councils assembled in Cincinnati in mid-November. Whig Congressman Kenneth Raynor of North Carolina proposed and got passed nearly unanimously a new degree of the Order by which members assented to maintain and preserve the union. While

Wilson and most of the Free Soil Know Nothings could endorse this provision, it later would be used in Northern states to attack antislavery sentiments.[17]

The participation of many of the Wilson faction in the Know Nothing movement offered a new opportunity to the conservative Free Soilers. Not only might they gain control of what was left of the party, but they would be working with men like Sumner and Howe, who, in contrast to the Adams faction, had commanded influence within the party because they had continued to labor for it. Bailey from Washington urged reorganization. Adams, Palfrey, Phillips, and Sumner talked, but they did not know what to do. Eventually a reluctant Stone was persuaded to call a meeting for December 27. A rally of old Liberty and Free Soil men under the old banner, Howe characterized the conclave. Adams, Phillips, Howe, Bird, Spooner, Keyes, E. L. Pierce, and Carter were among those in attendance. So were three Know Nothings—Kimball, Slack, and Stone. As might be anticipated, the majority favored keeping the organization. Otherwise they took no action. Stone thought they could count on 10,000 to 15,000 supporters. Whether they could attract more depended upon what the Know Nothings did. They met again two weeks later and designated a committee to plan strategy. With the Free Soil movement dead in other states and with the conservatives unhappy with the Republican party, they reestablished the committee of 1853. Phillips was to draw up an address to the public. But he delayed until April, when the time was inappropriate for a statement.[18]

A favorite topic of post-election speculation was the senatorship. Gardner had scarcely been nominated when a deal was alleged between his supporters and Wilson, the latter to be elected senator. The *Boston Advertiser* laughed that if it wasn't a deal, it was, to use Wilson's own word of 1851, a "programme." In his letter of withdrawal from the Republican nomination for governor, Wilson had denied he had made any arrangement. With the Know Nothing victory, the press concluded that the Wilson selection was assured. If there were any doubt, the *New York Herald* reporter said, Gardner's speech on election night corrected it. Sumner was convinced. But Wilson and his supporters were not as confident. According to Howe, Wilson and Wilder, the two major contenders, actively canvassed the legislators for votes. Adams declared such an activity in Massachusetts was unprecedented. Wilder was an ex-Whig and, like Wilson, had been president of the state Senate. As 1854 drew to a close the *Springfield Republican* prophesied a Wilson victory; his friends had been working hard for him and many ex-Whig Free Soilers favored him.[19]

The new General Court not only was composed of more men serving for the first time than ever before in the state's history, but it also lacked experienced legislative leaders. Only thirty-four representatives and six senators had held office before. Only eleven were lawyers. While all Know Nothing, the representatives had previously been divided among the three parties, so that none of the parties could control decisions. Caucuses were, of course, much larger than usual and experienced difficulty choosing the presiding officers and clerks of the two houses. The *Springfield Republican* reported that Wilson, to have more influence over decisions, slept in Boston instead of Natick.[20]

Governor Gardner's address was long, touching on a variety of state policies. He barely mentioned temperance. While he devoted only one out of eighteen pages to slavery, he demanded the restoration of the Missouri Compromise and spoke for the protection of civil rights, especially trial by jury and habeas corpus. The main thrust of the message was nativist. Gardner was concerned about four million immigrants entering Massachusetts in the 1850s and the problems they would create. He promised to disband military companies composed of men of foreign birth, recommended a law preventing voting by those who could not read and write English, and asked for an amendment to the state constitution, requiring twenty-one years' residence for naturalized citizens before they could vote.[21]

The General Court was expected quickly to elect a new United States senator. Wilder's support weakened in January and Alfred Ely of Boston, an early Know Nothing, became Wilson's chief opponent. Know Nothing lodges all over the state were canvassed to engender support for or against Wilson. Wilson was opposed by some former Free Soilers who were angry with his backing of the Gardner nomination. Others believed Wilson's election would endanger the growth of the party nationally, sending the wrong message to Southern Know Nothings. Many doubted Wilson was a true nativist. A senator had to be chosen by majority vote separately in each chamber of the General Court. Votes commonly were cast as decided by caucuses. Since all senators and almost all House members were Know Nothing, the caucus was all-important. By the second week of January Wilson supporters were confident of a majority in a joint caucus. But the opposition persuaded a number of senators to demand an independent caucus.[22]

The election became a bitter battle. One Boston lodge directed Slack to vote against Wilson. Slack resigned his office in the council and withdrew from the Order. On January 12 House Know Nothings in caucus selected Wilson, first by a majority of one on an informal poll, then with twenty-six more votes than he needed on the formal ballot. The opposition had no attractive alternate candidate, Ely securing only fifty-seven supporters. At an anti-Wilson meeting on the following Monday about one hundred legislators voted to try to postpone the election. Wilson's old opponent Devereaux, now a fellow Know Nothing, in the House attacked the candidate and challenged the haste of the caucus's decision. After a lengthy debate, the House, by a 62-vote majority, postponed its vote a week. The Senate, by a 19-to-13 vote, postponed until January 31. Both sides caucused after adjournment of the sessions. Stone assured Sumner that Wilson's partisans agreed to the change to attract even more support.[23]

The following day another caucus was called and approximately 350 attended. Even the press was allowed in. The character of Wilson was assailed and defended. His nativism came in for special questioning. He was not national enough, others said. The session was lengthy. Stone and Slack, the leaders of the Wilson forces, were trying to give every appearance of fairness. Two representatives said they had not voted for Wilson, but he was the candidate of the caucus and deserved support. Perry of New Salem had entered the caucus anti-Wilson, but was so unhappy with the charges he had heard, he would now support the man. The next day some of the Wilson opponents met again and agreed to endorse Bryant, not a man who could attract wide support. Continuing opposition by the Boston Whig press and by Southern Know Nothings were contributing to swing undecided representatives to Wilson.[24]

The House voted on January 23 as scheduled, with Wilson elected on the first ballot, obtaining 234 votes, 50 more than needed. Bryant had 85, Julius Rockwell 18, Ely 9, and 28 were scattered. The opposition still hoped it could prevent Senate action. The Boston Whig press kept up a constant attack, although Whig papers elsewhere preferred Wilson over the alternatives. The *Kennebec Journal* and the *Cincinnati Gazette* praised him. The *Albany Evening Journal* characterized Wilson as "a man of great ability," neither "impractical nor factious." To counter some of the opposition, Wilson chose to answer a letter from Robert Hall of Boston, who claimed that the issues of nativism were of "paramount importance" and that Wilson was alleged to have made speeches in the constitutional convention throwing into question his principles. Wilson replied in the *Boston Bee,* the Know Nothing newspaper, on January 23, the day of the House vote. The *Bee,* which had earlier opposed Wilson's selection, now supported him. The *Springfield Republican* believed Hall's letter had been contrived and that Wilson had ably smoothed over "the rough juts of his past political life with . . . ease and nonchalance."[25]

A large crowd assembled to witness the Senate ballot. Wilson won by one vote; he received 21, E. M. Wright 15, Rockwell 3, and Banks 1. Stone was so confident of victory that a report in several newspapers that five of Wilson's friends were going to change their vote to support him on the second ballot must have been true. Of the nineteen votes against Wilson, five were from his own Middlesex County, four from Suffolk.[26]

The press was incongruous in its response. A number of Know Nothing papers nationwide were unhappy with the selection. Some Free Soil publications were equally dissatisfied. The *National Era* attacked Wilson's reply to Hall and cited the *New York Herald* claim that the new senator had abandoned his antislavery beliefs and would enter Congress as a conservative Know Nothing. A Worcester reader criticized Bailey for his stance, characterizing the legislature as the most antislavery ever elected in Massachusetts. Wilson had backbone and would be faithful to liberty, he maintained. Massachusetts Free Soil papers were more pleased. The *Northampton Courier* called Wilson's election a "triumph for anti-slavery principles." The *Dedham Gazette* characterized it as no ordinary victory, in light of the unrelenting attacks of the Boston press. The Democratic *Boston Post,* unhappy with the selection, termed Wilson the most outspoken Free Soil man in the state. Massachusetts Whig papers regarded the election as a disaster, but, as the *Northampton Courier* pointed out, they had delivered "systematic abuse" of Wilson for seven years. The *New York Tribune* saw irony in its rejoicing at the election of a Know Nothing, but knew Wilson would be true to the slave. Its Washington correspondent reported Whigs and Republicans in the capital were delighted with the selection.[27]

The Boston elite varied in its response. Charles Eliot Norton complained Wilson had few qualifications for the post and was an intriguer, but he did have a "stiff backbone regarding slavery." Amos A. Lawrence called the election "too bad a joke to be true," but admitted Wilson might yet distinguish himself and honor the state. He had risen from the "cow yard to the Senate & therefore he may rise to great respectability by the use of his varied talent."[28]

Wilson's election was applauded by many abolitionists and Free Soilers. Long-time associate Whittier praised him: "a hard and close student, and no man better understands the history, laws, constitutions and political elements of the country. He is a fluent and forcible speaker, and his power as a controversial writer has been severely felt by some of his political opponents." Theodore Parker, preferring Phillips or Adams, because they had not sought the office, was nevertheless enthusiastic about Wilson. He was especially pleased by having a shoemaker in the Senate. Wilson would show the nation how a poor man could succeed. In the last seven years, Parker concluded, Wilson had done more than any other politician in New England "to liberalize and humanize the actions of the political parties." To Wilson was due the credit for organization of the Free Soil party, revolutionizing the "Fogyism" of Harvard College, and the election of Sumner. Other abolitionists, including Wendell Phillips and Garrison, while lamenting Wilson's Know Nothingism, approved of his election. Even Dana conceded Wilson would secure the voice of the state for antislavery.[29]

Other former associates were not as complimentary. An unforgiving Bird more than twenty years later was still charging this had been the only election ever won in Massachusetts by "truck and dicker." Adams in his diary expressed relief at Wilson's election, predicating it relieved him of difficulties by placing the two men on opposite sides. Even Sumner, according one biographer, was not too happy to have Wilson as a colleague, although the reason may have been the senior senator's opposition to nativism.[30]

The day after his election, Wilson accompanied Gardner to a Burlingame address at Tremont Temple. When the primary speaker had finished, the audience called for their new senator. Wilson did not have to take a controversial position. He could have said little of substance. Furthermore, as a freshman senator, he would not have to take an unpopular position in the month Congress would be in session before adjournment. Wilson must have wanted to reply to the charges of the *New York Herald* about his antislavery views. In his short remarks he commended the abolition sentiments of Burlingame's address. Wilson would not yield his abolition position, he declared. He would live and die with unrelenting opposition to slavery. The *Herald* responded by calling Wilson the "most fanatical and implacable abolitionist ever sent" to the Senate. It contended the Know Nothing State Council had to repudiate Wilson's views.[31]

Wilson's addition to the Senate was not the only change taking place as a result of the Kansas-Nebraska controversy and the collapse of the old political structure. The 1855 selections to the Senate were vital to the future success of those who opposed the extension of slavery. In several states the political picture was so chaotic, no choice could be made. In New York Seward and Weed had been wise to remain for another campaign within the Whig party. A Whig had been elected governor and he used his power to help with the senator's reelection. Seward was popular, particularly among those opposed to slavery. In Illinois Lincoln, a Whig, could not attract enough antislavery and anti-Nebraska Democratic votes to be elected, but those opposed to Douglas compromised on anti-Nebraska Democrat Lyman Trumball. In New Hampshire Know Nothing–Whig James Bell and Free Soil Hale were selected. Charles Durkee in Wisconsin and James Harlan in Iowa were also anti-Nebraska men.[32]

Wilson intended to leave for Washington on February 6. A snowstorm delayed his departure for two days. On February 5 twelve hundred of his friends and townspeople gathered in Natick to honor the community's most famous citizen. The hall was decorated with banners and a band provided music. More than ten speakers paid tribute. In his short reply Wilson noted how his public and private character had constantly been impugned. He denied making any arrangement with Gardner over the senatorship. He had followed his convictions. When he departed on the train from Boston for Washington, a large number of his friends, including some of the legislators, were at the station to see him off. Later other supporters assembled at the Worcester depot to express their best wishes.[33]

When Wilson took his Senate seat he was yet a young man, forty-three years old, 5 feet, 10 inches in height, and weighing about 165 pounds. He had blue eyes. People spoke of his vigorous frame. His health was excellent. He was described as having a "florid complexion, brown hair, ample brow, strong, clear voice . . . good natured and decidedly good looking." Several commentators use the word "ruddy" to describe his complexion. "A portly figure," more than one contemporary characterized him. He was "always clad," McClure tells us, "in elegant, but unostentatious apparel."[34]

One might presume Wilson would close his shoe business before he left for Washington; however, since he sold one-third the number of shoes he had the previous full year, he apparently continued with that employment until April, as Oliver Bacon wrote, with some relative or friend managing affairs. Wilson's worldly possessions, after sale of the business, amounted to his home and $2,500 in cash. He loaned $1,400 of that to a friend, who never repaid the debt. More than sixty others, in the small, rather poor community of Natick, paid higher taxes than

Wilson in 1856. Congressmen until 1855–1856 were paid by the day, which, critics charged, tended to lengthen the session. Thereafter, for a seven- or eight-month session one year, a three-month session the next, pay was $2,000, with $8.50 deducted for each day absent. Mileage was also allowed, with a Kansas Congressman collecting $17,000, while Wilson in the Thirty-fifth Congress (1857–1859) received $739. Wilson thus had $1,100 and a salary of $3,000 a year to live on, at least part of the time in one of the country's most expensive cities. He would spend the rest of his life with very little income; Wilson remarked to a friend a few weeks before his death in 1875 that he could sell all he owned for $8,000. During the 1850s he not only supported his wife and son, but his mother-in-law, as well. While there is no evidence, he probably also contributed money until their death to sustain his parents. Senator Henry B. Anthony of Rhode Island, in his memorial address in the Senate, asserted that Wilson carried his contempt for money to a fault. For all of this he had to have been, as Clerk of the House and Democratic leader John W. Forney characterized him, a man of simple tastes and frugal habits.[35]

In his eulogy at Wilson's death, long-time political associate Henry L. Dawes interestingly concluded that Wilson had "lived from infancy to the end as no other man has lived." He was "a creation, a force all by itself." That was a true appraisal of the man and his role in American history. What were the other characteristics of this man, who was about to become as important to the nation as he already had been to his state? Perhaps the quality most frequently alluded to was honesty. Other endowments often mentioned were loyalty and ambition. Yet newspaper editor and Republican leader Alexander J. McClure, a careful judge, contended Wilson never permitted friendship to deter him from duty. A number of commentators spoke of his "indomitable courage." As befitted one who had been often reminded of his humble origins, first by his state's Whig leadership, later by the Palfrey-Dana-Adams faction among the Free Soilers, Wilson was modest; at the same time he had come to appreciate his own abilities and accomplishments. He had already demonstrated in the state Senate and at the convention his distaste for arrogance and assumption.[36]

At the time of Wilson's election, the Boston *Congregationalist,* spoke of Wilson's high moral standing in his own community. He was a regular and devout attendant of church and a supporter of the town's religious institutions. He was kind-hearted, generous, and influential. Another religious publication declared Wilson made others wish there were more "Christian statesmen."[37]

Wilson was especially known for his kind treatment of others, whether friend or adversary. McClure was with him hundreds of times, he reported, but he had never heard Wilson utter a word that could give unreasonable offense to anyone. "Genial" is a term several commentators applied to him. "Gentle," "good-natured," "conciliatory" were other words used. Almost everyone liked Wilson and was attracted by the sympathetic warmth of his nature, Carl Schurz wrote. He was helped because he was a gentleman in both manners and address. He possessed a kindness of heart, no selfishness, envy, or hate, Dawes said. He was often the peacemaker, Senator Morrill reported. One would not realize from the Wilson portrayed in the papers of Adams, Palfrey, and Dana that he labored to avoid offense and was pained by strife. Forney remembered that Wilson was often the natural medium between quarreling associates. He could talk to an enemy as a friend. Wilson never seemed annoyed by harsh words, a *New York Tribune* obituary writer declared, but Wilson did remember them. Stephen Douglas is supposed to have said that if he had any favor to ask of the Republicans, he preferred going to Wilson, who did not allow political differences to interfere with the courtesies of life. As a result, once he got into the Senate Wilson was involved in few personal controversies and made few personal enemies.[38]

Many of his Washington and Massachusetts associates commented upon Wilson's continuing love of reading and knowledge. He had a respect for learning and a love of information, Robinson said. Senator Aaron H. Cragin characterized Wilson as a student all his life, adding that he read history and biography more than poetry and fiction. His biographer Nason recorded that Wilson might read or write fifteen or sixteen hours a day, much as he had worked in his shop that long. Mann declared he had a talent for original investigation and patient research. Forney and Banks were also impressed with his reading. Boutwell was less generous, remembering Wilson as having no extraordinary aptitude for scholarly pursuits, but endowed with a heroic determination to acquire knowledge.[39]

It was difficult to talk or write about Wilson and not mention his opposition to slavery. Even his detractors, like Dana, Palfrey, and Lawrence, on learning of his election as senator, recognized the slave had a new defender in high places. Some newspapers attempted to create political trouble by reporting his lukewarmness towards abolition, but compared to Sumner, Wilson was quick, once elected senator, in making his position known. "Antislavery sentiment filled his whole soul," Schurz wrote. He was a "hater of slavery," whose "war on these wrongs became a mission," according to Dawes. He had dedicated his life to emancipation, Banks declared, and that left him with a long and proud record as an abolitionist, a word which Wilson, in contrast to many of his associates, never shunned.[40]

Wilson knew what he thought about slavery, temperance, the union, and many other subjects. But if a topic were new, or the strategy he should pursue not clear, George Hoar recorded, Wilson could hesitate long. Boutwell called that vacillation. Garrison characterized Wilson as moving "carefully and circumspectly." People who did not know him would think he was indecisive, Hoar declared. Banks understood that Wilson was seeking the views of his constituency. Wilson would travel all over the state, Hoar revealed, spending a day visiting forty shops and factories near Boston, take an evening train to Springfield, get there at 2 or 3 a.m., call out of bed some politician, spend the night talking with him, then go on to Greenfield or Northampton to see some person whom most politicians did not even know, but whom Wilson had found understood the political sentiment of the area.

He might spend two or three weeks that way. Others would become angry with their senator. But when he made up his mind, Hoar continued, he would have all his own determination, sometimes moral fire and righteousness, behind his actions, and also the strength and power of public sentiment, which he knew.[41]

In his fifteen years in politics prior to election as senator Wilson had spoken to more people in his state than any other politician, about one-quarter of the population of Massachusetts. He "knew everybody from Barnstable to the Berkshires," the *New York Tribune* asserted. He understood the pulse of Massachusetts and later the North. The "keenest political prophet we ever had," the writer of Wilson's obituary in the *Independent* declared. The *New York Herald* concluded Wilson and Jackson had been the two best judges of popular sentiment in American politics. "Each had an unerring and almost intuitive perception of what the people wanted." His predictions about elections were usually very near the result. Any success at the polls elated him. "His step, always quick and firm," Mann wrote, "gained new speed & strength. His whole figure showed a transformation. His eyes flashed with unusual fire." On the other hand, when the 1856 Pennsylvania state election presaged a defeat for Fremont, Wilson could not hide his despondency from his young, inexperienced Republican associates.[42]

Two components of Wilson's ability to secure the will of the people are evident. The first is that he cared, not only because doing what the voters want gets a politician reelected, but because (1) he had not been separated from them by birth or breeding but was one of the people, and (2) he was sincere in his faith in the intelligence and integrity of the common person. Second, Wilson was tireless. Almost everyone commented on it. "Prodigious" was the word many used to characterize this energy. He would sit up all hours of the night, sometimes working, sometimes talking with others. He never slept, Forney declared. Swift is supposed to have said that the difference between Wilson and Burlingame was that Burlingame never got up and Wilson never went to bed. McClure in his long political life may have known more politicians than any other American; he had never met one who worked longer than Wilson, yet the man never seemed exhausted. This was possible because of another characteristic of Wilson frequently cited, the soundness and strength of his body. Journalist and abolitionist E. Z. Pangborn contended Wilson had never taken a day of recreation from the age of ten until his death at sixty-three. Boutwell thought his capacity to work was fortunate because Wilson had more obstacles to overcome than any other man he had known.[43]

Wilson possessed other qualities and habits of work which helped him to rise to leadership in the Senate and be elected time after time. He easily fell into conversation, comfortable with almost everyone. That helped keep him popular with his constituents, with politicians, and with his fellow senators. Senate records demonstrate he attended regularly; part of the reason for that was, of course, his good health. But also he was interested in the work of the body, he liked cooperating with others, and he was skillful at many duties asked of a senator. His power of concentration helped, so did his energy and extraordinary physical capacity. He had a tenacious memory. He not only was present, but he paid close attention to business. He possessed a clear head. He was quick to comprehend the directions of debate. In contrast to Sumner, he was eminently practical as a legislator. He was effective not only with public business, but did an immense amount of service for his individual constituents. Because Sumner was not performing his duties a good part of four years in the late 1850s, Wilson had extra work. Later, during the Civil War, only the chairman of the Finance Committee had nearly the labor Wilson had as chairman of the Military Affairs Committee.[44]

By the time Wilson entered the Senate, his style of speaking and understanding of how to influence others had been attained. Commentators were almost unanimous in their view that Wilson's speeches either in Congress or on the stump were not marks of eloquence by the standards, particularly among the well educated, of that day. An able public speaker, rather than an orator, his friend of twenty years, Senator Cragin of New Hampshire, characterized Wilson. "Loose and ramshackle in his manner of speech," Noah Brooks reported. His enunciation was indistinct, and he was often imprecise in his choice of words. Senator Morrill believed Wilson avoided flowery language because he wanted to be understood. Put another way, he was more interested in what he said than how he said it. Wilson was able to master the data of most political questions. Especially in major addresses in the Senate, he would muster evidence as few other speakers would. In fact, he was reluctant to address a subject he had not mastered. Another strength of Wilson's was the depth and earnestness of his convictions. His sarcasm could be telling.[45]

Before he entered the Senate, Wilson had obviously become a skillful and adroit manager. That had been a reason for his rise in politics. It had also been a reason some of the conservative Free Soilers disliked him. The *Independent* claimed he understood management and policy; above all, he was practical. Rather early in his senatorial career he divorced himself from the everyday politics of Massachusetts in a way a Chase in Ohio or a Simon Cameron in Pennsylvania did not. He turned his attention and skills to the national level. Wilson's knowledge of public men was more broad and intimate than that of any other man of his generation, the long-time political boss McClure recorded. Boutwell described Wilson as "chief of all chiefs" in the working and organizing of forces for the two national political contests of 1856 and 1860. Yet his return from congressional sessions was a political event, as his views were sought by allies who were running the party at home.[46]

When Everett arrived in Washington in late 1853, he commented on the changes which made his trip much easier than when he had first been sent as a congressman. Then, travel took a week: three days to New York City, two to Philadelphia, two more to Baltimore, and part of a day to the capital. But Everett in 1853 and Wilson fifteen months later could make the entire trip by railroad in a day, if they traveled by night. The cost was not high and it was much more comfortable. Soon Wilson would be undertaking the journey many times a year.[47]

On Monday, February 12, 1855, with less than three weeks remaining in the session, Wilson's credentials were presented by Sumner, the oath was prescribed, and Wilson took his seat. Senator Clayton, Whig and Know Nothing, had suggested Wilson be placed on the Whig side, while Sumner and Chase preferred he sit with the Free Soilers. Wilson ended up in a vacant chair alongside an anti-Nebraska Know Nothing, near Sumner and Chase. Several days later Parker wrote to him about the "dangers" of Wilson's new position. He warned him not to become overbearing and a braggart. He was concerned that Wilson intended to make his living from politics. But Parker was comforted that Wilson was "by nature" sympathetic with the people, and he knew Wilson would be faithful. He advised him to give up Know Nothingism. Wilson had not been in his new job long before he discovered Sumner had quarreled with almost all his Republican colleagues and was not speaking with many of them. Wilson realized he needed to find ways to bring together those who had broken with the two major parties.[48]

Although Sumner may not have been pleased with Wilson's election, the two quickly developed a relationship, both as friends and as senators from the same state, that was remarkable for its duration, strength, and effectiveness. It was possible because of the trust and integrity of the two men towards each other. They were a well-matched team, supplementing and complimenting one another. Congressman Clymer contrasted the two in his eulogy of Wilson. Sumner represented the cultivated, self-poised, admirable Boston society, Wilson represented a "warmer, more loveable, more American" Massachusetts. Sumner was a man of books, Wilson of men. Sumner evoked ideas, Wilson produced deeds. Sumner was a man of theories, Wilson of action. Sumner proceeded with indifference, if not contempt, towards the forces which existed in the political arena or in Congress, expecting to gain what he advocated sometime in the future. Wilson was much more aware of the real world and molded the influences around him, subordinating minor matters to accomplish some end he sought. Sumner could be dictatorial and impressive, Wilson genial and conciliatory. Sumner lacked the attributes of a practical statesman; after Wilson joined him, he had the luxury of being even more detached. Sumner could not be trusted to get bills enacted. Wilson was one of the most effective senators in accomplishing that. George Hoar concluded, "Wilson supplied almost everything Sumner lacked."[49]

Wilson was not a stranger to Washington, having made a number of trips, sometimes for visits of several weeks. The community had changed little since the 1830s, Forney wrote. The city was not very attractive. A "straggling village" with "dreary distances," Forney described it. Pennsylvania Avenue was a dirt road which crossed Tiber Creek on a wooden bridge. Most streets were poorly paved, almost impassable and poorly lighted at night. The city had no streetcars, only omnibuses which ran from the Capitol to Georgetown. On the Mall were the Smithsonian Institute, the Botanical gardens, and the uncompleted Washington Monument, almost 150 feet tall, inching towards completion. The Mall was neglected and unkempt. In 1855 plans began to erect a new dome on the Capitol. The early part of the decade was also marked with the construction of an aqueduct from the falls of the Potomac to a reservoir in Georgetown to free the city from the scourges of polluted wells. Just south of Pennsylvania Avenue the Chesapeake and Ohio Canals emptied into the Tiber, often called an open sewer. Along the Tiber were lumber and wood yards. Malaria was a constant problem. Allen had withdrawn after two terms as Congressman when his health would not take the Washington climate. And then there was slavery, a deplorable experience for some Northerners.[50]

During most of the year Washington was a quiet city. When Congress assembled it could be busy and gay, so that people of every class lived in expectation of the next session. The summer was hot, dusty, unhealthy, and dull; congressmen were eager to leave. The city's primary amusements were gambling houses, lottery offices, and a poor theater. As December approached, hotels and boardinghouses filled up, even clerks became more energetic. Most senators and distinguished guests stayed on "the avenue" at Willard's, Brown's, the Kirkwood House, the National, or the St. Charles. Boardinghouses were usually less expensive, but often more dreary. If the structure were as large as the National, with its capacity for 800 guests, one could not as carefully choose associates. But in general, residents tended to live near those who thought similarly to themselves, and by the middle 1850s, sectional lines especially were being drawn. Congressmen who owned their own homes, as Senators Douglas and Breckenridge did, were commonly located near one another in the northwest corner. Servants were still cheap, but rent and food prices were high.[51]

Social life was ruled by politicians with the position, prestige, and money to attract others or by the old aristocracy. In the 1850s both of these were controlled by Southern-sympathizers. President Pierce's entertaining was limited to necessary functions; the leading members of his cabinet either were uninterested in frequent social activities or had family difficulties which prevented entertaining. For most larger social functions, members of the diplomatic corps, cabinet officials, senators, representatives, and military and naval officers had to be invited. Yet the nonbusiness activities of many congressmen, especially those whose wives did not accompany them to Washington, were limited. Camaraderie in the cloakrooms and messes was valuable. Alliances at messes were important, and votes often were decided there. Four of the most powerful Republicans, who would dominate the economic affairs of the decade—Fessenden, Grimes, Justin Morrill, and Elihu Washburne—boarded in 1861 with Mrs. Shipman on Seventh Street.[52]

During the 1840s some of those with a common antipathy towards slavery began to meet at the home of Gamaliel Bailey, former physician, Cincinnati abolitionist and editor of the *Philanthropist,* and leader of the Liberty party. Bailey in 1847 had gone to Washington, a hotbed of slavery sentiments, to found an antislavery newspaper, the *National Era*, which after formation of the new party became the leading Free Soil journal. Mrs. Margaret Bailey, a Virginian by birth, was an intelligent, witty, enthusiastic, and gifted woman who presided over an active social circle. In the early 1850s the Baileys moved to a larger house on C Street, where their Saturday receptions became a regular attraction. These were "brilliant affairs." In the late 1840s and early 1850s men of all parties who were antislavery could reenforce one another, strengthen each other's resolve, and escape from the increasing ostracism of Washington society. By the late 1850s, of course, most of these people had become Republicans. Among those often at the Baileys' receptions were politicians Wilson, Seward, Sumner, Hale, Chase, Giddings, Julian, Allen, Wade, Durkee, Wilmot, King, Rantoul, Julian, Palfrey, Mann, and Thaddeus Stevens; even Corwin and Justice McLean; and Leavitt, Tappan, Whittier, Moncure Conway, and Harriet Beecher Stowe.[53]

Wilson was an untypical Massachusetts congressman in more ways than his politics. Between 1790 and 1850 two-thirds of the senators and more than half of the representatives had been lawyers. Most others had belonged to the professions or business. At least one senator at all times was a lawyer.[54]

The United States Senate was a body already with a long tradition and dignity. It was meeting in 1855 in a small room which before the end of the decade would be turned over to the Supreme Court. Open fires provided heat. If the winter were severe some of the older men, to keep warm, might spend more time at the open grates than listening to debates. Senators handled their own correspondence, for the government provided no secretaries. The Capitol building had no telegraph office, no barbershop, not even a bathroom. There was a post office and a restaurant. The Senate was sensitive about dignity and honor. Wilson soon became known as one of those most concerned. A page during the 1850s termed Wilson as "an index of decorum, always preserving an austere manner in the chamber." He cited one instance when Representative Farnsworth of Illinois seated himself in the Senate with his feet on a desk, a posture at variance with Senate traditions. Wilson, although a friend of Farnsworth, directed the page to tell his associate that his conduct was inappropriate in that chamber.[55]

The Senate consisted of sixty-two members. The Democratic majority controlled business. The power of the committee structure was in place by the mid-1840s; chairmanships went to the majority and the number of minority members of a committee was determined by the majority. Increasingly by the middle 1850s Democrats were expected to follow party caucus decisions. Although older and established Whigs like Crittenden and Bell were the exception, the majority Democrats had become domineering and offensive to members of the minority. On occasion members of the dominant party would go out of their way to seek controversies and assail senators among the minority.[56]

While he had been careful to reiterate his antislavery views, Wilson had also arrived in Washington as a senator elected by a Know Nothing–controlled legislature. He had an obligation to work with other members of and support the tenants of that party. Hoping to weaken the party, which had become the main Democratic opposition in his state, Senator Henry Wise of Virginia on February 5 launched a three-hour attack on the Know Nothings, latching on to Wilson's election as demonstrating the antislavery character of the party. To other Know Nothings it mattered what Wilson said and did. He was "courted and flattered," asked to forget or minimize his antislavery principles to assist in the growth of a national party. A Know Nothing candidate for governor of Georgia, declared Wilson, could determine the results of the Georgia election.[57]

Shortly thereafter, the editor of the *American Organ*, the capital's Know Nothing newspaper asked Wilson a series of questions which, by their nature, were intended to give the new senator the opportunity to proclaim his nationalism and thwart efforts to divide the party on the issue of slavery. Did Wilson recognize the power of a state to regulate slavery therein? Did Congress have the power to interfere with slavery in a state? Did Wilson accept the "higher law" doctrine and thereby ignore the constitution? Was slavery a subject the Know Nothing party in Massachusetts was formed to handle? These were questions Wilson wanted to answer. Chase, who had confided on February 9 to one of his closest friends that Wilson was "true as steel on the slavery question," helped him write the reply, to which Sumner assented.[58]

Wilson, who had always recognized the legality of slavery, could answer as some abolitionists could not. Slavery, he replied, was a state matter to be left to the legislature. Congress had no power to interfere with it in a state. Anyone who believed in God had to believe His law was paramount to "all human law," but he saw no conflict between the Constitution and the law of God. The American party in Massachusetts had not had the issue of slavery before it when it was formed, Wilson continued. On the other hand, the people of his state had very definite opinions about the institution. The national government, he added, should be relieved of all connections with slavery. He and those who supported him would not force their opinions on others, but they would not be dictated to about what they could believe or say. He had all the rights of any senator.[59]

Reaction varied. Bailey could not understand how the *American Organ* editor and Wilson could exist within the same party, but contended that this correspondence between the two had not dealt with the real issues of slavery, which would eventually divide the Know Nothings. The *American Organ's* editor thought Wilson's response should check the efforts of the enemies of Know Nothingism to divide the party. The Know Nothing *Boston Bee* praised the Wilson response as "clear, explicit and unmistakable," a justification of the *Bee's* support. The Free Soil *Northampton Courier* characterized the Wilson letter as "simply a reaffirmation of the old Free Soil doctrine." The *Springfield Republican*, long a detractor, termed the reply "manly, creditable and *right,*" but charged Wilson had abandoned his position of 1848 and had returned to the Whig view. Wilson himself was pleased, claiming his letter had done more for the antislavery cause than any other speech or act of his life.[60]

The new senator's first recorded votes were on amendments and procedural matters the day after he was sworn in. The same week he joined Fessenden, Sumner, and Wade in a losing cause to vote against increasing the salary of Supreme Court justices and providing appropriations to pay the Texas debt. Like Sumner, Wilson was to speak for the first time on an issue other than slavery. A bill to extend credit on iron imported by railroad companies was being considered when Senator Richard Brodhead of Pennsylvania stigmatized the intent of many Southern senators to vote for the bill as their abandonment of revenue tariffs; he asked support from easterners. Wilson declared he was opposed to tariffs on commodities necessary for a person's life or which the United States could produce as well as other nations. Massachusetts, he announced, was tending towards free trade and preferred providing for government expenses by other means. Brodhead shot back that Massachusetts had prolonged the slave trade by resisting its abolition. Wilson replied that his state regretted that and was now on the side of freedom. The *Boston Transcript* was horrified. A number of Massachusetts industries were depressed, it asserted. Massachusetts would be committing suicide advocating free trade. Was this what a Know Nothing believed? Yet in fact the state's views on tariff were changing. Most of the Massachusetts House delegation supported a rider to another bill providing for tariff reduction, and Wilson's position was applauded by the Whiggish *Springfield Republican.*[61]

Two days later, with only a week remaining, Wilson had an opportunity to speak about slavery, the only time the subject arose during the short session. Senator Isaac Toucey of Connecticut was in charge of a bill which would transfer to the federal courts cases against those who were attempting to enforce federal laws, meaning particularly the Fugitive Slave Act. Chase decided to challenge it. Fessenden, Seward, and Wade also ably attacked the proposal. Douglas in his remarks denied the 1854 elections had been a defeat for the Democrats; rather the Know Nothings had often won by combining people who otherwise had little in common. He maintained Wilson had not been elected as an antislavery man. Wilson made a short reply, agreeing, but emphasizing that no man in Massachusetts, of whatever party, could be elected to Congress unless he were antislavery.[62]

Later Wilson obtained the floor for an address of his own. His fellow senators and spectators listened with great attention, anxious to hear how a leading Northern Know Nothing stood and curious about the abilities of the new senator. Wilson had spoken with E. L. Pierce in planning his initial congressional abolition speech. The Massachusetts conservatives focused on Wilson's concern about what his fellow Know Nothings would think, but what was more important was that Wilson delivered the address. He declared he was obligated to reply to an attack by Senator

Jones of Tennessee who had called those from New England a "little band of traitors." Wilson said he had no intention of making war against Southern senators who represented one million people. He stood on the Virginia and Kentucky Resolutions, understanding states had powers. He would attack slavery where Congress had authority, in the territories and in the District of Columbia. He insisted the Fugitive Slave Act be repealed. Those who agreed with him would win a majority in Congress and vote Southerners down. Then he cleverly discussed resolutions framed by Hallett, who in 1855 was chairman of the Democratic National Committee, and passed by the Massachusetts Democratic Convention in 1849. These conventions claimed to be opposed to slavery in every form and color and affirmed slavery could exist in the territories only with congressional approval. Wilson spoke about his own strong nationalist position. He denied blacks as a race were inferior. He ably defended his views in a lively banter with Southern senators. While the bill passed the Senate 30 to 9, it never got to the floor of the House.[63]

Wilson created a problem for himself by his absence at the time of an important vote. Chase presented a group of petitions dealing with slavery and, for the first time, asked they be referred to a special committee. While he secured thirteen votes, Wilson's was not among them. The new senator had thought the session would begin at noon instead of 11 a.m. His opponents could claim that, as a Know Nothing, he was dodging taking a stand. That was nonsense, since he had clearly stated where he stood.[64]

Although presentation of petitions was more under the control of those who chose to send them than the congressional presenter himself, Wilson was able on March 1 to balance his two constituencies by introducing two petitions. One prayed for the repeal of the Fugitive Slave Act, the other for repeal of the naturalization laws. Both were, of course, laid on the table.[65]

Wilson also was highly criticized for his vote on the bill introduced by Douglas in the closing hours of the session, which would have authorized Oregon to begin actions which would lead to statehood. Many Southerners wanted to speak. Seward was anxious to move Oregon, likely to be a free state, forward. But Wilson wanted to be practical, he said; the bill could not be passed in the remaining hours. Only essential business should be conducted on a Sunday. It was better to deal with the civil and diplomatic appropriations bill. With Wilson's voting with the more extreme among the Southerners, the bill was tabled. The *National Era* tartly commented it was as necessary to admit new states as to provide for payments to a line of steamers. The Massachusetts press was also unhappy with Wilson's vote. Wilson later defended his actions by saying he would have supported the bill had it had a chance to pass. His explanation satisfied most of his Free Soil friends, including a highly critical Greeley.[66]

Wilson's first Senate session was over. Congress adjourned on March 3. Three days later Wilson returned to Massachusetts; the next morning the adroit politician visited the legislature. He spoke hopefully of the nation's future and maintained a triumph of the Know Nothings in 1856 would aid the cause of freedom. The *Boston Transcript* declared no public man had ever done so many "singular things" in such a short time. His "remarkable course" might be attributed to "greenness." Amasa Walker and David L. Child were somewhat more complimentary; Walker still bemoaned Wilson's Know Nothing position, Child could not understand the Oregon vote. Former adversary George Ashmun complimented him for his speeches and *American Organ* letter. Adams recorded that Sumner seemed to talk about Wilson alternately with pain and pleasure.[67]

Wilson understood the political scene better than his detractors. The Know Nothing movement was still a major force in American politics, particularly in Massachusetts. In the March town elections the Know Nothings were triumphant. In many communities no opposition candidates had been presented. Shortly thereafter the Know Nothings swept the New Hampshire polls. They won the governorship, more than two-thirds of the seats in the state legislature, and all congressional elections. Whigs and Free Soilers in the state commonly voted Know Nothing. In early April the Know Nothings, often combining with the Whigs, secured control of the Connecticut legislature by a large majority and won all major races in Rhode Island. The Connecticut Know Nothing gubernatorial candidate received a small plurality and the Democrats lost all congressional seats.[68]

Shortly after he returned to Massachusetts Wilson again used the reply-to-an-inquiry device to explain to the public his position. Writing on March 10 to Parker Pillsbury, Wilson emphasized his dedication to the slave for nineteen years. He discussed the attacks upon him during the legislature's deliberations for senator and the misrepresentations of his antislavery position in Washington. He explained what motivated his *American Organ* letter, his absence when the Senate was considering the Chase petitions, and his votes on the tariff and Oregon issues. He again convinced some of his audience of his good intentions.[69]

While the press and individuals, like Everett, who had long opposed him insisted upon regarding Wilson's initial Senate performance as a balancing act between Free Soilism and nativism, in fact his important contributions had been antislavery. Naturally, participating in Senate affairs would call for a different strategy to counteract the Slave Power than that used in Massachusetts. Wilson claimed he was alarmed at what he had seen. He found three alternatives for antislavery men in the Know Nothing movement: (1) they could ignore their principles and create a national party, (2) they could fight for what they believed in and impose their ideas on the party, in the process driving Southerners out, or (3) they could break up the emerging new party. He left Washington determined to get the Know Nothing June convention to adopt a moderate antislavery position and, if he failed, break up the party.[70]

He was so concerned that in the five months after Congress adjourned Wilson traveled nine thousand miles, wrote hundreds of letters, and devoted countless hours to consulting with those who were also opposed to slavery and the Slave

Power. Wilson began with a Boston address long planned. That winter a series of lectures on slavery which would attract many of the best speakers in the country was inaugurated in the city. Emerson, Burlingame, Frederick Douglass, Sumner, and Wilson spoke that year, while the succeeding winter's series provided two Southerners, including Senator Robert Toombs of Georgia, one of the nation's largest slaveholders. Wilson, whose health was always excellent, had to stop his March 23 address when a "rush of blood to his head" rendered it unsafe, in the opinion of physicians present, for him to continue. One can only speculate what had happened. Vertigo, one report said. Over-exertion, Wilson told Schouler. Whatever it was, it did not restrain him long, for he delivered the same lecture in Dorchester on March 29, Worcester March 30, and Westfield April 4, and then completed his Boston address on April 6.[71]

In his address Wilson declared he wanted to clarify his sentiments. He was "fully committed, in favor of the immediate and unconditional abolition of slavery." Wilson's tactic in the address was to contrast the antislavery movement of 1835 with that in 1855. He claimed the movement now controlled most Northern states and the House of Representatives; this had occurred on the wreckage of the former political system. Nevertheless, he was fearful the free states might not do their duty. The current danger was in the attempt to create a new national Know Nothing party. If it tried to repress antislavery sentiment, it also would die. An "able, generous and manly effort, . . . warmly applauded," *The Liberator* characterized the speech. A "violent free-soil lecture," Everett told Fillmore. "Little more than a political tirade," the *Boston Transcript* reported. Wilson may have wilted a while in Washington, the *New York Times* concluded, but he was now as strong a friend of abolition as ever.[72]

Charles Wright, a New York merchant residing in Hinsdale, Massachusetts, in the Berkshires, who would a decade later attack Wilson again, in March addressed a long letter to the same Parker Pillsbury to whom Wilson had written. Wright had participated in the 1852 Pittsburgh convention and served with Wilson on Free Soil committees in Massachusetts. He now accused Wilson of betraying his party by joining the Know Nothings and of having his friends persuade the state Republican committee to reject his resignation. Wilson was not fit to be senator and should resign, Wright declared. In May a petition from Hinsdale, signed by one hundred legal voters representing all four political parties, was delivered to the legislature and published in the *Springfield Republican*. It asked the General Court to request Wilson's resignation on the grounds that his election was secured by "complicated and slippery" acts. The lack of much support for the charges indicates that Wilson's Whig and Free Soil opponents were reconciling themselves to his new position.[73]

Wilson could hardly have defined his position better than by speaking during the anniversary week of national benevolent and reform societies, as part of the annual New York City meeting of the American Anti-Slavery Society. Wilson himself asked to speak before what was one of the most condemned abolition societies in the nation. Appearing under the auspices of this agency—technically for the New York City Anti-Slavery Society—clearly made a statement to both Northerners and Southerners. Furthermore, this was his first address on a New York stage. Wilson could have found other sponsors for such an important event to his future political career, had he wanted. What Wilson in two hours offered was essentially the same address, contrasting abolition in 1835 with 1855, he had been delivering all over Massachusetts.[74]

The North was changing. Only five years before a mob had driven the abolitionists from their meeting hall; for two years the society had been unable to obtain a room for its use. Henry Ward Beecher, in introducing Wilson, noted that the appearance of a senator from Massachusetts demonstrated how great a transformation had occurred since the senatorships of Webster and Everett. Although the weather was poor, five thousand people attended. The *New York Times* reporter characterized Wilson's speech as excellent and earnest; it received much applause. The less friendly *New York Herald* reported the speech was "rich in facts, pungent in satire, and highly suggestive as to the aims and objectives of the anti-slavery party." The New York correspondent of the *Boston Herald* was disgusted that Wilson and Sumner would appear on the same stage with Garrisonians. This address also demonstrates the confidence Wilson had developed in his own abilities, willing to allow a comparison, as the press made, with Sumner's classical, scholarly, and traditional oration the next evening.[75]

In the meantime the state's first Know Nothing legislature had produced a record about which contemporaries disagreed then and historians differ now. The old Whig elite were clear in their opinion that the legislature failed. Most contemporaries and historians agreed it was tempestuous in its operations. Furthermore, too many charges of petty graft were true. Yet this legislature passed and won approval of almost five hundred bills and more than eighty resolves. The *Northampton Courier* favorably concluded "no Legislature . . . for many years has embodied in its members more moral worth, integrity of purpose, and honest devotion to sound principle." Another newspaper two decades later complimented its "substratum of good sense and human purpose." The *Springfield Republican* concluded a majority of the legislature's members were honest and innocent but had fallen victim to a reckless minority. The *New York Times* characterized the Know Nothing legislature as courageous, determined, bold, but unrestrained.[76]

One historian termed the Know Nothing legislature "a resuscitation of the coalition." It had a remarkable record of progressive legislation, including establishing the first board of insurance commissioners; defining as larceny embezzlement of public property by county, city, and town officials; establishing a book fund for charitable institutions; requiring vaccination for public school children; overhauling the bankruptcy system and abolishing imprisonment for debt except for fraud; providing mechanics an improved lien law; permitting married women to own property; creating a state reform school for girls; forbidding employment of children under the age of fifteen unless they also attended school a minimum of eleven weeks a year; and empowering juries to interpret law in criminal cases. Since the state constitution's amending process required proposals to be passed in two successive years, the legislature agreed to the six amendments endorsed by the 1854 Whig General Court. With Whig and Know Nothing legislatures having passed the proposals and Free Soil and Democratic politicians having endorsed the ideas at the convention, a light vote on May 23 easily accepted them.[77]

The antislavery record was a good one. The Harvard Board of Overseers, now including appointees from the legislature, blocked the appointment of Judge Loring—of Anthony Burns fame—as a professor. Wilson was delighted, but reported the slaveholders in Washington were angry. Later in the term, the legislature considered a resolution requesting Governor Gardner remove Loring as judge of probate. Devereaux led the opposition. The resolution passed by large majorities. Even the governor's council, by a 7-to-2 vote, agreed. Gardner refused to act. The legislature also passed a personal liberty bill, which Gardner vetoed as unconstitutional. The Senate by a 32-to-3 vote, the House 229 to 76, repassed it over the veto. In addition to providing for due process, the bill declared no one could be both United States commissioner and hold a state office and prohibited, with penalties, state officers from participating in the rendition of fugitives. Another act forbade exclusion from the public schools on the basis of race, color, or religion. Resolutions to Congress protested violation of the Missouri Compromise, deplored the violence in Kansas, and asked for repeal of the Fugitive Slave Law. Theodore Parker characterized this as the strongest antislavery legislature the state had ever had.[78]

The Massachusetts Supreme Court in March had decided the sections of the 1852 temperance statute which authorized the seizure and destruction of liquors were unconstitutional. The legislature responded to temperance advocates with a stricter enforcement law prohibiting the sale of all intoxicating liquors, except for medical or sacramental purposes. Fines and imprisonment were provided for violators. Gardner addressed the annual meeting of the State Temperance Convention, strongly sustaining the new law. Wilson in subsequent years frequently characterized the law as imperfect, but with promise of effectiveness when properly enforced.[79]

The legislature's nativist activities engendered the greatest criticism. It authorized investigations, especially into convents and nunneries, which in the end made it appear foolish. One committee of inquiry charged its liquor bill to the state. The General Court ended up investigating its own committees. Legislators resigned and were expelled. Another committee examination was of Holy Cross College and of educational institutions at Lowell and Roxbury. The legislature required daily reading of the King James version of the Bible in the public schools. It removed a

Latin inscription above the Speaker's desk and banned foreign languages from the public school curriculum. Wilson was particularly unhappy with three proposed constitutional amendments. One would require a twenty-one-year residency of naturalized citizens for voting. Wilson did all he could to defeat it, but failed. But the law was poorly framed and had to be corrected by the next legislature. Two other proposals, barring naturalized and Catholic citizens from holding office, also passed, but each failed to get through the succeeding legislature.[80]

When the state Know Nothing Council assembled on May 1, the strength of the Wilson forces was remarkable. The conservatives, mostly from the Boston area, had tried to marshal their strength. Discussions were long and stormy. Jonathan Pierce, one of the original nativists, who had opposed Wilson's senator selection and was regarded as a Hunker, was replaced as president. Even a speech in which he denounced slavery did not save him. The presidency was first offered to Gardner, who declined, then to John W. Foster of Brimfield, an antislavery man whose authority would later be important to Wilson and his associates. Most officers were changed. Wilson himself was chosen delegate to the National Council. The tone of the meeting was antislavery. One approved resolution declared that, while the party recognized the right of states to regulate their own domestic affairs, the federal government should relieve itself from all connection with and responsibility for slavery. Wilson spoke in opposition to debarring from office all persons who were not native born.[81]

The New Hampshire state council, meeting the same week, defined its position on slavery as similar to that in Massachusetts. Slavery was supposed to have been temporary and sectional, their resolutions argued. The council protested against the Nebraska bill and the Fugitive Slave Law. But as important as the actions of these two state councils were, Orders in other states were not joining them.[82]

So within approximately six months the Massachusetts Know Nothing movement had accomplished most of those objectives Wilson had sought. It had swept the fall elections, winning the state House and sending antislavery congressmen to Washington. It had elected Wilson senator. It had passed a large package of reform legislation, most of which the coalition had previously advocated. It had adopted an acceptable antislavery stance. Of course, it had also undertaken an unfortunate program of nativist legislation and harassment of immigrants and Catholics. These six months had also demonstrated, however, that the Know Nothings could not be a national party unless some agreement could be reached on the subject of slavery. That was highly unlikely in the spring of 1855. Wilson next had to find out if North-South cooperation were possible and if it were not, what the alternative was for him and for those who believed in curtailing slavery through political actions.

12

Antislavery Versus Nativism

In the late spring of 1855, the political picture in the nation remained in the confusing state into which the passage of the Kansas-Nebraska bill and the rise of the Know Nothing party had thrown it. The Democratic party controlled the national government and was growing in strength in the South. It was not yet clear whether the Know Nothing movement would develop into the permanent opposition. Nor was it clear whether temperance or opposition to the expansion of slavery would become the cornerstone of a major national political party. While Wilson and his associates, working with the Gardner wing, had achieved endorsement of their antislavery position in Massachusetts, if they insisted upon the emerging national party's accepting their principles, the Know Nothings would split. Southern Americans would not, could not, accept a platform limiting the growth or endangering the health of slavery.

The Know Nothings in different states seemed concerned about different issues. In some Northern states antislaveryites and Know Nothings cooperated, in others the Whigs and Know Nothings worked together. In Massachusetts, despite the apparent unity at their May meeting, the American Know Nothings were in difficulty. The original nativists were angry at being thrust aside. The Gardner opportunist group would compromise on principles as long as nativism was not abandoned and their participation in governing continued. The movement was also becoming less secret. In Massachusetts Wilson in his frequent speeches was affirming everyone had a right to hear about issues of the day and react to what leaders proposed to do. The rituals and oaths of the Order were printed by the press.[1]

The weakness of the party in the South was demonstrated in the May 24 Virginia election. Henry A. Wise, Democratic candidate for governor, ran an excellent campaign, aided by superior organization. The Democrats widely publicized Wilson's various antislavery speeches, presenting him as the spokesman of the Northern Know Nothings. Since they could not deny his party affiliation or leadership in Massachusetts, the desperate Virginia Americans manufactured a newspaper report, from the *Boston Telegraph,* in which Wilson allegedly denounced the party. The Democrats, however, had enough time to demonstrate the article was fabricated. Wise was elected by more than a ten-thousand majority. Virginia Know Nothings were angry at Wilson for the result. The press concluded Know Nothings were now unlikely to capture the presidency in 1856 and could win in the South only where Whigs formerly had been very strong. In withdrawing as congressman from Georgia, former Whig leader Alexander Stephens contended he was opposed to a Know Nothing nomination both because the party proscribed Roman Catholics and because Massachusetts Americans had taken a position against slavery to which he could never agree.[2]

Wilson continued his heavy schedule of lectures, begun after his return from Washington. He spoke before the Know Nothing lodge in Gloucester, April 23, then repeated his slavery lecture the next week in Plymouth, West Newbury, and North Attleboro. After his endorsement at the state Know Nothing convention, Wilson returned to the lecture circuit. At Springfield on May 15, with the mayor presiding and members of the City Council on the platform, Wilson openly declared that if the American party placed itself against the antislavery cause, he would do all he could to defeat it. At Andover the following evening he was more emphatic, advocating an end of secrecy for the Order and insisting the party must take an antislavery position.[3]

Perhaps Wilson's most widely reported spring address was that at Brattleboro, Vermont; it well defined his position at this time. The Know Nothings of the state were in disarray and Wilson was sent as peacemaker. He first advocated all nominations be open. He then defined the nativist objectives of the party. Disclaiming all sympathy with a "narrow, bigoted, intolerant spirit that would make war upon a race of men because they happened to be born in other lands," terming such a spirit "un-American" and "devilish," Wilson declared the object of the American movement was not to halt foreign immigration, not even of felons and paupers. But Know Nothings were against naturalized citizens being organized in political blocs, he declared. To prevent that, naturalization laws might have to be more stringent or better enforced. The way to accomplish that, however, was not a constitutional amendment prohibiting naturalized citizens from voting for twenty-one years, as proposed in his own state. Finally, he argued that the greatest issue before the nation was slavery. The institution had to be defined as sectional and the national government should be divorced from it. He contended the Know Nothings had won elections when they cooperated with anti-Nebraska men and lost in New

York because the party there was controlled by the Silver Whigs. The recent defeat of the Americans in Virginia was a lesson not to unite with the slave oligarchy.[4]

Opposition to the Know Nothings among the Free Democrats of Massachusetts all spring failed to engender much support. Many of the Free Soilers who had opposed joining the nativist movement had maintained they were about to rout the Democrats when the Know Nothings intervened. The *Northampton Courier* in March interpreted these comments as an organized attack on the Know Nothings. The remnant of Free Soilers who had met in January did little for months. Phillips's assignment to define differences with the Know Nothings had not been undertaken by April and Adams thought the Order was declining so rapidly, the publication of an attack on them would make the Free Soilers look ridiculous. When the State Committee assembled on April 14, less sentiment was expressed in favor of action than in January; E. L. Pierce asserted the Know Nothings had become more antislavery and less intolerant. The growth of the Know Somethings was further confusing the issue. The Whigs still would not cooperate. The committee was unable to agree on how to proceed.[5]

The conservative Free Soilers were still unwilling to cooperate with the abolitionists, a contrast to Wilson's position. At the New England convention in early June Wendell Phillips attacked the Massachusetts gentry. In twenty years, he claimed, no clergyman of reputation, no officer of the state, no man of wealth or standing among the legal profession had ever participated in this annual meeting. When Higginson reminded him that Wilson had been there, Phillips replied that Wilson was so much the exception that he proved the rule.[6]

The long-expected meetings of the National Council of the Know Nothings were scheduled for Philadelphia, beginning June 5. The Order claimed to represent one and a half million voters. The objective of the convention was to formulate a national platform and lay plans for the 1856 presidential campaign. Each state was entitled to seven delegates, giving additional power to the smaller-populated South. All Southern delegations were proslavery, but free state representatives were divided on the issue. The Massachusetts Council had selected Wilson, Gardner, Foster, Congressman Edward Buffington, and three lesser-known delegates, and, at the instigation of the Wilson group, had directed them to urge the abandonment of most secrecy and to insist upon passage of resolutions in favor of abolition of slavery in the District of Columbia and the territories and in opposition to admittance of more slave states. Although the members of the Order were bound by their oaths of secrecy, the convention was fully reported. The *New York Tribune* engaged Samuel Bowles, already covering the proceedings for the *Boston Atlas* and his own *Springfield Republican*. Bowles was not a Know Nothing, so he was not present at the meetings. Wilson and Schuyler Colfax are believed to have been the sources of his information.[7]

Bowles reported that no one supposed the convention could harmonize its views. Delegations from four New England states and Indiana were determined to secure antislavery resolutions. Many Southern delegations were "maddened" by the loss in Virginia and angry at Wilson and the Massachusetts and New Hampshire Councils.[8]

The convention battled for three days before it could organize. Kenneth Raynor of North Carolina successfully led the fight to exclude Roman Catholics of Louisiana. Others, including the *Richmond Whig,* spokespaper of the Virginia Know Nothings, were determined that the credentials of the Massachusetts delegation, particularly those of Wilson, be rejected. On the opening day representatives from Arkansas, Ohio, and Massachusetts were excluded. The pretense for Massachusetts was that the Grand Potentate had no knowledge that Foster and E. C. Baker had been elected president and secretary and thus could certify the delegates. In the debates a Virginia representative launched a violent attack against Massachusetts and Wilson. Wilson coolly and forcefully replied, taking about an hour. Charged with endorsing Burlingame's Tremont Temple speech, Wilson asserted he did. Blacks and whites were equal in the sight of God; he saw no difference on earth than in heaven. He conceded to the states the power to direct their domestic affairs and repeated his adherence to the Virginia resolutions. But he denounced slavery and called for its abolition in the District of Columbia and the territories. He emphasized his devotion to the union. The attack against Wilson was so coarse it annoyed other Southerners. Some congratulated Wilson for his "frank boldness and admirable temper." The convention quickly backtracked and admitted the Northern delegations.[9]

Contemporary sources do not report a story which received frequent exposition later. During one of his speeches a Virginian approached Wilson with a pistol, denouncing and threatening him. Wilson continued speaking, however, declaring that he would not be intimidated, but he would "meet argument with argument, scorn with scorn, and, if need be, blow with blow." He told Parker a month after the council meetings that he had met "armed, drunken bullies of the Black Power." He had to let Southerners know, Wilson asserted, that their threats of disunion or civil war would no longer deter Northerners.[10]

While the Massachusetts delegation sought to be unified, efforts were widespread to weaken Northern determination. In contrast to their behavior towards most of the Massachusetts delegation, Southerners generally treated Gardner with respect. On June 7 over 450 people, including non–Know Nothings, attended the grand banquet, which was under the control of the proslavery element of the city. E. B. Ely, who had once been a power in the Order in Massachusetts, but who was not a council delegate, pledged at the banquet that Massachusetts would adhere to Know Nothing principles.[11]

With the controversy over credentials finally settled, the convention turned to the selection of its committees and officers. The current president Barker led on the first ballot for reelection with 56 votes; Gardner had 32. On the sixth ballot the Gardner supporters changed to E. B. Bartlett of Kentucky and elected him. Bowles reported the Massachusetts men were punishing Barker for his favoritism in presiding. The antislavery delegates were conspicuous in their opposition to him. Henry H. Rugg of Massachusetts was selected to be chaplain, but concern was so great that he was a Free Soiler that he subsequently resigned.[12]

The Massachusetts delegation offered antislavery resolutions, framed by Bowles and Wilson. The Committee on Resolutions rejected them by about a two-to-one majority. The primary hope for compromise lay with a call by Governor Johnson of Pennsylvania for restoration of the Missouri Compromise line. That was defeated almost unanimously, when the Northern delegations were as opposed as the Southern. What emerged from committee were two sets of resolutions. Representatives on the committee from twelve states signed the minority report. In addition, those from New Jersey and Delaware objected to only one clause. New York and the Minnesota Territory joined the slave states representatives in advocating the majority resolutions, passed 17 to 14. The majority disclaimed any responsibility of the American party for past actions of Whigs and Democrats, but contended the issue of slavery was so agitating that the nation's existence was threatened. Therefore, to bring peace, the party would submit to existing laws on the subject of slavery. In addition, Congress had no power to legislate about the institution in the states or exclude any state from the union because its constitution did or did not recognize slavery. Congress ought not to legislate on the subject of slavery in the territories. Any interference by Congress with slavery in the District of Columbia would be a violation of the agreement by which Maryland had ceded the land.[13]

By Monday, June 11 delegates from the Northern states were determined to bring matters to a head. The debate raged for three days, with recesses for caucusing. The second day's session continued until after 11 p.m., the third, until after midnight. Bowles declared that except for the treachery of New York delegates, the North could have won. Foster and Wilson, he reported, "spoke magnificently." Elsewhere he said, "Foster's speech was admirable. Wilson came down with crushing force on the New Yorkers, and Ford (of Ohio) swept the field." Gardner's support was of utmost importance; it was given. He told Southerners that not a city or town in Massachusetts would sustain the majority platform. When a New York delegate contended all Know Nothings were bound by the convention's actions, Gardner insisted the North was not.[14]

During the course of the debates a New York delegate delivered an impassioned attack on Massachusetts, especially on Wilson, accusing him of trying to break up the party. Wilson replied that he had uttered no words of unkindness. He had been treated well by many Southerners at the convention. He was in Philadelphia with 80,000 voters behind him, he noted, while the Know Nothings had failed to carry New York. No free state party could win on the platform being suggested. He would not accept it. He would trample on it. Massachusetts Know Nothings were for freedom. He had pledged himself in Washington nineteen years before to end slavery and he had not wavered from that position. He had expressed his antislavery convictions frequently and emphatically. Wilson dealt at length with the constitutional aspects of slavery, forecasting that Southerners one day would be happy to retreat to the position of the institution's municipal authority to exist. He spoke for an hour. Friends said it was his best speech.[15]

The *New York Tribune* in September of 1854, on the basis of statements by Southern leaders, had predicted the Order would become subservient to slavery. Fillmore would be its candidate in 1856 for the presidency. This was an astoundingly accurate analysis. Unfortunately, by the time of the council vote on the minority platform some Northerners had departed for home. They would have lost anyhow. The minority platform was beaten 51 to 92, compromise resolutions failed 44 to 97, and the next day the majority platform passed, 80 to 59. The council also abandoned secrecy.[16]

The morning following the council's decision on the platform, most Northern delegates met, with Wilson chairman. Bowles described them as spirited and determined not to look back. An "Address to the People of the United States" of four points, prepared by Foster, was signed. Two of the resolutions dealt with slavery and two, nativism. The *New York Tribune* praised the Address for its "strong" stand on Kansas, but in fact the antislavery positions had been diluted to win broader acceptance: unconditional restoration of the Missouri Compromise and protection by the president of settlers in the territories. Wilson also proposed a Declaration of Sentiments, which he withdrew because Gardner vigorously opposed it, declaring he would not be abolitionized. Fifty-three men, including all seven Massachusetts delegates, affixed their signatures to the Address. Maine, New Hampshire, Ohio, and Indiana delegations had been most stalwart in sustaining the Massachusetts position. Pennsylvania and New Jersey representatives, in addition to those of New York and the Minnesota Territory, did not leave the national party. While many of the representatives departed for Cleveland to join the Know Something convention, Maine and Massachusetts delegates left for home.[17]

The Northern press in general applauded the position of the seceders. The *New York Times* noted the unity of Southerners on the slavery issue. This had been the first time Northerners had accurately represented the sentiments of their constituents, the *Times* asserted. While it yet might win state and local elections, the Know Nothing movement was dead nationally. Massachusetts had created a North, the *Boston Telegraph* declared. Even the *Boston Atlas* praised Wilson, Gardner, and others for saving the nation from the contempt of the world. The Know Nothing–supporting *New York Herald* was happy with the split, concluding the party would be stronger. It hoped even in Massachusetts the Order could be reorganized.[18]

Wilson himself was often praised. No man went into the council with more mistrust directed towards him than Wilson, Bowles wrote. No one left with more fame. For more than a week he had led the Northern forces. Bowles particularly complimented Wilson's parliamentary skills. The former Wilson-basher went so far as to suggest that without the Massachusetts senator there would have been no fight. Oliver, the Boston correspondent of the *New York Tribune,* reported Wilson's actions were sustained in Massachusetts. People of the state were sick of representatives who would not stand up to slaveholders, Oliver insisted. Nothing Wilson had ever done was so applauded. Free Soilers and coalition Democrats, estranged from him by his affiliation with the Know Nothings, were now praising him. An editorial in the *New York Tribune,* acknowledging how often it had criticized Wilson, lauded his courage, calmness, and eloquence. Maine's *Kennebec Journal*, a Republican newspaper, commended the Massachusetts delegation, especially Wilson for his "bold and lofty bearing." Amasa Walker complimented his former political associate on his speech and declared Wilson had placed himself at the head of the political antislavery movement. A great responsibility rested on his shoulders, Walker added. The *National Era* continued to be displeased with Wilson, but agreed that he had become the leader of at least Northern Know Nothings and encouraged him to act.[19]

While the Know Nothings were meeting in Philadelphia, the Know Somethings had assembled in Cleveland. This group was anti-Catholic, but more circumscribed in its antiforeignism. It was antislavery. Slack, who had broken with his own chapter of the Order in February over his support of Wilson for senator, had become a Know Something. When Speaker of the House Ely had left to attend the New York City anniversaries in May, Slack had been elected to fill the vacancy. This action by the Massachusetts House speaks to the strength of the antislavery wing of the Know Nothing movement in the state. Slack was only thirty, one of the editors of the *Boston Telegraph*, and an acknowledged Free Soiler—three reasons he might lose the votes of some legislators. But, most important, he was an acknowledged Know Something. The new party's platform attacked the Nebraska bill, bemoaned the outrages in Kansas, opposed ecclesiastical interference in political affairs, recommended promotion of temperance by state action, spoke for federal support for internal improvements, supported free schools and free labor, and expressed a willingness to unite with others to attain the party's objectives.[20]

Wilson two decades later conceded that those who had left the Know Nothing Council were more optimistic than the facts warranted. The Know Nothing party was broken, but it was still strong enough to embarrass the Republican movement, win elections in three states, and enable the Democrats to recover control of four other states in the fall. After the seceders had left the council, the pro-Southern Know Nothings concluded a meeting in the city's Independence Square attended by between 10,000 and 15,000 people. In New York City several days later, 20,000 Know Nothings turned out to support their delegates and hear Barker quote Wilson's statement that the state's delegation had dug its political graves, but assert that he, Barker, felt very much alive. Many state councils simply ignored the actions of their delegates.[21]

Wilson returned to Massachusetts with determination and vigor. Fortunately, the *Boston Bee*, the chief Know Nothing journal, immediately endorsed the Northern platform. Over most of the state Know Nothing councils supported their delegates' Philadelphia positions. Only in some wards in Boston was there conflict. Wilson and Gardner reported to the Know Nothings of Boston's Eleventh Ward on June 23. Wilson, according to newspapers, declared that the Massachusetts delegates had tried to avoid the slavery question, but Southerners had been insistent. Wilson strongly attacked the New York delegation. He maintained that the states which had supported the majority plank would not vote Know Nothing in 1856.[22]

Political reorganization was again on Wilson's agenda. Wilson, Bowles, and Ezra Lincoln, the latter two former Whigs, immediately after the Know Nothing split met to determine what next should be done. They decided the time was appropriate to produce a stronger Free Soil party. They hoped to unite the few thousand Republicans, anti-Nebraska Democrats, Know Nothings, and Whigs. They agreed Winthrop was the man who could best lead the factions, and Lincoln and Bowles were urged to talk with him. What a strange action for Wilson to take, given Winthrop's past treatment of him! Charles T. Congdon, who in 1855 was a Whig editor in Boston, wrote that Wilson often spoke of Whig leaders who would not take positions to which their talents and private character entitled them. Whittier also urged Winthrop to get involved. Winthrop again refused. Worse, he wrote a letter on the fusion of parties, reemphasizing his support for tariffs and internal improvements and criticizing bargains. Thus, he alienated Democrats, coalitionists, and antislavery Know Nothings.[23]

Wilson contended time was essential. He and his friends would be generous and conciliatory. If the Whigs would join, the movement would succeed. The *Boston Telegraph* on June 19 pronounced the old issues dead and declared for unity among those who thought alike. More important, on the same date, the *Bee* endorsed fusion. The *Springfield Republican* in praising Wilson declaimed any regret for its past opposition, but attested to its readiness to join hands with him against slavery. Wilson had come home, it announced, pledged to inaugurate fusion.[24]

In other states, too, reorganization was being considered. The freemen of Vermont were scheduled to meet on June 27, while Ohio Know Nothings pointedly postponed making their nominations for office until after the Republican state convention. The *New York Tribune* thought there might be too much consultation. It recommended the Indiana method, in which the masses were asked to support a movement and a convention called. What other way was there when in most states the Know Nothings were rejecting cooperation, it asked. Pennsylvania would be particularly important. Its Republican convention on July 5 received a letter from Wilson, among others. He declared the state held the 1856 elections in its hands, an amazingly accurate forecast. If Pennsylvania would stand with the rest of the

North, Wilson asserted, then the Democrats could be overthrown. But even though the Know Nothing governor supported cooperation with other Northern Orders, the majority in the Pennsylvania Council sided with the Philadelphia platform, splitting the party and limiting the possibility of successful fusion.[25]

More than three hundred attended the convention of the State Council of the American party in Boston on June 28. The delegates were more divided in their sentiments than expected. Some wanted to accept the platform of the national meeting while rejecting the slavery planks. Others sought endorsement of the delegation. The Boston representatives particularly sought to remain national. The address adopted was bold. It termed the Philadelphia platform "utterly repugnant" in its views on slavery. The meeting approved the withdrawal by the Massachusetts delegates, abandoned secrecy, denounced the Kansas-Nebraska Bill, and severed relations with the national organization. Fusion with other political parties against the Democrats was virtually rejected. An evening ratification meeting was addressed by Wilson, Gardner, Foster, and others. Gardner called the national platform "an insult to the American people." When Wilson stepped forward, he was greeted with "thunderous applause." He reiterated his contention that Southerners had forced the slavery issue on the convention. His speech reasserted the principles the delegation had proposed in Philadelphia. This was the first national political convention, he declared, in which the North had stood up to the South. If the New Yorkers had voted with other Northerners, the South would have backed down. Separation now was "final and complete."[26]

Wilson was disappointed by the results of the meeting. The Boston correspondent of the *New York Post* had predicted a fusion convention would be held in July. Such diverse papers as the *Pittsfield Eagle* and the *Northampton Gazette*—both Whig partisans—and the *Greenfield Gazette, Springfield Republican,* and *Boston Atlas* had called for unity. The hour was not at hand, as Wilson had hoped only a few days before. Fusion of all those opposed to the Democrats was no nearer than a year earlier; neither the Whigs nor a large body of the Know Nothings would cooperate. Wilson continued his demanding speaking schedule. He was the leader of everything, Everett recorded, "bold, dexterous, unscrupulous, he has the trained art of a practiced political intriguer engrafted on the native stock of sly gypsy cunning." He would support Seward one campaign, Everett predicted, then seek the presidency himself. Replying to an invitation of the Massachusetts Anti-Slavery Society to join them for their annual July 4 celebrations, Wilson revealed he had two engagements in the Plymouth area on the day. He used the opportunity, however, to plead for cooperation of all those opposed to slavery. Wendell Phillips agreed they needed to respond in the same spirit and work together.[27]

Also willing to cooperate were the Know Somethings. Under the leadership of Slack and Stone, approximately 140 of them assembled in Worcester on July 10. They endorsed the Cleveland platform, adding a temperance plank. They were agreeable to fusion with other parties on the Nebraska issue, but believed the call for a meeting should come from another source.[28]

Oliver, the Boston reporter of the *New York Tribune*, dispatched an excellent analysis of the Massachusetts political scene in the beginning of July. None of the four parties were getting what they wanted, he asserted. The Know Nothings since January had lost some of their Hunker support, but had also gained other adherents by taking an antislavery stance. Oliver estimated the votes they could obtain at little different from the 80,000 they had attracted in the fall. The 20,000 Whigs of 1854 included about 6,000 Hunkers. Of the remaining 14,000, some were already Know Nothing; others might join a fusion movement. If they agreed to join, the Whig leaders would be excluded from the major offices of a victorious new party, since most of the congressional positions were held by Free Soil–Know Nothings and Gardner would remain as governor. Furthermore, the Whigs hated Gardner as much as Wilson. The 13,000 Democrats were half Hunker; the remainder were drifting to the Know Nothings. Of the 6,000 Free Soilers who had voted for Wilson, many were also Know Nothing. Fusion then would be impossible without the Know Nothings, a fact Adams as well as Wilson understood, but Bailey did not. With neither Hunker Whigs nor Democrats to be won over with an antislavery plank, only the Know Nothings could be attracted to an anti-Nebraska party. The Know Nothings at their June 28 meeting knew this; they also believed they could win state and local elections without having to accept stronger views on slavery or diluting their nativist platform through fusion.[29]

Bailey, in his ignorance of or naïveté about the Massachusetts scene, continued his attacks. On July 12 he charged Wilson and others had aroused the issue of antiforeignism, which they now could not control. Wilson, of course, had not generated the controversy and he was guiding it much better than those who had not joined the Order. Bailey charged for nine months the Wilson group had tried to bring the Americans to an antislavery stance and had failed. He asked if Wilson could endure the responsibility of preventing fusion. What Bailey could not grasp was what most Massachusetts Free Soilers, who had opposed the Know Nothings, did see: the creation of a meaningful anti-Nebraska party could occur only when large numbers of Know Nothings would join it.[30]

Wilson departed for the West to promote fusion there. Sumner already had gone, but not to speak or assist in organization of anti-Nebraska parties as much as to avoid the political choices he might have to make at home. Wilson first went to Cincinnati to speak, on July 11, and advocate the creation of a Republican party. For a year, Ohioan Chase had been promoting fusion with himself as candidate for governor. He avoided taking a strong Know Nothing position. But Chase could not win unless he obtained American support. Having a leading Northern Know Nothing like Wilson join him two days before the fusion convention would help. Wilson's address was his comparison of the abolition movements of 1835 and 1855, which he had been delivering since March. He added his analysis of the needs of the moment, a North willing to postpone other issues while it united in opposition to slavery. Two days later the Republican party of Ohio was born. By holding out the chief justice nomination to Know Nothing Jacob Brinkerhoff and the national Speakership to another Know Nothing Lewis D. Campbell, Chase outmaneuvered his opposition and obtained the nomination. All other positions on the ticket were won by Know Nothings.[31]

After his Cincinnati address, Wilson hurried to Indianapolis to participate in the largest convention that had ever been held in the state. Speaking before what was called the People's party, neither Free Soil nor Know Nothing, Wilson delivered what was described as an "eloquent speech." He maintained many of the Founding Fathers were antislavery, but the generation of the Compromise of 1820, for personal and political reasons, reversed the direction of the nation towards abolition. He emphasized the love of union among those present. Bemoaning the actions of a few Northerners at the Know Nothing national convention, he contended if his section had been unified, the upper South would have voted with it. No party then in existence could beat the Democrats. Only cooperation could produce a victory. Wilson was using both his Free Soil and his Know Nothing affiliations to advance fusion. He reported the meeting had been overwhelming in numbers and enthusiasm. Wilson had traveled a great distance to leave so soon; his address had to be scheduled so he could catch an afternoon train. He had returned to Boston by July 16. Oliver quoted one Know Nothing Hunker as saying of Wilson that "he has at least one quality of the Deity—he is omnipresent. If there is a Convention today in New-Hampshire, there will General Wilson be. If there is one to-morrow in Ohio, there also will General Wilson be. It seems that he contrives to be everywhere at once."[32]

Another reference to religion came from the *New York Herald,* which referred to Seward, Chase, and Wilson as the trinity out to disrupt the nation. Their work in Ohio was complete with Chase's nomination. They had done what no others had been able to do, bring the North and South into confrontation. They would, the *Herald* charged, kindle revolution.[33]

Wilson returned to a political climate in which efforts at fusion were still not working. Nativism was one obstacle. Many Know Nothings, whether they were antislavery or not, were still concerned about massive immigration and increasing Catholic influence, and many Free Soilers and Whigs were unwilling to accept nativism in order to advance antislavery principles. Gardner was another obstacle, a power because of his office, untrusted by many Free Soilers and temperance advocates. Then too, the American party, with the greatest mandate from the electorate any party in the state had ever held, was still popular. The *Springfield Republican* on July 7 declared that with the exception of two or three, all newspapers in the state favored fusion. It announced a private consultation of two or three hundred men would occur on July 21. But the date was too early—the Know Nothing Council was not to assemble until August 7.[34]

When the state council assembled in Springfield, Ely and his associates were pushing for a strong nativist statement and saw no need for fusion, although they would invite others to join the Know Nothing movement. The Wilson group was seeking a tough anti-Nebraska stance and authorization for fusion. Only about three hundred of the twelve hundred possible delegates attended. The debates were fierce. The *Boston Bee* said of Wilson's speech, "his language was eloquent, his reasoning forcible, his rhetoric clear and impressive, his manner calm and conciliatory." Wilson denied that the party was based upon bigotry and proscription. He spoke for suffrage laws which prohibited immigrants from voting until they understood American institutions. He would withhold diplomatic assignments to naturalized citizens, he opposed attempts by church authorities to acquire political power, and he would deny public money for sectarian schools. But he opposed the twenty-one-year naturalization amendment for suffrage. He advocated an end of all secrecy, declaring the American order was the only secret association he had joined, and would be the last. He contended the antislavery resolutions were not as strong as he would prefer, but they went as far as the people of the North would accept, so he would support them.[35]

Much of Wilson's speech was addressed to urging unification against the Slave Power, which, he noted, had occurred in Maine, Vermont, New Hampshire, Ohio, and Indiana. The American party nationally was controlled by the slaveholders, he reminded his audience. Massachusetts Know Nothings should not repeat their June mistake, but meet others halfway. A fusion movement would occur, whether the Know Nothings joined or not. He recalled his long antislavery position. He gave notice that if the Know Nothing party abandoned freedom, he would "shiver it to atoms with all the power he possessed."[36]

To avoid a split, the moderates crafted resolutions with both nativist and antislavery planks. Secrecy was abolished. The council rejected a proposal from its committee to admit naturalized Protestants. Clearly a majority favored both anti-Nebraska and nativist positions. The only nativist provision which Wilson did not support was one to prohibit an immigrant holding office until he had resided in the country for twenty-one years. The Free Soil components of the platform included the relief of the national government from contact with slavery, restoration of the Missouri Compromise and the rejection of any application from that area for admission as a slave state, and protection of the people in the territories in their use of the franchise. The convention would not, or could not, take a clear position on fusion. It instead authorized appointment of a committee of twenty-six to meet with other parties on the issue. Even this barely passed. Foster, Ely, DeWitt, and Timothy Davis were the only widely known men selected for the committee. One can debate whether the Wilson faction had been beaten or not. The nativist planks they expected. The antislavery provisions were weak, but acceptable. The fusion decision was most discouraging.[37]

In the meantime events in Kansas were altering the national political scene. Most eastern newspapers printed little about the early settlement of the territory opened by the passage of the Kansas-Nebraska Act. Nebraska, the largest part of the former free territory, was settled slowly by families from the free states and never became a major center of controversy. But Kansas, located directly west of slaveholding Missouri, became a battleground between those who were determined to make it free soil, and those who wanted to extend slavery. The Massachusetts Emigrant Aid Company was intended to aid the normal migration of people from the free states west and naturally aroused Southerners, particularly western Missourians, to respond. They were willing to use force. In the first months settlers from Southern states were in the majority in Kansas, and they elected a Missourian as territorial delegate to Congress. By mid-December, the *New York Tribune* and *Springfield Republican*, among other papers, were full of reports of injustices in Kansas. The *New York Times*, in contrast, virtually ignored these western events until June 1855. The second Kansas election, in March 1855, was characterized by illegal voting, especially by Missourians who crossed the border. This was unnecessary for proslavery success, for settlers from the Southern states at that moment outnumbered those from the North.

The government of Kansas began then as fraudulent and already an unfair test of Douglas's popular sovereignty. Pierce's first governor, Andrew Reeder, responded legalistically and allowed the disputed elections to stand. The territorial legislature thus chosen was manifestly so proslavery that even most Northern Democrats had difficulty defending it. It adopted, over the governor's veto, legislation not only to authorize and protect slavery, but to make it a crime to assist fugitive slaves or question the right to hold slaves in the territory. The majority expelled antislavery representatives chosen in a few districts in which Reeder had ordered reelections. Thus unrepresented, Free Soilers in the summer of 1855 moved to establish their own, unrecognized government. They also asked for and received from Massachusetts over three hundred modern rifles with which to defend themselves.

Now Massachusetts politicians had additional reasons to unite to halt the dominance of the Slave Power. Bowles labored as hard as Wilson in trying to promote fusion. Everyone was holding back, waiting for more to happen, the editor wrote Dawes on the eve of the state Know Nothing convention. The call for a meeting to consider fusion was eventually issued by a curious group, carefully varied in terms of geography and party affiliation, but hardly made up of leaders. It was headed by Bowles. Wilson contended this call emanated out of the July 10 Know Something convention.[38]

Whoever was invited, the meeting at Chapman Hall on August 16 was dominated by Free Soilers. Although it was well attended, few Democrats or city Whigs showed up. Among those present were Allen, Dana, Adams, Samuel Hoar, Kimball, Stone, S. C. Phillips, Walker, Swan, Slack, Goodrich, Increase Sumner,

Elizur Wright, Park, Keyes, Swift, George Bliss, Foster, and Boutwell. Bowles presided at the beginning. Walker was made temporary and Goodrich permanent president. Dana urged unification. Phillips wanted action; the nation had changed too little in twenty years, he declared. Foster delivered a strong antislavery speech. Bowles headed a business committee. Those assembled agreed to create a new party. Then they argued over what should be done next. One of the Know Nothing representatives wanted his party included en masse; Allen and Dana wanted individuals invited. Bowles offered the compromise: select a committee to call a mass convention and direct it to confer with committees of other organizations and the public. The Know Nothings' proposals were strongly antislavery. Wilson declared he was delighted the meeting had adopted a plan to unite. He wanted the majority of 1854 to be increased by 20,000 more votes. He had been working for years for a fusion of parties on one platform of freedom. One of the few Whigs there, Franklin Dexter, later declared the meeting had been too little a consultation and too much a Free Soil gathering; he could not "melt" his principles into Free Soilism. A large committee, headed by Samuel Hoar, was established to prepare for the mass convention and confer with other parties.[39]

On August 22 the Chapman Hall group reassembled at the United States Hotel to confer with representatives of the Republicans, led by Carter, Know Somethings, and Know Nothings. Each group first met separately. Consultation was then arranged, with each of the four groups appointing a committee of three. Bliss, Adams, and Boutwell were selected by the Chapman Hall group. The committees could agree that slavery was the primary issue. The Know Nothings insisted upon a delegate convention. As the strongest party in the state, they were unwilling to give up their independence unless assured of a controlling voice in the emerging reorganization. The Chapman Hall group was fearful the Americans were trying to force Gardner on them and would not agree. Others considered them dictatorial. After spending much of the day in consultation, in desperation the other groups united on a call, signed by Know Nothings, Know Somethings, Free Soilers, Democrats, Whigs, Republicans, and even several former Chapman Hall participants. That evening the Chapman Hall group met again and issued a call for a mass convention and recommended a delegate convention, both in Worcester, September 30. The *Boston Bee* subsequently announced the Know Nothings would not abandon their organization. The *New York Tribune* blamed Adams for preventing fusion.[40]

Whoever was to blame, the conservative former Free Soilers were, as the *Tribune* cited, being impractical. Adams and Allen represented no one, correspondent Oliver charged; at most one thousand people would follow them. True, a few more Whigs like Bowles, Dawes, and Goodrich had left their party and would join a new movement. Press support, even the *Boston Atlas*, looked promising for a fusion party. On the other hand, both the Whigs and Democrats intended to make separate nominations. A temperance party convention was scheduled for Worcester on August 30. Twelve hundred delegates opposed to the liquor law assembled the first week of September for their own nomination and chose the man who soon would also be the Democratic candidate for governor. No fusion party could do very well in this political atmosphere if the Know Nothings also were running separate tickets.[41]

In public Wilson was playing a minor role in the proceedings, perhaps because his participation would antagonize the Adams faction, perhaps because of his dual party connections, Know Nothing and Republican. He had promised since May that he would be a follower and let others lead, just as long as fusion were the result. While he attended the Chapman Hall meeting, the failure of most reports to list his presence, although his remarks were sometimes included, causes one to believe he arrived late. There is no record he was present at the first United States Hotel meeting, and he was campaigning in Maine when the second occurred. When the *Tribune* charged that Adams was preventing fusion, it explained he would not work with the Know Nothings because he was determined to exclude Wilson. Adams did not blame Wilson for the many attacks upon him. He credited the new senator with sincerity in attempting to break the Order and encourage fusion. Accidentally meeting him on August 27, Adams told the senator he had disapproved of him and his course for some years, but was not motivated in this matter by opposition to individuals. Wilson agreed the *Tribune* article was mischievous, and acknowledged some of his previous actions had engendered distrust in some of his former friends.[42]

On August 29 the twelve-man committee to create fusion tried again. The Chapman Hall contingent would not back down on its mass convention. More agreement was reached this time on a delegate meeting, accepting the call issued the previous week by the Republicans and Know Nothings. Samuel Hoar, Dana, Adams, Allen, and Kimball would not sign. But signers included Foster, president of the Know Nothings, P. M. Aldrich, president of the Know Somethings, S. C. Phillips, Increase Sumner, Congressmen Buffington, Comins, and Hall, Boutwell, Secretary of State E. M. Wright, and Wilson.[43]

The other parties met as if they had an opportunity of winning. The Democrats nominated Springfield lawyer Edward D. Beach, who had already been chosen by the anti–Maine Law convention. He was recognized as a strong candidate. They condemned the Maine law, endorsed the Pierce administration, and denounced the Know Nothings. After the Republican convention the Whigs, with two-thirds of the towns unrepresented, nominated Samuel H. Walley. Their platform ignored Kansas.[44]

Organization proceeded towards the Worcester meetings. The committee of the American party, chosen at the Springfield convention, directed the political units to assemble and elect delegates to the Republican convention. Issues of the *Northampton Courier* are full of reports of Republican and fusion gatherings. The *Boston Transcript* was impressed with how the "best men" were attending fusion meetings in many areas. But it feared in some communities the supporters of Gardner were controlling selection of delegates. It predicted the Maine elections would influence events in Massachusetts.[45]

Events in other states would, of course, affect Massachusetts. In the early elections in the South, the Democrats won convincingly, attracting Whigs to the party. The Know Nothings in many elections were the primary opposition, but, except in Kentucky, were beaten. Republican strength was growing in the upper mid-West. The Vermont gubernatorial winner in early September had both Republican and Know Nothing backing. Enthusiasm was strong in Pennsylvania when the Republicans held their convention, September 5. Wilson sent a letter of encouragement and support. Maine had three tickets, a Democratic-antiliquor law, a Whig, and an American-Republican. The last was antislavery and protemperance. Senators Wade, Hale, Bell, and Wilson were imported for the campaign. With an astonishingly large turnout Governor Anson Morrill won a plurality for reelection, but the Democrats won more legislative races and would combine with conservative Whigs to control the government. Temperance had beaten the Republicans. New York would be a determining state. There Weed worked with ex–Free Soil Democrat Preston King, Know Somethings, and others to call a Republican convention. The old Free Soilers had to ignore the Fugitive Slave Act and slavery in the District of Columbia to obtain fusion. But the Republicans lacked party organization and were hurt by the temperance issue.[46]

During the last few days of August, Wilson left for Vermont and Maine to lend his support. In six days he traveled 840 miles and delivered seven addresses. He returned to Massachusetts for only several days, then on September 7 departed for Michigan, expecting to be absent several weeks. He addressed the state convention at Kalamazoo at length. How he must have compared the unity of the Republican party in Michigan with the problems he had left behind in Massachusetts! He was announced to speak at the Republican state meeting in Syracuse on October 19, but preferred to return home for the Worcester conventions. Wilson would not have absented himself from Massachusetts had he believed his hand was necessary to assist in the formation of the fusion party. He both trusted his associates and recognized this was not the most propitious moment for his leadership.[47]

Gardner had not participated in the various meetings to plan for a new party. Trying to create trouble, the *New York Herald* contended the Chapman Hall meeting had been called by the "white kid gloves" group of Adams, Phillips, Dana, and Allen to prevent Gardner's reelection. The governor had long publicly advocated fusion of those who opposed slavery and had said so as early as his 1854 letters to Allen. His remarks and the prominence of his agreement with the other members of the Massachusetts delegation at Philadelphia, he maintained, might cost him the vice-presidential nomination in 1856. He offered to withdraw his name for governor if his candidacy would interfere with fusion. Gardner's many opponents believed he fully intended to have the nomination and his offers to withdraw were for public consumption. Shortly before the Worcester conventions, he angrily criticized Bowles for sustaining others who threatened to abandon the fusion movement if Gardner were nominated, but opposing Gardner's friends who stated they would do the same if he were not the candidate.[48]

As convention time approached, a split within the Know Nothings became more likely. Adams on September 17 attended a Quincy meeting to choose delegates and quickly concluded the Know Nothings would not permit his selection or that of any non-nativist. A fusion meeting in Boston on September 12 was stormy. Although the men selected represented various components of the movement, Gardner advocates considered this a defeat, since they had expected to capture most of the delegation. Carter in the *New York Tribune* predicted Gardner would not be nominated. The *Northampton Courier,* on the other hand, asserted Gardner's opponents had no viable alternative and his supporters were united. Foster and E. R. Hoar declined being candidates. On the eve of the conclave one newspaper correspondent from Worcester reported the fight would be bitter; Gardner's friends would bolt if he were not nominated, and others would leave if he were.[49]

On the night before the convention was to begin a mass rally was held at the Worcester city hall. Speeches were delivered by Congressman Mark Trafton, Goodrich, E. C. Baker, Wilson, and others. Baker spoke about nativism, the others about slavery. Wilson's remarks were characterized as calm and temperate and received with "much applause." He asserted the purpose of the meetings was union on the slavery issue. He asked people to put aside their past differences and jealousies. Although he agreed with Baker that the Know Nothing movement had been useful, he declared the time had arrived for a new party and the Republican was the only viable one. The Whigs were powerless, the Free Soilers too weak. He also declared that he had acted against every political party in the state and had abandoned a party whenever he had found another which would do more to carry out his principles.[50]

The Republican party was recreated at Worcester. Phillips was chairman of the mass convention of between two and three thousand people. Banks, Know Nothing but pro-fusion, agreed to preside over the delegate assembly. Members of Congress present were invited to take seats, but were not permitted to vote. Wilson stayed in the background. Adams and Sumner had refused to attend. The Resolutions Committee, chaired by Dana, recommended the party accept the Republican name, declared slavery was the most important political issue, and ignored nativism. It went beyond the Know Nothing and Whig platforms, which called for restoration of the Missouri Compromise line by opposing admittance of future slave states. His biographer later characterized Dana's participation as the most satisfactory episode of his political career.[51]

There were ironies in the selection of Rockwell as the candidate of those who opposed Gardner. He had not been active in the fusion movement. A Whig

Congressman for six years, he had been replaced in the Senate by Wilson, seemingly unacceptable then to any wing of the Know Nothing party. On the first ballot for the governorship, Gardner received 449 votes, Rockwell 305, Foster 122, Hoar 45, and 20 were scattered. A debate ensued about Gardner's support of fusion. One delegate asked if Gardner would stand with the Republican party or accept a Know Nothing nomination as well. He noted the Know Nothings had a convention already scheduled for October 3 and asked what Gardner's relationship was to that. Dana insisted Gardner be passed over unless he was willing to join the Republican party. On the second ballot Rockwell received 426, Gardner 395, Foster 13, others 5 votes. Rockwell had been narrowly nominated by 5 votes out of more than 800. Selections for the other state offices were by acclamation, all but one of them Know Nothing incumbents. Speeches of congratulation and ratification were delivered by S. C. Phillips, Eliot, Foster, Kimball, Wilson, and others.[52]

The Free Soil, the Whig, and some of the Know Nothing press applauded the Rockwell selection. Twelve of the western Massachusetts newspapers endorsed the Republican candidates; only three Democrat, two Know Nothing, and one Whig paper sustained the other parties. The *Atlas* was the most prominent of the old Boston dailies to endorse the Republicans. While ex-Whigs like Dana, Adams, Dawes, Bowles, Hoar, and Palfrey might be pleased with the nominee for governor and the platform, others might be less happy. Rockwell had until recently been a Whig leader. Furthermore, while the convention had selected nominees for state offices, the party had no state program. The mixture of ex-Whigs Rockwell and E. R. Hoar with incumbent Know Nothings presented a hybrid ticket. Those, like Wilson, whose main objective was to weaken the nativist movement and create a Massachusetts component of an antislavery party for 1856, could be satisfied. Those concerned about nativism would be unhappy.[53]

Who had engineered the candidate selections? We still do not know. Rockwell obviously attracted ex-Whigs and was preferred by the Free Soil–Dana group. Why did the Wilson-led Know Nothings accept him? Since the nativist wing of the party could not permit itself to become divided, it was unlikely to support any nominee of the fusion party, except Gardner. The Free Soil Americans therefore could hardly have offered a Know Nothing alternative to Gardner. Whigs or Democrats were not going to win. If Rockwell were elected, he would support antislavery actions in the state. His economic policies might not be as acceptable to former coalitionists, but that would have to be price to pay for winning. If he lost, it would be to a Know Nothing, likely Gardner, and the Free Soilers would be no worse off. Howe claimed Wilson himself in September was determined to be governor. The senator declared he could win 10,000 more votes than any other man. Wilson had asserted if Rockwell were nominated for governor and he for lieutenant governor, he would run far ahead. Howe had to confess Wilson was right. Whatever the conversation between the two, Wilson wasn't foolish enough to give up a safe

Senate seat for the unimportant lieutenant governorship or risk losing the election to the highest state position.[54]

Wilson declared his only purpose was fusion. He had been out of the state for most of four weeks after the first United States Hotel meeting, he stated in replying to charges he had been unfaithful to his party. He spoke at the convention only four times, never in support of any candidate. He attended no meeting at which arrangements were discussed. No one objected to the name Republican, and Know Nothings were prominent on the Resolutions Committee. He contended his role had been proper and uninfluential.[55]

But the nativists and the Gardner supporters were angered by the results at Worcester. Ely charged everything had been arranged the day before the convention opened. Know Nothing lodges in Boston and Charleston the night after the meetings denounced the deliberations and repudiated Rockwell. The *Bee* declared Wilson went to the convention on September 19 an ardent Gardner supporter. By the next morning he was wavering. By that evening he had endorsed Rockwell. Swift and Slack had arrived at Worcester favoring Gardner, then did not vote for him. The next day the editor of the same paper attacked the Adams-Dana wing of Free Soilers. He declared Know Nothings had participated in the August meetings with the understanding that all those present agreed on slavery issues. Every other point of view would be accepted. He contended those who refused to sign the Chapman Hall report—who said they would not support Gardner if nominated by the Worcester meeting—acted in bad faith. The paper even suggested a new fusion, with the Whigs.[56]

Foster, in contrast, submitted his resignation as president of the American State Council. He explained that Know Nothings were in the majority at Worcester and had acted in good faith. He endorsed the Rockwell nomination and pledged to abide by the result.[57]

Wilson continued to divorce himself from direct party organization and, following the Worcester convention, immediately left for speaking engagements in New York and Pennsylvania. The new party's state committee met on September 27 to organize. Henry S. Washburn, a Worcester Whig, was elected chairman and Webb, secretary. Of course, the latter was a longtime Wilson collaborator. Washburn soon declined and Goodrich accepted the position. The intent was to have an ex-Whig head the committee.[58]

Wilson and Goodrich after Worcester had gone together to Albany to address the county Republican convention on September 22. Wilson's speech was long, firm, humorous, and optimistic. He spoke of the need to save the union, the hopelessness after Philadelphia of Northerners' halting the advances of the Slave Power through the American party, the death of the Whig party, and the understanding New York Democrats, above all others, must have had that their party could never contain the slaveholders. Those opposed to slavery needed to realize this was their moment. He compared New Hampshire of twenty years before, when

Pierce was senator, with New Hampshire of 1855. He contrasted the mob attack upon the 1830s New York state antislavery meetings with the events of 1855. He noted the differences between the Ohio of 1835 and 1836, when Birney's press was thrown in the river, and in 1855, when Chase, Birney's supporter, could be nominated for governor. The Republicans could have a majority in the House in December, Wilson asserted. They could win the presidency in 1856. Wilson continued on to Philadelphia for another address on September 27.[59]

When he returned to Massachusetts, Wilson discovered that the Know Nothings opposed to the Worcester results were charging at meetings that their party had been betrayed by "political traitors and disunionists." Needing to correct the record, Wilson addressed a long letter to Baker, secretary of the party. He reviewed the positions, since the spring, of Know Nothing legislators, of state council meetings, of Baker himself, and of Gardner towards the issues of slavery and fusion. Baker and Gardner were shown to have been strong advocates of Know Nothing antislavery resolutions and Baker an active and influential participant in the fusion movement. Wilson minimized his own role in events since August, but professed his agreement with the results. Baker replied in writing, emphasizing Wilson's continued support of nativism at the Springfield convention and as late as September 19. He rejected Wilson's main argument that the Americans were bound in good faith not to oppose the Worcester nominations. Instead, he attacked Wilson and scrutinized the senator's political career. He also attempted to create additional friction within Republican ranks by reporting that Wilson had denounced Allen, Adams, and Dana to him.[60]

The Know Nothings who gathered in Boston on October 3 were those who had decided not to accept the results at Worcester. Baker presided. The "large and enthusiastic" conclave almost unanimously selected Gardner for governor. Since the other incumbents had accepted Republican nominations, the remainder of the ticket had to be new. In his speech before the convention Gardner attributed his defeat at Worcester to his refusal to surrender his nativist principles. The *New York Tribune* correspondent was struck that the speech, for a governor, was too characterized by attacks on individuals. Gardner called Bowles the father of the fusion movement, Dana the "master spirit" at Worcester. He pronounced fusion leaders to be traitors. He called Wilson "a political harlot." One delegate charged Wilson had joined the Know Nothing party for what he could get out of it and left when he got what he wanted. Another criticized Wilson and Foster for not defending Gardner from attacks.[61]

Many Republicans anticipated victory. Boutwell, not certain himself, recorded that the public at least thought election of Rockwell was a foregone conclusion. The *Northampton Courier* reported the Republican political meetings in October demonstrated they had marshaled forces of strength never seen before in the antislavery movement. Know Nothing chapters were in disarray. The Worcester auxiliary fell in membership to a little over 400, only 200 of whom had previously been members. Most of the men the party had raised to congressional or state office had abandoned it. On the other hand, within a week after the Know Nothing convention Bowles was worried about nativism's continued strength. Banks was wise enough that, while he supported Rockwell, he refrained from attacking Gardner and encouraged some of his own followers to work on behalf of the governor. In fact, the Americans were more united than the Republicans had anticipated; Hunker, nativist, and antislavery Know Nothings all supported the ticket. They waged an excellent campaign.[62]

Wilson and Foster addressed a Republican meeting in Worcester on October 5. The former replied to Gardner's attack in his Boston acceptance speech. Wilson contended he had never wronged nor spoken unkindly of the governor. Gardner's remarks were unbecoming of one in his office. The governor had long favored fusion, Wilson emphasized. Gardner had often spoken of his urging it on the Whig party in 1854 and being voted down. Wilson cited a long list of men with whom in conversation Gardner had expressed his commitment to fusion. Wilson respected Gardner's concern about nativism, but contended that if temperance, tariff, nativism, or other principles had been incorporated into the new party, many men would have refused to join.[63]

Four days later on October 9 Wilson returned for another speech in the Empire state campaign, this time before more than three thousand people at the Tabernacle in New York City. He had been invited to appear only the day before. He spoke of the union character of the Republican party; it was not in existence to make war on the South. He reiterated his belief in state powers. Republicans, he declared, were determined that Kansas and other territories would not be admitted as slave states. He attacked the Pierce administration and the Nebraska bill. He saw no hope of reorganizing the Whig party, which in bowing to slavery had died. In examining the history of the Know Nothing party, he portrayed it as having been antislavery in the North. He recalled the Philadelphia convention, his role there, and how the New York delegation had determined the results. "The first duty you owe to your country is to repudiate this baffled and defeated and disgraced faction," he asserted. Having traveled nearly 15,000 miles through thirteen states in the past seven months, he predicted Northerners would sustain the Republican platforms adopted in Massachusetts and New York. Those opposed to the Nebraska bill had carried the House in 1854 and had not endangered the union. They would elect an anti-Nebraska man president in 1856.[64]

The strength of the various parties was so different in the various Northern states that the October elections proved little. In Ohio the Republican ticket defeated the Democrats by 50,000 votes, although Chase, in a three-way race for governor, won only by a 15,000 plurality. The Republicans carried both houses of the legislature by large majorities. In the most important statewide race in Pennsylvania, for canal commissioner, the four anti-Democratic candidates were withdrawn shortly before the election, too late to prevent the Democrat from receiving a majority. In Indiana the Democrats also won.[65]

The new Massachusetts Republican party appeared to be well organized, but Webb feared they were less effective than the Know Nothings. Forty speakers, including Adams, Sumner, Banks, Boutwell, Hudson, Burlingame, Foster, Eliot, Goodrich, and Wilson were dispatched for addresses. Bowles and Webb were pleased with the "immense work" being done by Wilson. Rockwell received the greatest newspaper support, the Democrats second, and the Know Nothings least. Wilson participated in the campaign with zeal. Gardner called him "the grand leader" of the fusion movement, stumping the state, sometimes speaking twice a day. At Chicopee hundreds had to stand to hear him. A large crowd also appeared at Gloucester, but at the conclusion, three cheers were given for Gardner. One of the more amusing activities of Wilson was his participation in the Republican convention of his own Middlesex County, which adopted the Democratic resolutions drafted by Hallett in 1849 and the Whig resolutions of 1854.[66]

The results of the Massachusetts election were, as the *Boston Transcript* described them, a "brilliant victory" for the Americans. Gardner obtained more than 51,000 votes, Rockwell more than 36,000, Beach 35,000, and Walley 14,000. The Republicans had done poorer than their press had anticipated. Rockwell carried three counties but was without a majority in any. He did best in his own west, attracting especially former Whigs, in antislavery Worcester, and in the shoe towns of the east. The already weak Whigs of 1854 had declined by half. Beach, who carried only Hampden County, had benefited from his additional nomination by the antiliquor law party. Gardner attracted 30,000 fewer voters than a year before, but was comfortably elected. Of course, the governor would not have been reelected were this not the first time the new plurality rule was applied. Wilson's Middlesex County voted 9,000 for Gardner, 6,400 for Beach, 5,200 for Rockwell, and 2,600 for Walley.[67]

The state legislature would not again be so dominated by one party, but even there the Americans had done well. The Republicans had picked up all five Senate seats in antislavery Worcester County, two in Hampshire, and one in Franklin. Nantucket and Dukes had selected a Republican-American. The Democrats won two seats from Hampden. The remainder were Know Nothings, including all six positions from Suffolk County. Figures for the House are harder to arrive at, because of the confusing nature of party affiliations. The Americans were in a slight minority, if the other parties would work together, which they could not.[68]

The Whigs were shattered. Some of the traditional leaders had remained in the party because they opposed nativism or were incapable of understanding how weak and palsied their party had become. Many demonstrated such a hatred of Wilson and his associates that political issues no longer motivated them. In spite of the massive rejection of the Whigs, Everett was pleased with the results. He recorded that Sumner, Wilson, and Burlingame had spoken ten to twelve times each, yet after all their efforts, Rockwell's vote was little more than the 1853 anti-Whig number. The *Boston Advertiser* chose to count Democrat, Whig, and Know Nothing votes in mass and interpret that as a majority against Republican nullification. It claimed that Wilson and Sumner were senators unsupported by the electorate and recalled that John Quincy Adams in 1808 had resigned under those circumstances.[69]

The Know Nothing victory was undisputed. Gardner considered it a personal triumph, having received more votes than others on the ticket. "Oliver," the *New York Tribune* reporter, agreed. The governor had had arrayed against him the press of the state and virtually all the respected and well-known men, yet won, impressively. Many of the political leaders of the state had joined one movement: the conservative Free Soilers like Adams, Allen, and Dana; the loyalist Bird-Sumner wing of Free Soil–Republicans; the Wilson-Foster faction of the Know Nothings; most of the leading officeholders of the American party; Democrats like Banks and Boutwell who had held major state offices; and a large number of Whigs, including Rockwell himself, Dawes, Bowles, Child, Goodrich, and Eliot. Gardner particularly attacked Foster and Wilson. In truth, too, the electorate was not ready to make antislavery the issue, was suspicious of the Republican temperance position, and was more impressed with the Know Nothing reform legislation than disturbed by its anti-Catholic committee activities. The election was hardly over before the State Council convened and decided to send delegates, including Gardner, to a national convention at Cincinnati. There on November 22 representatives from seven states which had bolted at Philadelphia characterized the repeal of the Missouri Compromise as a violation of a trust, objected to coalescing with any party which wanted Americans to abandon their principles, and proposed reuniting with the national council.[70]

On election eve Giddings joined Wilson, Sumner, and others to await results. They were disappointed. Sumner was fearful that Gardner would replace him when his Senate term was complete. Dana was so deflated he again left politics for a year. Three days after the election Foster moved to Iowa. Elsewhere supporters were surprised or discouraged. William Birney wrote from Philadelphia that Wilson had led them to anticipate better results. Herman Kriesman in Chicago had also expected a better Republican showing. He supposed Wilson would feel the defeat more than others, for he had again placed himself in the minority. Yet Wilson had himself to blame, Kreisman believed, for he and Burlingame had led Free Soilers into the American party the year before and 15,000 of them had remained there to vote for Gardner. The *New York Tribune* correspondent tried to put up a good front, declaring the Republicans had fought a good fight and were not downcast. When the state committee assembled a group of leaders on November 16, the room was full, with a broad representation of former conservative Free Soilers, former Whigs, and former Know Nothings. Wilson was in western New York. They resolved to continue their party and work.[71]

Wilson's analysis was that Republicans, himself included, had overestimated the antislavery and underestimated the Know Nothing sentiment in the state. Furthermore, he blamed Dana for opposing consultation with other parties and for discouraging them from uniting with Republicans. Surely, Dana did not have that much influence other than for a day at the fusion convention. Wilson must have been using him as representative of a much wider-held, although minority, opinion. Second, Wilson was critical of the way the canvass had been waged. He and Foster had entered the campaign soon after the nominations. But against his advice, others had waited too long to get involved. Sumner had not spoken until eleven days before the election; Wilson had predicted then that they were already beaten. Not fewer than 12,000 former Free Soilers and at least 10,000 Whigs, he contended, had voted for Gardner. Wilson was fearful the defeat of the Republicans in Massachusetts and New York endangered the chances of victory in the presidential race in 1856.[72]

Elsewhere in the North in this off-year election the Republicans also had not fared as well as they had hoped. In New York the principal election was for secretary of state, with Preston King, the Republican, beaten by a Know Nothing. Know Nothings won other offices, with the Republicans second. The Republicans captured control of the state Senate, ran third for the Assembly. This was perhaps not a bad showing for a party in existence for only two months. In Wisconsin the Republicans captured control of the Senate, the Democrats of the House, and the governor's race was contested.[73]

As the end of 1855 approached the political antislavery movement had entered a new phase. Republican parties had been created in most Northern states and they had won control of several. In Indiana and Ohio Republicans were working uneasily with the Know Nothings. In three of the largest states—New York, Pennsylvania, and Massachusetts—the Know Nothings had beaten the Republicans. At the same time issues in the territories, especially in Kansas, were weakening the Democratic party. And the Whig party had collapsed as a national body, with former members holding on to skeleton organizations in a few states. Just as Wilson himself was now ready to turn more to national affairs so the future of the American political system was about to be determined more by national issues.

13

KANSAS, SUMMNER-BROOKS AND THE RISE TO REPUBLICAN SENATE LEADERSHIP

When Wilson returned to Washington for his first full term in the United States Senate, beginning December 3, 1855, he would be a part of a new Congress which would become one of the most contentious in the nation's history. This was the first meeting of the Thirty-fourth Congress, elected in the turmoil following Nebraska and the Know Nothings. Greeley, who was making his first visit to the capitol in four years, commented on the great turnover in personnel which had occurred in the New England and New York delegations. The Democrats had tried to ignore Republicans for committee assignments in earlier Congresses, claiming the Whigs were the minority party and thus entitled to assignments not set aside for the majority. Six senators, five from slave states, elected as Whigs, announced they now were separated from party organization. Of the sixty senators, fifteen were Republicans, one-quarter of the Senate, and the new minority party. But the Democrats carefully structured the committees so that they would dominate. They determined non-Democratic positions, assigning former Whig and Know Nothings so as to weaken the Republicans. "Slavery guards every pass," Greeley wrote. Wilson was placed on the less significant committees on Manufacturers and Private Land Claims.[1]

Life in Washington during his first full session was not as pleasant for Wilson as it was for many members of the majority party. He had predicted to Parker in the summer that the session would try their firmness. Sumner remarked in December that he had never seen such bad feelings, so little intermingling among those of different views. Seward, Sumner, and Wilson were the special objects of antipathy.

Wilson had neither a private home in the city nor was he living at one of the major hotels. He was the only senator staying at Mrs. Beveridge's on Pennsylvania Avenue, although Congressmen Buffington, Damrell, and Knapp were also residing there. Harriet had not accompanied him. In December Wilson took quite ill, according to the report, from pain in the face. He fell in his bathroom and lay insensible for a long time.[2]

Traditionally neither house proceeded very far with business until both were organized. Since only approximately one-third of the Senate was chosen at each national election and since the vice-president presided, the Senate was a continuing body rather quickly constituted. On the other hand, no party enjoyed a majority in the House of Representatives and thus choosing a Speaker became a formidable task. For two months the representatives argued. The Democrats selected William A. Richardson of Illinois, a close associate of Douglas, as their initial candidate. The others, a majority, included Northern Whigs, Republicans, antislavery Know Nothings, anti-Nebraska Democrats, and non-Democratic Southerners. They had little in common, except opposition to the Democrats. Most of them agreed to unite on Lewis D. Campbell of Ohio, a Know Nothing, with the understanding that if he failed to get a majority, they would turn to Banks.[3]

Wilson got heavily involved in the contest. The previous Congress had scarcely adjourned, when, in April 1855, he began work. Banks had Democratic, Know Nothing, and Free Soil affiliations, was personable and dignified, and was a veteran presiding officer. Campbell got as many as 80 votes out of 225, but he had been too much a leader in the anti-Nebraska fight, was temperamental, and was too nativist. Banks was then brought forward. One report asserted Burlingame, Greeley, and Wilson were "everywhere, cajoling, threatening, rounding up members for roll call votes." To attract Know Nothing support, the Democrats replaced Richardson with James L. Orr of South Carolina. As newspapers got caught up in the controversy, pressures mounted from home on representatives to stand firm. One wonders how Wilson survived financially during these nine weeks; members could not be paid until authorization was voted. The sergeant-at-arms of the previous House in late January procured funds from Pennsylvania banks to tide over some members.[4]

In late January the Democrats narrowly failed to get their man selected. Finally, a majority of the House agreed to accept a plurality choice and on February 3, after two months of balloting, Banks was chosen, 103 to 100 over William Aiken of South Carolina; 11 votes had been scattered. Wilson was actively involved in lining up support. Banks had been elected to Congress as a Know Nothing, and the long controversy dividing Southern and Northern Know Nothings had seriously damaged the nativist party. The anti-Nebraska men, on the other hand, had won their first important victory.[5]

On February 28 more than one hundred Massachusetts Republicans celebrated the House's decision and honored the new Speaker with a dinner. Wilson returned to Boston for the event and was seated at the head table. The usually negative Palfrey was pleased by the events. Since getting Adams and Palfrey to honor Banks was an accomplishment, "Warrington" was encouraged to hope for greater cooperation and conciliation. He reported Wilson was received cordially and spoke well. In his address the senator advocated union and harmony among anti-Nebraska men. He rebuked those from Massachusetts who had betrayed the North at the Know Nothing Philadelphia meetings. He made quite an impression, one of Sumner's correspondents reported. Adams unhappily recorded that he found himself with Wilson on his right and feared gossip if he did not on occasion converse with him. Both men delivered speeches, Wilson making Adams uncomfortable by referring to him several times as his friend.[6]

While the House tried to select a Speaker, the Senate either adjourned early, or occasionally considered matters within its own jurisdiction, or debated. In early February, because of the very severe winter, Senator Clayton of Delaware proposed a resolution taking money out of the Senate's contingency fund to provide firewood for the poor of Washington. The Senate establishment opposed the resolution, while Wilson voted in favor. Apparently Clayton or other supporters persuaded some of their colleagues of the need, for the next day, with Wilson again in favor, the Senate by a 28-to-21 vote set aside $1,500 for relief in the city and Georgetown. Wilson throughout his career took seriously his congressional responsibility for consideration and oversight of the District of Columbia.[7]

Off and on the Senate debated Central American affairs, prompted by a motion to refer to the Committee on Foreign Relations a letter of British Lord John Russell respecting interpretation of the 1850 Clayton-Bulwer Treaty. This treaty limited the right of Great Britain and the United States to exercise exclusive control over or fortify a canal built in Central America and ambiguously pledged the two not to control nations in Central America. On February 12 Wilson delivered his first important foreign policy address. It was strongly nationalistic. Wilson maintained the Pierce administration was using a foreign quarrel to divert attention from domestic issues. Cass had declared the controversy with Great Britain had reached a critical stage, Seward had suggested war was the solution. But Wilson maintained the problem was solvable. Neither American merchants nor the people in general were greatly concerned, he contended. But he was not about to allow the Democrats to present themselves as the defenders of American nationalism. He denied Clayton's claims that his treaty was clear. He understood why the British interpreted it to their own advantage. He recommended abrogating the agreement because of the differences in interpretation. If that left Great Britain in control of Central America, he did not think that the United States was thereby endangered. If the nation were better represented in Central America the problem could be solved. He charged the Democrats ever since President Jackson's day had been unwilling to sustain the Monroe Doctrine. He would never make an agreement with Great Britain or any other country which would limit American power to control any part of the continent. A "strong and sensible speech," Greeley declared. Wilson took "bold and decided ground," the *New York Times* correspondent reported. Douglas is supposed to have called it "the best speech yet on the subject."[8]

Since 1856 was a presidential election year, the time had arrived for creation of a national Republican party. Chase had been advocating this for months, dreaming of a presidential nomination for himself. Former Democratic leaders like Francis Blair and Gideon Welles had hoped before the summer of 1855 that one of their number who had distinguished himself in the congressional battles against the Nebraska bill, such as Benton or Houston, might be the first national nominee of a new party. Wilson was opposed to Houston, whom he said did not have "the principles or sense enough" to be president. On Christmas, 1855, at Blair's home outside Washington Sumner, Banks, Chase, King, Bailey, and Blair met to devise strategy. The next day Wilson urged Adams to accede to the plan. Five Republican state chairmen, including Goodrich of Massachusetts, subsequently issued a call for a meeting in Pittsburgh on Washington's birthday to establish organization for the new party and provide for a national delegate convention later.[9]

Wilson was one of the earliest instigators of the nomination of John C. Fremont, who for his exploring feats was known as the pathmarker of the West. Perhaps he was attracted to this nonpolitician because of Seward's tardy affiliation with the party or because the New Yorker did not at the end of 1855 seek the nomination. Wilson had a continuing correspondence with Chase, who wanted to be the candidate, but seems to have rejected him. Wilson told the governor that he understood pledges had been made before the Ohio election that Chase would not be a presidential nominee. Fremont, son-in-law of Benton, had already been contacted by several interested Democrats, but he would not agree to endorse the Fugitive Slave and Kansas-Nebraska Acts. Banks, a friend since 1853, became an unofficial adviser. One Republican claimed he, Wilson, and Fremont conferred about the nomination while Wilson was attending the Michigan convention in September of 1855. Then in November Wilson, Banks, Hale, and Joseph Palmer, a merchant, discussed the possible candidacy. Banks was heavily engaged throughout December in the promotion. Long before the February convention, party leaders and influential newspaper editors throughout the North had endorsed Fremont.[10]

The Know Nothings scheduled national meetings in Philadelphia the same week the Republicans were convening in Pittsburgh. Gardner had been trying to solidify his position in Massachusetts. The November election triumph had been followed only a month later by defeat. The Americans by two thousand votes had lost the Boston city elections to Citizens Party candidates. Similar alliances among Know Nothing oppositions had produced victory for citizen-type tickets in other Massachusetts communities. Furthermore, the continued losses of lodge membership were serious. The 1856 legislature was Know Nothing controlled, but many of its American members had been nominated by other parties as well, so that no nativist legislation could be passed. Yet the governor was shrewd. The State Council on February 5 endorsed the Cincinnati resolutions and, on Gardner's motion, chose delegates to Philadelphia.[11]

The governor overcame objections of the Ely wing and made a new slavery position a major issue for the national meeting. At Philadelphia the number of votes a delegation was entitled to was determined for the first time by the size of the state's congressional representation. The more numerous Northerners in the council were therefore able to get the objectionable Section Twelve dealing with slavery eliminated from the platform. But the convention defeated by a three-to-one majority a proposed antislavery plank. The statement on slavery was neutral enough to attract votes from both sections. The convention nominated former president Fillmore as its candidate for the fall elections. Gardner received little support for his vice-presidential candidacy.[12]

After the Philadelphia meetings, Gardner found himself in an increasingly uncomfortable position. The Fillmore nomination had been pleasing to conservative Whigs, but the longer many Massachusetts Know Nothings thought about their presidential candidate, the more unhappy they became. Fillmore was a late convert to nativism and had been unpopular as president with most Massachusetts voters. The State Council on March 5 postponed endorsement of the Philadelphia nominations and reiterated its support for the August 1855 platform. Having promoted reaffiliation with the national party and getting Fillmore as the nominee, Gardner endangered his own political power. The governor's national ambitions had been thwarted, so he turned to the senatorship, with pressure on the legislature to choose Sumner's successor a year early. But the Whig members of the General Court had no more fondness for Gardner than for Sumner, nor did the Democrats. Nor were some of the antislavery Know Nothings, including Speaker of the House Phelps, certain Gardner was their choice for senator. By April the governor had to abandon his plans.[13]

The Republicans assembled in Pittsburgh on February 22. The city was difficult to get to that time of year and Congress was in session, so many leaders of the party were not present. All free and eight slave states were represented. The more radical among the ex–Free Soilers were determined no compromise would be made with the Know Nothings and that the new party would focus upon slavery. The primary position, which would continue to characterize the party, was opposition to expansion of slavery in the territories.[14]

Events in Kansas had deteriorated steadily since the removal of Reeder as governor. Pierce, in August 1855, had appointed Wilson Shannon, former chief executive of Ohio. In the next six months the new governor consistently sided with the proslavery element. Believing they would not receive fair treatment from the territorial government, the Free Soilers held a convention at Topeka in midautumn. They drew up a state constitution, which was subsequently ratified by those participating in the election, and set up a state government of their own with

Charles Robinson as governor. At first the proslavery men in Kansas and Missouri treated the events as unworthy of notice. But soon they recognized the challenge was serious. The Free Soilers's so-called Topeka constitution was dispatched to Washington, where the House might respond to it favorably.

Both sides organized and prepared their legal cases. They almost came to war in December. The Free Soilers were well armed and trained and 1,200 Missourians were prepared to support the proslavery men of Kansas. An alarmed Shannon managed to intervene and cool down the controversy. A harsh winter also helped quiet affairs. However biased the legislature and governor were, they had the sanction of legality. Moderates among the Free Soilers had to control the hotheads like Lane from driving towards rebellion or sanctioning anarchy. In spite of some unwise actions by the Free Soil government, matters might have quieted had Pierce been objective and fair.

The time for a major debate over Kansas in Washington had arrived. Early in the session Hale presented a resolution calling for information from the president about the territory. On January 3 Wilson presented a similar, more specific proposal, seeking information in the president's possession about disturbances during Kansas elections Wilson asked by what authority armed men from Missouri were marching into Kansas, what steps the executive had taken to prevent those outrages, and what persons holding national office had participated in these events. On January 29 Pierce sent a message requesting appropriations to meet contingencies in Kansas and asking for legislation to authorize the people of the territory to take steps to form a state. In the argument over to which committee the requests should be referred, Seward dealt with technicalities, and former Whigs Bell and Clayton debated the Democrats; Wilson was the only Republican to attack the fundamental issues of Pierce's proposal. Shortly thereafter the Senate considered Pierce's nomination of Shannon, whose confirmation was anathema to the Republicans. On February 19, the same afternoon he began his major address on Kansas, Wilson in executive session attacked the governor and was insulted by three of his Senate colleagues in reply. The Senate confirmed the appointment, 30 to 12.[15]

Pierce replied to the resolutions requesting information on February 19. Since Wilson's remarks in executive session were not publishable, his speech in answer to Pierce's report was far more influential. Wilson had been preparing his address for weeks and he was the first of his party to speak. When the Senate adjourned, Wilson resumed the next day. The address was a "scathing rebuke" of the administration. The message and papers sent by Pierce were a distortion, he declared. The information provided was often little more than rumor. Describing with minuteness the outrages inflicted on antislavery people in Kansas, he especially attacked Shannon both for his personal habits and his inadequacies as governor. The territory's elections, excluding the first one for delegate to the House, had been a mockery, Wilson believed. He had a mass of statistics, some proving many more ballots had been cast than there were legal voters or even residents in a district. Of twenty-one federally appointed officers in Kansas, nineteen were slave state men; no fairness was being received from them. Wilson enunciated most of the sources for his information, including later senator Samuel C. Pomeroy and a lawyer from Lawrence, Kansas, who was present in the chamber. Wilson concluded that the administration was destroying popular sovereignty as a way to decide the question of slavery in a territory. He also defended the Emigrant Aid Society as legitimate and praiseworthy.[16]

The speech was a personal triumph. Wilson had become "the most active, outspoken and intrepid of all Northern Senators," *The Liberator* declared. He was not defensive, the Washington correspondent of the *New York Post* noted. He intended to break down his opponents by aggressive attacks. Sumner and Seward too often fired off heavy guns, and then rested, but Wilson would be a different kind of antagonist. Less likely to be favorable was the *New York Courier and Enquirer,* yet it reported the address had been "the ablest and most interesting exposition of Kansas affairs that has yet been heard in the Senate." When Nason and Russell published their biography of their friend, they devoted more space to this Kansas speech than to any other. More than ten thousand copies of the address were subscribed for by House members shortly after Wilson finished speaking. By mid-March nearly 100,000 copies had been printed and most of the antiadministration press of the North had published the address in full or part.[17]

Not everyone was as pleased. Henry Wise termed the effort a "harangue" and "a severe infliction to those who were obligated to listen to it." Wilson repeated himself, Wise reported; his language was "disjointed and ungraceful." He characterized Wilson as the least attractive speaker he had ever heard in the Senate. Although other reports indicate the size of his audience grew as Wilson continued, Wise claimed only about six or eight senators, most Republicans, listened. Typical of comments by the Democratic press were those of the Washington *Union,* which declared Wilson with that kind of speech would gain the reputation of a bully. The *New York Times* correspondent commented on the threats of personal violence Wilson had evoked, but thought he would be safe if he didn't stay out late at night.[18]

After Hale and Wade had also attacked the Kansas policy, four senators defended the administration, Jones of Tennessee and Toucey especially dealing in personalities. Hale accused some New England politicians, obviously Toucey, of crawling before slavery. Toucey termed Hale "mean and despicable." Wilson then objected to Toucey's personal attacks and to his making insinuations difficult to answer while avoiding direct charges. He intimated he considered Toucey "as beneath contempt." "Hot and spicy," Greeley termed the Toucey-Wilson encounter. Jones declared many of the most objectionable parts of Wilson's speech had been omitted or modified in print; he hoped that demonstrated the Massachusetts senator was not beyond redemption. Jones's remarks were intended to intimidate Wilson, one contemporary claimed. Sumner wrote that Wilson had "earned his senatorship." The speech had been "the great event of his life." The "slavemongers are very angry with Wilson," he reported.[19]

Between debates over slavery Wilson was defining his position on other issues. As might be expected from a former Whig and Free Soiler, he was making a record in favor of internal improvements, voting on March 17 for three geographically scattered river improvement appropriations. He was less supportive of the administration in two other areas. He opposed three million dollars for increasing armaments and munitions of war, claiming the president thereby was given too broad powers. While he would vote on specific amendments to the 1856 deficiency appropriations bill, he was not inconveniencing himself to participate in most votes, probably concluding the Democrats should have to assume the responsibility themselves for spending the money.[20]

Because of the multiparty structure in 1856, many of the congressmen, including Northern Know Nothings, who opposed the administration caucused to plan strategy. At a session on March 11 with eighty-five in attendance, Wilson, the first speaker, argued for a union of all Northerners in favor of freedom and pledged Massachusetts would sustain an anti-Nebraska candidate for the presidency. While they did not formally organize, they thereafter met almost weekly.[21]

The creation of a national party occupied the energies of people other than congressmen. Iowa and Connecticut Republicans organized in the spring. The national committee appointed at Pittsburgh sought to word the call for the nominating convention and to structure a platform to attract a broad spectrum of anti-Nebraska voters. The committee met four times with congressional leaders in Washington between March 27 and 29. An address to the people, prepared by Blair, was agreed to by the committee. It did not use the word "Republican," and articulated the committee's principles as opposition to slavery in the territories and admission of Kansas as a free state.[22]

The spring elections proved that the Republicans were still not a major party. In March in New Hampshire no party won. The Democrats had poured money liberally into the president's own state. The Opposition candidate for governor, Know Nothing more than Republican, defeated the Democrat but failed to procure a majority; the legislature would have to make the decision. The *Tribune* spoke of a Republican victory; if anything, it was a Know Nothing triumph. A month later in Rhode Island, the Know Nothing-Republican candidate for governor was chosen by almost 3,000 votes and both houses of the legislature were Opposition by almost three to one. In Connecticut the Republicans, just organized as a party, ran a separate ticket for governor, nominating Gideon Welles, a former Democrat and later Lincoln's secretary of the navy. He attracted only 10 percent of the vote. The Democratic nominee won a large plurality, but the opposition controlled the legislature. Know Nothings, Whigs, and Republicans elected an American governor. The Know Nothings might be struggling as a national party, but they yet were the principal challenge to the Democrats in the East.[23]

Wilson had become a central figure in the Kansas struggles. The East was flooded with the most important participants in the free state cause. First was Samuel C. Pomeroy, among the Massachusetts Emigrant Aid Society's initial party sent to the territory, who spent much of February and March speaking in New England communities, who furnished Wilson with a part of the evidence for his Kansas speeches, and who himself addressed an anti-Nebraska meeting on April 1 at a crucial moment in the debates. Then about April 1 Governor Robinson arrived. Charles Robinson also had been in Thayer's initial party of settlers, a founder of Lawrence, and an agent of the society. He had helped Shannon quiet affairs in December and as governor was careful and moderate. He and Wilson went to Boston the first week of April for conferences to engender money and support. Finally, Jim Lane came. Tireless, ambitious, unscrupulous, a captivating speaker, an officer in the Mexican War, Lane while serving as congressman from Indiana had voted for the Kansas-Nebraska Act. Now far more militant than Robinson, he sought to lead troops and influence territorial officials with force.[24]

As the Senate debated Kansas affairs, so did the House. A dispute between John W. Whitfield, chosen in the regular election, and Reeder, selected in the fall of 1855 by the Free State settlers, as to which was the delegate from the territory, was referred to the Elections Committee. After long debates, on March 19 the House authorized the Speaker to appoint a committee of three whose responsibilities were not only to seek evidence about elections in the territory but to investigate acts of violence and other disturbances. Banks appointed a former Whig who was recommended by the Democrats, Mordecai Oliver of Missouri, John Sherman of Ohio, and William H. Howard of Michigan. The latter two would subsequently become influential Republican senators. In addition, the committee was provided with clerical assistance and sergeants-at-arms. These appointments suggest a Wilson influence. They included George C. Fogg of Concord, a Republican national committeeman and editor, and S. P. Hanscom, another Republican, reporter of the 1853 convention, clerk in the Massachusetts State Department, and an active opponent of Gardner in the fall of 1855. It was an able committee, which not only sorted through evidence provided in Washington, but went to Lecompton, Lawrence, and Leavenworth in Kansas to hear testimony of fraud and violence.[25]

The Senate passed the better parts of three months debating Kansas affairs. Douglas, as chairman of the Committee on Territories, submitted a report which defended the territorial legislature, denounced the Topeka Convention and emigrant aid societies, and virtually ignored the activities of the Missouri Border Ruffians. In his speech he defined resistance to the actions of the legislature as treason and rebellion. Jacob Collamer of Vermont, in the minority report, stressed the duty of American citizens to employ their rights of free speech and assembly and the necessity for men whose democratic rights had been trampled, when they could receive no redress, to initiate the Topeka government. On March 20 Douglas replied with an able address, admitting, as most slave state senators would not, that fraud had occurred in Kansas, but contending the results with honest elections would have been the same. Two Kansas statehood bills were before Congress. Douglas would admit Kansas as a state whenever it attained 93,420 people, the current population figure for a representative in the House. That could take years; in the meantime, the people of the territory would be under the laws of the proslavery legislature as administered by appointees of Pierce and his successor. Seward's proposal would admit Kansas under the Topeka constitution, drawn up by an unauthorized convention controlled by one political element in the territory.

On April 9 Cass presented a petition given him by Lane from members of the Topeka legislature, asking for admission. Some of the signatures were in the same handwriting and there were erasures in the document. A lengthy debate ensued over printing the petition and referring it to the Committee on Territories. Butler characterized it as an insult to the South. Only Seward, Sumner, and James Harlan of Iowa supported the printing. Wilson did not vote; he may not yet have returned from his trip to New England. Lane persuaded Harlan that the disposal of the petition should not so easily be accomplished, nor the Free Soilers of Kansas so deserted by Republicans in Washington, and the Iowa senator found a way to revive the issue. In defending the petition, Wade got into an unpleasant exchange with Douglas.[26]

Wilson next obtained the floor. The freshman senator seemed to have no fear taking on one of the most effective debaters in Congress. Wilson admitted the memorial contained imperfections, then launched an attack on Douglas. He demonstrated that the Illinois senator had wanted the Nebraska Territory opened in 1853 without repealing the Missouri Compromise, but that Douglas altered his views the next year because he was afraid that, if he did not, Atchinson would replace him as chairman of the Committee on Territories. Wilson employed some of the evidence from his old address on the progress of antislavery between 1835 and 1855. Douglas maintained that Republican principles were sectional and no one could advocate them in a slave state. Wilson countered, undoubtedly gleefully, that he had spoken only the previous Friday in slave Delaware, had presented Republican principles fairly, and had been attentively listened to. He asked that the Democrats nominate a real leader of their party, one like Douglas himself, to make a clear position for the fall election campaign. He suggested Democrats no longer understood the North if they thought "Black Republican" and "abolition agitator" were sneering terms. The Republicans would vote against admission of a slave Kansas, and if they were defeated, they would turn to the people. They might this year be beaten there, too, but they would live to fight another day.[27]

This was not Wilson's best Senate speech. Greeley reported it was "spirited and vigorous" and one of Fessenden's correspondents praised Wilson's "dignified manner," which had raised his estimation of the senator. But the speech was disjointed and not well prepared when one contrasts it with his March effort. Most of the press had little to say about it.[28]

The Delaware address to which Wilson alluded had been delivered on April 11 in Wilmington to a "large and spirited" meeting called for the formation of the Republican party in the state. Wilson emphasized that Northerners did not intend to interfere with the domestic institutions of the South. Rather, they were opposed to the extension of slavery, a principle with which he believed many Southerners agreed. He associated the Republican party with the Declaration of Independence, the Constitution, and many of the Founding Fathers. The Whig party had collapsed, he told an audience primarily composed of former Whigs, and the American party was about to die, both for yielding to the Slave Power. The Democrats were under the control of that Power. If the Republicans were beaten, they would submit; they made no threats to leave the union. He also asserted that if the Republicans won, the slave states would not secede, for they would gain nothing by that. Wilson also delivered on March 21 the closing lecture of the Philadelphia antislavery series, entitled "The Position of the Slave Power and the Duties of the Free States in Regard to It."[29]

During the course of the April debates over Kansas, Wilson asked Senate permission to make a personal explanation. He and Hallett had long been quarreling over the 1849 resolutions of the state Democratic party and what they said. Wilson had quoted from them in his first important slavery speech in the Senate the previous February and had referred to them again just a year later. Hallett prepared a pamphlet, *A Question of Veracity for Senator Henry Wilson,* which was placed on the desks of Congressmen. This was taken from a speech by Hallett in New Hampshire during the fall campaign. The Democratic national chairman charged Wilson with "deliberate and repeated perversion" of the resolutions, of quoting half-sentences, and of disrespect. Wilson denied he had misquoted or been disrespectful. He explained how and under what circumstances he first saw the resolutions; he spoke of Hallett's anger in 1849 against Southern Democrats for deserting Cass, and the chairman's approval of coalition with the Free Soilers. Wilson quoted from his own 1855 speech to prove he had not garbled or falsified the extracts. Hallett was not chastened, for two months later, he released another pamphlet in reply to Wilson's explanation.[30]

Wilson continued to support Fremont for the Republican nomination. He met with the Pathmarker in mid-March to reassure himself about Fremont's position on Kansas. Wilson was pleased with how many Washington Republicans were backing him. By May 1 "Oliver" could report from Boston that 99 out of 100 Massachusetts Republicans endorsed Fremont. Fremont was the man for the moment: his Democratic antecedents and family connection with Benton helped, he was very acceptable to the Know Nothings, yet he attracted immigrant support as well. As Wade phrased it, Fremont was the strongest candidate he could think of. Bowles's *Springfield Republican* and Bailey's *National Era* were still not convinced in late April, but the alternatives—Seward, Chase, McLean, and Banks—did not seem to be right for 1856. Certainly the first three could not attract sufficient Know Nothing voters.[31]

The meeting of the anti-Nebraska caucus on April 21 discussed whether they could get through the House a bill for the admission of Kansas under the Topeka constitution. Those attending also established a committee whose purpose and subsequent activities today appear enigmatic. The *Springfield Republican* reported the committee was to cooperate with the popular movement for a presidential convention. The *National Era,* which opposed alliance with the Know Nothings, said it was to superintend the work of the canvass. How the committee's purposes were to differ from those of the already called Republican convention or how it was to relate to the national committee is not clear. Wilson and Jacob Collamer represented Senate anti-Nebraskans; five representatives were included. Shortly thereafter Wilson sought Seward's signature to a congressional call for a People's convention to nominate presidential candidates. While Seward recognized Know Nothing recalcitrance, he nevertheless considered himself a Republican and did not want to be associated with the proposed call.[32]

As Know Nothings departed from their party, unhappy with the Fillmore nomination or increasingly concerned about events in Kansas, what remained was more likely to be controlled by the nativist wing or motivated by personal political considerations. The New Hampshire Know Nothings repudiated the Fillmore nomination. The contest was close in Pennsylvania, but when the council accepted the decision of the national convention, some Know Nothings bolted. In Massachusetts only 149 councils were represented at the Order's May 6 meeting. A Fillmore supporter was elected president. Resolutions repudiating the national nomination and favoring a bolt were defeated. A minority left and a week later at their own conclave voted to select delegates for the June renegade national convention.[33]

As the congressional session had worn on, incivility, churlishness, even brutality had increased. An Arkansas member of Congress attacked a correspondent of a New York City newspaper, who was known to be a noncombatant. Another member, from California, murdered a waiter at Willard's Hotel. Greeley was assaulted for commenting too openly upon the conduct of a Southern politician. Wilson, in writing his history of the events of May 1856 almost two decades later, began his discussion of the Sumner-Brooks affair by comparing the assaults by the Border Ruffians in Kansas with the polemics of Southerners in Congress. Cries of secession were frequent, he attested. Proslaveryites were pressing vigorously to attain their objectives. Members of Congress were armed, some sitting with loaded revolvers in their desks, he recalled. In the streets, the hotels, and the capitol itself marauders often threatened to employ force to intimidate those who disagreed with them. The *New York Times* on May 7, reporting on an interchange between Senators Clement C. Clay of Alabama and

Hale, thought neither of the men had done well. Manners, especially in the Senate, were deteriorating.[34]

It was in this political climate that Charles Sumner arose on May 19 to deliver a long speech which he titled "The Crime Against Kansas." While the situation in the territory had been debated off an on for months, in the prior three or four weeks, Central America had primarily engaged the attention of the Senate. So Sumner chose to render this address at this time. It was carefully prepared. He would deliver "the most thorough & complete speech" of his life, he wrote Chase. "My soul is wronged by this outrage, & I shall pour it forth." Pour forth he did. He spoke for three hours the first day, recommenced the next. The galleries of the Senate were crowded. Carefully structured, perhaps committed to memory, full of allusions to antiquity, theatrical, immoderate, and abusive, the speech particularly impugned Douglas, Atchinson, Butler, and South Carolina. Wilson claimed the personal nature of the denunciation was in repayment for the men's own invective upon and disparagement of Sumner. Unlike Wilson, with his statistical and factual approach, Sumner was interested in effect. He was not speaking to the Senate at all, but to the intelligent public of the North and Great Britain.[35]

The Republicans, especially Sumner, had long been provoked, but this address needlessly offended. Wilson in his history of the age would later characterize the speech as elaborate, exhibiting great learning, forceful, exhaustive, bold, and unsparing. But at the time Wilson, Seward, Wade, and Hale disapproved of the personal attacks and the singling out of South Carolina. Seward, and probably also Wilson, had suggested Sumner eliminate the most objectionable parts. Still, what was said, as the subsequent investigation noted, was not unlawful, nor was Sumner ruled out of order by the presiding officer or his words even objected to by the senators. During the address, Douglas, James M. Mason, and others talked so loudly among themselves that Sumner more than once called on the sergeant-at-arms to restore quiet. Another example, the *Times* correspondent declared, of the "studied modes of insolence and overbearing arrogance . . . carried by the opposition." At the close Cass rose to express his regrets, terming the speech the most un-American and unpatriotic he had ever heard in the Senate. Douglas was angry, attacking the vulgarity and malignity of the speech, made worse by its careful preparation, and defended himself, the absent Butler, and his former colleague Atchinson. Mason was even more indignant. Sumner answered each of the men.[36]

The press differed in its evaluation of Sumner's oration. The *New York Times* correspondent characterized it as "one of surpassing eloquence and power." The effect was "electrical." An editorial in the same paper later termed the tone of the address "sharp and controversial," but within the limits of parliamentary propriety. The *Tribune* correspondent called it the "most masterly, striking and scathing production of the Session." Sumner had "never made such an impression in force, manner, and emphatic style." He was "animated . . . throughout, hurling defiance among the opposition." The *Springfield Republican* declared the speech "more than fulfill[ed] expectation and justifie[d] the long time consumed in preparation." President Pierce's own newspaper, the *New Hampshire Patriot*, insisted the address was "beyond comparison, the most malignantly abusive and personally insulting towards a number of Senators that was ever delivered in the Senate." The Southern press, of course, was infuriated, but the *Boston Courier* also called the address "intemperate and ill-judged."[37]

What would happen next? Representative John Bingham told Wilson that Sumner was in danger. Wilson insisted he should accompany his colleague home. Burlingame, Colfax, and Wilson waited for him at the end of the day, but Sumner left with Seward, with whom he was to dine, refusing to accept other aid. Wilson also feared Sumner might be attacked the next day.[38]

There is general agreement on what next transpired. On May 21 several Southerners discussed what should be done. Preston S. Brooks, a second-term congressman from South Carolina, an officer during the Mexican War, and a nephew of Senator Butler, concluded that he had to avenge the insults to his state and family. On May 22, after the Senate adjourned, Wilson remained a few minutes to finish a letter, then left; he saw Brooks, their eyes met, and they bowed to one another. The Senate was virtually empty. Sumner was busy writing at his desk and did not look up; he would not have recognized Brooks in any case. After expressing his anger in a few sentences, Brooks, quickly out of control, with his cane struck the seated Sumner repeatedly on the head. Sumner was blinded by blood and the blows, unable to rise because of his desk, and soon collapsed as congressmen and government employees nearby rushed to his aid. Some of those closest to the incident were prevented from intervening by Representative Lawrence Keitt, who had accompanied Brooks. Sumner was so injured that he did not return to his seat for any length of time for three and a half years. His enemies claimed he faked serious incapacity. He did, however, have immediate, grave physical injuries. They in time would heal, leaving him with psychosomatic shock, frequent and severe headaches, and insomnia.[39]

When Wilson heard of the assault, he rushed to the Senate, where he learned his colleague had been removed to the vice-president's room and was being attended by a physician. Wilson and Congressman Buffington took Sumner to a carriage and accompanied him to his lodgings. Wilson's own clothing was ruined from being soaked by Sumner's blood. A friend who saw Wilson that evening remembered his indignation and that she had never heard him use such strong language.[40]

Republicans were outraged and fearful. That evening the senators met at Seward's home to decide what to do. They agreed they should not make this a partisan question and that Massachusetts men should not take the lead. When the Senate convened the next day Wilson should call to the attention of the body what had happened. They hoped that someone in the majority party would move that a committee of investigation be appointed. If no one did, Seward would offer a motion. When the Senate assembled the next morning, the galleries were crowded. Wilson's speech was brief, factual, and unimpassioned. He first noted his colleague's seat was vacant for the first time in five years. He expressed his horror at the attack which had left Sumner senseless and unconscious. He called for prompt Senate response. He said he would make no motion, but await senior senators to suggest action to redress the wrongs. When no one rose to offer a motion, Seward was forced to present the resolution of inquiry, a committee of five, to be appointed by the president of the Senate. Had that been agreed to, the president would by custom select three members of the majority party and the other two would be the mover of the motion and probably another member of the minority or a Whig or Know Nothing. Mason of Virginia moved the committee instead be elected by the Senate. Republicans expected the majority party would control deliberations, but most Democrats voted only for their own. Neither Seward nor any member of Sumner's (and the minority) party was elected.[41]

Southern response was almost uniformly sympathetic to Brooks. Congressmen attempted to justify the action. The Southern press insisted Sumner deserved the treatment he had received. Southern groups purchased canes to replace the one Brooks had broken. This reaction was engendered partly by the release of frustration pent up within Southerners as a result of the continuing attack on slavery and their way of life. At least one Northerner, one of the best known and least liked, would now understand that this was unacceptable. The reaction was also a product of the Southern code of honor, which maintained that such a personal attack as Sumner's required a response. A gentleman could be challenged to a duel, but Sumner would not have accepted the challenge, and furthermore, he was not a gentleman by Brooks's standards.

Whatever reaction they had had to the speech, Northerners were almost as uniformly shocked and angered at the beating of a senator for something said during the course of Senate debates as Southerners were sympathetic. The assault "reverberates through the land," the *Tribune* declared. "A disgrace," said the Democratic *Providence Post*. President Pierce's own *New Hampshire Patriot*, after again attacking the speech, declared Brooks's action could not be defended; it was disgraceful and a gross outrage. Brooks "transgressed every rule of honor," declared the Whig *Boston Courier*. The largest meeting ever held in New York City's Tabernacle protested against the Brooks assault. The indignation of Massachusetts had never before been so aroused, Alley told Sumner.[42]

Indignation meetings in Massachusetts, hastily called, attracted capacity crowds and people of different political persuasions. The first, in Boston on May 23, was so well attended it had to be shifted from Chapman Hall to Tremont Temple. Wendell Phillips thanked God Wilson had been in Washington; he would not apologize as Everett had. This was perhaps too radical a fare for nonabolitionists and non-Republicans. The next evening a second gathering convened in Faneuil Hall. Governor Gardner presided, with the Know Nothing president of the state Senate, the Speaker of the House, the mayor, the last Whig candidate for governor, former governor Boutwell, Amos Lawrence, Hillard, and the editor of the Whig *Boston Advertiser* among the participants. Leading Hunker Democrats were conspicuously absent, as were Winthrop and Everett. Protests would continue throughout the state for the next three weeks. In the meantime the General Court established a special committee which soon recommended resolves in support of Sumner. They passed the Senate 28 to 0, the House 187 to 23.[43]

On the same day the Senate created its investigating committee, Campbell introduced a similar resolution into a House which agreed to it by only a 93-to-68 vote. Only two Southerners and no Democrats voted in favor. Banks appointed three Northern Republicans and two Southern Democrats. The Senate rather quickly concluded that, although Brooks's action had been "a breach of the privileges of the Senate," that body had no authority over a member of the other house. All that could be done was initiating court proceedings or providing information to the House. The House committee conducted a thorough investigation of the facts, including interviewing Sumner himself. The majority concluded the House had the power to punish its members and recommended expulsion of Brooks and censure of two other representatives who had known of Brooks's intentions and did nothing. The minority asserted the House had no authority over the "alleged" action; it could only discipline its members for disorderly behavior during its sessions. While a majority of representatives supported expulsion, a two-thirds vote was unattainable. Rather, Brooks and Keitt were censured, which required only a majority. The South Carolina congressman, insisting his actions had been a personal matter, promptly resigned but was almost as promptly reelected.[44]

Many in Washington were in a state of fear. They went into the streets, Wilson told Parker, with bloodthirsty eyes following them. Wilson and other Northern Congressmen were armed with revolvers. Informed that Campbell had been threatened for the part the congressman had taken in establishing the House investigating committee, Wilson offered his services, his "hand and life" at Campbell's command. He many years later told a friend that he became so accustomed to the situation, he was almost inclined to open fire. It was "almost civil war," Wilson wrote Hunt the last week of May, but Northern men would go to their graves rather than submit. Wilson's concern was justified. South Carolina Congressman James Orr, a believable source, in 1873 told Wilson that a secret meeting of a few radical Southerners had determined to attack him, and only Orr's intervention prevented violence. Two assaults would destroy the Democratic party, Orr argued to the Southern radicals. Representative Calvin C. Chaffee, while passing through Willard's Hotel, narrowly escaped attack by Brooks on May 30, the *Springfield Republican* correspondent reported. Wilson was concerned about what would happen to Harriet and Henry Hamilton. Alley and Claflin quickly assured him that, if necessary, they would take care of his family.[45]

Events in Kansas at this moment deepened antagonisms engendered by the Sumner-Brooks affair. While the House committee was investigating conditions in the territory, Judge Samuel D. Lecompte decided to instruct the grand jury to indict the members of the Topeka government for treason, and the jury responded with a number of bills against Free Soil leaders, two Lawrence newspapers, even the Free State Hotel. Reeder sought immunity as an official with the House committee and a contestant for the congressional seat.

On May 11 the federal marshal declared bodies of men were preventing process serving and asked for citizens to join him at Lecompton to support the law. This was just the excuse the most rabid proslaveryites needed. A large armed body of men, including many Missourians, soon collected. On May 21, the day before Brooks assaulted Sumner, Lawrence was surrounded. The men in the community who were sought by the marshal surrendered, the marshal dissolved the force, and some of the posse dined at the Free State Hotel. But part of the posse, recommissioned and led by the sheriff of Douglas County, turned into a mob. The hotel was blown up, the two newspaper offices were destroyed, Governor Robinson's property was burned, and a number of shops and homes were ravaged and looted. Fortunately, only one life was lost. Atchinson had been unable to halt the attacks. The Free Staters made no effort to resist; the defilement of civil liberties was committed by only one side. Wilson in his history of the era later described Kansas as "conquered, prostrate, powerless." The people were overawed, their presses destroyed, some of their leaders in exile, others in jail.[46] The timing of these events was also dreadful. Just before the attack on Sumner, Northerners heard of Governor Robinson's arrest. The sack of Lawrence was announced the day after the appearance of the news about Sumner.

But this was not all. John Brown had yet to be heard from. Brown was a man who inspired others to sustain his projects. In his mid-fifties at this time, he had been reared in a family which believed in church and abolition, but also had produced an unusual number of insane members. Brown had a life of migration from community to community, business failures, and litigations. Concerned about the welfare of blacks, he had participated in a scheme of Gerrit Smith's to establish a black colony in the vicinity of what is today Lake Placid, New York. A brooding man with a sense of personal relation to his God, he increasingly saw himself as an agent of God's plans, which included freeing of the slaves. Brown followed five of his sons to Kansas in the fall of 1855. He joined a volunteer band to protect Lawrence, but arrived too late. But he was aroused, determined, and vengeful. Brown and seven others, most of them family members, went to three homes along Pottawatomie Creek, hauled out five proslavery men, and shot or hacked open their bodies. The Pottawatomie Massacre joined the sack of Lawrence in American nomenclature. Furthermore, a sense of civil war had arrived. "Bleeding Kansas" came to describe the territory.

When the Senate resumed its session after the weekend recess, at first it was almost as if nothing had occurred. Pugh of Ohio chose to deliver his speech on the proposed Kansas statehood bill. On the following day Senators John Slidell of Louisiana, Toombs of Georgia, and Douglas spoke, attempting to clarify their roles during the Brooks assault, since Sumner in his testimony had mentioned he remembered seeing them nearby. Toombs declared Sumner had received the treatment he deserved. Butler spoke briefly, angering Wade, who replied. He told Toombs he would not be frightened, though outnumbered four to one. Wilson then spoke in behalf of Sumner, declaring his colleague had not intended to leave any incorrect impressions about the day, but had only reported what he recollected. A Senate page remembered Wilson as "provoked almost beyond utterance." He had a determination for duty, as he saw it. Wilson also denounced the attack as "brutal, murderous, and cowardly." Butler, who had returned to the city, called Wilson a liar; then, at the request of fellow senators, he withdrew the words so that they were not included in the official report of the day's debates. By voice vote debate was quickly ended.[47]

The rumor was that Wilson and Wade would be assaulted when the Senate adjourned. Their allies, however, were well armed and, for whatever reason, nothing happened. Wilson was accompanied by friends to the train station to leave for a speech at the New Jersey state Republican convention in Trenton. Of course, he there was the center of attention. He was speaking on free soil in behalf of free speech, he told the delegates. He promised to return to Washington and do the same. The only chance for freedom in Kansas was to overthrow the Democrats, he declared. That could only be done by uniting all antiadministration groups. He pointed out that no Southern Americans had voted for Banks for Speaker and only two had been willing to have the Sumner attack investigated. The city's Democratic newspaper interpreted that as an attempt to weaken the Fillmore candidacy. Its editor thought Wilson was "under restraint," his speech unlike his abolitionist pronouncements elsewhere.[48]

Before Wilson left Washington rumors were circulating that Toombs intended to challenge Wade, and Brooks would challenge Wilson, to duels. Giddings reported the "bullies" either had to back down or attack Wade. At 10:20 a.m. May 29, the morning Wilson returned, Colonel Joseph Lane of Oregon delivered a note from Brooks referring to Wilson's characterization of his conduct two days before as cowardly and issuing the challenge to meet somewhere outside the District of Columbia. Wilson immediately replied in a tone that Giddings, Colfax, and other friends urged against. Wilson affirmed his use of the words Brooks had cited and declared he still would characterize the attack on Sumner with those words. But he regarded dueling as a "lingering relic of a barbarous civilization" which the laws of the nation regarded as a crime; he refused the challenge. He did, however, believe in the right of self-defense if attacked. He dispatched his response by Representative Buffington and he continued armed. He telegraphed Harriet, "have declined to fight a duel, shall do my duty, and leave the rest with God. If assailed, shall defend my life, if possible at any cost. Be calm."[49]

The Massachusetts legislature in its resolutions of May 26 used language similar to Wilson's, terming the Brooks attack "brutal and cowardly." But it also characterized the action as a breach of parliamentary conduct, an attack on freedom of speech, and an indignity against the state of Massachusetts. It demanded a thorough investigation and an expulsion of Brooks. A bill to repeal the state's Personal Liberty Law, which had advanced to its third reading, was killed.[50]

Wilson received almost universal commendation in the North for his response to Brooks. Most Northerners abhorred dueling, but believed in self-defense. Lydia Maria Child was relieved that Wilson's fear of being termed a coward had not caused him to accept the challenge. He had handled the affair "wisely and bravely," she believed. The Philadelphia Female Anti-Slavery Society adopted resolutions commending the "fidelity and courage" of Wilson and Wade in rebuking the outrage against Sumner "at the peril of their lives." A correspondent from Illinois wrote Senator Trumball seeking copies of Wilson's remarks about Brooks. He admired Wilson's clear-headedness; if he had Wilson's intellect, he would stump Illinois until the day of election. Claflin reported people in Massachusetts had never been so happy Wilson represented them in Washington. If either Sumner or Wilson were up for election, all that would be needed would be to count the votes. The *Boston Transcript* was pleased with Wilson's "courage and dignity that do him honor." The Democratic *Boston Post* thought the response was manly and honorable. Several contemporaries later declared that Wilson's reply struck a blow to the system of dueling from which it never recovered. The *Natick Observer* reported that the story in Wilson's home town of his having shot Brooks was false, but declared if the South Carolinian did not keep his distance, he should be shot. The *Richmond Enquirer*, on the other hand, called Wilson "an ignorant Natick cobbler" whom someone needed to take for a beating.[51]

Wilson was increasingly concerned about Sumner's condition. Two days after the assault, he expected his colleague would soon return to his seat. He even was pleased Sumner had been hurt at the first blow; otherwise he might have fought back and in the process been shot. But a week after the attack Sumner continued to be seriously incapacitated. He was more injured than he would admit, Mrs. Seward wrote. Wilson was also critical of those who seemed unconcerned about his colleague's condition. At Trenton he noted all of the foreign ministers had called, but almost a week after the assault neither the president nor any member of his cabinet had gone to the senator's home.[52]

The day after his response to Brooks, Wilson left Washington for Massachusetts. This must have been arranged before, for no one seems have charged that he was fleeing from danger. Since so many Democrats had departed for their national convention in Cincinnati, only about fifteen senators and sixty House members remained to attend congressional sessions. When his train arrived in Natick on

Saturday, May 31, Wilson was welcomed by his neighbors and by a procession through the town. That evening a crowd went to his home to honor him. He shook hands all around, thanked those who had supported Harriet in her time of concern, and reiterated his condemnations of Brooks's conduct. On Monday he received an equally warm welcome in Boston. Tuesday evening he participated in a meeting called at Faneuil Hall to protest against the events in Kansas. The mayor, who presided, introduced Wilson as a guardian of liberty and as one who believed in his own defense. He was received "with a storm of enthusiasm." The Slave Power controlled the American government, Wilson told his audience. The conduct of the president and his cabinet towards Kansas was no more defensible than the conduct of Brooks. Brooks was only their representative.[53]

Republicans of Massachusetts assembled the next day at Worcester to elect state delegates to the national convention. More than 1,250 participated in what was generally reported to be a harmonious and enthusiastic meeting. Former Whigs were so numerous that Stone was unable to get Adams and Russell elected. Adams was in any case later chosen by his district meeting. Wilson arrived in town early in the morning and was escorted to a hotel by 400 to 500 people. He briefly spoke about events in Washington. Convention managers framed a resolution to be presented to a mass meeting, praising Wilson for his "manly and effective denunciation" in the Senate after the assault against Sumner and for his "wise and dignified" response to the challenge by Brooks. It was carefully worded, Adams believed, and he agreed to present it. The convention adjourned in midafternoon to the commons, where Wilson's appearance produced "the wildest storm of applause." As in his Faneuil Hall address, he gave a rather detailed description of the attack on Sumner and its aftermath and the Brooks challenge. He spoke about Southern newspaper response. He then turned to events in Kansas, especially denouncing Secretary of War Davis for interference by the government against Northern settlers. He noted the Democratic convention was unwilling to sustain the administration's Kansas policy in refusing to renominate the president.[54]

Wilson had attained a new height in popularity. Adams, while admitting they had had their differences, urged everyone at the convention to forget the past and unite with the senator. He praised Wilson for remaining both a patriot and a Christian during the difficult preceding two weeks. Old men leaped to their feet to cheer when Wilson appeared at the convention, the *Tribune's* correspondent reported. The moment must have repaid the speaker for his trying two-week experience. Even Boston's commercial State Street spoke well of him. Sumner's correspondence is full of letters from well-wishers who also applauded his colleague. Parker was glowing in his praise. "There is a North, a real North quite visible now," he proclaimed. "God bless you for your services. . . ." A former Whig opponent spoke of Wilson's calm, refinement, and steadfastness—most associates or opponents would previously have attributed none of these qualities to him.

Before he returned to Washington on June 10, Wilson spoke in Framington and again in Natick.[55]

The various parties met within a few days of one another. The Democrats assembled at Cincinnati, their first convention west of the Appalachians. Pierce hoped for endorsement, but, as Wilson wrote in his history of the era, they "had not dared to renominate him." Instead, the Democrats turned to James Buchanan of Pennsylvania, often an aspirant for the presidency. He was a more experienced man in national affairs than Pierce, he was from the crucial state of Pennsylvania, and he had been out of the country as minister to Great Britain during the tumultuous controversy over Kansas. He also had fewer enemies than the alternative, Douglas. To obtain border state support, John C. Breckenridge of Kentucky was selected for the vice-presidency. The platform attacked nativism and sought to straddle the slavery issue, endorsing the people of the territory making the decision, but suggesting that the decision to allow slavery should coincide with the territory's application for statehood.[56]

The Northern Know Nothing convention produced a dilemma for many Republicans and Americans. By meeting before the Philadelphia conclave, it could influence the Republican choice, compromising Fremont, if it selected him, and endangering an autumn victory for the Republicans if it nominated someone unacceptable to them. Republican managers hit upon the strategy of advocating Banks, who, after all, had been among the earliest and most prominent Fremont supporters. If Banks were nominated by the North Americans, he could withdraw after the Republicans made their choice. The plan worked. On June 16 the convention selected Banks, who, after the Philadelphia meeting, declined. A few delegates bolted and made their own nominations. The rest of the Northern Know Nothings reassembled and accepted Fremont, insisting upon their vice-presidential candidate to save face. He, too, however, soon withdrew. The Republicans had thus obtained Northern Know Nothing support without including in their platform nativist planks, which would have repelled foreign, particularly German, and antinativist voters. In the end, Wilson's Know Nothing strategy had worked.[57]

The Republicans assembled on June 17 in a revival-like atmosphere. All free states, two territories, the District of Columbia, and four slave states were represented. After the preliminaries of electing officers and establishing committees, Wilson was called for. He delivered a rousing political speech. In line with the direction of others by the summer of 1856, he attacked the Slave Power more than slavery. He called upon all those who opposed the administration to join the Republicans. Assailing Pierce, Douglas, and Buchanan, he maintained that a civil war was taking place in Kansas. There also was a struggle for freedom of speech in Congress. He managed to say good things about McLean, Fremont, Banks, Chase, and Seward. "A brilliant and searching review of the professions and practices of the pro-Slavery party," the *New York Times* correspondent characterized the speech. After a strong plea by Giddings, the convention refused to appoint a delegation to confer with the North Americans. The platform was short and emphasized the opposition to slavery in the territories and admission of Kansas as a free state. It denounced the Pierce administration's Ostend Manifesto which advocated the United States try to purchase Cuba and, if Spain would not sell, the United States would be justified in seizing the island. Buchanan had been one of its authors—and advocated government aid for the construction of a Pacific railroad by a central route.[58]

By the time the convention assembled, the contest for nomination appeared to be between Fremont and McLean, the latter supported by Pennsylvania and New Jersey delegates and often by former Whigs. Chase still wanted to be chosen, but his own delegation was divided. Ohio withdrew both McLean's and Chase's names before the voting began. On an informal ballot, Fremont received 359 votes, McLean 190. On the formal vote, Fremont was overwhelmingly selected. The most logical choice for the vice-presidential nomination would be someone from Pennsylvania, but the state's delegates could not agree on a man. Among those suggested were Banks, Wilmot, William L. Dayton of New Jersey, and Wilson. At the last minute, Illinois advocated Lincoln. On the first ballot, Wilson received 7 votes. Dayton led with 259, Lincoln had 110, Banks 46, Wilmot 43, Sumner 36, and other votes were scattered. Eliot, in behalf of the Massachusetts delegation, withdrew the names of Sumner, Banks, and Wilson. He noted the latter was present and was using his influence for another man. Dayton was selected, a choice which brought no strength to the ticket, in fact, antagonizing the Know Nothings.[59]

On the third day of the convention, various delegations responded to endorse the nominations. Wilson asked to speak in behalf of Massachusetts. He began by suggesting that a son of John Quincy Adams or Samuel Hoar should better speak than he. After congratulating the party on its nominees and platform, he delivered a rousing address, which engendered enthusiastic responses from the audience. The party had genius and talent, he declared; what it now needed was organization. Perhaps his most famous sentence was one in which he asked that the motto in the campaign be "free speech, free press, free men, free labor, and Fremont." Wilson should have been pleased. He had been one of the first to advocate Fremont and the platform was what he himself might have authored.[60]

Wilson's increasing reference to the Slave Power is significant, for the Republican party would ignore the abolition of slavery and concentrate upon slavery in the territories, the Fugitive Slave Act, and the unfair dominance by the Slave Power in national affairs. If one examines the platforms of 1856 and 1860 and Republican speeches in Congress treating issues of the Jacksonian years, like internal improvements at federal expense and free land, Republicans differed little from their Democratic competition. The Republicans' advantage would come from impolitic vetoes by Pierce and Buchanan of popular internal improvements and homestead bills. Because of their opposition to expansion of slavery, Republicans could carve out a separate foreign policy in reference to Cuba and Central America.

But the Slave Power and what it was doing to Northerners and the nation increasingly became the Republican thrust. Appropriately Wilson would later entitle his saga of the era, *History of the Rise and Fall of the Slave Power in America.* The Southern white worker and the Northern freeman were endangered by the Power and its control over labor, he wrote. The American system was corrupted by the Power's economic and political dominance in the South and in Washington and its ability to get its own way by threat, by intimidation, by bargains with suspect Northern Democrats. The very future of the nation was at risk because of a power that neither understood nor respected American institutions, but for decades had been strengthening itself at the same time nonslaveholders were increasing in numbers.

The Republicans were making a record with their support of internal improvements. Wilson declared the national government had a duty to protect and defend commerce and he would vote for bills necessary for naval, military, or commercial purposes. He noted how the Democratic press had presented Pierce in 1852 as a proponent of the development of the Northwest, but Pierce's vetoes had proven that wrong. Wilson on July 7 voted with the majority, 32 to –12, to override Pierce's veto of a bill to remove obstructions to the mouth of the Mississippi. A whole series of Great Lakes harbor improvement bills passed the Senate in July with similar votes, usually from 21 to 25 in favor and 10 to 12 opposed, generally Southern Democrats. In early August Wilson obtained appropriations for Boston Harbor, Plymouth, and New Bedford. He both believed in the national government's developing the country and was convinced the Republican party would benefit from this support.[61]

In the meantime, after the Democratic convention, the debates on the Kansas statehood bill reopened, with Butler on June 12 and 13 for three and a half hours delivering his major reply to Sumner's address and responding to the resolutions of the Massachusetts legislature. He was critical of the state, going as far back as its contributions in the Revolutionary War. This was not an approach either to quiet matters in Washington or defuse the Northern antagonism engendered by the Brooks assault. Butler also implied Sumner had been cowardly and was not badly injured. Wilson replied, beginning with what "painful and sad emotions" he had listened for two days. A man had been attacked on the Senate floor and the world was outraged. He noted the violence then occurring in Kansas, California, and New Orleans and concluded little could be expected when a senator for so long defended an attack on a colleague. He read from a report from Sumner's doctor to prove the seriousness of the injuries. He then vindicated Sumner's charges of aristocratic control of South Carolina, showing by constitutional provisions how limited the right to hold office and select officers was.[62]

Attempting to demonstrate that Butler had been the aggressor, not Sumner, Wilson recalled how during his first eight months in the Senate Sumner did not speak on the subject of slavery. When he asked for permission to deliver his first address, he was taunted by Butler for his desire to make "oratorical display" and he was denied the right to speak. Wilson referred to Sumner's February 1854 address on the Kansas-Nebraska bill, which had contained no allusion to Butler or South Carolina. Yet Butler replied two days later, bitter and taunting towards Northern men. After lengthy quotations, Wilson noted Sumner's replies only defended his state, not himself. Wilson next turned to Butler's assailing the petition of the three thousand Massachusetts clergymen and three months later a petition presented by Rockwell. He charged Butler had expressly tried to wound his colleague and called his remarks "unparalleled in the history of the Senate." Having defended his colleague's motivation, Wilson then turned to defending Sumner's speech. He characterized it as "severe," but parliamentary. Sumner had arraigned the crime in Kansas and in doing so, had to speak of those who sustained it. Butler himself had spoken frequently on the subject and his role had to be considered. David Donald, Sumner's biographer, concluded Wilson's argument was unconvincing; Sumner had been more offensive. In fairness to Wilson, Sumner's address was difficult to defend. Furthermore, it is difficult for those unprovoked to judge how long provocation should go unanswered and what degree of anger an answer may be expected to embody.[63]

Wilson also vindicated his state from charges of "sickly sentimentality." He declared Massachusetts did not have one thousand people, including federal officeholders, who were not outraged by the attack on their senator. The legislature fairly spoke the sentiments of its constituents. At the conclusion of the address, Butler engaged Wilson with charges about the contributions of Massachusetts during the Revolution. Wilson ably replied, maintaining so few battles were fought in the state because the British preferred fighting elsewhere, where they had more opportunity of winning. He said his state had contributed 69,000 men to the patriot armies, South Carolina 5,500. Paying tribute to South Carolina revolutionary leaders, he also recalled, with those leaders' records, the large number of Tories in the state. The nation hardly benefited from this type of debate. Wilson also got into a second controversy with Clay of Alabama.[64]

Seward, who was seldom so laudatory, termed Wilson's reply as "triumphant, . . . and the best possible vindication of Mr. Sumner." Sumner's contemporary biographer Pierce thought Wilson came out of the debates with honor, especially considering he was a freshman up against the veterans of the Senate.[65]

Following the Republican national convention, ratification meetings were held in Philadelphia on June 19. Wilson was a brief speaker at the Musical Fund Hall. He contrasted the economic health of the slave and free states and then asked whether slavery should be extended. He urged political organization to defend free speech and free press. He was scheduled to join others in speaking at the New York City ratification celebrations. But the House was considering the Sumner Committee report and the Kansas bill, so he cancelled his New York appearance to remain at the Capitol.[66]

Burlingame, frustrated that he had been unable to speak at length about Sumner, Brooks, and Kansas, managed to get the floor in the House on June 21. Wilson termed the address the "greatest oratorical effort of the session, yes of the last twenty years." More veteran members of Congress, like C. C. Washburne and Giddings, agreed. From his letters, one can conclude the speech was needed to restore Wilson's spirits. But Wilson also feared a duel would grow out of what Burlingame said.[67]

The Massachusetts political scene continued in ferment. Whigs in numbers joined the Republican movement, including Walley—the 1855 Whig gubernatorial candidate—and even the *Boston Advertiser* and *Boston Journal.* The *Worcester Palladium*, after the *Boston Post* the most influential Democratic paper in the state, also endorsed Fremont. The attack on Sumner and the bloodshed in Kansas accomplished what no other events had. A few old Whigs like Everett and Winthrop would refuse to endorse Fremont and could convince themselves that Fillmore, an ex-Whig, should again be president. This was in spite of their condemnation of Know Nothings for two years; they now would vote for one. The state's Americans met in a hastily called convention on July 11 in Springfield. Republican National Chairman Edwin Morgan dispatched Allen to induce the Americans to accept Fremont and Dayton. The Know Nothing Boston newspaper, the *Bee,* endorsed Fremont before the meeting. Country delegates tended to support him; eastern Massachusetts Know Nothings were more divided. Neither could win without Gardner's support and he was primarily concerned about his own renomination. On an informal ballot, Fremont barely won. On the formal vote, the Republican received 280 votes, Fillmore 197. But the convention would not accept Dayton. About a hundred Fillmore delegates bolted. Gardner termed the Fremont endorsement "unavoidable" and "wise."[68]

If the Democrats were to win the fall elections, they needed to convince more Southerners that Kansas was being treated fairly. On June 23 Robert Toombs of Georgia gave notice he would introduce a new bill. All of the previous proposals, he contended, just engendered more debate about what had happened in the past. His bill would authorize a new census to determine who was a resident and eligible to vote; that would both exclude Missourians and discourage other outsiders from going to Kansas to influence a later election. Second, the president would appoint commissioners to supervise the census and election. And third, the territory would move quickly to statehood, choosing delegates for a November constitutional convention. Kansas would be admitted as a state without meeting minimum population requirements. This was a genuine effort to solve the Kansas crisis. Douglas quickly reported the bill back from committee, but attached conclusions which Greeley characterized as savage on Free State men in the territory. To get the bill passed the Senate was kept in almost constant session during the first few days of July.[69]

The Republicans trusted neither Pierce appointees nor Douglas-sponsored territorial legislation. Wilson's response was to strike all substantive provisions and substitute a clause abrogating all acts passed by the territorial legislature. He attacked Governor Shannon, defended the Free State men, and charged the Kansas legislature had been forced on the people by the intercession of 4,900 Missourians. Later in the debates, Wilson "spoke with great energy and effect," arguing the committee proposal was intended to make Kansas a slave state. His amendment was rejected 35 to 8. Seward's alternative, to admit Kansas under the Topeka constitution, failed 36 to 11 and the Senate then passed a modified Toombs bill, 33 to 12. The House, which by a two-vote majority had just agreed to admit Kansas under the Topeka constitution, had no intention of seriously considering the Toombs proposal. Whether or not the Republicans were primarily motivated by the desire to have an election issue, they were representing the views of the Free State leadership. From prison, Robinson and others on July 5 wrote urging Wilson to save the territory from the "curse" of the Toombs bill. A week later a resolution from the Committee on Printing authorizing 20,000 copies of the Senate bill reopened the debate. Wilson said he was willing to have the bill go forth to the country as an electioneering document. He particularly emphasized the failure of popular sovereignty as a solution to the controversy over slavery in the territories. He also used the opportunity to defend the Emigrant Aid Company. While the session had almost two months to go, formal debates about Kansas now came to an end.[70]

Only his unusual stamina made it possible for Wilson to leave the all-night session of the Senate and catch the train for Independence Day celebrations in New England. He first joined Charles A. Dana of the *New York Tribune* to speak in New Haven, Connecticut. Wilson told the audience that he received an average of five letters a day from Southerners who claimed their section contained a strong element of antislavery sentiment, but the controls over freedom of thought and expression were so great, they could not speak. If the North would stop electing doughface politicians, Wilson asserted, Southerners would join with them to halt the spread of slavery in the territories. Wilson arrived in Springfield after the main celebration had closed, but his speech there attracted between 400 and 500 people. He continued on to Boston and returned to Washington on July 7.[71]

Brooks's antagonism toward the Massachusetts congressional delegation continued. On July 14 the House finally took up the motion to expel Brooks, failed to obtain the two-thirds majority, then censured him, and he resigned. Angry at Burlingame, he decided to act. Banks and Ashmun, in behalf of their colleague, met with several of Brooks's friends to resolve the matter. Burlingame addressed a note expressing personal regard for Brooks but condemning his actions. The *Tribune* correspondent characterized the wording as "most unfortunate." Brooks on July 21 issued a formal challenge. In contrast to Wilson, Burlingame accepted. Wilson recorded that he and Burlingame walked the Capitol grounds that evening, expecting the duel to take place nearby the next day. Burlingame asked Wilson to explain his conduct and defend his memory, if that became necessary. His second, Campbell of Ohio, then suggested the combatants meet on the Canadian side of Niagara Falls and fire rifles at fifty paces. Burlingame left immediately. Brooks, contending he could not safely travel through the North to Canada, refused to follow. But he did not suggest another site. Most of the Northern press criticized Burlingame for accepting the challenge, often comparing his response unfavorably with Wilson's.[72]

Having failed to defuse the Kansas issue with passage of the Toombs bill, Pierce sought to unburden the party of Shannon. His suggested replacement was John W. Geary of Pennsylvania, who, unlike his Northern predecessors, determined to be impartial in office. Geary had been a lawyer, civil engineer, officer in the Mexican War, and mayor of San Francisco. He was able, resourceful, and capable of exercising leadership. When his appointment came before the Senate in executive session, Wilson, tongue-in-cheek, was reported to have expressed surprise that Pierce would replace Shannon, who only six months before had been presented to the Senate as a perfect governor. Senator George W. Jones of Iowa cleverly replied that, since the senators had expressed this in secret session, Pierce had not learned about Shannon's true character.[73]

To create trouble for the Republicans, Senator William Bigler, from Buchanan's Pennsylvania, on August 11 raised the issue of Fremont's military accounts. Wilson called the subject political persecution. He wondered if the Senate this late in the session wanted to devote so much time to the topic. Both parties were divided on whether they did, but the Senate took up the matter, 29 to 14. Interestingly, Wilson carried the weight of the Fremont defense. The *New York Times* thought so highly of his speech that it gave two columns to covering it. Wilson recalled how Jackson, Harrison, Taylor, and Scott had all been harassed by some in Congress over their accounts. More telling, he declared the comptroller of the treasury in January 1854 had reported ninety-six pages of unpaid accounts, and Fremont's name was not among those listed. Furthermore, Congress had agreed the same year to pay Fremont $183,825 that it owed him, with no one claiming he was in debt to the government for anything. The *Springfield Republican* characterized Wilson's effort as "a good specimen of that senator's off-hand, vigorous, denunciatory style of speaking, when aroused to indignation by 'the tricks of the enemy.'"[74]

Congress was engaged in one of its longest sessions. By August 1 it still had not enacted many appropriations bills. Wilson would leave from time to time to visit Massachusetts or speak nearby. He had to cancel promised political appearances, such as at the Vermont Republican state convention, August 15. He was much in favor of a proposed bill to raise senators' pay to $2,500, a large increase. It passed the Senate, although it was later modified. Eventually all the legislation necessary for running the government was passed, except the army appropriations bill. The House included in the bill a provision forbidding use of money for enforcement of the acts of the Kansas legislature until Congress should pass legislation deciding whether the laws of that body were valid. Wilson, of course, supported the provision. Congress adjourned on August 18 after fifteen hours in continuous argument and Pierce called a special session for August 21 to pass an army bill. The Senate, safely under Democratic control, stood firm against the Kansas legislature provision. Wilson carried a good deal of the debating load for the Republicans. Only seven senators, Wilson included, opposed final passage. The House would constantly revote as personnel came and went or new pressures were applied to members whose party affiliations were not clear. In the end several Know Nothings abandoned their opposition and Congress adjourned again on August 30.[75]

14

A Year Dominated by Kansas

With the adjournment of Congress at the end of August 1856, Wilson was finally able to participate in the election campaign. The assignment for the Republicans in their first national contest was a challenging one. Since they could not hope to obtain any electoral votes from the South, they had to carry most of the free states. They were expected to win the northern tier—most of New England, New York, Michigan, Wisconsin, and Iowa. Ohio was assured as well. The Know Nothings could cause trouble in Massachusetts, Connecticut, and Rhode Island, but that had been worked out during the late summer. New Jersey and Pennsylvania in the East and Indiana and Illinois in the West would be the battleground.

The problems in the West were only partially resolved. The Know Nothings had been strong in Indiana and Democrats had been beaten prior to 1856 by creating a People's opposition. Those working together were not very trusting of one another or sufficiently cooperative in organizing a campaign. In Illinois the Whig leader Lincoln and the anti-Nebraska Democrat spokesman Trumball had resisted fusion into the Republican party until the spring of 1856. The Democrats continued to be so brazenly supportive of the Kansas-Nebraska bill, their opponents almost were compelled to unite. The number of foreigners was so large in the state that a new party would have to be careful how it handled the nativist question. The Republicans in the East concentrated upon Pennsylvania. New Jersey was neither in 1856 nor for years to follow comfortable with Republican tenets. The Republicans poured more money and energy into Pennsylvania than any other state. The Americans were strong and dominated the union ticket created in the spring, before events in Kansas and the capital altered the political scene in so many Southern states. Party leaders constantly quarreled. The Democrats, in contrast, possessed ample funds, unity, a favorite son as presidential candidate, and the organizing skill of John F. Forney.

Having accepted Fremont as their presidential candidate, the main body of Massachusetts Know Nothings reassembled in Boston on July 24. Many Fillmore supporters attended, hoping to reverse the party's decision. The convention, which Bowles called the "Faneuil Hall Mob," battled for fourteen hours just to elect officers. About 150 men then left. Ely decided the best way to get Fillmore accepted was for his group to win the governor's gratitude by supporting Gardner's renomination. But the assembly refused 290 to 215 to sustain Fillmore. Gardner in his acceptance letter again endorsed Fremont. The pro-Fillmore group would not accept the convention's decision at the council's quarterly meeting; with only about 150 out of 1,000 members present, Ely moved to endorse Fillmore. A substitute to accept Fremont and Johnston carried, 89 to 52. The Ely group produced a document from the national president revoking the Massachusetts charter on grounds the Order refused to support the national nominations. Ely was chosen president of the new state council. That faction convened another state convention in Boston on August 20. Their candidates were about two-thirds Know Nothing, one-third Whig. The Whig rump in early September, while endorsing Fillmore, ran its own nominee, Luther Bell, for governor.[1]

In midsummer political commentators differed in their opinions of what would happen. Giddings, whose heart usually conquered his head when he made political predictions, on July 2 heralded a Fremont victory unless the politicians of Pennsylvania failed. Wise reported on July 14 that Robert Walker, the astute Alabama Democrat, had just returned from a Northern tour convinced that Buchanan could not win and that Cass agreed. Fillmore might take Delaware and Maryland, and the election might then be sent to the House of Representatives to decide. Wilson demonstrated his usual political perspicacity about the task before them; he understood the Fillmore weakness nationwide. But he was overly concerned about the Know Nothings in Massachusetts. The Democrats, he predicted to Sumner on August 3, would be disappointed by the Fillmore vote in the free states. He hoped the Republicans could win, but he was prepared for defeat. If they could not carry Pennsylvania, then the best they could hope for would be a House election.[2]

The Republicans, of course, were eager to capture their own state. Webb was confident not only that Fremont would carry Massachusetts but that Republicans would elect their state ticket no matter whom they nominated. Bird and some of his friends were not as certain. To them Gardner had to be "killed off" to assure Fremont's capture of the state votes. Wilson must have been equally concerned. On August 11 he forwarded to Sumner two letters, each advocating Sumner be nominated for governor. The plan included selection of an able lieutenant governor in case Sumner's health did not improve sufficiently by January. Gardner could not stand against him. Sumner could serve in the Senate during December, the governor would appoint someone to the balance of Sumner's Senate term, and the legislature could reelect him. Gardner would be ousted, Sumner would be endorsed by the people and the legislature, the South would be rebuked, and Fremont would be aided.[3]

Whether Sumner refused to run for governor or the advocates of this plan had second thoughts, one cannot know. He was still talked about on the eve of the Republican convention. Certainly Sumner's health was not improving. Hale in early July visited him at Francis Blair's, where the senator was convalescing, and reported he looked poorly. Discussing his condition at dinner, Hale and Trumball concluded Sumner suffered from "mental anguish" and a wounded spirit. Wilson and Seward thought differently; Sumner gloried in his martyrdom and his weakened condition was physical in cause. Seward recorded that his colleague's mind was good, but his vigor gone; he moved like a man recovering from paralysis.[4]

The losers in the August state elections were the Americans. The Republicans captured both House seats in Iowa—one formerly had been Democratic—and, in absence of a gubernatorial race, took other statewide offices. They demolished the administration party in Vermont, capturing the governorship by a large margin and electing all three congressmen. On the other hand, the Democrats showed their strength on the border, the one area in which the Know Nothings most expected to do well. The regular Democrats defeated Know Nothing and Benton Democrats for the Missouri governorship; since Benton endorsed Buchanan, Missouri would choose a Democrat again in November. Kentucky, Tennessee, and North Carolina all voted Democratic, not American. Perhaps the two victories in the North made the Republican leadership overconfident. Both William Gienapp and Roy Nichols in their studies of the campaign are critical of the central organization. Fundraising began too late and was not very successful. Wilson must have early been aware of problems, for on August 8 in behalf of several others he asked for a meeting of the National Committee with Republican members of Congress. The lengthy congressional session interfered with early campaigning. Perhaps to get him out of Washington for safety reasons, but also because he was one of the party's most effective speakers and renowned figures, Burlingame began a campaign tour of the West in early August and then turned to the East in September.[5]

Political historians have generally agreed that the campaign of 1856 was the most exciting and energetic since 1840, Wilson's first. Seward, unhappy he did not receive the presidential nomination, initially did little. When Wilson, Hale, and others questioned his lack of participation, Seward abandoned plans to go to Europe and delivered a number of addresses in New York and Detroit.[6]

Wilson arrived in Natick on September 2. He left almost immediately for a speaking tour of Maine. Wilson had been concerned about the state. In early July he had written Webb to see if he could raise $200,000. Morgan managed to send Maine $7,000 from the National Committee. Republican chances in that state had improved. Hannibal Hamlin, longtime Democratic leader, in June had renounced his party affiliation and resigned his committee chairmanship and had since been nominated for governor. For once the temperance issue was avoided. Republicans poured in money—this was perhaps the only state in which they outspent the Democrats. Maine had voted for every Democratic presidential candidate since 1840. A minority of over 7,000 a year before, the Republicans now became a 19,000 majority. They won all congressional elections and would control the state Senate 30 to 1, the House 125 to 26.[7]

Wilson was supposed to go to Pennsylvania after Maine, but he instead stayed closer to home. Probably both his long absence from home and family and the impending state nominations caused him to make the decision. On September 9 the Fremont Club of Natick celebrated with an evening procession from the *Natick Observer* office to Wilson's residence and on to a meeting for several thousand people at the schoolhouse. The town's most illustrious citizen and George Woodman of Boston were the featured speakers. Longtime Wilson friends were officers of the meeting. Wilson was appreciative of the support he had received from Natick. He spoke about the Maine election and the troubles in Kansas. He attacked Brooks and praised Sam Houston. He also took the occasion to deny the rumor that Fremont was Catholic. The next day he joined Stanton and James F. Simmons at the largest political rally ever held in Providence. He was in Manchester and Needham on September 11; between 5,000 and 7,000 people participated in the former meeting, 2,000 in the latter. On September 12 between 25,000 and 30,000 people filled Boston's Tremont Temple and the nearby streets to honor the returning Burlingame. In his address the honored guest praised Wilson and confessed he would have been wiser had he followed his friend's example in replying to Brooks's challenge. Wilson that evening spoke to three different audiences.[8]

Sometime in the preceding month, Wilson concluded that since the Fremont election was of surpassing importance, to insure Massachusetts's votes, Gardner should be accepted as governor for another year. He and Banks became the foremost proponents of this strategy. Ex–Free Soilers as diverse as Adams, Hopkins, Alvord, and Bird opposed the step. The *Northampton Courier*, *Hampshire Gazette*, *Boston Telegraph*, *Worcester Spy*, and *Springfield Republican* all were unwilling to endorse Gardner. Their reasons are understandable. Not only was the governor objectionable for his nativism and political skullduggery, but he had manipulated patronage, ignored the Kansas crisis as much as he could, and vetoed important antislavery legislation. Bowles wrote Allen on August 26 that, if Sumner would not run, the Republicans had no candidate who could compete with the governor. He hoped Gardner would step aside and the two parties could agree on someone. Gardner had no intention of withdrawing. When the convention opened, those opposed to the governor tried to unite behind Sumner. Banks argued that a Sumner nomination would be disastrous; it would lose Pennsylvania for Fremont.[9]

The Republican convention, called not by the 1855 state committee, but by independent sources, met in Worcester September 16. The Fremont Americans gathered in the same city at the same time. During the day Banks and Wilson addressed both meetings. Wilson spoke to the Republicans with "even more than his usual power and directness, urging union (substantially) upon the Gardner state ticket," Bowles reported. Wilson's argument was that the party could afford to be liberal with a dying organization and accept Gardner one last time. They had a nation "to save." Bowles, who opposed that strategy, while admitting some of those who supported Gardner sought patronage, claimed most of those who favored the Wilson proposal did so for patriotic reasons, to defeat Buchanan. A majority would accept Gardner, but that nomination would split the fledgling party. Further complicating affairs, when Wilson arrived on the morning of the meeting, he brought along a message from Sumner declining unconditionally to be a candidate. The convention in the end made no choice for governor. But the two parties did agree to a joint national electoral ticket. A "skillful piece of strategy," "Byles" wrote to the *Tribune*. Robinson, Wilson's longtime colleague, was so angry at the decision to cooperate with Gardner that when he returned home, he grabbed an unframed picture of Wilson, pulled it off the wall, and threw it on the floor. A faction of the Republicans, led by Bird and Andrew, made their own nominations.[10]

The decision of the convention and Wilson's role are puzzling. When one examines the margin by which he won Massachusetts, one has to ask why Fremont needed additional aid from the Gardner Americans. Whatever happened, the number of Buchanan's supporters was not going to increase appreciably. Nor was Fillmore likely to attract very many more Americans in Massachusetts than he had. Fremont was going to carry the state. While the politically astute Wilson and Banks may have panicked, that is doubtful. Perhaps they were more concerned about getting the right men chosen for Congress; the Know Nothings in those elections would have been their primary opposition. Wilson propounded this view in his speech to the convention. But many of those first chosen in 1854 as Know Nothings were now Republicans and expected and deserved reelection. Furthermore, the Americans were so split among themselves that Republicans, with foresight and energy, could get good men nominated and chosen. Perhaps they were concerned about Sumner's reelection by the next legislature, again an argument Wilson employed in his speech urging unity. If so, they underestimated the political effect of Brooks's attack and underestimated their own and other Sumner supporters' effectiveness in propagandizing Sumner's sacrifice and the legislature's obligation to return him to Washington.[11]

By October 3 the Boston correspondent of the *New York Tribune* could report the coalition of Republicans and Fremont Americans was working well. Six congressmen, first elected as Know Nothings, had been renominated by both parties. DeWitt initially declined and was superseded by Thayer, who ran only as a Republican. Damrell's health was bad and his renomination was opposed, later accepted. While the Republicans were not enthusiastic about Davis, his district was the most Know Nothing in the state and they could not replace him. Opposition to Know Nothing Trafton in the west was so great that the Republicans selected their own man, Henry Dawes. Wilson's own Middlesex County achieved coalition for all offices. The *Tribune* correspondent credited Banks and Wilson for all this. Wilson had lived down the opposition and distrust toward him and even the *Boston Traveller* now spoke of his "excellent and careful management."[12]

When the Republican state convention adjourned, Wilson rushed to New York, Pennsylvania, and New Jersey for a month's speaking, with a short visit with Banks to Washington included. He began by delivering the main address at the New York City Tabernacle on September 17. He was already tired, having spoken twelve times in the preceding four days. He defended Fremont against the charges of misuse of government money and being a Catholic. He contended Buchanan was "a weak and vacillating man." He predicted Fremont could carry every town in Massachusetts and most of the states in the East. At Morristown, New Jersey, Wilson, one of four speakers, offered an analysis of the laws of Kansas, examined the inconsistencies of Southern doctrine, and disclosed that the Democrats hoped to win the presidency by dividing the opposition votes between Fremont and Fillmore. Almost 5,000 people turned out to listen to Wilson and Burlingame in Reading, Pennsylvania, on September 29. Wilson returned to New York City on October 4, sponsored by the Mechanics' and Workingmen's Central Republican Union. His approach there was to affirm free labor, rather than attack slavery, contrasting life in the free and slave states. He demonstrated that the national government, except for the House, was controlled by the South. In addition to Fremont's position on Kansas and the extension of slavery, Wilson emphasized the party's support for the Pacific railroad and other internal improvements.[13]

Pennsylvania was being lost, however, at least in part through inadequate funds and poor organization. Morgan had placed Stanton in charge of obtaining speakers and determining where they would appear. Stanton secured enough men, but did not always systemically dispatch them. The state committee was not helpful. Adams was quite unhappy with what he found in Philadelphia. With Wilson and three local Republicans on October 8 he went off in search of a meeting in the southern part of the city. He was so disappointed in the size and character of the audience, Adams declined Wilson's invitation to join him in speaking. After that meeting the two Massachusetts men parted, each to address another assembly. The next evening Adams, Wilson, and four local Republican leaders dined with Sumner, who was staying in the city. Then they left for an Independence Square assembly where Adams, Wilson, and Swan addressed about 25,000 people. In spite of his criticisms, Adams accepted the state party's expectation that they would win the October elections. Wilson closed his Pennsylvania campaign with former

Kansas governor Reeder before a large and enthusiastic audience at Easton on October 13.[14]

The results of the October elections were discouraging for the Republicans, although they had three more weeks to recover before the presidential balloting. They won overwhelmingly in Ohio, but even there the Democrats gained congressional seats. In the other two states, the tallies were so close the results were not known for several days. In Indiana the Democratic gubernatorial candidate won by 6,000 votes, the Democrats picked up four congressional seats, while the legislature would be divided between the two parties. In Pennsylvania, where the Democrats had boasted they would win by between 30,000 and 40,000 votes, the difference between the parties was only 3,000; fraud was rampant. Buchanan's party had apparently been able to attract former Whigs and Know Nothings. Morgan knew immediately they had been beaten and with Blair he hastened to Philadelphia. They conferred with Wilson, Simon Cameron, and Weed. Wilson was "enthusiastic and hopeful" and urged a "desperate effort" be made. What was now needed was cooperation with the Know Nothings, they concluded. Wilson undoubtedly was a strong advocate of that. With state elections over, cooperation should have been easier, since they were only dealing with presidential electors. They proposed a union ticket be established in any one of three or four ways. But their plan was rejected by the Americans, although a minority subsequently cooperated.[15]

The reaction was perhaps too negative. Perusal of the *Albany Argus* would cause one to conclude the Democrats must have swept Pennsylvania by 40,000 to 50,000 votes, rather than with under a 2 percent advantage. The *New York Tribune*, often regarded as the party's premier spokespaper in the East, on October 18 stated that the Democratic majority in Pennsylvania could be overcome, but then added that did not mean it would be. Since Greeley had been determined that cooperation with the Americans should be prevented, he did not or would not understand his own contributions to the October defeat. The paper, however, soon adopted the belief that the state could yet be carried in November and its editorials and news articles reported brightening prospects. Fremont and Blair still believed the Republicans could win. Wilson and Morgan likely departed from Philadelphia together for New York City. Morgan was after $100,000 and Wilson's friend Claflin contributed $1,000. While Morgan sought money, Wilson went to Poughkeepsie to speak on October 16 to about 15,000 people. The Know Nothings were regarded as more likely to influence events in New York, so he directed part of his attack against Fillmore. The Democrats, Wilson contended, were controlled by the slaveholders. He must have remained in the area for a week, for later he and Governor Robinson were scheduled to speak in Tarrytown.[16]

While working along the Hudson River, Wilson could also easily cross the border into the Berkshires area of his own state. Bowles was pleased; the southern Berkshires looked better for Fremont; "Wilson sowed good seed." Wilson also made a hurried trip to Natick, in time to arrive for a Fremont rally. To his townspeople he characterized the Pennsylvania election as "a fraud." He was scheduled to return to Pennsylvania and New Jersey for the remaining ten days of the campaign.[17]

In the midst of the important fall canvass, Wilson had to take time to defend Sumner from attacks by the Democratic press, especially in Indiana, which contended that the injuries inflicted by Brooks were not serious and that Sumner should have resumed his public duties. Wilson, in letters to the *New York Tribune* and the Philadelphia *North American,* repeated his condemnation of the assault and additionally denounced the Brooks apologists as "false, mean, and dastardly, with all the vileness of the original act." He recalled Sumner's excellent attendance record prior to the assault. And he included letters from three doctors, one who had attended Sumner for four days immediately following the beating, a second who had cared for him during his stay in Washington until the beginning of July, and a Philadelphia surgeon, identified as anti-Republican, under whose care the senator had been since. The latter prescribed seclusion. Sumner returned to Boston just before the election to be greeted by between 6,000 and 7,000 people, including Gardner, Banks, and Burlingame. He tried to respond to the governor's welcome, but before he proceeded very far, he had to stop and have a reporter read the remainder of his prepared address. In his remarks Sumner paid tribute to his "able, generous, and faithful colleague," Wilson. As a result of his own disabilities, he told the well-wishers, Wilson had the sole responsibility to represent the state in the Senate. He paid tribute to Wilson's "readiness, courage, and power, and his extraordinary energies equal to the extraordinary occasion."[18]

Buchanan was elected president by sweeping the South and carrying California, Indiana, Illinois, New Jersey, and Pennsylvania. He garnered 174 electoral votes to Fremont's 114. Voter turnout had been very high, with more voters in Indiana, Pennsylvania, and Ohio than in October. Buchanan secured 50 percent of the ballots in Pennsylvania, besting Fremont 231,000 to 148,000. The Republicans carried New York, while the Americans polled 124,000 votes for president, over 130,000 for governor, and emerged as the second party in the state Senate. Fillmore carried only Maryland, but attracted 44 percent of the popular vote in the slave states. The Know Nothing candidate had obtained 32 percent of the vote in California, 24 percent in New Jersey, 21 percent in New York, 16 percent in Illinois, 13 percent in Pennsylvania, and 10 percent in Indiana. If the party died, as appeared likely, what would those voters do in 1860? The two antiadministration candidates had 400,000 more ballots than the Democratic.[19]

Although the Republicans had lost, they had done very well for a party competing in its first presidential election. They were the majority party in eight states, almost the majority in Ohio, Iowa, and New York. In many states they had become the dominant party. In Maine, Connecticut, and New York they had attracted far more voters than their own leaders would have predicted six months before. Their accomplishments in one year were telling. They had established a platform; created party machinery; organized in every free state; eliminated, absorbed, or overwhelmed the Whigs; and crushed, neutralized, or subverted the Americans. Colfax said his party emerged from defeat "full of grit," and "full of more zeal than any defeated party I ever saw." Fessenden wrote Trumball that they had frightened the "rascals," who had to recognize they were doomed. What the Republicans needed in 1860 was to hold on to those states they had carried, and build effective party machinery in free states which the Democrats had won. Interestingly enough, during the party reorganization between 1851 and the end of 1856 Democrats were gaining adherents in the South and were not losing as many supporters in the North as one might expect. Free Soilers had almost all become Republican. A majority of Whigs and Know Nothings by 1856 also were voting for the new party; more would drift in as the decade moved along.[20]

In the largest turnout until that time, Massachusetts gave Fremont a plurality of 70,000 votes, a majority of 50,000. He carried every county, obtaining a majority in all but Suffolk. In his study of the state's political history of the Civil War era, Dale Baum has estimated that Fremont attracted almost all of those who had voted Free Soil and half of those who had cast Whig or Democratic ballots in 1848. A new two-party system appeared to have been created in Massachusetts. Fremont obtained more than 80 percent of the 1852-Scott Whig vote, indicating that the Winthrop-Everett leadership no longer had much influence. Former Democrats who had voted Know Nothing in 1854 now commonly supported Buchanan. Only in the Boston area race between Burlingame and Appleton were the congressional elections close, but even there the Republican won by a few votes. In most of the districts the Republican had impressively defeated a unity Democratic–Fillmore American nominee. Bowles's biographer insisted, however, that without the Republican-American cooperation, Chaffee and Dawes would have lost. Gardner won handily, but secured 13,000 fewer votes than Fremont. The Fillmore American candidate received only a little more than 10,000 votes, the Whig only 7,000, and Josiah Quincy, the anti-Gardner Republican, only 5,600. According to Baum, half of those who voted Republican in 1855 cast their votes for Gardner in 1856. The Fremont alliance captured all forty Senate seats and 286 House elections. Wilson's Natick had gone 476 for Fremont, 228 for Buchanan, and 129 for Fillmore; Gardner had received 25 fewer votes than Fremont.[21]

Despite the national loss, there was cause for Republican jubilation. Burlingame's followers celebrated with a procession through the streets to his Cambridge home. The reelected Representative was ill, but Wilson, among others, spoke to the crowd. Although he had earlier predicted a Republican victory, Whittier was not disappointed in the election results. Victory would be likely in 1860, he forecast. Republican newspapers *Northampton Courier* and *Worcester Spy* declared the results showed there had been no need for union with the North Americans; in those areas where the Republicans challenged the Know Nothings—the Dawes-

Trafton and DeWitt-Thayer races and Taunton, as examples—the Republicans had won.[22]

Wilson could now relax more than was his custom. He agreed to participate in a celebration in Montreal November 12 and 13, commemorating the opening of the Grand Trunk Railroad from that city to Toronto. Why he would be involved in this is not clear. The branch from Montreal to Portland, Maine, was already almost 300 miles complete. The trip to Montreal was uncomfortable in freezing quarters and the weather in the city unseasonably cold. Wilson accompanied Mayor Alexander H. Rice of Boston and ex-governor Kent of Maine. The festivities included an enormous procession and a banquet. Wilson was honored as the primary American representative on the dais and was asked to reply, oddly enough, to the toast to the American chief executive. He delivered enthusiastic remarks, endorsing goodwill between the two countries, cheering the development and prosperity in Canada, praising the interconnections between the two countries, and advocating an economic reciprocity treaty. His was reported to have been the best speech of the occasion. Following the activities, Wilson, E. C. Baker, *Boston Advertiser* editor Hale, and others took the Grand Trunk to Niagara Falls and returned to eastern Massachusetts through New York.[23]

Before the beginning of the congressional session, his supporters wanted to honor Burlingame. At a dinner in Faneuil Hall for 1,200 people on November 24 Wilson and other politicians spoke. Wilson praised those who had worked on Burlingame's campaign and proclaimed his confidence in the future of the defeated Republican party.[24]

The last session of the Thirty-fourth Congress, beginning December 1, would be short, but threatened to be explosive. Harriet this time accompanied her husband to the capital. They resided at the Washington House, at the corner of Third Street and Pennsylvania Avenue, along with Representatives Buffington of Massachusetts, King, William Kelsey, and Francis Edwards of New York, and Samuel Brenton of Indiana. The last winter of the Pierce administration was described as a gay one in the capital, with the White House, cabinet secretaries, and foreign ministers entertaining more than before. Speaker Banks and Senator Seward gave evening receptions and leading Republicans congregated at the tea parties at the Bailey residence. Seldom had the political complexion of a Congress changed so much during its two years in existence. Republican strength in the Senate now had reached one-quarter of the body. In the House the party lacked only eight votes of a majority, but counted on a few Northern Democrats and Americans for assistance. They soon discovered how tenuous the Republican position was: six Americans and four Democrats reversed their first session vote and Whitfield, the proslavery territorial delegate from Kansas, was admitted over Reeder. Congress's agenda was large: it included needed appropriations bills, a homestead act, tariff revision, a Pacific railroad bill, and settlement of the Kansas controversy before it endangered the administration of a second Democratic president.[25]

During the course of the summer Pierce had appointed Persifor F. Smith the new commander of the Department of the West and Geary as new governor. Before Geary departed, he talked with Wilson and showed him a bill he had framed to protect settlers. During August, between the resignation of Shannon and the arrival of Geary, territorial secretary Daniel Woodson openly and continually sided with the proslavery element. Several times in August and September serious outbreaks were barely prevented, although organized raids and murders continued. Governor Robinson was released from jail through the personal intervention of Amos and Abbott Lawrence with Pierce. This had the advantage of removing a political embarrassment for Northern Democrats. Following delivery of an able inaugural address on September 11, Geary set about quieting matters, persuading both sides that the governor's office sought fairness, dissolving the proslavery militia, and ordering irregular bands to disperse. He halted the invasion of a new Missouri army and persuaded Atchinson and others to withdraw while federal troops arrested and jailed a Free State organized band. Most Kansas settlers were hungry for peace and were eager to cooperate. As long as the campaign was going on, however, Republican newspapers were generally unwilling to recognize the improvements in Kansas, while the Democratic press conversely overplayed the importance of the pacification which was occurring.[26]

Although peace was restored, some of the more aggressive on each side would accept nothing less than control of the Kansas government. Judge Lecompte reopened wounds by allowing the murderer of a Free State man to be released on bail. To preserve the posture of the government's fairness, which he had labored so hard to achieve, Geary had the man rearrested, suspended LeCompte, and forced Marshal J. B. Donaldson's resignation. LeCompte retaliated with a writ ordering the governor to appear in court. Geary appealed to Pierce for support. The president had the opportunity both to promote peace during the closing three months of his administration and to quiet the debates in Congress over the territory. Instead, Congress had hardly assembled when Pierce's annual message arrived, which in great part was given over to an attack on the Republican party and a misrepresentation of the events in Kansas. A "shamelessly partisan message," the *New York Times* termed it. It "goes lower than any of his defenders . . . in misrepresenting and traducing those who have opposed his administration, and in belittling the outrages and sufferings in Kansas," the *Springfield Republican* declared.[27]

The message precipitated debate in both houses. Senator Albert G. Brown of Mississippi charged Fremont supporters with intending to abolish slavery in the states and referred especially to the views of Seward and Wilson. Wilson denied he had ever asserted that Congress had the power to abolish slavery in the states. When Brown referred him to a book by Spooner, Wilson said he had read the publication and disagreed with it; those who agreed with Spooner had voted for Gerrit Smith for president, about two thousand people. He also attacked Pierce's idea that the election had been an endorsement of the administration. The

Democrats themselves had repudiated Pierce by refusing to renominate him and by their stump speeches. He then carefully prepared a longer address while colleagues Collamer, Wade, and Fessenden delivered their own responses to the president.[28]

Because of his connections to the Emigrant Aid Society officers, his acquaintance with Kansas Free State leaders, his political capacities, and his speaking skills, Wilson had become a leader in the Kansas struggles. He was determined that his allies be legally correct. In early November Lawrence, Governor Robinson, and Wilson met with about twenty others concerned about Kansas to decide what should be done if Buchanan were elected. When Higginson advocated resistance to the government, Wilson joined Lawrence ardently to oppose that strategy. He also carefully distinguished between acceptable and unacceptable motives in reacting to a proposal in the Vermont legislature to provide monetary aid to Kansas. He would vote for it if he were a legislator, he asserted, but on the basis of charity to people in the territory, not, as the Vermont legislature affirmed, that a state had rights in the territory. As active as they otherwise were in the controversies over Kansas, Wilson and his wealthier close associates Claflin and Alley neither contributed much money to sustain the Emigrant Aid Company nor gave their energies to promote its activities.[29]

Wilson on December 19 for two and a half hours delivered his answer on Kansas to what he termed Pierce's "last will and testament." The *Times* correspondent reported the address was full of facts and effective, the *Tribune* used the words "bold" and "eloquent." Wilson began by quoting a Webster tribute to the wisdom of the Congress of the Confederation in passing the Northwest Ordinance. Massachusetts was consistent in its attitude toward slavery and both senators denied any attempt to interfere with the institution in the states. He quoted from a number of political opponents of slavery, North and South. After attacking Pierce for asserting the Republicans were engaged in a revolutionary movement, Wilson criticized Attorney General Cushing for his lack of better understanding of Northern sentiment. He denied a statement by Senator Pugh that Pierce was talking about abolitionists, not congressmen.[30]

While crediting them with self-sacrifices and ability, he demonstrated how the followers of Garrison and Smith differed from Republicans in their interpretation of the constitution and disunion sentiments. He had traveled more than 30,000 miles in fourteen free states since February of 1855 and had found no thinking that Congress possessed the power to abolish slavery in the states. The Republican was a states' rights party. Quoting from Toombs, Slidell, and Wise, Wilson contended that the charge of disunion came with ill grace from Pierce, when so many disunionists belonged to his party. Free laboring men seldom went South, he demonstrated; establish slavery in Kansas and they would be excluded from there, too. He noted that Benton and Toombs were lecturing in the free states, but antislavery Northerners could not speak in slave states. The South, he maintained, was an area of despotism; he cited examples of Fremont supporters denied the vote in Southern elections. Referring to an "ungenerous remark" by Cass about Sumner, he predicted his colleague would be reelected to his seat while Cass would be retired. The speech was considered so able that it was printed in pamphlet form.[31]

Several days later, as the debates continued, Brown read a statement of Wilson's asking Wendell Phillips's cooperation in abolishing slavery. Wilson replied, praising Phillips's character, talent, and oratorical skills, but explaining that Phillips had been asked to join Wilson and the Republicans and that Wilson did not support the Garrisonian's disunion. In a lengthy exchange between the two senators, Brown was unable or unwilling to see the distinctions Wilson was ably making. Brown also quoted Wilson as having stated at a local hotel that slaves would be justified in rising and murdering their masters. Wilson denied making the statement and others who overheard or participated in the conversation soon verified his interpretation of what had occurred. The debates over Kansas thereafter wound down.[32]

But the antagonisms reawakened by the president's annual message and the succeeding debates poisoned the capital scene. The day after his speech Wilson left for Natick for Christmas festivities and to deal with senatorial business. While there, attending the antislavery fair in Boston, he described to Lydia Maria Child "a frightful account of the state of things in Washington." As he passed through the streets, he told her, he encountered yells and curses from shops and saloons, advocating violence to Seward, Sumner, Burlingame, or himself. When he made his Kansas address, Democrats tried to insult him. One opponent brandished his cane over Wilson's head. His speech had offended many slavery advocates and he was told someone had vowed to reply as Brooks had answered Sumner. He never left his rooms to go to the Senate without wondering if he would return. Nor was Wilson's life easy financially; probably as a result of his months of fall campaigning, he had to borrow $800 from Sumner, to be paid back in early March at the end of the session.[33]

Wilson was naturally concerned about the reelection of his colleague. This was assured by the declining strength of the Know Nothings, the Brooks assault, and the ability and determination of Sumner's friends in Massachusetts. In early January the House voted for reelection 333 to 12 and the Senate unanimously, a marked contrast to the bitter battle Wilson had led six years before. Wilson urged his colleague to stay away from Washington as long as necessary, even visit Europe as his doctor suggested. Wilson was, however, finding the indefiniteness of Sumner's health and plans difficult to defend. But Sumner continued to remain quietly resting. He finally decided to return to the Senate during the last week of the session on February 26, not intending to speak, but summoned by Wilson to a vote on tariff revision, in which his participation made a difference.[34]

The relationship between Republican politicians and Garrisonian abolitionists had long been an uneasy one. Wilson was one of the few politicians willing to attend their antislavery meetings and otherwise publicly associate himself with them. When the split came in 1840 between the Garrisonians—who objected to separate political action and favored equality for women in the movement—and their opponents, a majority of abolitionists had either joined the rival American and Foreign Anti-Slavery Society or become involved with the Liberty party, or both. In the many states in which this happened politicians did not have to contend with the rigidity of principles and unpopularity of such a vocal, determined, and able group as the Garrisonians. Wilson was too young to have taken sides in the bitter controversies among abolitionists from 1838 to 1840. But of the Conscience Whig leaders of 1848 Wilson and Allen had retained the closest relationship with many abolitionists and had remained consistently outspoken in their objections to slavery.

Why some politicians were praised by the Garrisonians and others considered suspect is sometimes difficult to fathom. Hale developed a special relationship with the American Anti-Slavery Society. Sumner was a longtime friend of Wendell Phillips. Giddings, Chase, Julian, Tuck, and other politicians received frequent commendation in the Garrisonian press; in fact, the Garrisonians were more likely to think highly of politicians at a distance than within their own state. One is impressed with the wide-scale correspondence between Giddings and leading Massachusetts abolitionists, who at the same time had infrequent communication with Free Soilers or Republicans in their own state. Opinions change. During the controversial presidential campaign of 1872, when Sumner urged blacks to vote for Greeley and Wilson supported Grant, Garrison contended that Wilson had been actively opposed to slavery long before Sumner and he praised Wilson's participation in antislavery meetings. When Frederick Douglass wrote his autobiography, he differentiated between the services of the Garrisonians and the political abolitionists, including specifically Wilson, and declared both were necessary to achieve the end of slavery. In other words, a radical abolition attack on Wilson would have been less deserved than on almost any other Republican congressman.[35]

When Wilson came to write his history, he paused in his discussion of the election of 1856 to comment upon the lasting and beneficial influence of the American Anti-Slavery Society in helping swell Republican ranks. Many of their members didn't vote, he noted, but throughout the "seven years war" of 1850 to 1857, the Garrisonians denounced the attacks upon the rights of Americans and the integrity of the country. Wilson approved of their analysis and description of the evils of slavery. Julian and E. L. Pierce were less generous. In recalling events of forty years before, they in 1893 decided the Garrisonians had been able in their writing and speaking, but agreed with what Pierce remembered Wilson telling him in the 1870s: that he thought they had been an obstruction, too. The Garrisonians were cool toward the Republican party, which did not claim to be antislavery and which had welcomed and nominated to office men primarily concerned about the political and economic power of the South, keeping the territories open to whites, tariff, internal improvements, and other issues. If they were untrusting of radical

Republicans like Seward, Sumner, Wilson, Wade, and Trumball, what about more moderate men, like Lincoln, Doolittle, Banks, and Dawes, or more traditional political manipulators, such as Weed, Welles, or Cameron?[36]

Republicans were constantly forced to separate themselves from Garrisonian principles. The abolitionists left the Republicans little room in which to move. Garrison by the mid-1840s had burned a copy of the American constitution as a "covenant with hell." A Congressman had to take an oath of office. Under that oath, what could be done in opposing slavery and what was required in sustaining an institution authorized by the constitution, common law, or statutes of a sister state? Garrison's compatriot and longtime associate Oliver Johnson recognized this difficulty in his biography of his friend. He asserted Sumner, Chase, Hale, and Wilson had to find a way to "break through the web which the Constitution wove about them." The Democrats benefited by associating the Republicans with the abolitionists. The former could denounce the antislaveryites, whereas Republicans who did so might not be believed by voters. In cases like Wilson's, to denounce the abolitionists would both have political disadvantages and go against his own convictions. Alternatively, the politician might attempt to spell out the differences between himself and the abolitionist. This required more reflection than some voters were willing to give. So Wilson constantly had to disassociate himself from the disunion and unconstitutional beliefs of the abolitionists, much as he had done in his exchange with Brown in December.[37]

The Garrisonians backed a January 15 convention to consider the desirability of separation of the free and slave states. Called by citizens of Worcester, its planners hoped to attract a large number of participants. A few politically interested men, most important Higginson and Bird, discouraged by the return of the Democrats to power in the fall elections, organized the event. Estimates of people present vary between 90 and 300. Those planning for the event solicited Palfrey to preside (he declined) and sought letters from prominent opponents of slavery. Seventy responses were received. Theodore Parker endorsed the convention objectives; Adams and Giddings were noncommittal. Seward did not reply. That would have been a politic response for Wilson, accused so often of temporizing for his own benefit. Whether he was provoked by his constant need to defend himself and his party from charges of Garrisonian disunion or whether he had concluded that some Republican leader should take a strong national stance, Wilson dispatched a sharp protest. He claimed the convention could result in no good and might engender much evil. It would be seized upon by politicians to mislead and alarm. Americans loved their nation, he declared, and its preservation was essential. They would be repelled by calls for disunion. The convention could only weaken the efforts of those opposed to the extension of slavery. He was confident holding to constitutional and patriotic positions could attain more for the slave than dissolution of the union.[38]

Participants at the convention were infuriated. Bird's opening address attacked Republican interest in the territories, when most of the slaves were in the states. He primarily went after Wilson and his argument that slavery's continuance was to be determined by each individual state. Higginson claimed Wilson's letter was designed for its effect in Washington, not Worcester, since it had been published in the *Boston Traveller* before it was read to the convention. Phillips's speech also denounced Wilson and his letter. The convention reacted with "surprise, disgust, and indignation," Garrison's *Liberator* reported; Massachusetts deserved a better senator. The newspaper attacked Wilson not only in its report of the meeting's activities, but continued throughout January and February. Perhaps because the gathering had attracted so few people, its supporters overreacted against the man whose other beliefs often agreed with theirs but who now most openly opposed them. But the non-Garrisonian *Boston Telegraph* also thought Wilson had assailed the men at Worcester too hardily. If what they did was treason, it declared, then the government could act. Otherwise, the participants were entitled to freedom of speech.[39]

Wilson told Sumner the convention had "come down" on him. He had been asked to communicate his sentiments; he did, and was denounced. He was also irritated that Higginson had quoted remarks conveyed privately to him about the 1856 election. It would damage Sumner's position in Washington. Parker at a January 30 antislavery convention publicly defended Wilson. He asked his fellow abolitionists not to give up on the man because of one bad speech or letter; Wilson had personally sacrificed much for the cause of the slave. Parker believed Wilson was wrong to be concerned about states' rights protecting the institution. Privately, Parker wasn't as supportive. To Sumner he criticized Wilson for wanting to have "these negro discussions stop." Sumner replied that Parker was too harsh. He was undermining Wilson by furnishing arguments "to the luke-warm and the Hunkers." Wilson denied to Parker that he had written his letter for its effect in Washington; he had written it for the men to whom it was addressed. The Republicans had been beaten by disunion fears in 1856 and would be again, if they were not more careful. He claimed he took the criticism in "good spirit," but he lamented that Sumner and Giddings had left and every slave needing money was sent to him. Furthermore, while his detractors in Massachusetts complained about him, he had to walk the streets of Washington listening to the curses of men who hated him because he opposed slavery. He continued to be armed.[40]

Wilson was still unforgiven in May, when American Anti-Slavery Society met. Parker Pillsbury introduced a resolution attacking Banks, Hale, Wilson, and the *New York Tribune.* He was angry with Wilson for saying in the Senate that the Republicans were the party of states' rights and that slavery would be more secure under Fremont than under Buchanan. Until they repudiated their ideas, the resolution declared, the society should hold them and their party accountable and as more dangerous to the cause of liberty than any other party in the nation's history. Higginson in his address eulogized Garrison as a patriot and, producing much laughter, assigned as his source a speech six years before in which Wilson had extolled the abolitionist not for his courage, truth, or zeal, but for the "patriotism of the disunionist." Lydia Maria Child was more charitable. She wished the politicians of the 1830s had been as persevering as Wilson, Giddings, and Sumner now were. She was grateful for their support.[41]

The short congressional session did not turn out to benefit any of the political parties. The Know Nothings continued divided and were weakened further. The incoming president was embarrassed when the Democratic-controlled Pennsylvania legislature elected as senator Simon Cameron, former Democrat and political enemy, over Forney, Buchanan's primary editorial supporter and friend. Southerners were shocked by the sudden death in late January of Preston Brooks. Wilson was disgusted at the praise of Brooks's personal qualities and career in House elegies; Massachusetts Know Nothing Representative DeWitt had disgraced the state with his statements. On the day of the tributes, Wilson's thoughts were of Sumner and his condition and suffering. God, he believed, had taken revenge on Brooks. The Republicans were weakened when Giddings, their longtime leader in the House, collapsed. Wilson helped carry him to the Speaker's room and later to his lodgings.[42]

His votes and the resolutions which he introduced reveal much about the Wilson's values and vision for the country. For instance, a congressional committee investigating charges of corruption was unable to persuade a *New York Times* reporter to divulge sources from which he had obtained information. A bill was hurriedly sent through both houses and signed by the president, requiring the attendance of witnesses summoned by either house and compelling them to disclose testimony. Wilson asserted the Senate was panicking and the bill was too broad in scope and too loose in language. Some of those who supported the legislation did so as a way to retaliate against the press; others were afraid opposition would be viewed as screening corruption. Only Hale, Pugh, and Wilson in the Senate and thirteen others in the House were willing to cast negative votes. The ex-publisher recognized the need to protect sources; the friend of so many newspapermen was sympathetic to the need for confidentiality.[43]

Promotion of development and the West continued to win Wilson's support. He voted for a bill to expedite telegraphic communication for the government in its foreign intercourse. Furthermore, he was with the majority to provide appropriations for a telegraph line to the Pacific; the opposition was Democratic, primarily Southern. While he favored development, Wilson saw a distinction between selected government support for business and special favors which did not aid the nation and which injured western settlers. During the previous session Congress had granted twenty-one million acres of land for railroads. Wilson would withdraw the alternate sections of land from the market and sell them to people under the provision of an 1841 preemption rights bill. That, he argued, in the long run would also aid the railroads.[44]

Representative Galusha Grow of Pennsylvania had skillfully pushed through the House a bill authorizing the people of Minnesota to begin the statehood process. Senate opponents sought to forestall passage by adding a provision permitting only American citizens to vote for delegates to the constitutional convention. Wilson favored both the proposal and changes in American naturalization laws, but he would vote against the amendment to save the bill. Minnesota would be a free state and he would do nothing to delay its admission. The amendment was nevertheless added, 27 to 24, with the entire Southern delegation, except Toombs, in favor. With only nine days left in the session, the proposal was likely to fail, so Hale moved reconsideration. He spoke only ten minutes; the Southerners spoke for hours. With all Republicans in the majority, the Hale motion passed, 35 to 21. During the lengthy debate, adjournment motions were defeated twice. The Republicans, with Wilson very much involved, got the citizenship provision deleted, and then passed the House bill, 31 to 22. This was a sectional vote; included in the majority were the fourteen Republicans, thirteen free state Democrats, and four slave state senators. The *Boston Telegraph* characterized the Southern opposition as a "conspiracy of slaveholders and Know Nothings."[45]

The government had more money than it needed to undertake its responsibilities. Furthermore, the surplus was draining the economy of specie. Secretaries of the treasury for a number of years had been urging that the revenue be reduced. As the session moved to its close, Senator Robert T. M. Hunter of Virginia, chairman of the Senate Committee on Finance, pushed tariff revision provided for in a House bill. In his speech Wilson pronounced the issue the most important before Congress. The accumulation of precious metals by the government was dangerous, he declared; businessmen were concerned about a recession. He praised Campbell, chairman of the House committee, and revealed he had been working with him for weeks on the legislation. Wilson's concern was that the Senate would so alter the House bill, nothing could be passed.[46]

Since the issue became one of region rather than party, crafting an acceptable bill required skill. Ex-Whigs Wilson and Sumner (who attended only to vote on tariff proposals) and their Republican House colleagues joined the South Carolina Democrats in both houses to advocate decreased rates. Most of the South and southern New England favored lower duties; Pennsylvania and the West still sought protection. The real conflict occurred over wool. The woolen manufacturers did not need protection; the growers thought they did. Wilson, and most eastern senators, voted consistently in sustaining the House proposal. As the day wore on, Southern and Western Democrats joined to substitute, 26 to 24, a simple 25 percent tariff reduction for the basic House bill. Shortly thereafter, opponents won a reconsideration, 25 to 24. The wool issue, on Wilson's suggestion, was defused, 33 to 9, by admitting wool of lesser value duty free, the rest at between 20 and 23 percent. The Senate then accepted the new tariff proposal, 33 to 12. Former Whigs and the two Pennsylvania senators made up most of the minority.[47]

The old Congress adjourned, but the Senate of the Thirty-fifth Congress then convened to consider nominations of the new president. Republican ranks increased with the additions of Cameron, King of New York, Chandler of Michigan, Doolittle of Wisconsin, and James F. Simmons of Rhode Island. More controversial than approval of nominations was the assignment of committees. The Democrats filled most positions, then invited Republicans to appoint those left. The latter, given their numbers, should have received forty-three assignments; they were given thirty-three. The East had the bulk of the nation's commerce, but only two members on the Commerce Committee; not a senator from Massachusetts, Maine, or New York was selected for the Naval Committee. Many Republicans objected to the process, but Seward was cooperative. Wilson was assigned to committees on Military Affairs and Revolutionary Claims. The former appointment was fortuitous, giving Wilson the seniority and experience he would need to head that important committee during the Civil War.[48]

Wilson's public life was surprisingly quiet during the next five weeks. He appears not to have participated in the spring elections. In a light turnout in New Hampshire the Republicans won the governorship by a large majority and carried all three congressional contests. They repeated the success in Rhode Island, winning the governorship and both congressional seats, plus an overwhelming majority in both houses. Although the party captured control of the legislature, in Connecticut the Republicans barely won the governorship and the congressional delegation was divided. The primary political accomplishment in Massachusetts was approval of three constitutional amendments, one denying the right to vote, with some exemptions, to anyone who could not read the state constitution in English and write his name; a second reducing the size of the House to 240 members, elected by districts of similar population; and a third creating forty senatorial districts of nearly equal population. None of the many proponents of the town representation system in the 1853 convention now spoke for retaining it. The legislature had also considered a fourteen-year residency requirement before naturalized foreigners could vote. This had been recommended by Governor Gardner. Wilson would support a two-year requirement, but the proposal before the legislature, he wrote, would "disgrace the state." To quiet nativism, legislative Republicans accepted Wilson's position by passing for the first time the two-year provision.[49]

As senator and citizen Wilson actively participated in nonpolitical public affairs. He had scarcely returned from the senatorial session before he and Harriet were invited to a levee, concert, and ball at a new building owned by Walcott on Main Street on Natick. In 1857 the proprietors of the community's private library agreed to offer their books to the town, provided the town would contribute quarters, personnel, and funds to enlarge it. This was done; long interested in library affairs, Wilson thereafter provided the institution with public documents. On June 17 Everett delivered the address for the unveiling of a statute of Joseph Warren, a hero on the Revolution, on Bunker Hill. All members of the United States Senate were invited to attend. When James M. Mason, author of the Fugitive Slave Act, accepted, Winthrop was asked to introduce and host him. In his presentation Winthrop carefully spoke of the greatness of Virginia, and avoided praise for the guest. Nevertheless, he was attacked by the press. Wilson attended the event and with fairness complimented his frequent Massachusetts antagonist for his effort. Wilson also sadly attended the Salem funeral of his old associate, S. C. Phillips, who in June was drowned in the St. Lawrence River near Montreal.[50]

Although one might not surmise it from what was printed in the more radical Northern and Southern newspapers or from congressional debates, Geary's successful efforts at pacification in the fall of 1856 and the spring of 1857 had caused Kansas to gradually quiet. Buchanan in his inaugural address denounced the long agitation over slavery and called for allowing the people in the territories to decide the issue for themselves. That was good Democratic doctrine. But did the president mean the choice would be made by the territorial legislature—as Douglas, Cass, and many of their Northern brethren interpreted popular sovereignty—or did he mean the people would decide when their representatives drew up a constitution at the time a territory asked for statehood? When Buchanan delivered his inaugural address, he knew that the Supreme Court in the Dred Scott case was about to decree that slavery could exist in any territory and that the people possessed no power to prohibit it until they prepared for admission as a state. Accepting the Court's point of view would imply that the Republican party, with its opposition to slavery in the territories and its policy to exclude it by congressional action, would have little reason to exist. Furthermore, the solution of Cass and Douglas to the same issue—allowing the territorial legislature to establish or prohibit slavery—would also be unconstitutional.

What did the broad court interpretation signify for the immediate problem of Kansas? Fortunately for the Democratic party, Congress would not assemble again until December, so that the divisive issue would not immediately have to be debated or resolved. Fortunately for him, Buchanan had nine months to solve the Kansas problem without congressional interference. Surveyor General John Calhoun and his associates took over the proslavery leadership in the territory. In contrast to his deteriorating relations with the latter, Geary attained a state of comfortable truce with the Northerners. The Free State legislature agreed not to transact most business. Its members did dispatch a memorial, presented by Wilson, asking Congress to aid them in their struggle to maintain their constitutional rights.[51] Geary failed to persuade the Southern-controlled territorial legislature to repeal or reform its most objectionable acts. Rather, it passed legislation to provide for a census, a registry of voters, and a state constitutional convention. The implementation of these provisions was placed in the hands of proslavery officials.

The intention was not to submit the convention's work to the electorate for approval.

The die had been cast for renewed controversy over Kansas. Geary quite properly vetoed the bill as premature and partisan and in violation of the usual practice of popular ratification. The legislature passed it over his veto. Threats to assassinate the governor were frequent. Geary's appeal for military reinforcements was rejected by General Smith. Reacting to the deepening difficulties in Kansas, Wilson on February 28 submitted to the Senate a resolution asking the president to forward all Kansas correspondence with the governor not heretofore communicated. Geary in the meantime felt deserted, overworked, and increasingly unable to govern or fulfill the pledges he had made to protect civil rights and maintain peace. On March 4 he resigned. Buchanan was relieved to have the resignation, since Geary had become so unpopular among Southerners.[52]

The president's choice of a successor was Robert J. Walker of Mississippi, a longtime friend, an associate of Buchanan in Polk's cabinet, and a strong union man, so influential and able that he had been considered for secretary of state before Cass had been offered the position. This was no reward for a minor party functionary, but the selection of an able man, knowledgeable about politics, understanding the need to find a solution in Kansas, both for the health of the Democratic party and the future of the nation. Douglas was as enthusiastic about the choice as Buchanan was. Walker would never have taken the position if he were not certain he and the president saw eye to eye. Kansas had been the graveyard for three governors' political careers. Before accepting, Walker got Buchanan to agree that a political friend, former Representative F. P. Stanton of Tennessee, be appointed territorial secretary, the second in command, and that a new army commander acceptable to Walker be designated. Before he departed for the West, Walker published a letter including his perception of the views of the president and the cabinet and he asked Buchanan to look over Walker's proposed inaugural address and make changes if he disagreed. At a subsequent New York dinner in his honor, Walker pledged that the people of Kansas would have a fair referendum on a proposed constitution.

Walker was slow in traveling to his new assignment. Even before the appointments were made, the Free State leadership announced it would not cooperate with the territorial legislature, which included voting in the June elections for delegates to the constitutional convention. Secretary Stanton arrived first, determined to be neutral. The census and registry were complete but many of the Free Staters had been excluded and many ineligible proslavery men listed. Northerners would not participate in the election without revisions supervised by fair panels, a guarantee Stanton was not empowered to give. Still, they vowed to cooperate otherwise with the new governor. Walker arrived in Kansas in late May, too tardy to be able to persuade the proslavery leaders to provide necessary alterations to encourage their opposition to vote or to convince the Free Staters that participation in the elections would benefit them. His object was clear, however. He wanted to fashion Kansas into a Democratic state, as California was. The territory contained half the slaves and many more Northern immigrants than it had a year before. The largest political component was Free State Democrats. Walker intended to base his support on them and woo as many Republicans and proslavery Democrats as he could.[53]

Wilson also went to Kansas. On April 8, A. A. Lawrence, Adams, Howe, Wilson, and about twenty-five others met in Boston to listen to reports by visiting men from Kansas, including Judge M. F. Conway and John Brown. Conway, after talking with the new governor, had concluded that Walker wanted to be a peacemaker and would make Kansas a free state. Brown, on the other hand, wanted to raise a force of one hundred men to protect Northerners from unfair laws. Wilson must have decided soon thereafter, definitely by April 23, to go west, intending first to visit Kansas, Nebraska, and Minnesota and perhaps stay several months. Whether his original objective was fact-finding or influencing the elections in Kansas and Minnesota is not clear. Lawrence paid for at least part of the costs. Walker left New York on May 14, Wilson passed through the city the next day. Rather than taking the more obvious route through New York or Pennsylvania, Wilson went via Virginia, visited the grave of Henry Clay in Kentucky, and crossed Illinois. Wilson, Walker, Howe, and abolitionist minister John Pierpont found themselves on the same Missouri River steamboat.[54]

They left St. Louis on May 22 and arrived at Quindara two days later; this gave Wilson and Walker, both gregarious men, plenty of time to converse. They were invited to speak publicly on board; Walker declined, but his associate, E. O. Perkin of Tennessee, agreed. Wilson delivered a courageous address, considering he was in the middle of a slave state where a year before the people had blocked the passage of Northerners moving to Kansas. Wilson spoke of his hatred for slavery and his desire to prohibit it wherever he could. As usual, he acknowledged slavery had a right to exist where established by state law. He wished Southerners would visit the North more, so that they would find the objections to slavery came not from "wrath or hatred," but affection. Ever the politician, he predicted he would return wiser and more assured of the growing power of the nation. He also spoke of what labor could accomplish in the future. Perkin agreed with much of what Wilson had said and hoped the senator would have a "spirit of forbearance" when he reached Kansas. Former governor Robinson met the ship at Quindara to host Wilson on what was expected to be a three- or four-day excursion. Walker went to Leavenworth where he treated the men to $210 worth of whiskey and wine. One of his biographers claimed the governor intended to drink half the population into submission and pray the other half that way.[55]

The new arrivals quickly made their presence felt. The Republicans went to Lawrence, already the largest town in the territory. Pierpont delivered a temperance lecture on May 25; Wilson reluctantly spoke a few minutes, generally avoiding politics, but terming the Pierce administration a "page of infamy on the history of the country" and holding out little hope that Buchanan would be any better. The next evening about two thousand people turned out to listen to a series of speeches. Walker and his staff arrived during the day, were invited to attend, and did. The new governor declined to deliver a formal address, but referred the people to his forthcoming inaugural, and promised to protect the rights of all citizens. Among the speakers, Wilson related some of his impressions of Kansas after several days' visit and urged the people to make the territory into a free state. Stanton tried to conciliate the Free Staters. Robinson spoke hopefully of the new territorial administration and bluntly warned Walker of the difficulty of his work. Wilson continued the next day to Topeka for consultations and an address of over an hour to a crowded hall. Walker departed for LeCompton where on May 28 he delivered his promised speech, which recognized territorial laws and maintained they had to be executed. He urged all parties to participate in the elections for delegates to the constitutional convention, expected the completed document would be submitted to the people for ratification, contended the existence of slavery would ultimately be determined by climate, and hoped the controversy could be removed from Congress.[56]

Wilson emerged from his conversations with Walker en route to and within Kansas with an abiding distrust. It was so deep it would continue into the Civil War era, when the Southerner remained loyal to the union. This is critical to understanding the events concerning Kansas. Historians have often credited Walker with being a nationalist—able, reasonable, trying to guarantee peace and protection of civil rights, and with a sensible, if partisan, policy for Kansas. But Wilson, who could work so well with men of such different principles, objectives, and temperaments never would trust Walker again. He could forgive Winthrop, Adams, Allen, and Bird for their attacks upon him. He must have known more about Walker and his intentions than has ever been revealed.[57]

Wilson found the Kansas Free Staters disorganized, disagreeing with one another on tactics, and inactive. In his consultations he accepted their refusal to participate in the election of convention delegates, but he urged them to vote for members of the territorial legislature. The *New York Tribune* had been opposed to this, while the *National Era* had advocated it. Howe was undecided what should be done. Wilson knew Kansas would be free. What he sought to prevent was that it become Democratic and its elected officials sympathetic to the South. Too many Free Staters stood on principle, Wilson believed, insisting that to participate in elections would be to recognize the legality of the territorial legislature and betray the support already given to the Topeka government. Wilson urged them to appreciate the situation: they were confronted with a pro-Southern president and a Congress which would not accept the Topeka constitution. Wilson suggested the antislavery component in the territorial legislature organize, enunciate their principles, and denounce the convention. Next the Free Staters should vote down the proposed constitution. If they participated in the elections for a congressional delegate and new legislature, they could win, he maintained. Then the new legislature could repeal the invidious laws, abolish slavery, pass whatever legislation it thought desirable, and call another, more representative, constitutional convention.[58]

Wilson quickly altered his plan to continue to Minnesota and instead hastened East. Lawrence was puzzled as to how he could travel so fast and why he would return so rapidly after going so far. Wilson must have been confident that he had persuaded enough Free Staters that they should participate in the fall elections if they might win. What was needed more than anything else at the moment was money, between three and five thousand dollars, to carry the fall elections. En route down the Missouri he wrote letters to Kansas Free Staters with whom he had been unable to converse, urging them to vote and promising financial support if the Free State leadership agreed to participate. On May 31 he tried to see Frank Blair Jr. in St. Louis to report about affairs in the territory and seek his intervention with his father to use his influence with Morgan to collect money in New York City. He traveled continuously for five days, pausing only the one night in St. Louis to sleep. One doubts that Wilson could think a day or so would make much difference; perhaps his enthusiasm was getting the best of him.[59]

The next weeks were busy. The National Kansas Committee a few months before had been disbanded for lack of money and interest. Wilson thus had no organized agency through which to work. On June 4 he met in New York City with Morgan and Charles A. Dana, among others. By June 6 he was exhorting Lawrence to help obtain the money. On June 8 about thirty supporters, including Lawrence, Adams, Alley, Stearns, Howe, Bird, and Claflin, listened to Wilson's report. He insisted matters were going badly, the Free Staters were disillusioned and disorganized, and the administration might win Kansas if more outside assistance were not provided. He was convincing. Howe backed off his advocacy of violence as the only practical policy in Kansas. By mid-June Wilson had three thousand dollars pledged in Boston, Worcester, New Haven, and New York. On July 2 Thomas J. Marsh, the Republican candidate for state treasurer, was dispatched as agent to disperse the money and organize the cause. Although he traveled extensively at his own expense, Wilson was unable to raise the four thousand dollars he had hoped to obtain; the arrival of the Panic of 1857 in August in part dampened his chances.[60]

Controversy in and over Kansas first quieted, and then grew greater. The Kansas Free State leadership accepted the increasingly predominant Republican view and the advice of its own Kansas press that its defiance of the national government would be crushed. Walker worked hard to convince the Northerners that he sought fairness. As a result, when the Topeka legislature met on June 9, it contented itself with passing resolutions of principle and adjourned without taking action, which would have compelled the governor to react. The Free Staters were giving Wilson and Walker a chance. Within a week the elections for delegates to the constitutional convention took place. Half of the Free Staters could not vote, having not been registered or having arrived in the massive immigration of the previous few months; others stayed away; not more than 2,200 participated. Through faulty census and registration procedures, gerrymandering and malapportionment of election districts, and the Free Staters' refusal to vote, the radical Southern element would control the convention.

Even before the vote, proslaveryites had told Walker they would not dispatch the constitution to the people for ratification, no matter what he had promised. In spite of the recognition of most people in both Border Ruffian territory and throughout the North that the Free Staters were now in the overwhelming majority in Kansas, the radical Southern leadership and press strengthened their Kansas allies by denouncing Walker. He had not been in office for six weeks before Southern governors, Congressmen, party conventions, and editors were calling for his replacement. Buchanan was still sustaining his governor in early July, but as he feared Southern threats of secession were truthful, he began to waver.

With such divisions in the nation and without vocal support by his party leaders and the cabinet, Walker's authority was weakened. In early July the governor denounced an effort by people in Lawrence to set up their own city government, unauthorized by either the governor or the Topeka legislature. When Walker asked for troop reinforcements to handle the situation, the cabinet opposed him. Several weeks later Lane, under the auspices of the Topeka government, issued a proclamation setting up militia companies. To alienate Free Staters further, Robinson was brought to trial, but did not claim to be governor and was acquitted. A "poor creature," Wilson characterized Walker. Nor could the governor count on the support of the Democratic element in the state; while its July meeting favored submission of the constitution to the people, Walker increasingly doubted the proslavery-dominated convention would permit that. The convention met briefly in September and ominously elected Calhoun president. Committees were appointed to draft sections of the document, with the delegates to return October 19.[61]

As the summer of 1857 drew to a close the future of Kansas was as unclear as it had been since the passage of Douglas's bill of territorial organization. Wilson had tried, but he was not certain whether he had raised enough money or persuaded enough Kansas leaders to participate in the fall territorial elections. The hope that Governor Walker could establish peace and justice in Kansas was waning. He was obviously losing control of events in the territory and Buchanan was not likely much longer to back him. The proslavery element controlled the existing legislature and the convention and probably would not submit the proposed constitution to the people for ratification, no matter what the custom had been or the governor had promised. The victory of the Democrats in 1856 and their increasingly militant control of Congress boded ill for Wilson and Republican objectives.

15

In Power in Massachusetts Gaining in the Nation

Wilson in 1857 was still a power in Massachusetts politics. He now was to demonstrate he had as great an influence as he'd had during the convention in 1853, directing political affairs in 1854, and preventing a nomination in 1856. Gardner had alienated Republicans even more by refusing to remove Judge Loring and by vetoing a grant for the School for Idiot Children. What remained of the once powerful Know Nothing party was a minority of the voters. In the political disorganization about half of the members of the General Court were not certain to which party they belonged. Without the necessity of attracting Know Nothings for a presidential or congressional campaign, the Republicans enjoyed more freedom of choice in their gubernatorial selection. The time for political reorganization had finally arrived. The Wilson faction thus concluded their party should select its own candidates for state office. Wilson, Bowles, and many others favored Banks for the gubernatorial nomination; he might attract many Know Nothings permanently to the Republican party and would assure both the political demise of Gardner and a Republican triumph. Their objective was not as much victory—that was likely anyhow—but creating a Republican party in the state that was broad in appeal, so that it would become permanently one of the two major parties. Wilson had sufficient time between his return from Washington and his departure for Kansas to participate in the plans for the direction of party activities in the state. The Republicans were called to assemble June 24, two and a half months earlier than conventions in the state usually met.[1]

Bird led the Republican opposition to Banks. He had battled against the election of Rockwell in 1855 and had secured the alternative nomination of Josiah Quincy in 1856. While he was a former state chairman and was admired for his integrity and hard work, Bird often occupied too radical a position. Furthermore, he had no chance of overthrowing the Banks-Burlingame-Wilson faction. In part, too, he had to depend upon the influence of men like Adams, Hoar, and Palfrey, whom Bird himself had opposed in the early 1850s and who had already demonstrated their lack of skill to develop a large political party. Unfortunately for his own aims, Bird also objected to alternative candidates to Banks, such as Boutwell or Goodrich. When Adams joined about twenty others at a last-minute consultation called by Bird on June 11, he had to admit Wilson already had established the time frame of the campaign and those assembled lacked common objectives, save opposition to Banks's nomination. One newspaper correspondent commented on how many of those at Bird's meeting a year and a half before had spoken at the banquet honoring Banks. More telling, he noted they sought to purify the party by driving out 90 percent of its members.[2]

The former Free Soil *Worcester Spy*—the principal press voice of the Bird faction—shortly before the Republican convention attacked Wilson for his role in the union 1856 nominations. Wilson in reply not only defended his stance of the year before, but declared he sought the votes for the 1857 Republican state ticket not only from all those who had supported Fremont, but also from the twenty thousand who had voted for Fillmore and the forty thousand for Buchanan. Wilson went to Washington so he would not be in Massachusetts while the convention met.[3]

Know Nothings were uncertain how to respond. His supporters sought Gardner's renomination. But the governor was unpopular even among the faction that remained, including the *Boston Bee* and many country Know Nothing newspapers. Although Wilson had advocated no opposition to Gardner in 1856, this had not been because of friendship, political affinity, or ability to work together; Wilson in mid-1857 had not spoken to the governor for two years. The Know Nothings decided to call their convention a week before the Republicans so that they might preempt the Banks nomination. If the Republicans did not want to accept a man nominated by another party, the Know Nothings might win with a veteran and well-known candidate with nativist, Democratic, and Republican antecedents. If, on the other hand, the Republicans also selected Banks, the new governor would then be beholden to both parties. The convention nominated Banks almost unanimously. He accepted. The Gardner faction, however, would not consent to the results and both the state party chairman and secretary called the meeting "bogus" and unauthorized.[4]

The Republican nomination was not in doubt. Palfrey and Dana failed to be elected as delegates. Burlingame assured the convention that Banks was a Republican. Boutwell, Goodrich, and Eliot were the primary alternatives. Banks received 63 percent of the votes on an informal ballot, 78 percent on the official tally. By November Adams admitted the selection of Banks had been a good tactic. Bird, Pierce, Hopkins, and others were not as willing to acquiesce. Unfortunately, the two parties chose different candidates for other state offices. In late July Goodrich resigned his chairmanship of the state committee because he could not sustain Banks; Wilson's close friend Alley took over.[5]

By mid-July the Gardner faction decided to go ahead on its own. Before a crowd of supporters the governor in late August launched his attack against Banks. Fillmore Know Nothings, led by Wilder, began to offer their support. While the Democrats prepared for a convention of their own, Cushing ominously met with the governor. If he could attract five thousand Whigs, one correspondent predicated, Gardner might defeat Banks. Wilson was not worried; no combination could be made which would reelect the governor, he told Sumner. Both the Fillmore and Gardner Know Nothings met on the same day; Gardner was nominated by both. Wilson's old antagonist Devereaux attacked the Republicans as too narrow a party in philosophy and maintained Banks's course did not merit American support. Bowles, who had taken over the *Boston Traveller*, and combined the *Atlas*, *Telegraph*, and *Chronicle* with it, sold out and the Gardner element thereby obtained a needed Boston press voice. They tried unsuccessfully to purchase the influential *Boston Bee*. The governor's weakness was his inability to appeal to Democrats. Still, Gardner and Cushing were working together. Furthermore, former Whig leaders Winthrop and Alexander K. Bullock endorsed the governor.[6]

Having held their state convention in June, the Republicans needed some other device to launch their fall campaign, so they called a Young Men's Convention in Worcester, September 8. Banks and Wilson were the featured speakers. Wilson, who was greeted with "tumultuous applause," urged the assembled to hate slavery. He advocated prohibiting the domestic slave trade and slavery in the District of Columbia and in the territories and reversing the Dred Scott Decision. Asserting he had played no role in the nomination, he maintained the Americans and Republicans had both selected Banks and he deserved to be supported. He compared the nominee's antislavery stance with Fremont's, credited him with a major role in Sumner's election, and praised his effectiveness as Speaker of the House. Banks departed from the custom of a candidate's keeping silent. In his address he opposed the extension of slavery and admission of any more slave states, favored guarding the ballot box from use by foreigners, and promised economical administration of state government. *The Liberator* contrasted Wilson's strong antislavery speech with Banks's limited objectives.[7]

Republican opposition to the Banks nomination weakened. Many of those who had grumbled all summer—including Goodrich, Alvord, Hopkins, and the *Dedham Gazette*—faced with the possibility of a Gardner victory or a weakened Republican party in future national contests, endorsed Banks. On October 8 and 9 Republican and Banks American leaders assembled to create a coalition ticket for other state offices. But Republicans who could support Banks were unhappy with the qualifications and principles of several of the other nominees. Bird and the editor of the *Worcester Spy* were experiencing difficulties in providing a Banks alternative. Neither Howe nor Andrew would run. A convention called for September 30 had to be postponed to October 15; then Swan was nominated for governor. Only Bird, Robinson, Stone, Charles G. Davis, and Henry L. Pierce, of the leading Republicans, participated. They started their own weak newspaper, the *Straight Republican*, edited by Robinson.[8]

The correspondent of the *New York Tribune* characterized the campaign as proceeding "lazily," with few meetings and poor attendance. Only Banks, Wilson, and Burlingame could attract audiences, he claimed. Gardner spoke primarily at agricultural and military shows. One of Banks's major addresses was in Boston on October 15, when Wilson also spoke briefly. Two nights later Wilson delivered his primary campaign address in Worcester and followed that by a Faneuil Hall speech, October 24. Although suggesting earlier that he hoped to participate in the campaigns in Illinois and Indiana, Wilson limited his appearances to Massachusetts.[9]

Election results were mixed, but more encouraging to the Democrats than to the Republicans. The administration swept the Southern states, even those which prior to 1852 had strong Whig parties. The Republicans captured the early elections in Vermont and Maine. They also won in Iowa, but by diminished majorities. The two Indiana congressional seats were divided. Chase sneaked in by a little over a thousand votes in Ohio, the Democrats barely won in Minnesota. The greatest Republican defeat was in Pennsylvania, Wilmot losing by more than 40,000 votes and the Democrats capturing both houses of the legislature. The *Tribune* was despondent. The *Times* declared the Republicans had lost ground everywhere; the party, it declared, was almost extinguished in Pennsylvania, and virtually defeated in Ohio. The *National Era* was more encouraged; the Republicans had carried five New England states so far and would pick up a new senator in Iowa. In November the Democrats improved their performance in Wisconsin and, with an impressive showing by the Know Nothings, captured minor state offices in New York; its legislature would have no majority party. As one historian has pointed out, in Pennsylvania and New York, states in which the Republicans were unwilling to unite sufficiently with the Know Nothings, the Democrats won. Massachusetts, under Wilson's guidance, did not make that mistake.[10]

Banks swept Massachusetts with almost 60,000 votes to 38,000 for Gardner and 31,000 for Democrat Erasmus Beach. Swan received only 200. For the first time the Republicans would control the General Court; they won 32 in the Senate, with the Americans 4 and the Democrats 3, and 166 in the House, with the Democrats 36 and Americans 34. Banks secured every county but three, although he had a majority in only Worcester, Franklin, and Hampden. "An astounding Republican victory," the *New York Times* correspondent declared. Gardnerism was dead. More important, Banks could permanently meld free soil and mildly nativist voters into the new majority. In three campaigns he would never really obtain half of the 1855 Know Nothing vote, but he secured enough—for as the separate nativist movement declined in strength, the Democrats, the only alternative, were unable to attract very many nativists. Wilson's tactics had worked. As victory became evident a crowd went to the Revere House to cheer Banks. Wilson introduced the new governor and Burlingame, Hamlin, Banks, and Wilson all spoke. The newspapers commented during the next few weeks on the restraint of the Republican press and the muteness of the vanquished. On November 10 his Waltham neighbors threw a banquet to honor the governor-elect. Most of the state's congressional delegation was present. Wilson was one of the five speakers.[11]

Gardner soon thereafter wrote a curious letter to Wilson. He thanked the senator for sending so many materials from Washington, then declared the election results had provided him real satisfaction! He praised his opponent's antislavery position and claimed his own candidacy had not hurt Banks. Given their lack of communication for years and press speculation that Gardner had been after Wilson's Senate or Burlingame's House position, one wonders what prompted this note.[12]

Wilson was able to relax for about a month, but still participated in two widely reported public events. He was now strengthening his support of temperance and on November 19 he presided over an immense gathering at the Tremont Temple to honor Neal Dow, the Maine-law proponent, on his return from Europe. Both Dow and Wilson spoke. Perhaps in part from Wilson's influence, two of his closest political associates, Swift and Russell, affiliated themselves with the movement. In 1858 his Natick friends would name their chapter the Wilson Division of the Sons of Temperance; by 1860 it would have five hundred members. Earlier the same day Wilson, Banks, Phelps, and others met Sumner when his ship from Europe docked. They escorted the still incapacitated senator to his mother's home, where Sumner spoke briefly and Wilson more extensively. The latter told the several hundred people who had assembled that Sumner would go to Washington to speak in the people's behalf.[13]

Throughout the summer arguments had continued among Free Staters in Kansas whether or not to vote in the fall elections, as urged by Wilson. Conway, for example, was still unconvinced in early August. Some Free Staters expected simply to gain control of the legislature and govern, repealing objectionable laws, passing new ones; others argued in favor of taking over, then adjourning *sine die,* and leaving legislative functions to the Topeka government. Walker and Stanton were able to produce a peaceful election day with a large turnout. The Free Staters won the territorial delegate election by about a two-to-one majority. Legislative returns were confusing. In two districts with few registered voters, more than a thousand ballots had been cast. Walker and Stanton visited the two counties, threw out the returns, and the Free Staters had won. This was not the result Walker had sought. Fraud was so evident, however, that if he hadn't interfered he would have destroyed the creditability of the Democratic party in the North. His own plan of engendering and strengthening a middle ground between the radical proslavery faction and the more militant Free Staters had been subverted. On the other hand, Wilson's summer analysis and advice had been vindicated and his labors for financial support had achieved their end; no non-Kansas Republican politician had played a more important role.[14]

The response to the Kansas events differed by section and party. Republicans, of course, applauded the great victory and Wilson must have been gratified at the major role he had played. Had the Buchanan administration's unhappiness with Walker been known before the November elections, the Republicans would have done much better. The Democrats were more divided in their reactions. Douglas, the architect of the bill creating Kansas and the Democratic spokesman of the Northwest, understood that the majority had spoken. He publicly pronounced in the press that the voters had decided for a free state. The convention had to recognize that voice, although it could frame the constitution however else it chose. Southern leaders and press thought otherwise. They were angry and dismayed. More radical papers like the *Charleston Mercury* and *Savannah Georgian* were vehement in their denunciations of Walker.[15]

While the votes for the legislature were being counted and the qualifications of the voters examined, the constitutional convention reconvened. An overwhelming majority of the delegates had migrated from slave states. Unrepresentative and selected at a rigged election, they were determined to create a document which would guarantee a framework of government for the kind of state they wanted. In session less than two weeks, they created a constitution similar in many ways to those of other western states. Crucial was their decision to provide for slavery. They argued over whether to (1) send their document directly to Washington or (2) devise some method by which either a restricted, and friendly, electorate could register its approval, or the electorate could respond to just one provision—with slavery guaranteed one way or the other. Leading national Southern politicians urged some recognition by the convention of the people's right to be heard.

The most radical in the convention barely were beaten. In the end, the constitution was not to be submitted for ratification; the people were permitted to choose between two alternatives, the constitution with slavery, or the constitution protecting slavery, but with a provision that no additional slaves could be imported. In either case, the state legislature could not emancipate slaves, free blacks were to be excluded, and the Fugitive Slave Act would be enforced. No section of the document could be amended prior to 1864. If a voter did not like other important provisions of the constitution, he had no way to register his objections. Also included was a curious addition providing an end to federal officeholders'—including the governor's—authority on December 1, establishing a provisional government, and authorizing Calhoun, as its head, to supervise an election for new state officers, including determination of the validity of the returns. Calhoun also would select those who would establish precincts and supervise the polls by which eligible voters on December 21 would determine the degree of slavery to be permitted in the constitution.

The response was immediate. Lane and Robinson spoke of organized resistance. Not only Kansas Republican journals but most Democratic editors denounced the convention and its constitution. The Lecompton constitution did more to unite Free Staters politically than any other event. Throughout the North newspapers were almost unanimous in attacking the convention's refusal to submit its work to the people. Douglas's organ, the *Chicago Times,* was outraged. Even Buchanan's former closest editorial supporter, Forney, denounced the Lecompton fraud. In contrast, the Southern press was as firm in its insistence that the work of a legally constituted convention had to be sustained by Congress. Walker, who a month earlier had requested permission for a leave, departed on November 19 for Washington. Pressures upon him had become unbearable; he needed to get away. Members of Buchanan's cabinet and the Southern Democratic leadership talked of secession if Kansas were not accepted under the Lecompton constitution. When Walker met with the cabinet, an impasse resulted which the press immediately disseminated. Timid, unimaginative, swayed by his cabinet, ignorant of the depth of feelings in the North, Buchanan determined to be as strong as Presidents Jackson and Polk had been and force his party and Congress to accept Lecompton. The fall elections had encouraged firmness, even rashness, in the administration.

The Democratic party was being broken in two. Outside of Pennsylvania, most of Buchanan's closest political friends had long been Southerners. The president now accepted the cabinet's views, and in his annual message to Congress, later delivered on December 8, endorsed the convention, contended the question of slavery was being fairly referred to the electorate, and urged the people of Kansas to vote. Before he delivered the message, Buchanan met with Douglas in an angry confrontation. Douglas in July had sustained Walker's promise that the Kansas constitution be approved or rejected by the voters. In their meeting the author of the Kansas-Nebraska Act declared he would oppose the Lecompton constitution and Buchanan asserted he would make support of the document a test of party loyalty. In Kansas itself, Stanton, trying to prevent a renewal of bloodshed, called the new legislature into session for December 7 and recommended it authorize a second election in which the voters could accept or reject the entire constitution. The legislature agreed. Before Buchanan heard of the acting governor's action, but too late to prevent Stanton from signing the authorization bill for the second election, the president removed the governor from office.[16]

The Republicans gathered for the Thirty-fifth Congress with twenty senators, a steadily growing group. Every New England state but Rhode Island had chosen two Republicans; only Indiana, among Northern states, was unrepresented by the party. Wilson continued to occupy a back row seat, with Hale and Seward on his left, and the empty Sumner seat on his right. Committees were again carefully packed, with Wilson once more assigned to Military Affairs and Revolutionary

Claims. Jefferson Davis's chairmanship of the former committee provided Wilson with a continuing working relationship with the future president of the Confederacy and at least some idea how the man thought. Hamlin, unsuccessful Republican candidate for president *pro tempore*, launched his party's complaint over committee organization. Senator William Gwin of California replied, contending the House Republicans the last session had badly discriminated against the Democrats. Wilson immediately countered, demonstrating that an equal number of Republicans and opposition had been placed on House committees, that most committees had been controlled by the majority only five to four, that several Democrats had been given chairmanships, and that the Democrats even had controlled the Commerce Committee. He objected to the sectional more than the partisan structure of the Thirty-fifth Congress's organization, citing three Southerners on the Library Committee, when most renowned American writers were from the North.[17]

Wilson returned to the Washington House, again the only senator residing there. Buffington was the only other Massachusetts congressman at the same address, although ten additional representatives lodged there. Most of the Massachusetts delegation lived at Willard's Hotel and its environs. Harriet accompanied her husband this term.[18]

Wilson again had the duties normally performed by two senators. Sumner would not and should not resign, in spite of his inability to serve during the first month of the session, Wilson told a correspondent. On the one hand, Wilson asked Sumner when he thought he could return. On the other, he assured his friend that restoration of his health was paramount. He had been "stricken down on the field of conflict," Wilson wrote, and he had the right to demand time for recovery. As conflicts between the administration and the Republicans deepened, Wilson telegraphed Sumner on February 1 to come to Washington. But whenever the senator returned to the capital, his old symptoms reappeared. Wilson himself urged his colleague to leave. Sumner did not serve on committees or participate in debates. An April relapse limited his activities even further. So on May 22 he left again for Europe, not returning until November 1859.[19]

Douglas was determined to challenge the Lecompton proceedings. He knew he could not prevent the Senate's acceptance of Kansas admission, but a lengthy and effective debate might invigorate Northern public opinion and force enough House Democrats to desert the president to compel some new election. Douglas occupied himself during December planning strategy with Northern House Democrats and establishing friendlier relations with Republicans, including Wilson. The day after the president's message, Douglas rose to deliver one of his finest speeches, powerful, skillfully reasoned, impassioned, and effective—as even the pro-Buchanan press conceded. Senator A. G. Brown of Mississippi congratulated Wilson on his "new Republican ally." Most Southern senators were angry and bitter.[20]

The Republican leaders were not leading. For once Wilson did not know how to advise his friends in Kansas. In late November he did not see how they could vote in the convention-sponsored referendum on the degree of slavery in the state. But if the constitution were approved, he urged them to vote for state officers and congressmen. He did not think the Lecompton document could be accepted by Congress, but he was sagacious enough to recognize the great powers an administration had to persuade and buy congressmen. When Congress convened, Buchanan had a replacement for the dismissed Stanton, the Commissioner of Indian Affairs J. W. Denver. With Governor Walker absent, an immediate appointment was needed. On December 10 the Senate quickly confirmed Denver, with Douglas among the twenty-nine votes in support. Walker, working with Douglas, penned an effective analysis of Kansas affairs and a resignation, dated December 15. But what dominated the first three weeks of the session was the attack and defense by Douglas. By Christmas it was clear only Democrats David Broderick of California and Charles A. Stuart of Michigan were joining the revolt. At first Illinois Republicans rejected Douglas's eagerness to cooperate, but by mid-December he had thrown his state's politics into chaos. Republican senators were willing to work with him, but they were conscious that Douglas's motives were self-serving and his stance on outlawing slavery in the territories had not changed.[21]

In Kansas the Free Staters were amazingly unified in their refusal to vote in the convention-called election. The administration and many Southern leaders hoped for tactical reasons the people would select the provision to end slave importation. But so few Northerners participated and the Southern element was so radical that Kansas as an unlimited slave state passed, 6,226 to 569, although about 40 percent of the ballots were fraudulent. Two weeks later, at the second referendum, more than 10,200 voters rejected the Lecompton document, while 138 would accept it without slavery, and 24 favored it with slavery. Wilson sent his approval of the Free Staters's actions. Kentucky's Crittenden was impressed enough to add his influence to Senate opposition to the Kansas admission under the Lecompton constitution. Acting Governor Denver told Buchanan that Congress would be going against the wishes of the people of Kansas if it admitted the state under Lecompton. One is amazed how often proslavery officials were selected for Kansas, yet they were forced by a substance of fairness to take a position different from what the Pierce and Buchanan administrations wanted, and their wise advice was then rejected. On February 2, 1858, Buchanan forwarded a message to Congress recommending admission of Kansas as a state under the Lecompton constitution.[22]

In the meantime the relationship between Douglas and the Republicans and Douglas's role in Illinois, where he was up for reelection, was threatening to divide the young party. Almost all eastern Republicans were anxious to cooperate with him. Greeley was so enthusiastic about the split among the Democrats that he was urging Republicans in Illinois to nominate the "Little Giant." Most practical

Republican politicians recognized that to win in 1860 they had to attract more supporters, either Democrats or remaining Whigs and Know Nothings. The addition to the cause of a man of Douglas's abilities and national reputation would be devastating to the Democrats throughout the North. Yet Douglas had never retreated from his support of popular sovereignty, not even defining the idea in a way more palatable to the Republicans; nor did he believe in congressional exclusion of slavery in the territories, the cornerstone of the Republican party. Wilson was widely recognized as supporting Douglas, but little evidence exists to sustain the idea that be believed Douglas would become a Republican or, this early in 1858, that he advocated a Douglas Senate nomination. He told Parker in late February that Douglas would be with them in the future, as much as Chase, Seward, and Sumner. Douglas favored crushing the Slave Power and he would continue to attack the administration, Wilson contended. Wilson hoped the controversy would weaken the Democratic party. That did not mean Douglas would become a Republican. About the same time, Wilson wrote to Schouler that he had no faith Douglas would join them; nevertheless, they should "deal kindly" with "these men."[23]

The Illinois Republicans were concerned. Most had little trust in Douglas, who had been their longtime and most vocal antagonist. Lincoln, the leader of the party in the state, protested to Trumball. Trumball admitted the difficulty which the praise of Douglas by Republican politicians and newspapers would create in Illinois. Some had acted like fools in flattering Douglas, he wrote. Douglas had encouraged Wilson, Seward, Burlingame, and others to confer with him. The Republicans had purposely let Douglas and the Democrats lead, since no legislative proposal was yet before them. Some believed Douglas was politically ruined as a Democrat and would have to join them. But Trumball was as opposed as Lincoln to accepting Douglas as a leader.[24]

When Buchanan in February submitted his message on Kansas, Trumball opposed even allowing it to be printed, prompting a strong reply from Toombs. The next day, when the Senate reassembled, Wilson sought to add to the referral motion instructions to the committee on territories to investigate Kansas affairs, including the circumstances involving the call of the Lecompton convention and an inquiry into the voting. In defense of his motion, Wilson reviewed the history of the Kansas controversy. He asserted the territorial government had been captured by an invasion of Missourians and in protest the people had instituted the Topeka government, but it had never tried to enforce laws and thus had never been in rebellion. He charged the president with ignorance about Kansas affairs and spoke of Walker's appointment and purposes in Kansas and their arrival in the territory together. He contended Walker was a proslavery man on a proslavery mission. Kansas was quiet when he arrived. Walker thereafter had engendered rebellion and had moved the army on Lawrence. The new governor had promised a free vote on the constitution and there had been none. Wilson noted that the Lecompton constitution was more than even Douglas and Wise could swallow. He also carefully drew a distinction between the Republican stance and that of Douglas. Neither of his latter two remarks would lead to political unification of the Douglas Democrats and the Republicans.[25]

The debate continued the next day. Wilson entered the discussion again to deal with Brown of Mississippi's argument that the nation needed to return to the equality of free and slave states provided for in the Compromise of 1850. Wilson could not see why seven million Southern men should to be equal to seventeen million Northern freemen. He also attacked Brown and the Democratic record in Kansas while providing a defense of the Emigrant Aid Society. Letting his emotions get away from him, Wilson contended that no man deserved a "traitor's death" more than John Calhoun, the proslavery Kansas leader. The speech was full of facts and, since it could not have been prepared, it testified to Wilson's grasp of the subject and increasing skill in debate. After three days of controversy the amendment failed by a majority of six, the Republicans joined by Whigs Crittenden and Bell and Democrats Douglas, Broderick of California, and Pugh of Ohio. Douglas soon thereafter sought approval of a resolution simply asking for information about Kansas from the president. That was first avoided, then defeated, 24 to 23, the three renegade Democrats and Bell joining the Republicans.[26]

The Democrats set aside Lecompton debates to turn to an equally controversial issue, the army appropriations bill. This would give the administration time to engender additional support in the House. A proposal in the latter body to establish a special committee to investigate Kansas affairs passed by only three votes, showing a deterioration of Free State strength. Democratic Speaker James L. Orr selected a majority from those who opposed the motion. The administration claimed it wanted to enlarge the army to control affairs in Utah, but Jefferson Davis was frank about needing more men in Kansas. When the House would not agree to this provision, the administration came back with a separate request, more limited to Utah, to provide for first five, later three, new volunteer regiments. Hale, perhaps best representing Republican reaction, asserted he opposed giving additional power to *this* president. Wilson spoke for the bill and in the process revealed his opinions about the insurrection. He would treat the Mormons as a tribe of Indians, he declared; attempt to purchase their lands and encourage them to leave the United States for another part of North America. Since that was not being done, since their lands were strategically located and they were in rebellion, the government needed the resources to control the territory. The bill passed with Seward, Cameron, Harlan, and Wilson joining the Democrats.[27]

Two other issues occupied Senate time, both initiated by the Republicans. Douglas wanted to consider the admission of Minnesota. While likely to be Democratic, it would be a free state. Southern Democrats sought to couple its admission with that of slave Kansas. While acknowledging irregularities had occurred in the Minnesota voting, Wilson maintained the situation was quite different from that in Kansas. The people of Minnesota clearly sought statehood under the constitution, which had been ratified 30,000 to 500. He also replied to Mason, who had suggested postponing action on Minnesota until they could see how the Republicans voted on Kansas. There was no need to wait, Wilson declared; Republicans would do all in their power to keep Kansas with the Lecompton constitution out of the union. The other issue was the validity of the election of Senators Graham N. Fitch and Wright of Indiana. Both elections had been protested in 1857; the men had been temporarily seated and the challenge carried over. The Republicans sought to settle the cases, hoping to oust both senators and even replace them with Republicans. The Democrats, however, preferred stalling, and suggested allowing collection of testimony in Indiana. That took until June, when the key vote to exclude the senators failed, 30 to 23.[28]

The Senate committee took only two weeks before reporting back in favor of the admission of Kansas under the Lecompton constitution. Douglas and Collamer each had a minority report. Mustering its forces, the administration brought in sixteen Kansas officials, including the surveyor general, district attorney, and a judge. A provoked Wilson sought to persuade the Senate to pass a resolution asking the president why so many government employees were absent from their posts. Beginning March 1 virtually all of Senate time was devoted to the subject. By mid-March Wilson took over from Hale management of the Republican strategy. Particular attention was given to addresses by Whigs Crittenden and Bell, both longtime representatives from border states who condemned the process in Kansas. Seward deepened the antagonism with a personal and fierce attack on Buchanan and the Supreme Court. Bigler was embarrassed when Wilson asked if he had not in the summer in Kansas expressed his support for submission of a constitution to the vote of the people.[29]

One of the most widely reported speeches was by James H. Hammond of South Carolina, a newcomer who delivered a disunionist and extremely proslavery address. Hammond maintained all societies contain a class to do the drudgery. The South was fortunate to have the blacks for that. He countered Seward's assertion that the world had abolished slavery, declaring the South had kept it in name, but the North had its slaves. Northern laborers were the "mudsills of society." People in the North were hired for the day, uncared for at night. The South had actually elevated its blacks. The struggles for labor unions and homesteads in the North were marks of Northern wage slaves out to get what they wanted. Some historians have downplayed the speech as untypical of Southern views, but it was widely reported and praised in the slave states. Through all of these days, full of formal speeches unlikely to affect votes, Wilson was silent, but he was determined to use his opportunity to answer Hammond.[30]

Both Broderick and Hamlin defended Northern labor, but the primary reply to Hammond was delivered by Wilson, in what was perhaps his most famous speech. He was indignant. Hammond, Wilson charged, had not even examined the

Kansas issue, but had chosen to speak in defense of slavery. Wilson attacked Hammond's King Cotton theme, laughing at the idea that agricultural societies could control the economies and policies of the great commercial and industrial powers and proving neither Western Europe nor the North was dependent upon cotton production. If Southerners had more carefully listened to Wilson's presentation that day, they might not have been as disillusioned when European powers did not come to their support after secession. Wilson next showed that South Carolina had been in the vanguard of the defense of slavery and nullification of federal actions for decades, but he lamented that most other Southern states had once repudiated that position and no longer did.[31]

Wilson also attacked Hammond's claim for the superiority of Southern soil, climate, and institutions. He contrasted the two sections by examining a number of sources including census reports and statements of Southern leaders in their speeches and writings. Much as Hinton Helper was doing in his widely circulated study, *The Impending Crisis of the South: How to Meet It*, Wilson compared areas of life—manufacturing, commerce, education, literature, charitable institutions, and religion—and concluded the South was in these "a mere dependency of the North." The free states had seven times as many religious newspapers, twelve times as many scientific journals, and 90 percent of the nation's publishers. Of the authors in the *Cyclopaedia of American Literature*, 87 were natives of the slave, 403 of the free states. New York had more scholars in its public schools than all the slave states together; state laws forbade the education of more than four million Southerners (slaves). The free states had fifteen thousand libraries, the slave states seven hundred. Only in politics was the South superior. He quoted eminent men of two hundred years before to demonstrate how fertile the soil of Virginia and South Carolina had been and contrasted the soil of 1857, exhausted by slave labor. Yet New England farms were comparatively rich.[32]

After dealing with the contrasts between free and slave labor, Wilson turned to the effects of slavery upon the nonslaveholding whites, with statements by Southerners as his sources. He rebuked Northern Democrats for not defending laborers in their section. He noted he was the son of a manual laborer, now seventy years old. He had been a worker himself and he never felt "galled by degradation," as Hammond had characterized labor. He always had thought of himself as the peer of his employer. He had employed hundreds of workmen. Some of them then, others subsequently, possessed more property than Wilson. Some were better educated than he was or other senators were. Workers in Massachusetts iron mills received thirty dollars a month, he noted, while free workingmen in South Carolina were paid fifteen. He scoffed at Hammond's idea that slaves were well paid.[33]

Wilson had been "thorough," "eloquent," and "statistical," the *Times* correspondent reported. The speech assured his reelection. His array of facts was overwhelming, Bartlett of the *Springfield Republican* contended. The best speech Wilson ever made, one of Sumner's correspondents recorded. The *Tribune* agreed.

Wilson was "audacity personified, and yet he is not unparliamentary, or even uncourteous." The most effective address she had ever heard in the Senate, a Wilson admirer wrote in 1879. Seward and Wilson had delivered the most esteemed anti-Kansas speeches of the session, the *New York Times* correspondent later concluded. Nason and Russell, Wilson's 1870s biographers, emphasized his "bold invective."[34]

Wilson spoke on March 20, others followed. The situation became more complicated for the administration when Calhoun publicly admitted the contested election for members of the state legislature had been won by the Republicans; soon thereafter Buchanan removed him as surveyor general. The Senate majority had concluded it would accept no amendments, nor would it support a Crittenden substitute to provide for a third Kansas election under strict guidelines. The Senate passed the bill, 33 to 25. The three renegade Northern Democrats, plus Pugh, instructed by the Ohio legislature to vote negatively, broke with their party.[35]

The months of talking had reinvigorated the North. In the March New Hampshire elections, the Republicans won the governorship by an increased majority. The *New Hampshire Patriot* characterized the results as "overwhelming" and claimed Lecompton had destroyed the Democratic party in the state. Shortly thereafter the Republicans carried the governorship and legislature in Connecticut, by a rather large margin for that state. In Rhode Island the Republican gubernatorial candidate attracted more than double the ballots of his Democratic opponent, while the administration party was almost eliminated from representation in the state legislature. Municipal elections in the West also commonly went Republican.[36]

Throughout the East cooperation with Douglas and his wing of the party was encouraging Republicans to believe unity was possible and desirable. The Republican party was being foolish in not gaining Douglas's support, Connecticut Senator James W. Dixon told Gideon Welles in March. Union between Douglas and the Republicans was "complete," he wrote on April 2. Senators Fessenden, Hale, King, Washburn, Foster, Cameron, and one or two others agreed with him. Only Trumball was holding out, he reported. William H. Herndon, Lincoln's law partner, departed for Washington, New York, and Boston to investigate the political scene and protest against outside interference in Illinois political affairs. Herndon reported he saw a number of Republican leaders, including Seward and Wilson, and was satisfied with their views and their determination "to stem the rising tide of Douglasism."[37]

By March the Illinois party was united; while two-thirds of the Democrats had deserted the administration, they would not be permitted to capture control of the Republican party. Trumball was told to inform outsiders that they could not dictate to Illinois; Lincoln would be the Senate candidate. A month later Herndon remarked on the change in sentiment in the state since the winter; Illinois Republicans would rebel against outside interference asking for a leadership role for Douglas. The leadership, meeting in early April, determined to hold its own, separate convention. His supporters later the same month nominated Douglas for senator, but the Buchanan Democrats would not accept that decision and each faction uttered bitter remarks about the other. Furthermore, the Douglas supporters, by endorsing the 1856 Democratic platform, separated themselves from the Republicans.[38]

The House had been in chaos throughout much of the session whenever issues dealing with Kansas were considered. Arguments in both houses threatened to turn violent, with altercations between James S. Green and Cameron in the Senate and Grow and Keitt in the House. The administration, after Senate action, still hoped it could carry the House. Douglas supporters lost their jobs whenever the administration could use its influence effectively. Few legislative proposals in the nation's history have engendered such an outpouring of administrative time and energy. Among the opposition, Wilson "threw himself among the revolting Democrats. He consulted with us and encouraged us; he traveled far and near to effect co-operation and organization," Forney later recorded. He worked night and day on the Kansas question, his friend Jonathan Mann wrote. Wilson, Wade, Colfax, Burlingame, John Covode, and one or two others were authorized by the Republicans to confer with the anti-Lecompton Democrats. Douglas, of course, had the greatest influence with Northern House Democrats. Wilson had always regarded the result as close and had been aware of the power an administration in the 1850s had. A last-minute attempt to compromise in the House was defeated by the radical Southerners.[39]

When the House voted on April 1, a modified Crittenden proposal (sponsored by Representative William Montgomery of Pennsylvania) was substituted for the Senate resolution. The Lecompton constitution would be submitted again to the people of Kansas and if they rejected it, a new constitutional convention would be authorized. The administration and the Democratic majority in the Senate refused to accept the House compromise. A conference committee was agreed to only by the Speaker's casting his tie-breaking vote. The committee reported out a bill, partially the work of the Indiana Congressman William H. English, submitting the entire Lecompton constitution to the Kansas electorate. The bill promised a generous land grant and immediate admission, if the constitution were ratified, and denied the grant and established the requirement of 93,000 inhabitants for admission, if the voting results were negative. The bill established one set of conditions for admission as slave state, another for free, charged Howard of Michigan, a minority member of the conference committee. "A conglomeration of bribes, menaces, and meditated frauds," claimed Wilson. The government had already advertised thousands of acres of land for sale in July, and if the people of Kansas rejected the constitution, they would lose their share of the land sales, he added.[40]

It appeared the Democratic majority had found the solution. Walker and Stanton both urged passage of the bill. Even Douglas wavered, at first agreeing to support it, then retreating when Broderick, Stuart, part of the anti-Lecompton faction in the House, and his mail from voters all insisted he must stand firm. Wilson by April 23 was convinced the proposal would pass. He was critical of Republicans in districts represented by Democrats who had not been supportive and cordial enough to their political opponents. They failed to see the objective should be to deprive the Democrats of strength, he declared. When the Senate returned to the debate, Green, the committee chairman, naturally directed matters for the Democrats, but Wilson, who was not a member of the Committee on Territories or the conference committee, managed affairs for the opposition. In his speech Wilson reviewed Kansas affairs at length and with particular effectiveness, demonstrating how Buchanan had removed the honest officials and permitted the others to remain. He attacked those Democrats who had opposed the Lecompton constitution for four months and now advocated this proposal. He predicted the people of Kansas would reject the land bribe. Eleven of the twenty-three House Democrats switched to produce a 112 to 103 majority. Two senators changed their votes and the English proposal passed, 31 to 22.[41]

The English bill had enabled the administration to save face and retain the support of a majority of Southerners. But the long controversy over Kansas, particularly over the Lecompton constitution, both split the Democratic party and weakened it substantially in the North. The able Maryland Democratic leader, Reverdy Johnson, termed the administration's policy "extraordinary," discouraging to Democrats in the free states, and likely to engender "unfortunate results." Failure to submit the constitution to the people had been a "fraud." An even greater blunder, Johnson continued, was denouncing all those who had the manliness and honor to say so.[42] The Republican party had won new adherents. Wilson's prediction came true: in August the Kansas voters by an almost 10,000 majority rejected statehood under the Lecompton constitution. Kansas remained in territorial status with Buchanan-appointed executive and judicial officials and a populace and legislature dominated by Northern-oriented views. Kansas would not receive statehood until Southern congressmen began to leave Washington in 1861.

Since Wilson has been so frequently connected by historians with efforts to encourage Douglas to become a Republican or force Illinois Republicans to accept their longtime enemy as their leader and candidate for senator, a final word needs to be said about this subject. Wilson's cautious acceptance of cooperation with Douglas in December and January and his assuring Herndon in the winter that he recognized Douglas's character and motives have been noted. Even Trumball wanted to cooperate with Douglas at the time. But in the longer run the need to defeat Lecompton and the desire to strengthen the state party and advance its principles would be prioritized differently in Washington and Illinois. By March cooperation between the Douglas faction and the Republicans in Congress was extensive and almost daily, but only on Lecompton issues. Wilson was a leader in that. But Wilson recognized Douglas's duplicity. Most of those who have written about the matter have tended to make too general of statements, selecting a quotation from Wilson or others made at a specific time, especially Wilson's February 28 letter to Parker. These writers too often have ignored the development of events and the changes which would have occurred in a man's mind over time.

What was Wilson trying to accomplish in addition to the defeat of Lecompton? Lincoln's friend and biographer, Ward H. Lamon, declared that Wilson believed Douglas "devoutly." The question is, believed what? That Douglas would fight Buchanan and Lecompton? If so, Wilson was right. That Douglas would accept Republican principles? That is doubtful. Wilson was concerned about the 1860 presidential election; Illinois had gone Democratic in 1856; carrying it was critical for victory. If Douglas, with all his ability and influence, could not carry the state, who could, Wilson asked? Wilson later wrote in his history of the era that "we had to believe him to be in earnest, and that he would be practically fighting their battles in the coming Presidential contest." Douglas's repeated declarations to Wilson and others caused them to favor his return to the Senate "in the confident expectation that it would tend to divide and disrupt the Democratic party." However, when the Illinois Republicans made their position clear in April, when Douglas would not modify his stance on the issue of slavery in the territories, and when Douglas considered supporting the English bill, a wise Wilson should have recognized the limits of cooperation.[43]

Instead, Wilson appears to have concluded that splitting the Democrats was all important and that it could be advanced by reelecting Douglas. Herndon has been presented as undertaking only one investigative trip east, but he may have been there both in the late winter and again in May. He reported in May that Wilson, Banks, Greeley, and others still wanted Douglas back in the Senate. Newspaperman Z. K. Pangborn in 1860 also declared Wilson in 1858 believed the nomination of Lincoln was "a fatal mistake" and Representative William Kellogg of Illinois that same year provided extensive evidence that Wilson had wanted Illinois Republicans to endorse Douglas. Historian George Milton recorded eighty years later that Wilson "never became altogether reconciled to Lincoln's aspirations." But Wilson was not concerned about Lincoln; he sought a Republican victory in 1860, not 1858.[44]

Just when Republicans should have abandoned the Little Giant—after the Republican leadership took its position, after the state convention on June 16 attached to the platform the nomination of Lincoln, and after the near desertion of Douglas over the English bill—Wilson appears to have advocated the nomination of or acquiescence to Douglas by Illinois Republicans. Since election would be by the state legislature, that meant nominating Republicans or coalitionists willing to vote for Douglas, or permitting Douglas Democrats to run unopposed. Perhaps the acceptance of the English bill by a portion of the anti-Lecompton Democrats in the

House, prompting about one-third of the party in Illinois to sustain the administration ticket, motivated Wilson. When he wrote his history of the era, Wilson himself remarked how the nomination of Lincoln ended the possibility of union with Douglas, yet at the time Wilson continued to advocate changing the decision. In that history he did criticize the Douglas campaign as "pandering to the prejudice against color" and being strongly in favor of popular sovereignty. In any case, Lincoln's close associates, John C. Nicolay and John Hay, reported Lincoln never questioned the motives of those who sought to displace him with Douglas, but also never thought of following their advice or regretted he had not. Likewise, Representative Kellogg also pronounced Wilson's motives pure and credited him with being moved by conviction.[45]

Following its March passage of the bill to accept Kansas under the Lecompton constitution, Douglas persuaded the Senate next to consider the admission of Minnesota. One section of the proposal would have given the new state three House seats. Although this would have added three more free state representatives, Wilson contended the census had been faulty and that the number should be one. He eventually moved an amendment and, with only Trumball from his own party supporting him, got that provision added, 22 to 21. Before he voted for the final bill, Wilson expressed his disapproval of the state constitution's suffrage section. The former Know Nothing objected to unnaturalized citizens' voting; the abolitionist opposed the section prohibiting black franchise. Minnesota statehood, however, was held hostage in the House until the English bill was passed.[46]

Wilson played a curious role in another free state admission bill, for Oregon. When Douglas sought to take up the bill, Senator Andrew Johnson of Tennessee moved to postpone so that homestead legislation could be considered. This lost, with the vice-president breaking a tie vote. Wilson supported consideration while most Southerners, the Indiana Democrats, Bigler, and Trumball opposed it. A motion to postpone consideration until December lost 16 to 38. During the debates Wilson attacked the provision in the Oregon constitution prohibiting admission of blacks or mulattoes into the state, forbidding their owning property or making contracts. It was unconstitutional, inhuman, and unChristian, he declared. When asked how Massachusetts treated blacks, Wilson admitted prejudice existed in the state, but he praised blacks, reporting they held many good jobs and had played important roles in the state's wars. Wilson in the end joined those who had voted for postponement to oppose passage of the bill. He lost, 35 to 17. Massachusetts Republicans Thayer and Comins had no trouble voting for admission under these conditions. Garrison's *Liberator* subsequently praised Wilson's position.[47]

Wilson, who commonly supported most internal improvements, had a different position on the Pacific Railroad Bill. If Congress could not now agree, the bill was unlikely to be passed during the three-month session of 1858–1859. The measure was under the sponsorship of Douglas and William Gwin of California and advocated by Buchanan. The route was open, providing its western terminus be at San Francisco and its eastern near the Big Sioux and Kansas rivers where they emptied into the Missouri. Contractors would make the choice of route based on feasibility, distance, and economy. Claiming that Massachusetts and he supported the idea of the bill and did not care which route was selected, Wilson nevertheless argued that the nation was too much in debt to undertake construction at this moment; it would cost over two hundred million dollars and would not pay its running expenses for years. He doubted capitalists could be found to invest in it. Why pass it, he argued, if neither the government nor private sources would or could provide funds. In a sectional vote, with New Englanders and Southerners joining together, a motion to postpone passed, 25 to 22. Lawrence approved of Wilson's speech, both for its opposition to the expenditure of government money and for bringing the Northeast and South together on a vote.[48]

Both his desire for economy and his unwillingness to assist the Buchanan administration caused Wilson to object to several bills dealing with authorization of funds. Yet he was not recalcitrant. In December, for example, when the administration asked for authority to issue Treasury notes to cover debts, Wilson recalled that when Congress had last met the government had an overflowing treasury. The administration was not willing to recommend increasing revenue, just temporary expedients, he charged. He thought the solution was to increase tariff duties on iron, cotton, and woolen goods. A series of amendments, most of which Wilson supported, failed. While most Republicans voted against the bill, Wilson reluctantly supported it. He was willing to apply his belief in economy to his own state, opposing $75,000 to improve the defenses of Boston harbor. Throughout the debates on the annual Post Office appropriations bill, he sought to add amendments awarding printing and other consignments to the lowest bidder rather than as a result of patronage.[49]

Wilson had the sole responsibility in the Senate of defending the interests of Massachusetts. In May the Senate considered a bill which would repeal all laws or parts of laws allowing bounties to vessels employed in the bank or codfish industries. In his speech Wilson noted his constituents had half the vessels, half the capital, and half the number of persons engaged in cod fishing in the nation. He defended the bounties not as gifts to people but as promoting commercial activities and therefore being in the interest of the whole nation. Admitting the annual cost would be as much as $150,000, he maintained other areas of the nation benefited from special interest bills; the nation paid twelve million annually on duties to protect Louisiana sugar. Attempts by Hamlin to postpone the implementation date seven, then five years failed, 28 to 27; Wilson attempted to postpone it until 1862 and failed, 26 to 30. This was virtually a party measure, with almost all the 28 Democrats in favor.[50]

As the session drew to a close Andrew Johnson attempted again to secure Senate consideration of a homestead bill. Southern senators, however, were unwilling to support legislation which would encourage rapid western settlement. When Johnson finally called up the bill on May 27, a motion was presented to postpone until January. In a sectional vote, Northern Democrats and Republicans, including Wilson, were in the minority, 30 to 22. The two Maine and two Connecticut senators and Pennsylvania's Bigler joined the Southerners.[51]

Not all opponents of slavery were willing to trust to legal solutions the problems in Kansas. While a majority of Republicans in the territory had accepted Wilson's urgings to participate in the autumn territorial elections, John Brown had decided the best response was force. Brown sought financial support from eastern abolitionists. He had begun organizing as early as the autumn of 1857 and engaged Colonel Hugh Forbes, an English adventurer who had fought with Garibaldi in Italy, to help him. The men were too unlike; they quarreled, and Forbes left. In early 1858 Brown went east to visit Gerrit Smith. He wrote George L. Stearns, Frank B. Sanborn, Parker, and Higginson to help raise money and asked Howe, Stearns, and Sanborn to meet him. Only Sanborn came. Brown explained his plans and sought one thousand dollars. Recognizing the difficulty and character of the scheme, his listeners tried to disabuse him. Brown was unbudgeable. In March Brown visited Boston to discuss his plans to invade Virginia. A secret committee was to obtain funds and mid-May was established as the date. Forbes in the meantime went to Washington where, on the floor of the Senate, during a recess, he told Wilson of the wrongs Brown had perpetuated against him and warned him that Brown and his supporters should be disarmed. He also told Bailey, Seward, and Hale that arms furnished by the Massachusetts Kansas Committee were to be used by Brown for illegal purposes.[52]

Wilson's program of union, nationalism, and political and constitutional means to overthrow slavery was being challenged again. Concerned that Brown might attack Missouri from Kansas and at the request of Seward and Bailey, Wilson wrote to Howe on May 9, revealing what Forbes had told them, asserting this would hurt those who were working for the defense of Kansas, and asking Howe to recover the weapons. Stearns wrote the reply, maintaining that Brown was unauthorized to undertake any operation outside Kansas and that Brown had been urged a few days before to leave for the territory to help in the election campaign. He called Forbes "a disappointed and malicious man." A week later Howe assured Wilson prompt measures would be taken to prevent use of the arms for purposes of which "their subscribers of the fund would disapprove and vehemently condemn." Howe was being partially truthful, trying to convince Wilson that Brown was being controlled, while withholding the information that a secret committee of six was now cooperating with his schemes.[53]

The plans were not abandoned. On May 14 Stearns wrote to Brown, enclosing a copy of Wilson's letter, and reminded Brown he had the arms to defend Kansas and he should not use them for other purposes. That would provide proper cover. Brown, who was in Canada, had already heard of Forbes's Washington activities.

On May 24 the secret committee met in Boston, where they determined to postpone the attack until the spring of 1859 and sought to obscure the issue Wilson had raised by transferring ownership of the rifles from the Kansas committee to Stearns. Brown, a week later, got the word and was persuaded to cooperate, receiving custody of the arms from Stearns, five hundred dollars, and the promise of more money. He contended Wilson had intimidated the committee of supporters. Still, he departed for Kansas. Wilson could believe he had successfully prevented an unwise and unlawful action from occurring.[54]

The most interesting position of Wilson on foreign affairs during the 1858 session was his nationalistic stance denouncing British aggressions against American vessels in the Gulf of Mexico and Caribbean. British officers were overeager to halt the slave trade. A Senate committee investigating the matter reported the British had stopped American vessels bound from one American port to another and had searched American ships in Cuban ports. Hale, Seward, and Wilson delivered especially impassioned speeches, convinced that Southerners were maneuvering to represent Republicans as on the British side so that they could classify them as traitors and descendents of those who had participated in the 1814 Hartford Convention. Wilson declared his section of the country was more greatly concerned about the matter than perhaps any other. He was ready to adopt strong measures to halt these infringements and assure indemnities. He would support arrest of British officers who had violated American sovereignty. He used the opportunity to attack prostitution of the American flag by slavers off the coasts of Africa and near Cuba and demanded ships be sent there. The Buchanan administration was not doing enough to cooperate with the British in controlling the African slave trade, he charged. Wilson's tactics surprised the Democrats and forced them to proceed with more caution. Since the resolutions were only a reflection of Senate opinion, they did not much endanger the nation.[55]

As Congress worked towards a June adjournment, tempers flared. The long Kansas debates had engendered ill will and the rush to complete routine appropriations bills, interwoven with postponed and controversial issues—such as the Pacific railroad, a homestead bill, admission of new states, and creation of new territories—required lengthy sessions and exacerbated personal antagonisms. Even the weather was uncooperative; May was usually a beautiful month in Washington, but in 1858 was characterized by one rainy day after another. Douglas and Slidell had a major argument "over virtually nothing" in the beginning of the month and Green and Johnson engaged in angry dispute. Seward was irritated at the time he was spending trying to make peace between Republicans and Southern radicals. Yet when Senator Josiah J. Evans of South Carolina died, Wilson and Hale joined Hammond and Benjamin in tribute. Wilson had worked with Evans in committee and had come to "respect, to admire, to love him." Evans had done many acts of kindness to him, Wilson related. Parker was angry; Evans had assaulted Sumner, he declared. Sumner himself was hurt by Wilson's tribute. Wilson replied no one had regretted the Brooks attack more than Evans. A man could be kind and generous and still be a slaveholder. Furthermore, he and Sumner could not agree on everything.[56]

But Wilson also got involved in serious controversy. He was speaking on June 10 about the government being plundered in California when Gwin interrupted to remark Wilson spoke like a demagogue. Wilson replied he would rather be a demagogue than a thief. Gwin demanded an explanation for the remark and Wilson said he had none to give. Gwin called Wilson a liar and coward. Gwin, Southern-born, had been a member of the California constitutional convention and had then been elected the state's senator. Rumors were frequent about his political corruption, his quarters in Washington allegedly paid for by a company from which Gwin should not have received payments. The next morning Wilson received via Senator Fitch a challenge from Gwin. Wilson replied with almost the same words he had used in response to Brooks two years before. Seward again tried to be peacemaker. Gwin, having challenged, couldn't ask for an explanation or retreat. Wilson couldn't explain what he meant after having received a challenge. Seward offered to speak in Wilson's behalf, but the latter's friends believed that would ruin him. The New Yorker then attempted to draw up explanations in writing, but each was injurious either to Wilson, the party, or Seward himself. For two days Seward did little else and, with Congress about to adjourn, Gwin threatened to assault Wilson in the streets. Wilson would have to initiate any proposition and he did. Davis and Seward then called in Crittenden and the adversaries were persuaded to refer the matter for arbitration to the three.[57]

The controversy was settled when Gwin agreed he had made objectionable and unparliamentary remarks by imputing unworthy motives to Wilson, but these did not warrant Wilson's reply. The latter declared he did not imply any want in the personal integrity of Gwin, but had reflected upon his course in legislation dealing with California, which Wilson termed extravagant and wasteful. The *New York Post* correspondent commented that Gwin had challenged a man on record as opposing duels and had ignored others who equally condemned him, implying he really didn't want to fight. Wilson's constituents again supported his position.[58]

In the meantime, in Massachusetts, Wilson's strategy to create a permanent, majority party was on its way to fruition. The remaining antislavery Know Nothings were uniting behind Banks with the Republicans. Sumner was unhappy with the new governor's message, which he declared had no particle of antislavery sentiment in it. But Banks's actions were what was needed. Again both houses urged the governor to remove Judge Loring. Banks, in contrast to Gardner, complied. Buchanan then selected Loring for the Court of Claims and Wilson could not prevent his confirmation. Banks pleased some of the most influential party members, like Adams, Lincoln, and Boutwell, by inviting them to a session with legislative leaders to plan tactics. The governor proceeded to reorient the courts, with able, but distinctly antislavery, appointees. Longtime colleagues of Wilson were especially favored. Other veteran Free Soilers were rewarded, Swift with the position of pilot commissioner and DeWitt with that of bank commissioner.[59]

Sometime between 1857 and 1859 a division occurred between the radicals who tended to congregate around Bird and Andrew and the moderates who followed Banks's leadership. There had been divisions over the nomination of Banks for governor, the disunion convention, support for John Brown and Kansas activities, and how best to achieve antislavery objectives. The Bird Club dinners, attended by some friends of Banks, often were held at the Parker House at the same time as the Banks dinners. Burlingame and Charles Hale, editor of the *Boston Advertiser;* Phelps; Swift; and Train participated in the latter. Wilson attended both. But by 1860 Banks's influence was declining and with the nomination and election of Andrew as governor, the Bird Club would come to dominate Massachusetts politics for the succeeding decade.[60]

Up for reelection Wilson needed to be concerned about events at home. The problem was, as the state's only voice in the Senate, he could not be absent from Washington very long. He returned to Massachusetts for a quick trip in early May and repaired relations with Robinson. He confessed to the editor he had gone too far in his support of Know Nothings. "Warrington" admitted that while Wilson liked office, he was nevertheless one of the nation's most unselfish politicians. Less than a week after the special session of the Senate adjourned, Wilson on June 22 participated in a conference to lay plans for the party's future course. Many of the state's congressmen had been elected first as Know Nothings and returned for some of the same reasons Gardner had been supported by the Republicans in 1856. Damrell was in ill health and expected to retire; Wilson himself sought to replace Davis with his good friend Alley. He was warned to back off or he might lose the nomination for Alley and endanger his own chances for reelection. Almost everyone expected a renomination of Banks and reelection of Wilson.[61]

Unlike during the long congressional session of 1856, Wilson was able to employ his months away from Washington traveling widely over the commonwealth. He as usual attended the July 4 festivities of the Garrisonian abolitionists at Framingham. But he was unwilling to participate in an early August picnic at Waverly Grove, organized by Parker. Chase, making the best of opportunities prior to the presidential conventions of 1860, arrived in Boston in late July; Banks, Wilson, and four representatives honored him at a dinner. Wilson also participated in a celebration in Braintree July 29; while Adams would never have admitted it, Wilson's presence at an event in which Adams was delivering the major address supported his detractor's candidacy. Wilson assisted Buffington as well, with a visit to Fall River.[62]

In July the Republican and Banks-American state committees agreed to sign a call for a single September state convention. Alley, chairman of the Republican committee, maintained that was the best way for the Americans to save face. One political commentator noted that since 1854 the votes received by Know Nothings had declined from 80,000 to 51,000 to 40,000. In 1857 20,000 had supported Gardner, 10,000 Banks. Selection of delegates to the state convention confirmed the changes taking place. Swan, candidate of the Bird faction, and E. H. Kellogg, a Gardner man in 1857, were both chosen. When the convention assembled, Wilson was conveniently campaigning in Maine. The whole ticket was renominated and Wilson's reelection by the legislature was "enthusiastically endorsed." Two of Wilson's closest political associates were chosen to the most important positions on the new state committee, Alley as chairman, Claflin as secretary.[63]

Restless and ever willing to speak, Wilson began the fall campaign in Maine, making seven appearances in one county. For the first time Wilson was on a campaign with a female speaker, Susan B. Anthony. Kansas was making itself felt. The Republicans swept the state, electing the governor, all six members of Congress, thirty of thirty-one senators, and two-thirds of the lower House. Earlier the Republicans had swept Vermont. The party also did well in the October elections. It won minor state offices in Ohio by about 20,000 votes and captured fifteen House seats to six for the Democrats. In Indiana the party took eight Congressional seats, the Democrats only three. The Democrats, however, salvaged statewide offices. Both houses of the legislature were equally divided, but each contained several anti-Lecompton Democrats. Buchanan was clearly repudiated in his own state. Only two of twenty-five Pennsylvania congressmen would support him. While the state Senate would be almost equally divided, the House would be overwhelmingly opposition. The administration had suffered a "disastrous defeat," the *Boston Transcript* concluded. A victory for free labor, Wilson maintained.[64]

Wilson was especially concerned about New York, where national party chairman Morgan was running for governor. Wilson had hoped for a 100,000-vote majority and election of twenty-eight or twenty-nine Congressmen. That was impossible by mid-September, he declared, but money, workers, and speakers could still produce a victory. With amazing accuracy, he predicted the Democrats could attract between 220,000 and 230,000 votes. Thousands of Whigs would finally have to choose their new party and he feared many would become Democrats. Papers and orators needed to avoid attacks on the Americans, whose support was needed, he cautioned. Wilson's major speech in the state was delivered to a large audience on September 27. Two years before the people had been asked to rally around freedom, Wilson asserted, and New York by a majority of 80,000 had responded. Free men again had a duty to themselves and their nation. Every department of the government was under slave control. Contrasting the antislavery stand of the Founding Fathers with 1858, he declared the Democratic party had been the instrument of the change. In November Morgan won by about 20,000 votes. Both houses of the legislature were safely Republican. The Republicans captured twenty-seven House seats, the Democrats five.[65]

Wilson devoted most of his time to Massachusetts. He won special approbation for an October 13 address at Charleston. Jefferson Davis, who had spoken in the state, had been praised by the Southern press, the *Courier* and the *Post.* Wilson asserted that to listen to these reports, one would assume that the 108,000 men who had voted in 1856 for Fremont were ignorant and fanatical, without character or property. Quite the contrary, he declared. Eighty percent of the educated men in the state, 90 percent of the members of Protestant churches, had voted for Fremont. Other speakers had been ignoring Beach, the Democratic candidate for governor; Cushing; Hallett; and other opposition leaders, "Warrington" reported, but Wilson had launched an attack which should end "Democratic nonsense." The "best speech of the campaign," the *New York Times* correspondent characterized it; "it is wonderful how the General improves."[66]

Despite Adams's long distrust and dislike, Wilson was a vigorous and effective supporter for Adams's ambitions for Congress. Damrell, the Know Nothing incumbent, had been in ill health. Adams could not, as usual, blame Wilson for his failure to be selected or the difficulty in obtaining the nomination. But neither can the choice of Adams be credited to Sumner, as Charles Francis Adams Jr. later suggested. Sumner was abroad and in 1858 was not that breed of politician who could influence nominations in a congressional district. Wilson characterized the selection of Adams as a "triumph," the perceptive Pierce wrote Sumner. He immediately offered to speak in any town in the district where he could help. A ratification meeting was called for Dedham on October 26 with Wilson demonstrating his support in attendance. In his address Wilson paid tribute to Adams's early opposition to slavery. No man had more loyalty to the principles of 1848 than Adams. Wilson attacked the two hundred Massachusetts Whigs who had recently announced they were reorganizing their party for 1860. He noted they were opposing ex-Whigs Rice, Adams, and Burlingame. Boston business leaders were collecting money to elect Burlingame's Democratic opponent. Wilson launched a lengthy attack on conservatives who were uniting with Democrats.[67]

Wilson was busy almost every day from mid-October until the election, often speaking more than once in a day. Adams and Wilson frequently were on the same platform—in Dorchester on October 21, Dedham October 26, and Braintree on October 27. At the latter Adams recorded Wilson had given him "a profusion of compliments." Burlingame's district was the most severely contested. Democrats would clearly support their nominee, most former Know Nothings could back Burlingame, and so former Whigs were the crucial element. On October 22 Wilson, Banks, Burlingame, and Thomas Russell spoke in Cambridge. Faneuil Hall was the site of an October 27 meeting with Wilson and Hamlin among the speakers. The next evening in the same building Gardner severely attacked Burlingame and Wilson, especially condemning the latter's alleged tariff stance as not protectionist enough. Wilson replied the next evening at Cambridge and was critical of Gardner's temperance position. He poked fun at the former governor's political predictions and attacked his support for Burlingame's opponent, who was antitariff. A whole lineup of addresses in Burlingame's district were arranged for Monday before the election, with Wilson scheduled for three appearances. He concluded by proposing a vote of thanks to Gardner for endorsing the Democrat and thus helping elect Burlingame.[68]

The Republicans swept the state, electing their full ticket and all eleven congressmen. Victories for the latter ranged from 4,800 votes to Burlingame's 435. With only four congressmen renominated, and only Buffington and Burlingame veterans of the 1854 Know Nothing sweep, those opposed to the expansion of slavery had finally captured control of the Massachusetts House delegation. Banks carried every county, although he had only a plurality in three. The Republicans would control the Senate 37 to 3, the House 197 to 29. They would choose the next senator. The Republicans also won in Michigan, Wisconsin, New York, and Illinois. In the latter, however, because of apportionment, the Democrats would control the legislature and be able to reelect Douglas to the Senate. While the Democrats of Illinois captured five congressional seats to the Republicans's four, this was not a pro-Buchanan, but a pro-Douglas, vote. Most surprising was New Jersey, where the opposition won all five congressional seats and control of the lower house. The Democrats had never done so poorly in the North.[69]

After the election in the two Boston districts was assured, a procession went to the Parker House to honor Burlingame. Wilson and the reelected representative both spoke. Wilson chose to single out Robert Winthrop among the Democratic supporters. Wilson noted Winthrop had advocated retiring antislavery agitators. Rather than furloughing Burlingame, the people of Massachusetts had given Winthrop a permanent discharge, he maintained to loud cheering. He noted how over and over again they had invited Winthrop to join them and had suggested important positions for him. Winthrop had scornfully turned them down. He had condemned those who resisted the demands of the Slave Power, before which Winthrop trembled. He deserved retirement. The people then went on to the Revere House, where Wilson, Banks, and Pangborn spoke.[70]

To congratulate one another the Republicans gathered in Boston on November 11. Wilson was among the leaders present. Adams characterized the men as ranging from old Liberty party adherents to the most recent converts. He was amazed at the goodwill manifested towards him. Also to celebrate their victory the Republicans of East Boston held a banquet with Wilson the main speaker. In his address the senator looked at the South, which, he asserted, lacked free speech, a free press, and a free franchise. Slavery, he insisted, was intended to be temporary. But the South controlled the national government. He complimented those who had begun the antislavery movement and maintained they only had to continue agitating to be assured of success. He urged his audience to take all constitutional and legal steps to obtain control of the federal government. That would end slavery everywhere.[71]

Wilson had not recanted in his belief that Illinois Republicans should have supported Douglas. It was a great political mistake, he told E. L. Pierce. If they had sustained him, Douglas would have assured the Republicans the North as a unit and yet would not have been a leader of the party. Pierce, and most Northern Republicans, by this time did not agree. The Illinois political leader N. B. Judd was disgusted; he hoped Wilson was proud of his protégé. Herndon was more forgiving. When Wilson was reelected to the Senate, Herndon was pleased and wished him success.[72]

Before leaving for Washington, Wilson participated in several other activities. Giddings, in poor health anyhow, had failed to be renominated in his district of Ohio. Wilson said he could not become reconciled to the change. He urged Giddings now that he had less pressing duties to undertake a history of the antislavery movement. About seventy supporters gathered at the Parker House on December 2 to honor the veteran. Wilson, the presiding officer, spoke highly of his friend, terming him the man who had earliest warned others of the dangers of the Slave Power. The next evening Wilson prudently sponsored a dinner of men interested in the tariff so that he might benefit from their views. Lawrence had already sought his support for a Chinese commercial treaty. Wilson joined Pierce and A. G. Browne in urging Sumner to stay in Europe during the short session so that he would be prepared for the longer session in 1859–1860.[73]

16

Consolidation and Preparation for 1860

Although the second session of the Thirty-fifth Congress would be only three months long, the Senate took its time organizing and then adjourned between December 23 and January 4. Harriet did not accompany her husband this session, so Wilson lived at Willard's Hotel along with six of the Massachusetts House delegation and seven other senators. In his December 6 annual message the president expressed pleasure that the Kansas issue had been settled, asked for tariff revisions and authorization for a Pacific railroad, and adopted a bellicose foreign policy towards Mexico, Cuba, and Central America. Since the Northern electorate had clearly voted against the administration and the people of Kansas had settled the controversy there, Buchanan would have been well advised to make peace with Douglas and his supporters. Instead, the president favored isolating the anti-Lecompton Democrats. The senators in caucus quarreled over session assignments and finally Douglas, who had headed the committee since 1847 and who had made a name for himself in that influential position, was removed as chairman of the Committee on Territories. This decision was over the objection of not only Northern Democrats like Stuart and Bigler, but Toombs, Brown, Thomas L. Clingman, and Green. Douglas himself had gone to visit the South after the election and then continued on to Cuba, apparently waiting for his reelection by the Illinois legislature before proceeding to Washington.[1]

Wilson was returned to the Military Affairs Committee, but shifted from Revolutionary Claims to an area in which he had much more interest, the District of Columbia Committee. His first act after the Senate convened was to give notice of his intention to introduce a bill to appropriate one million acres of public lands for support of the schools in the District. He had introduced similar bills in the preceding two sessions. The previous May he had strongly supported a provision in an appropriations bill which would have provided $20,000 for schools in the district. Andrew Johnson called the provision unconstitutional. Congress had a terrible record providing for education, Wilson contended. As late as 1842 Washington had only two schools and two teachers; in 1858 it contained twenty-four schools and thirty-seven teachers. Yet only 22 percent of the children were in public schools. He insisted Congress needed to do more.[2]

The principal issue before the Senate during much of December and January was a Pacific railroad bill. It would authorize the president to contract for the transportation of the mails, troops, seamen, munitions of war, and other governmental needs and services on a railroad from the Missouri River to San Francisco. Wilson sought to amend the bill to limit the route to between certain parallels, so as not to be too far North or South, and twice agreed to change the location to obtain more votes. He supported an amendment requiring the iron rails to be American made. In his major speech on the issue, Wilson asserted the time had passed when Congress should be arguing whether to build a railroad or not; the only issue was the details. He had advocated a railroad in seventeen states during the past seven years, he declared. He accused Davis, when secretary of war, of drawing unjustified conclusions from reports of suggested routes. He also attacked Iverson for wanting a Southern route so it would be available to a possible slave confederacy. More importantly, Wilson could not imagine why private business would be willing to undertake construction, with no possibility of profit for years. He would have the government build on a central route. That location by that agency was the only way a railroad would get constructed. He noted how frequently privately-funded railroad business had failed in better locations, yet the improved transportation had benefited the people.[3]

Northern correspondents declared Wilson had never given a better speech and had badly damaged the prospects of a Southern or desert route. He had demonstrated a company as a carrier of passengers and freight simply could not pay its own costs. Most Republicans soon thereafter supported a Harlan proposal, which lost, to require the road to be further North than specified in Wilson's amendment. But Wilson's proposal also was defeated, 31 to 23. Wilson then got added an amendment to provide for land to a railroad in eastern parts, money rewards in central and western sections. Wilson even suggested $40,000 per mile in the center. Attempts, primarily supported by Southerners, to lay the matter on the table were beaten back, with Wilson among those wanting a bill passed. A combination of Southern and New England interests was preventing passage. Securing a majority seemed impossible. Simmons finally effected a substitution, opposed by Wilson, providing for construction of three roads; the strongest advocates of a transcontinental railroad declared it undid virtually all the efforts of six weeks. The bill finally passed with the substitution, with Wilson in the majority, providing $3,000 for expenses, advertising by the secretary of interior, and the results to be submitted to the next Congress. Wilson declared it was better than no bill.[4]

Wilson was also supportive of another measure, which would be passed during the Civil War, after Southerners had left Congress—a House bill to provide public lands to support agricultural colleges. Stuart had twice attempted to obtain Senate consideration in December, with Wilson in support, but had failed. In early February, with most Southern Democrats in opposition, Wade tried again, failed, then two days later succeeded, always with Wilson's vote. Buchanan vetoed the bill on constitutional grounds.[5]

When one remembers the controversy over Wilson's first election to the Senate, his reelection was anticlimatic. Obviously some of those who opposed his Know Nothing affiliation, his support of Gardner in 1856, or his maneuvering for a Banks nomination in 1857 would have preferred someone else. On the other hand, Wilson had for several years done the work of two senators and had ably defended Sumner's and the state's reputation. A Sumner supporter could not easily object to him. Old Whigs and Gardner-faction Know Nothings had little influence. In addition, who might those opposed to Wilson support? The old Adams-Palfrey-Dana group had limited influence; Phillips was dead, Allen's health not up to the demands of the senatorship. Furthermore, the Wilson faction controlled the governorship and the state party machinery. Even Howe, long disdainful of Wilson's principles and abilities and recently thwarted by Wilson's interference in John Brown's plans, had concluded Wilson was performing "very well . . . all things considered." There was no doubt Wilson would be reelected, Stone wrote Sumner in May of 1858. By September rumors circulated that Americans and Democrats were trying to unite on General Court nominations in order to defeat Wilson, but few politicians believed the Republicans could lose. One rumor was that Goodrich was to be substituted for the lieutenant governor, so that Banks, with an excellent replacement, could be sent to the Senate. That is doubtful; the antislavery group was too strong in the party to accept Banks as senator.[6]

Wilson's reelection was visibly an issue in the fall campaign. The Republican convention endorsed him. The finance committee, in seeking money, declared he had "by his efforts the past few years, earned re-election." Whittier in a public letter declared Wilson had shown himself equal to any emergency and had protected the state's interests. When the fall election was over, the *Boston Transcript* praised Wilson. His speeches in defense of the state and his attacks on political opponents had evinced power. "No politician in New England shows more knowledge of the popular heart or possesses greater ability as the leader of masses of men," it asserted. Wilson had worked in the campaign "with zeal and an ability that surprised even his own friends," the Boston correspondent of the *New York Tribune* reported. His future was assured and thus he was laboring for the election of others.[7]

The Massachusetts legislature had not been in session many days before it turned to the senatorship. The Senate on January 11 voted 35 for Wilson, 3 for Boutwell, 1 for Cushing, and 1 for Everett. There had not even been a caucus, so two Republicans felt free to vote for Boutwell. The House gave Wilson 190 votes, to 25 for Cushing, 9 for Amos Lawrence, and 2 for Ben Butler. Wilson's election was "expected," because of his rising national reputation, the *Boston Journal* declared. The *Atlas and Bee* was "gratified." No man had encountered fiercer opposition and better lived it down; "no man has suffered more from baseless prejudice, and surely none has better sustained and survived its burden," it continued. In forwarding official notice of the reelection, Governor Banks included a personal note, recalling how the two had met as members of the House in 1849 and had worked together for ten years. The governor noted that Wilson had the respect not only of his political associates, but of his opponents as well. Seward on January 17 presented Wilson's credentials of reelection.[8]

Life might be demanding in Washington, and his long battle to end slavery might be frustrating, but Wilson revealed his satisfaction with life in a January 13 letter to Harriet. Here was a man who liked challenges, who was comfortable with his personal life, and who had been overwhelmingly endorsed by his party for his political services. He was thankful to God for His goodness. "Sustained with such unanimity by my state, applauded by my personal and political friends, out of debt with a home for the wife and son I love so much and blessed with health and strength surely I ought to be grateful. . . ."[9]

When Douglas finally reached the capital, he participated in the Democratic caucus. He angered some of his former Lecompton supporters by strongly sustaining Buchanan's foreign policy. But administration supporters were not to be placated. Appointments in Illinois were made without consultation with the party's only senator. Charges inside and outside the Senate were insolent and intended to be intimidating. Douglas employed a bodyguard. The Democratic party was saved by the shortness of the session, however; by late February Davis, Mason, Brown, Hunter, Clay, Green, and Gwin had repudiated popular sovereignty and demanded that the 1860 Democratic platform guarantee protection of slavery wherever it might exist in the territories. They also demanded the return of fugitives. A candidate running on a popular sovereignty plank could not obtain an electoral vote in the South, Davis and Mason declared. Northern Democrats Douglas, Broderick, Stuart, and Pugh, on the other hand, defended squatter rights.[10]

With the failure to get effective Pacific railroad and agricultural colleges bills enacted into law, the primary matters before Congress in so short a session should have been passage of the usual appropriations bills and dealing with the government's lack of income. Instead, Congress was heavily involved with foreign affairs. Buchanan's request to send troops into northern Mexico was refused. So was another to use the army and navy wherever the president thought proper in the republics south of the United States. He sought thirty million dollars in negotiations for Cuba, but even the Democratic-controlled Senate would not approve that. Wilson was out of humor. Republican senators had come to this session hoping to avoid extraneous issues, he declared on February 9. When Buchanan became president the treasury contained twenty-five million dollars; it was now empty and forty million had been borrowed. Why were they debating Cuba when in three weeks they had 500 private bills to consider plus the appropriations legislation and need for retrenchment? Slidell, in charge of the Cuban bill, accused the Republicans of obstruction, which Wilson, among others, denied. Wilson charged Hunter and the Finance Committee with talking retrenchment and doing little. Eventually the Cuban proposal had to be abandoned. While he played little role with most appropriations bills, for some reason Wilson was very active in negotiating a group of amendments which sought to reduce post office expenditures.[11]

Wilson's public appearances were limited because of senatorial duties. His only speech reported in the newspapers was in early February to the hide and leather dealers of New York. Following adjournment of Congress, a special session of the Senate met from March 4 to 10 and nineteen senators, including Wilson, were sworn in. Wilson was unavailable to speak during the New Hampshire campaign. He could, however, participate in Connecticut, about which in late January he expressed concern and volunteered to speak. From March 22 through the first week of April Wilson delivered addresses in ten Connecticut communities. Although the Democrats poured money into the state and the Republicans at first appeared disorganized, the voters responded as Wilson had hoped. The Republicans, who sought to gain control of the last New England state, won the governorship, both houses of the legislature, and all four congressional seats. When he returned to Massachusetts, Wilson was one of the speakers at a Jefferson Day dinner at the Parker House.[12]

Wilson became a leader in opposition to limiting the franchise for the foreign-born. Under nativist influence, the Massachusetts legislature had considered amending the constitution first by providing for a twenty-one-year standard of citizenship before one could vote, then had turned to fourteen years, and finally to two. Massachusetts Democrats, led by Cushing, attacked the restriction. Republicans in the West, dependent upon the German vote for carrying their states in 1860, also urged defeat. It was the former Know Nothing Wilson who assumed leadership among Republicans against the proposal. Banks carefully dodged. In a reversal of roles, Adams supported the amendment on the grounds that native Americans, for all they had given the Republican party, deserved this limited concession. Wilson and E. L. Pierce invited Carl Schurz, a hero of the German revolts of 1848 and spokesman for the Germans of the West, to Massachusetts, ostensibly to participate in the Jefferson birthday celebration but actually to speak against the amendment. About two thousand people attended Schurz's Boston address, with Wilson introducing the guest. Schurz also spoke in Worcester.[13]

In general, however, Massachusetts Republicans tended to sustain the two-years proposal. The *Boston Bee, Boston Journal,* and *Worcester Transcript* urged ratification. Wilson promised Schurz and Pierce he would write a letter opposing the amendment. But something caused Wilson to delay or reconsider. Perhaps he agreed with Pierce that the proposal would be ratified anyhow. Schurz grew impatient and urged Pierce to "give Wilson no rest" until the work was done. On April 20, in a letter to Francis Gillette of Connecticut, who had expressed concern that Massachusetts adoption of the amendment would prejudice the party's success in the nation, Wilson took his stand. He noted that many others had a view similar to Gillette's. He agreed with that position. The amendment was intended to correct an admitted evil, men being hunted up to vote. He would support a one-year proposal and better enforcement of naturalization laws. Defining what the Republican party stood for, he pronounced the amendment a violation of equal rights. Antislavery was the great cause, he declared, and other issues should be subordinated to it. The two-years proposal was "indiscreet and ill-timed."[14]

The *Springfield Republican* praised the candor of Wilson's letter and agreed that he had ably presented the case for voting against the amendment. "Generous and timely," the *New York Post* characterized the epistle. The letter won general approval, the Boston correspondent of the *New York Tribune* reported. Wilson was a man of expedients, like most politicians, he asserted, but nothing he did would harm him as long as he remained faithful to the antislavery cause. Bailey commended Wilson's "wise and liberal course." The *Boston Bee* and the *Boston Atlas,* on the other hand, launched an onslaught on the letter.[15]

Amasa Walker replied, publicly attacking Wilson's position, precipitating a second letter vindicating Wilson's consistency. Wilson declared during his affiliation with the Americans he had not endorsed propositions that would degrade or make unequal any class of people. He had opposed the twenty-one- and fourteen-year proposals, the provision which would make foreign-born men ineligible for office, the reading-and-writing amendment, and the expulsion of foreigners in poverty. He noted he had traveled 40,000 miles in seventeen states during the past five years and had found few Republicans outside Massachusetts who would sustain the proposed two-year requirement of citizenship before a man could vote. But the issue did not seem to arouse most people. While more than 110,000 ballots had been cast in November, only 35,000 voters showed up to vote in this election, and the amendment was approved approximately 20,700 to 15,100. Western Massachusetts was opposed. In spite of the number of Democratic and foreign-born voters, the eastern counties favored the proposal. Western Republican papers praised Wilson's position. Banks emerged from the controversy politically damaged as a national figure; Wilson was widely praised.[16]

The lengthy time between congressional sessions, without a major state political campaign, provided Wilson his most leisurely period in years. He visited and spoke at important meetings frequently. With Governor William A. Buckingham of Connecticut he attended the conclave of the National Typographical Union in Boston in early May. Wilson had become so prominent a speaker that he was included on the program May 9 to 16 of the Grand Horticultural School Festival of famous orators. He continued to defy elite opinion by attending the New England Anti-Slavery Convention and speaking at the Church Anti-Slavery Society meetings, on May 25 and September 29, respectively. As senator he was invited to a dinner honoring the English politician Richard Cobden. With Thayer he visited the New Hampshire legislature June 14. On Independence Day he was the featured speaker at day-long festivities in Lawrence. Most of his lengthy address was the usual patriotic praise for the Founding Fathers and contrasts between Britain and the United States, but he also expressed concern about the dangers facing the republic in 1859, especially slavery and the possible reopening of the foreign slave trade.[17]

Because of his prominence, Wilson was either asked to assume certain positions or he chose to reap the political benefits of leading certain causes. Upon the death of Horace Mann, Wilson met with others to make arrangements for erection of a monument to the educator and former politician. Wilson pledged one hundred dollars from his own community. In Natick two meetings of testimonial were held, with the senator one of five appointed to a committee to obtain subscriptions. In the summer Wilson was elected captain of the Natick Guard; his ambition "must now be very nearly satisfied," the *Springfield Republican* commented. This was more than an honor, for Wilson directed his troops in an outside drill on September 24 and entertained at a levee and fair on October 12. While Banks and his Democratic gubernatorial opponent Ben Butler made major political capital out of the activities of the September state militia encampment, Wilson, Boutwell, the Executive Council, and others also visited the site. At the first annual meeting of the Massachusetts Temperance Society, in Boston on September 13, Wilson presided. On the other hand, Wilson was conspicuously absent from a celebration at the dedication of Webster's statue in the State House grounds three days later.[18]

Wilson continued to be concerned about the welfare of old friends. Gamaliel Bailey was in ill health by 1859 and Chase was seeking money to purchase a lot in Chicago for the publisher. When the Pierce brothers gave their fifty dollars and asked the stock certificates be awarded to Wilson, the latter signed his interest over to Bailey. He also was concerned to aid the continued publication of the *National Era*. He seldom asked for political favors, but in February 1858 he sought the intervention of Claflin and Alley with the executive committee of the state party and with the secretary of state to retain his former pastor, E. D. Moore, in office. He described Moore as his friend when he first arrived in Natick, when he had no other. Wilson had obtained Moore's appointment in the secretary's office in 1855. He suggested his six to eight weeks of campaigning entitled him to make the request. Since Moore owed the senator $230 Wilson had even more reason to want the minister to be employed.[19]

Wilson had decided on his candidate a year before the presidential election of 1856; in contrast, he was reluctant to back anyone for 1860. There would be time enough to decide, he told Schouler in February 1858. He at that moment preferred Chase, Seward was his second choice, and Banks was young enough to wait. In November he repeated his advice to do nothing, this time to Amos A. Lawrence, but he added he did not believe Seward would lead to "unity and victory." Republicans were not speaking about presidential candidates during the congressional session, Wilson in January 1859 told Stansbury. In the spring of 1859 the former-Whig Silver Greys were out to halt a Seward nomination and were pushing Banks as the best alternative. Wilson and some of his associates were unsympathetic to the Banks movement, and the two-year residency amendment controversy strengthened their position. By September, according to Pierce, Wilson thought Banks or Read would be the candidate. His fascination with John M. Read, a Pennsylvania judge and former minister to China, was a strange one. In an October speech he included Read's name among six possible candidates and in December he predicted that, if not blocked by Cameron, Read would be the candidate; Fessenden was the leading alternative.[20]

Wilson was doing what he could to aid the party. He continued to correspond with Robinson in Kansas. He believed a mistake had been made in organizing a Republican party before Kansas was admitted as a state. The Democrats appeared stronger than he had anticipated. He urged Robinson to make certain the Republicans won. Heavily involved in collecting funds for the Minnesota election, Wilson claimed to be responsible for $3,000. while the Massachusetts committee had obtained only $520. The money helped; the Republicans won the governorship and both houses of the state legislature and could anticipate election of a Republican senator.[21]

When the Republicans met in Fitchburg on September 20, Banks's renomination was a foregone conclusion. No contest developed for any state office. "Warrington" pronounced the convention as marking the final absorption of other elements into the Republican party and the restoration after more than a decade of a two-party system in the state. Wilson did not attend the meetings.[22]

In contrast to most years Wilson undertook no speaking tours for the September and October elections. This may have been because both Henry's father and Harriet were ill. The Republicans won in Iowa by a greater, yet small, margin and increased their gubernatorial majority and House numbers in Maine. More important, the opposition won the three minor offices at stake in Pennsylvania and captured control of the legislature by approximately a two-to-one margin. Wilson was in the state a few days before the election. In contrast to 1857 the Republicans in Ohio won the governorship and both houses of the legislature, assuring election of a Republican to replace one of the few remaining Northern Democratic senators.

The people of Kansas endorsed the Republican-sponsored state constitution. All in all, not only had the administration been beaten, but, since the state Democratic parties had emphasized popular sovereignty, so had the Douglas Democrats.[23]

In the meantime John Brown had again complicated the future of the Republican party and the life of Wilson. Brown had left Massachusetts in June of 1858 with his plans put on hold, but with money in his pocket. His backers set out to "decoy" Wilson, Seward, and others, while permitting Brown to go ahead with his plans. The weapons, once transferred to Stearns's ownership, had been given to Brown; the Massachusetts Kansas Aid Committee dissolved. Brown returned to Kansas, where he quickly engaged in whatever offensive actions against proslavery men he could. Perhaps most famous was his December invasion of Missouri, freeing slaves, looting homes, and killing one man. So outraged were the Free Staters of Kansas that Brown left and slowly transported the slaves to Canada. The enthusiasm for him in Northern communities through which he traveled and his doing something, while others could find little to accomplish in the Buchanan years, encouraged both Brown and his eastern backers to continue their planning for another offensive action.[24]

Brown's last appearance in eastern Massachusetts was in late May and early June, 1859, when he collected more money, lectured, and attended sessions of the New England Anti-Slavery Convention, at which Wilson was also present. He revealed to a number of listeners his intention to strike at a Southern community and instigate a slave revolt. At a dinner of about a dozen people, Wilson and Brown were introduced. The latter commented that he understood Wilson did not approve of his course and Wilson replied he did not; he regarded violence as injurious to the antislavery cause. Brown was equally firm in defending his actions. In July Brown moved to southern Pennsylvania.[25]

His plans are not clear, probably because they were irrational. With so few supporters he could accomplish little; he expected slaves to join him in numbers. He chose a difficult-to-defend site, in a heavily populated agricultural community, without cutting communications to the outside world, and with no or poor plans for retreat. In any case, on the night of October 16 the Brown forces took over the armory and arsenal at Harper's Ferry and captured some hostages. The townspeople themselves, plus men from neighboring communities, soon surrounded the area; state troops, and quickly United States marines, joined them. Most of the raiders were killed before the marines stormed the building. Brown was wounded, taken captive, and a week later placed on trial. A week of testimony resulted in a decision by the jury of guilt on all three counts. Governor Wise of Virginia permitted the sentence of hanging to be carried out, thus creating a martyr. As Governor Wise marched troops back and forth across Virginia, stimulating Southern anger, many Northerners praised Brown's motives. The South was inflamed, believing slaveholding communities thereafter would be subjected to raids by bands of assailants.

The response of Wilson and much of the Massachusetts press was similar. Brown's raid was "an insane and villainous scheme," the *Boston Transcript* declared. The leader was "monomanic." The folly of an insane man, crazed by the murder of two sons in Kansas, the *Springfield Republican* declared. The scheme was so foolhardy, in an area of too few slaves, it was incredible that it was inspiring so much fear. Important Democratic papers blamed both the Republicans and the abolitionists.[26]

Wilson was fearful Brown had caused untold damage to Republican chances in 1860. People would not understand what Brown had been trying to do and how few Republicans agreed with those tactics, he told Pangborn. Brown was a "d----d old fool," Thayer quotes Wilson as saying. He quickly sought out Garrison, whose nonresistant views made him an opponent of Brown's actions. Yet while the *Liberator* condemned the violence, Garrison assured Wilson the affair would be all for the best. The abolitionist sympathized with Brown's feelings for the slave and would attend a memorial service the day Brown was hanged. Wilson also visited Amos Lawrence, who condemned Brown's murders but nevertheless viewed him as brave and likely to die a martyr. As Know Nothing candidate for governor in 1858, Lawrence was unlikely to sympathize much with Wilson's distress over what Harper's Ferry had done to the Republican party. Wilson was indignant with Howe and Stearns, who had deceived him; he allegedly declared he did not care if the two were hanged.[27]

While Wilson had played little role prior to the October elections, he now was scheduled for a major speaking tour of New York. He began with an appearance before the Young Men's Republican Committee of the city on October 25. He had hardly begun, however, when he was felled with what was termed "vertigo." He fell back on his seat, but soon he was able to walk again, and he was led to his carriage and returned to his rooms at the Astor House. The illness was short-lived, for the next evening he addressed a large Republican rally in Brooklyn. The United States Senate, Supreme Court, and Democratic party were owned by slaveholders, he told his audience. He responded to John Cochrane's speech of the previous night, attacking the Republicans as behind Harper's Ferry. Cochrane, a nephew of Gerrit Smith, once had supported the irrepressible conflict concept, but now he was condemning Republicans on that theme. Wilson contended the Republican party was strongest where education, religion, and refinement flourished. The Democrats were more numerous where poverty, squalor, and bad morals existed. The Republican party was being denounced as hostile to the union, while Democratic governors were preaching disunion. It was Cochrane who was connected with Toombs, Slidell, Mason, Brooks, John Floyd, and Wise, Wilson asserted. Had Missourians not attempted to force slavery on Kansas, Brown would never have gone to Harper's Ferry. He appealed to the people of the state to stay Republican; they would elect a man in 1860 opposed to the expansion of slavery, whether it be Seward, Banks, Chase, Judge Read, Fessenden, or Wade.[28]

As Wilson continued his tour, he increasingly had to defend his party against accusations of being responsible for Brown. Harper's Ferry, Wilson contended at Syracuse, was the natural outgrowth of outrages in Kansas. Just as the French Revolution was a reaction to blind oppressions of government, so Kansas was inevitable because of government policies. If anyone were responsible for Brown, it was those "who drove him to madness by burning his dwelling, murdering his children, and justifying deeds of oppression upon his neighbors and friends." In Watertown Wilson spoke of the laborer and his conflict with the slave system. He noted how few voices remained in the South against slavery; where were the Bentons, Clays, and Jeffersons now, he asked? He recalled that Pierce had declared the slavery question ended in 1853 and then the South and Democrats had reopened it. He charged Buchanan had retreated from Walker's pledges and had tried to destroy all those who would not bow before him. He wondered how 350,000 slaveholders could control a nation, and suggested they could because Northerners let them. He contrasted the proslavery advisors of Pierce and Buchanan with those of Washington, who was surrounded by antislavery men such as Adams, Jefferson, Hamilton, Jay, and Morris. Wilson launched a strong attack against New York Democrats, many of whom had sustained the administrations in Kansas, jeered Sumner, and voted for the English bill. Between October 28 and November 2 Wilson spoke in Syracuse, Rome, Watertown, Geneva, Lowville, and Auburn.[29]

Wilson concluded his efforts with an address in Paterson, New Jersey, on November 4 and in East Brooklyn on November 5. In a throwback to the campaign in 1840, in which both men first emerged as powerful speakers, Corwin and Wilson were the primary out-of-staters imported by New York Republicans. On election day the Democrats carried three state offices, the Republicans others; more important, the Republicans won control of the state Senate 23 to 9 and the assembly 91 to 37. The once powerful Americans had made no separate nominations.[30]

The November elections in the North went well enough for the Republicans. They won in Michigan and Wisconsin, and the Democratic candidate for governor lost in New Jersey—although that party captured control of both houses of the legislature. Massachusetts had a dull campaign with a low turnout. Natick was now clearly Republican: Banks attracted over 400 votes, Butler 214, and the American-Whig candidate, 106.[31]

Wilson had returned home just before the elections and had delivered a lengthy political address to his townspeople; he included his thoughts about Harper's Ferry. A few of those present disagreed with their senator's evaluation of Brown and they invited the radical, veteran Garrisonian abolitionist Henry C. Wright to speak. Wright offered a resolution that slaves possessed the right and duty to resist their masters and that the North had the duty to incite them to resistance and aid them when they did revolt. Wright urged his audience to treat slaveholders as they would robbers, murderers, or pirates. He eulogized the raiders at Harper's Ferry. At the close of the address a resolution was adopted by what Wilson described as fifteen or twenty persons out of the seven or eight hundred who attended. The evening's events would soon cause Wilson trouble.[32]

Wilson and Harriet left for Washington on November 30. Hamilton remained in Natick. The Wilsons resided at a Mr. Joy's at the corner of Eighth Street and Pennsylvania Avenue. Wilkinson of Minnesota was the only other senator there; five House members, including Owen Lovejoy of Illinois and Sherman of Ohio, would also board with the Wilsons. Sumner finally returned, although he did not speak for months. Washington was a hostile environment; E. L. Pierce reported that bitterness between the two sections had deepened in the three years Sumner had been gone. Only formal and official recognition took place between most Southerners and Republicans; foreign ministers had to invite guests with extreme care. Mrs. Roger A. Pryor, wife of a Virginia Congressman, remembered feelings as so intense that Southern ladies, trained to be good conversationalists, found they could only speak about trivialities. The Buchanan-Douglas differences made socializing additionally difficult. Yet within the factions or political clans, life could be pleasant. In contrast to the Pierce years, the president and members of his cabinet gave lavish entertainments. Seward offered frequent dinner parties, including gatherings on Friday evening open to whomever wanted to call. Adams entertained often and Blair kept open house for Republicans.[33]

Wilson was gaining seniority; he moved to the second row in the Senate, with Wade on his right and Solomon Foot of Vermont on his left. In spite of the increasing number of Republicans, Senate Democrats again carefully crafted the major committees of seven members, only two on each committee of which were Republican; Wilson was reassigned to Military Affairs and the District of Columbia. The Massachusetts delegation of two senators and eleven representatives was now Republican rather than Know Nothing. Ten of the men were Massachusetts natives; ten had attended college, but only two Harvard; eight were lawyers; most were self-made men; and most were former Whigs.[34]

While the Senate was soon organized, the House was unable to select a Speaker. In the complicated political shadings of the winter of 1859–1860 party affiliation was sometimes difficult to determine. The *New York Post* tallied 113 Republicans, 92 administration Democrats, 9 anti-Lecompton Democrats, and 23 Southern opposition. For eight weeks the Republicans supported John Sherman, who was usually able to attract four or five votes of the needed majority. Wilson, as might be expected, got so heavily involved, especially in the first few weeks, that he had to deny charges of interference. The controversy had hardly begun when Representative J. B. Clark of Missouri proposed a resolution that no man who had endorsed the doctrines of Hinton Helper's *The Impending Crisis of the South* should be Speaker. Sherman had never read the book but was among almost seventy Republicans who had signed a circular seeking funds to permit wide distribution of it. Wilson also was a partisan of Helper. In his March 1858 speech answering Hammond, Wilson had cited Helper's work as an authoritative picture of Southern society. Senator Asa Briggs of North Carolina had replied on April 5 with an attack on Helper's character. To help clear himself of charges of theft Helper provided testimony and documents for Wilson, who in December 1859 in the Senate demonstrated that the author had been falsely charged.[35]

The work of government ground to a halt as the House debates continued throughout December and January. Southerners utilized obstructionist tactics, preventing votes. The House became an armed camp. The clerk was unable to maintain order. Southerners knew their best weapon was intimidation, Adams recorded. "We carry on forms of deliberation seated on a volcano." The Republicans were willing to accept John Forney, Buchanan's former primary newspaper supporter, as clerk. He would become an important addition to the cause. Forney maintained as an editor he had to be free to advocate whatever he thought desirable. He credited Wilson with being most responsible for persuading the party to accept their former adversary without pledges. In late January on the thirty-ninth ballot a combination of Democrats and Southern Americans almost selected a North Carolina Know Nothing as Speaker, but Sherman entered the voting to produce a tie. The Republicans then dropped their candidate and accepted William Pennington of New Jersey, previously a Whig, now representative of the People's party. He had been governor of New Jersey from 1839 to 1844, but was only in his first term in Congress. While Pennington turned out to be a poor Speaker, he permitted the organization of the House to be dominated by Republicans.[36]

In the meantime, on the second day the Senate was in session—even before it was organized—Mason proposed creation of a special committee to investigate what had happened at Harper's Ferry. This provoked a lengthy and broadening debate, with the Republicans emphasizing the people of the North held no sympathy for the invasion of Virginia. In supporting the Mason resolution Wilson declared the immediate response in the free states to the events in Virginia had been regret. Several misguided New York City newspapers had sought to make political capital out of the affair, which excited Northern opinion. He had spent two or three weeks in New York and New Jersey, where he found everyone was saddened by the attack. On the other hand, he declared Brown by his courage and words had engendered sympathy and Governor Wise had created sentiment for the condemned man by his mishandling of the affair. When Wilson had finished, Senator Brown asked about the resolution passed in Natick following the Wright speech. Had Wilson attended the meeting, Brown asked, and had he resisted passage of the statement by advice or any other action?[37]

Immediately following the Natick meeting Wright had addressed a letter to John Brown, sending copies to the keeper of the jail and to Wise. Wright told Brown about the resolution and added it included a provision that "resistance to tyrants is obedience to God." He noted both a United States senator and the postmaster had attended the meeting. Brown's death, Wright assured the prisoner, would urge others on to conflict. His execution would be the beginning of a death struggle. In his letter to Wise, Wright pointedly identified the community where the resolution was passed as the "residency of the Hon. Henry Wilson." Wright also dispatched on the same date the resolution and an inflammatory letter to the *Richmond Enquirer*. This time he added "though our Senators and Representatives in Congress dare not avow this as their opinion in Washington, at home, among their constituents, they countenance and sustain it by direct advocacy, or by silence." His remarks antagonized not only Southerners, but Northern Christians as well. The sin of the country would be taken away not by Christ, Wright asserted, but by John Brown. Christ had failed, Brown had shown greater power. A second letter to Wise accused the governor personally of killing Brown. Slaves had as much right to perpetuate murder, robbery, and rape on Southern whites as the latter had to perpetuate them upon blacks, the abolitionist contended. Wright soon published these letters in pamphlet form.[38]

Wilson saw little need to defend his own actions but recognized anew the Republican party had to stand in the public mind for union and a constitutional solution to the controversy over slavery. Wilson must have expected someone to raise the issue and was prepared to answer. He quoted from an article in the *Boston Journal,* written by Jonathan Mann probably for Wilson's subsequent use. Wilson contended the Wright meeting was not unusual; itinerant preachers often came to Natick. In Massachusetts speakers had a right to be heard and many Natick people, including Wilson, listened. "Senators should remember that the right to hold meetings, and to utter opinions upon all matters of public concern, is an acknowledged right in my section of the country." Wilson noted no one else spoke and few voted. Neither he nor others saw any reason to reply to Wright or to comment upon the resolution. Wilson further declared he had fully condemned the Harper's Ferry episode in many speeches during the campaign in New York and New Jersey and again only a few nights earlier in Natick. He also made known that the community's postmaster, a Democrat subservient to the Buchanan administration and the South, had said nothing at the meeting.[39]

The following day Trumball debated with the Southerners, but Wilson obtained the floor again. Southern arguments, he maintained, were based on some idea that the nation was in peril. He saw no danger; the invaders of Virginia were in jail or in graves. Slaves were bringing even higher prices. He reemphasized his condemnation of any man who justified the raid on Harper's Ferry, but reported sentiment in Massachusetts was almost unanimously sympathetic to Brown. Senator Alfred Iverson of Georgia was horrified that no one had rebuked treason. But the debate with Brown and Iverson was primarily over freedom of speech and Massachusetts's willingness for anyone to speak. Senator Brown claimed to believe in the right, but avowed no one in his state would be permitted to advocate the election of Fremont or Seward, because of what they stood for. Wright continued to harass Wilson, with a letter on December 10 providing his version of the conditions under which the Natick meeting had been called, what had been decided, and Wilson's role. Wright maintained the conclave was not advertised as a lecture and that Wilson was specifically invited to comment. People came to the meeting, Wright contended—undoubtedly correctly— not out of curiosity, but out of sympathy for Brown. He agreed with Iverson that Wilson's silence sanctioned the resolution. He denied statements by Republican senators that Brown's actions engendered "regret and condemnation" in the North. As proof, Wright cited speeches in the Massachusetts legislature and at a Tremont Temple meeting attended by three thousand people the night Brown was hanged.[40]

Wilson, of course, was reflecting the views of not only most people, but most Republicans of Massachusetts, in condemning the inciting of slaves to arms. For example, Sumner and Thayer were far apart in their degrees of racism, although both were opposed to slavery and both were Republicans. Sumner termed Brown "almost mad," believed "his act must be deplored," and yet admired the man's courage. Thayer recorded while a few congressmen would have placed Brown in an asylum rather than execute him, "not one" regarded his punishment as unjust. One man, an editor of Wisconsin's *Spartan Herald,* who had known Brown well for twenty-five years, aptly described him to Doolittle, Republican member of the Mason committee: "in many respects he was a good man, in others he was exceedingly peculiar and untoward." The editor employed such language as "visionary," "hopeful temperament," "shrewd," "kind," "sternly severe in what appeared to him duties," "devotedly pious," but with "peculiar views of Christianity." Wright represented a small minority. [41]

The Massachusetts press, on the other hand, experienced difficulty drawing distinctions. The *Natick Observer* termed Wilson's explanations an "apology which was condescendingly accepted" and criticized him for not telling his accusers to mind their own business. "Warrington" agreed that Wilson should have stated the facts of the meeting, but he was critical of the senator's implications that the machinations of Tammany Hall and Governor Wise's mishandling had prompted the pro-Brown demonstrations. Rather, Brown's piety, courage, and concern for slaves were what attracted Northerners. While Wright sought to keep the issue alive, the Massachusetts press rather soon forgot Harper's Ferry.[42]

Wilson believed he needed to respond to Wright and did so on December 27. He objected to being placed in the position in which Wright's letters to Brown and Wise had placed him. "I have no words to characterize this act of personal unkindness and of wrong towards one who has never wronged you," he told Wright. Senator Brown's question in the Senate was courteously asked, and courteously answered. In his explanation he had not cast aspersions on Wright. He repeated his version of what had happened and quoted from the notice for the meeting to prove it was a lecture. Defending his record of fifteen years of political life, Wilson asserted he had traveled more than fifty thousand miles in seventeen states, been often quoted in the press, and written extensively, and had consistently "stood for peaceful, legal, and constitutional opposition to slavery." "Warrington" criticized Wilson for defending himself in the "hated" *New York Herald.* The *Springfield Republican* termed Wright's attempts to implicate Wilson "mean and shabby," an attempt to "make trouble for him at Washington." Wright replied on February 2. His charges were still strongly worded, but more respectful and kind. The lecturer could not make Wilson responsible for Wright's own words simply because the senator was present, the *Natick Observer* declared in reporting the existence of Wright's new publication. "Everybody in Natick knows that Mr. Wilson did not agree with Wright, Wright knows it, and he has known it all along."[43]

The Garrisonians understood the distinctions Wilson and the Republicans were making; while opposed to the violent solution to slavery which Brown had come to personify, Garrison simply did not agree with Wilson's position. At the annual meeting of the American Anti-Slavery Society in January, Garrison attacked the Republicans. Among the party's governors, he contended, Morgan was willing to agree to the extension of slavery and Banks and Chase had ignored the subject entirely in their addresses to the state legislatures. The Republican party was "a time-serving, a temporizing, a cowardly party." It had spent too much time and effort simply opposing the extension of slavery. No Fremont supporter could have stood on Southern soil except at the peril of his life; "if Henry Wilson had dared to go down South and advocate his [Fremont's] election to the Presidency, he would have gone there as a man goes to his grave, and never would have come back to Massachusetts alive." Garrison admitted opposition to extension of slavery was better than nothing, but he could not find logic in making a distinction on the rights of man based upon geography. The Republican party was temporary and would have to be broken up and a higher position taken, he concluded.[44]

Wendell Phillips was more denunciatory and personal. James Freeman Clarke assured the senator that not all abolitionists agreed with Phillips. He understood one was much safer in Massachusetts than on the front line in Washington. Wilson replied that he was sensitive. He had tried to keep his mouth shut when attacked, but he had felt the injustice. As he looked back on twenty-four years, he claimed, he could not recall any day when he failed to take the strongest antislavery position he could to accomplish the most practical good. He simply did not have the time to turn away from the slave to attack those who attacked him. The Southerners were men of talent. They were determined to excite the nation and through fear defeat the Republicans in the fall. It required patience and self-control to stand against them.[45]

The Senate debated slavery for the first two weeks of the session under the guise of establishing a committee to investigate Harper's Ferry. Northern Democrats had rushed to persuade their Southern brethren of their condemnation and of Republican support; Wilson himself had sympathized with Brown in his Syracuse speech, the chairman of the Democratic Central Committee wrote

Virginia Senator Hunter. The South was buttressing its defenses against black insurrection or further outside attack with vigilant patrols, new legislation restricting black actions, and strengthened militias. Garrison was so irate at the new limitations on civil rights and human dignity that he issued a pamphlet titled *The New Reign of Terror.* Trumball proposed an amendment that would expand the assignment of Mason's proposed Harper's Ferry committee to include investigation of the 1855 attack on the Missouri arsenal. The amendment failed by almost a party vote, 32 to 22, and the Mason motion then passed 55 to 0, Wilson voting. Several days later (December 20) Wilson left for home, summoned because of family illness, but perhaps also anxious to persuade the Brown backers they needed to testify when called by the Mason committee. While there he lectured at the Natick Lyceum. The Senate, in any case, recessed for most of the period between December 23 and January 3. Then the upper house debated the contents of the president's speech and a motion dealing with several territorial governments. Wilson did not speak. He later recorded the Republicans had decided not to participate in debates over disunion and treason.[46]

The silence could not continue. Speaking in executive session to consider the nomination of Charles J. Faulkner to the French mission, Wilson charged the candidate had recommended resistance if a Republican were elected president. Wilson would vote for no man who professed those opinions. Doolittle concurred, calling the remarks treasonable. But Mason replied that most Virginians and most Southerners would agree with Faulkner. Clingman the same week declared the election of a Republican would be cause for secession.[47]

Brown introduced a resolution which provided Wilson the opportunity to deliver a major and carefully prepared speech on slavery. Brown would have the Senate instruct its Committee on Territories to insert in any bill for organization of a new territory a clause declaring the territorial legislature had the duty to enact laws for the protection of all kinds of property recognized by the constitution of the United States or held under the laws of any state. If that were not done, Congress had the duty to interfere and pass appropriate laws. Wilson began with an attack on slavery and a review of its history since 1620. He sought to prove the Founding Fathers were antislavery. He then demonstrated that the Slave Power controlled the national government and had forced Northern Democrats to bow to its demands in 1850 and 1854 and even to abandon popular sovereignty in 1857. Northern Democrats had lost influence in their own section and in party councils. The Republican party had been formed, he maintained, to "arrest the aggressive policy of slave propaganda, which is perverting the Constitution, subverting the institutions, disturbing the repose of the country, endangering the stability of the Union, and bringing reproach upon the American name." He followed with commentary on the expansion of slavery in numbers and power.[48]

Wilson continued by characterizing Southern Democrats as disunionist, quoting at length from their speeches, especially of those present. Clay interrupted to contend these were Southern, not Democratic, statements, but Wilson countered: while that might be true in Alabama, in many states many members of the opposition were not disunionist. He attacked Northern Democrats for not having rebuked sentiments of disunion and charged the Northern Democratic press was too busy assailing those who defended the union. He made an effective argument against the Democratic position, concluding with Andrew Jackson's statement, "the Federal Union, it must be preserved." Clingman replied by attacking Massachusetts and citing outrages which he claimed Northerners had committed against Southerners. Davis, attacked the concept of a Slave Power and characterized Wilson as a pupil of Garrison. The Southerners maintained Massachusetts was the offender by trying to nullify the Fugitive Slave Act.[49]

The next day Wilson, obviously angered, began again. He thought he had proved his case concerning disunion. He sought to demonstrate the Republicans were a national party, willing to stand on a platform which the Founding Fathers could have sustained. Not only would a Southern state in 1860 not send a Madison, Patrick Henry, or Luther Martin to Congress, because they were too antislavery, but not even a Jackson or Clay, for they were too nationalist. He defended his tribute to the Garrisonians, much as he differed from them on constitutional grounds. He then justified his use of the term "Slave Power," citing a long list of actions that spanned more than two decades, including limitations on the right of petition, interference by Southern postmasters with the mails, the Mexican War, refusal for months to admit California, the Fugitive Slave Act, repeal of the Missouri Compromise, invasion of Kansas, attempts to acquire Cuba, and South Carolinian limitations on the rights of black seamen. Wilson got into a lengthy debate with Hammond and James Chestnut over whether Massachusetts had committed any "aggression" which had provoked South Carolina's treatment of Hoar and whether that state denied rights to Massachusetts citizens. He especially came off well in a dispute with Davis. When he challenged any Southern Senator to say whether the union would be dissolved if a Republican were elected president, Fitch of Indiana replied by declaring the Northwest would separate from the Northeast if the slaveholding states seceded.[50]

The Washington correspondent of the *New York Tribune* reported the speech was a "forcible vindication" of Republican principles, an "unanswerable arraignment" of the disunion purposes of Southern Democrats, and it produced "a decided impression on the Senate." The correspondent termed Wilson's efforts of the second day as more effective than those of the first. Wilson "brought up one act after another, explaining, apologizing, and extenuating to the great amusement of the galleries." Another reporter from the same paper claimed Wilson had vindicated the position of his party "with great care." His reply to Clingman had been "terribly severe." When Wilson had told Southerners "with cool, measured tones, . . . and firm gesture," his finger pointing straight at Clingman, that those who had struggled so often in the past for their nation would do so again, the Senate chamber was "silent as a tomb." One of Wilson's "best efforts," the *Springfield Republican* editorialized. "Good" and "aggressive," "Warrington" commented, and needed after the "disgraceful Republican apologies of December." A "noble speech," one of Sumner's correspondents declared. It was the "most manly" that had been made, a friend of Dawes wrote. The *Springfield Republican* and the *Boston Atlas and Bee* predicted correctly the address would become an effective campaign document. So great was the immediate demand, the *Bee* published an extra and within a week 40,000 copies had been sold.[51]

The Mason committee investigating the John Brown affair called numerous witnesses. Wilson's advice to the conservative Lawrence was to keep quiet and answer questions only if requested. On the grounds they would be unsafe, Sanborn, Stearns, and Howe initially resolved not to go to Washington, although they would meet with the committee in Massachusetts. They wrote Wilson and Sumner asking them to propose that strategy; Sanborn believed Wilson would risk unpopularity at home if he did not sustain them. Stearns hoped Wilson would lead the fight to prevent the committee from requiring him and his associates to testify. Instead, at a meeting in Boston on December 24 Wilson expressed his anger about the Harper's Ferry affair and urged those asked to appear to comply. They would by law be required to testify, Wilson declared, although that appearance would relieve them of judicial charges in national courts. The committee would "cast a dragnet" over the North, he told Higginson; Mason expected to uncover "a great plot." Wilson was "behaving very badly" and acting in a "craven way," Sanborn told Higginson. Sanford fled to Canada rather than appear. Howe testified, hoping to redeem his reputation, but he was irritated that not a single senator had protested against instituting the investigation. Collamer, a Republican member of the committee, claimed Mason didn't want to uncover illegal activities beyond Brown's immediate supporters; he preferred just to embarrass the Republicans. Whittier hoped Wilson would make no apologies for his state, which had not been responsible for Brown.[52]

Wilson's testimony before the Mason committee on February 1 was brief. He explained Forbes's contact with him in May of 1858 and his intervention with Howe to prevent rifles intended for Kansas from being used for other purposes. At the time his greatest fear was that Brown might invade Missouri from Kansas, he avowed. After he was assured by Howe that money intended for weapons for Kansas was not being misused, Wilson concluded the Forbes-Brown affair was only a personal controversy and he thought no more about it. When asked if he had ever met Brown, he told of their encounter at the Parker House in May or June of 1859 and of his seeing Brown a few nights later at the Tremont Temple meeting.[53]

Testimony increasingly indicated that the Republican party and its representatives had not been associated with the Harper's Ferry raid, although few Southerners were open minded enough on the subject to pay much attention. Brown's so-called secretary of state, an Englishman named Richard Realf, was particularly helpful to Wilson. By March the committee was damaging its own cause in the North by broadening its net and asking extraneous questions. The *New York Times* objected to the discussion over the abstract rights of government that took place during the interrogation of Giddings and to questions about the Sumner-Brooks affair which arose while Andrew was testifying. On February 15 Mason sought permission to issue warrants for John Brown Jr., Sanborn, and Redpath. By a vote of 46 to 4, with Toombs and three Republicans opposed, the Senate agreed. Wilson did not vote. On February 21 Mason sought to add Thaddeus Hyatt to the list, kindling a debate, but again the Senate agreed, 43 to 12. This time Wilson and eight of his Republican colleagues voted negatively.[54]

Family and financial problems made life for Wilson more difficult. Harriet had been in poor health when they went to Washington. After a time in January under the care of Sumner's Philadelphia physician, she felt better. Yet she never was good enough to venture out in the evening and her life outside their quarters was limited to short walks, carriage rides, and routine social calls. Fortunately, she enjoyed living at the boarding house. She wrote occasionally for the *Natick Observer* about affairs in Washington, under the pseudonym "Melvina." In early February Wilson's father died and he hurried to Natick to attend the funeral. As usual, Wilson had to borrow money until his Senate pay began; since the House did not organize until February, congressmen were not paid until much later than usual. Wilson's relations with Adams were improving. As a freshman representative, Adams had little to do during the two months' struggle over the Speakership, so he attempted to enhance his own influence through entertaining and social contacts. He called on Wilson at his quarters in mid-December, an unusual step when one remembers Adams's long and harsh criticism. Since they were often invited to the same dinners, their relationship perhaps had to change. The first Senate address Adams ever went to hear was Wilson's slavery speech on January 25. Adams even invited his former adversary to dinner.[55]

As the presidential election year began, the direction of the contest was becoming clearer. The continued estrangement between the Buchanan administration and Douglas, and debates among Democrats in Congress encouraged Republicans to anticipate a divided opposition. In Massachusetts the remnant of the conservative Whigs might have opposed Banks in 1859, but their only chance of winning was to unite with the Democrats. The latter remained more interested in federal patronage than winning and their gubernatorial nominee Ben Butler was too radical economically and socially to attract the conservatives. The latter were revived by Harper's Ferry. Morton, Gardner, Clifford, Lincoln, Briggs, and the Appleton brothers called a meeting for Faneuil Hall on December 8 to demonstrate that many Northerners were not anti-South. In spite of his conviction that the South would be satisfied only with "total surrender" of Northern principles, Everett, who had not voted in three years, concluded the nation's situation was so critical he should reenter public life. The leadership in the deep South, however, recognized how few others these men represented. Samuel Hooper told Lawrence the Democrats had to be beaten nationally and dividing the opposition was no way to do that. Nevertheless, by spring Lawrence was convinced a new conservative political movement was possible, even without Democratic support. Crittenden would be his presidential choice; the Banks faction of Republicans might support the new party's gubernatorial nominee.[56]

Wilson remained undecided about the Republican presidential candidate. He was opposed to Banks, who had alienated the foreign vote, and perhaps also to Seward. As late as December he was still talking about Judge Read. On his return from his Christmas trip to Natick, Wilson made a curious call upon Winfield Scott in New York City. The general was a Virginian, Southern in sympathy, but loyal to the nation. Wilson proposed a public dinner in Scott's honor, which the general understood was to be the first step towards a presidential nomination. For some reason Wilson put the offer in writing. Scott, who barely knew the senator of five years, was impressed with Wilson's "manliness and conservatism." He quickly told Crittenden about the meeting. If he were again nominated for the presidency, Scott wrote, he would run on no platform but the constitution and his own record in public life. He declined the dinner in writing, declaring in the present state of the nation, he needed to stand aside from politics. Wilson did not pursue the matter further. He was opposed to Southern Whigs Crittenden and Bell. In congratulating Chase on February 5 on his election to the Senate Wilson claimed if he had his way, Chase would be the nominee.[57]

The Republican choice became complicated with the candidacy of Edward Bates, a Missouri Whig, endorsed by Greeley. The *New York Tribune* would accept either Chase or Seward, the leading nominees, an editorial said on February 20. But if they were not electable, as was often claimed, then neither were Banks, Fessenden, Dayton, Cameron, or Lincoln. Bates was the "coming man," Griswold told Wilson; he would unite the party and likely carry Missouri, Delaware, and Maryland. The party was weaker than in 1856, Griswold declared, and therefore had to attract moderates. When the Republican convention should be held became a controversial issue. Morgan asked the Executive Committee of the Republican National Committee to reconsider the June choice. Wilson claimed to represent most Republicans in Washington in advocating a change. The new Union party, scheduled to meet May 7, could convert thousands before the Republicans even chose their man, he wrote Morgan; in addition, it might ominously influence the Republican choice. The Democrats also would have six weeks to organize and flood the country with speakers. Wilson won his point and the convention was rescheduled for May 16. When the Massachusetts delegates were selected in March, eight favored Seward, two Chase, and two Banks. Ten of the twelve, however, were expected to vote for Seward on the first ballot.[58]

Wilson instigated an inquiry into the "outrages" engendered by slavery upon the rights of people and freedoms of press and speech; he hoped the information could be used in the presidential campaign. He asked Stearns on a Washington visit to find someone to undertake the work and David L. Child consented. Wilson was asked to provide names of reliable Southerners willing to furnish information.[59]

Anticipating that the spring state elections might influence the presidential choice, both the Republicans and Democrats poured in money and manpower. Franklin Pierce's New Hampshire had become so solidly Republican by 1860, congressmen did not have to be called from Washington to campaign. The incumbent Republican governor was reelected on March 16 by an additional thousand votes and both houses of the legislature were Republican by about two-to-one majorities. Connecticut and Rhode Island were another matter. The latter election was complicated by fusion tickets uniting conservative Republicans and Democrats. Both parties poured speakers into Connecticut. The people had the opportunity to hear all shades of political views. Wilson arrived on March 24 and in the week spoke at Newton, New Milford, Hartford, Woodbury, Winsted, Wolcottville, and Watertown. On March 27 Corwin and Wilson participated in Hartford in the largest political rally in the state since 1840. Wilson talked about the threats of disunion in Congress. He recalled that Cushing had advised the people of Maine to convert their property and money to be ready for a revolution. The people of New Hampshire had nevertheless voted their convictions and the Connecticut electorate should, too. The Republican party was committed to the union.[60]

The Rhode Island election was a Republican defeat, but not a Democratic victory. The more radical Republicans had insisted upon nominating their own man and others seceded. The Fusion governor candidate won by 1,400 votes; the Republicans barely carried the Senate; the Fusionists captured the House by a comfortable margin. With a large turnout Governor Buckingham squeaked through for another term in Connecticut over a strong opponent; the legislature would be controlled by the Republicans. Cities generally went Democratic while the Republicans carried the interior towns, in which Wilson campaigned.[61]

Congress, which was to adjourn in mid-June, accomplished very little. The House got to work after its lengthy two-month contest over the Speaker, but the Senate, engaged in almost endless debates, would consider an issue, then postpone it. The fall campaign was primary in most senators' minds. On February 2 Davis introduced seven resolutions which sought to commit the Democratic party to the doctrine that the constitution protected slavery everywhere, that the people of a territory had no power to prohibit or restrict slavery, that the national government was obligated to protect it in the territories, and that state laws interfering with the return of fugitive slaves were subversive. He met opposition not only from Douglas Democrats, but from Southerners who disagreed either with the philosophy, the practicality, or the wisdom of passing such resolutions in a presidential election year. The Democratic caucus engaged in heated debates over the proposals, then adopted them by a large majority.[62]

Wilson did not deliver a major speech on this issue. When it came time to vote, he asserted he could agree with some of the proposals separately, but because he opposed them as a whole, he would not vote for any. On one, recognizing the right of new states to be admitted whether they established slavery or not, Wilson attempted to substitute a statement that slavery was against natural rights and Congress had the duty to prevent its extension; he could secure only nine votes for that. After all the resolutions had been considered, Wilson, who had voted with fellow Republicans to replace one of Davis's proposals with one by Clingman, moved reconsideration. The Clingman substitute declared no need existed for Congress to protect slavery in the territories. Wilson had decided his party should not be responsible for any of the resolutions. Radical Southerners and Republicans joined to defeat the Clingman proposal.[63]

Kansas provided another cause for debate. The territorial legislature in February 1859 had passed a resolution calling for a constitutional convention. A free state document was subsequently adopted in July and ratified by the people in October. The Senate in February would not agree to admission, Douglas among those in opposition because the proposed constitution permitted blacks to vote and hold office. After the House passed an admission bill, the subject returned to the Senate. Sumner, who had not delivered an address since his caning, spoke on June 4 for four hours on "The Barbarism of Slavery." He virtually ignored the issue being considered. The speech was not conceived to win votes for Kansas. "Severe in denunciation" and "personal in application," the *Springfield Republican* report declared of the speech. While Adams thought the address had been "strong, clear and in part eloquent," he also termed it "fierce, harsh, and . . . calculated rather to harden the hearts of his opponents than to soften or convince them."[64]

Violence against Sumner was anticipated. Wilson, Representatives Burlingame and Lovejoy, and Senators King and Kinsley S. Bingham sat near him while he spoke. Wilson, Burlingame, and E. L. Pierce accompanied Sumner home. Wilson was armed, Pierce reported, and Burlingame may have been. Nothing happened immediately, but four days after the speech a Southerner appeared at Sumner's home and berated the senator. When ordered to leave, he promised to return. Sumner sent for Wilson. Shortly thereafter another man appeared, but when informed Sumner was not alone, the man would not enter. Later three additional men called and asked for a private interview. Wilson and several others guarded the residence. Wilson and Burlingame accompanied Sumner to the Senate the next day, and when Sumner dined with Adams on June 9 and 10, he had a bodyguard. The Washington mayor, who investigated the first threats, concluded the man had been drunk and Sumner was asked to accept an apology. South Carolina Senator Chestnut, in his reply to Sumner's speech, declared there would be no more caning and Southerners would ignore the address. The Senate on June 7 defeated 26 to 32 the Kansas admission bill.[65]

On March 31 the District of Columbia Committee, of which Wilson was a member, proposed that fines and forfeitures collected by the federal government in the District be given to the city of Washington for school purposes. In addition, the city authorities would be authorized to collect for the benefit of the schools a property tax which would be matched by the national Treasury, up to $25,000 per year. When debate resumed on the proposal, Wilson tried to attach an amendment, similar to a bill he had introduced two months before, which would donate one million acres of land to Washington and Georgetown, the proceeds from rental of the land to be available for instruction of free children. When Grimes of his own party objected to the idea, not wanting to take so much land off the tax roles, Wilson withdrew his proposal. Polk of Missouri sought to delete the matching provision. Wilson maintained the national government prevented half of the land in the city from being taxable and laid out such broad avenues it raised the cost of city government. With 51 percent of the city children not in schools, the national government owed the city aid and needed to help schools, Wilson declared. Polk's amendment failed only 20 to 22. Wilson had in January presented a petition from citizens of Washington, asking for the establishment of a District of Columbia normal school; it, of course, never got out of committee.[66]

Only a few days before, during debates on a homestead bill, Wilson had defended free blacks from attacks by Mason. The eight to nine thousand Massachusetts blacks, Wilson declared, were intelligent, industrious, and could read and write. They differed little from others. He thought this was true elsewhere in the Northeast. Because so much prejudice was shown against them, he was surprised they had done as well as they had. They had achieved remarkable progress in the previous twenty years. Where was there a more law-abiding people than the twelve to thirteen thousand blacks of Washington, he asked. They yearly improved their education and increased their property.[67]

The Republicans sought an amendment to the District school funding bill which would permit public money also to be used for black schools. As the debate continued, Wilson expressed anger that every time Republicans sought to help unfortunate blacks, they were charged with seeking racial equality. He did not think the two races were equal, but that had nothing to do with educating them. Wilson and Iverson argued over whether Southern laws prohibited teaching blacks to read and write. Wilson had the evidence to silence his opponent. Wilson then took on Davis; he contended that while mental and physical characteristics of the races made them unequal, they were equal in rights. Davis declared he didn't have to sit there and listen to doctrines of black equality. Wilson answered Davis either had to listen or leave the chamber. The two were soon engaged in a spirited exchange. Wilson was no gentleman because he insulted his associates in the Senate and would give them no satisfaction, Davis said at one point. Wilson's reply was "pungent and powerful," "defiant and determined," demanding an apology on the spot. Wilson "bore on" Davis "very hard," one correspondent reported. Wilson demonstrated the days of slaveholding domination were over, said another. Harlan and Wilson carried most of the Republican message.[68]

During debates on June 13 Mason of Virginia echoed Davis's judgment that Wilson was not a gentleman. The *Boston Transcript* noted that, since Hammond's characterization of Northern laborers as wage slaves, the farmers and mechanics of Massachusetts had been considering the Southern views about them. The legislature had its say, also. It passed a series of resolutions including commendation of Sumner's speech and thanking Wilson for "his able, fearless, and always prompt defence of the great principles of human freedom while acting as a senator and as a citizen. . . ."[69]

Wilson had special concern about the African slave trade. Although historians today would not agree with such a high figure, Wilson in his *History of the Rise and Fall of the Slave Power in America* claimed eighty-five vessels departed from New York City alone in seventeen months in 1859—1860, and that between 30,000 and 60,000 Africans a year were being transported out of Africa by American-owned vessels—most, of course, not to the United States. In any case, Republican newspapers at the time reported an increase in the foreign slave trade. On March 13, 1860, Wilson introduced a resolution to direct the Committee on Foreign Relations to inquire into the subject and report whether the treaty with Great Britain for suppression of the slave trade was being executed. A few days later he introduced two other bills, one for construction of five sloops of war for service on the African coast and the other to provide for better right of search of vessels presumed engaged in the slave trade. In April he introduced an improved bill, increasing the bounty to informers, relieving naval officers from liability when they mistakenly captured legitimate vessels, and broadening the concept of piracy. Commodore Andrew H. Foote wrote to the senator, agreeing with his objectives, and suggesting modification of the bill to make it more practicable.[70]

On May 21 Wilson called his resolution from the table, an action which permitted him to deliver a fifteen-minute explanation, printed in the record as a lengthy speech. He claimed the western world condemned the slave trade and the United States had once led efforts to end it. Now, however, some Americans were getting wealthy from the trade, juries were refusing to convict those accused of violating slave trade laws, and politicians were seeking to make the trade once again legal. In a history of American opposition, he quoted Southerners. He must not have expected his proposals to pass in the climate of 1860. The speech was soon issued in pamphlet form to be used in the campaign. The bill never came to a vote. In the closing days of the session Wilson sought to amend the naval appropriations bill, adding $300,000 to provide for three sloops to be used off the African coast to implement the Webster-Ashburton Treaty. When Toombs claimed the nation had enough vessels in African waters, Wilson responded by impugning the type and location of those vessels; he claimed to have the names of nine ships engaged in the slave trade since the first of the year. Mason attacked the treaty;

Green moved an amendment to abrogate it. Wilson declared the United States stood convicted before the world for its refusal to enforce its own laws against slavers. His proposal failed by a party vote.[71]

With the Democrats to convene their national nominating convention the third week of April and the Republicans the third week of May, an effort was made to recess Congress from April 18 to May 22. This failed 20 to 31 in a nonparty vote, with Wilson supporting the recess. The houses met, restricted in their conduct of business, the Senate sometimes unable to obtain a quorum. Wilson himself went home in late April. He was soon back in Washington, without Harriet, who was in poor health. He wrote Hamilton, begging him to be "very kind to your dear Mother," who was "very weak—she can not bear much trouble."[72]

Each side spent much of the year maneuvering on the issues, hoping thereby to attract votes in November. Republicans in the Senate sought to pass a House bill providing for free homesteads. Many Southerners wanted to kill the idea, an action Northern Democrats, including Douglas and those from Minnesota, could not permit. On May 10 Wade failed by a five-vote majority, with Wilson in support, to substitute the House bill. The latter was a "real homestead bill," Wilson proclaimed. But he wanted something, so he would vote for the Senate proposal. Southern Democrats filibustered half a day, deserting their seats, delivering lengthy speeches, interposing whatever obstacles they could. Hammond openly proposed preventing a final vote by leaving. Eventually the Senate approved the bill, 44 to 8. The Southern hope was that the conference committee of the two houses would not be able to agree, but just before adjournment, it did. The Senate on June 19 accepted the conference committee bill, 36 to 2. President Buchanan, however, vetoed the legislation. Southerners failed to prevent a veto override vote, 19 to 26, but Republicans and Northern Democrats together, 32 to 18, could not muster the two-thirds majority necessary for passage over a veto. In mid-June the Republicans also sought tariff revision, which by almost a party vote was postponed until December. Democratic Senator Bigler, of high tariff Pennsylvania, asked for reconsideration on June 20. Wilson called that political grandstanding, but voted affirmatively. Wilson was right. Under Senate rules, the motion was dropped from the agenda when Bigler left town and thus the Republicans were unable to move to take up the debate.[73]

Wilson presented resolutions on a broad range of subjects that indicate something of his value system. He sought to substitute imprisonment for life for the death penalty. He would restore the acts and duties of the office of Indian Affairs from the Interior to the War Department. He abandoned his opposition to the franking privilege, which allowed congressmen free use of the mails for official government business. He contended no clamor existed among the people for its abolition, it did not cost the government much money, and it provided the people the benefits of communication with their representatives. He also was willing to depart from his colleagues when he thought he was right. He joined the administration to sustain creation of a new regiment to prevent the drift into war with Mexico and better control the Indians.[74]

Wilson had an opportunity to take a position in a divisive shoemakers' strike in eastern Massachusetts in the spring of 1860. Mechanization in the 1850s had increased the capacity to produce shoes beyond demand. In a depressed market the manufacturers had cut wages and the shoemakers, including thousands in Lynn, more than five hundred in Natick, went on strike for two months. Some employers gave in; others stood firm and the strikers eventually, sometimes bitterly, returned to work. In Lynn police from outside helped maintain order and militia were called forth. Northern Democrats asserted the cause of the strike was a Southern boycott of Northern goods; they could easily side with the workers. The Republicans were more divided, although most Massachusetts leaders concluded wages were too low. Wilson had been a shoemaker himself, he had claimed to understand the aspirations and needs of the laboring people, and he had often contrasted the aristocratic Southern society which belittled labor with that in Massachusetts. Even his close associate Alley, the wealthy Lynn businessman, held a similar view about the harmony of capital and labor. The Free Soil and Republican parties had both tried to win the laboring man's vote. Philip S. Foner, in his history of the American labor movement, declared no party before in history had so consciously sought workers' votes as the Republicans in 1860. Yet Wilson avoided taking any position on the issues and never even alluded to the events in his speeches.[75]

17

The Election of Lincoln and Secession

The election of Abraham Lincoln and Hannibal Hamlin as president and vice-president of the United States precipitated secession. It mattered little, however, who the winners were, for those seven states which claimed to leave the union between December, 1860, and February, 1861, were responding to a Republican, not a Lincoln, victory at the polls. The election was a contest among four candidates. The Democrats assembled first, at Charleston. Since they expected to carry all the slave states, California, and Oregon, they needed only to add New York, or Pennsylvania, or Indiana and Illinois for victory. None of those four states, however, could be carried with a proslavery platform, and seven Southern state delegations resolved to withdraw unless the convention adopted such a plank. A nomination with a proslavery platform, however, was useless to Douglas. After a decade of controversy and a week of sometimes intentionally offensive remarks, the convention could find no statement on slavery acceptable to all delegations. Some Southerners withdrew. Although Douglas, ballot after ballot, obtained a majority, no candidate could secure two-thirds of the votes of all (including seceding) delegates. The convention adjourned to meet again in Baltimore. There, after a contentious week, more Southerners walked out. Douglas was nominated by those left. The bolters assembled at Richmond, approved a slavery plank, and selected Vice-President John C. Breckenridge of Kentucky as their presidential nominee.

Between the Democratic conventions, a new party had come into existence. Strongest in the upper South, attracting primarily former Whigs and Know Nothings, the Constitutional Unionists sought to avoid the frictions over slavery by ignoring the issue. The party could win only if, with the Democrats divided, no candidate obtained a majority of electoral votes. It selected two former Whigs, John Bell of Tennessee and Everett, as its candidates. Wilson emphasized in his history of the era that slaveholder Bell asked in his acceptance letter to be judged on his record, which included voting to protect slave property, favoring extension of slavery, holding slavery to be "in accordance with the law of Nature and the will of God," and claiming that emancipation was against the interests of both the master and the slave. In discussing the antecedents of the party's adherents, Wilson ignored any connections with the Know Nothings.[1]

Wilson was strangely detached from the Republican presidential process. Having abandoned Judge Read in the winter, believing Banks and Seward, and perhaps Chase, were likely losers, he did not advocate any contender. If he could consider Scott, perhaps other moderates like Bates might have attracted him. His speaking in Connecticut influenced his thinking. The Washington correspondent of the *New York Tribune* reported the state election had sobered most of those who participated in it; they had concluded they needed a conservative nominee for November. Wilson himself wrote on April 16 that the party could not win without the votes of "moderate men." On the one hand, he declared, the cause should "not be sacrificed to men or to the interests of any class of men"; the nominee should be fully committed to Republican principles. On the other hand, they needed men "not so mixed up in the conflict as to lose the support of the more moderate." In his history Wilson recalled the autumn 1859 and spring 1860 elections had not been encouraging. Shortly before the convention assembled, in reporting the leaders supporting various candidates, the Washington correspondent of the *New York Times* asserted Wilson, "with more impulse than prudence, will pitch in on his own hook for whoever will win." Wilson did not attend the convention.[2]

Wilson himself was occasionally mentioned for the presidential nomination. The Boston correspondent of the *New York Times* in 1858 predicted Wilson's senatorial reelection and added he would serve six years unless he received the presidential nomination. D. W. Bartlett, Washington correspondent of the *New York Post* and the *Independent,* compiled in 1859 a book of 360 pages containing sketches of prominent candidates for the presidency. Twenty-one men were included, including three of the four nominees. Lincoln was not mentioned. The length of the biographies was determined in part by the availability of information. Seward and Douglas naturally received the most space, forty-four pages, but Wilson was next with forty-three.[3]

Wilson recorded in his history that most people thought Seward would be nominated. So assured was the New Yorker of his selection, he left the Senate for home and told Wilson he did not expect to return. Wilson quoted Seward as telling him that, considering their antecedents and their good professional and personal relations, Wilson should have been supporting his nomination more than any other senator. Wilson replied that if he could elect a president he would choose Seward or Chase and he hoped one day Seward would be elected. But victory for the cause was most important and Chase and Seward had by their ability and long opposition to slavery antagonized too many people and awakened conservative fears in important states. Wilson reported Seward nevertheless was confident he would be nominated and elected.[4]

Historians have noted the vast difference between the first Republican convention in 1856 and its successor in 1860. In the intervening years the professionals had taken over in the states and the convention itself was conducted more formally. The meeting was held in Chicago. George Ashmun, who only a few weeks before had expressed to Wilson his surprise at being selected as a delegate, was made permanent chairman. The convention adopted a platform which opposed extension of slavery into the territories, attacked reopening of the African slave trade, demanded the immediate admittance of Kansas as a free state, and reaffirmed the truths of the Declaration of Independence. This platform was broader than that of 1856: it called for free homesteads, a Pacific railroad, internal improvements, and tariff revision. Seward remained the leading candidate.[5]

Lincoln's selection came as a surprise to Republicans in Congress. He was viewed as a thorough-going Whig, the Washington correspondent of the *Tribune* reported. Lincoln could carry Illinois over Douglas. Sumner was disturbed at the failure to select Seward; Adams asserted the party owed Seward the nomination. But Wilson enthusiastically supported the nomination. He reported in Washington the decision "takes well—the West will go with it with a rush." The Republican press was enthusiastic about Lincoln's availability and integrity. Republicans in Washington held a ratification meeting on May 28 before a large crowd. Wilson, among the eight congressmen speaking, asserted the Democrats had failed to nominate at Charleston and were torn asunder. The Republicans, in contrast, had selected a son of the soil, a man behind whom the masses would rally. He predicted a Lincoln-Hamlin victory. When Seward returned to the capital, the New Yorker wrote his wife, several Northern senators greeted him kindly, most others were embarrassed, having to make courteous remarks. Only Wilson, he recorded, went to him a half a dozen times, sat down with him, and waited for Seward to open a conversation on what had occurred at Chicago.[6]

Wilson returned to Massachusetts in late June. He had over a month to tend to quasi-official duties and rest before a hectic campaign. He, as often before, ventured into the lion's den by attending the annual Fourth of July celebration of the Massachusetts Anti-Slavery Society in Farmingham. The emerging black leader, H. Ford Douglass, in his speech was critical of the Founding Fathers and of the political leaders of the day, concentrating his attack on Lincoln and the Republicans. Among his criticisms of Lincoln was that Lincoln had introduced in 1849 a bill to abolish slavery in the District of Columbia combined with an improved process for the return of fugitive slaves in the federal district. Douglass also attacked Massachusetts Republicans, singling out Wilson for opposing black equality in his mid-April debate with Jefferson Davis. The presiding officer was about to introduce the next speaker when Wilson asked to be heard. He had admired much of Douglass's speech, but he needed to correct the record. He defended Lincoln, claiming his attempt, as representative of a Southern-oriented district of Illinois, to end slavery in the District of Columbia was commendable, not an act for censure.[7]

Wilson, who usually bore the attacks of the abolitionists with no response, also defended himself. He had been an antislavery man since 1836, he told his abolitionist audience. Because of his slavery stance, he had acted with and against all parties. He explained his racial views. He had answered blacks and whites were not equal, but he saw no reason to wrong a man because he was different from another. Whoever was not his equal intellectually or physically was in greater need of defense of his rights. All men were equal before the law. He noted he had attended abolition meetings for a quarter of a century; they agreed on hatred of slavery and love of liberty. He challenged anyone to report any unkind words he had uttered against abolitionists. Wilson also spoke for his party. While opposition to the extension of slavery might appear to be a limited position, Republicans could end slavery simply by no longer giving it favor, he contended. If Republicans controlled the national government, slavery would die. The party recognized state powers; slavery was a local institution. But there was no power in the constitution for the national government to promote it. He explained how difficult the last session of Congress had been, the hostility directed towards them, the accusations of treason, the determination of their opposition to create fear. But Republicans had stood firm and had been effective in resisting slaveholding domination. He was confident of victory in November.[8]

Wilson received a favorable response. Mrs. Foster asked Wilson how the Whig party of 1848 differed from the Republican of 1860. Wilson's saw little difference on the state level, but the Republicans stood for the Wilmot Proviso, a stance the Whigs nationally would never take. The Whigs of 1848 had no platform, he declared; in 1852 they took a position in favor of the Compromise of 1850. Garrison and Parker Pillsbury both good-naturedly replied to Wilson's statements. Pillsbury was pleased such an important Republican was present, praised the senator for his frequent attendance at antislavery meetings, and noted his own collections were always larger when Wilson attended Pillsbury's lectures in Natick. The correspondent of the *National Anti-Slavery Standard* also commended the senator for his frequent appearance at abolition gatherings and for the antislavery character and spirit of his Framingham remarks. Wilson had offered an excellent enunciation of Republican principles, the usually critical *Liberator* reported. Wilson four days later in Natick debated with abolitionists S. S. Foster and J. H. Stevenson on whether the national government had the constitutional power to abolish slavery in the states. Wilson, of course, asserted it did not.[9]

On July 10 Wilson began the political campaign in Watertown. In reviewing the platforms and records of the candidates, he declared Douglas had become so pro-Southern, even Jefferson Davis had to rebuke him. Douglas claimed when addressing Southern audiences that popular sovereignty would assure slavery in New Mexico, Arizona, and additional lands likely to be acquired from Mexico. Wilson predicted a Republican victory. Douglas, he asserted, would not get an electoral vote; more accurately, he maintained the contest was between Breckenridge and Lincoln. Douglas had just completed a swing through New England. Had he been around much longer, the *Springfield Republican* commented, he would have become antislavery; in his Springfield speech Douglas had praised New England migrants to Kansas, in contrast to his earlier denunciations of them. Wilson, noting the hope of Douglas supporters to do well in Maine, wrote Israel Washburn in early July how important it was for Republicans in September to carry his state by a good majority. Douglas, of course, was weakened throughout the North because Breckenridge Democrats controlled patronage and usually party machinery. Even before leaving Massachusetts Douglas told Wilson and Burlingame that Lincoln would be elected.[10]

On July 18 Wilson, the former circumscriber of Harvard, sat on the platform with Governor Banks, Douglas, Sumner, Everett, and members of the corporation for college commencement activities. How values must have changed for A. A. Lawrence to identify them as "all men of mark." That evening Wilson attended and delivered an address at a reception in honor of Congressman Charles R. Train. Wilson also joined Burlingame and Moses Kimball on July 23 for addresses at the dedication of a Lincoln-Hamlin Club headquarters in Boston. Before he left for New York he spoke July 24 at a celebration of two thousand members of the Sons of Temperance of twelve towns. In truth, Wilson was not needed in Massachusetts, which was solidly Republican. Antagonisms between Breckenridge and Douglas Democrats in the state strengthened the Republican position. But while the *New York Tribune* predicted Lincoln would carry New York by a 100,000 majority, campaign strategists were not as confident; they established an elaborate speaking program there and called for Wilson.[11]

Wilson opened in New York with Congressmen John Cavode and Roscoe Conkling speaking at Herkimer on August 1. The Democratic *Albany Atlas and Argus* reported only one thousand people showed up—one-third of them Douglas supporters—and pronounced the effort a fizzle. The next day Wilson, Cavode, and Representative William A. Howard of Michigan addressed in Batavia what a correspondent of the *Albany Evening Journal* characterized as the best meeting he'd ever attended. Free trains were provided to get people there. Wilson spoke with "fervor and eloquence." About ten thousand people showed up, another *Journal* report asserted; five other counties were represented, farmers left their harvest to attend, it was the largest and most brilliant political demonstration ever held in that county. No more than two thousand people participated, the *Atlas and Argus* contended. It was the wrong time of year to attract people in an agricultural area. Wilson spoke to women and children and empty benches. He "appeared much chagrined." Wilson continued on to Lockport and Buffalo. He closed before eight thousand people in Oswego on August 6.[12]

Before continuing his campaigning, Wilson returned to Massachusetts to rest. On August 13 he joined about four thousand others at a hastily called public reception in Boston to honor Seward, who had just arrived from speaking in Maine. Wilson, Adams, and Banks spoke, Wilson praising his colleague's strength in bearing misrepresentation so well. Wilson then hastened to Maine, beginning at a Republican county mass meeting in Bangor on August 16. Douglas had spoken there a few days before. The crowd was so large, Wilson addressed one gathering, Hale another. Twenty to thirty thousand people showed up, one newspaper reported; the size probably never had been equaled before in the state. Wilson first attacked the anti–popular sovereignty record of Douglas's vice-presidential running mate, Herschel Johnson of Georgia, and then compared Johnson's position to that of Hamlin. He undertook a long review of Douglas's support of or silence toward administrative activities in Kansas from 1854 to 1857. He insisted other interests of the country, including tariff reform and a Pacific railroad, had been sacrificed as a result of Douglas's stance. Douglas had claimed the Republicans, in supporting the 1857 Crittenden amendment, had abandoned their principles and endorsed his. Wilson declared Douglas to him had commended the consistency of Republican actions, but when asked why he had stated in his 1858 debates with Lincoln what he knew to be false, had responded that he had to save his political life.[13]

Wilson continued longer in Maine. The state offices and three of the six congressional seats were not in doubt; the other three were contested. The election-day turnout was the largest on record. Emory Washburn was elected by 18,000 votes, all six congressional seats were taken by Republicans, the state Senate would be Republican, 31 to 0, the House Republican, 128 to 23. Vermont had already gone overwhelmingly Republican, with about one-third of that party's adherents not even bothering to vote. Earlier, Democratic Oregon had repudiated the Breckenridge vice-presidential nominee Joseph Lane by electing a Republican legislature.[14]

When he returned to Massachusetts, after traveling more than four thousand miles and delivering nineteen addresses in four weeks, Wilson wrote Lincoln, expressing his concern about overconfidence and faulty organization. He was pleased with the mass meetings, but they were relied upon too much, he claimed. Too little progress had been made in the preceding ninety days. Work was needed especially in the smaller towns and school districts. Lincoln answered promptly, but hardly in a tone to inspire confidence. He appreciated what Wilson was saying, yet described the work as "irksome" and "dry" and, in a detached way, mentioned he did what he could to help with organization.[15]

Wilson returned to Massachusetts in time to have participated in the machinations to determine who would be the new governor. There is no evidence, however, he played any role; he did not attend the state convention. Banks had decided not to run again and accepted the presidency of the Illinois Central Railroad. For a time he tried to keep his decision quiet so that Dawes might be his successor; western Massachusetts believed it was entitled to the nomination. Claflin, chairman of the state committee, found out about Banks's plans and told others. Bird, Robinson, Pierce, and Sumner determined to push Andrew. Because the Republicans were assured of carrying the state, someone as radical as Andrew would be no hindrance to winning. The platform was more conservative than the nominees, emphasizing the party's devotion to the union, its recognition of slavery in the states, and its opposition to slavery in the territories.[16]

Wilson stayed in Massachusetts and New Hampshire throughout September. He began at Exeter on September 4, joined Burlingame at Wolfboro, New Hampshire, on September 6, and spoke in Boston; Manchester, New Hampshire; Lowell; Lawrence; and Southboro on successive days, September 10 through 14. With the Democrats so divided, Wilson used the Bowdoin Square meeting of September 10 to examine the Constitutional Union party, the only one, he charged, which would not take a stand on the issue of slavery in the territories. But if the platform was silent, members of the party had not been, Wilson continued, and he reviewed the position of its Southern adherents as exemplified by votes in Congress and by statements of Bell. He predicted the vote for the party in Massachusetts would not exceed that for Fillmore in 1856. The next evening thousands turned out for a torchlight parade and ratification meetings in the Music Hall. Although Wilson had spoken earlier in the day in New Hampshire, he delivered a lengthy address in the upper hall and repeated parts of it downstairs. The mission of the Republican party was twofold, he told the audiences: to overthrow the Slave Power and to secure the territories for freedom. Wilson attacked George Lunt, editor of the *Boston Courier,* the primary press supporter of the Bell-Everett ticket. Lunt was seeking coalition with the Democrats, Wilson contended.[17]

Mass rallies were scheduled almost every day the following week. On Tuesday, September 18, Wilson, Sumner, Andrew, and others spoke at Myrick's Station, near New Bedford. Ten thousand people attended. Wilson delivered a devastating attack on a recent speech by Stevenson in support of Bell. Stevenson had contended the presidential candidate regarded slavery as "a dreadful evil." Where had Stevenson been during the past fifteen-year battle against the Slave Power, Wilson asked. He cited a long list of actions in Congress: Bell had voted against the right of petition, sought admission of slave Texas, restricted rights of alleged fugitives, repealed the Missouri Compromise, and sustained the Border Ruffians. Bell's Northern supporters had faltered on the admission of Texas and in sustaining the Compromise of 1850 and had vied with Democrats in their fidelity to the Slave Power. The address was quickly published in pamphlet form. The next day Wilson gave two speeches, the first in Springfield. He went into detail about the principles of the Republicans towards labor, contrasting them with the Democrats, whose slavery advocates looked with scorn on workingmen. He severely criticized a recent Cushing speech in Boston. Characterizing the views of Douglas and Johnson as proslavery, he contended votes for Bell and Everett were wasted. Wilson delivered in Natick much the same speech he had given at Myrick's Station in Springfield; far more turned out than the Universalist church could hold.[18]

The party nationally was united as Lincoln's opponents for the nomination accepted the convention's choice and worked. Morgan was chairman of the Republican National Committee and Wilson's friend George G. Fogg of New Hampshire was an able secretary. One is impressed with the number of speeches made and the geographical distance covered by leading orators. Wilson the third week of September left Massachusetts to confer with the leaders in New York and to speak widely in New Jersey, a state virtually ignored in most campaigns. Wilson, Cummings, Stanton, and Forney agreed that Pennsylvania was not sufficiently aroused, Weed wrote Morgan on September 26; he feared the money the Bell supporters had been able to raise. Friends in Pennsylvania were alarmed, Wilson wrote Sumner in trying to get his colleague to speak more widely. Wilson would go there to look over the field for himself.[19]

Wilson, with his radical reputation, was a strange choice to speak in conservative New Jersey. No other Northern state had so consistently sustained state powers. While the Democrats lost the governorship in 1857, they controlled the legislature, except for the assembly one year, throughout the 1850s. The Republican party hardly existed, with Know Nothings, Whigs, and Republicans all in an Opposition coalition. Wilson stayed close to the New York City area. He gave three speeches, one reviewing the recent record of the Republican party, one discussing the presidential candidates, especially the record of Bell, and one contrasting the Republican support of the workingman with the Democratic advocacy of slavery. Wilson opened his state campaign in Jersey City, then between September 25 and 28 he delivered addresses in Morristown, Belleville, Patterson, and Newark. His Newark speech was number forty in the yet young campaign. Before returning to Natick on October 6 Wilson delivered a parting address to the Republican Young Men's Union Association in New York City. He emphasized what would happen to the rights of workingmen with a Democratic victory. The type of man sent by Congress from the South had changed, he asserted; that section was now represented by "bold, arrogant, domineering public men" who defended slavery as a positive good. When Northern Democrats sold themselves to the slaveholders, the party had ceased to advocate the rights of labor. Vermont and Maine had spoken; he predicted a Republican victory the next week in Pennsylvania.[20]

Most contemporaries agreed that, with the Republican victory in the October state elections in Indiana and Pennsylvania, Lincoln would become president. As diverse political leaders as Everett, Cushing, and the Alabama fireeater William L. Yancey expressed that view; so did the Democratic *New York Herald* and the realistic *Springfield Republican.* In a large turnout Andrew G. Curtin won the Pennsylvania governorship by more than 30,000 votes. The state Republicans swept both houses of the legislature and elected eighteen national House members to six Democrats. In Indiana, state offices went Republican by about 10,000 votes, congressional seats would be 7 to 4 Republican, and the legislature would be safely Republican. Democratic senators Bigler and Bright would not be reelected. In Ohio the decision was less impressive, the Republicans electing thirteen out of twenty-one congressmen. The most optimistic hope for the anti-Republicans for November was a unity electoral ticket in New York. Wilson's withdrawing from his scheduled engagements in New York therefore seems strange.[21]

The reason was not Wilson's ill health, for during the three weeks before the presidential election he was actively engaged in Massachusetts. This activity may have been unnecessary. Lincoln was going to carry the state, only two Boston congressional districts were in doubt, and many others, including Sumner—who would not campaign outside Massachusetts—were available for speaking. Wilson began at a mass meeting of between four and five thousand people at Harmony Grove, Framingham, on October 11. Four days later he delivered his now perfected lecture on the workingman's vote to a large crowd in East Boston. The next evening he sat with Burlingame, Rice, Adams, and others on the platform to view a monster torchlight procession of between eight and ten thousand people. A visit of the Prince of Wales occupied Wilson's attention for the next four days, including a reception on October 17, a grand ball on the eighteenth, and accompanying the prince on the Portland train as far as Salem on October 21. Important as these events might have been to the son of an alcoholic farmer, they were not pressing enough to have distracted Wilson from the campaign trail had he been really needed.[22]

The congressional contest in the Worcester district was a problem for Wilson and many other Republicans. Unwilling any longer to tolerate Thayer's conservatism and racism, the party there had made another nomination. Thayer ran anyhow. Wilson was disgusted with Thayer's congressional stance, but reluctant to interfere. With two weeks left before the election, first Boutwell, then Wilson, attacked Thayer, and others soon followed. Wilson then went to New York City to consult on and assist with organizational matters. En route on October 23 he addressed several thousand "greasy mechanics" and "mud-sills" in Bedford, Westchester County. His advice to Sumner for the final week of the campaign in Massachusetts was to concentrate upon the Boston congressional districts. He returned on October 30, confident his party would carry New York and New Jersey and win all the congressional seats in Massachusetts.[23]

The electorate was ready to decide. Wilson's remaining campaign addresses were at Natick, Woburn, and Roxbury, October 31 and November 1 and 2. He predicted Lincoln's election, but at the last minute became concerned about New York. Wilson's last campaign day was spent at a series of meetings in Boston to secure more votes for congressional candidates Rice and Burlingame. He attacked fusion efforts among the other parties to defeat the Republican nominees. Lincoln was elected nationally with 180 electoral votes to 72 for Breckenridge, 39 for Bell, and 12 for Douglas. Douglas, however, was second in popular votes, with 500,000 more than Breckenridge. In Massachusetts Lincoln secured 106,000 votes to 34,000 for Douglas, 23,000 for Bell, and 6,000 for Breckenridge. More surprising were the results in some other states. Lincoln obtained 63 percent of the vote in formerly Democratic Minnesota, 56 percent in Pennsylvania, 54 percent over three opponents in Connecticut, a 13,500 majority in Indiana, and a 50,000 majority in New York. In Massachusetts the gubernatorial candidates were within 2,000 votes of the presidential. Lincoln received a majority in every county but Suffolk and a plurality there. The Republicans captured 38 of 40 state Senate races and did equally as well in the House. Burlingame was the only Republican to lose a congressional race, that by a few hundred ballots. Thayer was defeated by 2,000 votes.[24]

The Republican press was, of course, jubilant. Northern opposition papers were tempered in their response. The *New York Herald,* which had been extravagant in its predictions of disunion in the case of a Lincoln victory, now wanted the dust to settle and people to forget politics and busy themselves with their jobs. The *New York Express* spoke of citizens' duty to make the best of a new situation. The Trenton, New Jersey, *Daily True American's* apprehension was tempered by the knowledge Lincoln would be "bound hand and foot—with both branches of Congress against him"; that should calm the nation. The Democratic *Boston Post* claimed the closeness of the election would force the new administration to be moderate and conciliatory. On the other hand, reports immediately circulated of meetings in the South to consider secession. Douglas had been fearful of Southern secession and had campaigned in the border states from July on, as much against secession as for the presidency. After the Pennsylvania state elections, he risked his health by traversing the lower South to forestall disunion. But within three days of the election, South Carolina called a secession convention. Mississippi, Alabama, and Georgia were astir with secession advocates.[25]

In Boston the Republicans celebrated on November 9 with Wilson among the speakers. He was angry that Burlingame had been defeated by so few votes, especially because of false charges of drunkenness. But, he rejoiced, the country, which had been controlled by the Slave Power—which had destroyed the Whig party, corrupted the American party, and used the Democratic party—would now be returned to what the Founding Fathers had intended. He praised Lincoln and spoke "defiantly" about Southern threats of secession. "Go on, if you dare," he said to the South. The Republican party had won with principles and they would demonstrate to the world they could stand by them. Four nights later Moses

Kimball entertained Wilson, Andrew, Alley, Adams, Burlingame, Gooch, Rice, and Claflin, among others, at a political dinner to discuss the nation's situation. The Republican press in the state and nation seemed to be ignoring events and attitudes in the South. No cause for panic, the *New York Times* editorialized; South Carolina would stand alone. The *Springfield Republican* agreed. Trumball believed Southerners were up to their usual threats; there would be no secession or war. Welles called the threats "harmless ebullitions of excited demagogues." Seward expected Southern unionists would quiet the secessionists.[26]

Wilson later wrote that Republicans, while enthusiastic about their victory, recognized its limits. The Senate remained Democratic, they had failed to carry the House, and the Court was dominated by Southerners. Slaveholders, he continued, better understood the significance of the election: an executive, armed with patronage, could accomplish much. Cushing, in a major address at Newburyport on November 26, charged the North, especially the Republicans, with responsibility for engendering revolution, but at least he was realistic enough to assert that the nation was drifting towards destruction and that the lower South would not retreat. He attacked Wilson for declaring in his Boston speech that the Republicans would crush the Slave Power under their feet. On November 23 a Republican levee in Cambridge honored the senator. In his remarks Wilson was willing to repeat his Boston statement, claiming the opposition was trying to misrepresent Republican beliefs. He did not mean to say the Republicans had their heels on the South, only on the Slave Power, he explained.[27]

Yet prudence demanded the victors also be cautious. For the first anniversary of the hanging of John Brown, some of the abolitionists intended to hold a commemorative meeting. Although invited to speak, both Wilson and Andrew declined. Ignoring an opportunity to explain his absence by his congressional responsibilities, Wilson in a letter reaffirmed his hatred of slavery and his determination to use all constitutional means to end it by prohibiting it wherever Congress could and by persuading others to alter their mistaken views in its favor. He credited Brown with sincerity of motive and courage, but condemned his invasion of Virginia. Wilson was "utterly opposed to all appeals by whomsoever made, to force and violence." Since they lived in a government of constitutions and laws, friends of the slave should appeal not "to the rifle, nor the pike" but to "the heart, the conscience, the reason, and the enduring interests of the people of the slave states, upon whom rests the responsibility of slavery in the States." Blaming abolitionists for the problems of the nation, a broadcloth crowd, led by Amos Lawrence, disrupted the meeting. Police sided with the antagonists and the mayor closed the hall. Mobs appeared at speeches of Wendell Phillips on both January 20 a February 17, but Governor Andrew and local authorities made certain peace was maintained.[28]

Wilson and Harriet ate Thanksgiving dinner on November 29 with their family, and then left Natick for New York City. On December 1 they settled at the

Washington House along with Senators Clark of New Hampshire and Bingham of Michigan; thirteen House members also lodged there, none from Massachusetts. Harriet had agreed again to write for the Natick paper. Wilson, of course, was concerned about the makeup of the first Republican government and the strategy his party would pursue in this short winter session. On the day he arrived, he quickly consulted Seward. The latter, and his chief associate Weed, through editorials and letters, had been encouraging a conciliatory tone towards the South. The *New York Times* and many other Republican journals also urged concessions. Yet when Weed argued for restoration of the Missouri Compromise line, a clear retreat from the party's platform, the anti-Republican *New York Herald* characterized his proposal as insufficient. When Republican senators caucused, Seward was asked if he supported Weed's opinions. His response was that that each man was independent of the other, a lie. The caucus declared it would make no compromise with men or states that were violating the constitution or the laws. But the New Yorker was able to persuade the meeting to adopt a conciliatory policy, including silence about the major sectional differences over slavery and, instead, attention to public business.[29]

The Senate's opening session was, according to the *Times* correspondent, marked with decorum and calm. After listening to the president's message the next day, Clingman delivered an attack on the North and was chastised by a dismayed and eloquent Crittenden. The Republicans remained silent. Most Northern newspapers regretted Buchanan's failure to rise above politics in the crisis. His address was "an arraignment of the Free States," declared the moderate *Boston Transcript*. Seward, who feared Hale was determined to respond, asked Wilson, Adams, and others to dissuade him. Wilson reported back Hale would not reply, but Hale did, noting Lincoln might be a minority president, but so were Polk and Buchanan, and warning the losers of the fall election that they either had to submit or face war. Amazingly, Sumner kept quiet throughout the month. The House, with Republicans badly divided, responded to the president's message and the crisis with creation of the Committee of Thirty-three, a member from each state, to consider the crumbling condition of the nation.[30]

When the Senate reassembled on December 10, Powell of Kentucky proposed a resolution to create a special committee to study the state of the union. During the next two days Northern and Southern Democrats debated about the slavery issue. While Iverson and Wigfall condemned the North in unparliamentary terms, Davis was more dignified. Still, United States senators were voicing their determination to destroy the union. The Connecticut senators responded so moderately that many of their colleagues were unhappy with them. By mid-December, with secession conventions called in a number of states, something needed to be done to halt the increasingly obvious direction of Southern actions. The *Springfield Republican* and the departing Governor Banks urged that Massachusetts repeal its Personal Liberty Laws as an act of good faith, but doing so would have produced little change in

Southern public opinion. Adams, who was assuming leadership of House Republicans on the Committee of Thirty-three, asked Wilson on December 16 for his views; he did not record what answer he got. In any case, the Senate passed the Powell resolution for the special committee. Vice-President Breckenridge selected five Republicans to the Committee of Thirteen, Collamer to represent New England.[31]

Wilson was quiet during these weeks, following the caucus advice to make no Senate speeches. E. L. Pierce many years later listed Wilson among the senators who stood firm. Some Republicans were weak, Wilson wrote Chase on December 15, most were strong; they had to stand by their principles. Because of their nonresistance beliefs, their desire to be separated from slavery, or their unwillingness to force a people to remain in a union they no longer wanted, a number of leading Northerners—including Howe, Whittier, Clarke, Garrison, Rockwell Hoar, Pierpont, and Greeley—spoke about allowing the seceding states to depart. House Republican moderates delivered conciliatory remarks; Sherman proposed solving the problem by admitting all territories as states. Guarantees of return of fugitive slaves or compensation for their loss, extension of the Missouri Compromise line to the Pacific, and security for the interstate slave trade were all acceptable to some Republicans. Massachusetts itself was concerned; in the December municipal elections coalition or Democratic candidates won in Boston, Springfield, New Bedford, Lynn, Newburyport, and Worcester.[32]

In his history written more than a decade later Wilson blamed Northerners for encouraging secessionists to believe they could get away with their plans. "They would never have ventured upon the rash experiment" otherwise, he asserted. Men like Horatio Seymour, Franklin Pierce, and Fernando Wood had declared civil war would occur in the North if the Republican administration attempted to coerce seceding states. Wilson also was critical of the too moderate stance of Weed and Greeley. He described four classes in the North: (1) Breckenridge supporters who would have agreed to the demands of the secessionists, (2) mainly Douglas and Bell men who favored new concessions and more compromise, (3) Republicans, "representing largely the mercantile, manufacturing and monied interests, who were in favor of making calm and conciliatory appeals to the excited exponents of Southern opinion," and (4) most of the Republican masses who adhered to the principles of the party platform, believed in union, and supported the authority of the government, including putting down rebellion by arms, if necessary.[33]

The president-elect and the majority of the Republican senators were in agreement. Lincoln had generally remained silent. He endorsed a late-November speech by Trumball, conciliatory in tone, but offering no concessions. He adopted a similar view in private conversations, some of which were widely reported in the press. Wilson wrote Herndon, asking for assurance as to how firm the president-elect would be. Herndon replied on December 21 that his law partner was "a man of heart . . . yet of strong will" who could be unyielding where principle was involved.[34]

Wilson devoted considerable time to composing an answer to Cushing's late-November speech. He began with an excellent review contrasting Cushing's opposition to slavery in the 1830s with his position in 1860. Wilson effectively demonstrated with election returns that Pierce's former attorney general was discredited in his own state and spoke for virtually no one. At a time of crisis, Wilson asserted, people expected statesmanship and instead they got a political response from a former leader. Wilson was willing to concede his remarks about crushing the South had been "unpremeditated, unguarded," but charged Cushing had twisted their meaning. He also replied to Cushing's declaration that the Republican party was opposed to states' making decisions concerning slavery by citing statements of Seward, Lincoln, and himself. Wilson examined the 1860 Republican platform and demonstrated both Seward and Lincoln had publicly sustained it. Cushing was unjust and unwise to charge Wilson with efforts to override a state's authority to allow slavery, when few politicians had been as consistent and as outspoken in recognizing that power. Wilson in his letter very ably recalled how in the press, in the Senate, and in public addresses he had consistently defended the doctrine of states' powers and disavowed aggressions upon the rights of states to regulate their internal affairs. An "emphatic crusher," the *Atlas and Bee* declared.[35]

Governor-elect Andrew had hoped to stiffen Northern backbone by a trip to Washington soon after the session opened, but illness prevented his going. He joined seven other Northern and eastern governors in New York City on December 20 to urge the party to make no compromise of its principles, then he hastened on to Washington. He met with those of the state's House delegation who had not gone home. On Christmas eve he conferred with Wilson, Sumner, Trumball, and Doolittle. He was asked to continue his antislavery position and stand firm. Republicans by then were less uncertain what stance to take. Andrew returned to Massachusetts convinced he should prepare for the worst while avoiding any action by which he or his state could be accused of instigating further secession or promoting war. Why Wilson remained in Washington as long as he did, and why he decided to make a quick trip home, is not clear. In any case, he was in Natick, was involved in consultations with colleagues, was called on by several Constitutional Union men, and was back in Washington by December 30, declaring sentiment was against compromise and in support of enforcement of the law.[36]

Wilson was able to be a part of planning strategy for the party in Massachusetts. Governor Banks delivered an unusual departing speech in which he called for the repeal of the state's Personal Liberty Law, and Benjamin R. Curtis drew up an address, signed by former governors Gardner, Clifford, and Washburn, among others, asking for the same action. The party leadership knew where it stood. Andrew was firm but dispassionate in his inaugural address and opposed to repeal.

Speaker Phelps and Senate President Claflin, longtime Wilson associates, emphasized Massachusetts's willingness to submit to judicial decisions, but its determination to guard the liberties of its citizens. Privately from Washington another close associate, Alley, told Bird, "a revolution is upon us. . . . Now is the time for stout hearts & clear heads. . . . This union must be preserved & maintained—if it shall cost rivers of blood. . . . I would not be rash—but firm." At Seward's suggestion, via Adams, Andrew called for a special celebration January 8 of the birthday of Andrew Jackson, who had stood up to Southern threats during the nullification crisis of 1833.[37]

On December 20 the South Carolina convention adopted an ordinance of secession. The votes in some of the elections demonstrated much more opposition to secession than the subsequent decisions by the conventions. Between Mississippi's action on January 9 and Texas's on February 1, Florida, Alabama, Georgia, and Louisiana by large convention majorities claimed to leave the American union. The states agreed to meet at Montgomery, Alabama, on February 4 to create a new nation. Within three days they had drawn up and adopted a provisional constitution, and on February 9 they chose Jefferson Davis as their new president.

The executive branch of the government was vacillating and uncooperative. Buchanan had so alienated himself from Republicans and the Douglas-majority wing of his own party in the North that he could not function effectively as a president in a crisis. Always influenced excessively by his cabinet, he found it unable to agree on advice. Southern members and the aging and often inert Secretary of State Cass resigned. Attorney General Jeremiah S. Black became secretary of state and Edwin Stanton was appointed attorney general; with Joseph Holt, recently promoted from postmaster general to secretary of war, they urged greater action by the president. To reenforce federal troops at Fort Sumter in Charleston harbor, Buchanan was persuaded to send a chartered steamer, *Star of the West*, which, on arrival on January 9, was fired upon and retreated. The army commander in the area, Major Robert Anderson of Kentucky, and the South Carolina governor arranged a truce. In the next three months secessionist military strength in the Charleston area grew while Buchanan and Anderson pretended they were preserving peace and maintaining the *status quo*.

Wilson's own analysis of the crucial winter of 1860–1861 in his history, while admittedly written long after the fact, is revealing. The period was marked by a "confusion of ideas, the conflicts of purposes, and the lack of any well-defined plans that received the advocacy and support of any considerable number," he declared. He quoted Representative Montgomery as declaring day after day was devoted to speaking and much of what was said only increased the nation's problems. Wilson wondered whether a generation of hearing about human rights had educated very many people. He asserted that three factors were basic to understanding the period. The first was the dominating belief in the South in slavery and its preservation. One wonders whether those who today think compromise should have been possible sufficiently give weight to that factor. Second, according to Wilson, was the steadfast faith in the North in union. Events of the next four years were to demonstrate how pervasive that was. Third, as Wilson saw it, were the people involved. Some were ambitious or sought revenge. Others lacked firmness, persistence, and wisdom. How much better we might comprehend the months he was discussing if only he would have told to whom he was alluding and what they did and did not do and think.[38]

The House Committee of Thirty-three, with a tactful and conciliatory Corwin as chairman, sought a solution. With moderate Republicans joining Southerners, it passed a resolution regretting Southern discontent and favoring concessions. This was followed by another, asking states to reconsider their personal liberty laws, coupled with a subcommittee to consider revisions to the Fugitive Slave Act. The Republicans unanimously opposed extending the Missouri Compromise line. Wilson's influence would have to come though Adams, the Massachusetts representative on the committee. Fortunately, their communication was now frequent. Between Christmas and New Year's Adams and a majority of committee Republicans bought the suggestion of Maryland's Henry Winter Davis and determined to support the admission of New Mexico as a slave state, as a needed substitute for Crittenden's proposals and a tactic to encourage divisions within the South. Three of the more conservative Massachusetts House members, Train, Delano, and Rice, supported him, but so did Wilson. Adams was not selling out to the enemy, as some charged, for, after lengthy consultations with Dana on the constitutionality of the Massachusetts Personal Liberty Laws, he urged Andrew to oppose repeal and to strengthen the state militarily.[39]

The key proposal in the Committee of Thirteen was from Crittenden. One of its provisions, the most important—reestablishment of the Missouri Compromise line—would have been an abandonment of the Republican territorial position. The party had won the election and any solution to the secession crisis should have its approval. Wilson in his history declared the resolutions were not a compromise at all, but were entirely one-sided; even the concession for stricter enforcement of the prohibition of the foreign slave trade, he declared, would please the border slave states. Since the committee required a majority of Republicans and a majority of Southern Democrats to agree to any proposal to be recommended to the Senate, the Crittenden resolutions were rejected. So were a number of other proposals. When the Senate reconvened, the committee reported back that it could reach no conclusion. Crittenden now sought to get the Senate to accept his resolutions, reinforced by two more proposed by Douglas. In debate Benjamin attacked Massachusetts for electing Andrew governor after he had endorsed the John Brown raid. The people had also sent senators whose "only business has been, year after year, to insult the people of the South," Benjamin continued, "to call them thieves, murderers, violators; charge them of being criminals. . . ." Wilson tried to interrupt, but could not get recognized.[40]

Harriet on January 5 wrote to the *Natick Observer*, reporting Congress lacked its usual good feeling. The city was filled with the "most intense excitement and anxiety." But, at least, she continued, changes in the cabinet had improved the state of feeling. She spoke of Benjamin's "strong session speech," Edward Baker's reply, and Douglas's disappointing "compromising" speech.[41]

Lincoln made some of the major decisions about his cabinet personnel a few days after the election. Republican leaders argued over who should be selected and attempted to influence the choices, and Lincoln reconsidered. Wilson appears initially to have played no role in this. He did write Chase, encouraging him to accept a cabinet offer and he probably anticipated Seward would be chosen. Furthermore, he had talked with Senator Dixon just before Christmas and had agreed on cabinet recommendations; since Vice-President Hamlin was from New England, and Connecticut favored a position for Gideon Welles, Wilson was apparently supporting Welles and accepting that Massachusetts might not be rewarded. But the state wanted to be represented and Wilson was delegated to telegraph the president-elect on January 4, asking him to suspend his decision until he heard from them. Adams was the man being pushed, although some of the delegation were unenthusiastic or privately opposed. Seward, who had accepted the secretary of state position, wanted Adams for the treasury. Sumner and Wilson both objected, Sumner unhappy with Adams's bonds with Seward and hoping for an appointment himself. Wilson's letter to Lincoln is revealing. Not willing to counter the decision of the state's delegation, he wrote about the "propriety" of making any recommendation. If Massachusetts received an appointment, Adams should be the man, but Lincoln did not have to reward the state. Then Wilson praised Welles.[42]

Adams was heavily criticized by many Republicans for his support of New Mexico statehood, even though the proposal seemed to be achieving its end, division within the slave states. Wilson was reported as angry at the treatment of his colleague. In his history of the era, however, Wilson was less supportive, declaring Adams thought Southern discontent was without reason, but "counseled moderation and every reasonable effort to stem and turn the rising current of secession." The usually radical "Warrington" termed the proposal simply an enabling act and declared Adams knew full well it would not be passed. The idea divided the Republican party, however, and Adams himself subsequently voted against the proposal; the committee reported in mid-January without endorsing any plan. In his minority report Adams declared no compromise would be satisfactory to the seceding states which did not protect the extension of slavery, an assurance he could never give.[43]

Fears were often expressed by Northerners that Southerners in government were engaged in a conspiracy to weaken the union. The usually non-alarmist Adams in early January feared rebels would take possession of the government, perhaps within thirty days. Wilson in his history concluded a plan existed to take the city, but it was contingent upon the secession of Maryland, which, of course, did not occur. Washington, after all, had slavery; the District was surrounded by two slave states; the social elite was Southern; government offices and the military were dominated by the Southern-born. In the area were three to four hundred marines and about one hundred enlisted men at the arsenal. In addition there were a few volunteer battalions. The city had no natural protection. Fortunately, the commanding general of the army, Virginian Winfield Scott, recognized his duty to the nation and knew how to perform it. The size of the force steadily grew.[44]

"You can have no idea of the intense excitement and anxiety that prevails here, in view of . . . the warlike position of the Southern States, and the danger of invasion and insurrection in this city," Harriet wrote Mrs. Claflin. Some ladies were preparing to depart and Wilson did not believe she would be safe much longer. Harriet, however, was unwilling to leave her husband. There were three or four fights every night. Rumors circulated that the Washington House, where they and other Republicans lived, would be burned. The Wilsons expected trouble when the electoral votes were counted. Harriet praised Scott for taking "strong measures," but she and her husband regarded half the militia as secessionist.[45]

Seward and Adams urged Andrew to raise a military force to handle a conspiracy in Maryland or the District. On January 12 Andrew, via Wilson—chosen because of his former services with the militia—wrote Scott asking for advice on preparing Massachusetts aid to the federal government. The general was embarrassed by the request, he stated in his answer to Wilson. The matter should have been addressed to the president or secretary of state. He did not think volunteers beyond those in the District would be called for soon. The *Springfield Republican* throughout January and February opposed any actions to prepare the militia. But the Massachusetts governmental leaders did not give up. The general told Sumner how Washington was defended and stated he would accompany Lincoln to the inauguration. The next day in behalf of both senators Sumner suggested to Andrew ways in which money could be made immediately available to the new administration. Wilson on February 1 wrote his old friend Schouler, now in command of Massachusetts's military forces, that Scott was doing all he could, that the state should put its forces "in good order," and that it should prepare to finance a war.[46]

With less than two months remaining in the congressional session, the Senate spent two days of the second week of January debating a Pacific railroad bill. When some senators questioned whether enough time remained to consider such a controversial bill, in the midst of the need for passing appropriations and responding to secession, Wilson replied there was and urged support for Polk of Missouri's motion to make Kansas City the eastern terminus of the railroad. The issue continued on the Senate agenda on many succeeding days. In his speech, Wilson declared his willingness to go for either two or three routes; the important matter was to agree to some bill. When the vote came on January 29, Wilson supported striking out all but a central route, but was with the minority. He voted with the majority for the final bill.[47]

When Buchanan informed Congress that South Carolina commissioners wanted to meet with him, Howard sought to refer the matter to a special committee. That provided Davis with an opportunity for a major speech on January 10, which Wilson in his 1870s history gave thorough coverage. On Saturday, January 12, Seward delivered his long-awaited address. Wilson in his history declared the future secretary of state's conciliatory tone proved the Republicans were not trying to force secession, but were willing to compromise, and some were even willing to make perpetual guarantees of slavery in the states. At the time he apparently approved. On the other hand, Sumner, who had seen the draft of the address before it was delivered, was much opposed to it. The *Anti-Slavery Standard,* which in the past had often praised the New Yorker, characterized the speech as a surrender. Republican radicals, in general, lost faith in the New Yorker. The next evening Republicans caucused for three hours, taking a stand against concessions. When the Senate reassembled on Monday, it took up the arsenals bill. Wilson then sought to return to the Pacific railroad issue and the admission of Kansas, while Crittenden pushed, and was beaten, on continuing the debate of the state of the union issue. The next day, after Green spoke, the Republicans unanimously supported railroad discussion and won, 27 to 21.[48]

The postponement of discussion these two days and the January 16 substitution of the Clark resolutions, 25 to 23, for the Crittenden proposals, Congressman Cox later asserted, were the most important 1861 Senate actions. On the substitution, every Republican voted in favor; six Southern senators did not vote. Two days later, Crittenden won reconsideration, 27 to 24. On some of the days which followed, however, speeches of a single senator occupied most of the time, not in any way helping solve the crisis. The compromise was dead, Colfax assured Carter.[49]

On January 18 the Senate also turned to the admission of Kansas. Crittenden and four Northern Democrats helped defeat Southern attempts to postpone the subject. After three days of debate and after the withdrawal of five more Southern senators, Kansas on January 21 was voted in, 36 to 16.[50]

When a state convention passed an ordinance of secession, generally its senators and representatives would withdraw. Wilson had enjoyed "kind personal relations" with Davis, the men serving together on the Military Affairs Committee. The story was told that after Davis resigned, he walked across the chamber, took Wilson's hand, and expressed a desire that they would meet again in calmer times. A Natick friend of Wilson's in 1879 claimed the senator related to her that Davis expressed his hope to be able to control the secession movement. The Senate could not decide the status of those who had left; some had not resigned, but simply given departing speeches. On January 22 the Senate unanimously agreed to fill the vacant positions on committees. But when Vice-President Breckenridge asked whether the resignations should be noted in the journal and the names called for votes, some, including Wilson, maintained the Southerners were still members of the Senate; they might reconsider their action and return. Douglas, on the other hand, termed their step irrevocable. Eventually, on Seward's motion, the matter was tabled, 32 to 22, and not settled until the special session in mid-March.[51]

What possibilities were available to either the Buchanan administration or its successor? One reporter suggested repealing the acts admitting seceding, non-original states (such as Alabama) into the union or seizing all vessels trying to enter the ports of seceding states. The reporter added that Wilson thought "such treatment would cure secession and treason quicker than more violent measures."[52]

Efforts to compromise continued in the border states and by Northern Democrats and Constitutional Unionists. Many Northern businessmen were deeply concerned. Reputable newspapers, including the *Providence Journal*, *New York Times*, *Ohio State Journal*, and *Boston Advertiser* urged concessions. Meetings in a number of Massachusetts communities, including Natick, called for accepting the Crittenden compromise. Following a large public assemblage in Boston in late January, Everett, Lawrence, and Winthrop were dispatched to Washington with a petition signed by 15,000 voters seeking compromise. They spoke with the president and vice-president, Justice McLean, Cass, Douglas, Virginia Senators Hunter and Mason, Scott, Wilson, and others. Winthrop was pleased with the conciliatory spirit he found in Adams and Seward. The latter two often voted with their fellow Republicans, but were working to find some way out of the impasse. The Boston city council on February 7 passed a resolution declaring Sumner was not representing Boston's views.[53]

When those opposed to major concessions tried to counter the compromisers, they ran into difficulty. At the first session of the Massachusetts Anti-Slavery Society, January 24, Phillips was shouted down. The mayor subsequently closed Tremont Temple to prevent violence. Five thousand people gathered to make certain it would not be reopened. Police protected Phillips's home.[54]

Sumner, as representative of those unwilling to propose much in the way of compromise, broke politically and personally with Adams, a leader among those seeking to demonstrate to moderates and the border states that the Republican party was trying to save the union, that it was working to gain time until the government could be placed in the hands of friends. "There was a scene, . . . the details of which were not known," Pierce later wrote. The two men seldom spoke again. Wilson's relations with Adams, on the other hand, continued to improve. On January 23 the Adamses entertained the Wilsons, among others, for dinner. Wilson was not being wooed by the flattery of moderates, but sincerely believed Republicans needed to demonstrate to the border states that they were flexible and were not Garrisonian abolitionists. He could not sit near the border state men and listen to their pleading, some with tears in their eyes, and not respond. On the other hand, he publicly declared the conservative Boston delegation did not represent the sentiment of the state, but only of the city.[55]

The crisis in the South and in the capital, of course, did not prevent politicians, including the cabinet, from being concerned about patronage. Wilson's friend Fogg was dispatched, on January 20, with a message from Wilson attesting to Fogg's ability to convey the sentiments of Republican senators. Whom Fogg was supporting or opposing is not clear. Sumner was increasingly unhappy. With Welles representing New England, he would get no cabinet appointment. He wanted to be designated as minister to Great Britain, and the thought that Adams might be selected instead increased his distress.[56]

The decision of the Virginia convention against seceding had quieted the situation in Washington temporarily. This prompted Seward on February 4 to suggest Adams telegraph Andrew that troops were not immediately needed. At that time Colonel Harrison Ritchie, of Andrew's staff, was in the capital to consult with Wilson, Sumner, Seward, and others. Wilson told him that Massachusetts's primary responsibility would be to furnish money. Scott was quoted on February 13 as stating he had no intention of calling on Massachusetts for troops. Wilson joined Colfax and other Republican congressmen in a "committee of vigilance" to protect the capital and each other. In the meantime, Attorney General Stanton had begun his regular consultations with Republican leaders, including Wilson, which assured them that the administration would not engage in treason, yet left them discomforted at the administration's lack of action.[57]

The Senate during much of February in its debates almost ignored the events of secession. Republicans were encouraged when Tennessee, Kentucky, and Virginia took no action to secede and the counting of electoral votes proceeded without interference. Two big balls were held on February 11. Everyone in Washington was now "cheerful and hopeful," Harriet reported. For almost the entire month, the Senate occupied itself with appropriations, private bills, and consideration of tariff revision. Wilson declared Massachusetts was generally happy with the Tariff of 1857 and uninterested in change. An increase in iron duties would injure its shipping and railroad interests. Increases in other items would protect and "raise up rivals at home," as injurious as foreign competition. Greater protection might also permit the cotton states to hold out additional reasons for border states to secede. But he did see a need for greater revenues and would support increases which might produce that result. In the end, Wilson joined other Republicans in voting for the bill.[58]

Missouri senator Green, a Democrat and chairman of the committee on territories, was eager to organize Colorado, Nevada, and Dakota into territories. While Douglas could charge that without the Wilmot Proviso attached, the Republicans were abandoning their platform and endorsing his popular sovereignty ideas, the Republicans were willing to create more territories, at least some of them as a counterweight to admitting New Mexico as a state. Neither house recorded its votes.[59]

Lincoln continued to remain silent. On February 1 he did respond to an appeal from Seward and rejected the Crittenden plan, although he was willing to accept the New Mexico proposal and guarantees for slavery in the South. Seward was out to destroy the party, Giddings wrote. Herndon reported that Lincoln was distressed by the position of Adams and Seward. The president-elect wrote his inaugural address in early February, emphasizing his party's opposition to the expansion of slavery in the territories and his obligation to enforce the law; secession was constitutionally impossible. On February 11 he left for Washington by a time-consuming, energy-draining, and circuitous route. What he said often angered Southerners, and distressed Seward and Adams, as well.[60]

As Congress seemed unable to solve the secession crisis, the Virginia governor and legislature called a special convention to meet in Washington on February 4. Most Democrats, Whigs, and Americans of the North and upper South were supportive of the call. Republicans were more divided, some fearful about what might ensue if their voices were not heard, others willing to pursue possibilities which could prevent division or civil war, others regarding the convention as unconstitutional or an effort to undo their November political victory. Bird, Robinson, Sanborn, and Wright were, as might be predicted, opposed. The *Boston Advertiser*, perhaps more representative of Massachusetts thought, doubted the conference could accomplish anything, but declared the crisis was too great not to try. Wilson and all other members of the Massachusetts delegation, except Sumner, favored sending delegates. Andrew and a majority of the Massachusetts Senate at first opposed participation, but yielded to the advice from their Washington representatives. The radicals were unhappy the state was cooperating; the conservatives disapproved of who was selected. Wilson's advice was to send "no Hunkers but able and firm" men like Allen, Boutwell, Hoar, and Dana. The appointments, which included Allen, Boutwell, and Goodrich, were agreed to so late that the assembly had been in session several days before the Massachusetts men arrived.[61]

The peace conference, with twenty-one states represented, met for three weeks. It was, of course, an extra-constitutional assemblage. Wilson in his 1870s history devoted an entire chapter to the conference, which he characterized as "strongly conservative" and "decidedly . . . southern." In fact, some of the delegates had come simply to prevent action they opposed. Had the conference been able to find a solution, consideration by Congress would have been necessary; how even a conservative body could have produced a plan acceptable to the already-seceded states remains a mystery. But what solution was there? Amendments to the constitution, similar to the Crittenden compromise, were proposed and presented to Congress three days before the assemblage was to adjourn. The extension of the Missouri Compromise line to the Pacific had carried, eight states to seven.

Congress itself seemed relieved the problems of secession were being considered by a different body.[62]

In the midst of general business on appropriations bills, the Senate met on the evening of February 21 before crowded galleries for Wilson to deliver his long-postponed speech on slavery and the Crittenden compromise. Although he had agreed several times to delay his remarks to help the Senate get on with its business, why only Wilson felt called upon to debate these issues at this time is not clear. He regarded his address as important, for when he came to write his history, Wilson devoted more space to this speech than to any other. Wilson began by quoting George Mason, complimenting the Virginian's stance three-quarters of a century before. Noting how frequently "treason" had been talked of in Congress in 1860, he declared those utterances were now deeds. He spoke of his dreams about the nation and how appalling the current situation was. He wondered what the president-elect had done to justify breaking up the union. He went to great lengths to demonstrate that the people of the North did not hate those of the South. Republican speakers had over and over again emphasized their intention to use constitutional means to arrest the extension of slavery and to disclaim their hostility toward the South. His state's personal liberty law was to protect its inhabitants, not to interfere with the execution of the Fugitive Slave Act.[63]

Defending Massachusetts from attacks, Wilson showed how Virginia and South Carolina had mistreated Massachusetts citizens. Particularly antagonized by Benjamin, whose speech had provoked this response in the first place, he defended Andrew's views on the John Brown affair. He further commented upon the addresses of Wigfall, Douglas, and Crittenden. While he complimented the latter for his good intentions, Wilson declared that agreeing to those proposals could only result in a permanent guarantee of slavery. He attacked most parts of the Crittenden proposal, unable to find anything the North would gain in exchange for concessions to the slave states. Confronting headlong a provision which would have prohibited voting by blacks, he noted the long record of political participation by members of that race in some states, including Massachusetts. He recorded a list of blacks who had ably served their nation. He would not be a party to their degradation. He also was repelled by a provision which would have authorized the national government to acquire lands in Africa or South America for colonization of free blacks and mulattoes. While he could agree to assist those who wanted to leave the United States, he termed the Crittenden proposal a proslavery scheme. Furthermore, he did not see how compromise was possible while Southerners occupied their current stance.[64]

The speech was "most vigorous," and "remarkable for its uncompromising adherence to true Republican principles," the *New York Tribune* declared. The "best ever made by him," the *Natick Observer* commented, ranking it beside those of Seward and Adams. Whittier immediately complimented his friend for his "manly, frank and dignified" effort; he especially liked Wilson's tribute to blacks.

"Eloquent, able, true, brave words," Lydia Maria Child wrote. "Much as I have admired several of your former speeches, you have never so completely gained my heart as in this last one." Gerrit Smith and Amasa Walker were equally complimentary. The best defense of Massachusetts institutions and beliefs anyone could have made, *The Liberator* pronounced; yet it also bemoaned that the state treated slaveholders so courteously, Wilson's speech only proving his state's hypocrisy. Garrison personally wrote Wilson to express his "great pleasure" with the address, applauding the senator for his defense of the state. The Union Progressive Association, a literary society of young blacks, thanked Wilson for his able analysis of the compromise and his "manly recognition" of the contributions of their revolutionary forefathers.[65]

After his arrival in Washington, President-elect Lincoln was taken to Congress by Seward and Trumball on February 26 for introductions. Wilson called upon him on both February 26 and 27. Controversy over cabinet positions and initial efforts to get other important appointments must have involved Wilson, as well as others.[66]

When the peace conference adjourned on February 27, Congress had only four days to respond to its report. The House even on that day debated the Corwin proposals. The New Mexico statehood resolution was tabled. The House more profitably considered a thirteenth amendment to the constitution, which failed by ten votes to get the two-thirds necessary. This would have provided that no amendment could be added to permit Congress to abolish or interfere with any state's domestic institutions, including slavery. Greeley and Giddings, among others, devoted two days to lobbying against compromise measures. The next day, however, four Pennsylvania representatives changed their minds and the Corwin proposal passed by one vote, but with a large majority of Republicans opposed. When the peace conference report reached the Senate, the Republicans objected to its consideration, but after a long debate, were beaten, 26 to 23. March 1 was devoted to the issue, then over Crittenden's objections, by a 23-to-22 vote, the Senate adjourned. Wilson wrote that the efforts of the conference, "brought forth with so much labor and anxiety, if they did not fall still-born, were left to sleep. . . ." But the following day the Democrats, joined by five Republicans, by a 20-to-16 vote suspended the rules, enabling the Senate to take up the House's proposed constitutional amendment. The vote to consider it was 25 to 11, Wilson among those opposed, as were Mason of Virginia, Clingman of North Carolina, and Bayard of Delaware. Sumner was absent all day and Seward played no role on either March 2 or 3.[67]

Congress's close was extraordinarily quiet, the rowdies absent, D. W. Bartlett of the *Springfield Republican* reported. The Senate met much of the night. In Wilson's short remarks, he asserted he would vote from "deepest convictions." He never believed the federal government had the power to interfere with or abolish slavery in the states. He did not want to give Congress that power. But, on the other hand, he was unwilling to make the whole nation responsible for the institution. He would stand by the constitution as it was and would therefore oppose the amendment. Before it adjourned, the Senate passed, with exactly the two-thirds majority needed, the House-approved amendment. All those opposed, including Wilson and Sumner, were Republicans. Congress took no other action dealing with secession. Wilson later asserted in his history that the Crittenden resolutions in the end failed not because of Republican votes, but because of Southern. Many slave state senators had withdrawn, six others did not participate; the resolutions lost by only one vote. If all Southerners had been present even a two-thirds majority for an amendment would have been possible.[68]

The day was cloudy and chilling, but the *New York Tribune* reported the largest crowd thus far for an inauguration—as many as 100,000 people; Bartlett reported the figure as 25,000 to the *Springfield Republican.* In his address Lincoln rejected the constitutionality of secession, but employed conciliatory language. The choice between war and peace would be that of Southerners. "Kind, temperate, genial, patriotic," Wilson characterized the speech. "Able, candid, patriotic," were the words Harriet used in her "Melvina" letter. The Senate was in special session to handle appointments and did not adjourn until March 28. Radical Republicans—Fessenden, Chandler, Wade, Sumner, Trumball, Hale, and Wilson—were chosen to head the important committees. Wilson was made chairman of the Military Affairs Committee, the position in which he would make his greatest contribution to his nation's history.[69]

Much of Senate time was given over to unreported executive sessions. Debates were held over whether to expel Senator Wigfall of Texas and whether to recognize the seats of certain Southern senators as vacant. Wilson played no part. Slave state senators advocated resolutions urging the president to withdraw troops from the seceded states and dealing with the status of forts there. Wilson's only speech, on March 15, was short and made in what Douglas characterized as a "petulant" tone, in response to the Illinois senator's remarks. He was angry with Douglas, who, he declared, was more alarmed than the country and whose own speech had been mischievous and unpatriotic. Douglas, he continued, represented no one. Yet he had set himself up to interpret the president's address and now sought from the Senate a resolution asking the administration what it intended to do. Congress, the armed forces, the country was full of traitors. The administration had just taken over and needed time to decide what to do. In the meantime, Wilson declared, offering no proof, "matters are clearing up. The skies brighten." While angry with Wilson, Douglas ignored the rebuke and continued to offer his unsolicited advice.[70]

Reward time had arrived for those who had labored so long in the antislavery, Free Soil, and Republican causes. No one could know the number of government positions would increase from 50,000 to 150,000 in the next four years of expansion. For as political an animal as Wilson always had been, he had been almost uninvolved with issues of presidential appointments for four months, and continued to lay low. In contrast, Sumner, who had seldom shown much interest in the subject, now became a major advocate of appointment of longtime Republicans to office. Andrew had his preferences, too. He hoped Sumner could get Palfrey sent out of the country so that with "his freaks and whims and his qualms," he wouldn't destroy the party. Cabinet nominations were quickly confirmed on March 5. Goodrich received the important collector of the Port of Boston position and Amos Tuck of New Hampshire and later Phelps were nominated as surveyor. Sumner was unhappy that most of the Massachusetts House delegation left for home before deciding on the state's recommendations. Congressmen Alley, Rice, Buffington, and Delano met in Boston on March 15 to attempt to agree on their preferences, which they carried to Washington later that week. On April 3 a second Boston meeting, including all of the Massachusetts delegation but three, divided the spoils. In spite of the fact that others—probably including Wilson—preferred Phelps or Pangborn for the position, Adams and Sumner got Palfrey selected as postmaster of Boston. Wilson, Alley, and Train returned to Washington to make certain the selections were agreed to by the administration.[71]

For diplomatic posts, Seward had the primary responsibility, while Lincoln would intervene on occasion. Sumner, as the new chairman of the Senate Foreign Relations Committee, would exercise special influence. Andrew threw his support behind the appointment of Sumner to the British ministry, but Wilson on March 14 told the governor that either Adams or Dayton would be selected. Adams, in spite of Sumner's views, received the London post and Burlingame was rewarded for his long services by nomination to Austria. When the Austrians rejected Burlingame Wilson and Sumner got Motley chosen.[72]

The voters of Connecticut and Rhode Island had the opportunity to respond to events since November in the early April elections. Wilson's presence was hardly needed in Washington, but the frequent campaigner did not participate. The results were as confusing as the national scene was. Voting was light in Connecticut; its Republican governor was reelected, and the Republican majority in the state legislature increased, but the party lost two congressional seats. In Rhode Island an anti-Republican coalition won both congressional seats, the state offices, and control of the legislature. Yet the new governor had promised to sustain the Lincoln administration.[73]

In his history Wilson quoted from a foreign correspondent, noting the quiescence in the North in the six weeks after the inaugural. The president was overly involved with patronage. Wilson in his book was equivocal on Seward's role. But Seward was convinced he had to save the union and the way to maintain the peace was to abandon the remaining forts in the seceded states, even promising Southern commissioners it would be done. Scott, Welles, and Holt agreed with Seward. Reports circulated that Lincoln was softening his position. He had made no effort to recapture the lost forts and he was doing nothing to collect customs duties where they were not being obtained. Shortly after the new president's inauguration, he had been informed that Major Robert Anderson, commander of American forces at Fort Sumter, had provisions adequate only for four to six more weeks. Twenty to twenty-five thousand troops would be needed to reinforce the fort. No record exists of what advice, if any, Wilson was giving Lincoln during these weeks. But while the president first appeared to be indecisive, he subsequently determined to prepare relief expeditions for both Fort Sumter in South Carolina and Fort Pickens in Florida. When orders got confused in aiding Pickens, Lincoln was forced to make his move at Sumter, carefully notifying the South Carolina governor of his limited intentions.[74]

The Confederate government had already determined to take over the forts whenever that could be done successfully and with minimum loss of life. It now believed it had been deceived by Seward's promises and had to respond. Instead of permitting its commander in Charleston to follow previous orders and prevent the landing of a relief expedition's supplies, it ordered Fort Sumter be taken before the naval force arrived. Thus, the Confederacy would become the aggressor and fire on the American flag. When Major Anderson refused a demand for evacuation, the Confederates on April 12 began shelling the fort; a day and a half later, it was surrendered. It all those hours, not a single man was killed. In attacking Northern forces, the South "was guilty of the very madness the North had deemed impossible," Wilson wrote in the 1870s; "and the North revealed the grateful fact that its love of country, though long dormant, was real." War was the result, but no one in mid-April could know how long, broadly encompassing, and bloody that war would be.[75]

The years of the Civil War arguably would be the most significant in American history. In thirty years Wilson had been unable to achieve his most important objective, the abolition of slavery; he would be able to accomplish that in the five years that followed the attack on Fort Sumter. Unfortunately, that achievement would come at the cost of thousands of deaths, North and South, and the destruction of whole sections of the nation. In addition, during the next decade and a half, Wilson would be one of the most influential men in the nation, as chairman of Senate Military Affairs Committee, leader in securing legislation and constitutional amendments to protect blacks, and the most frequent speaker in the nation at political events. He would end his career as vice-president of the country.

NOTES

Chapter 1

1. U.S., Congress, Senate, *Congressional Record*, 44th Cong., 1st sess., 1876, 4, pt. 1: 532.
2. Ibid., p. 533.
3. Benjamin P. Thomas, *Abraham Lincoln, a Biography* (New York: Alfred A. Knopf, 1952), p. 4.
4. Jonathan B. Mann, *The Life of Henry Wilson, Republican Candidate for Vice-President, 1872* (Boston: James R. Osgood and Company, 1872), pp. 1–2; *National Era*, Oct. 20, 1853; Charles S. Phelps, *Life and Public Services of Ulysses S. Grant, from His Birth to the Present Time, and a Biographical Sketch of Hon. Henry Wilson* (Boston: Lee Shepard and Dillingham, 1872), p. 350.
5. Elias Nason and Thomas Russell, *The Life and Public Services of Henry Wilson, Late Vice-President of the United States* (Boston: B. B. Russell, 1876), p. 14; Mann, *Life of Wilson*, pp. 1–2; John G. Whittier, "Henry Wilson," *Appleton's Cyclopaedia of American Biography*, ed. James G. Wilson and John Fiske, 6 vols. (New York: D. Appleton and Company, 1888–1889), 5: 548–49; Elias Nason, "Biographical Sketch of Henry Wilson, Late Vice-President of the United States," *New England Historical and Genealogical Register* 32 (July 1878): 261–62; *New York Times*, Dec. 12 and 15, 1875; *Boston Journal*, Sept. 22, 1875; *Natick Bulletin*, Nov. 26, 1875; Feb. 26, 1892; "First Congregational Church Records, Rochester, N.H. Marriages by Rev. Joseph Haven," *New Hampshire Genealogical Record* 5 (Oct. 1908): 146; Oliver N. Bacon, *A History of Natick from Its First Settlement in 1651 to the Present Time* (Boston: Damrell and Moore, 1856), p. 144.
6. *Natick Bulletin*, Feb. 26, 1892; Oct. 19, 1906.
7. U.S., Congress, Senate, *Congressional Globe*, 35th Cong., 1st sess., Appendix, p. 173; J. Daniel Loubert, "The Orientation of Henry Wilson, 1812–1856," (Ph.D. diss., Boston University, 1952), p. 2; Henry Wilson, *Speech on Prohibition, Tremont Temple, Apil 15, 1867* (New York: American Tract Society, 1867), p. 1; *Natick Bulletin*, Oct. 19, 1906.
8. *New York Tribune*, Nov. 24, 1875; *New York Times*, Nov. 23, 1875; Mann, *Life of Wilson*, p. 1; Loubert, p. 2; Nason and Russell, p. 15.
9. *Boston Transcript*, Aug. 10, 1866.
10. Nason and Russell, p. 15.

11. Mann, *Life of Wilson*, p. 2.
12. *New York Tribune*, Nov. 24, 1875.
13. Charles Wright, *Our Political Practice* (Boston: Alfred Mudge & Son, Printers, 1864–1865), pp. 73–74; *New York Herald*, July 15, 1866; diary, Nov. 1, 1858, Edward Everett Papers, Massachusetts Historical Society, Boston, hereafter cited as MHS; Dana to Richard Henry Dana III, Nov. 22, 1875, Richard Henry Dana Jr. Papers, MHS; *New York Times*, Dec. 15, 1875.
14. Duane H. Hurd, ed., *History of Rockingham and Strafford Counties, New Hampshire* (Philadelphia: J. W. Lewis & Co., 1882), p. 630; Mann, *Life of Wilson*, p. 1; *Natick Bulletin*, Nov. 12, 1909.
15. John Farmer and Jacob B. Moore, *A Gazetteer of the State of New-Hampshire* (Concord: Jacob B. Moore, 1823), pp. 134–35, 272; Alonzo J. Fogg, *The Statistics and Gazetteer of New Hampshire* (Concord: D. L. Guernsey, 1874), pp. 156–57; Timothy Dwight, *Travels in New-England and New-York*, 4 vols. (New Haven, Conn.: T. Dwight, 1821–22), 4: 158–59.
16. Mann, *Life of Wilson*, p. 1.
17. Farmer and Moore, pp. 134–35; Hurd, *Rockingham and Strafford Counties*, p. 621; Mann, *Life of Wilson*, p. 1; Nason and Russell, pp. 14–16; *New York Times*, Nov. 17, 1872; Nov. 23, 1875; *Natick Bulletin*, Feb. 26, 1892; Jonathan B. Mann, *Henry Wilson's Boyhood* (South Natick, Mass.: Historical Collections, Natural History and Library Society, 1910), p. 27; Nason, "Sketch of Wilson," pp. 261–62.
18. Henry Wilson, *Stand by the Republican Colors! Speech of Hon. Henry Wilson, of Massachusetts, at Great Falls, New Hampshire, February 24, 1872* (Washington, 1872), p. 4.
19. Mann, *Life of Wilson*, pp. 1–2; Nason, "Sketch of Wilson," pp. 261–62; Phelps, p. 350; Nason and Russell, pp. 14, 17; *National Era*, Oct. 20, 1853; *New York Times*, Nov. 23, 1875; *Natick Bulletin*, Feb. 26, 1892; Feb. 14, 1902; *Henry Wilson, 18th Vice President of the United States Serving under President U. S. Grant, Born in Farmington, New Hampshire, February 16, 1812* (Farmington, N.H.: Farmington-New Durham Historical Society, 1954), p. 2.
20. Nason and Russell, p. 15; *Natick Bulletin*, Feb. 14, 1902; Nason, "Sketch of Wilson," p. 262; *Henry Wilson, 18th Vice President*, p. 6.
21. Nason, "Sketch of Wilson," pp. 262–63; Hurd, *Rockingham and Strafford Counties*, pp. 601, 620–21, 625, 628–29; John Scales, *History of Strafford County, New Hampshire* (Chicago: Richmond-Arnold Publishing Co., 1914), pp. 41, 505; Mann, *Life of Wilson*, pp. 3–6; Mann, *Henry Wilson's Boyhood*, pp. 27–35; Nason and Russell, pp. 16–19; Alexander K. McClure, *Colonel Alexander McClure's Recollections of Half a Century* (Salem, Mass.: Salem Publishing Company, 1902), p. 287; Phelps, p. 351; *Natick Bulletin*, Oct. 29, 1870; Feb. 26, 1892; Nov. 19, 1909; *Commonwealth*, Sept. 24, 1853; *National Era*, Oct. 20, 1853; *New York Times*, Nov. 23, 1875; *Boston Journal*, Sept. 22, 1875; *Henry Wilson, 18th Vice President*, p. 2.
22. Farmer and Moore, pp. 51–53, 134–35, 272; Fogg, p. 157.
23. Mann, *Life of Wilson*, pp. 3, 7; Phelps, pp. 350–51; Nason, "Sketch of Wilson," pp. 262–63; Bacon, *History of Natick*, p. 144; Wilson, *Republican Colors*, pp. 2, 4; *New York Tribune*, Nov. 24, 1875; *Natick Bulletin*, Dec. 31, 1875; Nov. 26, 1875; Feb. 26, 1892; *Natick Citizen*, Mar. 4, 1881; Mann, *Henry Wilson's Boyhood*, pp. 28–33; Nason and Russell, pp. 17–19; *Henry Wilson, 18th Vice President*, p. 8; *National Era*, Oct.

20, 1853; *Independent*, May 21, 1868.

24. Wilson, *Republican Colors*, p. 4; Mann, *Life of Wilson*, p. 5; *Natick Bulletin*, Nov. 12 and 19, 1909; Mann, *Henry Wilson's Boyhood*, pp. 30–31.
25. *Natick Bulletin*, Feb. 26, 1892; Nov. 12, 1909; Mann, *Henry Wilson's Boyhood*, p. 31; Mann, *Life of Wilson*, p. 3; *Boston Journal*, May 2, 1868.
26. Mann, *Henry Wilson's Boyhood*, pp. 34–35; Wilson, *Republican Colors*, p. 4; *New York Tribune*, Nov. 24, 1875; *Natick Bulletin*, Feb. 26, 1892; Nov. 26, 1909; *Commonwealth*, Sept. 24, 1853; *National Era*, Oct. 20, 1853; Mann, *Life of Wilson*, pp. 7–8; Mann, *Henry Wilson's Boyhood*, pp. 34–35; *Natick Citizen*, Mar. 4, 1881; *Boston Journal*, May 20, 1869; *Congressional Globe*, 41st Cong., 1st sess., 1871, p. 363; Nason and Russell, pp. 19–20.
27. Mary B. Claflin, *Under the Elms* (Boston: Thomas Y. Crowell, 1895), pp. 43–44; *Natick Bulletin*, Feb. 24, 1882.
28. New Hampshire, House of Representatives, Journal, at Their Session, Holden at the Capitol in Concord, Commencing Wednesday, June 5, 1833 (Concord: State of New Hampshire, 1833), pp. 28, 29; New Hampshire, Laws of the State of New Hampshire; Passed June Session, 1833 (Concord: Horatio Hill & Co., 1833), pp. 489–90; New Hampshire, Laws: Volume Ten, Second Constitutional Period, 1829–1835 (Concord: Evans Printing Company, 1922), pp. 128–29.
29. Bacon, *History of Natick*, pp. 143–44; Whittier, *Appleton's Cyclopaedia*, 5: 548; *Natick Bulletin*, Nov. 26, 1875, quoting from the *Boston Herald*; *New York Tribune*, Nov. 23, 1875; *Army and Navy Journal*, Nov. 27, 1875; *New York Times*, Dec. 12, 1875.
30. Nason and Russell, p. 20.
31. Natick Bulletin, Feb. 26, 1892.
32. Ibid.; Mann, *Life of Wilson*, pp. 5–6; *New York Times*, Nov. 25, 1875; Dec. 12, 1875; Nason and Russell, p. 20; Blanche Evans Hazard, *The Organization of the Boot and Shoe Industry in Massachusetts before 1875* (Cambridge: Harvard University Press, 1921), pp. 68–70, 213–18.
33. Mann, *Life of Wilson*, p. 8; *Natick Bulletin*, Nov. 26, 1909; *Boston Journal*, May 2, 1868; Wilson, *Republican Colors*, p. 4; Mann, *Henry Wilson's Boyhood*, pp. 34–35; Nason and Russell, pp. 20–2l.
34. Mann, *Life of Wilson*, pp. 6, 8; Mann, *Henry Wilson's Boyhood*, p. 34; Nason and Russell, p. 22–23.
35. Albert B. Hart, ed., *Commonwealth History of Massachusetts*, 5 vols. (New York: Russell & Russell, 1900), 4: 74–76, 281–82; Arthur B. Darling, *Political Changes in Massachusetts, 1824–1848* (New Haven: Yale University Press, 1925), pp. 2, 7, 22–26; Ronald P. Formisano, *The Transformation of Political Culture: Massachusetts Politics, 1790s–1840s* (New York: Oxford University Press, 1983), pp. 177–96.
36. Formisano, *Transformation of Political Culture*, p. 282; Francis X. Bloun, *The Boston Region, 1810–1850, a Study in Urbanization* (Ann Arbor: UMI Research Press, 1978), pp. 1–78.
37. Bacon, *History of Natick*, pp. 7, 9, 108, 124, 128–29, 134, 149–5l, 162–64; D. Hamilton Hurd, comp., *Middlesex County*, 3 vols. (Philadelphia: J. W. Lewis & Co., 1890), 1: 512–13, 525, 553–54; Michael J. Crawford, *History of Natick, Massachusetts, 1650–1976* (Natick: Natick Historical Commission, 1976), pp. 42, 46, 48; Edward P. Conklin, *Middlesex County and Its People*, 5 vols. (New York: Lewis Historical Publishing Company, 1927), 1: 598–600; Nason and Russell, p. 24.

38. Bacon, *History of Natick*, p. 151; Crawford, *History of Natick*, pp. 42–43; Bloun, pp. 43, 50–51; Hurd, *Middlesex County,* 1: 554; Paul G. Faler, *Mechanics and Manufacturers in the Early Industrial Revolution: Lynn, Massachusetts, 1780–1860* (Albany: State University of New York Press, 1981), p. 18; Nason and Russell, pp. 24–25; *Natick Bulletin*, Oct. 29, 1870.
39. Hazard, pp. 3–63; Faler, pp. 12–13, 17–24; Hart, 4: 403, 414–16; Alan Dawley, *Class and Community: the Industrial Revolution in Lynn* (Cambridge: Harvard University Press, 1976), pp. 17–20, 25–27; Mary H. Blunett, "The Sexual Division of Labor and the Artisan Tradition in Early Industrial Capitalism: the Case of New England Shoemaking, 1780–1860," in *"To Toil the Live-Long Day": America's Women at Work, 1780–1980,* ed. Carol Groneman and Mary Beth Norton (Ithaca: Cornell University Press, 1987), pp. 36–40.
40. Faler, pp. 26–27, 58–61; Hazard, pp. 42–49; Bacon, *History of Natick,* p. 152; Dawley, pp. 26–31, 42–44; Blunett, p. 40.
41. Hazard, p. 54.
42. Cawford, *History of Natick*, pp. 3, 49; Hurd, *Middlesex County*, 1: 559; Bacon, *History of Natick*, p. 152; Hazard, pp. 53–54; Bloun, pp. 155–65; Nason and Russell, pp. 24–26.
43. Hurd, *Rockingham and Strafford Counties,* p. 635; *Natick Citizen*, Mar. 7, 1879; *Natick Bulletin*, Oct. 29, 1870.
44. Bacon, *History of Natick*, pp. 146–48; Hurd, *Middlesex County*, 1: 554, 565–66; Wilbur H. Siebert, "The Underground Railroad in Massachusetts," *Proceedings of the American Antiquarian Society*, n.s., 45 (1935): 48–49.
45. *Natick Bulletin*, Oct. 29, 1870; *Natick Citizen*, Jan. 31 and Mar. 7, 1879; *National Era*, Oct. 20, 1853; *Commonwealth*, Aug. 28, 1869; Bloun, pp. 155–60; Mann, *Life of Wilson*, p. 10; Nason and Russell, pp. 23–25; *Henry Wilson, 18th Vice President*, p. 10; Hurd, *Rockingham and Strafford Counties*, p. 635; Alonzo Travis, "Felchville: Its Past, Present and Future," *Historical Collections of the Historical, Natural History and Library Society* 2 (1910): 88; Hurd, *Middlesex County*, 1: 554.
46. Hazard, pp. 73–74; *Henry Wilson, 18th Vice President,* p. 10; Nason, "Sketch of Wilson," p. 263; Mann, *Life of Wilson*, p. 10; *Natick Bulletin*, Oct. 29, 1870; *Natick Citizen*, Jan. 31, 1879.
47. Jonathan B. Mann, "Rambling Thoughts: From Scraps of History by J. B. M. in 1884: Henry Wilson at Twenty-Two," clipping file, Morse Institute, Natick, Massachusetts; *Natick Bulletin*, Feb. 26, 1892.
48. Mann, *Life of Wilson*, pp. 10–11.
49. *Natick Citizen*, Jan. 31, 1879; *Natick Bulletin*, Mar. 11, 1892, quoting from the *Rochester (N.H.) Leader;* Feb. 14, 1902; *New York Times,* Nov. 23, 1875; Mann, *Life of Wilson*, p. 11; Mann, "Rambling Thoughts."
50. *Natick Citizen*, Jan. 31, 1879.
51. Nason and Russell, p. 26.
52. Ibid., p. 24.
53. Ibid., pp. 29, 38; Wilson to Claflin, Feb. 1, 1858, William Claflin Papers, Rutherford B. Hayes Library, Fremont, Ohio; *Fourth Annual Report of the American Anti-Slavery Society* (New York: American Anti-Slavery, 1837), pp. 19, 127; *First Congregational Church, Natick, Mass., The Confession of Faith, . . . with an Historical Sketch and List of Members* (Boston: Congregational House, 1877), pp. 67–68; Bacon, *History of Natick*, p. 72; Hurd, *Middlesex County*, 1: 89, 541; Wilson and Fiske, eds.,

Appleton's Cyclopaedia, 4: 380; Crawford, *History of Natick*, p. 50; *National Era*, Aug. 5, 1847; E. D. Moore, *On Living Peaceably with All Men, a Farewell Sermon* (Boston: David H. Ela, 1842), *passim*.

54. *Natick Bulletin*, May 5, 1876; Sept. 18, 1903; *Natick Observer*, May 28, 1859; July 7, 1860; Mann, *Life of Wilson*, p. 12; Nason and Russell, p. 27.
55. Harriet F. Bacon, "Personal Recollections of Natick," *Historical Collections of the Historical Natural History and Library Society* 1 (1909): 36; *Natick Observer*, May 28, 1859; July 7, 1860; *Natick Bulletin*, Sept. 18, 1903.
56. *Natick Bulletin*, May 5, 1876; Sept. 18, 1903; *Natick Observer*, July 7, 1860; *Boston Journal*, Sept. 29, 1875; Hurd, *Rockingham and Strafford Counties*, p. 636; Crawford, *History of Natick*, p. 49; Nason and Russell, p. 27; Bacon, *History of Natick*, pp. 141–42; Allen Johnson and Dumas Malone, eds., *Dictionary of American Biography*, 21 vols. (New York: Charles Scribner's Sons, 1937–1944), 18: 401–2.
57. *Natick Bulletin*, May 5, 1876; Sept. 18, 1903; *Natick Observer*, July 7, 1860.
58. *Natick Bulletin*, May 5, 1876; Mann, *Life of Wilson*, p. 12; Nason and Russell, pp. 27–28; Bacon, *History of Natick*, p. 144; *Henry Wilson, 18th Vice President*, p. 11; *Memorial Addresses of the Life and Character of Henry Wilson, (Vice-President of the United States,) Delivered in the Senate and House of Representatives, January 21, 1876, with Other Congressional Tributes of Respect* (Washington: Government Printing Office, 1876), p. 8.
59. *Natick Observer*, July 7, 1860; Mann, *Life of Wilson*, p. 12; *Natick Bulletin*, May 5, 1876.
60. Mann, *Life of Wilson*, p. 12; Phelps, p. 353; *Natick Bulletin*, Feb. 5, 1876; *Proceedings of the American Anti-Slavery Society at Its Third Decade, Held in the City of Philadelphia, Dec. 3d and 4th, 1863* (New York: American Anti-Slavery Society, 1864), p. 102; Jacob M. Manning, *Sermons and Addresses* (Boston: Houghton, Mifflin and Company, 1889), p. 535; *Fourth Annual Report of the American Anti-Slavery Society*, pp. 19, 127; *Fifth Annual Report of the American Anti-Slavery Society* (New York: American Anti-Slavery Society, 1838), p. 135.
61. Mann, *Life of Wilson*, p. 13.
62. Hubbard Winslow, *The Young Man's Aid to Knowledge, Virtue, and Happiness* (Boston: D. K. Hitchcock, 1837), p. v.
63. Ibid, pp. 13–24, 32, 38–41, 68–72.
64. Ibid, pp. 87–116.
65. Ibid, pp. 277–319, 349–356, 382–398.
66. Wilson, *Republican Colors*, p. 4.
67. Mann, *Life of Wilson*, p. 14.
68. *Natick Bulletin*, Nov. 26, 1875, quoting from *Boston Herald; Commonwealth*, Sept. 24, 1853; Bacon, *History of Natick*, p. 144; *Natick Citizen*, Jan. 31, 1879; Mar. 4, 1881, quoting from *Providence Journal*; Nason and Russell, pp. 25–26, 29; *Natick Observer*, Nov. 10, 1860; *Henry Wilson, 18th Vice President*, p. 11; Nason, "Sketch of Wilson," p. 263.
69. *Henry Wilson, 18th Vice President*, p. 11; Nason and Russell, pp. 29–32; Bacon, *History of Natick*, p. 144; Phelps, p. 354; Linus P. Brockett, *Men of Our Day* (Philadelphia: Zeigler, McCurdy & Co., 1868), p. 390; *Natick Bulletin*, Nov. 26, 1875, quoting from *Boston Herald; Commonwealth*, July 14, 1852; Sept. 24, 1853; *National Era*, Oct. 20, 1853; *American Anti-Slavery Society at Its Third Decade*, pp. 102–3; *Congressional Globe*, 34th Cong., 1st sess., 1856, Appendix, p. 394.

70. *Henry Wilson, 18th Vice President*, p. 11; Farmer and Moore, pp. 51–53; Fogg, p. 377; Dwight, 4: 158–63; Whittier, *Appleton's Cyclopaedia*, 5: 548; Bacon, *History of Natick*, p. 144.
71. *Henry Wilson, 18th Vice President*, p. 11; Whittier, *Appleton's Cyclopaedia*, 5: 548; Bacon, *History of Natick*, p. 144; Nason, "Sketch of Wilson," p. 264; *Natick Bulletin*, Mar. 11, 1892; *National Era*, Oct. 20, 1853; Nason and Russell, pp. 32–34; *New York Tribune*, Nov. 24, 1875; Wilson to John R. French, Feb. 29, 1868, Wilson Papers, South Natick Museum.
72. P. C. Headley, *Massachusetts in the Rebellion* (Boston: Walker, Fuller and Co., 1866), p. 46; *Henry Wilson, 18th Vice President*, p. 11; Bacon, *History of Natick*, p. 144; *New York Tribune*, Nov. 24, 1875; Nason, "Sketch of Wilson," p. 264; *Natick Bulletin*, Mar. 11, 1892; *National Era*, Oct. 20, 1853; Mann, *Life of Wilson*, p. 14; Wilson to John R. French, Feb. 29, 1868, Wilson Papers, South Natick Museum; Nason and Russell, pp. 34–35.
73. John L. Myers, "The Beginning of Antislavery Agencies in New Hampshire, 1832–1835" *Historical New Hampshire* 25 (Fall 1970): 3–25; idem, "The Major Effort of Antislavery Agents in New Hampshire, 1835–1837," *Historical New Hampshire* 26 (Fall 1971): 3–27.
74. *Liberator*, Mar. 6, 1846.
75. Wilson to French, Feb. 29, 1868, Wilson Papers, South Natick Museum; *Natick Bulletin*, Nov. 26, 1875; Mar. 11, 1892, quoting from *Rochester Leader*; *Herald of Freedom*, Aug. 26, 1875; *New York Tribune*, Nov. 24, 1875; Nason and Russell, p. 34; Brockett, p. 390.

Chapter 2

1. Nason and Russell, p. 35; Mann, *Life of Wilson*, pp. 14–15; *Henry Wilson, 18th Vice President*, p. 11; *National Era*, Oct. 20, 1853.
2. Hazard, pp. 54, 63–76, 210–11; Bloun, pp. 1–48; Bacon, *History of Natick*, pp. 152–53; Nason and Russell, p. 35; *Boston Journal*, May 16, 1870.
3. Faler, pp. 58–64, 74–75.
4. Hazard, pp. 53–54, 68–70, 80–81, 213–18; Faler, pp. 59–61, 75; Bloun, *passim*; Nason and Russell, p. 36; Mann, *Life of Wilson*, pp. 14–15; *Natick Observer*, Nov. 10, 1860.
5. Hazard, pp. 68–70, 213–18; ledger, Wilson Papers, South Natick Museum.
6. Hazard, pp. 68–70, 213–18; Hurd, *Middlesex County*, 1: 554; *National Era*, Oct. 20, 1853; *Natick Observer*, Nov. 10, 1860; *Natick Bulletin*, Nov. 29, 1870; Wilson to Schouler, Aug. 5, 1841, William Schouler Papers, MHS; ledger, Wilson Papers, South Natick Museum; Mrs. J. D. Macewen, "Henry Wilson," clipping file, Morse Institute; Mann, *Life of Wilson*, p. 18.
7. Bacon, *History of Natick*, pp. 152–54; Crawford, *History of Natick*, p. 46; Hurd, *Middlesex County*, 1: 554.
8. Dawley, pp. 50–56; Faler, pp. 153–63.
9. Hazard, pp. 68–70; Bacon, *History of Natick*, p. 153; Mann, *Life of Wilson*, pp. 18–19.
10. Loubert, pp. 16–18; Mann, *Life of Wilson*, p. 19; Nason and Russell, pp. 35–36; *National Era*, Oct. 20, 1853; *Boston Journal*, Sept. 22, 1875; ledger for 1845 and 1846, Wilson Papers, South Natick Museum; Harriet Beecher Stowe, *Men of Our*

Times (Hartford, Conn.: Hartford Publishing Co., 1868), p. 271; *Congressional Globe*, 35th Cong, 1st sess., Appendix, p. 173.

11. *Boston Transcript*, Nov. 22, 1875.
12. Bacon, "Personal Recollections of Natick," p. 36.
13. First Congregational Church, *Natick*, pp. 68–70; Hurd, *Middlesex County*, 1: 542; Bacon, *History of Natick*, p. 89; Wilson and Fiske, eds., *Appleton's Cyclopaedia*, 3: 318; Frank M. Bishop, *300th Anniversary of the First Congregational Church, Natick, Massachusetts* (Boston: Lincoln & Smith, 1951), p. 19; *Commonwealth*, Jan. 2, 1869; Mar. 15, 1873; *Natick Bulletin*, Feb. 2, 1877; Mary Howe to Caroline C. Howe, July 7, 1850, Wilson Papers, South Natick Museum; Wilson to Hunt, May 29, 1856, Hunt to "My Dear Babies," Mar. 2, 1870, and clipping, review of *A History of the Rise and Fall of the Slave Power in America*, vol. 3, from the *Friend*, Samuel Hunt Papers, John Hay Library, Providence, R.I.; Nason and Russell, pp. 39–41; *Boston Journal*, Dec. 2, 1875.
14. Writings on tombstones of Harriet Howe Wilson and Mary T. Howe in Dell Park Cemetery, Natick; Thomas W. Baldwin, comp., *Vital Records of Natick, Massachusetts to 1850* (Boston: F. H. Gilson & Co., 1910), p. 197; clipping booklet, Morse Institute, 7.3; Nason, "Sketch of Henry Wilson," p. 264; Nason and Russell, pp. 42, 439n; Mary Ann Munroe to Caroline C. Howe, July 14 [no year given], Harriet Wilson to Caroline C. Howe, June 29, 1851, and legal papers for Nov. 8, 1859, and Apr. 3, 1863, sale and gift of lots, Wilson Papers, South Natick Museum; *Commonwealth*, Nov. 4, 1865; *Natick Bulletin*, Sept. 2, 1881.
15. Nason and Russell, p. 398; Mann, *Life of Wilson*, p. 18; Macewan, "Henry Wilson," clipping file, Morse Institute.
16. Nason and Russell, p. 397; Wilson to Henry Hamilton Wilson, May 2, 1860, Wilson Papers, South Natick Museum; Blanche Glassman Hersh, *The Slavery of Sex: Feminist-Abolitionists in America* (Urbana: University of Illinois Press, 1978), p. 175.
17. Nason and Russell, p. 42.
18. Ibid, p. 398; J. W. Buel, *Heroes of the Plains* (St. Louis: Historical Publishing Company, 1884), p. 108.
19. *Independent*, June 23, 1870.
20. *Natick Bulletin*, June 4, 1870.
21. Nason and Russell, pp. 396–99.
22. Ibid, pp. 42, 396–99.
23. Keith E. Melder, *The Beginnings of Sisterhood* (New York: Schocken Books, 1977), pp. 7–8; Barbara Welter, "The Cult of True Womanhood," *American Quarterly* 18 (Summer 1966): 151–52; Hersh, pp. 1–4.
24. Nason and Russell, pp. 42, 397–99.
25. *New York Times*, Nov. 23, 1875; *Natick Observer*, Feb. 11, 1860.
26. Wilson to Schouler, June 3, 1843, Schouler Papers; Nason and Russell, pp. 42–43; *Commonwealth*, Nov. 4, 1865; Mann, *Life of Wilson*, pp. 14, 18; Hazard, pp. 69, 215; warranty deed, Wilson Papers, South Natick Museum; Middlesex County, Southern District, Cambridge, Mass., Registry of Deeds, book 414, p. 279; diary, Nov. 10 and 11, 1843, Adams Family Papers, MHS.
27. Wilson to Bancroft, Feb. 16, 1843, George Bancroft Papers, MHS.
28. *Boston Journal*, Sept. 22, 1875; Dec 2, 1875; *Natick Bulletin*, Nov. 26, 1875.

29. *Boston Journal,* Jan. 1, 1872; *Henry Wilson, 18th Vice President,* p. 12; *Henry Wilson, Speech at the First New England Temperance Convention, Boston, October 3rd and 4th, 1866* (Boston: S. M. Usher, 1866), pp. 1–3; Wilson, *Speech on Prohibition,* p. 1; Nason and Russell, pp. 43, 54–58; Bacon, *History of Natick,* pp. 164–65, 178–81.
30. Robert L. Hampel, *Temperance and Prohibition in Massachusetts, 1813–1852* (Ann Arbor: UMI Research Press, 1982), pp. 14–17, 30–32, 49–51, 54–57, 79–87; George F. Clark, *History of Temperance Reform in Massachusetts, 1813–1883* (Boston: Clark & Carruth, 1888), pp. 18, 25, 34–40; *Boston Post,* Mar. 7, 1839; Sept. 30, 1839; *Commonwealth*, Mar. 1, 1852.
31. *Boston Journal,* Sept. 22, 1875; *National Era*, Oct. 20, 1853; *Henry Wilson, 18th Vice President,* p. 12; Bacon, *History of Natick,* p. 145; Nason and Russell, pp. 43–44.
32. *National Era*, Oct. 20, 1853; *Commonwealth*, Sept. 24, 1853; *Boston Journal*, Sept. 22, 1875.
33. Mann, *Life of Wilson*, pp. 5–6; Mann, *Henry Wilson's Boyhood*, pp. 32–35; Scales, p. 505; Hurd, *Rockingham and Strafford Counties*, pp. 628–29.
34. *Indianapolis Journal,* Aug. 5, 1872.
35. *National Era,* Oct. 20, 1853; *Boston Journal,* Sept. 22, 1875; Bacon, *History of Natick,* p. 145; Nason and Russell, p. 44; Hurd, *Middlesex County*, 1: 528.
36. Hart, 4: 77–93; Darling, pp. 40–82, *passim* to 156, 182–83, 214–19, 239–41, 288–90, 301–13; Oscar Handlin and Mary F. Handlin, *Commonwealth, a Study of the Role of Government in the American Economy: Massachusetts, 1774–1861*, rev. ed. (Cambridge: Harvard University Press, 1969), p. 200; Joseph G. Rayback, *Free Soil, the Election of 1848* (Lexington: University of Kentucky Press, 1970), pp. 77–78; Formisano, pp. 197–261; *Tribune Almanac,* 1841, p. 8.
37. William R. Brock, *Parties and Political Conscience: American Dilemmas, 1840–1860* (Millwood, N.Y.: KTO Press, 1979), pp. 53–63, 67.
38. Hart, 4: 74–76; Ronald Story, *The Forging of an Aristocracy* (Middletown, Conn.: Wesleyan University Press, 1980), *passim*; Edward Pessen, *Riches, Class, and Power before the Civil War* (Lexington, Mass.: D. C. Heath and Company, 1975), *passim*; Darling, pp. 2, 7, 12–17, 40–53, 173; Thomas H. O'Connor, *Lords of the Loom* (New York: Charles Scribner's Sons, 1968), pp. 28–35; Formisano, pp. 175–96; Kinley J. Brauer, *Cotton versus Conscience: Massachusetts Whig Politics and Southwestern Expansion, 1843–1848* (Lexington: University of Kentucky Press, 1967), pp. 12, 7–19; Handlin and Handlin, *Commonwealth*, pp. 183–86; Frederic C. Jaher, *The Urban Establishment* (Urbana: University of Illinois Press, 1982), pp. 44–56, 61–75.
39. Hart, 4: 81–83, 90–91; Darling, pp. 85–87, 96, 127–28, 156–57; Handlin and Handlin, *Commonwealth,* p. 202; Reinhard O. Johnson, "The Liberty Party in Massachusetts, 1840–1848: Antislavery Third Party Politics in the Bay State," *Civil War History* 28 (Sept. 1982): 237–43.
40. Darling, pp. 202–42, 251–70; Brauer, pp. 16–19.
41. Mann, *Life of Wilson*, pp. 14–15; *Boston Atlas*, Mar. 25, 1840; *Boston Post,* Mar. 30, 1840; *Natick Citizen*, Mar. 16, 1883.
42. *Boston Post*, Mar. 30, 1840; *Boston Atlas,* Mar. 25, 1840; *Natick Citizen*, Mar. 16, 1883.
43. *Natick Citizen*, Mar. 16, 1883; *Boston Atlas*, Mar. 25, 1840; *Boston Post*, Mar. 30, 1840; Mann, *Life of Wilson*, pp. 15–16.

44. *New York Times*, Oct. 30, 1875; *Natick Bulletin*, May 5, 1876; Jan. 22, 1897; *Boston Atlas*, Apr. 8, 1840; Nason and Russell, p. 45; James R. Munroe, *A Life of Francis Amasa Walker* (New York: Henry Holt and Company, 1933), pp. 10–15, 23; Henry Wilson, *A History of the Rise and Fall of the Slave Power in America*, 3 vols. (Boston: Houghton Mifflin Company, 1872–77), 2: 344.
45. *Natick Bulletin*, Jan. 22, 1897; *Boston Post*, Apr. 13, 1840; *Boston Atlas*, Apr. 8, 1840; Apr. 16, 1840; Mann, *Life of Wilson*, p. 16.
46. Robert G. Gunderson, *The Log Cabin Campaign* (Louisville: University of Kentucky Press, 1957), p. 201.
47. Ibid, p. 216.
48. Ibid, pp. 201–02, 207–08; McClure, *Recollections*, p. 4; *Boston Atlas*, June 18 and 19, 1840.
49. McClure, *Recollections*, pp. 287–88; William S. Robinson, *"Warrington" Pen Portraits* (Boston: Lee and Shepard, 1877), p. 20; Mann, *Life of Wilson*, p. 17; Phelps, p. 354; George S. Boutwell, *Reminiscences of Sixty Years in Public Affairs*, 2 vols. (New York: McClure, Phillips, 1902), 1: 79; Charles T. Congdon, *Reminiscences of a Journalist* (Boston: James R. Osgood and Company, 1880), p. 70; Ernest McKay, *Henry Wilson, Practical Radical* (Port Washington, N.Y.: Kennikat Press, 1971), pp. 18–19.
50. *Natick Bulletin*, Feb. 5, 1876; May 5, 1876; Feb. 2, 1877; *New York Tribune*, Nov. 23, 1875; Mann, *Life of Wilson*, pp. 17–18; Bacon, *History of Natick*, p. 145; Nason and Russell, pp. 45–46; *Commonwealth*, Sept. 24, 1853; Congdon, p. 70.
51. Memorial Addresses, pp. 101–102.
52. *Natick Bulletin*, Apr. 17, 1903.
53. *Boston Post*, May 22, 1840.
54. Wilson, *Rise and Fall*, 1: 424.
55. *The Tribune Almanac for the Years 1838 to 1880, Inclusive* (New York: New York Tribune, 1881), 1843: 38; Nason and Russell, p. 46; Mann, *Life of Wilson*, p. 18.
56. Natick Bulletin, Feb. 2, 1877; June 12, 1896; Bacon, "Personal Recollections," pp. 36–37; Levi S. Gould, *Ancient Middlesex with Brief Biographical Sketches of the Men Who Have Served the County Officially Since Its Settlement* (Somerville, Mass.: Somerville Journal Print, 1905), p. 177; Mann, "Rambling Thoughts."
57. Massachusetts, General Court, House, Journal of the House of Representatives of the Commonwealth of Massachusetts, 1841, *passim*, Appendices; Boutwell, *Reminiscences*, 1: 71.
58. Massachusetts, General Court, House, Journal, 1841, p. 33; *Henry Wilson, 18th Vice President*, p. 12; Nason and Russell, pp. 46–47; Mann, *Life of Wilson*, pp. 19–20.
59. Mann, *Life of Wilson*, pp. 19–20; *Springfield Republican*, May 8, 1858.
60. *Commonwealth*, Nov. 2, 1872; Robinson, *"Warrington,"* p. 527; *Emancipator and Republican*, May 10, 1849; *Boston Journal*, Oct. 25, 1872; *Springfield Republican*, May 8, 1858.
61. Nason and Russell, pp. 45–46.
62. *Boston Transcript*, Nov. 27, 1875; Boutwell, *Reminiscences*, 1: 79.
63. Wilson to Bancroft, Feb. 16, 1843, George Bancroft Papers; *Natick Bulletin*, Feb. 2, 1877; Wilson to Schouler, June 3, 1842, Schouler Papers; Robinson, *"Warrington,"* p. 401.

64. Massachusetts, General Court, House, Journal, 1841, Appendices 1—11, and House Legislative Document 15; *Commonwealth*, July 14, 1852; *Springfield Republican*, Feb. 3, 1855, quoting from *Cincinnati Gazette*.
65. Mann, *Life of Wilson*, pp. 19–20; *Boston Journal*, Sept. 22, 1875; *National Era*, Oct. 20, 1853; Massachusetts, General Court, House, Journal, 1842, House Document 22.
66. Massachusetts, General Court, House, Journal, 1842, House Document 37 and Appendices 3 and 4.
67. Wilson to Schouler, July 5, 1861 [actually 1841] and Aug. 5, 1841, Schouler Papers.
68. Mann, *Life of Wilson*, p. 25; Nason and Russell, p. 48; Wilson to Garrison, Dec. 30, 1865, William Lloyd Garrison Papers, Boston Public Library, hereafter cited as BPL; *Commonwealth*, July 14, 1852; Wilson to Schouler, July 5, 1861 [1841], Schouler Papers.
69. *Commonwealth*, July 14, 1852; Brauer, pp. 30–48; Mann, *Life of Wilson*, pp. 24–25.
70. O'Connor, pp. 45–49; Brauer, pp. 22–23.
71. Louis Ruchames, "Race, Marriage, and Abolition in Massachusetts," *Journal of Negro History* 40 (1955): 250–73; Wilson, *Rise and Fall*, 1: 489–92; Massachusetts, General Court, House, Journal, 1841, Appendix 3; idem, Journal, 1842, Appendix 7; *Boston Journal*, Feb. 15, 1842; *Liberator*, Feb. 24, 1842; *Commonwealth*, July 14, 1852; Nason and Russell, p. 48.
72. Massachusetts, General Court, House, Journal, 1842, pp. 52, 76, 83; *Boston Journal*, Jan. 20, 1842.
73. Mann, *Life of Wilson*, p. 25.
74. Nason and Russell, p. 48; Bacon, *History of Natick*, p. 145.
75. *New York Times*, Nov. 23, 1875; Mann, *Life of Wilson*, p. 23; Nason and Russell, p. 49; Massachusetts, General Court, Senate, Journal, 1844, pp. 11, 16; diary, Nov. 10 and 11, 1843, Adams Papers.
76. Springfield Republican, Feb. 3, 1855, quoting from the *Cincinnati Gazette*; Mann, *Life of Wilson*, p. 23; *Boston Journal*, Sept. 22, 1875; *New York Times*, Nov. 23, 1875; Hurd, *Middlesex County*, 1: 528; *Henry Wilson, 18th Vice President*, p. 13; Nason and Russell, pp. 51–54.
77. Mann, *History of Wilson*, p. 23; *New York Times*, Nov. 23, 1875; Thomas F. Edmands, "The Massachusetts Militia," *New England Magazine* 6 (Feb. 1895): 770–76; Massachusetts, General Court, Senate, 1844, Document 28.
78. Massachusetts, General Court, Senate, Legislative Documents, 1844, p. 34; idem, Journal, 1844, p. 316, and Document 28; Nason and Russell, pp. 49, 52; Mann, *Life of Wilson*, p. 23; Edmands, "The Massachusetts Militia," p. 770; diary, Feb. 16, 1844, Adams Papers.
79. Nason and Russell, pp. 53–54; *Boston Transcript*, Nov. 28, 1875.
80. Karl F. Kaestle, Pillars of the Republic: Common Schools and American Society, 1789–1860 (New York: Hill and Wang, 1983), p. 153; Hart, 4: 173.

Chapter 3

1. Brauer, pp. 43–48.
2. Wilson, *Rise and Fall*, 1: 424.
3. Wilson to Schouler, June 3, 1842, Schouler Papers; Hamilton A. Hill, *Memoir of Abbott Lawrence* (Boston: Wilson and Son, 1883), pp. 74–75; Brauer, pp. 77–80.

4. Hart, 4: 93; Brauer, pp. 77–84, 91; James Schouler, "The Whig Party in Massachusetts," *Proceedings of the Massachusetts Historical Society* 50 (Nov. 1916): 42–44; *Tribune Almanac*, 1844, p. 43; Darling, pp. 282, 288–89, 309–10; O'Connor, pp. 62–63; Formisano, pp. 298–301.
5. Brauer, pp. 55–57, 61; Hart, 4: 295.
6. Brauer, pp. 84–87, 92; Wilson to Schouler, June 2, 1842, Schouler Papers; diary, Feb. 16, 1844, and Charles Francis Adams to John Quincy Adams, Feb. 18, 1844, Adams Papers; Nathan Appleton, "Memoir of Abbott Lawrence," *Collections of the Massachusetts Historical Society*, 4th ser., 4 (1858): 500.
7. *Boston Journal,* Jan. 24, 1844; Brauer, pp. 62–63; *Boston Courier,* Feb. 4, 1844; Stowe, p. 272.
8. *Boston Courier,* Feb. 4, 1844.
9. Massachusetts, General Court, Senate, Journal, 1844, Document 27 and p. 75; *Thirteenth Annual Report of the Massachusetts Anti-Slavery Society*, (Boston: Massachusetts Anti-Slavery Society, 1845), pp. 4–6; Hart, 4: 295; *Boston Advertiser*, Feb. 21, 1844; *Boston Courier*, Feb. 24, 1844; diary, Feb. 20, 1844, and Charles Francis Adams to John Quincy Adams, Feb. 18, 1844, Adams Papers; Nason and Russell, p. 61; Wilson, *Rise and Fall*, 1: 482, 485.
10. Legislative Documents of the Massachusetts Senate, 1844, Senate Document 27; diary, Feb. 20 and 29 and Mar. 7, 1844, and Adams to his mother, Apr. 4, 1844, Adams Papers; *Boston Courier,* Feb. 24, 1844; Brauer, pp. 27, 60–63; Nason and Russell, p. 61; *Boston Advertiser,* Feb. 21, 1844; *Thirteenth Annual Report of the Massachusetts Anti-Slavery Society,* pp. 5–6; Wilson, *Rise and Fall,* 1: 482, 485.
11. Diary, Mar. 8 to 16, 1844, Adams Papers.
12. Brauer, pp. 64–66; Winthrop to Appleton, Feb. 21, 1844, and Winthrop to Lawrence, Feb. 21, 1844, Robert Winthrop Papers, MHS; Hudson to "Sir," Mar. 13, 1844, and Hudson to an unidentifiable person in Boston, Mar. 19, 1844, Charles Hudson Papers, American Antiquarian Society, Worcester, Mass.
13. Diary, Mar. 20 to 23, 1844, Adams Papers; Brauer, pp. 68–70; Frank O. Gatell, "Palfrey's Vote, the Conscience Whigs, and the Election of Speaker Winthrop," *New England Quarterly* 21 (June 1858): 219.
14. *Boston Courier*, Apr. 24, 1844; diary, Mar. 22 to Apr. 12, 1844, Adams Papers; Brauer, pp. 70–72.
15. *Boston Courier,* Apr. 24, 1844; Brauer, pp. 73–76; John Quincy Adams to Charles Francis Adams, Apr. 12, 1844, Adams Papers.
16. Wilson to Schouler, June 3, 1842, Dec. 17, 1843, and Apr. 16, 1844, Schouler Papers; *Natick Bulletin*, Feb. 2, 1877; John Quincy Adams to Charles Francis Adams, Apr. 12, 1844, Adams Papers; Hill, *Abbott Lawrence,* p. 76; *Boston Courier*, Apr. 24, 1844.
17. Diary, June 19, 1844, Adams Papers; Wilson to Schouler, Aug. 17, 1844, Schouler Papers; *Natick Bulletin,* Feb. 2, 1877.
18. Diary, *passim* summer 1844, particularly Aug. 22 and Sept. 30, 1844, and Adams to his mother, June 2, 1844, Adams Papers; Brauer, pp. 88–89, 93–96; David L. Child, *An Appeal from David L. Child, Editor of the Anti-Slavery Standard to the Abolitionists* (Albany: Albany Evening Journal, 1844).
19. W. Dean Burnham, *Presidential Ballots, 1836–1892* (Baltimore: Johns Hopkins Press, 1955), pp. 510–12; Darling, pp. 284–86, 316–19; Brauer, pp. 95–97; Johnson, "Liberty Party in Massachusetts," pp. 241–42; William G. Bean, "Party Transformations in Massachusetts, with Special Reference to the Antecedents of

Republicanism, 1848–1860" (Ph.D. diss., Harvard University, 1922), pp. 4–5.

20. Brauer, pp. 106–8; Robert C. Winthrop Jr., *A Memoir of Robert C. Winthrop* (Boston: Little, Brown and Company, 1897), p. 38; O'Connor, pp. 63–64.
21. Brauer, pp. 105–6; diary, Jan. 4, 1845, Adams Papers; Wilson, *Rise and Fall*, 1: 622.
22. Moorfield Storey and Edward W. Emerson, *Ebenezer Rockwood Hoar, a Memoir* (Boston: Houghton Mifflin Company, 1911), p. 39; Brauer, pp. 108–109; O'Connor, p. 65; *Fourteenth Annual Report of the Massachusetts Anti-Slavery Society*, (Boston: Massachusetts Anti-Slavery Society, 1846), pp. 29; Wilson, *Rise and Fall*, 1: 578–80.
23. Brauer, pp.108–109; *Fourteenth Annual Report of the Massachusetts Anti–Slavery Society*, pp. 29–32; Hart, 4: 339–40; diary, *passim*, Jan. and Feb., particularly Jan. 9, 1845, Adams Papers; Massachusetts, General Court, Senate, 1845, Document 31 and p. 369; Wilson, *Rise and Fall*, 1: 585.
24. Brauer, pp. 108–10; Charles Wiltse, ed., *The Papers of Daniel Webster: Correspondence*, ser. 1, 6 vols. (Hanover, N.H.: University Press of New England, 1974–1984), 6: 69; *Fourteenth Annual Report of the Massachusetts Anti–Slavery Society*, pp. 8–9; diary, Jan. 9, 13, 24, 25, and 31, 1845, Adams Papers; Wilson, *Rise and Fall*, 1: 622; Hart, 4: 295.
25. Brauer, pp. 101–2; O'Connor, p. 66; Darling, pp. 325–26; diary, Jan. 29, 1845, Adams Papers.
26. Diary, Jan. 8–11, 14, 22, and 27, 1845, Adams Papers; Brauer, pp. 114–18; *Boston Advertiser*, Jan. 30, 1845; Wilson, *Rise and Fall*, 1: 622.
27. Notice of a "Convention of the People," Letters Received, Adams Papers; *Boston Advertiser*, Jan. 24 and 27, 1845; *Fourteenth Annual Report of the Massachusetts Anti-Slavery Society*, p. 9; Brauer, pp. 117–19.
28. Brauer, pp. 118–26; diary, Jan. 22, 1845, and Adams to his mother, Jan. 24, 1845, Adams Papers; *Emancipator and Republican*, Oct. 18, 1849; *Commonwealth*, July 14, 1852; Wilson, *Rise and Fall*, 1: 637.
29. J. W. McIntyre, ed., *Writings and Speeches of Daniel Webster*, 18 vols. (Boston: Little Brown & Company, 1903), 16: 429; Wilson, *Rise and Fall*, 1: 623; *Commonwealth*, July 14, 1852; Apr. 22, 1871; *National Era*, Apr. 8, 1852; *Emancipator and Republican*, Oct. 18, 1849; George F. Hoar, "Charles Allen of Worcester," *Proceedings of the American Antiquarian Society*, n.s., 14 (Oct. 1901): 344–46; Nason and Russell, p. 62; diary, Jan. 29, 1845, and Adams to his mother, Jan. 31, 1845, Adams Papers.
30. *Boston Advertiser*, Jan. 30 and 31, 1845; Brauer, pp. 119–20; *Fourteenth Annual Report of the Massachusetts Anti-Slavery Society*, p. 9; *Emancipator*, Feb. 5, 1845; *Emancipator and Republican*, Oct. 18, 1849; Nason and Russell, p. 62; diary, Jan. 29 and 30, 1845, Adams Papers; Wilson, *Rise and Fall*, 1: 623.
31. *Emancipator*, Feb. 5, 1845; *Fourteenth Annual Report of the Massachusetts Anti-Slavery Society*, pp. 9–10; Wilson, *Rise and Fall*, 1: 623; diary, Jan. 29 and 30, 1845, Adams Papers; Brauer, pp. 120–25.
32. *Fourteenth Annual Report of the Massachusetts Anti-Slavery Society*, pp. 9–10; Brauer, pp. 123, 125–26; Wilson, *Rise and Fall*, 1: 623; diary, Feb. 10, 11, and 13, and Mar. 5, 1845, and S. C. Phillips to Adams, Mar. 3, 1845, Adams Papers.
33. Winthrop, pp. 38, 43; Brauer, pp. 104–8; Wilson, *Rise and Fall*, 1: 613–15.
34. Wilson, *Rise and Fall*, 1: 622; *Commonwealth*, July 14, 1852; *Liberator*, May 18, 1845; Massachusetts, General Court, Senate, Journal, pp. 285, 293, 318; diary, Feb. 14, 15, and 18, 1845, Adams Papers; *Fourteenth Annual Report of the Massachusetts*

Anti-Slavery Society, pp. 8–9, 29–33.

35. Massachusetts, General Court, Senate, Journal, 1845, p. 367; Brauer, pp. 110, 125–26; *Liberator*, May 16, 1845; S. C. Phillips to Adams, Mar. 3, 1845, and Adams to Palfrey, July 11, 1851, Adams Papers; Wilson, *Rise and Fall*, 1: 636; David Donald, *Charles Sumner and the Coming of the Civil War* (New York: Alfred A. Knopf, 1960), pp. 136–38; *Fourteenth Annual Report of the Massachusetts Anti-Slavery Society*, pp. 29–33.
36. Brauer, pp. 111–13; Wilson, *Rise and Fall*, 1: 636; diary, Mar. 7, 10, 14, 15, 25, and 26, 1845, Adams Papers; *Liberator*, May 16, 1845; Mar. 21, 1845.
37. *Boston Journal,* Mar. 19, 1845; *Liberator,* May 16, 1845; Wilson, *Rise and Fall,* 1: 636–37; *Fourteenth Annual Report of the Massachusetts Anti-Slavery Society,* pp. 29–33.
38. William P. Garrison and Francis J. Garrison, *William Lloyd Garrison, the Story of His Life Told by His Children,* 4 vols. (New York: Century Company, 1885–1889), 3: 136.
39. *Liberator*, Mar. 7, 1845; *Boston Post*, Feb. 21, 1845; Wilson, Slave Power, 1: 495–98; Nason and Russell, pp. 49–50.
40. Diary, Jan. 24, 1845, and Adams to his mother, Feb. 24, 1845, Adams Papers; Massachusetts, General Court, Senate, Journal, 1845, pp. 31–37 and *passim*.
41. Diary, Mar. 26, 1845, Adams Papers; ledger, Wilson Papers, South Natick Museum.
42. Brauer, pp. 127–32; Wilson, *Rise and Fall,* 1: 638; *Liberator*, July 25, 1845; Phillips, Allen, and Adams to "Dear Sir," June 25, 1845, Adams Papers; Winthrop, pp. 44–45.
43. Wilson, *Rise and Fall*, 1: 646–47; Brauer, p. 131; diary, Sept. 24, 1845, and Adams to Palfrey, July 11, 1851, Adams Papers.
44. Greeley, July 21, 1845, Wilson, July 10, 1845, Robinson, Aug. 6, 1845, and many others between July 1 and mid-August, 1845, all to Phillips, Allen, and Adams, Adams Papers.
45. *Lowell Daily Courier,* Aug. 4, 1845; *Liberator,* July 11, 1845; July 18, 1845; July 25, 1845; Aug. 8, 1845; diary, Aug. 25, 1845, Adams Papers; Wilson, *Rise and Fall*, 1: 638–41; Nason and Russell, pp. 62–63.
46. *Liberator,* Sept. 19, 1845; Sept. 26, 1845; Oct. 3, 1845, quoting from *Boston Post*; Wilson, *Rise and Fall*, 1: 641–43; Robinson, *"Warrington,"* p. 29; Storey, *Hoar*, pp. 40–41; *Emancipator*, Sept. 17, 1845; Sept. 24, 1845; Oct. 1, 1845; *Commonwealth*, July 14, 1853; diary, Sept. 17 and Oct. 2, 1845, and Adams to Wilson, Sept. 15, 1845, Adams Papers; Samuel T. Pickard, *Life and Letters of John Greenleaf Whittier,* 2 vols. (Boston: Houghton Mifflin and Company, 1899), 1: 662–63; James B. Stewart, "The Aims and Impact of Garrisonian Abolitionism, 1840–1860," *Civil War History* 15 (Sept. 1969): 201–2; Nason and Russell, p. 63; Garrison and Garrison, 3: 140–41.
47. *Liberator*, Sept. 26, 1845; Wilson, *Rise and Fall*, 1: 642; Storey, *Hoar*, p.40; *Emancipator and Republican,* Oct. 18, 1849.
48. *Liberator*, Sept. 26, 1845; Oct. 10, 1845; Wilson, *Rise and Fall,* 1: 642–43; *Emancipator*, Sept. 17, 1845; Sept. 24, 1845; Oct. 8, 1845; Elizur Wright to Adams, Sept. 13, 1845, and circular, Samuel Sewell and Elizur Wright to "Dear Friend," Oct. 10, 1845, Adams Papers; *Emancipator and Republican,* Oct. 18, 1849.
49. *Liberator*, Oct. 10, 1845; Oct. 31, 1845; Nov. 14, 1845; Jan. 30, 1846; *Emancipator*, Nov. 5, 1845; *Lowell Daily Courier*, Oct. 22, 1845; *Commonwealth*, July 14, 1853; Wilson, *Rise and Fall*, 1: 643–44; Storey, *Hoar*, pp. 41–42; diary, Oct. 9, 10, 20–22, 30—31, and Nov. 7, 1845, and Sewell to Adams, Oct. 8, 10, and 16, 1845, Wright to Adams, Oct. 13 and 27, 1845, Hoar to Adams, Oct. 24, 1845, an eleven-page tract

with an Address to the Friends of Free Institutions in Massachusetts and Other Free States issued by the Committee appointed at the Oct. 21, 1845, Cambridge meeting, Adams Papers; Frank O. Gattel, *John Gorham Palfrey and the New England Conscience* (Cambridge: Harvard University Press, 1963), p. 126; Brauer, pp. 141–45; *Fourteenth Annual Report of the Massachusetts Anti-Slavery Society*, pp. 9–11.

50. Charles Sumner, *The Works of Charles Sumner*, 15 vols. (Boston: Lee and Shepard, 1870–1883), 1: 143.

51. Diary, Oct. 31 and Nov. 1, 3, 4, and 6, 1845, Sewell to Adams, Oct. 24, 1845, Wright to Adams, Oct. 27, 1845, Palfrey, Phillips, and Adams to John Quincy Adams, Adams Papers; Stanton to Smith, Nov. 5, 1845, Gerrit Smith Papers, Syracuse University Library; Storey, *Hoar*, p. 42; Garrison and Garrison, 3: 142–43; Wilson, *Rise and Fall*, 1: 645; *Emancipator*, Nov. 12, 1845; *Liberator*, Oct. 31 and Nov. 7, 1845; *Fourteenth Annual Report of the Massachusetts Anti-Slavery Society*, p. 11.

52. *Lowell Daily Courier*, Nov. 13, 1845; *Liberator*, Oct. 31, 1845; Nov. 14, 1845; Nov. 21, 1845; Dec. 5, 1845; Dec. 19, 1845; Jan. 30, 1846; Wilson, *Rise and Fall*, 1: 646; *Free State Rally*, Dec. 6, 1845; *Fourteenth Annual Report of the Massachusetts Anti-Slavery Society*, pp. 11–12; *Commonwealth*, July 14, 1852; diary, Nov. 15, 17, 18, 21, and 22, 1845, Adams to Lawrence, Nov. 13, 1845, and Lawrence to Adams, Nov. 17, 1845, Adams Papers; E. L. Pierce, ed., *Memoir and Letters of Charles Sumner*, 4 vols. (Boston: Roberts Brothers, 1877–1893), 3: 103.

53. Diary, Nov. 25, 26, 28, and 29, and Dec. 6 and 16, 1845, and Whittier to Adams, Dec. 12, 1845, Adams Papers; John B. Pickard, ed. *The Letters of John Greenleaf Whittier*, 3 vols. (Cambridge: Harvard University Press, 1975), 1: 680–82; Whittier, *Appleton's Cyclopaedia*, 5: 548; Albert Mordell, *Quaker Militant: John Greenleaf Whittier* (Boston: Houghton Mifflin Company, 1933), p. 14; *Liberator*, Jan. 30, 1846; *Emancipator and Republican*, Oct. 18, 1849.

54. Wilson, *Rise and Fall*, 1: 647; *Emancipator and Republican*, Oct. 18, 1849; John Pickard, 1: 683; diary, Dec. 18, 1845, Adams Papers; *Liberator*, Jan. 30, 1846.

55. Stanton to Smith, Dec. 18, 1845, Smith Papers; Gattel, *Palfrey*, p. 127; Wilson, *Rise and Fall*, 1: 649; *Emancipator and Republican*, Oct. 18, 1849; *Liberator*, Jan. 30, 1846; *Free State Rally*, Jan. 12, 1846; diary, Nov. 28 and Dec. 2, 9, 12, 13, 18, 20, 23, 25, and 30, 1845, and Adams to his mother, Dec. 15, 1845, Adams Papers; *Fourteenth Annual Report of the Massachusetts Anti-Slavery Society*, pp. 10–12; Arthur H. Rice, "Henry B. Stanton as a Political Abolitionist," (Ph.D. diss., Columbia University, 1968), pp. 261–62; Brauer, pp. 156–58.

56. Slade to Adams, Dec. 24, 1845, Adams Papers.

Chapter 4

1. Brauer, pp. 132–33, 149–50; Hurd, *Middlesex County*, 1: 528; *Reunion of the Free Soilers of 1848, at Downer Landing, Higham, Massachusetts, August 9, 1877* (Boston: Albert J. Wright, 1877), p. 20; Formisano, pp. 33–34; *Boston Post*, Oct. 2, 1845; Brockett, p. 392; Nason and Russell, p. 65.

2. Diary, Jan. 8, 19, 27, and 28, 1846, Adams Papers; Brauer, p. 164; Martin B. Duberman, *Charles Francis Adams* (Boston: Houghton Mifflin Company), p. 110.

3. *Liberator*, Feb. 13, 1846; *Fourteenth Annual Report of the Massachusetts Anti-Slavery Society*, p. 96.

4. George L. Austin, *The History of Massachusetts from the Landing of the Pilgrims to the Present Time* (Boston: B. B. Russell, 1876), pp. 445–46; Mann, *Life of Wilson,* pp. 26–27; *Liberator,* Feb. 6, 1846; Wilson, *Rise and Fall,* 2: 115; *Boston Courier,* Jan. 31, 1846; *Fifteenth Annual Report of the Massachusetts Anti-Slavery Society,* pp. 12–13.
5. Nason and Russell, pp. 65–66; Massachusetts, General Court, House, Journal, 1846, pp. 175, 184, 224, 280–81; Wilson, *Rise and Fall* 2: 115–16; *Boston Courier*, Feb. 4, 1846; Feb. 19, 1846; *Emancipator*, Feb. 11, 1846; Feb. 25, 1846; *Liberator,* Feb. 20, 1846; Mar. 6, 1846; *Fifteenth Annual Report of the Massachusetts Anti-Slavery Society,* pp. 12–14.
6. Nason and Russell, pp. 66–86; *The Liberator*, Mar. 6, 1846; *Boston Courier*, Feb. 19, 1846.
7. *The Liberator*, Feb. 20, 1846; Mar. 6, 1846; Apr. 10, 1846; Apr. 17, 1846; Apr. 24, 1846; *Fifteenth Annual Report of the Massachusetts Anti-Slavery Society,* pp. 12–14; Massachusetts, General Court, House, Journal, pp. 280–81, 318, 335, 563, 591, 602, 624, and House Report, No. 89; *Emancipator*, Feb. 25, 1846; Apr. 29, 1846; *Boston Courier*, Feb. 19, 1846; Feb. 21, 1846; *Commonwealth*, July 14, 1852; Wilson, *Rise and Fall*, 2: 116–18; Storey, *Hoar*, pp. 43–44; Pierce, 3: 106; Mann, *Life of Wilson,* pp. 27–28.
8. Diary, Apr. 18, 1846, Adams Papers; Mann, *Life of Wilson*, p. 27; *Emancipator*, Apr. 22, 1846.
9. *Liberator*, Mar. 13, 1846; *Boston Journal*, Feb. 27, 1846; Nason and Russell, p. 87.
10. George H. Haynes, *Charles Sumner* (Philadelphia: George W. Jacobs & Company, 1909), p. 103; Charles Francis Adams Jr., *Charles Francis Adams* (Boston: Houghton Mifflin and Company, 1900), pp. 50–51; journal, pp. 196–98, John Gorham Palfrey Papers, Houghton Library, Harvard University, Cambridge, Mass.; Pierce, 3: 47–48, 106; diary, Dec. 25, 1845, May, *passim*, June 6, 16, 19, and 20 and Aug. 25, 1846, quotation by Wilson is May 19, Adams to Louisa Catherine Adams, July 5, 1846, and Louisa Catherine Adams to Adams, May 23, 1846, Adams Papers; *Boston Whig*, June through Sept., *passim*, 1846.
11. Diary, June 26 and 27, July 3, 18, 21, 22, 25, 28, 30, and 31, and Aug. 6 and 22, 1846, Adams Papers; *Boston Whig*, July 23, 1846.
12. Irving H. Bartlett, *Daniel Webster* (New York: W. W. Norton & Company, 1978), pp. 229–32; Hoar, "Charles Allen," p. 347; Winthrop, p. 51; Pierce, 3: 107–11; *Boston Whig,* June 5, 1846; Wilson, *Rise and Fall,* 2: 118; Brauer, pp. 170–72.
13. Adams, *Adams*, p. 63; diary, July 1, 15, 16, and 27 and Aug. 3, 10, 11, 14, and 20, 1846, Adams Papers; journal, p. 198, Palfrey Papers; Pierce, 3: 107–17; Winthrop, pp. 51–57; *Boston Whig, passim*, July and early Aug., 1846; Aug. 14, 1846; Aug. 19, 1846; *Liberator,* May and June, 1846, *passim*; Wilson, *Rise and Fall*, 2: 118; Winthrop to Sumner, Aug. 17, 1846, Appleton to Sumner, Aug. 10 and 20, 1846, and Buckingham to Sumner, Sept. 30, 1846, Sumner Papers, Houghton; Brauer, pp. 168–80.
14. Diary, May 16 and July 25 and 28, 1846, Adams Papers; *Boston Whig*, July 9, 1846; Aug. 19, 1846.
15. Brauer, pp. 167–68; *Boston Whig*, July 31, 1846.
16. Lawrence to Davis, Sept. 10, 1846, John W. Davis Papers, American Antiquarian Society, Worcester, Mass.; diary, Sept. 9, 10, 14, 21, and 23, 1846; Pierce, 3: 122.
17. Diary, Sept. 4, 5, and 19–22, 1846, Adams Papers.

18. Pierce, 3: 123; Sumner, 1: 313–14; diary, Sept. 23, 1846, Adams Papers; *Boston Whig*, Sept. 24, 1846; Sept. 26, 1846; *Boston Courier*, Sept. 24, 1846; Sept. 25, 1846; *Emancipator and Republican*, Oct. 18, 1849; *Boston Journal*, Aug. 16, 1869; *Emancipator*, Sept. 30, 1846; *Commonwealth*, July 14, 1852; Henry B. Stanton, *Random Recollections*, 3d ed. (New York: Harper & Brothers, 1887), pp. 149–50; Whittier to Sumner, Sept. 25, 1846, Whittier-Pickard Papers, Houghton; Wilson, *Rise and Fall*, 2: 118–21; Robinson, *"Warrington,"* pp. 30–31, 404–5; Bartlett, p. 230; Duberman, *Adams*, pp. 114–18.
19. Wilson, *Rise and Fall*, 2: 120–22; *Boston Whig*, Sept. 25, 1846; diary, Sept. 24, 25, and 28, and Oct. 1, 1846, Adams Papers; Appleton to Sumner, Oct. 1, 1846, Sumner Papers; Pierce, 3: 119, 123; Duberman, *Adams*, p. 119; *Boston Advertiser*, Sept 28, 1846; Sept. 29, 1846.
20. Wilson, *Rise and Fall*, 2: 122; diary, Sept. 28 and 29, Oct., *passim*, and Nov. 5, 7, and 10, 1846, Adams Papers; Pierce, 3: 134–38; Winthrop, p. 56; *Boston Whig*, Oct. 30, 1846; *Boston Atlas*, Oct. 31, 1846; Laura E. Richards, ed., *Letters and Journals of Samuel Gridley Howe* (Boston: Dana Estes & Company, 1909), pp. 248–49; Brauer, pp. 199–204.
21. *Lowell Courier*, Oct. 7, 1846; Storey, *Hoar*, p. 46; diary, Oct. 7, 8, and 12 and Nov. 10, 1846, Adams Papers; *Boston Advertiser*, Nov. 10, 1846; *Boston Whig*, Nov. 11, 1846; Nov. 12, 1846; *Boston Courier*, Nov. 10, 1846; Nov. 11, 1846; Palfrey to Hoar, Sept. 30, 1846, and Hoar to Palfrey, Oct. 1, 1846, Palfrey Papers.
22. Brauer, pp. 204–5; *Boston Advertiser*, Nov. 10, 1846; *Boston Atlas*, Nov. 10, 1846; diary, Nov. 10–12 and 27 and Dec. 3, 1846, Adams to Giddings, Dec. 16 and 30, 1846, and Feb. 22, 1847, and Giddings to Adams, Dec. 11, 1846, Adams Papers.
23. Adams to Palfrey, Feb. 14, 1847, and Adams to Giddings, Feb. 22, 1847, and Giddings to Adams, Feb. 26, Apr. 16, and Sept. 12, 1847, Adams Papers; Josiah Morrow, ed., *Life and Speeches of Thomas Corwin* (Cincinnati: W. H. Anderson & Co. 1896), pp. 47–51; Norman Graebner, "Thomas Corwin and the Election of 1848," *Journal of Southern History* 17 (May 1951): 162–64, 172–73; Francis P. Weisenberger, *The Life of John McLean* (Columbus: The Ohio State University Press, 1937), pp. 112–13; Wilson to Giddings, Feb. 6, 1847 and Greeley to Giddings, Apr. 24 and May 5, 1847, Joshua Giddings Papers, Ohio Historical Society, Columbus, Ohio.
24. *Boston Whig*, Mar. 27, 1847; Wilson to Giddings, Feb. 6, 1847, Giddings Papers; Morrow, pp. 47–51; Weisenberger, pp. 113–14.
25. Wilson to Schouler, Nov. 26, 1846, Schouler Papers; Nason and Russell, p. 88; diary, Dec. 16, 1846, Adams Papers; Baldwin, p. 101; Mary Ann Munroe to Caroline C. Howe, July 14 [no year given], and Lowly Ann Coolidge to Howe, June 21, 1847, Wilson Papers, South Natick Museum.
26. *Natick Bulletin*, June 12, 1896; Hazard, pp. 213–16; Baldwin, pp. 27, 129.
27. Crawford, pp. 46–49; Bacon, *History of Natick*, pp. 107–8, 124; Conklin, 2: 600, 602; Hurd, *Middlesex County*, 1: 528, 560; Annual Report of the Circle of Industry for 1845, Wilson Papers, South Natick Museum; Lucie M. Child, "West Central Street: Its Trees and Residences," *The Historical Collections of the Historical Natural History and Library Society*, 3 vols. (South Natick, Mass.: The Historical Natural History and Library Society, 1919–1930), 2: 36–37; John W. Bacon, "Natick Public Libraries and Their Origin," *The Historical Collections of the Historical Natural History and Library Society*, 2: 42; *Commonwealth*, Aug. 28, 1869; Wilson to Schouler, Oct. 31, 1846, Schouler Papers; Wilson to Convers Francis, Dec. 21, 1846,

Chamberlain Papers, BPL.

28. *Sixteenth Annual Report of the Massachusetts Anti-Slavery Society*, (Boston: Massachusetts Anti-Slavery Society, 1848), pp. 15–17; *National Era,* May 13, 1847; *Northampton Courier,* May 1, 1847; Pierce, 3: 140; diary, Apr. 16, 23, 24, and 28, 1847, Adams Papers; Brauer, pp. 210–13; Bartlett, pp. 232–34.
29. Diary, Mar. 15 and Apr. 7, 1847, Adams Papers; Wilson to Giddings, Apr. 10, 1847, and Adams to Giddings, May 19, 1847, Giddings Papers; *Emancipator*, Apr. 21, 1847; June 16, 1847.
30. *Boston Whig*, June 17, 1847; June 12, 1847; diary, June 23 and 25 and July 3, 1847, Adams Papers.
31. Diary, Aug. 3, 5, 9, 11, 12, 16, 19, and 21, 1847, Adams Papers; *Boston Whig*, Aug. 18, 1847; *National Era*, Sept. 30, 1847.
32. Corwin to Giddings, Aug. 18 and 19, 1847, Adams to Giddings, Sept. 7, 1847, and Adams to J. C. Vaughan, Oct. 21, 1847, Giddings Papers; Corwin to Sumner, Sept. 2 and 20 and Oct. 25, 1847, Sumner Papers; Graebner, "Thomas Corwin," pp. 165–73; *National Era*, Sept. 30, 1847; diary, Sept. 6, 25, and 28, 1847 and Adams to J. C. Vaughan, Oct. 21, 1847, Adams Papers; Sumner to Chase, Oct. 1, 1847, Salmon P. Chase Papers, Library of Congress, Washington, D.C., hereafter LC.
33. Diary, Aug. 25 and Sept. 22, 24, 25, and 27, 1847, Adams Papers; *Liberator*, Sept. 24, 1847; *Commonwealth*, July 14, 1852; *Boston Whig*, Sept. 28, 1847; Sept. 29, 1847.
34. Diary, Sept. 15, 22, 24, 25, and 27–29, 1847, Adams Papers; *Liberator*, Sept. 24, 1847; *Boston Advertiser*, Sept. 30, 1847; *Boston Courier*, Sept. 30, 1847; Oct. 1, 1847; Pierce, 3: 143–46; *Commonwealth*, July 14, 1852; *Emancipator and Republican,* Oct. 18, 1849; *Boston Whig*, Oct. 1, 1847; Oct. 2, 1847; Oct. 16, 1847; Winthrop, p. 65; Wilson, *Rise and Fall*, 2: 123–24; Sumner to Giddings, Oct. 1, 1847, Giddings Papers; journal, pp. 204–5, Palfrey Papers.
35. *National Era*, Apr. 8, 1852; Brauer, pp. 217–19; *Boston Advertiser*, Sept. 30, 1847; *Boston Courier*, Oct. 1, 1847; *New York Tribune*, Oct. 2, 1847; George S. Merriam, *The Life and Times of Samuel Bowles,* 2 vols. (New York: The Century Company, 1885), 1: 48–49; Wilson, *Rise and Fall*, 2: 124; Sumner to Chase, Oct. 1, 1847, Chase Papers, LC; diary, Sept. 29 and Oct. 12, 1847, Adams Papers.
36. Darling, pp. 342–46; Brauer, pp. 218–19; Rayback, pp. 77–78; diary, Nov. 2–4, 9, 15, and 20, 1847, Adams Papers; *Liberator*, Dec. 3, 1847; *National Era*, Jan. 20, 1848.
37. *National Era*, Dec. 9, 1847; Winthrop, pp. 68–73; Brauer, pp. 219–22; diary, Nov. 5, 12, 15, 20, and 30 and Dec. 7, 8, 14, 15, and 18, 1847, Adams to Palfrey, Dec. 11 and 17, 1847, Adams to Giddings, Feb. 17, 1848, Adams Papers; Adams to Schouler, Nov. 18, 1847, and Schouler to Adams, Nov. 18, 1847, Schouler Papers; Sumner to Giddings, Dec. 10, 1847, Giddings to Joseph A. Giddings, Dec. 25, 1847, and *passim,* early February, 1848, Giddings Papers; Charles R. Corning, *Amos Tuck* (Exeter, N.H.: The News Letter Press, 1902), pp. 32, 52–54.
38. Frederick J. Blue, *The Free Soilers: Third Party Politics, 1848–1854* (Urbana: University of Illinois Press, 1973), pp. 39–41, 44–46; Brauer, pp. 223–24.
39. Diary, Jan. 20 and 21, 1848, and Adams to Giddings, Dec. 30, 1847, and Jan. 24, 1848, and Adams to Palfrey, Feb. 12, 1848, Adams Papers; *Emancipator,* Dec. 9, 1846; Sumner to Chase, Feb. 7, 1848, Chase Papers, LC.
40. *Boston Whig,* Dec. 22, 1847; *National Era,* Jan. 20, 1848; *Liberator*, Jan. 21, 1848; Adams to Palfrey, Jan. 19 and Feb. 2, 1849, Adams to Giddings, Feb. 8, 1848, and Wilson to Adams, Jan. 3, 1848, Adams Papers; *New York Tribune*, Apr. 1, 1848;

Springfield Republican, Feb. 24, 1848; Feb. 28, 1848; Apr. 5, 1848.

41. *New York Tribune*, Feb. 29, 1848; Mann, *Life of Wilson*, p. 29; Palfrey to Sumner, Feb. 28, 1848, Palfrey Papers; diary, Mar. 9, 14, and 15, and Apr. 4, 1848, Adams Papers; Wilson to Mann, Mar. 17, 1848, Mann Papers; *Emancipator*, Mar. 22, 1848; *National Era*, Apr. 13, 1848; Oct. 20, 1853; *Boston Journal*, Sept. 22, 1875.
42. Wilson, *Rise and Fall*, 2: 124; Mann, *Life of Wilson*, pp. 29–30; Frank O. Gatell, "Conscience and Judgment: the Bolt of the Massachusetts Conscience Whigs," *The Historian* 21 (Nov. 1958): 20; *Springfield Republican*, Apr. 6, 1848; Apr. 29, 1848; *National Era*, Oct. 20, 1853; *Emancipator*, Mar. 22, 1848; *Boston Whig*, Apr. 29, 1848; *Commonwealth*, July 14, 1852; Adams to Palfrey, Mar. 14, 1848, Adams Papers; Charles Allen to Palfrey, May 22, 1848, Palfrey Papers.
43. *National Era*, Apr. 8, 1852; *Commonwealth*, July 14, 1852.
44. Pierce, 3: 164; diary, Apr. 20, 21, and 29, May 1, 18, 23, and 27, 1848, and Adams to Wilson, Sept. 2, 1870, Adams Papers; *Natick Bulletin*, Mar. 17, 1899; Sumner to Palfrey, Apr. 22, 1848, Palfrey Papers; Gattel, "Conscience and Judgment," p. 24; *Commonwealth*, Mar. 1, 1852; *Liberator*, Mar. 12, 1852. In 1870 when Wilson, then seeking information for his history of *The Rise and Fall of the Slave Power*, asked Adams for his recollections of events of this month, Adams ignored Wilson's May 18 visit and gave primary credit to Allen for instigating the May 27 meeting.
45. Diary, May 15, 27, and 30 and June 1, 1848, Adams to Palfrey, May 26 and 30, 1848, Adams to Wilson, Sept. 2, 1870, and Hoar to Adams, June 5, 1848, Adams Papers; Pierce, 3: 165; *Natick Bulletin*, Mar. 17, 1899; Keyes to Sumner, May 27, 1848, Sumner Papers; Wilson, *Rise and Fall*, 2: 125; *Reunion of the Free Soilers, 1877*, p. 15; Storey, *Hoar*, p. 52; Sumner to Palfrey, June 8, 1848, Palfrey Papers.
46. Gattel, "Conscience and Judgment," pp. 22–23; Sumner to Palfrey, May 24, 1848, Palfrey Papers; *Emancipator*, Apr. 26, 1848; *Commonwealth*, Mar. 1, 1852; July 14, 1852; *Liberator*, Mar. 12, 1852; *National Era*, Apr. 8, 1852; Winthrop, pp. 82–83; diary, June 2, 3, 7, and 9, 1848 and Adams to Palfrey, May 30 and 31, 1848, Adams Papers.
47. Diary, June 4 and 9, 1848, Adams Papers; *Northampton Courier*, June 14, 1848; June 24, 1848; *National Intelligencer*, June 8–12, 1848; *New York Tribune*, June 10, 1848; June 12, 1848; *National Era*, June 15, 1848; Gattel, "Conscience and Judgment," p. 25; Wilson, *Rise and Fall*, 2: 135–37; Holman Hamilton, *Zachary Taylor, Soldier in the White House* (Indianapolis: The Bobbs-Merrill Company, 1951), p. 88.
48. *National Intelligencer*, June 12, 1848; *Northampton Courier*, July 1, 1848; *Seventeenth Annual Report of the American Anti-Slavery Society* (New York: American Anti-Slavery Society, 1849), pp. 16–17; *Commonwealth*, July 14, 1852; *New York Tribune*, June 10, 1848; June 13, 1848; *National Era*, Oct. 20, 1853; *Springfield Republican*, June 12, 1848; *Boston Whig*, June 12, 1848; *New York Post*, Jan. 7, 1853; Hoar, "Charles Allen," pp. 351–52; Wilson, *Rise and Fall*, 2: 135–36.
49. *Springfield Republican*, June 12, 1848; *Boston Whig*, June 12, 1848; *Liberator*, June 16, 1848; *National Intelligencer*, June 12, 1848; *New York Tribune*, June 10, 1848; Wilson, *Rise and Fall*, 2: 136–38; *National Era*, Oct. 20, 1853; *Reunion of the Free Soilers, 1877*, p. 15; McClure, *Recollections*, p. 288.
50. *New York Tribune*, June 10, 1848; *Springfield Republican*, June 12, 1848; June 14, 1848; Wilson, *Rise and Fall*, 2: 137; Oliver Dyer, *Great Senators of the United States Forty Years Ago* (New York: Robert Bonner's Sons, 1889), pp. 38–39, 78; O'Connor, pp. 78–79; Hale to his mother, June 11, 1848, Nathan Hale Jr. Papers, Smith College

Library, Northampton, Mass.; A. E. Eastman to Lawrence, June 14, 1848, Amos A. Lawrence Papers, MHS; diary, June 10, 1848, Adams Papers; Gattel, "Conscience and Judgment," p. 25; Brauer, pp. 234–35.

51. Wilson, *Rise and Fall*, 2: 142–43; *Commonwealth*, July 14, 1852; Stanley Matthews to Chase, June 12, 1848, Chase Papers, LC.
52. Rayback, pp. 182–83; Bailey to Sumner, May 31, 1848, Sumner Papers; diary, June 4, 9, and 10, 1848, and Adams to Stanton, June 8, 1848, Adams Papers; *Boston Whig*, June 10, 1848; *Liberator*, June 23, 1848; Wilson, *Rise and Fall*, 2: 145.
53. *Reunion of the Free Soilers, 1877*, pp. 12–13, 73; Bartlett, pp. 237–39; *Commonwealth*, Mar. 1, 1852; Mann, *Life of Wilson*, p. 31; Sumner to Giddings, June 8, 1848, Giddings Papers; Sumner to Palfrey, June 8, 1848, Palfrey Papers; diary, June 14–17, 1848 and Adams to Palfrey, June 10, 1848, Adams Papers; McIntyre, 16: 495, 496, 498; *Springfield Republican*, June 14, 1848; Gattel "Conscience and Judgment," pp. 28–29.
54. *Boston Transcript*, June 9, 1848; *Boston Whig*, June 17, 1848; *Springfield Republican*, June 14, 1848; June 15, 1848; June 27, 1848; June 28, 1848; *New York Tribune*, June 22, 1848; June 25, 1848; Wilson, *Rise and Fall*, 2: 145; Robinson, "*Warrington*," p. 37; J. N. Brewer to Schouler, May 21, 1848, Schouler Papers.
55. diary, June 12, 17, 19, and 21–27, 1848, Adams Papers; Adams to Giddings, June 15, 1848 and Sumner to Giddings, June 17, 1848; Giddings Papers; Allen to Sumner, June 17, 1848, Sumner Papers; Sumner to Palfrey, June 21, 1848, Palfrey Papers; Sumner to Mann, June 21, 1848 and Wilson to Mann, June 22, 1848, Mann Papers; Gattel, "Conscience and Judgment," pp. 27–28, 38.
56. *Reunion of the Free Soilers, 1877*, pp. 57, 63; Hoar, "Charles Allen," pp. 356–58; *Liberator*, June 30, 1848; *Emancipator*, June 28, 1848; Wilson, *Rise and Fall*, 2: 145; Allen to Sumner, June 17, 1848, Sumner Papers.
57. *Northampton Courier*, July 1, 1848; Wilson, *Rise and Fall*, 2: 144–45; Pickard, *John Greenleaf Whittier*, 2: 103; *Liberator*, June 30, 1848; *Reunion of the Free Soilers, 1877*, p. 15; Pierce, 3: 165; Mann, *Life of Wilson*, p. 30; *Springfield Republican*, June 24, 1848; *Boston Transcript*, June 22, 1848; Thomas N. Brewer to Mann, June 15, 1848, Mann Papers; Giddings to his daughter, June 30, 1848, Joshua Giddings–George W. Julian Papers, LC.

Chapter 5

1. Gattel, *Palfrey*, p. 164; idem, "Conscience and Judgment," p. 33; Pierce, 3: 166; *New York Tribune*, June 30, 1848; *National Era*, July 13, 1848; Sumner, *The Works of Charles Sumner*, 2: 81; *Emancipator*, July 5, 1848; *Springfield Republican*, June 29, 1848; *Boston Transcript*, June 29, 1848.
2. Gattel, "Conscience and Judgment," pp. 29–34; Austin Willey, *The History of the Antislavery Cause in State and Nation*, (New York: Negro Universities Press, 1969), p. 340; diary, June 28, 1848, Adams Papers; *Emancipator*, July 5, 1848; *Northampton Courier*, July 1, 1848; *Springfield Republican*, June 29, 1848; *New York Tribune*, June 30, 1848; *Liberator*, July 7, 1848; *Boston Whig*, June 30, 1848; Wilson, *Rise and Fall*, 2: 145–46; Sumner, *The Works of Charles Sumner*, 2: 81; Frank P. Stearns, *Life and Public Services of George Luther Stearns* (Philadelphia: J. B. Lippincott Co., 1907), p. 59; *Reunion of the Free Soilers, 1877*, pp. 30–34, 68–69; Robinson, *"Warrington,"*

pp. 183–85.

3. *Springfield Republican*, June 30, 1848; Sumner, *The Works of Charles Sumner*, 2: 81; Gattel, "Conscience and Judgment," pp. 29, 33; Nathan Appleton to Sumner, July 4, Aug. 17, and Sept. 4, 1848, and Sumner to Appleton, July 8, and Aug. 12 and 31, 1848, Sumner Papers; *Boston Atlas*, June 30, 1848; July 3, 1848; *Northampton Courier*, July 3, 1848; *Emancipator*, June 28, 1848.
4. *Reunion of Free Soilers, 1877*, pp. 18–19; George F. Hoar, *Autobiography of Seventy Years*, 2 vols. (New York: C. Scribner's Sons, 1903), 1: 152; Hoar, "Charles Allen," pp. 353–54.
5. *Springfield Republican*, June 29, 1848; June 30, 1848; *Liberator*, July 7, 1848; July 14, 1848; *Northampton Courier*, July 1, 1848; Wilson, *Rise and Fall*, 2: 145; *Boston Transcript*, July 1, 1848; diary, June 30 and July 1, 1848, Adams Papers; Giddings to his daughter, June 30, 1848, Giddings-Julian Papers; Giddings to Joseph A. Giddings, July 7, 1848, Giddings Papers; Samuel Shapiro, *Richard Henry Dana, Jr., 1815–1882* (East Lansing: Michigan State University Press, 1961), pp. 32–34.
6. Gattel, "Conscience and Judgment," p. 31; Rayback, pp. 205–14; Blue, pp. 54–58; Willey, p. 340; Wilson, *Rise and Fall*, 2: 140–44; *Springfield Republican*, June 29, 1848; *passim*, June 20–30, 1848; diary, June 23, 1848, Adams Papers.
7. *Northampton Courier*, July 1, 1848; *Springfield Republican*, June 29, 1848; June 30, 1848; Wilson, *Rise and Fall*, 2: 146–48; *Commonwealth*, Mar. 1, 1852; July 14, 1852; *National Era*, Apr. 8, 1852; *Reunion of the Free Soilers, 1877*, pp. 72–73; Nason and Russell, p. 90; Bean, "Party Transformation," pp. 24–26; diary, June 27, 1848, Adams Papers; Wilson to Mann, July 10, 1848, and Sumner to Mann, July 2, 1848, Mann Papers; Sumner to Palfrey, July 4, 1848, Palfrey Papers; Darling, pp. 350–52.
8. Rayback, pp. 201–7, 215–17; Gattel, "Conscience and Judgment," pp. 42–44; Blue, pp. 54–69; journal, pp. 211–12, Palfrey Papers; Sumner to Chase, June 12, 1848, and July 7, Chase Papers, LC; Giddings to Joseph A. Giddings, July 30, 1848, Giddings Papers; diary, July 11, 14, and 15, 1848, and Adams to E. I. Hamlin, July 12, 1848, and Adams to Palfrey, July 30, 1848, Adams Papers.
9. Diary, July 2, 6, 10, 24, and 25 and Aug. 1, 2, and 4, 1848, and Adams to Palfrey, July 6, 23, and 30, 1848, and Adams to S. F. Lyman, July 21, 1848, Adams Papers; Storey, *Hoar*, p. 62; *Emancipator*, July 12, 1848; *National Era*, July 20, 1848; Aug. 17, 1848; *Northampton Courier*, July 15, 1848; *New York Tribune*, July 19, 1848.
10. Journal, August 8–11, 1848, Dana Papers; *Reunion of the Free Soilers, 1877*, pp. 51–53, 57–59, 69; *Northampton Courier*, Aug. 22, 1848; Oliver Dyer, *Phonographic Report of the Proceedings of the National Free Soil Convention, . . . 1848* (Buffalo: G. H. Derby & Company, 1848), pp. 6, 27–32; diary, Aug. 8–10, 1848, Adams Papers; Pierce, 3: 168–70; Chase to "My Dear Taylor," Aug. 15, 1848, Salmon P. Chase Papers, Historical Society of Pennsylvania, hereafter referred to as HSP; William Jackson to Mann, Aug. 19, 1848, Mann Papers, MHS; Rayback, pp. 218–29; Blue, pp. 70–71, 76–79.
11. Oliver C. Gardiner, *The Great Issue* (Westport, Conn.: Negro Universities Press, 1970), pp. 137–40; *Reunion of Free Soilers, 1877*, p. 17; Eric Foner, *Free Soil, Free Labor, Free Men* (London: Oxford University Press, 1970), p. 83; Pierce, 3: 168–70; Dyer, pp. 12; Rayback, pp. 225–26; Blue, pp. 71–75.
12. Wilson, *Rise and Fall*, 2: 150–56.

13. Gardiner, p. 138; Jackson to Mann, Aug. 19, 1848, Mann Papers; *Reunion of Free Soilers, 1877*, p. 43; Garrison to Edmund Quincy, Aug. 10, 1848, Garrison Papers, Smith College Library, Northampton, Mass.; *Emancipator*, Aug. 2, 1848; Aug. 16, 1848; Aug. 23, 1848; Aug. 30, 1848; *National Era*, Aug, 17, 1848; Wilson, *Rise and Fall*, 2: 150–56; Richard H. Sewell, *Ballots to Freedom: Antislavery Politics in the United States, 1837–1860* (New York: Oxford University Press, 1976), pp. 189–99.
14. Diary, Aug 25 and 28 and Sept. 1 and 2, 1848, Adams Papers; *Emancipator*, Aug. 30, 1848; Sept. 13, 1848; *Northampton Courier*, Aug. 29, 1848; Sept. 12, 1848; *Boston Advertiser*, Sept. 8, 1848; Sumner to Giddings, Sept. 3, 1848, Giddings Papers; Gattel, *Palfrey*, p. 173; Wilson, *Rise and Fall*, 2: 157.
15. *Boston Transcript*, Sept 12, 1848.
16. *National Era*, Sept. 7, 1848; Darling, pp. 350–52; *Northampton Courier*, Oct. 1848, *passim*; *Emancipator*, Nov. 8, 1848; *Boston Transcript*, Nov. 1, 1848.
17. Nason and Russell, p. 90; *Commonwealth*, Sept. 24, 1853; *Emancipator*, June 28, 1848; *Henry Wilson, 18th Vice President*, pp. 13–14; Robinson, "*Warrington*," p. 38; diary, Apr. 5 and 8–11, Aug. 24, and Sept. 12, 1848, and Adams to Palfrey, June 18 and July 9, 1848, Adams Papers; Loubert, pp. 74–75.
18. Nason and Russell, p. 91.
19. Ibid., pp. 90–91; *Emancipator*, Aug. 23, 1848; *Emancipator and Free Soil Press*, Sept. 20, 1848; Nov. 8, 1848; *Emancipator and Republican*, Nov. 23, 1848; Feb. 9, 1848; *passim*, Nov. 1848 to July 1849; Headley, p. 46; Loubert, pp. 74–75.
20. Diary, Jan. 10, 16, 20, and 22, 1849, and Adams to Palfrey, Jan. 23, 1849, Adams Papers; Estes Howe to Palfrey, Feb. 13, 1849, Palfrey Papers; Robinson, "*Warrington*," p. 42; Loubert, p. 76; *Emancipator and Republican*, Jan. 26, 1849; Feb. 2, 1849; Feb. 9, 1849; Dec. 26, 1850; *Boston Chronotype*, Feb. 8, 1849.
21. Nason and Russell, pp. 90–91; *Emancipator*, Aug. 23, 1848; Robinson, "*Warrington*" pp. 38–42; Loubert, pp. 74–76; Adams to Palfrey, Jan. 23, 1849, Adams Papers; Estes Howe to Palfrey, Feb. 13, 1849, Palfrey Papers; *Boston Transcript*, Feb. 7, 1849; *Emancipator and Republican*, Nov. 17, 1848; Dec. 26, 1848; Feb. 9, 1849; May 31, 1849; Dec. 26, 1850; *passim*, Jan. to July 1849.
22. *Natick Observer*, Nov. 10, 1860; *Natick Bulletin*, Oct. 29, 1870; Nason and Russell, p. 37; Bacon, *History of Natick*, p. 153; Hazard, pp. 68–70; Faler, pp. 77–79, 91–92.
23. *Natick Bulletin*, June 26, 1896; H. C. Fisher to Mann, Aug. 2, 1848, Mann Papers.
24. Storey, *Hoar*, pp. 73–77; Sumner to Giddings, Nov. 10, 1848, Giddings Papers; *National Era*, Oct. 20, 1853; *Boston Telegraph*, Jan. 30, 1855; *Emancipator*, Sept. and Oct. 1848, *passim*; *Northampton Courier*, Oct 11, 1848; Oct. 1848, *passim*; Donald, *Sumner*, p. 168; Pierce, 3: 171–74.
25. Diary, July 3 and 5, Sept. 18 and 25, and Oct. 4 and 13, 1848, Adams Papers; *Boston Transcript*, Oct. 20, 1848.
26. Dyer, *Great Senators*, pp. 104–5; John T. Morse Jr., *Memoir of Colonel Henry Lee* (Boston: Little, Brown and Company, 1905), p. 54; Pierce, 3: 177–79; *National Era*, Nov. 16, 1848; Blue, pp. 131; Brauer, p. 243; Rayback, p. 245.
27. Svend Peterson, *A Statistical History of the American Presidential Elections*, (New York: Frederick Ungar Publishing Company, 1963), p. 29; Sewell, *Ballots*, pp. 167–68; *Northampton Courier*, Nov. 21, 1848; Rayback, pp. 279–88; Blue, pp. 134–37; James G. Blaine, *Twenty Years of Congress*, 2 vols. (Norwich, Conn.: Henry Bill Publishing Company, 1884–86), 1: 77; Pierce, 3: 175.

28. Peterson, p. 29; Burnham, pp. 510–12; *Tribune Almanac*, 1849, pp. 42, 48; Marcus Morton to Sumner, Aug. 26, 1848, Sumner Papers; *Emancipator and Republican*, Jan. 5, 1849; Bean, "Party Transformation," pp. 27–31; Darling, pp. 352–53; Duberman, *Adams*, p. 157; Rayback, p. 299; Kevin Sweeney, "Rum, Romanism, Representation, and Reform: Coalition Politics in Massachusetts, 1847–1853," *Civil War History* 22 (June 1976): 117–18.
29. Pierce, 3: 183–84; Sewell, *Ballots*, pp. 167–68; Schouler, "The Whig Party in Massachusetts," pp. 48–49; *Northampton Courier*, Nov. 21, 1848; Sumner to Giddings, Nov. 10, 1848, Giddings Papers; Sumner to Chase, Nov. 16, 1848, Chase Papers, LC; Hoar, "Charles Allen," pp. 357–61; Blue, pp. 109–17, 134; *National Era*, Nov. 16, 1848; Robinson, "Warrington," pp. 482–83; *Emancipator and Republican*, Jan. 12, 1849.
30. Clare Taylor, British and American Abolitionists: an Episode in Transatlantic Understanding (Edinburgh: Edinburgh University Press, 1974), pp. 332–33.
31. Adams, *Adams*, p. 100–101; Duberman, *Adams*, pp. 158–59; diary, Dec. 7, 1848, Adams Papers.
32. Blue, pp. 152–78; John Mayfield, *Rehearsal for Republicanism: Free Soil and the Politics of Anti-Slavery* (Port Washington, N.Y.: Kennikat Press, 1980), *passim*; Boutwell, *Reminiscences*, 1: 115; *Northampton Courier*, Apr. 10, 1849; May 8, 1849; June 5, 1849; Thomas H. Brown, "George Sewell Boutwell: Public Servant (1818–1905)," (Ph.D. diss., New York University, 1979), pp. 41–42; Sewell, *Ballots*, pp. 145–46, 167–68, 204–6, 218–19; Wilson, *Rise and Fall*, 2: 337–41; Rice, pp. 311–15; Stanton to Chase, Feb. 24, 1849, and Sumner to Chase, Nov. 16, 1848, and Feb. 7 and 27, 1849, Chase Papers, LC; Hans L. Trefousse, *The Radical Republicans* (New York: Alfred A. Knopf, 1969), pp. 34–35.
33. *Emancipator and Republican*, May 17, 1849; June 7, 1849; June 14, 1849; *Northampton Courier*, Apr. 10, 1849; May 8, 1849; June 5, 1849; diary, Feb. 19 and 23, Apr. 4, and June 2, 1849, Adams Papers.
34. Diary, Feb. 19 and Apr. 10, 1849, Adams Papers; *Chronotype*, Mar. 5, 1849; *Liberator*, Apr. 6, 1849; *Emancipator and Republican*, May 17, 1849; Sumner to Giddings, July 3, 1849, Giddings-Julian Papers.
35. *Emancipator and Republican*, June 28, 1849; July 26, 1849; *Northampton Courier*, June 26, 1849.
36. Sumner to Giddings, June 29 and Aug. 20, 1849, Giddings-Julian Papers; diary, Sept. 1, 1849, Adams Papers; E. R. Hoar to Palfrey, June 24, 1849, Sumner to Palfrey, Aug. 31 and Sept. 13, 1849, and Estes Howe to Palfrey, Sept. 13, 1849, Palfrey Papers.
37. Diary, June 1, 6, 7, and 19, 1849, and Adams to Gamaliel Bailey, June 15, 1849, Adams Papers; *Emancipator and Republican*, Aug. 16, 1849; Aug. 23, 1849; Sept. 20, 1849.
38. James A. Whitson to Sumner, July 27, 1849, Sumner Papers; Pierce, 3: 185; Moorfield Storey, *Charles Sumner* (Boston: Houghton, Mifflin and Company, 1900), p. 76; Donald, *Sumner*, pp. 178–81; Blue, pp. 208–11; Bean, "Transformation," pp. 34–35; Sweeney, p. 120; Charles Francis Adams Jr., *Richard Henry Dana, a Biography*, 2 vols. (Boston: Houghton, Mifflin and Company, 1890), 1: 169; diary, Sept. 12, 1849, Adams Papers.
39. Morton to F. A. Hildreth, May 11 and Aug. 18 and 29, 1849, Marcus Morton Papers, MHS; Marcus Morton Jr. to Adams, May 31, 1849, Adams Papers; *Northampton Courier*, Sept. 11, 1849.

40. *Emancipator and Republican*, Aug. 23, 1849; Oct. 18, 1849; Sweeney, p. 120.
41. *Emancipator and Republican*, Aug. 30, 1849; Sept. 6, 1849; Sept. 20, 1849; Oct. 4, 1849; Oct. 18, 1849; *Chronotype*, Aug. 24, 1849; Sept. 13, 1849; *Northampton Courier*, Sept. 18, 1849; *National Era*, Sept, 27, 1849; diary, Sept. 8, 11, 12, and 15, 1849, Adams Papers; *Commonwealth*, Sept. 24, 1853; Donald, *Sumner*, pp. 181–82.
42. *Chronotype*, Sept. 20, 1849; *Northampton Courier*, Sept. 25, 1849; Morton to "My Dear Sir," Aug. 25, 1849, Morton Papers; *Boston Post*, Sept. 19, 1849; Boutwell, *Reminiscences*, 1: 113; Pierce, 3: 188; Wilson, *Rise and Fall*, 2: 338–39; Benjamin F. Hallett, *Mr. Hallett's Reply to Mr. Wilson's "Personal Explanation" "A Question of Veracity" Evaded by Senator Wilson and Again Settled Against Him* (1856), *passim*; Bean, "Transformation," pp. 35–37; Thomas Brown, pp. 41–42; *Emancipator and Republican*, Sept. 27, 1849.
43. *Emancipator and Republican*, Sept. 27, 1849; Oct. 4, 1849; Rice, pp. 314–16; Sumner to Chase, Sept. 18, 1849, and Stanton to Chase, Oct. 1, 1849, Chase Papers, LC; S. A. Maynard to Sumner, Sept. 23 and Oct. 19, 1849, Sumner Papers; Sumner to Giddings, Oct. 19, 1849, Giddings Papers; *Northampton Courier*, Sept. 25, 1849; Oct. 23, 1849; Wilson, *Rise and Fall*, 2: 338–41; diary, Sept. 15 and Oct. 4, 1849, Adams Papers.
44. *Northampton Courier*, Sept. 25, 1849; Stanley Harrold, *Gamaliel Bailey and Antislavery Union* (Kent, Ohio: Kent State University Press, 1986), p. 146.
45. *Boston Courier*, Oct. 15, 1849, quoting from *Lowell American*; Oct. 16–20, 1849, *passim*; Oct. 25, 1849; Nov. 2, 1849; *Northampton Courier*, Oct. 30, 1849; Dec. 6, 1853, quoting from *Plymouth Rock*; *Emancipator and Republican*, Oct. 18, 1849; Nov. 1, 1849; diary, Oct. 4, 11, 13, 15, 17, and 31 and Nov. 1, 1849, Adams Papers; Wilson, *Rise and Fall*, 2: 345; Hoar, *Autobiography*, 1: 171; Duberman, *Adams*, pp. 160–62; Sumner to Giddings, Oct. 19 and Nov. 3, 1849, Giddings Papers; journal, Oct. 1849, Dana Papers; *Boston Transcript*, *passim*, Oct.–early Nov., 1849; Blue, p. 210–12.
46. *Emancipator and Republican*, Oct. 18, 1849.
47. *Boston Transcript*, Nov. 9, 1849; *Emancipator and Republican*, Oct. 18, 1849; Nov. 1, 1849; *Northampton Courier*, Oct. 30, 1849; *Chronotype*, Oct. 30, 1849.
48. *Natick Bulletin*, June 26, 1896; *Emancipator and Republican*, Dec. 6, 1849.
49. Sumner to Giddings, Nov. 3, 1849; diary, Nov. 13 and 17, 1849, Adams Papers; *Boston Transcript*, Nov. 13 and 15, 1849; *Northampton Courier*, Nov. 13 and 20, 1849; *Tribune Almanac*, 1850, p. 42; *Emancipator and Republican*, Nov. 1, 1849; Nov. 15, 1849; Nov. 22, 1849; *New York Evening Post*, Jan. 7, 1853; Boutwell, *Reminiscences*, 1: 115; Wilson, *Rise and Fall*, 2: 339; Pierce, 3: 188; Blue, pp. 211–12.
50. *Emancipator and Republican*, Dec. 20, 1847; Dec. 27, 1847; Winthrop, p. 97; Sumner to Giddings, Nov. 29, 1849, and Giddings to his wife, Dec. 2, 1849, Giddings Papers.
51. *Boston Transcript*, Nov. 9, 1872.
52. S. A. Maynard to Sumner, Oct. 19, 1849, Sumner Papers; diary, Nov. 15, 1849, Adams Papers; Sumner to Giddings, Oct. 19, 1849, Giddings Papers; Duberman, *Adams*, p. 453n; *Emancipator and Republican*, Nov. 15, 1849; Nov. 22, 1849; Dec. 13, 1849; *Chronotype*, Nov. 16, 1849; *Northampton Courier*, Nov. 20, 1849.
53. *Emancipator and Republican*, Aug. 9, 1849; Oct. 18, 1849; *Boston Transcript*, Oct. 17, 1849; Oct. 31, 1849; Nov. 8, 1849.

54. *Emancipator and Republican*, Jan. 10, 1850; Jan. 17, 1850; Massachusetts, General Court, House, 1850, Legislative Documents, p. 57; *Commonwealth*, Sept. 24, 1853; *Chronotype*, Jan. 3, 1850; *Northampton Courier*, Jan. 8, 1850; Jan. 15, 1850; *Boston Transcript*, Jan. 9, 1850.
55. Bean, "Transformation," pp. 39–40; Sweeney, p. 122.
56. *Emancipator and Republican*, Mar. 22, 1849; Apr. 19, 1849; Pierce, 3: 223; Bean, "Transformation," pp. 39–40.
57. *Emancipator and Republican*, Jan. 17, 1850; Jan. 24, 1850; *Boston Transcript*, Jan. 14, 1850; Jan. 19, 1850; *Northampton Courier*, Jan. 22, 1850.
58. *Emancipator and Republican*, May 2, 1850; *Boston Transcript*, Apr. 27, 1850; *Northampton Courier*, Apr. 23, 1850; Apr. 30, 1850; Bean, "Transformation," p. 39.
59. *Emancipator and Republican*, Jan. 31, 1850; Feb. 28, 1850; *Northampton Courier*, Jan. 29, 1850; Bean, "Transformation," pp. 39–40; *Boston Transcript*, Jan. 26, 1850.
60. *Boston Transcript*, Jan. 22, 1850; Jan. 28, 1850; Feb. 18, 1850; *Emancipator and Republican*, Jan 24, 1850; Jan. 31, 1850; Feb. 14, 1850; Feb. 21, 1850; Feb. 28, 1850; Mar. 14, 1850.
61. Massachusetts, General Court, House, 1850, Journal, p. 733, Appendix 26, and House Legislative Document No. 153; *Chronotype*, *passim*, Sept., 1849; Oct. 10, 1849; Blue, pp. 128–29.
62. *Northampton Courier*, Jan. 22, 1850; Hoar, *Autobiography*, 1: 29; *Emancipator and Republican*, May 2, 1850.
63. *Emancipator and Republican*, Mar. 7, 1850; *Boston Transcript*, Mar. 1, 1850.
64. Massachusetts, General Court, House, Journal, 1850, pp. 203, 318, 323, 335 and Appendix 9; *Emancipator and Republican*, Feb. 21, 1850; Feb. 28, 1850; Mar. 7, 1850; *Boston Transcript*, Feb. 7, 1850; Feb. 22, 1850; Mar. 1, 1850; *Dedham Gazette*, Mar. 2, 1850; Mar. 30, 1850.
65. *Emancipator and Republican*, Feb. 7, 1850.
66. Northampton Courier, Jan. 22, 1850; Massachusetts, General Court, House, 1850, Appendix 16.

Chapter 6

1. *Boston Transcript*, Mar. 6, 1850.
2. Massachusetts, General Court, House, Journal, 1850, pp. 47, 53, 56, and 103 and Document No. 33; diary, Jan. 9, 1850, Adams Papers; *Emancipator and Republican*, Jan. 17, 1850; *Northampton Courier*, Jan. 15, 1850; *Chronotype*, Jan. 12, 1850; *Boston Transcript*, Jan. 11, 1850; Wilson, *Rise and Fall*, 2: 247; *Nineteenth Annual Report of the Massachusetts Anti-Slavery Society* (Boston: Massachusetts Anti-Slavery Society, 1851), p. 49.
3. Diary, Jan. 11, 21, and 28, 1850, Adams Papers; *Emancipator and Republican*, Jan. 31, 1850; Adams to Giddings, Jan. 27, 1850, and Giddings to Joseph A. Giddings, Jan. 20, 1859, Giddings Papers.
4. Wilson, *Rise and Fall*, 2: 250.
5. Diary, Feb. 2, 4, 5, 14, 15, and 26–28, and Mar. 1, 1850, Adams Papers; journal, Feb. 27, 1850, Dana Papers; *Emancipator and Republican*, Feb. 14, 1850; Feb. 28, 1850; *Dedham Gazette*, Feb. 16, 1850; Mar. 2, 1850; *Northampton Courier*, Mar. 5, 1850; *Boston Transcript*, Feb. 13, 1850; Feb. 27, 1850; *Liberator*, Mar. 8, 1850; Wilson,

Rise and Fall, 2: 249–52; Pierce, 3: 221.

6. Wilson, *Rise and Fall*, 2: 248–50; *Liberator*, Feb. 8, 1850; Mar. 1, 1850; *Northampton Courier*, Feb. 19, 1850; *Emancipator and Republican*, Feb. 7, 1850; Mar. 28, 1850; Bean, "Transformation," p. 42; Massachusetts, General Court, House, Journal, 1850, pp. 181, 237, 340–45, 353–54; idem, Document No. 33; Loubert, pp. 84–86.
7. *Liberator*, Feb. 22, 1850; Massachusetts, General Court, House, Journal, 1850, pp. 245, 254, 266, 267, 304, 351; idem, Appendices 5, 6, and 8.
8. *Emancipator and Republican*, Mar. 7, 1850.
9. Ibid.; Apr. 25, 1850; *Northampton Courier*, Mar. 12, 1850; *Dedham Gazette*, Mar. 2, 1850; Bean, "Transformation," pp. 40–41.
10. *Emancipator and Republican*, Mar. 14, 1850, including one article from the *Boston Post*; Mar. 21, 1850; Apr. 11, 1850; Apr. 25, 1850; *Northampton Courier*, Mar. 12, 1850; Mar. 19, 1850; *Boston Transcript*, Mar. 12, 1850; Apr. 6, 1850.
11. *Emancipator and Republican*, Apr. 11, 1850; Apr. 18, 1850; Apr. 25, 1850.
12. Diary, Sept. 15 and 20, 1849 and Jan. 31, 1850, Adams Papers.
13. Ibid., Jan. 5, 1850.
14. Ibid., Mar. 4, 12, and 25 and May 20, 1850, and White to Adams, Mar. 21, 1850, and T. W. Higginson to Adams, May 23, 1850; Higginson to Palfrey, Aug. 21, 1850, Palfrey Papers; *Northampton Courier*, June 11, 1850.
15. Davis to Briggs, Mar. 3, 1850, George N. Briggs Papers, American Antiquarian Society.
16. Wilson, *Rise and Fall*, 2: 241–42, 249; Bartlett, p. 245; Hamilton, p. 31; Winthrop, pp. 111–13.
17. Bartlett, pp. 245–50; Pierce, 3: 195–201; Hamilton, pp. 307–10.
18. Godfrey T. Anderson, "The Slavery Issue as a Factor in Massachusetts Politics from the Compromise of 1850 to the Outbreak of the Civil War," (Ph. D. diss., University of Chicago, 1944), pp. 6–7; diary, Apr. 2, 1850, Everett Papers; O'Connor, pp. 83–85; Sumner to Chase, Mar. 9, 1850, Chase Papers, LC; Giddings to Joseph A. Giddings, Mar. 8 and 16, 1850, and Sumner to Giddings, Apr. 9, 1850, Giddings Papers; Bean, "Transformation," pp. 44–46; *Nineteenth Annual Report of the Massachusetts Anti–Slavery Society*, pp. 12–13; Pierce, 3: 204–6; Donald, *Sumner*, pp. 183–85; *Boston Atlas*, Mar. 13, 1850; *Boston Transcript*, Mar. 20, 1850; *Northampton Courier*, Mar. 19, 1850; Charles R. Williams, ed., *Diary and Letters of Rutherford B. Hayes*, 5 vols. (Columbus: Ohio State Archaeological and Historical Society, 1922–1926), 1: 296.
19. Pierce, 3: 204–6; Anderson, pp. 1–6; *Boston Transcript*, Mar. 11, 1850.
20. *Boston Transcript*, Mar. 11, 1850, quoting from the *Boston Post.*
21. O'Connor, pp. 84–85; Anderson, pp. 10–11, 14; *Nineteenth Annual Report of the Massachusetts Anti-Slavery Society,* pp. 12–13; Giddings to Joseph Giddings, Apr. 11, 1850, Giddings Papers; *Emancipator and Republican*, Apr.11, 1850.
22. William Jackson to Mann, Mar. 22, 1850, Mann Papers; diary, Apr. 4 and 8, 1850, Adams Papers; Bean, "Transformation," p. 51.
23. *Emancipator and Republican*, Mar. 14, 1850.
24. *Dedham Gazette*, Mar. 16, 1850; Wilson, *Rise and Fall*, 2: 241–42.
25. Robinson, *"Warrington,"* pp. 404–5; Mann, *Life of Wilson*, p. 32–33; Nason and Russell, pp. 91–93; Wilson, *Slave Power*, 2: 341; Fred H. Harrington, *Fighting Politician, Major General N. P. Banks* (Philadelphia: University of Pennsylvania

Press, 1948), pp. 9–11.

26. *Reunion of the Free Soilers*, 1877, p. 73.
27. Ibid., p.76.
28. Hoar, *Autobiography*, 1: 132.
29. Archibald H. Grimke, *The Life of Charles Sumner, the Scholar in Politics* (New York: Funk & Wagnalls Company, 1892), p. 202.
30. Haynes, *Sumner*, p. 125.
31. Mann, *Life of Wilson*, p. 31.
32. Diary, Nov. 22, 1875, Adams Papers.
33. *Natick Bulletin*, June 26, 1896; Loubert, p. 78.
34. Wilson, *Rise and Fall*, 2: 254.
35. Diary, Mar. 11, 15, 18, 21, and 22, 1850, Adams Papers; Massachusetts, General Court, House, Journal, 1850, pp. 445, 471, 480, 486–87 and Appendices 10 and 11; Wilson, *Rise and Fall*, 2: 252–55; *Boston Transcript*, Mar. 20, 1850; *Emancipator and Republican*, Mar. 21, 1850; Mar. 28, 1850; *Northampton Courier*, Apr. 2, 1850; *Nineteenth Annual Report of the Massachusetts Anti-Slavery Society*, pp. 49–51.
36. Massachusetts, General Court, House, Journal, 1849, pp. 492–93, 498–99, 7l0 and Appendices 12 and 13; Wilson, *Rise and Fall*, 2: 255; *Emancipator and Republican*, Apr. 11, 1850; May 2, 1850; *Northampton Courier*, May 7, 1850; *Liberator*, Apr. 19, 1850; May 17, 1850.
37. Wilson, *Rise and Fall*, 2: 256; *Liberator*, Mar. 22, 1850; Mar. 29, 1850; *Boston Transcript*, Mar. 26, 1850; William Jay to Sumner, Mar. 14, 1850, and Francis Jackson, Wendell Phillips, and Samuel G. Howe to Sumner, Mar. 21, 1850, Sumner Papers.
38. Calvin Fairbank, *Rev. Calvin Fairbank during Slavery Times* (New York: Negro Universities Press, 1969), p. 71.
39. *Emancipator and Republican*, Apr. 18, 1850; May 2, 1850; Wilson, *Rise and Fall*, 2: 257–58, 341; *Boston Transcript*, May 1, 1850; May 4, 1850; *Dedham Gazette*, May 4, 1850; Haynes, *Sumner*, p. 125; Anderson, p. 9; Claude M. Fuess, *Daniel Webster*, 2 vols. (Hamden, Conn.: Archon Books, 1963), 2: 224–27.
40. Wilson to Palfrey, Apr. 20, 1850, Palfrey Papers; diary, Apr. 11 and 13 and May 15, 18, 22, 28, and 29, 1850, Adams Papers; Bigelow to Sumner, May 24, 1850, Sumner Papers; *Emancipator and Republican*, May 23, 1850; May 30, 1850; June 6, 1850; Duberman, *Adams*, p. 168.
41. *Emancipator and Republican*, May 2, 1850.
42. *Emancipator and Republican*, July 4, 1850; Leet [?] Coolidge to Caroline C. Howe, June 6, 1850, and Harriet Wilson to Caroline Howe, July 30, 1850, Wilson Papers, South Natick Museum.
43. *Emancipator and Republican*, Aug. 30, 1849; Sept. 6, 1849; Sept. 27, 1849; Aug. 29, 1850; Sept. 5, 1850; Sept. 19, 1850.
44. Ibid., June 6, 1850; June 20, 1850; Pierce, 3: 209; Francis Bowen to Palfrey, Nov. 26, 1849, Palfrey Papers; McIntyre, 16: 548.
45. *Emancipator and Republican*, July 18, 1850.
46. McIntyre, 16: 557, 559.
47. *Emancipator and Republican*, Aug. 1, 1850; Aug. 15, 1850; Aug. 22, 1850; diary, July 28 and Aug. 2, 13, 19, and 23, 1850, Adams Papers; Sumner to William Bates and James M. Stone, Aug. 12, 1850, Miscellaneous Collection, BPL; Pierce, 3: 207–8; *Commonwealth*, July 14, 1852; O'Connor, p. 86; Bean, "Transformation," p. 49.

48. *Commonwealth*, July 14, 1852; Bean, "Transformation," pp. 45–46, 50–52, 59–60; Hart, 4: 474; Winthrop, p.136.
49. Adams to Sumner, 1850, Adams Papers.
50. Sweeney, pp. 117–22.
51. *Emancipator and Republican*, Aug. 8, 1850; Aug. 22, 1850; Aug. 29, 1850; *Northampton Courier*, July 30, 1850; Aug. 13, 1850; diary, July 20 and 23 and Aug. 10, 1850, Adams Papers; Sumner to Chase, Aug. 29, 1850, Chase Papers, LC; Duberman, Adams, pp. 170–71; Donald, *Sumner*, p. 186; Wilson, *Slave Power*, 2: 341; Nason and Russell, pp. 92–93.
52. *Northampton Courier*, Sept. 3, 1850; Sept. 10, 1850; *Emancipator and Republican*, Sept. 5, 1850; Duberman, *Adams*, pp. 171–72; diary, Aug. 27 and 31 and Sept. 2, 5, and 7, 1850, Adams Papers; Wilson, *Slave Power*, 2: 342–43; Sumner to Chase, Aug. 29, 1850, Chase Papers, LC.
53. Adams, *Dana*, 1: 176; journal, Sept. 1, 1850, and Dana to R. H. Dana Sr., Sept. 11, 1850, Dana Papers; diary, Sept. 2, 5, and 10, 1850, and May 5 and 20, 1873, and Adams to Wilson, Sept. 20, 1873, Adams Papers; Pierce, 3: 221–23; Wilson, *Rise and Fall*, 2: 342–43; Nason and Russell, p. 92; Haynes, *Sumner*, pp. 125–26; Bean, "Transformation," p. 54; Loubert, pp. 96–97.
54. Diary, Mar. 21, 1874, Adams Papers; Pierce, 3: 222; Donald, *Sumner*, pp. 186–87.
55. Claude M. Fuess, *The Life of Caleb Cushing*, 2 vols. (Hamden, Conn.: Archon Books, 1965), 2: 98; Wilson, *Rise and Fall*, 2: 343; *Reunion of the Free Soilers, 1877*, p. 44; Nason and Russell, p. 92; Loubert, p. 97; *Emancipator and Republican*, Sept. 19, 1850; Oct. 3, 1850; *Northampton Courier*, Sept. 24, 1850; *National Era*, Oct. 24, 1850.
56. Stearns, *Cambridge Sketches*, pp. 162, 172–73; *New York Tribune*, Mar. 10, 1860; *Commonwealth*, Aug. 5, 1865; Oct. 29, 1870; *Cincinnati Gazette*, July 19, 1865; *Bird, a Biographical Sketch*, pp. 32–34; Pearson, 1: 60–61.
57. *Emancipator and Republican*, Oct. 3, 1850; Phelps, p. 356.
58. *Emancipator and Republican*, Oct. 10, 1850; *Boston Transcript*, Oct. 3, 1850; *Chronotype*, Oct. 4, 1850; *Northampton Courier*, Oct. 8, 1850; *National Era*, Oct. 10, 1850; Wilson, *Rise and Fall*, 2: 343–44; diary, Oct. 2, 3, and 7, 1850, Adams Papers; S. C. Phillips to Sumner [early Oct., 1850], Sumner Papers; Pierce, 3: 224.
59. Harrington, *Fighting Politician*, p. 10; Fuess, *Cushing* 2: 98; Bean, "Transformation," pp. 57–58; Benjamin P. Butler, *Butler's Book: Autobiography and Personal Reminiscences* (Boston: A. M. Thayer & Co., 1892), pp. 92–94; Hans L. Trefousse, *Ben Butler: the South Called Him Beast* (New York: Twayne Publishers, 1957), pp. 34–35; *New York Post*, Jan. 7, 1853; Hart, 4: 475–76; Pierce, 3: 224.
60. Wilson, *Rise and Fall*, 2: 345.
61. *Emancipator and Republican*, Sept. 26, 1850; Oct. 3, 1850; Oct. 10, 1850; Dana to Ned Dana, Nov. 12, 1850, Dana Papers; diary, Oct. 8–9, 1850, Adams Papers; *Northampton Courier*, Oct. 15, 1850; *Chronotype*, Oct. 9, 1850; *National Era*, Oct. 24, 1850; *New York Tribune*, Oct. 21, 1850; Trefousse, *Butler*, p. 262n.
62. *Chronotype*, Oct. 15, 1850; *Northampton Courier*, Oct. 15, 1850; diary, Oct. 8, 11, and 12, 1850, Adams Papers; Dana to Ned Dana, Nov. 12, 1850, Dana Papers; *Emancipator and Republican*, Oct. 17, 1850.
63. Journal, Oct. 15 and 16, 1850, and Sumner to Palfrey, Oct. 15, 1850, Palfrey Papers.
64. *Northampton Courier*, Oct. 29, 1850; Wilson, *Rise and Fall*, 2: 345–46; Pierce, 3: 227; *Emancipator and Republican*, Oct. 24, 1850.

65. Diary, Oct. 14, 16, 25, and 31, 1850, and Adams to Wilson, Sept. 20, 1873, Adams Papers; Dana to Ned Dana, Nov. 12, 1850, Dana Papers; *Emancipator and Republican*, Oct. 17, 1850; *Northampton Courier*, Nov. 5, 1850; Wilson, *Rise and Fall*, 2: 344–45; Shapiro, Dana, p. 56.
66. Wilson to Mann, Oct. 31, 1850, Mann Papers; Dana to Ned Dana, Nov. 12, 1850, Dana Papers.
67. *Liberator*, Oct. 18, 1850; diary, Oct. 12, 14, and 15, 1850, and Adams to Wilson, Oct. 11, 1873, Adams Papers; *Nineteenth Annual Report of the Massachusetts Anti-Slavery Society*, pp. 42–43; Wilson, *Rise and Fall*, 2: 306–8; *Emancipator and Republican*, Oct. 10, 1850; Oct. 17, 1850; Oct. 24, 1850; Robinson, *"Warrington,"* pp. 45–46; Pierce, 3: 208.
68. *Emancipator and Republican*, Oct. 31, 1850.
69. Sewell, *Ballots*, pp. 211–30; Rice, pp. 321–26; Blue, pp. 162–83, 187, 231; Harrold, pp. 144–46.
70. *Northampton Courier*, Dec. 6, 1853, quoting from *Plymouth Rock*; *Emancipator and Republican*, Oct. 10, 1850; Oct. 17, 1850; Oct. 24, 1850; Oct. 31, 1850; Nov. 7, 1850; Haynes, *Sumner*, p. 127; Pierce, 3: 227; *Dedham Gazette*, Oct. 26, 1850; *Chronotype*, Oct. 28, 1850; Wilson to Higginson, Oct. 28, 1850, Thomas Wentworth Higginson Papers, Houghton.
71. Wilson, *Rise and Fall*, 2: 308, 346; Pierce, 3: 227–29.
72. Winthrop to Hoar, Aug. 13, 1879, George Frisbie Hoar Papers, MHS.
73. McIntyre, 16: 560, 573, 575; *Commonwealth*, July 14, 1852; *Emancipator and Republican*, Oct. 17, 1850.
74. *Tribune Almanac*, 1851, p. 40; Hart, 4: 477; Pierce, 3: 230; Anderson, p. 36; Blue, p. 217; Gattel, *Palfrey*, p. 193; *Northampton Courier*, Dec. 3, 1850; *National Era*, Nov. 21, 1850; *Boston Transcript*, Nov. 30, 1850; Sweeney, pp. 123–24.
75. O'Connor, pp. 87–88; Harrington, *Fighting Politician*, p. 10; *Emancipator and Republican*, Oct. 31, 1850; *Boston Advertiser*, Nov. 15, 1850; Nov. 17, 1850; Nov. 18, 1850; Nov. 20, 1850; Sweeney, p. 123; Blue, p. 217; Winthrop, pp. 142–43; *Nineteenth Annual Report of the Massachusetts Anti-Slavery Society*, pp. 30–32; *Boston Transcript*, Nov. 27, 1850; *Chronotype*, Nov. 27, 1850; Wilson, *Rise and Fall*, 2: 317.
76. *Chronotype*, Nov. 12, 1850; *Northampton Courier*, Dec. 9, 1851; *National Era*, Nov. 21, 1850; Whittier to Wilson, Nov. 18, 1850, Henry Wilson Papers, New York Public Library, New York City; Webb to Sumner [no date, about Nov. 8 or 9, 1850], Sumner Papers; Henry Adams, *The Education of Henry Adams: an Autobiography* (Boston: Houghton Mifflin Company, 1918); *Emancipator and Republican*, Nov. 21, 1850; *Dedham Gazette*, Nov. 16, 1850.
77. Swan to Sumner, Nov. 26, 1850, Sumner Papers.
78. Whittier to Wilson, Nov. 18, 1850, Wilson Papers, New York Public Library.

Chapter 7

1. Winthrop, p. 140–41; diary, Sept. 10–13 and Oct. 7, 1850, and Stephen Higginson to Adams, Sept. 4, 1850, Adams Papers.

2. Diary, Nov. 19 and 23 and Dec. 22, 1850, and Jan. 2, 1851, Adams Papers; Richards, pp. 327–31, 341; Howe to Mann, Dec. 29, 1850, Howe Family Papers, Houghton; Nason and Russell, p. 91; *Emancipator and Republican*, Dec. 5, 1850; Dec. 26, 1850; *Boston Transcript*, Jan. 3, 1851; *Springfield Republican*, Jan. 1, 1851; *Northampton Courier*, Jan. 7, 1851; *Commonwealth*, Jan. 1, 1851; Jan. 3, 1851; Gattel, *Palfrey*, p. 201; journal, pp. 223–25, Palfrey Papers.
3. *Emancipator and Republican*, Dec. 26, 1850; *Commonwealth*, Jan. 1, 1851; *National Era*, Oct. 20, 1853; Nason and Russell, p. 91.
4. *National Era*, Nov. 21, 1850; *New York Post*, Jan. 7, 1853; *Reunion of the Free Soilers, 1877*, p. 44; Pierce, 3: 234; Whittier to Wilson, Nov. 18, 1850, Wilson Papers, New York Public Library; Swan to Sumner, Nov. 26, 1850, Sumner Papers; Donald, *Sumner*, pp. 186–89; diary, Nov. 14, 1850, Adams Papers.
5. Pierce, 3: 231; *Emancipator and Republican,* Oct. 17, 1850; Nov. 7, 1850; *Lowell Journal and Courier,* Oct. 21, 1850; *Boston Transcript,* Nov. 10, 1850; John Albree, ed., *Whittier Correspondence from the Oak Knoll Collections, 1830–1892* (Salem, Mass.: Essex Book and Printing Club, 1911), pp. 22–23n; E. M. Wright to Dawes, Nov. 27, 1850, Henry L. Dawes Papers, LC; diary, Nov. 16 and Dec. 21, 1850, Adams Papers; Winthrop, p. 145; *New York Tribune,* Dec. 8, 1850; Mills to Sumner, Dec. 10, 1850, Sumner Papers.
6. Donald, *Sumner*, pp. 188–89, 192–93; Morton to Frederick Robinson, Nov. 11, 1850, and Morton to B. V. French, Nov. 22, 1850, Marcus Morton Papers.
7. Diary, Nov. 14 and 19, 1850, Adams Papers; *Emancipator and Republican*, Nov. 14, 1850; Nov. 21, 1850; *Northampton Courier*, Dec. 20, 1853; Donald, *Sumner*, p. 192; Whittier to Wilson, Nov. 18, 1850, Wilson Papers, New York Public Library; Michael C. Hodgson, "Caleb Cushing, Attorney General of the United States" (Ph. D. diss., Catholic University, 1955), pp. 40–51; Boutwell, *Reminiscences*, 1: 119–21.
8. Diary, Nov. 19 and 22 and Dec. 27, 1850, Adams Papers; Leavitt to Sumner, Dec. 18, 1850, Sumner Papers.
9. *Emancipator and Republican*, Dec. 12, 1850; Dec. 19, 1850; *Dedham Gazette*, Dec. 7, 1850; *Northampton Courier*, Dec. 17, 1850; *Commonwealth*, Jan. 30, 1851.
10. Howe to Mann, Dec. 29, 1850, Howe Papers; diary, Dec. 27 and 28, 1850, and Jan. 4, 1851, Adams Papers; Dana to Ned Dana, Mar. 2, 1851, Dana Papers; *Dedham Gazette*, Jan. 11, 1851; *Boston Transcript*, Jan. 4, 1851; Jan. 7, 1851; *Springfield Republican,* Jan. 1, 1851; Jan. 6, 1851; Jan. 8, 1851; *Commonwealth*, Jan. 8, 1851; Jan. 13, 1851; Wilson, *Rise and Fall,* 2: 347.
11. Horace B. Davis, "The Occupations of Massachusetts Legislators, 1790–1950," *New England Quarterly* 24 (Mar. 1951): 94–95; Formisano, p. 353; *New York Tribune,* Feb. 13, 1851; *Northampton Courier*, Jan. 7, 1851; Massachusetts, General Court, Senate, Legislative Documents, p. 46.
12. *Emancipator and Republican*, Jan. 26, 1850; *Commonwealth*, Jan. 2, 1851; Jan. 30, 1851; Feb. 18, 1851; *Boston Post*, Feb. 7, 1851; *Boston Transcript,* Jan. 1, 1851; *Springfield Republican,* Jan. 1, 1851; Jan. 2, 1851; *Northampton Courier*, Jan. 7, 1851; Pierce, 3: 234; Massachusetts, General Court, Senate, Journal, 1851, p. 3; diary, Dec. 21 and 30, 1850, Adams Papers; Nason and Russell, pp. 94–95.
13. Mann, *Life of Wilson,* p. 33; Pierce, 3: 234; Boutwell, *Reminiscences,* 1: 115; *Commonwealth*, Jan. 2, 1851; Jan. 7, 1851; Jan. 30, 1851; Feb. 18, 1851; *Springfield Republican*, Jan. 1–10, 1851; *Boston Transcript*, Jan. 2, 1851; Jan. 10, 1851; *Boston Post*, Feb. 7, 1851; *Northampton Courier,* Feb. 18, 1851; Hart, 4: 478; Dana to Ned

Dana, Mar. 2, 1852, Dana Papers; Fuess, *Cushing*, 2: 100–101; Benjamin R. Curtis Jr., ed., *A Memoir of Robert Benjamin Curtis, with some of His Professional and Miscellaneous Writings*, 2 vols. (New York: DaCapo Press, 1970), 1: 138–40; Wilson, *Rise and Fall*, 2: 348; diary, Jan. 1, 7, and 8, 1851, Adams Papers; Keyes to Sumner, Jan. 4, 1851, Sumner Papers.

14. Pierce, 3: 230; diary, Dec. 21 and Jan. 9, 10, and 12, 1850, Adams Papers; H. W. Hawley to Dawes, Jan. 11, 1851, Dawes Papers; Phillips to Sumner, Jan. 9, 1851, and J. W. Thompson to Sumner, Jan. 10, 1851, Sumner Papers; Boutwell, *Reminiscences*, 1: 216–17; *Commonwealth*, Jan. 11, 1851; Jan. 13, 1851; Jan. 30, 1851; Feb. 18, 1851; *Northampton Courier*, Jan. 14, 1851; *Boston Transcript*, Jan. 11, 1851; *Springfield Republican*, Jan. 11, 1851; Jan. 13, 1851.
15. *Springfield Republican*, Jan. 8, 1851; Jan. 10, 1851; Jan. 14, 1851; *Boston Transcript*, Jan. 3, 1851; *Commonwealth*, Jan. 8, 1851; Jan. 15, 1851; Jan. 30, 1851; Feb. 18, 1851; Wilson, *Rise and Fall*, 2: 348; Boutwell, *Reminiscences*, 1: 116; Pierce, 3: 234.
16. *Commonwealth*, Jan. 14, 1851.
17. *Springfield Republican*, Jan. 17, 1851; *Boston Transcript*, Jan. 16, 1851; *Commonwealth*, Jan. 20, 1851; Jan. 23, 1851; Pickard, 1: 352; diary, Jan. 16 and 17, 1850, Adams Papers.
18. *Commonwealth*, Jan. 14–20, 1851; *Springfield Republican*, Jan. 16, 1851; Jan. 17, 1851; Jan. 23, 1851; *Boston Transcript*, Jan. 16, 1851; Jan. 17, 1851; Jan. 18, 1851; Jan. 22, 1851; Massachusetts, General Court, Senate, Journal, 1851, pp. 58, 70, 71; Wilson, *Rise and Fall*, 1: 348; *Dedham Gazette*, Jan. 18, 1851; Curtis, 1: 140–41.
19. Pierce, 3: 237; Whittier to Sumner, Jan. 15, 1851, Whittier-Pickard Papers; Dana to Ned Dana, Mar. 2, 1851, Dana Papers; John Bigelow, *Retrospections of an Active Life*, 5 vols. (New York: The Baker & Taylor Co., 1909–1913), 1: 106–7; *Northampton Courier*, Jan. 21, 1851; *National Era*, Jan. 16, 1851, quoting from *Washington Union*.
20. *Commonwealth*, Jan. 18, 1851.
21. Pierce, 3: 238; *Commonwealth*, Jan. 20, 1851; *Boston Post*, Jan. 20, 1851; diary, Jan. 31, 1851, Everett Papers; O'Connor, pp. 87–89; diary, Feb. 6, 1851, Adams Papers.
22. *Boston Transcript*, Jan. 16, 1851, quoting from *Boston Courier*; *Springfield Republican*, Jan. 17, 1851.
23. *Northampton Courier*, Jan. 21, 1851; *Commonwealth*, Jan. 16, 1851; *Boston Transcript*, Jan. 18, 1851, quoting from *Worcester Spy*; *National Era*, Jan. 30, 1851; Wilson, *Rise and Fall*, 1: 349; *Springfield Republican*, Jan. 25, 1851; *New York Tribune*, Jan. 23, 1851.
24. *Springfield Republican*, Jan. 21, 1851; Jan. 22, 1851; Jan. 24, 1851; Jan. 25, 1851; *Commonwealth*, Jan. 23–25, 1851; Gattel, *Palfrey*, pp. 196–97.
25. *Springfield Republican*, Jan. 28–31, 1851; Massachusetts, General Court, Senate, journal, 1851, pp. 87, 92–93; *Boston Transcript*, Jan. 30, 1851; Jan. 31, 1851; *Commonwealth*, Jan. 29–31, 1851.
26. *Commonwealth*, Jan. 30, 1851; Wilson to E. A. Stansbury, Jan. 31, 1851, Wilson Papers, LC; *Springfield Republican*, Jan. 31, 1851; Feb. 1, 1851; Curtis, 1: 143.
27. *Commonwealth*, Feb. 7–15, 1851; *Springfield Republican*, Feb. 8, 1851; *Boston Post*, Feb. 7, 1851; Feb. 17, 1851; *Northampton Courier*, Feb. 18, 1851, quoting from *Greenfield Democrat*.
28. *Commonwealth*, Jan. 28, 1851; Jan. 29, 1851.

29. *Liberator*, Jan. 31, 1851; Garrison, *Garrison*, 3: 313–20; Nason and Russell, pp. 95–96; Wilson to E. A. Stansbury, Jan. 31, 1851, and clippings in the Wilson Papers, LC; *Commonwealth*, Jan. 30, 1851.
30. Harriet Wilson to Caroline C. Howe, Jan. 29, 1851, Wilson Papers, South Natick Museum.
31. *Commonwealth*, Feb. 8, 1851; Feb. 12–14, 1851; *Springfield Republican*, Feb. 8, 1851; Feb. 13, 1851; Feb. 14, 1851; Wilson, *Rise and Fall*, 2: 348–49; diary, Feb. 12 and 13, 1851, Adams Papers; Pierce, 3: 239–40; Sumner, 2: 430; Donald, *Sumner*, pp. 196–98; S. C. Phillips to Sumner, Feb. 26, 1851, Sumner Papers.
32. Richards, p. 338.
33. Ibid., pp. 335, 341; Wilson, *Rise and Fall*, 2: 348 *Springfield Republican*, Feb. 14, 1851; Feb. 19, 1851; *Commonwealth*, Feb. 21, 1851.
34. *Commonwealth*, Feb. 18, 1851; *New York Tribune*, Nov. 23, 1875.
35. *Commonwealth*, Mar. 19, 1851.
36. Ibid., Feb. 27, 1851; Mar. 13, 1851; Mar. 20, 1851; *Springfield Republican*, Feb. 27, 1851; Mar. 13, 1851; *Northampton Courier*, Mar. 25, 1851; *Boston Transcript*, Mar. 13, 1851; diary, Mar. 12 and 19, 1851, Adams Papers; Fuess, *Cushing*, 2: 103; Hart, 4: 99; Wilson, *Rise and Fall*, 2: 348; Mann, *Life of Wilson*, pp. 34–35; Pierce, 3: 242.
37. *Commonwealth*, Mar. 12, 1851; Mar. 18, 1851; Mar. 25, 1851, quoting from *Burlington Courier*; *Northampton Courier*, Apr. 1, 1851, quoting from *Worcester Palladium*; *Springfield Republican*, Mar. 21, 1851.
38. Letters of Morton to Sumner, Mar. 12, to the editors of the *Commonwealth*, Mar. 19, to Alley, Mar. 21, to Lyman W. Dean and to Amasa Walker, Mar. 22, to Robinson, Mar. 24, to Edward Kadbearsm, Mar. 25, to William C. Tabor and to George Steed, Mar. 26, to George Austin, Mar. 27, and to Dean, Mar. 31, 1851, Marcus Morton Papers.
39. *Commonwealth*, Apr. 1, 1851; Apr. 3, 1851; *Springfield Republican*, Apr. 2, 1851; Apr. 3, 1851; *Northampton Courier*, Apr. 8, 1851, quoting from *Dedham Gazette; New York Tribune*, Apr. 3, 1851.
40. Anderson, pp. 19, 44; *Springfield Republican*, Feb. 18–20, 1851; *Commonwealth*, Feb. 18–22, 1851; diary, Feb. 27 and 28, 1851, Adams Papers.
41. *Commonwealth*, Mar. 28, 1851; Apr. 5–9, 1851; *Northampton Courier*, Apr. 1, 1851; *Boston Transcript*, Apr. 8, 1851; *Springfield Republican*, Apr. 9–10, 1851; Wilson, *Rise and Fall*, 2: 334–36; diary, Apr. 8, 1851, Adams Papers.
42. *Liberator*, Apr. 18, 1851; *Commonwealth*, Apr. 10, 1851; Apr. 16, 1851.
43. Massachusetts, General Court, Senate, Journal, 1851, pp. 315, 324, 364, 446–47, 504 and Document No. 51; Joseph T. Buckingham, *Personal Memoirs and Recollections of Editorial Life*, 2 vols. (Boston: Ticknor, Reed, and Fields, 1852), 2: 245; *Northampton Courier*, Apr. 1, 1851; *Commonwealth*, Jan. 23, 1851; Mar. 25, 1851; *Springfield Republican*, Mar. 25, 1851; Mar. 29, 1851; Apr. 5, 1851; Apr. 7, 1851; Bean, "Transformation," p. 94; Anderson, pp. 27–28.
44. *Commonwealth, passim*, Mar. to Apr. 15, 1851; *Springfield Republican*, Mar. 8, 1851; Mar. 14–17, 1851; Mar. 20, 1851; Mar. 29, 1851; *Northampton Courier*, Mar. 18, 1851; Oct. 28, 1851; Michel Brunet, "The Secret Ballot Issue in Massachusetts Politics from 1851 to 1853," *New England Quarterly* 25 (Sept. 1952): 354–56; Formisano, pp. 143–47; Massachusetts, General Court, Senate, Journal, 1851, pp. 82, 195, 228, 236–37, 245, 260, 270–72, and Documents 28, 37, and 39.

45. *Springfield Republican*, Mar. 28, 1851; Apr. 15, 1851; Apr. 18, 1851; May 7, 1851; *Commonwealth*, Apr. 15, 1851; Apr. 17, 1851; Apr. 22, 1851; *Northampton Courier*, Apr. 22, 1851; May 13, 1851.
46. Story, pp. 136–39; Bean, "Transformation," pp. 80–81; Pierce, 3: 1–5; Formisano, pp. 290–92.
47. Bean, "Transformation," pp. 85–86; Story, p. 141; *Northampton Courier*, Oct. 28, 1851; *Commonwealth*, Jan. 13, 1851; Jan. 20, 1851.
48. Nason and Russell, pp.110–14; *Commonwealth*, Feb. 7, 1851; Story, p. 141.
49. *Commonwealth*, Feb. 21, 1851; Mar. 7, 1851.
50. *Northampton Courier*, Apr. 15, 1851; *Commonwealth*, Apr. 8, 1851; Gattel, *Palfrey*, pp. 196—97.
51. *Commonwealth*, Apr. 16, 1851; Apr. 23, 1851; Apr. 26, 1851; Apr. 29, 1851; *Northampton Courier*, Apr. 22, 1851; *Springfield Republican*, Apr. 23, 1851; Wilson, *Rise and Fall*, 2: 335; *Twentieth Annual Report of the Massachusetts Anti-Slavery Society* (Boston: Massachusetts Anti-Slavery Society, 1852), pp. 24–25.
52. Diary, Apr. 21, 1851, Adams Papers; Richards, pp. 343–44; *Commonwealth*, Apr. 24, 1851; Apr. 25, 1851; *Boston Courier*, Apr. 24, 1851; *Boston Transcript*, Apr. 23, 1851; Apr. 24, 1851; *Springfield Republican*, Apr. 24, 1851; Apr. 25, 1851; *Northampton Courier*, Apr. 29, 1851; *New York Tribune*, Apr. 24, 1851; Apr. 25, 1851; Pierce, 3: 242–43; Wilson, *Rise and Fall*, 2: 349; *Connecticut Courant*, Jan. 30, 1869; Butler, pp. 116–17.
53. *Liberator*, May 21, 1851; *Boston Transcript*, Apr. 25, 1851; *Northampton Courier*, Apr. 29, 1851; *Commonwealth*, Apr. 25–29, 1851; Pierce, 3: 243; Wilson, *Rise and Fall*, 2: 349; diary, Apr. 24 and 25, 1851, Adams Papers; Adams, *Education of Henry Adams*, p. 51; *New York Tribune*, Apr. 26, 1851.
54. *Commonwealth*, May 1, 1851; May 2, 1851.
55. *Commonwealth*, May 15, 1851.
56. *Springfield Republican*, Apr. 25, 1851; *Boston Transcript*, Apr. 24, 1851; Apr. 25, 1851; *Boston Advertiser*, Apr. 25, 1851; Apr. 26, 1851; *Boston Courier*, Apr. 25, 1861; Apr. 26, 1851; diary, Apr. 24, 1851, Everett Papers; Hart, 4: 480; *Boston Post*, Apr. 25, 1861.
57. *Commonwealth*, May 3, 1851; Wilson, *Rise and Fall*, 2: 350; Pierce, 3: 249; Nason and Russell, pp. 93–94.
58. Mann, *Life of Wilson*, p. 3; Nason and Russell, p. 93; Pierce, 3: 249; *Connecticut Courant*, Jan. 30, 1869; Carl Schurz, *Charles Sumner, an Essay* (Urbana: University of Illinois Press, 1951), p. 57.
59. Walter G. Shotwell, *Life of Charles Sumner* (New York: Thomas Y. Crowell & Company, 1910), p. 235; Donald, *Sumner*, p. 202.
60. Curtis, 1: 143–48.
61. Stuart J. Davis, "Liberty before Union: Massachusetts and the Coming of the Civil War" (Ph. D. diss., University of Massachusetts, 1975), p. 26; *Commonwealth*, Apr. 29, 1851; May 1, 1851; May 6, 1851; May 20, 1851; May 21, 1851; May 24, 1851; May 27, 1851; *Northampton Courier*, May 27, 1851; Oct. 28, 1851; *Springfield Republican*, May 8, 1851; May 13, 1851; May 14. 1851; May 19–22 1851; May 26, 1851; Massachusetts, General Court, Senate, 1851, Document 46.
62. *Northampton Courier*, May 27, 1851; Oct. 28, 1851; *Springfield Republican*, May 6, 1851; May 8, 1851; May 13, 1851; May 23, 1851; May 26, 1851; *Boston Transcript*, May 26, 1851; *Commonwealth*, May 5, 1851; May 7, 1851; May 8, 1851; May 22,

1851; May 23, 1851; May 27, 1851; *Dedham Gazette,* May 31, 1851; *New York Post,* Jan. 7, 1853; Nason and Russell, p. 96; Bean, "Transformation," pp. 76–80; Sweeney, pp. 124–25.

63. *Northampton Courier*, May 27, 1851; Oct. 28, 1851; *Boston Transcript*, May 26, 1851; *Commonwealth*, May 6, 1851; May 10, 1851; May 12, 1851; *Springfield Republican,* May 22, 1851; Fuess, *Cushing*, 2: 104–5; Nason and Russell, p. 96; Story, p. 140–41; Bean, "Transformation," pp. 85–86.

64. *Commonwealth,* Apr. 30, 1851; May 3, 1851; May 8–12, 1851; *Northampton Courier*, May 13, 1851; *Springfield Republican*, May 8, 1851; Massachusetts, General Court, Senate, Journal, 1851, p. 504.

65. *Commonwealth,* May 8, 1851; May 14, 1851; May 16, 1851; May 17, 1851; May 21, 1851; *Northampton Courier*, May 20, 1851; May 27, 1851; *Springfield Republican,* May 14, 1851; May 16, 1851; May 19, 1851; May 24, 1851; Massachusetts, General Court, Senate, Journal, 1851, pp. 504, 567–72.

66. *Springfield Republican*, May 23, 1851; Bean, "Transformation," p. 92; *Commonwealth*, May 23, 1851; May 24, 1851; May 27, 1851; *Twentieth Annual Report of the Massachusetts Anti-Slavery Society,* pp. 37–39.

67. Massachusetts, General Court, Senate, Journal, 1851, p. 678; *Commonwealth,* May 26, 1851; *Northampton Courier*, May 27, 1851; Nason and Russell, pp. 96–97.

68. *Northampton Courier*, May 20, 1851; Gattel, *Palfrey*, p. 199; *Commonwealth*, May 15, 1851; May 17, 1851; *Liberator*, May 23, 1851; *National Era*, June 5, 1851; Sumner to Palfrey, May, 1851, and Wilson to Palfrey, May 19, 1851, Palfrey Papers; Wilson to Stansbury, May 8, 1851, Norcross Family Collection, MHS.

69. *Springfield Republican*, May 27, 1851; *Northampton Courier*, May 27, 1851; June 3, 1851; *Commonwealth*, May 27, 1851; *National Era*, June 5, 1851; Gattel, *Palfrey*, p. 200; E. R. Hoar to Palfrey, May 27, 1851, Palfrey Papers.

70. Duberman, *Adams,* pp. 175–76; Shapiro, *Dana*, p. 56; journal, pp. 224–26, Palfrey Papers.

71. Wilson to Hoar, Henry Claflin and W. H. Chamberlain, June 5, 1851, Hoar Papers; Wilson to Stansbury, May 8, 1851, Norcross Family Collection; *Liberator*, June 20, 1851; *Commonwealth,* June 2, 1851; June 10, 1851; June 18, 1851; July 18, 1851; *New York Tribune*, June 19, 1851; *Springfield Republican*, May 31, 1851.

72. *Northampton Courier,* July 8, 1851; July 29, 1851; *Commonwealth*, July 7, 1851; *Dedham Gazette,* July 12, 1851; July 19, 1851; *Liberator*, July 18, 1851.

73. McIntyre, 14: 610–12; *Commonwealth, passim* July and Aug., 1851; Aug. 8, 1851; diary, July 24 and 30, 1851, Adams Papers; Winthrop to Davis, Sept. 2, 1851, Davis Papers; Bean, "Transformation," pp. 97–99.

74. *Northampton Courier,* July 1, 1851, quoting from *Democratic Standard*; Dec. 20, 1851, quoting from *Greenfield Democrat;* Aug. 26, 1851; *Springfield Republican*, June 25, 1851; Bean, "Transformation," p. 94; *Dedham Gazette*, July 26, 1851; *Boston Transcript,* Aug. 20, 1851; Aug. 21, 1851; *Commonwealth*, Aug. 22, 1851; *Worcester Spy*, Aug. 22, 1851; Butler to Hallett, Aug. 25, 1851, Benjamin F. Butler Papers, LC.

75. *Boston Advertiser*, Sept. 11, 1851; *Northampton Courier*, Sept. 16, 1851; *Dedham Gazette*, Sept. 12, 1851; *National Era*, Sept. 4, 1851; Sept. 18, 1851; *Commonwealth*, Sept. 12, 1851; Winthrop, p. 147.

76. *National Era*, Sept. 4, 1851; Pierce, 3: 253; *Northampton Courier*, June 3, 1851; *Commonwealth,* July 19, 1851; July 24, 1851; diary, July 21, Aug. 5 and 27, and Sept. 13 and 16, 1851, and Wilson to Adams, Aug. 22 and 26, 1851, Adams Papers.

77. *Boston Transcript*, Aug. 29, 1851; *Commonwealth*, Aug. 29, 1851; *Northampton Courier*, Sept. 2, 1851.
78. *Northampton Courier*, Sept. 9, 1851, one article quoting from *Adams Sentinel*; Duberman, *Adams*, p. 176; diary, Sept. 15 and 22, 1851, Adams Papers; Gattel, *Palfrey*, pp. 203–4; Blue, p. 227; *Liberator*, Sept. 9, 1851; *National Era*, Sept. 25, 1851.
79. *Liberator*, Sept. 9, 1851; *New York Weekly Tribune*, Sept. 20, 1851; *National Era*, Sept. 25, 1851; *Commonwealth*, Sept. 17, 1851; *Boston Transcript*, Sept. 16, 1851; diary, Sept. 19 and 22, 1851, Adams Papers.
80. *Commonwealth*, Sept. 10, 1851; Sept. 16, 1851.
81. Bacon, *History of Natick*, pp. 32–39; *Commonwealth*, Oct. 11, 1851.
82. *Boston Transcript*, Sept. 16–20, 1851; *Commonwealth*, June 20, 1851; Sept. 18–20, 1851; Frank H. Severance, ed., *The Millard Fillmore Papers* (Buffalo: Buffalo Historical Society, 1907), 1: 421; Mann, *Life of Wilson*, pp. 27–30; Nason and Russell, p. 98.
83. *Commonwealth*, Sept. 23, 1851.

Chapter 8

1. *Commonwealth*, Oct. 2, 1851; Oct. 6, 1851; *New York Weekly Tribune*, Oct. 4, 1851; *Northampton Courier*, Oct. 7, 1851; Oct. 28, 1851; *Boston Transcript*, Oct. 2, 1851.
2. *Commonwealth*, Oct. 5, 1851; Oct. 6, 1851; Oct. 11, 1851, quoting from *Boston Atlas;* Oct. 14, 1851, quoting from *Boston Bee*.
3. *Commonwealth*, Sept. 25, 1851; Oct. 1, 1851; Oct. 10, 1851; Oct. 14, 1851; Oct. 17, 1851; Oct. 18, 1851; Oct. 20, 1851; Oct. 21, 1851; Sumner to Chase, Sept. 15, 1851, Chase Papers, LC; *Northampton Courier*, Oct. 14, 1851; Oct. 21, 1851.
4. *Northampton Courier*, Oct. 21, 1851; *New York Weekly Tribune*, Oct. 18, 1851; *Dedham Gazette*, Oct. 25, 1851; *Commonwealth*, Oct. 27, 1851.
5. Wilson to Hoar, Oct. 31, 1851, Hoar Papers; *Commonwealth*, Oct. 17, 1851; Oct. 24, 1851; Oct. 28, 1851; Nov. 1, 1851; Loubert, p. 139; *New York Times*, Nov. 4, 1851.
6. *Commonwealth*, Oct. 30, 1851.
7. Diary, May 31, June 11 and 14, Sept. 24 and 29, Oct. 3, and Nov. 20, 1851, Adams Papers.
8. Diary, Oct. 3, 13, 17, and 24, 1851 and Wilson to Adams, Oct. 16, 1851, and Bird to Adams, Oct. 17 and 30, 1851, Adams Papers.
9. Diary, Sept. 15 and Nov. 1 to 8, 1851, Adams Papers; Adams to Wilson, Oct. 31, 1851, Chamberlain Papers.
10. *Commonwealth*, Oct. 18, 1851; Oct. 31, 1851; Nov. 6, 1851; *Northampton Courier*, Nov. 4, 1851; diary, Nov. 1, 1851, Adams Papers; Winthrop to Davis, Sept. 30, 1851, Davis Papers; *Boston Pilot*, Nov. 8, 1851.
11. *Northampton Courier*, Oct. 28, 1851; Nov. 18, 1851; Jan. 6, 1851; *Boston Transcript*, Nov. 11, 1851; Nov. 12, 1851; Nov. 17, 1851; Nov. 18, 1851; Dec. 23, 1851; *Commonwealth*, Nov. 11–15, 1851; Nov. 17, 1851; Nov. 19, 1851; Dec. 3, 1851; *Tribune Almanac*, 1852, p. 37; Bean, "Transformation," pp. 109–10; Winthrop to Davis, Nov. 15, 1851, Davis Papers; Winthrop, pp. 150–51, 157–58; diary, Nov. 11 and 14, 1851, Adams Papers; Butler, p. 114; Pierce, 3: 253; Anderson, pp. 41–42.

12. *Commonwealth,* Nov. 12, 1851; Nov. 21, 1851; Nov. 22, 1851; Nov. 25, 1851; Nov. 26, 1851; Dec. 3, 1851; *Liberator,* Nov. 28, 1851; *Boston Transcript,* Nov. 26, 1851; *New York Weekly Tribune,* Dec. 6, 1851; *Northampton Courier,* Nov. 18, 1845; Nov. 25, 1851; Formisano, pp. 284–86; *Tribune Almanac,* 1852, p. 37.
13. *Commonwealth,* Nov. 26, 1851; *Northampton Courier,* Nov. 25, 1851, quoting from *Worcester Palladium*; Cushing to Boutwell, Dec. 5, 1851, Emory Washburn Papers, MHS; Richards, p. 353; journal, Nov. 16 and 26, 1851, Dana Papers.
14. *Commonwealth,* Mar. 15, 1851; Sewell, *Ballots,* pp. 204–11, 231–33, 240–42; Patrick W. Riddleberger, *George Washington Julian, Radical Republican* (Indianapolis: Indiana Historical Bureau, 1966), p. 84; Harrold, pp. 145–46; *Northampton Courier,* Sept. 23, 1851, quoting from *Salem Freeman.*
15. *Commonwealth,* Dec. 13, 1851; Jan. 8, 1852; Jan. 10, 1852; Jan. 14, 1852; Wilson to Sumner, Jan. 5, 1852, Walker to Sumner, Jan. 3, 1852, and Alley to Sumner, Jan. 3, 1852, Sumner Papers; diary, Dec. 27, 1851, and Jan. 5, 8, and 9, 1852, and Adams to Sumner, Jan. 1, 1852, Adams Papers; Sumner to Wilson, Jan. 10, 1852, Wilson Papers, LC; *Liberator,* Jan. 16, 1852; *Boston Transcript,* Jan. 7, 1852; Jan. 10, 1852; Jan. 13, 1852; Jan. 14, 1852; *Northampton Courier,* Jan. 13, 1852; Jan. 20, 1852; *New York Tribune,* Jan. 8, 1852.
16. *Boston Transcript,* Jan. 15, 1852; Feb. 9, 1852; *Northampton Courier,* Jan. 20, 1852; Feb. 3, 1852; Feb. 10, 1852; *Commonwealth,* Jan. 16, 1852; Jan. 17, 1852; Feb. 10, 1852; Brown, p. 71; Massachusetts, General Court, Senate, 1852, Legislative Documents, p. 46.
17. *Northampton Courier,* Jan. 13, 1852; Jan. 20, 1852.
18. *Boston Courier,* Feb. 4, 1844; *Chronotype, passim,* Jan. to Mar., especially Feb. 16 and 17 and July through early Aug., 1849; *Emancipator and Republican,* Jan. 19, 1849; Clark, pp. 89, 187–88, 238–39; *Commonwealth,* Jan. 30, 1851; *Northampton Courier,* Oct. 7, 1851.
19. Hampel, p. 147; Clark, pp. 89–90; *Northampton Courier,* Jan. 27, 1852; Feb. 3, 1852; Wilson to Sumner, Feb. 17, 1852, Sumner Papers; *Boston Transcript,* Jan. 29, 1852; Nason and Russell, p. 98.
20. *Commonwealth, passim,* Feb. through Apr., 1852; *Liberator,* Mar. 12, 1852; Bean, "Transformation," pp. 113–15; Hampel, pp. 159–63; *Boston Transcript,* Feb. 16, 1852; Feb. 24–26, 1852; Mar. 3, 1852; Mar. 4, 1852; Mar. 10, 1852; Mar. 18, 1852; Mar. 23–Apr. 14, 1852; *Northampton Courier,* Feb. 24, 1852; Mar. 9, 1852; Mar. 30, 1852; Apr. 6, 1852; Apr. 20, 1852; Apr. 27, 1852; May 11, 1852; May 18, 1852.
21. Massachusetts, General Court, Senate, 1852, Documents 149 and 150; Bean, "Transformation," p. 114; *Commonwealth,* Apr. 15, 1852; Apr. 17, 1852; Apr. 19, 1852; May 20–25, 1852; Brown, p. 72; Clark, p. 91; *Boston Traveller,* June 8, 1852; *Boston Transcript,* May 18, 1852; May 19–22, 1852; *Northampton Courier,* May 25, 1852.
22. Richards, pp. 360–63; Sweeney, pp. 128–29; *New York Post,* Jan. 7, 1853; Bean, "Transformation," pp. 115–18; *Northampton Courier,* June 1, 1852.
23. *Twenty-first Annual Report of the Massachusetts Anti-Slavery Society* (Boston: Massachusetts Anti-Slavery Society, 1853), p. 32; Formisano, pp. 185–86; Brunet, p. 355; *Northampton Courier,* Feb. 17, 1852; Feb. 24, 1852; Mar. 2, 1852; Mar. 9, 1852; Apr. 27, 1852; Bean, "Transformation," pp. 118–19; *Commonwealth,* Mar. 8, 1852; Mar. 16–18, 1852; May 17, 1852; May 27, 1852.

24. *Emancipator and Republican*, June 14, 1849; Aug. 16, 1849; *Commonwealth*, Sept. 16, 1852; Sewell, *Ballots*, p. 183.
25. *Emancipator and Republican*, Apr. 26, 1849; Sumner to Bird, Mar. 29, 1849, Bird Papers, Houghton; Wilson to David L. Child, Sept. 16, 1858, Anti-Slavery Papers, BPL.
26. *Commonwealth*, Mar. 8, 1852; Mar. 12, 1852; Mar. 13, 1852; Mar. 19, 1852; Bean, "Transformation," pp. 116–17; *Northampton Courier*, Mar. 16, 1852; Mar. 23, 1852; *Boston Transcript*, Apr. 22, 1852.
27. *Emancipator and Republican*, *passim* July and August, 1849; Donald S. Spencer, *Louis Kossuth and Young America* (Columbia: University of Missouri Press, 1977), pp. 1–120; *New York Weekly Tribune*, Oct. 11, 1851; Dec. 13, 1851; *New York Times*, *passim*, Oct. and Nov. 1851 and Jan. 1852.
28. Wilson to Sumner, Jan. 5, 1852, Sumner Papers; Massachusetts, General Court, Senate, 1852, journal, pp. 17, 184; *Northampton Courier*, Jan. 13, 1852; *Commonwealth*, Jan. 8, 1852; Jan. 9, 1852; *Boston Transcript*, Jan. 7, 1852; Jan. 8, 1852; Jan. 15, 1852; *Kossuth in New England*, (Boston: John P. Jewett & Co., 1852), pp. 1–2, 6.
29. Spencer, pp. 51–59, 95–154; *Kossuth in New England*, pp. 10–46; *New York Times*, *passim* Jan.–Apr., 1852; Massachusetts, General Court, Senate, 1852, journal, pp. 537, 561, 666–67, 671; *Boston Transcript*, Apr. 24, 1852; Apr. 26, 1852; Apr. 27, 1852; *Northampton Courier*, Apr. 13, 1852; Apr. 27, 1852; *Commonwealth*, Apr. 27, 1852; Nason and Russell, pp. 98–101; Pierce, 3: 272.
30. Spencer, p. 154; *Kossuth in New England*, pp. 46–124; *Boston Transcript*, Apr. 27–May 1, 1852; *Northampton Courier*, May 4, 1852; *New York Tribune*, Apr. 28–May 1, 1852; May 17, 1852; *Liberator*, Apr. 30, 1852; May 7, 1852; *Commonwealth*, Apr. 28–May 1, 1852; Nason and Russell, p. 101.
31. *Boston Transcript*, *passim* May 3 to 17, 1852; *Commonwealth*, *passim* May 4–12, 1852; May 19, 1852; *New York Tribune*, May 20, 1852; Spencer, pp. 155–68; *Kossuth in New England*, pp. 128–285; Richards, p. 376.
32. *New York Tribune*, May 21, 1852; *Northampton Courier*, May 25, 1852; Massachusetts, General Court, Senate, 1852, journal, pp. 802, 806, 826; Pierce, 3: 272; Wilson to Sumner, May 4, 1852, and Albert G. Browne to Sumner and John Andrew to Sumner, May 17, 1852, Sumner Papers, Houghton; *Commonwealth*, May 21, 1852.
33. Spencer, pp. 65–81; *Liberator*, Apr. 30, 1852; *New York Times*, Jan. 31, 1852; diary, Apr. 27, 1852, Everett Papers; Bean, "Transformation," pp. 124–25; "Literary Notes and Criticism, Kossuth in New England," *Brownson's Quarterly Review* 14 (Oct. 1852): 556; Richards, pp. 370, 376; diary, Apr. 27 and 28 and May 4–6, 1852, and Sumner to Adams, Apr. 21, 1852, Bird to Adams, Apr. 28, 1852, and Wilson to Adams, May 4, 1852, Adams Papers; Nason and Russell, p. 101.
34. *Commonwealth*, Jan. 28, 1852; May 21, 1852; *Northampton Courier*, May 25, 1852; Massachusetts, General Court, Senate, 1852, journal, p. 840; Nason and Russell, pp. 101–2.
35. *Northampton Courier*, May 28, 1852; Dec. 20, 1853; *Liberator*, May 28, 1852; *Boston Transcript*, June 8, 1852.
36. Pierce, 3: 266–70, 273–74; Sumner to Mrs. Adams, Jan. 2, 1852, and Sumner to Adams, Feb. 1, 1852, Adams Papers; John Jay to Sumner, Dec. 10, 1851, Stone to Sumner, Dec. 11, 12, and 16, 1851, Dana to Sumner, Dec. 11, 1851, Webb to Sumner,

Dec. 12, 1851, and Wilson to Sumner, Dec. 15, 1851, Sumner Papers; Winthrop to Davis, Dec. 13, 1851, Davis Papers.

37. Sumner to Adams, Feb. 1, 1852, Adams Papers; *Commonwealth*, Mar. 24, 1852; Mar. 25, 1852; Rayback, p. 265; Donald, *Sumner*, pp. 222–23; Pierce, 3: 272; Wilson to Sumner, Feb. 3, 1852, Samuel E. Sewell to Sumner, Mar. 19, 1852, and Alley to Sumner, Mar. 23, 1852, Sumner Papers.
38. *Commonwealth*, Mar. 25, 1852; Mar. 26, 1852; Apr. 16, 1852; Wilson to Sumner, Mar. 27, 1852, and James W. Stone to Sumner, Apr. 19, 1852, Sumner Papers.
39. Stone to Sumner, Apr. 19, 1852, Bowditch to Sumner, Apr. 22, 1852, Phillips to Sumner, Apr. 27, 1852, and Wilson to Sumner, Mar. 9, May 4, and June 29, 1852, Sumner Papers; diary, May 22, 1852, Adams Papers; Sumner to Wilson, Apr. 15, 1852, Miscellaneous Papers, BPL; Wilson, *Rise and Fall*, 2: 353–54; Haynes, *Sumner*, p. 147; Pierce, 3: 288.
40. Giddings to Julian, June 30, 1852, Giddings-Julian Papers; diary, July 6, 1852, Everett Papers; Sumner to Palfrey, July 2, 1852, Palfrey Papers; Haynes, *Sumner*, p. 147; Sumner to Mrs. Adams, July 23[?], 1852, and Sumner to Adams, July 27[?] and Aug. 5, 1852, Adams Papers; journal, Sept. 11, 1852, Dana Papers; Wilson, *Rise and Fall*, 2: 353–59; Sumner to Carter, Aug. 3, 10, and 14, and two August letters undated, 1852, Robert Carter Papers, Houghton; John Weiss, *Life and Correspondence of Theodore Parker*, 2 vols. (New York: D. Appleton & Company, 1864), 2: 214; *Commonwealth*, July 29–Aug. 2, 1852; *Boston Transcript*, Aug. 2, 1852.
41. Wilson, *Rise and Fall*, 2: 358; Howe to Carter, undated, 1852, Carter Papers; diary, Aug. 27, 1852, Adams Papers; Weiss, 2: 215; Pierce, 3: 307; Wilson to Sumner, Sept. 5, 1852, Sumner Papers; *Commonwealth*, Aug. 28, 1852; Aug. 30, 1852; Sept. 1, 1852.
42. Diary, Dec. 9, 1851, and Adams to Bailey, Feb. 2, 1852, Adams Papers; Sumner to Wilson, Jan. 10, 1852, Wilson Papers, LC; Alley to Sumner, Jan. 3, 1852, and Wilson to Sumner, Dec. 15, 1851, and Jan. 5, Feb. 17, and June 23, 1852, Sumner Papers; Sumner to Bird, Feb. 8, 1852, Francis W. Bird Papers, Houghton; Pierce, 3: 314.
43. Wilson to Sumner, Feb. 3 and 17, Mar. 9, and May 4 and Stone to Sumner, Apr. 5, 1852, Sumner Papers; diary, Mar. 26 and May 23, 1852, Adams Papers.
44. Stone to Sumner, June 2 and 6, 1852, Sumner Papers; diary, June 2 and 9, 1852, and Adams to Sumner, June 11, 1852, Adams Papers; Duberman, *Adams*, p. 180; Pierce, 3: 314.
45. Wilson, *Rise and Fall*, 2: 360–71; Bean, "Transformation," pp. 130–31; Bartlett, pp. 273–76; Pierce, 3: 312–15; John Andrew to Sumner, May 17, 1852, Sumner Papers; Rice, pp. 340–45, 352–53; Sumner to Adams, June, 1852, Adams Papers; *Northampton Courier*, Dec. 20, 1853; Blue, pp. 235–38.
46. Allan Nevins, *Ordeal of the Union,* 2 vols. (New York: Charles Scribner's Sons, 1947), 2: 29, quoting from Washington *Union.*
47. *Northampton Courier*, June 22, 1852; *Commonwealth*, June 23, 1852; Stone to Sumner, June 2 and 9, 1852, Sumner Papers; diary, June 22, 1852, and Sumner to Adams, June, 1852, Adams Papers.
48. Diary, June 5, 19, and 21, 1852, and Adams to Bailey, Apr. 3, 1852, Adams to Sumner, Apr. 7 and June 23, 1852, and Adams to Hopkins, June 23, 1852, Adams Papers; R. M. Devens to Wilson and others, Aug. 12, 1852, Mann Papers; Wilson to Sumner, June 23 and 29, 1852, and Adams to Sumner, June 23, 1852, Sumner Papers.

49. Stone to Sumner, June 2 and 6, 1852, Sumner Papers.
50. *Boston Traveller*, June 8. 1852; *Northampton Courier*, June 15, 1852; *Commonwealth*, June 28, 1852; diary, June 26 and 30, 1852, Adams Papers; Stone to Sumner, July 3, 1852, Sumner Papers.
51. *Commonwealth*, June 29, 1852; July 2, 1852; July 3, 1852.
52. Ibid., July 7, 1852.
53. Ibid.
54. *Northampton Courier*, July 20, 1852.
55. *National Era*, July 15, 1852; *Northampton Courier*, July 13, 1852; July 20, 1852; *Liberator*, July 9, 1852; *Commonwealth*, July 7, 1852; July 8, 1852; *New York Tribune*, July 7, 1852.
56. *National Era*, July 15, 1852; *Boston Transcript*, July 7, 1852, quoting from *Boston Advertiser*; *New York Tribune*, July 7, 1852.
57. Wilson to Sumner, July 7, 1852, Sumner Papers; *Commonwealth*, July 14, 1852; *passim*, July, 1852.
58. *Commonwealth*, July 14, 1852; July 19, 1852, quoting from *Boston Times;* July 24, 1852, including one article quoting from *Worcester Spy*; July 26, 1852, quoting from *Greylock Sentinel.*
59. *Commonwealth*, July 20, 1852; diary, July 28, 1852, and Sumner to Adams, June, 1852, Adams Papers; Pierce, 3: 315–16; Wilson to Sumner, July 7 and 22, 1852, and Stone to Sumner, July 7, 1852, Sumner Papers; Wilson to Seward, July 8, 1852, William H. Seward Papers, University of Rochester, Rochester, New York.
60. *Commonwealth*, July 26, 1852, quoting from *Greylock Sentinel*; Wilson, *Rise and Fall*, 2: 373; *Northampton Courier*, Aug. 17, 1852; *National Era*, Aug. 19, 1852; Aug. 26, 1852; *New York Tribune*, Aug. 11, 1852; Aug. 16, 1852; diary, Aug. 11, 1852, Adams Papers; Stone to Sumner, Aug. 15, 1852, Sumner Papers; Blue, pp. 239–41.
61. *Commonwealth*, Aug. 12, 1852; *Northampton Courier*, Aug. 17, 1852; *National Era*, Aug. 19, 1852; *Liberator*, Aug. 20, 1852; *New York Tribune*, Aug. 13, 1852; diary, Aug. 11, 1852, Adams Papers; Wilson, *Rise and Fall*, 2: 373–74; Eric Foner, "Politics and Prejudice: the Free Soil Party and the Negro, 1849–1852," *Journal of Negro History* 50 (1965): 250–53; Schuyler C. Marshall, "The Free Democratic Convention of 1852," *Pennsylvania History* 22 (January 1955): 149–53; Sewell, *Ballots*, pp. 244–45.
62. *New York Tribune*, Aug. 13, 1852; *Commonwealth*, Aug 13, 1852; Aug. 14, 1852; Sept. 14, 1852; *National Era*, Aug. 26, 1852; *Boston Transcript*, Aug. 12, 1852; Wilson to Hawley, July 31, 1852, Joseph R. Hawley Papers, LC; Stone to Sumner, Aug. 15, 1852, Sumner Papers; diary, Aug. 10, 1852, Adams Papers; Richard H. Sewell, *John P. Hale and the Politics of Abolition* (Cambridge: Harvard University Press, 1965), pp. 147–48; *Liberator*, Sept. 6, 1852; *New York Times*, Aug. 14. 1852.
63. Diary, Aug. 12, 1852, Adams Papers; Riddleberger, *Julian*, pp. 85–86; George W. Julian, *Political Recollections, 1840 to 1872* (New York: Negro Universities Press, 1976), pp. 123–25; Lewis to Julian, Aug. 19, 1852, Giddings-Julian Papers; Sewell, *Ballots*, pp. 243–45.
64. Rantoul to Butler, June 13, 1852, Butler Papers.
65. Bean, "Transformation," pp. 125–27; Robert Rantoul, *Memoirs, Speeches and Writings of Robert Rantoul Jr.*, ed. Luther Hamilton (Boston: John P. Jewett and Company, 1854), p. 811; Sumner to Adams, June, 1852, Adams Papers; *Northampton*

Courier, Aug. 10, 1852; *Commonwealth,* Aug. 11, 1852.

66. Journal, Aug. 26, 1852, Dana Papers; Donald, *Sumner*, p. 240; Stone to Sumner, 2 letters both Oct. 19, 1852, and Wilson to Sumner, Sumner Papers; *Commonwealth*, Sept. 16, 1852; Walter M. Merrill and Louis T. Ruchames, eds., *The Letters of William Lloyd Garrison,* 4 vols. (Cambridge: Harvard University Press, 1970–1975), 4: 206; *Memorial Addresses*, p. 103.
67. *Commonwealth*, Aug. 28, 1852; Sept. 6, 1853; Sept. 7, 1853; Sept. 9, 1852; Sept. 21, 1852; *Boston Transcript*, Aug. 26, 1848; Aug. 28, 1848; *Northampton Courier*, Aug. 10, 1852; Sept. 14, 1852; Wilson to Sumner, Sept. 6, 1852, Sumner Papers; Erastus Hopkins to Hawley, Sept. 6, 1852, Hawley Papers.
68. *Commonwealth*, Sept. 11, 1852, quoting from *Worcester Spy;* Sept. 21, 1852; *Northampton Courier*, Sept. 14, 1852; Sept. 21, 1852, quoting from *Worcester Palladium*; Sept. 28, 1852; Oct. 12, 1852.
69. *Commonwealth*, Sept. 2, 1852; Sept. 3, 1852; Sept. 9, 1852; Bean, "Transformation," pp. 128–29.
70. *Commonwealth*, Sept. 8, 1852; diary, Sept. 6, 9–11, 13, and 14, 1852, Adams Papers; journal, Sept. 6 and 15, 1852, manuscript autobiography, pp. 227–30, E. R. Hoar to Palfrey, Sept. 7, 1852, and Higginson to Palfrey, Sept. 18, 1852, Palfrey Papers; journal, Sept. 15, 1852, and Dana to his father, Sept. 17, 1852, Dana Papers; Gattel, *Palfrey*, pp. 207–9.
71. Diary, Sept. 11, 1852, Adams Papers.
72. Ibid., Sept. 6, 10, 11, 14, and 15, 1852; Gattel, *Palfrey*, pp. 208–9; journal, Sept. 15, 1852, and Dana to his father, Sept. 17, 1852, Dana Papers; *Commonwealth*, Sept. 10, 1852; Sept. 14, 1852; *Boston Transcript,* Sept. 14, 1852.
73. *Commonwealth*, Sept. 14, 1852; *Boston Transcript*, Sept. 14, 1852; Sept. 15, 1852; manuscript autobiography, pp. 228—29, and Higginson to Palfrey, Sept. 18, 1852, Palfrey Papers; diary, Sept. 6, 13, and 14, 1852, Adams Papers; journal, Sept. 15, 1852, Dana Papers.
74. *Northampton Courier*, Sept. 21, 1852; *Boston Transcript*, Sept 15, 1852; Sept. 16, 1852; *National Era*, Sept. 23, 1852; *Commonwealth*, Sept. 15, 1852; Sept. 16, 1852; *Liberator*, Sept. 24, 1852; diary, Sept. 14 and 15, 1852, Adams Papers; Bean, "Transformation," pp. 133–34.
75. *Commonwealth*, Sept. 17, 1852; diary, Sept. 15, 1852, Adams Papers.
76. Diary, Sept. 15–21, 25, 29, and 30 and Oct. 5, 19, 21, and 22, 1852, Adams Papers; *Northampton Courier*, Oct. 26, 1852; diary, Oct. 20, 1852, and Dana to his father, Sept. 17, 1852, Dana Papers; manuscript autobiography, pp. 229–30, Palfrey Papers; Gattel, *Palfrey*, p. 209; *New York Post,* Nov. 7, 1853.
77. *Northampton Courier*, Sept. 28, 1852.
78. Ibid.; *Commonwealth,* Sept. 23–25, 1852; Sept. 30, 1852; Oct. 2, 1852; *Boston Transcript*, Sept. 25, 1852; Sept. 28, 1852.
79. *Commonwealth*, Sept. 28, 1852; Sept. 30, 1852; *Boston Transcript*, Sept. 28, 1852.
80. *Boston Journal*, Sept. 22, 1875; *Commonwealth*, Oct. 22, 1852; Wilson to Smith, Oct. 11, 1852, Smith Papers.
81. Wilson to Carter, Sept. 29, 1852, Carter Papers.
82. Wilson to Sumner, Aug. 23, 1852, Sumner Papers; *Commonwealth*, Oct. 12, 1852, one article quoting from the *Milwaukee Free Democrat; Northampton Courier,* Oct. 19, 1852; *New York Tribune,* Oct. 13, 1852; Wilson to Smith, Oct. 11, 1852, Smith Papers.

83. *Commonwealth*, Oct. 13, 1852; Oct. 22, 1852; *Boston Transcript*, Oct. 13, 1852; *New York Tribune*, Oct. 13, 1852.
84. *Commonwealth*, Oct. 22, 1852.
85. Robinson, "*Warrington*," p. 56; diary, Oct., *passim*, Adams Papers; *Commonwealth*, Oct. 1, 1852; Oct. 4–8, 1852; Oct. 13, 1852; Oct. 16, 1852; Oct. 18, 1852; Oct. 22, 1852; Oct. 27, 1852; Nov. 2, 1852.
86. *Northampton Courier*, Oct. 19, 1852.
87. Bartlett, pp. 289–95; *Commonwealth*, Oct. 30, 1852; Dec. 1, 1850; *Springfield Republican*, Oct. 27, 1860.
88. Robinson, "*Warrington*," p. 40; *Northampton Courier*, Oct. 19, 1852; Oct. 26, 1852; Nov. 9, 1852; *Commonwealth*, Oct. 21, 1852.

Chapter 9

1. Burnham, pp. 510–12; Peterson, p. 31; William E. Gienapp, *The Origins of the Republican Party, 1852–1856* (New York: Oxford University Press, 1987), pp. 20–30; Dale Baum, *The Civil War Party System: the Case of Massachusetts, 1848–1876* (Chapel Hill: University of North Carolina Press, 1984), pp. 17, 25–26; Pierce, 3: 316; *Commonwealth*, Nov. 3, 1852; Nov. 5, 1852.
2. *Liberator*, Nov. 12, 1852; *Boston Transcript*, Nov. 6, 1852; Nov. 18, 1852; *Northampton Courier*, Nov. 16, 1852; *Commonwealth*, Nov. 9, 1852; Nov. 10, 1852; Bean, "Transformation," p. 134; Sweeney, p. 132; Baum, pp. 26–27; *Tribune Almanac*, 1853, p. 36.
3. *Commonwealth*, Nov. 3, 1852; Nov. 4, 1852; Wilson, *Rise and Fall*, 2: 376.
4. *Northampton Courier*, Nov. 16, 1852; *Boston Post*, Nov. 10, 1852; *Boston Pilot*, Nov. 6, 1852.
5. *Commonwealth*, Nov. 5, 1852; Nov. 6, 1852.
6. Ibid., Nov 12, 1852; Nov. 15, 1852.
7. Gienapp, pp. 44–60, 488; *Commonwealth*, Apr. 10, 1852; Nov. 11, 1852; Nov. 25, 1852; *Northampton Courier*, Nov. 30, 1852; *Boston Pilot*, Nov. 10, 1852; *Boston Post*, Nov. 10, 1852; *New York Tribune*, Apr. 8, 1852; Pierce, 3: 317; diary, Nov. 8 and 24, 1852, Adams Papers.
8. Bean, "Transformation," p. 135; Loubert, pp. 134–35; Blue, p. 260; Bird to Sumner, Dec. 15, 1852, Adams Papers.
9. *Commonwealth*, Nov. 23–25, 1852; *Northampton Courier*, Nov. 30, 1852; Dec. 28, 1852; *New York Tribune*, Nov. 25, 1852; *Tribune Almanac*, 1853, p. 4; Sweeney, p. 132; *New York Post*, Jan. 7, 1853.
10. *Commonwealth*, Dec. 6, 1852; Dec. 9–11, 1852; Dec. 13, 1852; Dec. 16, 1852; Dec. 22, 1852; Jan. 1, 1853; diary, Dec. 10, 15, and 31, 1852, Adams Papers; Nason and Russell, p. 97; *Boston Pilot*, Nov. 20, 1852; *Boston Post*, Dec. 11, 1852; Dec. 16, 1852; Griswold to Butler, Dec. 2, 1852, Butler Papers; Robinson, "*Warrington*," p. 401; Pierce to Sumner, Dec. 5, 1852, and Stone to Sumner, Dec. 27, 1852, Sumner Papers; *Twenty-first Annual Report of the Massachusetts Anti-Slavery Society*, p 32.
11. *National Era*, Dec. 2, 1848; Dec. 16, 1848; Pickard, 2: 202.
12. Diary, Nov. 25–27, 1852, Adams Papers; Pierce to Sumner, Dec. 5, 1852, Sumner Papers; Pierce, 3: 317; *Commonwealth*, Nov. 24, 1852; Dec. 20–23, 1852; Donald, *Sumner*, p. 241.

13. Robinson, "*Warrington*," p. 401; diary, Dec. 27 and 28, 1852, Adams Papers; Richards, pp. 389; *Commonwealth*, Feb. 12, 1853; Mar. 24, 1853; Willey, pp. 405–6.
14. Diary, Nov. 3 and 10, 1852, and Feb. 2, 1853, Adams Papers; Sweeney, p. 132; Gienapp, pp. 31–35; *Dedham Gazette*, Jan. 22, 1853; O'Connor, pp. 90–91; *New York Post*, Jan. 7, 1853; Pierce, 3: 323–24; Stone to Sumner, Dec. 27, 1852, Sumner Papers; *Commonwealth*, Jan. 26–31, 1853; Bean, "Transformation," pp. 138–39.
15. *Commonwealth*, Jan. 28, 1853; Feb. 4, 1853; Feb. 5, 1853; Feb. 7, 1853; Feb. 16, 1853; Feb. 19, 1853; Feb. 21–28, 1853; Mar. 1, 1853; Mar. 3, 1853; May 26, 1853; *Northampton Courier*, Feb. 15, 1853; *New York Post*, Jan. 15, 1853; Feb. 28, 1853; Mar. 30, 1853; *Boston Transcript*, May 16, 1853; Bean, "Transformation," pp. 140–45; Brunet, pp. 355–59.
16. *Commonwealth*, Jan. 28, 1853; Feb. 8, 1853; Feb. 19, 1853; Mar. 12, 1853; Mar. 31, 1853; Apr. 29, 1853; May 13, 1853; *Northampton Courier*, Feb. 15, 1853; Apr. 12, 1853; Apr. 19, 1853; *New York Tribune*, Mar. 18, 1853; *New York Post*, Jan, 18, 1853; *Boston Transcript*, May 26, 1853; Bean, "Transformation," p. 145.
17. *Official Report of the Debates and Proceedings in the State Convention . . . to Revise and Amend the Constitution of the Commonwealth of Massachusetts*, 3 vols. (Boston: White & Potter, 1853), hereafter cited as *State Convention*, 1: 3–4; Pierce, 3: 326; Jean C. Kenney, "An Analysis of Political Alignments in Massachusetts as Revealed in the Constitutional Convention of 1853" (M.A. thesis, Smith College, 1951), pp. 1–3; James Schouler, "The Massachusetts Convention of 1853," *Proceedings of the Massachusetts Historical Society*, 2d series, 18 (1903–1904): 30–35.
18. *Commonwealth*, Feb. 1, 1853; Feb. 8, 1853; Feb. 9, 1853.
19. *Northampton Courier*, Feb. 1, 1853; *Dedham Gazette*, Jan. 29, 1853; *Commonwealth*, Feb. 16, 1833; Jan. 26, 1853; Kenney, pp. 23–25.
20. Diary, Feb. 10 and 11, Mar. 3, 5, 7, 9, and 16, 1853, and George White to Adams, Mar. 4, 1853, and F. W. Bird to Adams, Mar. 2, 1853, Adams Papers; Wilson to Lunt, Feb. 26, 1853, Carter Papers; Pierce, 3: 326; Robinson, "*Warrington*," p. 401; diary, Feb. 23, 1853, Dana Papers; Shapiro, *Dana*, p. 70; Boutwell, *Reminiscences*, 1: 218–19; Samuel Shapiro, "The Conservative Dilemma: the Massachusetts Constitutional Convention of 1853," *New England Quarterly* 33 (June 1960): 211; Howe to Sumner, Feb. 8, 1853, Howe Papers, Houghton; Albert G. Browne to Sumner, Feb. 18, 1853, and Wilson to Sumner, Mar. 5, 1853, Sumner Papers; *New York Post*, Nov. 7, 1853; *Commonwealth*, Feb. 21, 1853.
21. Diary, Feb. 10 and 12 and Mar. 9, 16, and 26, and Apr. 20, 1853, and White to Adams, Mar. 4, 1853, and Bird to Adams, Mar. 2, 1853, Adams Papers; Samuel Downer to Mann, Feb. 16, 1853, Mann Papers; Pierce, 3: 326–27; *Commonwealth*, Mar. 12, 1853; Apr. 22, 1871, from *Springfield Republican*; Shapiro, "Conservative Dilemma," p. 211; Boutwell, *Reminiscences*, 1: 216–17.
22. Mann, *Life of Wilson*, p. 37; Boutwell, *Reminiscences*, 1: 218–19; diary, Feb. 10, 1853, Adams Papers; *Commonwealth*, Mar. 9, 1853; Nason and Russell, p. 106.
23. *New York Tribune*, Mar. 18, 1853; *Northampton Courier*, Mar. 15, 1853; *Commonwealth*, Mar. 9, 1853; *New York Post*, Mar. 8, 1853; Mar. 30, 1853.
24. *State Convention*, 1: 3–4; Boutwell, *Reminiscences*, 1: 225; Mann, *Life of Wilson*, p. 36; Hoar, *Autobiography*, 1: 178; *Commonwealth*, Mar. 1, 1853; Mar. 8, 1853; *New York Post*, Mar. 9, 1853; *Springfield Republican*, Feb. 9, 1856; Nason and Russell, p. 105.

25. *Northampton Courier*, June 21, 1853; Davis, "Occupations of Massachusetts Legislators," p. 92.
26. *Liberator*, May 13, 1853; *New York Herald*, May 7, 1853; *Commonwealth*, May 6, 1853; Pierce, 3: 324; diary, Apr. 13 and May 5 and 7, 1853, Adams Papers; Willey, p. 410.
27. *Boston Transcript*, Apr. 20, 1853; *New York Post*, Apr. 27, 1853.
28. *State Convention*, 1: 3, 9–10, 12, 35, and 43; *Commonwealth*, Apr. 23, 1853; May 5, 1853; diary, May 4, 1853, Dana Papers; *New York Post*, Apr. 27, 1853; May 3–5, 1853; *Northampton Courier*, May 10, 1853; Robinson, "*Warrington*," pp. 57–58; Harrington, *Fighting Politician*, p. 16; Nason and Russell, p. 106; Kenney, p. 32.
29. *State Convention*, 1: 10, 12, 35, 43, 88; *Northampton Courier*, May 10, 1853; May 17, 1853; May 24, 1853; *New York Post*, May 7, 1853; May 10, 1853; May 14, 1853; May 19, 1853; May 21, 1853; *New York Herald*, May 22, 1853; *Commonwealth*, May 5, 1853; May 17–20, 1853.
30. *New York Post*, May 14, 1853; May 19, 1853; May 21, 1853; *State Convention*, 1: 178–82; *Commonwealth*, May 19, 1853; May 20, 1853.
31. *State Convention*, 1: 190, 196, 322, 327; Austin, pp. 466–67; *New York Post*, May 23, 1853; *Boston Post*, June 3, 1853; Mann, *Life of Wilson*, pp. 38–39; *Commonwealth*, May 30, 1858; June 2–4, 1853; June 6, 1853; *Northampton Courier*, June 14, 1853; *New York Post*, June 13, 1853.
32. *Commonwealth*, May 30, 1853.
33. *State Convention*, 1: 159, 310–13, 385–96, 419–24; *New York Post*, May 30, 1853; *Commonwealth*, May 30, 1853; June 2, 1853; *Boston Post*, June 3, 1853; *Northampton Courier*, May 31, 1853.
34. *State Convention*, 1: 319, 348–49, 478, 514–17, 522–33; *Commonwealth*, June 2–4, 1853; June 6, 1853; *Northampton Courier*, June 14, 1853; *New York Post*, June 13, 1853.
35. *Commonwealth*, June 1, 1853.
36. *State Convention*, 1: 581–87, 701–2, 744–46; *Commonwealth*, June 8–11, 1853; *New York Post*, June 13, 1853; *Northampton Courier*, June 14, 1853.
37. *Northampton Courier*, June 14, 1853; *New York Herald*, June 6, 1853; *New York Times*, June 21, 1853; *Commonwealth*, May 31, 1853; Dawes to his wife, June 19, 1853, Dawes Papers; *State Convention*, 2: 220.
38. *Northampton Courier*, June 21–July 12, 1853; *New York Post*, June 25, 1853; July 5, 1853; July 14, 1853; Aug. 4, 1853; *Commonwealth*, June 13, 1853; June 14, 1853; June 17, 1853; June 24, 1853; June 25, 1853; June 29, 1853; July 2, 1853; July 12, 1853; *State Convention*, 2: 420, 424, 450, 464, 466, 558–59, 633–37; Pierce, 3: 325–26.
39. Pierce, 2: 422–24, 427, 450.
40. Ibid., 2: 17–18, 66–68, 75, 78–81; *Commonwealth*, June 24, 1853; Mann, *Life of Wilson*, p. 40; Phelps, p. 357; Nason and Russell, p. 107.
41. *State Convention*, 1: 783–86; *New York Post*, Aug. 4, 1853.
42. *State Convention*, 2: 258–59, 260, 266; *New York Post*, July 20, 1853.
43. *State Convention*, 2: 295–96, 306, 312–13; *Commonwealth*, July 11, 1853; *New York Post*, July 20, 1853.
44. *State Convention*, 2: 498–501; 517; journal, June 26 and July 17, 1853, Dana Papers; *Commonwealth*, June 27, 1853; Mann, *Life of Wilson*, pp. 41–42.

45. *State Convention*, 2: 530–31; 3: 247–48, 254–64; *New York Post*, July 20, 1853; *Commonwealth*, Jan. 28, 1852; Feb. 20, 1852; Feb. 23, 1852; July 22, 1853; Nason and Russell, pp. 109–14; Story, pp. 141–42.
46. *State Convention*, 2: 267, 330–32; 3: 50, 100, 125–29, 219; diary, June 2 and 4, 1853, Adams Papers; journal, Aug. 2, 1853, Dana Papers; *Commonwealth*, July 16, 1853; *Northampton Courier*, July 26, 1853; Nason and Russell, p. 107.
47. *State Convention*, 3: 229–36; 437–65, 515–17, 697, 701–7, 828–32; *Commonwealth*, July 13, 1853; July 15, 1853; July 21, 1853; July 22, 1853; *New York Post*, July 14, 1853; July 18, 1853; July 20, 1853; July 28, 1853; Aug. 4, 1853; *Northampton Courier*, July 26, 1853; journal, July 17 and Aug. 2, 1853, Dana Papers.
48. *State Convention*, 2: 703–7.
49. Ibid., 3: 405–16, 474.
50. Ibid., 2: 738, 760–75; *Northampton Courier*, July 19, 1853; Robinson, "*Warrington*," p. 403; Nason and Russell, pp. 108–9.
51. *State Convention*, 3: 131, 134–36, 140–48, 278, 287–89, 611–12; *Northampton Courier*, July 26, 1853; Aug. 2, 1853; *New York Post*, July 28, 1853; Aug. 4, 1853; *Commonwealth*, July 30, 1853; *New York Tribune*, Aug. 4, 1853; Bean, "Transformation," p. 154.
52. *New York Post*, Aug. 4, 1853; Boutwell, *Reminiscences*, 1: 220–22; journal, Aug. 2, 1853, Dana Papers; Shapiro, "Conservative Dilemma," p. 218; Brown, p. 81.
53. Journal, Aug. 2, 1853, Dana Papers; Schouler, "Massachusetts Convention," pp. 36–37; Donald, *Sumner*, pp. 245–46; Pierce, 3: 327–28, 331–32; manuscript autobiography, pp. 234–35, Palfrey Papers.
54. Pierce, 3: 327–28.
55. *Commonwealth*, June 11, 1853, quoting from *New Bedford Standard*.
56. *National Era*, Oct. 20, 1853.
57. Boutwell, *Reminiscences*, 1: 228; *Commonwealth*, Sept. 24, 1853; Mann, *Life of Wilson*, p. 43.
58. Kenney, p. 32.
59. Donald, *Sumner*, pp. 244–46.
60. Blue, pp. 275–77; Kenney, pp. 68–72; *New York Tribune*, Jan. 13, 1853; *Commonwealth*, *passim*, Apr. 5 to May 13, 1853.
61. Schouler, "Massachusetts Convention," pp. 41–45.
62. *Northampton Courier*, Aug. 2, 1853; Aug. 9, 1853; diary, July 27, 1853, Adams Papers; *Boston Transcript*, Aug. 1, 1853; *Commonwealth*, July 30, 1853; Aug. 3, 1853.
63. Pierce, 3: 335; *Northampton Courier*, Sept. 6, 1853; Sept. 13, 1853, quoting from *Boston Times*; Carter to Adams [1853], Adams Papers; *Commonwealth*, Aug. 31, 1853; Sept. 3, 1853; Sept. 5, 1853; Sept. 10, 1853; diary, Sept. 1, 1853, Everett Papers.
64. *Henry Wilson, The New Constitution. Address Delivered by Hon. Henry Wilson, to His Constituents, Explanatory of the Proposed Constitutional Amendments* (Boston: White & Potter, 1853).
65. *Commonwealth*, Aug. 11, 1853; *Boston Transcript*, Aug. 17, 1853; Wilson to Sumner, Sept. 1, 1853, Sumner Papers.
66. *Northampton Courier*, Aug. 2, 1853; Aug. 9, 1853; Aug. 23, 1853; Aug. 30, 1853; *Commonwealth*, Aug. 5, 1853; *New York Tribune*, Aug. 11, 1853.

67. Adams to Wilson, Aug. 6, 1853, Carter to Adams [1853], and Stone to Adams, Sept. 13, 1853, and diary, Sept. 8, 12, and 13, 1853, Adams Papers.
68. *Commonwealth*, Sept. 8, 1853; *Boston Transcript*, Sept. 2, 1853; *New York Post*, Sept. 5, 1853.
69. *New York Tribune*, Sept. 16, 1853; Sept. 19, 1853; *Northampton Courier*, Sept. 20, 1853; Sept. 27, 1853; Pierce, 3: 335–36; *New York Post*, Sept. 17, 1853; *Commonwealth*, Sept. 16, 1853; Sept. 17, 1853.
70. *Northampton Courier*, Oct. 4, quoting from *Dedham Gazette*; Oct. 11, 1853, quoting from *Greylock Sentinel; Commonwealth*, Sept. 16, 1853; Sept. 17, 1853; *Liberator*, Sept. 23, 1853.
71. *Northampton Courier*, Sept. 27, 1853, quoting from cited newspapers; *Commonwealth*, Sept. 21, 1853, quoting from *Boston Journal*.
72. *National Era*, Oct. 20, 1853.
73. *New York Post*, Oct. 1, 1853; *Boston Post*, Sept. 5, 1853; Oct. 2, 1853; Wilson to Sumner, Sept. 1, 1853, Sumner Papers; *Commonwealth*, Sept. 21, 1853; *Northampton Courier*, Aug. 30, 1853; *Boston Transcript*, Aug. 17, 1853; Sept. 28, 1853; Sept. 29, 1853; *New York Tribune*, Sept. 30, 1853.
74. Wilson to E. A. Stansbury, Sept. 24, 1853, Wilson Papers, LC; *New York Tribune*, Sept. 30, 1853.
75. *Commonwealth*, Oct. 14, 1853; Oct. 21, 1853; Oct. 31, 1853; *passim*, October; *Boston Transcript*, Oct. 31, 1853; Nov. 3, 1853.
76. *New York Post*, Sept. 16, 1853; Oct. 17, 1853; *New York Times*, Oct. 12, 1853; *Commonwealth*, Oct. 11, 1853.
77. *Boston Advertiser*, Oct. 4, 1853; *Commonwealth*, Oct. 5, 1853; *New York Post*, Sept. 16, 1853; Hill, *Abbott Lawrence*, p. 121; *New York Times*, Oct. 12, 1853.
78. *Commonwealth*, Oct. 17, 1853; Shapiro, "Conservative Dilemma," pp. 222–23; diary, Oct. 20, 1853, Everett Papers.
79. Pierce, 3: 336–38; *New York Post*, Sept. 20, 1853; Oct. 22, 1853; *Commonwealth*, Oct. 28, 1853; Oct. 29, 1853; diary, Sept. 29 and Oct. 6, 1853, Adams Papers.
80. *Dedham Gazette*, Oct. 29, 1853; *Commonwealth*, Nov. 1, 1853; *Northampton Courier*, Nov. 1, 1853; *New York Post*, Nov. 3, 1853.
81. *Commonwealth*, Oct. 18, 1853; Oct. 27, 1853; Oct. 28, 1853; diary, Sept. 29 and Oct. 8, 1853, Adams Papers; Gatell, *Palfrey*, pp. 212–13; *Boston Transcript*, Oct. 25, 1853; *New York Post*, Nov. 7, 1853.
82. Gatell, *Palfrey*, pp. 214–15; *New York Post*, Nov. 7, 1853.
83. *Commonwealth*, Oct. 31, 1853; Nov. 12, 1853; Pierce, 3: 338; diary, Oct. 27 and 28, 1853, Adams Papers; *New York Post*, Nov. 7, 1853.
84. Pierce, 3: 338; diary, Sept. 29, Oct. 6, 7, 23, 27, and 28 and Nov. 2, 5, 8, 10, and 14, 1853, Inquiry from 12 citizens from Quincy to Adams, Oct. 28, 1853, Adams to Josiah Bingham and others, Oct. 31, 1853, and Adams to Everett, Nov. 1, 1853, Adams Papers; diary, Sept. 29, 1853, Dana Papers; *Boston Courier*, Nov. 8, 1853; *Commonwealth*, Oct. 20, 1853; Nov. 7, 1853; *Boston Transcript*, Nov. 7, 1853; *New York Post*, Nov. 7, 1853; Nov. 15, 1853.
85. *Boston Transcript*, Oct. 6, 1853; Nov. 3, 1853; Nov. 5, 1853; Nov. 8, 1853; *Commonwealth*, Nov. 12, 1853; Pierce, 3: 339; Fuess, *Cushing*, 2: 139–43; Boutwell, *Reminiscences*, 1: 233; *Boston Pilot*, Nov. 5, 1853; Nov. 12, 1853; *New York Tribune*, Nov. 1, 1853; Nov. 4, 1853; *New York Post*, Nov. 1, 1853; Nov. 7, 1853.

86. Stone to Carter, Nov. 7, 1853, Carter Papers; *New York Post*, Oct. 27, 1853; Nov. 8, 1853; Nov. 15, 1853; *Commonwealth,* Nov. 2, 1853; Nov. 3, 1853; Nov. 11, 1853; *New York Tribune*, Nov. 4, 1853; *Boston Transcript*, Nov. 12, 1853.
87. *New York Post*, Nov. 2, 1853; Nov. 3, 1853; Nov. 15, 1853; *Boston Advertiser, passim,* Nov., 1853; *New York Tribune*, Nov. 12, 1853; *Commonwealth*, Nov. 11, 1853; Nov. 12, 1853; Hoar to Palfrey, Oct. 7, 1853, Palfrey Papers; Storey, *Hoar*, pp. 101–4; *Boston Transcript*, Nov. 10, 1853; Shapiro, "Conservative Dilemma," p. 221.
88. *Tribune Almanac,* 1854, p. 40; *State Constitution*, 3: 756; *Commonwealth*, Nov. 15, 1853; Kenney, pp. 84–85; Bean, "Transformation," pp. 173–79; Sweeney, pp. 134–36; Baum, pp. 28–30.
89. *New York Post*, Nov. 16, 1853; Nov. 18, 1853; *Commonwealth,* Nov. 17, 1853; Sumner to Adams, Nov. 21, 1853, Adams Papers.
90. Joshua Leavitt to R. H. Leavitt, Nov. 17, 1853, Joshua Leavitt Papers, LC; Albree, pp. 121–22; *New York Post*, Nov. 16, 1853; *Northampton Courier*, Nov. 22, 1853, one article quoting from *Dedham Gazette*; Everett to Mrs. Charles Eames, Nov. 15, 1853, Everett Papers; diary, Nov. 19 and 30, 1853, Adams Papers; *Commonwealth*, Nov. 23, 1853.
91. *New York Tribune*, Nov. 17, 1853; *Commonwealth*, Nov. 17, 1853; Nov. 22, 1853; May 2, 1854; *Northampton Courier*, Nov. 22, 1853, quoting from *Dedham Gazette*; *Liberator*, Nov. 18, 1853; Butler, p. 119.
92. Leavitt to R. H. Leavitt, Nov. 17, 1853, Leavitt Papers; Weiss, 2: 232–34; Schouler, "Massachusetts Convention," pp. 41–43; Hart, 4: 59.
93. *National Era*, Dec. 15, 1853; Pierce, 3: 340.
94. Hart, 4: 25–26; Schouler, "Massachusetts Convention," pp. 46–47.
95. Manuscript autobiography, p. 237, Palfrey Papers; diary, Nov. 15 and 17, 1853, and Adams to Robinson, Nov. 21, 1853, Adams Papers; Albree, p. 279.
96. Diary, Nov. 18 and 19, 1853, Adams Papers; *Boston Advertiser*, Nov. 15, 1853; Pierce, 3: 341–42; *Commonwealth*, Dec. 9, 1853; Albert Browne to Sumner, Dec. 14, 1853, Sumner Papers.
97. *New York Tribune*, Nov. 19, 1853; *New York Post*, Nov. 18, 1853; *Commonwealth*, Nov. 30, 1853.
98. Pierce, 3: 342; *New York Post*, Dec. 7, 1853; *Commonwealth*, Dec. 2, 1853.

Chapter 10

1. Bacon, *History of Natick*, p. 153; *Natick Bulletin*, Oct. 29, 1870; *Natick Observer*, Nov. 10, 1860; Pierce, 3: 342; Hazard, pp. 80–81; *Dedham Gazette*, Oct. 29, 1853; *Cincinnati Gazette*, Feb. 3, 1865.
2. Nason and Russell, pp. 42–43; warranty deed, Apr. 20, 1853, Wilson Papers, South Natick Museum; Joseph P. Ridley, *Ridley's Directory of Natick (*Worcester, Mass.: Edward R. Fiske & Co., 1873), p. 113; Middlesex County, Southern District, Cambridge, Registry of Deeds, book 624, p. 112.
3. Bacon, *History of Natick*, pp. 8, 107–8, 124; *Congressional Globe*, 35th Cong., 1st sess., 1858, Appendix, p. 173.
4. Johnson and Malone, *Dictionary of American Biography*, 13: 389–90; Nason and Russell, pp. 39–41, 103–5; *First Congregational Church, Natick*, pp. 70–71, 107; Bacon, *History of Natick*, pp. 95–96; Mary Howe to Caroline C. Howe, July 7, 1850,

Wilson Papers, South Natick Museum; Hurd, *Middlesex County*, 1: 542.

5. Stone to Sumner, Dec. 31, 1853, and Wilson to Sumner, Jan. 5, 1854, Sumner Papers; *New York Post*, Dec. 15, 1853; Jan. 11, 1854; *Commonwealth, passim*, Dec., 1853; Jan. 10, 1854; Mar. 1, 1854; Pierce, 3: 345; Haynes, *Sumner*, p. 164; Austin, p. 469; *New York Tribune*, Apr. 20, 1854; Apr. 21, 1854.
6. Sewell, *Ballots*, pp. 251–52; Gienapp, pp. 47, 55–59; Blue, pp. 271–80.
7. *Commonwealth*, Jan. 9, 1854; *New York Tribune*, Jan. 5, 1854; Jan. 25, 1854; Pierce, 3: 363; Wilson, *Rise and Fall*, 2: 407; *New York Post*, Jan. 25, 1854; Jan. 31, 1854; Howe to Sumner, Jan. 18, 1854, Howe Papers, Houghton; *New York Times*, Jan. 24, 1854; Jan. 31, 1854.
8. Wilson to Sumner, Jan. 5 and 18, 1854, and Howe to Sumner, Jan. 29, 1854, Howe Papers, Houghton.
9. *Boston Atlas*, Jan. 26, 1854; *New York Tribune*, Feb. 3, 1854; Howe to Sumner, Jan. 25 and 29, 1854, Howe Papers, Houghton.
10. *Commonwealth*, Jan. 31, 1854.
11. Howe to Sumner, Jan. 25 and Feb. 16, 1854, Howe Papers, Houghton; Dana to Sumner, Feb. 26, 1854, Sumner Papers; diary, Feb. 4, 8, 11, 13, 16, and 17, 1854, and E. R. Hoar, John B. Alley, Charles Davis, and James Stone to Adams, Feb. 4, 1854, Adams Papers.
12. Howe to Sumner, Feb. 16, 1854, Howe Papers, Houghton; Albert G. Browne to Sumner, Feb. 22, 1854, Sumner Papers; diary, Feb. 4 and 11, 1854, Adams Papers; Pierce, 3: 342.
13. *Commonwealth*, Jan. 31, 1854, and *passim* Feb. 2 to 11, 1854, particularly Feb. 8; Feb. 15, 1854; Feb. 20, 1854; *Dedham Gazette*, Feb. 4, 1854; *New York Post*, Feb. 4, 1854; Feb. 7, 1854; *Boston Transcript, passim*, Feb. 3 to 14, 1854; *New York Tribune*, Feb. 16, 1854; Pierce, 3: 363.
14. *Commonwealth*, Feb. 15, 1854; Winthrop to Everett, Feb. 6, 1854, and Fillmore to Everett, Feb. 8, 1854, Everett Papers; Wilson, *Rise and Fall*, 2: 386–87; *New York Tribune*, Feb. 16, 1854; Adams to Sumner, Feb. 26, 1854, Adams Papers; Wilson to Sumner, Feb. 26, 1854, and T. P. Chandler to Sumner, Mar. 8, 1854, Sumner Papers.
15. *Commonwealth*, Feb. 14, 1854; *New York Tribune*, Feb. 16, 1854.
16. *Commonwealth*, Feb. 17, 1854; *New York Times*, Feb. 18, 1854; *New York Tribune*, Feb. 17, 1854; Feb. 20, 1854; *Liberator*, Feb. 24, 1854.
17. *New York Times*, Feb. 18, 1854; *Commonwealth*, Feb. 17, 1854; Wilson to Sumner, Feb. [no day given], 1854, Sumner Papers.
18. *Boston Atlas*, Feb. 24, 1854; *New York Tribune*, Feb. 24, 1854; *Commonwealth*, Feb. 24, 1854; *Liberator*, Feb. 24, 1854; Mar. 4, 1854.
19. *New York Tribune*, Feb. 22, 1854.
20. Pierce, 3: 357; Wilson to Sumner, Feb. 14 and 26, 1854 and Feb. [no day given], 1854 and T. P. Chandler to Sumner, Feb. 26, 1854, Sumner Papers; Sumner to Adams, Mar. 14, 1854, Adams Papers; *New York Times*, Mar. 7, 1854; *New York Tribune*, Mar. 4, 1854; Mar. 6, 1854; diary, Mar. 2, 3, and 7, 1854, Everett Papers.
21. Diary, Feb. 21, Mar. 9, 14, and 20, Apr. 12, 13, and 29, and May 3–6 and 12, 1854, and Everett to Mrs. Charles Eames, Mar. 21, Apr. 21, and May 5, 16, and 22, 1854, Everett Papers; *Commonwealth*, Mar. 23, 1854; Mar. 24, 1854; Wilson to Sumner, Mar. 15, 1854, Sumner Papers; *Boston Advertiser*, May 20, 1854.
22. Wilson to Sumner, Feb. 26 and Mar. 1 and 22, 1854, Sumner Papers; Sewell, *Ballots*, pp. 263–64.

23. *Commonwealth*, Mar. 2, 1854; Mar. 15, 1854; Mar. 17, 1854; *New York Tribune*, Mar. 17, 1854; Mar. 27, 1854; Apr. 7, 1854; Wilson to Sumner, Mar. 15 and 22, 1854, Sumner Papers; Pierce, 3: 357; *National Era*, June 29, 1854; *Boston Transcript*, Apr. 4, 1854; *New York Post*, Mar. 9, 1854; Hurd, *Middlesex County*, 1: 529; Wilson, *Rise and Fall*, 2: 408–9; *National Era*, June 29, 1854; C. M. Seeter to Hawley, Apr. 11, 1854, and Edmund Tuttle to Hawley, Apr. 12, 1854, Hawley Papers; *Northampton Courier*, May 23, 1854.
24. Bird to Sumner, Apr. 16, 1854, Sumner Papers; Bird to Adams, May 3, 1854, Adams Papers.
25. *Commonwealth*, Mar. 10, 1854; *New York Post*, Mar. 10, 1854; Mar. 11, 1854; Mann, *Life of Wilson*, p. 43; Pierce, 3: 365; *Northampton Courier*, Mar. 21, 1854; *New York Tribune*, *passim*, Apr., 1854.
26. *National Era*, June 8, 1854; Harold Schwartz, *Samuel Gridley Howe: Social Reformer, 1801–1876* (Cambridge: Harvard University Press, 1956), p. 197; Richards, p. 416n; William Lawrence, *Life of Amos A. Lawrence* (Boston: Houghton Mifflin Co., 1888), pp. 77–78, 87; O'Connor, p. 102; diary, May 27 and 31 and June 2 and 10, 1854, Everett papers.
27. Anderson, pp. 103–10.
28. *New York Post*, May 9, 1854; May 23, 1854; *Commonwealth*, May 12, 1854; Mann, *Life of Wilson*, p. 43; Nason and Russell, p. 117; *New York Tribune*, May 8, 1854; May 9, 1854; May 22, 1854; *New York Times*, May 17, 1854; Wilson to Seward, May 28, 1854, Seward Papers; Gienapp, pp. 77–84.
29. *Commonwealth*, May 24, 1854; *New York Times*, May 29, 1854.
30. Wilson, *Rise and Fall*, 2: 378.
31. Anderson, pp. 87–90; *Congressional Globe*, 38th Cong., 1st sess., 1864, p. 139; Wilson, *Rise and Fall*, 2: 435–41; *Commonwealth*, May 27–31, 1854; George W. Smalley, *Anglo-American Memories* (London: Duckworth & Co., 1911), pp. 28–29.
32. Anderson, pp. 87–102; Alley to Sumner, June 5, 1854, Sumner Papers; *New York Post*, June 5, 1854; diary, May 27, 1854, Everett Papers; Wilson, *Rise and Fall*, 2: 441–43; *Commonwealth*, June 3, 1854; June 5, 1854, quoting from *Boston Atlas*; June 19, 1854; *New York Times*, June 1, 1854; June 3, 1854; *Boston Transcript*, May 27 to June 3, 1854; Smalley, p. 27.
33. *Commonwealth*, June 7, 1854.
34. Ibid., June 1, 1854; *Dedham Gazette*, June 3, 1854; June 10, 1854; *National Era*, June 8, 1854; Wilson, *Rise and Fall*, 2: 414; Alley to Sumner, June 5, 1854, Sumner Papers.
35. *Commonwealth*, June 2, 1854; *Liberator*, June 9, 1854; June 30, 1854.
36. Wilson, *Rise and Fall*, 2: 410–11, 413; Wilson to Seward, May 28, 1854, Seward Papers; Wilson to Washburn, Israel Washburn Jr. Papers, LC.
37. *National Era*, June 1, 1854; *Northampton Courier*, June 20, 1854; *Commonwealth*, Apr. 27, 1854; June 14, 1854; June 21, 1854; *New York Tribune*, June 30, 1854; Gordon S. P. Kleeberg, *The Formation of the Republican Party as a National Political Organization* (New York: Moods Publishing Company, 1911), pp. 14–15; Wilson, *Rise and Fall*, 2: 410–11.
38. Alley to Sumner, June 5, 1854, Sumner Papers; Wilson to Washburn, May 28, 1854, Israel Washburn Papers; Mann, *Life of Wilson*, pp. 44–45; Wilson, *Rise and Fall*, 2: 414.

39. Bean, "Transformation," pp. 188–89; Duberman, *Adams,* p. 191; *New York Tribune,* Aug. 10, 1854; *New York Post,* June 27, 1854; *Commonwealth,* July 1, 1854; William Jackson to Sumner, July 1, 1854, Sumner Papers; diary, May 22 and 31, 1854, and Adams to Parker, June 4, 1854, Adams Papers.
40. *National Era,* June 8, 1854; Everett to Mrs. Eames, May 26, 1854, Everett Papers; *Boston Transcript,* May 20, 1854; *Commonwealth,* May 25, 1854; June 8, 1854.
41. Stone to Sumner, July 14, 1854, Sumner Papers; *Boston Transcript,* July 3, 1854; *Commonwealth,* June 19, 1854; July 6, 1854; *New York Herald,* June 21, 1854.
42. Hoar, *Autobiography,* 1: 30; *Commonwealth,* June 29, 1854; *National Era,* July 6, 1854; diary, June 1 and July 22, 1854, Adams Papers; Wilson to Moses Cartland, June 24, 1854, Cartland Family Papers, MHS.
43. *Northampton Courier,* June 27, 1854; *Commonwealth,* July 8, 1854; July 11, 1854; *Boston Transcript,* July 8, 1854; *New York Tribune,* Aug. 10, 1854; Pierce, 3: 398–99; Frank A. Flower, *History of the Republican Party* (Springfield: Union Publishing Company, 1884), pp. 192–93.
44. *New York Post,* July 6, 1854; *Springfield Republican,* July 21, 1854; *New York Tribune,* Aug. 10, 1854; Webb to Sumner, July 14, 1854, Sumner Papers.
45. *Northampton Courier,* July 25, 1854; Aug. 1, 1854; *Commonwealth,* July 21, 1854; *New York Tribune,* Aug. 10, 1854; *Springfield Republican,* July 21, 1854; *New York Herald,* July 21–24, 1854.
46. *Springfield Republican,* July 24, 1854; Aug. 2, 1854; *Commonwealth,* July 24, 1854; July 29, 1854.
47. *Northampton Courier,* July 25, 1854; Aug. 1, 1854; *Springfield Republican,* July 21, 1854; *Commonwealth,* July 24, 1854; July 27, 1854; *National Era,* Aug. 3, 1854; *Dedham Gazette,* July 29, 1854; Flower, p. 193.
48. *Northampton Courier,* June 20, 1854; Wilson to Sumner, July 2, 1854, Sumner Papers; *Commonwealth,* June 20, 1854; June 27, 1854; July 1, 1854; July 26, 1854; *Dedham Gazette,* July 29, 1854; Pierce, 3: 398; *Springfield Republican,* July 24, 1854.
49. Wilson, *Rise and Fall,* 2: 408, 415; Mann, *Life of Wilson,* p. 46; Nason and Russell, pp. 118–19.
50. The story of the nativist movement and Know Nothing party in Massachusetts and the nation may be found in Ray A. Billington, *The Protestant Crusade* (New York: Rhinehart & Company, 1952); Tyler Anbinder, *Nativism and Slavery* (New York: Oxford University Press, 1992); Humphrey J. Desmond *The Know-Nothing Party* (Washington: The New Century Press, 1904); Louis D. Scisco, *Political Nativism in New York,* Columbia University Studies in History, Economics and Public Law, no. 13 (New York: The Columbia University Press, 1901); John R. Mulkern, "The Know-Nothing Party in Massachusetts," (Ph.D. diss., Boston University, 1963); Ira Cross, "Origin, Principles, and History of the American Party," *Iowa Journal of History and Politics,* 6 (1906): 526–53; George H. Haynes, "A Know-Nothing Legislature," *Report of the American Historical Association* 1 (1896): 177–87; idem, "The Causes of Know-Nothing Success in Massachusetts," *American Historical Review* 3 (Oct. 1897): 67–82; Harry J. Carman and Richard H. Luthin, "Some Aspects of the Know Nothing Movement Reconsidered," *The South Atlantic Quarterly* 39 (Apr. 1940): 213–34; Oscar Handlin, *Boston's Immigrants, 1790–1865* (Cambridge: Harvard University Press, 1941); Gienapp, pp. 60–67, 92–94; Bean, "Transformation," pp. 234–41; idem., "Puritan Verses Celt, 1850–1860," *New England Quarterly* 7 (Mar. 1934): 70–89; *New York Post,* Aug. 11, 1854.

51. Haynes, "Causes of Know-Nothing Success," pp. 73, 77; Bean, "Transformation," pp. 195–98.
52. Desmond, pp. 10–11; Scisco, p. 243; Anbinder, pp. 3–15.
53. This follows the history in Billington, pp. 1–158.
54. Desmond, pp. 91–93; Anbinder, pp. 10–13.
55. *Boston Transcript*, Mar. 14, 1854; *New York Tribune*, Aug. 10, 1854; *New York Post*, Aug. 11, 1854; Stone to Sumner, Mar. 15, 1854, and Winslow to Sumner, May 5, 1854, Sumner Papers.
56. Diary, July 2 and 5 and Aug. 30, 1854, Adams Papers; Winthrop, pp. 167–68; Nason and Russell, pp. 119, 139; *Liberator*, June 29, 1855; Pierce, 3: 401; *New York Tribune*, Aug. 31, 1872.
57. Wilson to Sumner, July 2, 1854, and Webb to Sumner, July 14, 1854, Sumner Papers; *New York Herald*, July 31, 1854; *Springfield Republican*, Aug. 1, 1854.
58. *Northampton Courier*, Aug. 1, 1854; Aug. 8, 1854; Aug. 29, 1854; *Commonwealth*, Aug. 3, 1854; Aug. 5, 1854, quoting from *Newburyport Herald*; *Boston Transcript*, Aug. 2, 1854, quoting from *Boston Herald*; *New York Tribune*, Aug. 10, 1854.
59. *Northampton Courier*, Aug. 15, 1854; *New York Tribune*, Aug. 10, 1854; Aug. 14, 1854; Aug. 22, 1854; *New York Post*, Aug. 17, 1854; Moses Kimball to Dawes, Aug. 24, 1854, Dawes Papers; *Commonwealth*, June 27, 1854; Aug. 17, 1854.
60. *New York Post*, Aug. 30, 1854; *New York Herald*, Sept.10, 1854; Sept. 27, 1854.
61. *New York Herald*, Aug. 27, 1854; *Boston Transcript*, July 29, 1854; *Commonwealth*, Sept. 4–8, 1854; diary, Aug 31 and Sept. 2, 1854, Andrew to Adams, July 22 and August 30, 1854, Bird to Adams, Sept. 1 and 7, 1854, and Adams to Andrew, Sept. 2, 1854, Adams Papers; Gattel, *Palfrey*, p. 221; Hoar, *Autobiography*, 1: 30; Pierce, 3: 398; Mann, *Life of Wilson*, p. 45; *Dedham Gazette*, Sept. 9, 1854; *Springfield Republican*, Sept. 8, 1854.
62. *New York Herald*, Sept. 24, 1854; Bird to Adams, Sept. 7, 1854, Adams Papers; *Springfield Republican*, Sept. 8, 1854; *Northampton Courier*, Sept. 12, 1854; *Boston Advertiser*, Sept. 8, 1854.
63. Diary, Sept. 7, 9, and 15, 1854, Adams Papers.
64. *Springfield Republican*, Oct. 3, 1854; *Boston Telegraph*, Oct. 3, 1854; *New York Tribune*, Oct. 5, 1854.
65. Bean, "Transformation, p. 246; *New York Herald*, Aug. 24, 1854; *Springfield Republican*, Sept. 9, 1854; Winthrop, p. 168; *Boston Advertiser*, Sept. 8, 1854; *New York Tribune*, Sept. 27, 1854; Pierce, 3: 398.
66. *Springfield Republican*, Aug. 21, 1854; *Boston Transcript*, Oct. 17, 1854; *New York Tribune*, Oct. 18, 1854; Pierce, 3: 398; Alvord to Carter, Sept. 30, 1854, Carter Papers.
67. Mulkern, pp. 81–83; Wilson, *Rise and Fall*, 2: 415, 419–20.
68. *New York Tribune*, July 3, 1872; *Natick Bulletin*, Apr. 17, 1896; Schouler to Wilson, July 30, 1872, Schouler Papers.
69. Nason and Russell, pp. 66–67; Foner, *Free Soil*, p. 113.
70. *Natick Bulletin*, Apr. 17, 1896.
71. *New York Tribune*, July 3, 1872; Robinson, "*Warrington*," pp. 544–45.
72. Massachusetts, General Court, Journal, 1845, pp. 216, 243, 297, 298, 355, and Document 44; *Emancipator and Republican*, May 3, 1849.
73. Phelps, p. 360; *Boston Bee*, Jan. 23, 1855; Wilson to ?, Aug. 12, 1859, Simon Gratz Autograph Collection, Historical Society of Pennsylvania, hereafter cited as HSPa.

74. Mulkern, p. 82–84; Haynes, "Causes of Know-Nothing Success," p. 82.
75. Anderson, p. 116; James F. Hambleton, *A Biographical Sketch of Henry A. Wise* (Richmond: J. W. Randolph, 1856), p. 132; William G. Bean, "An Aspect of Know-Nothingism—the Immigrant and Slavery," *South Atlantic Quarterly* 23 (Oct. 1924): 321–22; Mulkern, p. 17.
76. *Francis William Bird, a Biographical Sketch* (Boston: privately printed, 1897), p. 47; Hoar, *Autobiography*, 1: 189; Trefousse, *Radical Republicans*, pp.83–85; *National Era*, Oct. 12, 1854; Nov. 2, 1854.
77. *National Era*, Sept. 28, 1854; diary, Aug. 4 and Sept. 21, 1854, Adams Papers; Richards, p. 401.
78. Sewell, *Ballots*, pp. 164–65; *New York Tribune*, Aug. 17, 1854; Aug. 19, 1854; Sept. 9, 1854; Sept. 25, 1854; *National Era*, Sept. 28, 1854; Andrew W. Crandall, *The Early History of the Republican Party, 1854–1856* (Boston: R. G. Badger, 1928), pp. 21–22; Gienapp, pp. 121–22, 129–33.
79. *National Era*, Oct. 19, 1854; Oct. 26, 1854; *New York Times*, Oct. 12, 1854; Oct.20, 1854; *New York Tribune*, Oct. 14, 1854; Oct. 18, 1854; Oct. 27, 1854; Gienapp, pp. 107–19, 139–47; Sewell, *Ballots*, pp. 265–70.

Chapter 11

1. *Boston Telegraph*, Oct. 5, 1856; *Northampton Courier*, Oct. 17, 1854; *Springfield Republican*, Oct. 12, 1854; Oct. 13, 1854; *Boston Courier*, Oct. 18, 1854; *Dedham Gazette*, Oct. 28, 1854; *New York Herald*, Oct. 22, 1854; *Boston Transcript, passim*, Oct., 1854.
2. *New York Tribune*, Sept. 7, 1854; *New York Herald*, Sept. 24, 1854; Sept. 27, 1854; Oct. 22, 1854; *New York Post*, Oct. 7, 1854; *Boston Transcript*, Sept. 29, 1854; *Springfield Republican*, Oct. 3, 1854; *Boston Telegraph*, Oct. 11, 1854; Oct. 14, 1854; Oct. 17, 1854.
3. *Boston Courier*, Oct. 31, 1854; *Boston Telegraph*, Oct. 19, 1854; *New York Post*, Oct. 26, 1854; *New York Herald*, Oct. 27, 1854; *New York Times*, Oct. 19, 1854; Oct. 20, 1854; *Northampton Courier*, Oct. 31, 1854; *Springfield Republican*, Oct. 19, 1854; Oct. 21, 1854; Oct. 24, 1854; Dec. 13, 1856; Robinson, "*Warrington*," p. 543; Mann, *Life of Wilson*, p. 46; Austin, p. 475.
4. *New York Post*, Oct. 21, 1854; *New York Herald*, Oct. 27, 1854; Everett to Mrs. Eames, Nov. 4, 1854, Everett Papers; *Boston Telegraph*, Oct. 26, 1854, quoting from *Cincinnati Gazette; Springfield Republican*, Oct. 21, 1854; *Boston Transcript*, Oct. 6, 1853; Oct. 13, 1854; Hoar, *Autobiography*, 1: 189.
5. Harrington, *Fighting Politician*, pp. 22–24; Pierce, 3: 401; Davis, "Liberty before Union," pp. 30–31; Haynes, "Know Nothing Legislature," p. 178.
6. Diary, Oct. 24, 1854, and Adams to Bird, Oct. 16, 1854, Adams Papers; Donald, *Sumner*, p. 267; Chase to Sumner, Oct. 21, 1854, Sumner Papers; *Dedham Gazette*, Nov. 11, 1854; *New York Herald*, Oct. 27, 1854; *Boston Courier*, Oct. 31, 1854; *New York Post*, Oct. 26, 1854.
7. *New York Post*, Oct. 27, 1854; *Springfield Republican*, Nov. 1, 1854; *New York Times*, Oct. 27, 1854.
8. *Springfield Republican*, Oct. 30, 1854; Nov. 1, 1854; *New York Tribune*, Oct. 25, 1854; *New York Post*, Nov. 2, 1854; *New York Herald*, Nov. 5, 1854.

9. *Boston Transcript*, Nov.4–8, 1854; *Boston Post*, Nov. 8, 1854; *Springfield Republican*, Nov. 6, 1854; Nov. 8, 1854.
10. *Boston Telegraph*, Nov. 2, 1854; Nov. 4, 1854; Henry G. Pearson, *The Life of John A. Andrew, Governor of Massachusetts, 1861–1865*, 2 vols. (Boston: Houghton, Mifflin and Company, 1904), 1: 65; *New York Tribune*, Nov. 3, 1854; *Springfield Republican*, Nov. 2, 1854; Nov. 3, 1854; Nov. 10, 1854; Nov. 13, 1854; Mann, *Life of Wilson*, p. 46.
11. Anderson, p. 131; *New York Post*, Nov. 15, 1854; *Boston Transcript*, Jan. 8, 1855; Pierce, 3: 401; Bean, "Transformation," pp. 243–44; Mann, *Life of Wilson*, pp. 46; Gienapp, p. 137.
12. *Boston Courier*, Nov. 15, 1854; *Dedham Gazette*, Nov. 18, 1854; Everett to Mrs. Eames, Nov. 13 and 16, 1854, Everett Papers; *Boston Telegraph*, Nov. 14, 1854; *Boston Post*, Nov. 16, 1854; *Pilot*, Nov. 25, 1854; *Northampton Courier*, Nov. 21, 1854; Howe to Mann, Nov. 14, 1854, Howe Family Papers.
13. Haynes, "Causes of Know Nothing Success," p. 81n; Phillips to Sumner, Nov. 15, 1854, Sumner Papers.
14. Mulkern, pp. 113–14; Handlin, *Boston's Immigrants*, pp. 210–11.
15. *Northampton Courier*, Nov. 21, 1854; *Liberator*, Nov. 24, 1854; Howe to Mann, Nov. 14, 1854, Howe Family Papers.
16. *Boston Telegraph*, Nov. 25, 1854; *New York Post*, Nov. 29, 1854; *Springfield Republican*, Nov. 31, 1854; *New York Herald*, Dec. 1, 1854.
17. Wilson, *Rise and Fall*, 2: 420–22.
18. Diary, Nov. 16 and 23, Dec. 27, 1854, and Jan. 10, 13, and 17 and Apr. 14, 1855, Adams to Phillips, Nov. 16, 1854, Adams to Bailey, Dec. 9, 1854, and Jan. 20, 1855, and Bailey to Adams, Dec. 5, 1854, Adams Papers; Gattel, *Palfrey*, pp. 223–24; Stone to Sumner, Dec. 22 and 29, 1854, Sumner Papers; Richards, p. 408; *New York Post*, Dec. 29, 1854; *Northampton Courier*, Jan. 2, 1855; Jan. 16, 1855; Duberman, *Adams*, pp. 198–201.
19. *Boston Advertiser*, Nov. 8, 1854; *Boston Telegraph*, Nov. 4, 1854; Nov. 20, 1854; *Pilot*, Nov. 25, 1854; *Boston Telegraph*, Nov. 20, 1854; *New York Herald*, Nov. 20, 1854; diary, Nov. 19 and Dec. 7, 1854, Adams Papers; *New York Tribune*, Dec. 19, 1854; *Northampton Courier*, Dec. 12, 1854; *Springfield Republican*, Nov. 21, 1854; Dec. 28, 1854.
20. *Springfield Republican*, Dec. 28, 1854; Jan. 3, 1855; Jan. 4, 1855; Mulkern, pp. 121–25; Haynes, "Know-Nothing Legislature," pp. 178–79; *New York Post*, Dec. 29, 1854.
21. *Boston Telegraph*, Jan. 9, 1855; Bean, "Transformation," pp. 263–64; Mulkern, pp. 125–31.
22. *Boston Telegraph*, Jan. 9, 1855; *Springfield Republican*, Dec. 28, 1854; Jan 8–10, 1855; Jan. 12, 1855; Jan. 15, 1855; *Boston Transcript*, Jan. 13, 1855; *New York Tribune*, Jan. 10, 1855; *Northampton Courier*, Jan. 23, 1855; Haynes, "Know-Nothing Legislature," p. 180; Bean, "Transformation," pp. 268–70.
23. *Boston Telegraph*, Jan. 13, 1855; Jan. 17, 1855; Jan. 18, 1855; *Springfield Republican*, Jan. 15–17, 1855; *Boston Transcript*, Jan. 15, 1855; Jan. 17, 1855; *Lowell Journal and Courier*, Jan. 15–17, 1855; *Northampton Courier*, Jan, 23, 1855; Stone to Sumner, Jan. 13 and 20, 1855, Sumner Papers.

24. *Northampton Courier*, Jan. 16, 1855; Jan. 23, 1855; *Boston Telegraph*, Jan. 16, 1855; Jan. 17, 1855; Jan. 19, 1855; Jan. 20, 1855; Jan. 22, 1855; *Springfield Republican*, Jan. 19, 1855, one article quoting from *Providence Journal*; Jan. 20, 1855; Jan. 22, 1855; *Boston Transcript*, Jan. 19, 1855; *Lowell Journal and Courier*, Jan. 22, 1855; Jan. 23, 1855; *Dedham Gazette*, Jan. 20, 1855.
25. *Boston Transcript*, Jan. 23, 1855; *Boston Telegraph*, Jan. 27, 1855; *Northampton Courier*, Jan. 30, 1855; *Boston Bee*, Jan. 23, 1855; Robinson, *"Warrington,"* p. 542; *Springfield Republican*, Jan. 24, 1855.
26. *Lowell Journal and Courier*, Jan. 27, 1855; *New York Tribune*, Jan. 31, 1855; *New York Times*, Jan. 31, 1855; Stone to Sumner, Jan. 29, 1855, Sumner Papers; *Boston Transcript*, Feb. 2, 1855; *Springfield Republican*, Feb. 2, 1855.
27. *National Era*, Feb. 1, 1855; Feb. 8, 1854; *Boston Telegraph*, Jan. 24, 1855; *Dedham Gazette*, Feb. 3, 1855; *Northampton Courier*, Feb. 6, 1855; *Boston Post*, Jan. 24, 1855 *New York Tribune*, Jan. 24, 1855; Feb. 2, 1855.
28. Sara Norton and M. A. DeWolfe Howe, eds., *Letters of Charles Norton*, 2 vols. (Boston: Houghton Mifflin Company, 1913), 1: 120; Lawrence to his wife, Feb. 1, 1855, Lawrence Papers.
29. *Northampton Courier*, Feb. 20, 1855; Parker to Wilson, Feb. 15, 1855, Wilson Papers, LC; Irving H. Bartlett, *Wendell Phillips, Brahmin Radical* (Boston: Beacon Press, 1961), pp. 189–90; *Liberator*, Feb. 2, 1855; journal, Feb. 9, 1855, Dana Papers.
30. *Reunion of the Free Soilers*, p. 29; diary, Jan. 13, 1855, Adams Papers; Donald, *Sumner*, p. 269; diary, Feb. 9, 1855, Everett Papers; *Boston Telegraph*, Feb. 9, 1855.
31. *Boston Telegraph*, Feb. 2, 1855; Feb. 5, 1855, quoting from *New York Herald*; *Boston Transcript*, Feb. 2, 1855; *New York Times*, Feb. 5, 1855; *Liberator*, Feb. 9, 1855.
32. Gienapp, pp. 174, 176–79; Scisco, pp. 129–32; *National Era, passim* Jan., 1855; Feb. 15, 1855; Chase to Edward S. Hamlin, Feb. 9, 1855, Chase Papers, LC.
33. *New York Times*, Feb. 6, 1855; *Liberator*, Feb. 9, 1855; Harriet Wilson to her sister, Feb. 11, 1855, Wilson Papers, South Natick Museum; *Northampton Courier*, Feb. 13, 1855; *Boston Transcript*, Feb. 9, 1855; *New York Tribune*, Feb 9, 1855; *Boston Telegraph*, Feb. 8, 1855; diary, Feb. 9, 1855, Everett Papers.
34. *Henry Wilson, 18th Vice President*, p. 15; *Boston Journal*, Sept. 22, 1875; Noah Brooks, *Washington, D. C., in Lincoln's Time* (New York: Collier Books, 1962), p. 40; Nason and Russell, pp. 104, 122; Manning, p. 533; *New York Weekly Tribune*, Dec. 15, 1855; McClure, *Recollections*, p. 288.
35. *Springfield Republican*, Feb. 3, 1855; Bacon, *History of Natick*, p. 153; *Natick Bulletin*, Oct. 29, 1870; *Natick Observer*, Aug. 9, 1856; Aug. 23, 1856; *Cincinnati Gazette*, Feb. 3, 1865; *New York Times*, Dec. 10, 1875; *New York Tribune*, July 25, 1860; July 26, 1860; Mann, *Life of Wilson*, p. 120; *Memorial Addresses*, p. 69; John W. Forney, *Anecdotes of Public Men*, 2 vols. (New York: DaCapo Press, 1970), 1: 341; *Boston Transcript*, Nov. 26, 1875; *Boston Journal*, Nov. 23, 1875; McClure, *Recollections*, p. 293.
36. *Memorial Addresses*, pp. 72, 96, 153; *Commonwealth*, Sept. 24, 1853; Carl Schurz, *Reminiscences of Carl Schurz*, 3 vols. (New York: The McClure Company, 1907–1908), 2: 117; Forney, 1: 342; *Independent*, Feb. 11, 1869; Nov. 25, 1875; *New York Tribune*, Nov. 23, 1875; *Boston Transcript*, Nov. 29, 1875; Boutwell, *Reminiscences* 1: 228; McClure, *Recollections*, p. 292; *Natick Citizen*, Mar. 14, 1879.
37. *Northampton Courier*, Feb. 13, 1855, quoting from the *Congregationalist*; Nason and Russell, pp. 103–5; *Independent*, Nov. 25, 1875; *Memorial Addresses*, p. 15.

38. McClure, *Recollections*, p. 288; Brooks, p. 40; James McCabe, *Behind the Scenes in Washington* (New York: Continental Publishing Company, c. 1873), p. 154; Nason and Russell, pp. 104–5; Manning, p. 532; Schurz, *Reminiscences*, 2: 118; Brockett, p. 39; *Memorial Addresses*, pp. 47, 80, 97; Forney, 1: 342–43; *New York Tribune*, Nov. 23, 1875; Frances W. Granger to Harriet Wilson, Sept. 14, 1868, Wilson Papers, LC.
39. Robinson, "*Warrington*," p. 545; *Memorial Addresses*, p. 34; Nason and Russell, p. 104; *Natick Bulletin*, Nov. 20, 1885; Forney, *Reminiscences*, 1: 342; *Boston Transcript*, Nov. 27, 1875; *Congressional Record*, 44th Cong., 1st sess., 1876, 4, pt. 1: 532.
40. Schurz, *Reminiscences*, 2: 117; *Memorial Addresses*, p. 75; *Boston Transcript*, Nov. 27, 1875; Nov. 29, 1875; *Independent*, Feb. 11, 1869; *Boston Telegraph*, Jan. 30, 1855; Boutwell, *Reminiscences*, 1: 228; *Congressional Record*, 44th Cong., 1st sess., 1876, 4, pt. 1: 532.
41. Nason and Russell, p. 122; Hoar, *Autobiography*, 1: 217; Boutwell, *Reminiscences*, 1: 228; *Boston Transcript*, Nov. 27, 1875; Nov. 29, 1875.
42. Elliott C. Cowdin, *Tribute to the Memory of Henry Wilson, Late Vice-President of the United States* (New York: Union League Club of New York, 1875), p. 6; Boutwell, *Reminiscences*, 1: 228; *Commonwealth*, Sept. 24, 1853; *Independent*, Nov. 25, 1875; *Boston Journal*, Nov. 24, 1875, quoting from *New York Herald; Natick Bulletin*, Nov. 20, 1885.
43. *Independent*, Feb. 11, 1869; *Boston Journal*, Nov. 23, 1875; Nason and Russell, p. 104; Forney, 1: 342; McClure, *Recollections*, p. 292; *New York Times*, Nov 29, 1875; Dec. 10, 1875; *New York Tribune*, Jan. 15, 1859; *Commonwealth*, May 7, 1870; *Boston Transcript*, Nov. 29, 1875; *Congressional Record*, 44th Cong., 1st sess., 1876, 4, pt. 1: 532.
44. *Boston Journal*, Nov. 23, 1875; *New York Tribune*, Jan. 15, 1859; *Natick Bulletin*, Nov. 20, 1885; Nason and Russell, pp. 103–5, 122; Forney, 1: 342; Cowdin, p. 7; *Boston Transcript*, Feb. 11, 1873; *Boston Journal*, Nov. 23, 1875.
45. Brockett, p. 394; *Memorial Addresses*, pp. 34, 45; Nason and Russell, p. 122; Brooks, p. 40; *New York Tribune*, Jan. 15, 1859; McCabe, p. 157; Manning, p. 537; Boutwell, *Reminiscences*, 1: 229; *Congressional Record*, 44th Cong., 1st sess., 1876, 4, pt. 1: 532; McClure, *Recollections*, p. 188; *Natick Citizen*, Mar. 14, 1879.
46. *Boston Telegraph*, Jan. 30, 1855; *Independent*, Nov. 25, 1875; *Commonwealth*, Mar. 23, 1872, quoting from *New York Mail*; McClure, *Recollections*, pp. 292–93; *Congressional Record*, 44th Cong., 1st sess., 1876, 4, pt. 1: 53; *Natick Bulletin*, Nov. 20, 1885.
47. Diary, Nov. 20, 1853, Everett Papers.
48. *Congressional Globe*, 33d Cong., 2d sess., 1855, 1, pt. 1: 657; *National Era*, Feb. 15, 1855; *New York Times*, Feb. 12, 1855; *Springfield Republican*, Feb. 13, 1855, quoting from *New York Post;* Parker to Wilson, Feb. 15, 1855, Wilson Papers, LC; *Independent*, Nov. 15, 1865.
49. Brooks, p. 40; *Congressional Record*, 44th Cong., 1st sess., 1876, 4, pt. 1: 545; Hoar, *Autobiography*, 1: 214.
50. Forney, 1: 230–33; Percival G. Melbourne, ed., *Memoirs of a Senate Page, 1855–1859* (New York: Broadway Publishing Company, 1909), pp. 15–17; Nevins, *Ordeal*, 2: 52–53; Hoar, "Charles Allen," pp. 362–63.

51. McCabe, pp. 46–47; Nevins, *Ordeal*, 2: 49, 52, 57–58; Forney, 1: 232; *New York Weekly Tribune,* Dec. 15, 1855; *Boston Journal*, Jan. 16, 1872.
52. Nevins, *Ordeal*, 2: 54–55; Parker, *Morrill*, p. 114.
53. Josiah B. Grinnell, *Men and Events of Forty Years* (Boston: D. Lothrop Company, 1891), p. 52; Hoar, "Charles Allen," p. 365; Charles E. Hamlin, *The Life and Times of Hannibal Hamlin* (Cambridge: Riverside Press, 1899), pp. 276–77; Grace Greenwood, "An American Salon," *Cosmopolitan* 8 (1890): 437–47; *New York Times,* Mar. 18, 1874; 1850s *passim*, Giddings-Julian Papers; Claflin, pp. 28–29; Harrold, pp. 133–34.
54. Davis, "Occupations of Massachusetts Legislators," pp. 89–91.
55. Melbourne, pp. 5–10, 19–22; Greenwood, p. 440.
56. David J. Rothman, *Politics and Power: the United States Senate, 1869–1901* (Cambridge: Harvard University Press, 1966), pp. 13–14; *Congressional Globe*, 41st Cong., 2d sess., 1872, p. 113.
57. *Boston Telegraph,* Feb. 9, 1855; Wilson to Parker, July 23, 1855, Parker Papers; Nason and Russell, pp. 129–31; diary, Mar. 28, 1855, Everett Papers.
58. *Boston Telegraph*, Feb. 21, 1855; Mar. 13, 1855; *National Era*, Mar. 1, 1855; Chase to Edward S. Hamlin, Feb. 15, 1855, Chase Papers, LC; Wilson to Carter, Feb. 20, 1855, Carter Papers.
59. *Boston Telegraph*, Feb. 21, 1855; *National Era*, Mar. 1, 1855.
60. *Boston Telegraph*, Feb. 21, 1855; Mar. 13, 1855; *National Era*, Mar. 1, 1855; *Boston Bee*, Feb. 23, 1855; *Northampton Courier*, Feb. 27, 1855; *Springfield Republican*, Feb. 22, 1855; Wilson to Carter, Feb. 28, 1855, Carter Papers.
61. *Congressional Globe*, 33d Congress, 2d sess., 1855, pp. 698, 718, 742, 855, 861; *New York Times,* Feb. 22, 1855; Mar. 2, 1855; David L. Child to Sumner, Mar. 15, 1855, Sumner Papers; Mann, *Life of Wilson*, pp. 60, 64–65; *Boston Transcript,* Feb. 23, 1855; *Springfield Republican*, Mar. 24, 1855; *Boston Telegraph*, Mar. 13, 1855.
62. *Congressional Globe*, 33d Cong, 2d sess., 1855, Appendix, p. 216; *New York Tribune*, Feb. 27, 1855; *New York Times*, Feb. 24, 1855; *National Era*, Mar. 1, 1855; Robert W. Johannsen, *Stephen A. Douglas* (New York: Oxford University Press, 1973), pp. 469–70.
63. *Congressional Globe,* 33d Cong., 2d sess., 1855, Appendix, p. 237–40; *National Era*, Mar. 8, 1855; Mar. 15, 1855; Pierce, 3: 410–12; Wilson, *Rise and Fall*, 2: 453–58; *Northampton Courier*, Mar. 20, 1855; Mann, *Life of Wilson*, pp. 60–62; Nason and Russell, pp. 123–25; *New York Tribune,* Feb. 27, 1855; Mar. 5, 1855; *New York Times*, Feb. 24, 1855.
64. *National Era,* Mar. 8, 1855; *Boston Transcript*, Feb. 24, 1855; *Boston Telegraph*, Mar. 13, 1855; Wilson to Carter, Feb. 28, 1855, Carter Papers.
65. *Congressional Globe*, 33d Cong., 2d sess., 1855, p. 1047.
66. Ibid., p. 1050; *National Era*, Mar. 22, 1855; *New York Tribune,* Mar. 6, 1855; Mar. 27, 1855; Child to Sumner, Mar. 15, 1855, Sumner Papers; *Boston Telegraph*, Mar. 13, 1855; Mar. 28, 1855; diary, Mar. 28, 1855, Everett Papers.
67. *Boston Transcript*, Mar. 7, 1855; Mar. 10, 1855; *Springfield Republican*, Mar. 8, 1855; Walker to Sumner, Mar. 12, 1855, and Child to Sumner, Mar. 15, 1855, Sumner Papers; Nason and Russell, pp. 126–27; diary, Mar. 11, 1855, Adams Papers.
68. *Springfield Republican*, Mar. 8, 1855; Apr. 4, 1855; *New York Times*, Mar. 18, 1855; Apr. 4, 1855; *New York Tribune*, Mar. 15, 1855; *Tribune Almanac*, 1856, p. 40.

69. *Boston Telegraph,* Mar. 13, 1855; *New York Tribune,* Mar. 27, 1855; *Springfield Republican,* Mar. 31, 1855.
70. Wilson to Parker, July 23, 1855, Parker Papers; Wilson, *Rise and Fall*, 2: 423.
71. Wilson to Parker, July 23, 1855, Parker Papers; Mann, *Life of Wilson,* p. 47; Anderson, p. 157; diary, Mar. 24, 1855, Adams Papers; Wilson to Chase, Apr. 16, 1855, Chase Papers, HSPa; *Boston Transcript*, Mar. 24, 1855; *National Era*, Mar. 29, 1855; *Boston Telegraph*, Mar. 24, 1855; Mar. 30, 1855; Wilson to Schouler, Apr. 15, 1855, Schouler Papers; *Springfield Republican*, Mar. 30, 1855; *Northampton Courier*, Mar. 27, 1855.
72. *National Era*, Apr. 19, 1855; *Boston Telegraph*, Mar. 24, 1855; Mar. 30, 1855; Apr. 7, 1855; *Liberator*, Apr. 13, 1855; Everett to Fillmore, Apr. 4, 1855, Everett Papers; *Boston Transcript*, Apr. 7, 1855; *New York Times,* Mar. 30, 1855.
73. *Springfield Republican*, Apr. 7, 1855; Charles Wright, *Our Political Practice* (Boston: Alfred Mudge & Son, 1864–1865); *Boston Transcript*, May 5, 1855; *Northampton Courier*, May 8, 1855; *New York Tribune*, May 14, 1855.
74. Oliver Johnson to Sumner, Apr. 17, 1855, Sumner Papers; *National Anti-Slavery Standard,* May 12, 1855; May 19, 1855; *National Era,* May 17, 1855, quoting from the *New York Post*; *New York Times,* May 9, 1855; Nason and Russell, pp. 132–35.
75. *New York Weekly Tribune,* May 19, 1855; *New York Times,* May 9, 1855; May 10, 1855; *New York Herald,* May 9, 1855; *National Anti-Slavery Standard,* May 12, 1855; *Liberator,* May 25, 1855, quoting from *Boston Herald.*
76. Bean," Transformation," pp. 266–68; Hart, 4: 491; Haynes, "Know Nothing Legislature," p. 181; Mulkern, pp. 153–54, 156–57; Anderson, pp. 132–33; *Northampton Courier*, May 29, 1855; *Springfield Republican,* May 24, 1855; *Commonwealth*, Feb. 15, 1873; *New York Times*, May 25, 1855.
77. Bean, "Puritan vs. Celt," p. 84; idem, "Transformation," p. 266; Handlin, *Boston's Immigrants*, pp. 209–11; Austin, p. 477; Mulkern, pp. 140–46; Formisano, pp. 332–35; *Northampton Courier*, May 8, 1855; May 29, 1855; *Boston Transcript*, May 22, 1855; May 24, 1855; *Springfield Republican,* May 12, 1855.
78. Wilson, *Rise and Fall*, 2: 444; Story, pp. 142–43; Wilson to Carter, Feb. 20, 1855, Carter Papers; *Springfield Republican*, Mar. 23, 1855; Wilson to Chase, Apr. 16, 1855, Chase Papers, HSPa; *Commonwealth*, Feb. 15, 1873; *New York Tribune*, May 21, 1855; *New York Weekly Tribune*, May 26, 1855; Mann, *Life of Wilson,* p. 47; Mulkern, pp. 136–38; Anderson, pp. 132–37.
79. *Boston Transcript*, Mar. 13, 1854; May 1, 1855; May 8, 1855; *Commonwealth*, Mar. 14, 1855; Clark, p. 92; Wilson, *Speech on Prohibition*, p. 4; *National Era*, Sept. 10, 1857.
80. *New York Tribune, passim*, Apr. 1855; Haynes, "Know Nothing Legislature," pp. 182–83; "A Know-Nothing Legislature," *Brownson's Quarterly Review* 17 (July 1855): 393–411; *Springfield Republican, passim,* 1855; Mulkern, pp. 147–53, 162–87; *Northampton Courier*, Apr. 24, 1855; Wilson to Schouler, Apr. 15, 1855, Schouler Papers.
81. *Boston Telegraph*, May 2, 1855; May 3, 1855; *Northampton Courier*, May 8, 1855; *New York Herald*, May 7, 1855; *New York Tribune*, May 12, 1855.
82. *Boston Transcript*, May 3, 1855; *National Era,* May 10, 1855.

Chapter 12

1. *Springfield Republican,* Apr. 13, 1855; *New York Times,* Apr. 24, 1855; Apr. 30, 1855, quoting from *Pittsburgh Gazette*; *New York Herald,* May 7, 1855; *National Era, passim,* Apr. and May, 1855.
2. *Boston Telegraph,* May 4, 1855; *New York Times,* May 28, 1855; Hambleton, pp. 212–13, 236–45; *New York Weekly Tribune,* May 26, 1855; May 29, 1855.
3. *Northampton Courier,* Apr. 24, 1855; *Springfield Republican,* May 16, 1855; May 22, 1855; *New York Tribune,* May 21, 1855; *Boston Telegraph,* May 15, 1855.
4. *New York Weekly Tribune,* June 9, 1855; *Springfield Republican,* June 5, 1855; *National Era,* June 7, 1855; *New York Times,* June 5, 1855; Mann, *Life of Wilson,* p. 48; Nason and Russell, pp. 135–38; Wilson, *Rise and Fall,* 2: 424.
5. *National Era,* Feb. 22, 1855; *Northampton Courier,* Mar. 6, 1855; diary, Apr. 14, 19, and 21, May 24, and June 10, 1855, and Adams to Bailey, Apr. 15, 1855, Adams Papers; Richards, p. 409.
6. *Liberator,* June 8, 1855.
7. *New York Weekly Tribune,* May 5, 1855; Wilson, *Rise and Fall,* 2: 423; *Boston Telegraph,* May 3, 1855; *New York Times,* June 4, 1855; June 5, 1855; Merriam, 1: 137; Richard Hooker, *The Story of an Independent Newspaper* (New York: Macmillan Company, 1924), pp. 72–73; Peter A. Isely, *Horace Greeley and the Republican Party, 1853–1861* (New York: Octagon Books, Inc., 1965), pp. 116–17.
8. *Springfield Republican,* June 6, 1855; June 7, 1855; Wilson, *Rise and Fall,* 2: 422–23.
9. *New York Times,* June 4, 1855; June 8, 1855; *Boston Telegraph,* June 9, 1855; *Springfield Republican,* June 6–9, 1855; Wilson, *Rise and Fall,* 2: 425; *New York Weekly Tribune,* June 9, 1855; *New York Tribune,* June 7, 1855; *New York Herald,* June 8, 1855.
10. *Henry Wilson, 18th Vice President,* pp. 15–16; Nason and Russell, p. 138; Headley, p. 47; Wilson to Parker, July 23, 1855, Theodore Parker Papers, MHS.
11. *Springfield Republican,* June 6, 1855; June 8, 1855; June 9, 1855; *New York Weekly Tribune,* June 9, 1855; *New York Times,* June 9, 1855; Wilson, *Rise and Fall,* 2: 425; *National Era,* June 14, 1855.
12. *Springfield Republican,* June 9, 1855; June 11, 1855; *New York Weekly Tribune,* June 16, 1855; Wilson, *Rise and Fall,* 2: 425; Hooker, p. 73; Merriam, 1: 138.
13. *Springfield Republican,* June 11, 1855; June 12, 1855; *New York Herald,* June 12, 1855; *New York Weekly Tribune,* June 16, 1855; William D. Overdyke, *The Know-Nothing Party in the South* (Baton Rouge: Louisiana State University Press, 1950), pp. 131–32; Wilson, *Rise and Fall,* 2: 425.
14. *Springfield Republican,* June 13–15, 1855; *New York Weekly Tribune,* June 16, 1855; *New York Times,* June 25, 1855; *New York Herald,* June 13, 1855; Wilson, *Rise and Fall,* 2: 427–28.
15. *Springfield Republican,* June 14, 1855; *Boston Bee,* June 27, 1855; *Liberator,* June 29, 1855; Wilson, *Rise and Fall,* 2: 428; Nason and Russell, pp. 139–40; Mann, *Life of Wilson,* p. 53.
16. *New York Tribune,* Sept. 27, 1855; *New York Weekly Tribune,* June 16, 1855; *Springfield Republican,* June 15, 1855; *New York Herald,* June 13–15, 1855; Wilson, *Rise and Fall,* 2: 427–31.

17. *Springfield Republican*, June 15, 1855; June 16, 1855; *New York Herald*, June 13, 1855; Wilson, *Rise and Fall*, 2: 431; Mulkern, p. 202; *Boston Bee*, June 16, 1855; *Liberator*, June 22, 1855; *New York Weekly Tribune*, June 23, 1855.
18. *New York Times*, June 15, 1855; *Boston Telegraph*, June 15, 1855; *Liberator*, June 29, 1855, quoting from *Boston Atlas; New York Herald*, June 15–18, 1855.
19. *New York Weekly Tribune*, June 23, 1855; *New York Tribune*, June 11, 1865; *Springfield Republican*, June 21, 1855; *Kennebec Journal*, June 22, 1855; Nason and Russell, pp. 140–41; *National Era*, June 21, 1855.
20. Gienapp, pp. 180–81; *New York Tribune*, May 12, 1855; *New York Weekly Tribune*, June 16, 1855; June 23, 1855; *New York Times*, June 14, 1855.
21. Wilson, *Rise and Fall*, 2: 433–34; *New York Times*, June 18, 1855; June 19, 1855; *New York Weekly Tribune*, July 14, 1855.
22. *Boston Bee*, June 19, 1855; June 25, 1855; *New York Tribune*, June 22, 1855; *New York Herald*, June 24, 1855; *New York Times*, June 22, 1855; June 25, 1855; *National Era*, June 28, 1855.
23. Wilson, *Rise and Fall*, 2: 433; Merriam, 1: 139; Winthrop, pp. 170–79; Francis Curtis, *The Republican Party*, 2 vols. (New York: G. P. Putnam's Sons, 1904), 1: 222; Winthrop to Bowles, June 21, 1855, Samuel Bowles Papers, Yale University Library; Boutwell, *Reminiscences*, 1: 118; Congdon, pp. 86–88; Mann, *Life of Wilson*, pp. 53–54.
24. Wilson to Bowles, June 23, 1855, Bowles Papers; *Boston Telegraph*, June 18, 1855; June 19, 1855; *Boston Bee*, June 19, 1855; *Springfield Republican*, June 21, 1855.
25. *Boston Telegraph*, June 19, 1855; Wilson, *Rise and Fall*, 2: 416; *New York Tribune*, July 7, 1855; *National Era*, Sept. 20, 1855; *New York Times*, July 6, 1855.
26. *Boston Bee*, June 29, 1855; *New York Herald*, June 29, 1855; July 4, 1855; *New York Times*, June 30, 1855; *New York Tribune*, June 29, 1855; July 4, 1855; *Northampton Courier*, Oct. 9, 1855; *Springfield Republican*, June 29, 1855; Anderson, p. 142.
27. *Boston Transcript*, June 16, 1855, quoting from *New York Post*; *New York Tribune*, June 29, 1855; July 4, 1855; Wilson to Parker, July 23, 1855, Parker Papers; *Northampton Courier*, June 26, 1855; Wilson to Bowles, June 23, 1855, Bowles Papers; Everett to Mrs. Eames, July 5, 1855, Everett Papers; *Liberator*, July 13, 1855; Mann, *Life of Wilson*, pp. 53–54.
28. *New York Times*, July 11, 1855; *Boston Transcript*, July 11, 1855; *New York Weekly Tribune*, July 21, 1855; *New York Tribune*, July 12, 1855; Bean, "Transformation," pp. 312–13.
29. *New York Tribune*, July 4, 1855.
30. *National Era*, July 12, 1855.
31. Donald, *Sumner*, p. 272; *Liberator*, Sept. 14, 1855; Gienapp, pp. 192–200; *New York Times*, July 16, 1855; *Cincinnati Gazette*, July 9, 1855; July 12–14, 1855; Mann, *Life of Wilson*, p. 54; *National Era*, July 19, 1855.
32. *New York Tribune*, July 14, 1855; July 16, 1855, quoting from *Cincinnati Columbian*; July 19, 1855; *Boston Transcript*, July 14, 1855; *National Era*, July 19, 1855; *Indianapolis Journal*, July 7, 1855; July 13, 1855; July 18, 1855; *Albany Journal*, July 16, 1855; Mann, *Life of Wilson*, p. 54.
33. *New York Herald*, July 25, 1855.
34. *New York Tribune*, July 28, 1855; *Springfield Republican*, July 7, 1855.

35. *Boston Bee*, Aug. 9, 1855; Aug. 16, 1855; Aug. 18, 1855; *Boston Transcript*, Aug. 8, 1855; *New York Tribune*, Aug. 10, 1855; *National Era*, Aug. 30, 1855; Nason and Russell, pp. 142–46.
36. *National Era*, Aug. 30, 1855; *Boston Bee*, Aug. 16, 1855; Mann, *Life of Wilson*, p. 55; Nason and Russell, pp. 142–45.
37. *Boston Transcript*, Aug. 7, 1855; Aug. 8, 1855; *Boston Bee*, Aug. 8, 1855; Aug. 9, 1855; *New York Tribune*, Aug. 10, 1855; Aug. 11, 1855; Mulkern, pp. 215–17; *National Era*, Aug. 23, 1855; *Northampton Courier*, Aug. 14, 1855; Oct. 9, 1855.
38. Stowe to Dawes, July 30, 1855, and Bowles to Dawes, Aug. 6, 1855, Dawes Papers; *New York Tribune*, Aug. 15, 1855; *Northampton Courier*, Oct. 9, 1855.
39. Wilson, *Rise and Fall*, 2: 416–17; *New York Tribune*, Aug 15, 1855; *Boston Journal*, Aug. 16, 1855; Aug. 17, 1855; *Boston Transcript*, Aug. 15–17, 1855, last quoting from *Boston Advertiser*; *New York Times*, Aug. 17, 1855; *Northampton Courier*, Aug. 21, 1855; Oct. 9, 1855; Merriam, 1: 141; journal, Aug. 16, 1855, Dana Papers; diary, Aug. 15 and 16, 1855, Adams Papers; Hoar, *Autobiography*, 1: 30.
40. Diary, Aug. 20, 22, 23, 25, and 26, 1855, Adams Papers; journal, Aug. 22, 1855, Dana Papers; *New York Herald*, Aug. 21, 1855; Merriam, 1: 140–41; *Boston Journal*, Aug 22, 1855; Aug. 23, 1855; Aug. 30, 1855; *New York Tribune*, Aug. 24, 1855; *New York Weekly Tribune*, Aug. 25, 1855; *New York Times*, Aug. 23, 1855; *National Era*, Aug. 30, 1855; *Northampton Courier*, Aug. 28, 1855; Oct. 9, 1855; *Boston Transcript*, Aug. 23, 1855.
41. *New York Tribune*, Aug. 24, 1855; Sept. 4, 1855; *Boston Transcript*, Aug. 15, 1855.
42. *Boston Bee*, Aug. 30, 1855; *New York Herald*, Aug. 21, 1855; diary, Aug. 27, 1855 and Adams to Bailey, Sept. 2, 1855, Adams Papers.
43. *New York Times*, Aug. 30, 1855; *New York Weekly Tribune*, Aug. 25, 1855; Sept. 1, 1855; *Boston Bee*, Aug. 30, 1855; *Boston Transcript*, Aug. 29, 1855; Aug. 30, 1855; *Northampton Courier*, Sept. 4, 1855; Wilson, *Rise and Fall*, 2: 417; Dana to R. H. Dana Sr., Aug. 30, 1855, Dana Papers; diary, Aug. 29, 1855, Adams Papers.
44. *New York Weekly Tribune*, Sept. 8, 1855; *Boston Transcript*, Sept. 6, 1855; Oct. 3, 1855; Oct. 5, 1855; *Liberator*, Oct. 5, 1855.
45. *Northampton Courier*, *passim*, Sept., 1855; Sept. 11, 1855; Oct. 9, 1855; *Boston Transcript*, Sept. 14, 1855; *New York Tribune*, Sept. 4, 1855; Sept. 15, 1855.
46. *New York Times*, *passim*, Aug. and Sept., 1855; Crandall, pp. 31, 37; Francis Curtis, 1: 219; *Kennebec Journal*, Aug. 17, 1855; Sept. 14, 1855; Sept. 28, 1855; *New York Tribune*, Aug. 15, 1855; Sept. 6, 1855; Sept. 10, 1855; *New York Weekly Tribune*, Aug. 11, 1855; Sept. 15, 1855; *Boston Transcript*, Sept. 13, 1855; Willey, pp. 461–63; Gienapp, pp. 203–8, 223–31; Stanton, p. 184.
47. *Northampton Courier*, Oct. 9, 1855; *Liberator*, Sept. 14, 1855; *New York Tribune*, Sept. 11, 1855; Sept. 20, 1855; *National Era*, Sept. 26, 1855; *Jackson American Citizen*, Sept. 5, 1855; *Boston Transcript*, Sept. 14, 1855; H. Kreisman to Sumner, Sept. 18, 1855, Sumner Papers; *New York Times*, Sept. 18, 1855.
48. *New York Herald*, Aug. 21, 1855; Gardner to Bowles, Aug. 17 and Sept. 17, 1855, Bowles Papers; diary, Sept. 3, 1855, Adams Papers.
49. *New York Tribune*, Sept. 15, 1855; *Northampton Courier*, Sept. 18, 1855; *Boston Transcript*, Sept. 19, 1855; Sept. 20, 1855; *New York Times*, Sept. 20, 1845.
50. *Northampton Courier*, Sept. 25, 1855; *Boston Bee*, Sept. 24, 1855; *Boston Transcript*, Sept. 20, 1855.

51. Harrington, *Fighting Politician,* p. 25; *Boston Transcript,* Sept. 20, 1855; *New York Weekly Tribune,* Sept. 29, 1855; Boutwell to Dana, Sept. 22, 1855, Dana Papers; Wilson, *Rise and Fall*, 2: 417; Shapiro, *Dana*, p. 100.
52. *New York Tribune*, Sept. 15, 1855; *New York Weekly Tribune*, Sept. 29, 1855; Gienapp, pp. 217–18; *National Era*, Sept. 27, 1855; *Boston Transcript*, Sept. 21, 1855; *New York Times*, Sept. 21, 1855; *Northampton Courier*, Sept. 25, 1855; Shapiro, *Dana*, p. 100; Wilson, *Rise and Fall*, 2: 417; *Liberator*, Sept. 28, 1855.
53. *Boston Transcript*, Sept. 21, 1855; *Northampton Courier*, Oct. 2, 1855; *National Era*, Oct. 4, 1855; Bean, "Transformation," pp. 321–23.
54. Richards, 2: 409.
55. Northampton Courier, Oct. 9, 1855.
56. *Boston Bee*, Sept. 21, 1855; Sept. 24, 1855; Sept. 25, 1855; *New York Times,* Sept. 24, 1855; *Northampton Courier*, Oct. 2, 1855.
57. *Boston Transcript,* Sept. 27, 1855.
58. Ibid., Sept. 27, 1855; Oct. 1, 1855; Oct. 6, 1855.
59. *New York Times,* Sept. 24, 1855; *Albany Journal*, Sept. 22–24, 1855; *New York Tribune*, Sept. 28, 1855; *Northampton Courier*, Oct. 9, 1855.
60. *Northampton Courier*, Oct. 9, 1855; *Boston Bee,* Oct. 9, 1855.
61. *Boston Transcript*, Oct. 4, 1855; *New York Times,* Oct. 4, 1855; *National Era*, Oct. 11, 1855; *Northampton Courier,* Oct. 9, 1855; *New York Tribune,* Oct. 8, 1855; *Boston Bee,* Oct. 4, 1855; Oct. 8, 1855.
62. Boutwell to Dana, Sept. 22, 1855, Dana Papers; *New York Tribune,* Sept. 24, 1855; Nov. 9, 1855; *Northampton Courier*, *passim,* Oct. 1855; George H. Haynes, "A Chapter from the Local History of Know-Nothingism," *New England Magazine* 15 (Sept., 1896): 86; Bowles to Dawes, Oct. 10, 1855, Dawes Papers; Harrington, *Fighting Politician*, p. 25; Bean, "Transformation," p. 324.
63. *Northampton Courier,* Oct. 9, 1855.
64. *New York Weekly Tribune,* Oct. 13, 1855; *Boston Transcript,* Oct. 11, 1855.
65. *Tribune Almanac*, 1856, pp. 42, 44; *Cincinnati Gazette*, Oct. 11, 1855; Oct. 12, 1855; Wade to Washburn, Oct. 13, 1855, Israel Washburn Papers; Giddings to Stansbury, Sept. 4, 1855, Gidddings-Julian Papers; *New York Times,* Oct. 12, 1855; Oct. 17, 1855; Oct. 30, 1855; *National Era*, Oct. 18, 1855; *New York Tribune,* Oct. 11, 1855; *Indianapolis Journal*, Oct. 10–12, 1855; Gienapp, pp. 208–13.
66. *National Era*, Oct. 25, 1855; *New York Tribune,* Oct. 29, 1855; *Boston Transcript*, Oct. 12, 1855; Oct. 31, 1855; Nov. 2, 1855; Nov. 3, 1855; Webb to Bowles, Oct. 9 and 10, 1855, Bowles Papers; Shapiro, *Dana*, p. 101; Pierce, 3: 421; diary, Oct. 16 and 19 and Nov. 2, 3, and 5, 1855, and Adams to Webb, Oct. 2, 1855, and Adams to Palfrey, Oct. 31, 1855, Adams Papers; Gardner to Morton, Nov. 17, 1855, George R. Morton Miscellaneous Papers, Rutherford B. Hayes Library, Fremont, Ohio; Mann, *Life of Wilson*, p. 57; *Boston Bee*, Oct. 10, *passim* Oct. 18–25, 1855; Oct. 31, 1855; *Northampton Courier,* Oct. 30, 1855; Hallett, p. 4.
67. *Boston Transcript,* Nov. 7, 1855; *Tribune Almanac*, 1856, p. 40; *New York Tribune*, Oct. 29, 1855; Mulkern, p. 231; *Boston Bee*, Nov. 7, 1855; Nov. 8, 1855; Boutwell, *Reminiscences*, 1: 119.
68. *Boston Transcript*, Nov. 5, 1855; Nov. 7, 1855; *Tribune Almanac*, 1856, p. 40; *Boston Bee,* Nov. 7, 1855; Nov. 8, 1855.

69. Anderson, p. 151; diary, Nov. 7, 1855, and Everett to Mrs. Eames, Nov. 7, 1855, Everett Papers; Pierce, 3: 423–24; *New York Tribune*, Nov 9, 1855; Nov. 12, 1855; *Boston Advertiser*, Nov. 10, 1855.
70. Gardner to Morton, Nov. 17, 1855, George R. Morton Miscellaneous Papers, Hayes Library; *New York Tribune*, Nov. 9, 1855; *Boston Transcript*, Nov. 14, 1855; Nov. 22, 1855; *New York Times*, Nov. 14, 1855; Crandall, p. 39; Mulkern, pp. 230–35.
71. Giddings to Molly, Nov. 7 1855, Giddings-Julian Papers; diary, Nov. 9, 1855, Adams Papers; Gardner to Morton, Nov. 17, 1855, George Morton Papers; Shapiro, *Dana*, p. 100; William Birney to Sumner, Nov. 7, 1855, and Herman Kreisman to Sumner, Nov. 13, 1855, Sumner Papers; *New York Tribune*, Nov. 12, 1855; *Northampton Courier*, Nov. 20, 1855; diary, Nov. 9, 1855, Adams Papers.
72. Wilson to Chase, Nov. 17, 1855, Chase Papers, HSPa.
73. *Tribune Almanac*, 1856, pp. 41, 49; Scisco, pp. 163–70; Gienapp, pp. 229–33.

Chapter 13

1. *New York Weekly Tribune*, Dec. 8, 1855; Dec. 15, 1855; *New York Tribune*, Dec. 6, 1855; Dec. 7, 1855; Dec. 14, 1855; Pierce, 3: 425; *New York Times*, Dec. 14, 1855; *Congressional Globe*, 34th Cong., 1st sess., 1856, pp. 17–20; idem, 41st Cong., 2d sess., 1869, p. 111.
2. Burlingame to Jennie Burlingame, Dec. 12, 1855, Burlingame Family Papers, LC; *Congressional Directory for the First Session of the Thirty-fourth Congress of the United States of America* (Washington: G. S. Gideon, Printer, 1856), pp. 50–52; *Northampton Courier*, Dec. 18, 1855; Wilson to Parker, July 23, 1855, and Sumner to Parker, Dec. 14, 1856, Parker Papers.
3. *New York Weekly Tribune*, Dec. 8, 1855; Crandall, pp. 53–54; Fred H. Harrington, "The First Northern Victory," *Journal of Southern History* 5 (May 1939): 186–87.
4. Wilson to Schouler, Apr. 16, 1855, Schouler Papers; Harrington, "First Northern Victory," pp. 194–97; Crandall, p. 54; *New York Times*, Jan. 28, 1856.
5. Crandall, pp. 55–58; Harrington, "First Northern Victory," pp. 198–204; Perley B. Poore, *Reminiscences of Sixty Years in the National Metropolis*, 2 vols. (Philadelphia: Hubbard Brothers, Publishers, 1886), 1: 448; *New York Times*, Feb. 4, 1856; Giddings to his daughter, Feb. 1 and 3, 1856, Giddings-Julian Papers.
6. *Springfield Republican*, Feb. 29, 1856; Mar. 1, 1856; Palfrey to Sumner, Mar. 1, 1856, Palfrey Papers; T. P. Chandler to Sumner, Mar. 3, 1856, Sumner Papers; diary, Feb. 28, 1856, Adams Papers.
7. *Congressional Globe*, 34th Cong., 1st sess., 1856, pp. 355, 364; *National Era*, Feb. 14, 1856.
8. *Congressional Globe*, 34th Cong., 1st sess., 1856, Appendix, pp. 84–87; Henry Wilson, *The Central American Question* (Washington: Buell & Blanchard, 1856); *New York Times*, Feb. 13, 1856; Feb. 15, 1856; *National Era*, Feb. 21, 1856; *New York Tribune*, Feb. 13, 1856; *Northampton Courier*, Feb. 19, 1856.
9. Sewell, *Ballots*, p. 277–78; Harrington, *Fighting Politician*, pp. 34–35; Crandall, pp. 43–52; Wilson to Chase, Apr. 16, 1855, Chase Papers, HSPa; diary, Dec. 26, 1855, Adams Papers; *New York Tribune*, Jan. 17, 1856; Gienapp, pp. 248–53.

10. Wilson to Chase, Jan. 15, 1856, Chase Papers, HSPa; William E. Smith, *The Francis Preston Blair Family in Politics,* 2 vols. (New York: Macmillan Company, 1933), 1: 342–43; *Ohio State Journal*, Sept. 1, 1856; Ruhl J. Bartlett, *John C. Fremont and the Republican Party* (New York: DaCapo Press, 1970), pp. 14–15; Allan Nevins, *Fremont, Pathmarker of the West,* new ed. (New York: Longmans, Green and Co., 1955), pp. 423–27.
11. *Boston Transcript, passim*, Dec. 3–11, 1855; Haynes, "Know-Nothing Legislature," p. 186; Stone to Sumner, Jan. 25, 1856, Sumner Papers; Mulkern, pp. 234–36.
12. *Springfield Republican,* Feb. 4, 1856; Feb. 20–26, 1856; Mulkern, pp. 238–39; Wilson, *Rise and Fall*, 2: 508; Overdyke, pp. 134–35; Cross, pp. 540–41; Scisco, pp. 171–73.
13. Webb to Sumner, Mar. 19, 1856, Stone to Sumner, Mar. 20, 26, and 28, 1856, and Alley to Sumner, Mar. 14, 1856, Sumner Papers; Thomas J. Marsh to Banks, Mar. 19, 1856, Nathaniel Banks Papers, LC; *Springfield Republican*, Mar. 3, 1856; Mar. 5, 1856; Mar. 6, 1856; Mar. 8, 1856; Apr. 8, 1856; *New York Tribune,* Apr. 7, 1856; Mulkern, pp. 243–44; Gienapp, pp. 260–63.
14. Charles W. Johnson, ed., *Proceedings of the First Three Republican National Conventions of 1856, 1860, and 1864* (Minneapolis: Charles W. Johnson, 1893), pp. 8–11; Gienapp, pp. 254–56; *Northampton Courier*, Feb. 19, 1856; *New York Times,* Feb. 26, 1856; Feb. 27, 1856; Harrington, *Fighting Politician,* pp. 35; George W. Julian, "The First Republican National Convention," *American Historical Review* 4 (1899): 315–21; diary, Feb. 14 and 18, 1856, Adams Papers; Trefousse, *Radical Republicans*, pp. 95–98.
15. *Congressional Globe*, 34th Cong., 1st sess., 1856, pp. 136, 289–92; Wilson, *Rise and Fall*, 2: 474–75; *Boston Telegraph*, Feb. 25, 1856, quoting from *New York Post*; *Boston Transcript*, Feb. 20, 1856.
16. *Congressional Globe,* 34th Cong, 1st sess., 1856, pp. 89–95; Henry Wilson, *"State of Affairs in Kansas." Speech of Henry Wilson in the Senate, February 18, 1856* (Washington: Republican Association of the District of Columbia, 1856); *National Era*, Feb. 21, 1856; Mar. 6, 1856; Wilson, *Rise and Fall*, 2: 475; Nason and Russell, pp. 150–83; (Washington) *Union*, Feb. 20, 1856; Pierce, 3: 430; *Liberator*, Feb. 29, 1856; Mar. 7, 1856; *Springfield Republican*, Feb. 19, 1856; *New York Tribune*, Feb. 18–23, 1856.
17. *Liberator*, Mar. 7, 1856; *Boston Telegraph,* Feb. 25, 1856 quoting from *New York Post*; *New York Tribune*, Feb. 20, 1856; *Springfield Republican,* Mar. 14, 1856; *Northampton Courier*, Feb. 26, 1856, quoting from *New York Courier and Enquirer;* Mar. 11, 1856; Nason and Russell, pp. 150–83.
18. Henry A. Wise to Everett, Feb. 20, 1856, Everett Papers; (Washington) *Union*, Feb. 20, 1856; *New York Times*, Feb. 22, 1856.
19. Pierce, 3: 430–32; *Boston Transcript*, Feb. 20, 1856; *New York Times,* Feb. 26, 1856; Mar. 6, 1856; *New York Tribune*, Mar. 6, 1856; *Congressional Globe*, 34th Cong., 1st sess., 1856, p. 591; *National Era*, Mar. 13, 1856.
20. *Congressional Globe*, 34th Cong., 1st sess., 1856, pp. 618, 665, 682, 704, 738, 743; *National Era,* Mar. 20, 1856; *New York Times*, Mar. 11, 1856.
21. *New York Times, passim*, Jan. to Mar., 1856, especially Mar. 12; *National Era*, Mar. 20, 1856; Mar. 27, 1856; *New York Weekly Tribune*, Mar. 15, 1856.
22. *National Era*, Mar. 20, 1856; *New York Tribune,* Mar. 28, 1856; Mar. 29, 1856; Crandall, pp. 177–78; Gienapp, pp. 264–68, 278–79.

23. *New York Times*, Mar. 15, 1856; Mar. 20, 1856; Apr. 4, 1856; Apr. 9, 1856; *New York Tribune*, Mar. 14, 1856; Apr. 4, 1856; *Tribune Almanac*, 1857, pp. 44–45; Gienapp, pp. 263, 273–77.
24. *Boston Transcript*, *passim*, Feb. and Mar., 1856; Apr. 1–3, 1856; *Northampton Courier*, Apr. 8, 1856; Wilson to Andrew H. Reeder, Mar. 31, 1856, C. E. French Papers, MHS.
25. *New York Times*, Mar. 29, 1856.
26. Ibid., Apr. 10, 1856; Apr. 15, 1856; Apr. 16, 1865; *Congressional Globe*, 34th Cong., 1st sess., 1856, p. 864 and Appendix, pp. 390–95; *New York Tribune*, Apr. 15, 1856; Johannsen, pp. 500–1; Johnson Brigham, *James Harlan* (Iowa City: State Historical Society of Iowa, 1913), pp. 98–99.
27. *Congressional Globe*, 34th Cong., 1st sess., 1856, pp. 393–95; Nason and Russell, pp. 183–87; Mann, *Life of Wilson*, pp. 65–66; Julia Ward Howe, *Reminiscences, 1819–1899* (New York: Negro Universities Press, 1969), p. 178.
28. *New York Tribune*, Apr. 15, 1856; Edward Stabler to Fessenden, Apr. 16, 1856, William P. Fessenden Papers, LC.
29. *Boston Telegraph*, Apr. 22, 1856, quoting from *Wilmington Journal and Statesman*; *New York Tribune*, Apr. 14, 1856; *National Anti-Slavery Standard*, Mar. 29, 1856.
30. *Congressional Globe*, 34th Cong., 1st sess., 1856, p. 982; Hallett, *Mr. Hallett's Reply to Mr. Wilson's "Personal Explanation"*; Mann, *Life of Wilson*, pp. 61–63.
31. Wilson to Webb, Mar. 10, 1856, Chamberlain Papers; *New York Tribune*, Apr. 26, 1856; May 1, 1856; Colfax to Alfred Wheeler, Apr. 11, 1856, Schuyler Colfax Papers, LC; Wade to his wife, Mar. 20, 1856, Benjamin Wade Papers, LC; *Springfield Republican*, Apr. 25, 1856.
32. *New York Times*, Apr. 22, 1856; *Springfield Republican*, Apr. 23, 1856 *National Era*, May 1, 1850; Frederick W. Seward, *Seward at Washington, Senator and Secretary of State*, 3 vols. (New York: Derby and Miller, 1891), 2: 270.
33. *Northampton Courier*, May 13, 1856; May 20, 1856; *Springfield Republican*, May 7, 1856; May 8, 1856; May 15, 1856; Bean, "Puritan Versus Celt, 1850-1860" New England Quarterly 7 (March 1934): 85; Mulkern, pp. 244–45.
34. *New York Times*, May 7, 1856; May 23, 1856; *New York Tribune*, May 24, 1856; Wilson, *Rise and Fall*, 2: 478–79.
35. Sumner to Chase, May 15, 1856, Chase Papers, LC; *New York Times*, *passim*, May 1 to 20, 1856, especially May 7, 1856; Wilson, *Rise and Fall*, 2: 479–80; *New York Tribune*, May 21, 1856.
36. Wilson, *Rise and Fall*, 2: 479–81; Donald, *Sumner*, p. 288; diary, June 18 and 19, 1856, and Wise to Everett, May 21, 1856, Everett Papers; *Alleged Assault upon Senator Sumner*, (United States, Congress, House Report, No. 182, 34th Cong, 1st Sess., 1856), p. 2; *New York Times*, May 21, 1856; May 23, 1856; *New York Tribune*, May 21, 1856.
37. *New York Times*, May 23, 1856; May 24, 1856; *New York Tribune*, May 20, 1856; May 21, 1856; *Springfield Republican*, May 21, 1856; *New Hampshire Patriot*, May 28, 1856; *Boston Courier*, May 29, 1856.
38. *Alleged Assault*, pp. 25, 42–44; Grimke, p. 277; *Boston Telegraph*, May 24, 1856.
39. *Alleged Assault*, pp. 1–4; Wilson, *Rise and Fall*, 2: 481; *New York Times*, May 24, 1856; Pierce, 3: 469–70; *Congressional Globe*, 34th Cong., 1st sess., 1856, pp. 1254, 1258; *New York Tribune*, May 23, 1856.

40. Wilson, *Rise and Fall*, 2: 481; *New York Tribune*, May 23, 1856; *New York Times*, May 24, 1856; Pierce, 3: 475–76; Nason and Russell, p. 187; Phelps, p. 362; *Alleged Assault*, pp. 26, 42; *Natick Citizen*, Mar. 14, 1879.
41. Wilson, *Rise and Fall*, 2: 482–84; *Congressional Globe*, 34th Cong, 1st sess., 1856, pp. 1279–80; Pierce, 3: 476–77; Seward, 2: 271; *New York Tribune*, May 23, 1854; May 24, 1856; *New York Times*, May 24, 1956; *National Era*, May 29, 1856.
42. *New York Tribune*, May 24, 1856; *Boston Transcript*, May 23, 1856; *Northampton Courier*, May 27, 1856, quoting from *Providence Post* and *Boston Courier; New York Times*, May 31, 1856; Alley to Sumner, May 24, 1856, Sumner Papers.
43. *New York Tribune*, May 24, 1856; May 26, 1856; *New York Times*, May 24, 1856; May 26, 1856; *Boston Transcript*, May 26, 1856; *passim*, late May, early June, 1856; *Springfield Republican, passim* May 24–31, 1856; diary, May 25, 1856, Everett papers; Winthrop, pp. 182–84; *Boston Telegraph, passim*, May 24 to 31, 1856; *Boston Advertiser*, May 26, 1856; May 27, 1856; *National Era*, May 29, 1856; Anderson, pp. 173–76.
44. Wilson, *Rise and Fall*, 2: 484; Pierce, 3: 478; *Congressional Globe*, 34th Cong., 1st sess., 1856, pp. 279, 317; *Alleged Assault*, pp. 1–9, 14, 76–79; *New York Tribune*, May 23, 1856; *New York Times*, May 24, 1856; May 29, 1856; *National Era*, May 29, 1856.
45. Wilson to Campbell, May 24, 1856, Lewis D. Campbell Papers, Ohio Historical Society, Columbus, Ohio; Blanche Butler Ames, *Chronicles from the Nineteenth Century: Family Letters of Blanche Butler and Adelbert Ames*, 2 vols. (Clinton, Mass.: Colonial Press, 1937), 1: 283; Poore, 1: 464; Wilson to Parker, May 25 and 26, 1856, Parker Papers; *Natick Citizen*, Mar. 21, 1879; Wilson to Hunt, May 29, 1856, Henry Wilson Papers, John Hay Library, Brown University; *Boston Journal*, Nov. 22, 1875; Wilson, *Rise and Fall*, 2: 486; Giddings to his daughter, May 28, 1856, Giddings-Julian Papers; *Springfield Republican*, May 31, 1856; Claflin to Wilson, May 27, 1856, Wilson Papers, South Natick Museum.
46. Wilson, *Rise and Fall*, 2: 502.
47. *National Era*, May 29, 1856; *Liberator*, May 30. 1856; *Congressional Globe*, 34th Cong., 1st sess., 1856, pp. 1304–6; Pierce, 3: 480–81; Wilson, *Rise and Fall*, 2: 486; Melbourne, p. 96; Wilson to Parker, May 25, 1856, Parker Papers; Giddings to his daughter, May 28, 1856, Giddings-Julian Papers; *New York Times*, May 28, 1856; *New York Tribune*, May 28, 1856.
48. *New York Times*, May 29, 1856; *New York Tribune*, May 28, 1856; June 3, 1856; Wilson to Parker, May 25, 1856, Parker Papers; (Trenton, N.J.) *Daily True American*, May 29, 1856.
49. Giddings to his daughter, May 28, 1856, Giddings-Julian Papers; Brooks to Wilson, May 27, 1856, Autograph File, Beinecke Library, Yale University; *New York Tribune*, May 28, 1856; *Springfield Republican*, May 29, 1856; *Boston Transcript*, Sept. 2, 1873; Nason and Russell, p. 188; *New York Times*, May 28–30, 1856; *Liberator*, June 13, 1856; Wilson, *Rise and Fall*, 2: 486; Pierce, 3: 494; Cowdin, pp. 9–10.
50. *Congressional Globe*, 34th Cong., 1st sess., 1856, pp. 629–30; *New York Times*, May 27, 1856; *National Era*, June 5, 1856.
51. *Liberator*, June 13, 1856, one article quoting from the *Richmond Enquirer* and *passim*, Aug. 1856; Nason and Russell, pp. 188–89; Milton Meltser and Patricia G. Holland, eds., *Lydia Maria Child, Selected Letters, 1817–1880*, (Amherst: University of

Massachusetts Press, 1982), p. 284; George A. Smith to Trumball, Lyman Trumball Papers, LC; Sarah Pugh to Wade, June 18, 1856, Wade Papers; Claflin to Wilson, May 27, 1856, Wilson Papers, South Natick Museum; *Boston Transcript,* May 31, 1856; Cowdin, p. 11; Mann, *Life of Wilson*, p. 69; *Natick Observer*, May 31, 1856.

52. Wilson to Parker, May 25, 1856, Parker Papers; *New York Times*, May 29, 1856; Seward, 2: 274; *Liberator*, June 13, 1856.
53. *New York Times*, June 3, 1856; *Boston Telegraph*, June 2, 1856; *Natick Observer*, June 7, 1856; *Northampton Courier*, June 3, 1856; *Springfield Republican,* June 4, 1856; *Liberator*, June 6, 1856.
54. Diary, June 4, 6, and 7, Adams Papers; *New York Tribune*, June 7, 1856; June 9, 1856; *Boston Transcript,* June 4, 1856; June 5, 1856; *Springfield Republican*, June 5, 1856; *New York Times,* June 7, 1856.
55. *Boston Transcript*, June 5, 1856; *New York Tribune,* June 9, 1856; June 11, 1856; July 8, 1856; *Northampton Courier*, June 17, 1856, quoting from *Newburyport Herald*; Browne to Sumner, June 6, 1856, Sumner Papers; Parker to Wilson, July 7, 1856, Wilson Papers, LC; Taylor, pp. 423–25; *Natick Observer*, June 14, 1856.
56. Wilson, *Rise and Fall*, 2: 502, 515–517.
57. *Passim*, May and June, 1856, Banks Papers; *Springfield Republican*, June 13, 1856; June 16, 1856; June 17, 1856; Fred H. Harrington, "Fremont and the North Americans," *American Historical Review* 44 (July 1939): 842–48; Gienapp, pp. 331, 344–45.
58. *New York Times*, June 18, 1856; *New York Tribune*, June 18, 1856; Johnson, *First Three Conventions,* pp. 15–53; *Springfield Republican,* June 18, 1856; Wilson, *Rise and Fall,* 2: 511–13; Giddings to his daughter, June 18 and 20, 1856, Giddings-Julian Papers.
59. *New York Tribune*, June 17, 1856; June 19, 1856; Johnson, *First Three Conventions,* pp. 52–58, 64; Harrington, *Fighting Politician*, p. 36; Gienapp, pp. 338–44; Sewell, *Ballots,* pp. 282–84; *New York Times,* June 25, 1856; diary, June 18, 1856, Adams Papers.
60. *New York Times,* June 20, 1856; Johnson, *First Three Conventions*, pp. 77–79; Curtis, *Republican Party*, p. 262; Wilson, *Rise and Fall*, 2: 514.
61. *Congressional Globe,* 34th Cong., 1st sess., 1856, pp. 1307–12, 1542–44, 1076–77, 1700, 1723, 1743, 1848–49, 1904.
62. *National Era*, June 19, 1856; *Congressional Globe*, 34th Cong., 1st sess., 1856, pp. 1399–1400 and Appendix, pp. 625–35; Nason and Russell, pp. 190–93.
63. Congressional Globe, 34th Cong, 1st sess., 1856, pp. 1400–3; *Henry Wilson, Personalities and Aggressions of Mr. Butler Speech of Hon. Henry Wilson, of Massachusetts, in the Senate of the United States, June 13, 1856* (Washington: Buell & Blanchard, 1856); Nason and Russell, pp. 193–202; *New York Times,* June 14, 1856; June 17, 1856; Donald, Sumner, p. 310n; (Washington) *Union,* June 17, 1856.
64. *Congressional Globe*, 34th Cong, 1st sess., 1856, pp. 1399–1405 and Appendix, pp. 625–35; Nason and Russell, pp. 203–6.
65. Seward, 2: 277; Pierce: 3: 483.
66. *New York Times*, June 20, 1856; June 25, 1856; *New York Tribune*, June 26, 1856.
67. *Boston Transcript,* June 24, 1856; June 25, 1856; Wilson to Parker, June 21, 1856, Parker Papers; Burlingame to Jennie Burlingame, May 31, 1856, C. C. Washburne to Isaac Livermore, June 21, 1856, and Wilson to Livermore, June 21, 1856, Burlingame Family Papers; Wilson to "Dear Will," June 21, 1856, Wilson Papers, New York

Public Library.

68. Webb to Sumner, June 14, 1856, Sumner Papers; *Northampton Courier*, July 1, 1856; Roy Nichols, "Some Problems of the First Republican Presidential Campaign," *American Historical Review* 28 (Apr. 1923): 493; *Springfield Republican*, July 1, 1856; July 2, 1856; *New York Times*, July 2, 1856; Mulkern, pp. 249–52.
69. *Congressional Globe*, 34th Cong, 1st sess., 1856, p. 1439 and Appendix, p. 749; *New York Times*, July 1, 1856; *New York Tribune*, July 1, 1856; July 3, 1856.
70. *Congressional Globe,* 34th Cong., 1st sess., 1856, Appendix, pp. 761–75, 792–94, 803–5; 840–41, 852–53; *New York Times*, July 1–4, 1856; July 10, 1856; *New York Tribune,* July 3, 1856; July 4, 1856; *Springfield Republican*, July 19, 1856; Nason and Russell, pp. 207–9.
71. *Springfield Republican*, July 3, 1856; July 5, 1856; July 7, 1856; *Liberator*, Aug. 22, 1856, quoting from *Genesee Valley Free Press*; *Natick Observer*, July 12, 1856.
72. *New York Tribune,* July 23, 1856; July 30, 1856; *New York Times*, July 22–24, 1856, one article quoting from *Boston Traveller;* Wilson, *Rise and Fall,* 2: 491–92; *Northampton Courier*, July 22, 1856; *Liberator*, *passim*, Aug., 1856; Lawrence A. Gobright, *Recollections of Men and Things at Washington* (Philadelphia: Claxton, Remser & Haffelfinger, 1869), pp. 155–56; Bigelow, 1: 165–70.
73. Wilson, *Rise and Fall*, 2: 535–36; *New York Tribune*, Aug. 2, 1856.
74. *Congressional Globe,* 34th Cong., 1st sess., 1856, pp. 2019–22; *New York Times*, Aug. 13, 1856; Aug. 14, 1856; *Springfield Republican*, Aug. 16, 1856.
75. *Springfield Republican*, Aug. 1, 1856; Aug. 5, 1856; Aug. 19, 1856; *Natick Observer*, July 12, 1856; Aug. 2, 1856; *Congressional Globe,* 34th Cong., 1st sess., 1856, p. 2081 and Appendix, pp. 1089–90, 1101–3; idem, 2d sess., pp. 30, 35–36, 44, 78; *New York Tribune,* Aug. 8, 1856; Aug. 14, 1856; Aug. 18, 1856; Aug. 19, 1856; Aug. 23, 1856; *National Era*, Oct. 9, 1856; *New York Times,* Aug. 19, 1856.

Chapter 14

1. *Springfield Republican*, July 24–26, 1856; July 30, 1856; Aug. 6, 1856; Aug. 21, 1856; *New York Times,* July 26, 1856, quoting from *Boston Times*; July 30, 1856; Mulkern, pp. 253–57.
2. Giddings to Joseph A. Giddings, July 2, 1856, Giddings Papers; Wise to Everett, July 14, 1856, Everett Papers; Wilson to Sumner, Aug. 3, 1856, Sumner Papers.
3. Webb to Sumner, Aug. 5, 1856, E. L. Pierce to Sumner, July 28, 1856, Wilson to Sumner, Aug. 11, 1856, including two enclosures, and J. D. Baldwin to Sumner, Aug. 20, 1856, Sumner Papers.
4. Hale to his wife, July 3, 1856, John P. Hale Papers, New Hampshire Historical Society, Concord; Seward, 2: 282.
5. Gienapp, pp. 377–80; Nichols, "First Republican Presidential Campaign," pp. 494–95; James A. Rawley, "Financing the Fremont Campaign," *Pennsylvania Magazine of History and Biography* 75 (Jan. 1951): 27–34; Wilson to Morgan, Aug. 8, 1856, Edwin D. Morgan Papers, State Library, Albany; *Springfield Republican*, Aug. 20, 1856.
6. Glyndon van Deusen, *William Henry Seward* (New York: Oxford University Press, 1967), pp. 178–79.

7. *Boston Transcript*, Sept. 2, 1856; *Natick Observer*, Sept. 6, 1856; Wilson to Webb, July 11, 1856, Simon Gratz Autograph Collection; *Springfield Republican*, Sept. 5, 1856; Sept. 9, 1856; Gienapp, p. 389; *Tribune Almanac*, 1857, p. 44.
8. *Springfield Republican*, Sept. 5, 1856; Sept. 11, 1856; Sept. 13, 1856; *Natick Observer*, Sept. 13, 1856; *New York Weekly Tribune*, Sept. 11, 1856; *New York Times*, Sept. 11, 1856; *Liberator*, Sept. 19, 1856; *Boston Transcript*, Sept. 13, 1856.
9. Merriam, 1: 173; diary, Sept. 15, 1856, Adams Papers; Mulkern, pp. 257–58; *Springfield Republican*, Sept. 12, 1856; Sept. 15–17, 1856; *Boston Telegraph*, Sept. 16, 1856.
10. Merriam, 1: 155–56, 175; diary, Sept. 16, 1856, Adams Papers; *Springfield Republican*, Sept. 5, 1856; Sept. 12, 1856; Sept. 17, 1856; *Boston Telegraph*, Sept. 16, 1856; Sept. 18, 1856; Mulkern, pp. 259–62; *New York Tribune*, Sept. 20, 1856; Robinson, "*Warrington*," pp. 63–64.
11. *Boston Telegraph*, Sept. 18, 1856.
12. *New York Tribune*, Oct. 6, 1856; *Springfield Republican*, *passim*, late Sept. to Oct. 8, 1856; diary, Aug. 30, 1856, Adams Papers.
13. *Springfield Republican*, Sept. 17, 1856; Oct. l, 1856; *New York Times*, Sept. 18, 1856; Sept. 20, 1856; Oct. 6, 1856; *Natick Observer*, Sept. 27, 1856; Oct. 4, 1856; *New York Weekly Tribune*, Oct. 11, 1856.
14. Nevins, *Ordeal*, 2: 505; Rawley, pp. 27–34; diary, Oct. 8, 9, 12, 15, and 16, 1856, Adams Papers; Rice, pp. 361–62; Gienapp, pp. 379–80, 394–401; *Springfield Republican*, Oct. 11, 1856; *New York Times*, Oct. 15, 1856.
15. *Tribune Almanac*, 1857, pp. 47, 56–58; Gienapp, pp. 394–407; Emma Lou Thornborough, *Indiana in the Civil War Era, 1850–1880* (Indianapolis: Indiana Historical Bureau, 1965), pp. 76–77; *New York Times*, Oct. 20, 1856; Morgan to Welles, Oct. 15 and 18, 1856, Gideon Welles Papers, LC; Chace to Morgan, Oct. 24, 1856, Morgan Papers; McClure, *Recollections*, p. 45.
16. *Albany Argus*, *passim*, Oct. 20–15, 1856; Gienapp, p. 411; box 43, Morgan Papers, fundraising efforts, 1856; *New York Tribune*, Oct. 17, 1856; Oct. 18, 1856; Oct. 20, 1856; Oct. 23, 1856; Oct. 27, 1856; *Boston Transcript*, Oct. 17, 1856.
17. *Springfield Republican*, Oct. 18, 1856; Merriam, 1: 175; *Natick Observer*, Oct. 25, 1856.
18. *New York Weekly Tribune*, Oct. 11, 1856; *National Era*, Oct. 6, 1856; Sumner, 4: 378–85.
19. *Tribune Almanac*, 1857; Peterson, p. 34; Gienapp, pp. 413–21.
20. *Tribune Almanac*, 1857; Peterson, p. 34; Colfax to Wheeler, Nov. 13, 1856, Colfax Papers; Fessenden to Trumball, Nov. 16, 1856, Trumball Papers.
21. *Springfield Republican*, Nov. 6, 1856; Baum, pp. 17, 38–40; Merriam, 1: 155; *Tribune Almanac*, 1857, p. 44; *Boston Transcript*, Nov. 5, 1856; Anderson, pp. 220, 224, 227; *Natick Observer*, Nov. 8, 1856.
22. *Boston Transcript*, Nov. 5, 1856; Pickard, *Whittier Letters*, 2: 308–9; *Northampton Courier*, Nov. 11, 1856; Nov. 18, 1856, quoting from *Worcester Spy*.
23. *Springfield Republican*, Nov. 14, 1856; Nov. 17, 1856; Nov. 18, 1856; *New York Times*, Nov. 14, 1856; Nason and Russell, pp. 222–24.
24. *Boston Transcript*, Nov. 25, 1856; diary, Nov. 24, 1856, Adams Papers; *Liberator*, Nov. 28, 1856.
25. *Springfield Republican*, Nov. 29, 1856; *Congressional Directory*, 34th Cong., 3d sess., 1856, pp. 32, 51–56; Poore, 1: 490; *New York Times*, Dec. 10, 1856.

26. Wilson, *Rise and Fall*, 2: 536; Lawrence, pp. 110–11.
27. *New York Times*, Dec. 5, 1856; *Springfield Republican*, Dec. 3, 1856.
28. *New York Times*, Dec. 3, 1856; *New York Tribune*, Dec. 3, 1856; *National Era*, Dec. 11, 1856.
29. Reeder to Washburn, Aug. 11, 1856, Israel Washburn Papers; Lawrence, pp. 105–6; Wilson to Parker, Dec. 5, 1856, Parker Papers; Thayer to F. P. Rice, Feb. 4, 1889, Eli Thayer Papers, John Hay Library.
30. Nason and Russell, pp. 211–22; *Congressional Globe*, 34th Cong, 3d sess., 1856, pp. 62–69; *New York Times*, Dec. 20, 1856; *New York Tribune*, Dec. 20, 1856.
31. Nason and Russell, pp. 211–22; *Congressional Globe*, 34th Cong., 3d sess., 1856, pp. 62–69; Henry Wilson, *Defence of the Republican Party. Speech of Hon. Henry Wilson, of Massachusetts, on the President's Message, in the United States Senate, December 19, 1856* (Washington: Buell & Blanchard, 1857); *National Era*, Dec. 25, 1856; Jan. 22, 1857.
32. *New York Times*, Dec. 23, 1856; *New York Tribune*, Dec. 24, 1856; *Congressional Globe*, 34th Cong, 3d sess., 1856, Appendix, pp. 95–96.
33. *Boston Transcript*, Dec. 26, 1856; *Springfield Republican*, Dec. 30, 1856; L. M. Child to Whittier, Jan. 2, 1857, Lydia Maria Child and John Greenleaf Whittier Papers, LC; L. M. Child to D. L. Child, Jan. 7, 1857, Lydia Maria Child Papers, Anti-Slavery Collection, Cornell University; Wilson to Sumner, Jan. 13 and 19, 1857, Houghton.
34. Pierce, 3: 516, 518; Donald, *Sumner*, p. 321; Wilson to Sumner, Jan. 6 and 19, 1856; *Congressional Globe*, 34th Cong, 3d sess., 1857, Appendix, p. 344; Weiss, 2: 218; *New York Tribune*, Mar. 6, 1857.
35. *Passim*, Giddings Papers; *Letters of William Lloyd Garrison, Wendell Phillips, and James G. Blaine* (Concord, 1872), pp. 3–5; Frederick Douglass, *Life and Times of Frederick Douglass* (New York: Pathway Press, 1941), p. 536.
36. Wilson, *Rise and Fall*, 2: 518; Pierce to Julian, Dec. 2, 1893, Julian-Giddings Papers.
37. Oliver Johnson, *William Lloyd Garrison and His Times* (Boston: B. B. Russell & Co., 1879), pp. 338–39; Lawrence J. Friedman, *Gregarious Saints: Self and Community in American Abolitionism, 1830–1870* (Cambridge: Cambridge University Press, 1982), p. 234.
38. Garrison, 3: 448–53; Higginson to Palfrey, Dec. 30, 1856, and Jan. 17, 1857, Palfrey Papers; *New York Tribune*, Jan. 10, 1857; Russel B. Nye, *William Lloyd Garrison and the Humanitarian Reformers* (Boston: Little, Brown and Company, 1955), p. 165; *Twenty-fourth Annual Report of the American Anti-Slavery Society* (New York: American Anti-Slavery Society, 1857), pp. 90–97.
39. Tilden G. Edelstein, *Strange Enthusiasm: A Life of Thomas Wentworth Higginson* (New Haven: Yale University Press, 1968), pp. 197–98, 201; *Twenty-fourth Annual Report of the American Anti-Slavery Society*, p. 97; Higginson to Palfrey, Jan. 17, 1857, Palfrey Papers; *Liberator*, Jan. 23, 1857; Jan. 30, 1857; Feb. 13, 1857; Feb. 27, 1857; *New York Times*, Jan. 16, 1857; Jan. 20, 1857; *New York Tribune*, Jan. 17, 1857; *Boston Telegraph*, Jan. 17, 1857.
40. Wilson to Sumner, Jan. 19 and 29, 1857, Sumner Papers; *Liberator*, Feb. 27, 1857; Weiss, 2: 218; Wilson to Parker, Mar. 14, 1857, Parker Papers; Walker to Higginson, Jan. 30, 1857, Higginson Papers.
41. *New York Times*, May 13, 1857; May 14, 1857; Harriet W. Sewell, ed., *Letters of Lydia Maria Child*, 4th ed. (Boston: Houghton, Mifflin and Company, 1884), p. 308.
42. Wilson to Sumner, Jan. 13, 19, 27 and 29, 1857, Sumner Papers.

43. *New York Times*, Jan. 23–27, 1857; *National Era*, Jan. 29, 1857.
44. *National Era*, Jan. 29, 1857; *Congressional Globe*, 34th Cong., 3d sess., 1857, pp. 568–69 and Appendix, pp. 294, 298; Nason and Russell, pp. 224–25.
45. *Congressional Globe*, 34th Cong., 3d sess., 1857, p. 813; *National Era*, Mar. 12, 1857; *Boston Telegraph,* Mar. 3, 1857.
46. *New York Times*, Feb. 4, 1857; *Congressional Globe*, 34th Cong., 3d sess., 1857, Appendix, pp. 328–44; Richard Hofstadter, "The Tariff Issue on the Eve of the Civil War," *American Historical Review* 24 (Oct. 1938): 50; *National Era*, Mar. 5, 1857.
47. *New York Times*, Feb. 4, 1857; *Congressional Globe*, 34th Cong., 3d sess., 1857, Appendix, pp. 328–58; *National Era*, Mar. 5, 1857; Hofstadter, pp. 50–53; *New York Tribune*, Mar. 6, 1857.
48. *Congressional Globe,* 34th Cong., special Senate session, 1857, pp. 371, 379, 384, 398; *New York Tribune*, Mar. 10, 1857; *Northampton Courier*, Mar. 17, 1857.
49. *Tribune Almanac*, 1858, p. 51; *New York Times*, Mar. 11, 1857; Apr. 2, 1857; May 10, 1857; *New York Tribune*, May 2. 1857; *Northampton Courier*, Apr. 28, 1857; Wilson to Pierce, Apr. 12 and 23, 1857, Edward L. Pierce Papers, Houghton; Mulkern, pp. 270–74.
50. *Natick Observer*, Mar. 28, 1857; John W. Bacon, pp. 42–43; Winthrop, pp. 197–98; *Liberator*, June 3, 1857.
51. *Congressional Globe*, 34th Cong., 3d sess., 1857, p. 677.
52. Ibid, p. 1016.
53. Allan Nevins, *The Emergence of Lincoln,* 2 vols. (New York: Charles Scribner's Sons, 1950), 1: 146–53; Wilson to F. P. Blair Jr., May 31, 1857, Morgan Papers.
54. Diary, Apr. 8, 1857, Adams Papers; letterbook 4, Apr. 23, 1857, p. 53, Amos A. Lawrence Papers; Wilson to Pierce, Apr. 23, 1857, Pierce Papers; *Boston Transcript,* May 8, 1856; *New York Tribune*, May 8, 1857; May 12, 1857; May 14, 1857; May 16, 1857; *New York Times,* June 4, 1857; Wilson, *Rise and Fall*, 2: 537.
55. *New York Times,* June 4, 1857; *New York Tribune,* June 2, 1857, quoting from *Cincinnati Commercial*; June 4, 1857, one article quoting from *Chicago Tribune*; *National Era,* June 11, 1857; James P. Shenton, *Robert John Walker, a Politician from Jackson to Lincoln* (New York: Columbia University Press, 1961), p. 153.
56. *New York Times,* June 1, 1857; June 4, 1857; June 6, 1857; *New York Tribune*, June 2, 1857, one article quoting from *Cincinnati Commercial*; June 4, 1857; June 8, 1857; *National Era*, June 11, 1857; Shenton, p. 153.
57. Wilson to Blair, May 31, 1857, Morgan Papers; *New York Tribune*, Oct. 31, 1857; Wilson, *Rise and Fall*, 2: 537; *Boston Transcript*, June 5, 1857.
58. Mann, *Life of Wilson*, p. 118; Trefousse, *Radical Republicans*, p. 110; Richards, p. 431; Jeffrey Rossbach, *Ambivalent Conspirators: John Brown, the Secret Six and a Theory of Slave Violence* (Philadelphia: University of Pennsylvania Press, 1982), p. 126; Wilson to Blair, May 31, 1857, Morgan Papers; *New York Tribune,* Oct. 31, 1857; Wilson, *Rise and Fall,* 2: 537–38.
59. *New York Tribune*, June 5, 1857; Oct. 31, 1857; Mann, *Life of Wilson*, p. 118; Lawrence to Robinson, June 6, 1857, Charles Robinson Papers, University of Kansas, Lawrence; Wilson to Blair, May 31, 1857, Morgan Papers; Wilson to Trumball, June 28, 1857, Trumball Papers; M. F. Conway to George L. Stearns, May 29, 1857, Samuel Gridley Howe Papers, MHS; Richards, p. 431.

60. *New York Tribune*, June 5, 1857; Oct. 31, 1857; Wilson, *Rise and Fall*, 2: 538; Wilson to Trumball, June 28, 1857, Trumball Papers; Richards, p. 431; Rossbach, pp. 126–27; Lawrence to Robinson, June 6 and Aug. 17, 1857, Robinson Papers, University of Kansas; diary, June 8, 1857, Adams Papers; Wilson to Robinson, June 15, 1857, Charles Robinson Papers, Kansas State Historical Society, Topeka; Wilson to Sumner, Aug. 26, 1857, Sumner Papers; Wilson to Morgan, July 22 and Aug. 9 and 26, 1857, Morgan Papers.
61. Wilson to Sumner, Aug. 26, 1857, Sumner Papers.

Chapter 15

1. Mulkern, pp. 275–76; *New York Tribune,* May 8, 1857; June 3, 1857; June 10, 1857; *New York Times,* June 11, 1857; Apr. 29, 1858.
2. *New York Tribune*, May 8, 1857; June 10, 1857; June 11, 1857; June 15, 1857; *New York Times,* June 11, 1857; Bird to Sumner, June 8, 1857, Sumner Papers; diary, June 11 and 18, 1857, Adams Papers.
3. *Boston Transcript*, June 20, 1857; Wilson to Carter, June 25, 1857, Carter Papers; Wilson to Colfax, July 25, 1857, Colfax Papers.
4. *New York Tribune*, June 10, 1857; June 11, 1857; Fish to Gardner, Feb. 9, 1857, Hamilton Fish Papers, LC; Mulkern, pp. 276–77; *Northampton Courier*, June 16, 1857; June 23, 1857.
5. Diary, June 18, 20, 23, and 24, Aug. 20, and Nov. 4, 1857, and Adams to Sumner, June 26, 1857, Adams Papers; *New York Tribune*, July 2, 1857; *Northampton Courier*, June 30, 1857; July 4, 1857; July 21, 1857, July 28, 1857; *Boston Transcript*, June 24, 1857; June 25, 1857; *New York Times,* July 28, 1857; *National Era*, July 2, 1857; July 9, 1857; Wilson to Colfax, July 25, 1857, Colfax Papers.
6. *New York Tribune*, July 17, 1857; Sept. 11, 1857; Oct. 7, 1857; Oct. 19, 1857; *New York Times,* Sept. 1, 1857; Sept. 5, 1857; Sept. 11, 1857; Sept. 19, 1857; *Northampton Courier*, July 21, 1857; Sept. 1, 1857; Sept. 15, 1857; Sept. 29, 1857; Wilson to Sumner, Aug. 26, 1857, Sumner Papers; Mulkern, pp. 280–87; Merriam, 1: 179–80; *National Era*, Oct. 8, 1857; J. F. Marsh to Banks, Oct. 19, 1857, Banks Papers.
7. *Boston Transcript*, Sept. 8, 1857; Sept. 9, 1857; *New York Times*, Sept. 9, 1857; *Liberator*, Sept. 18, 1857.
8. *Northampton Courier*, Sept. 1–Oct. 27, 1857; *New York Times*, Sept. 1, 1857; *Bird, a Biographical Sketch*, p. 148; *New York Weekly Tribune*, Sept. 12, 1857; *New York Tribune*, Oct. 19, 1857; Pierce to Sumner, Sept. 1857, Sumner Papers.
9. *New York Tribune*, Oct. 24, 1857; *Boston Transcript*, Oct. 16, 1857; *New York Times*, Oct. 26, 1857; Wilson to Trumball, June 28, 1857, Trumball Papers; Wilson to Colfax, July 25, 1857, Colfax Papers.
10. *Tribune Almanac*, 1858, pp. 51–63; *New York Times*, Oct. 17, 1856; *National Era*, Nov. 5, 1857; Foner, *Free Soil*, pp. 254–55.
11. *Tribune Almanac,* 1858, p. 51; *Boston Transcript*, Nov. 4, 1857; Nov. 11, 1857; Dec. 5, 1857; *Northampton Courier*, Nov. 3, 1857; Baum, p. 42; Mulkern, pp. 286–87; *New York Tribune*, Nov. 6, 1857; *New York Times*, Nov. 4, 1857; Nov. 6, 1857; Nov. 11, 1857; *Liberator*, Nov. 6, 1857; Nov. 20, 1857.
12. Gardner to Wilson, Nov. 25, 1857, Banks Papers.

13. *Boston Transcript*, Nov. 20, 1857; *Northampton Courier*, Nov. 24, 1857; *Natick Observer*, Mar. 10, 1860; *Liberator*, Nov. 27, 1857; Pierce, 3: 556.
14. Conway to Howe, Aug. 7 and 23, 1857, Howe Papers, MHS; *New York Times*, Aug. 24, 1857; Sept. 16, 1857; Oct. 1, 1857; Wilson, *Rise and Fall*, 2: 538–40.
15. *New York Times*, Nov. 6, 1857.
16. Robert W. Johannsen, ed., *The Letters of Stephen A. Douglas* (Urbana: University of Illinois Press, 1961), p. 386; *passim*, Nov. 21 to Dec. 1, 1857, Trumball Papers; *New York Times*, Dec. 1, 1857; Dec. 3, 1857.
17. *Congressional Globe*, 35th Cong, 1st sess., 1857, pp. 1, 39–42; Poore, 1: 528; *National Era*, Dec. 17, 1857; Dec. 24, 1857; Mann, *Life of Wilson*, p. 71.
18. *Congressional Directory*, 35th Cong., 1st sess., 2d ed., 1858, pp. iv, 40–47, 54.
19. *New York Times*, Jan. 6, 1858; Wilson to Sumner, Jan. 8 and 18, 1858, and telegram, Feb. 1, 1858, Sumner Papers; Pierce, 3: 558–60, 594, 599; Donald, *Sumner*, pp. 332–33.
20. *Congressional Globe*, 35th Cong, 1st sess., 1857, pp. 14–22; *New York Times*, Dec. 9–11, 1857; Poore, 1: 530; C. H. Ray to Trumball, Nov. 24, 1857, Trumball Papers; Don E. Fehrenbacher, *Prelude to Greatness: Lincoln in the 1850's* (Stanford: Stanford University Press, 1962).
21. Wilson to Robinson, Nov. 26, 1857, Charles Robinson Papers, Kansas State Historical Society; *New York Times*, Dec. 10, 1857; Dec. 15–17, 1857; *New York Tribune*, Dec. 11, 1857; Wilson, *Rise and Fall*, 2: 542–45; correspondence until mid-month favored staying clear of Douglas; then confusion: *passim*, Dec. 1857, Trumball Papers.
22. Lawrence to Robinson, Jan. 2, 1858, Lawrence Papers.
23. Sewell, *Ballots*, pp. 344–53; Merriam, 1: 232; Joseph F. Newton, *Lincoln and Herndon* (Cedar Rapids, Iowa: The Torch Press, 1910), p. 148; Wilson to Parker, Feb. 28, 1858, Parker Papers; Wilson to Schouler, Feb. 19, 1858, Schouler Papers.
24. Trumball to Lincoln, Jan. 3, 1858, Robert Todd Lincoln Papers, LC; William H. Bissell to Trumball, Jan. 9, 1858, Trumball Papers; Merriam, 1: 232.
25. *Congressional Globe*, 35th Cong., 1st sess., 1858, pp. 521–53; *National Era*, Feb. 11, 1858; Wilson, *Rise and Fall*, 2: 545; *New York Post*, Feb. 5, 1858.
26. *Congressional Globe*, 35th Cong., 1st sess., 1858, pp. 570–76, 621; *National Era*, Feb. 11, 1858; Feb. 18, 1858; Mann, *Life of Wilson*, pp. 75–76; Wilson, *Rise and Fall*, 2: 245.
27. *New York Times*, Feb. 4, 1858; Feb. 8, 1858; Feb. 9, 1858; *New York Post*, Feb. 11, 1858; Feb. 13, 1858; *Boston Transcript*, Feb. 9, 1858; Feb. 12, 1858; *Congressional Globe*, 35th Cong., 1st sess., 1858, pp. 1431–33.
28. *National Era*, Feb. 4, 1858; *Congressional Globe*, 35th Cong., 1st sess., 1858, pp. 497–98, 698, 720–24, 861–67, 2923, 2981; *New York Times*, Feb. 2, 1858; Sumner to Trumball, Sat. morning [Feb. 1858?], Trumball Papers.
29. *Congressional Globe*, 35th Cong, 1st sess., 1857, pp. 755, 1036, Appendix, p. 102; *New York Post*, Feb. 22, 1858; Mar. 15, 1858; Mar. 18, 1858; Mark J. Stegmaier, "Intensifying the Sectional Conflict: William Seward versus James Hammond in the LeCompton Debate of 1858," *Civil War History* 31 (Sept. 1985): 198–210.
30. *Congressional Globe*, 35th Cong., 1st sess., 1858, pp. 959–64, 1025–35; Stegmaier, pp. 210–15; *New York Post*, Mar. 8, 1858; Wilson to Sumner, Mar. 8, 1858, Sumner Papers.

31. Nason and Russell, pp. 231–32; *Congressional Globe*, 35th Cong., 1st sess., 1858, Appendix, pp. 167–69; McClure, *Recollections*, p. 293; Stegmaier, p. 215; *New York Post,* Mar. 8, 1858.
32. *Congressional Globe*, 35th Cong., 1st sess., 1858, Appendix, pp. 169–71; Nason and Russell, pp. 232–38.
33. *Congressional Globe*, 35th Cong, 1st sess, 1858, pp. 1002–6, 1087, and Appendix, pp. 172–73; Wilson, *Rise and Fall*, 2: 551; *New York Post,* Mar. 8, 1858; Mar. 22, 1858; Nason and Russell, pp. 238–46.
34. *Springfield Republican*, Mar. 25, 1858; May 22, 1858; *Liberator*, Apr. 18, 1858; A. B. Johnson to Sumner, Mar. 25, 1858, Sumner Papers; *New York Weekly Tribune,* Apr. 10, 1858; *Natick Citizen,* Mar. 14, 1879; Nason and Russell, p. 229.
35. *Congressional Globe*, 35th Cong, 1st sess., 1858, pp. 1258–64 and Appendix, pp. 174–214; *New York Times,* Mar. 22, 1858; *New York Post,* Mar. 23, 1858; Wilson, *Rise and Fall*, 2: 557.
36. *New Hampshire Patriot*, Mar. 10, 1858; *Tribune Almanac*, 1859, pp. 44, 56; *New York Post*, Apr. 8, 1858.
37. Dixon to Welles, Mar. 6, 8, 17, 19, and 24, Apr. 2, and May 7, 1858, Welles Papers; Newton, pp. 149–56; William H. Herndon and Jesse W. Weik, *Herndon's Life of Lincoln,* ed. Paul M. Angle (Cleveland: The World Publishing Company, 1965), pp. 319–20; Emanuel Hertz, *The Hidden Lincoln: from the Letters and Papers of William H. Herndon* (New York: Blue Ribbon Books, 1940), p. 114.
38. Judd to Trumball, Mar. 7 and 19, 1858, C. H. Ray to Trumball, Mar. 9, 1858, Herndon to Trumball, Apr. 12 and 26, 1858, Trumball Papers; Pierce, 3: 557.
39. Forney, 1: 342; Wilson to Parker, Feb. 28, 1858, Parker Papers; Wilson to Sumner, Jan. 18, 1858, Sumner Papers; Mann, *Life of Wilson*, p. 75; Wilson, *Rise and Fall,* 2: 562–63, 567; Ovando J. Hollister, *Life of Schuyler Colfax* (New York: Funk & Wagnalls, 1886), p. 119; *New York Times*, Apr. 29, 1858; Giddings to Grotius R. Giddings, Apr. 2, 1858, Giddings Papers; Giddings to his daughter, Apr. 30, 1858, Giddings-Julian Papers.
40. Wilson, *Rise and Fall,* 2: 558–65; *New York Post*, Apr. 2, 1858; *Congressional Globe,* 35th Cong., 1st sess., pp. 1858, 1874–80.
41. *New York Times,* Apr. 24, 1858; Apr. 26, 1858; *National Era*, May 6, 1858; Wilson, *Rise and Fall,* 2: 563–64; *Congressional Globe*, 35th Cong, 1st sess., 1858, pp. 1786–1805, 1855, 1874–80, 1898–99.
42. Johnson to "My Dear Governor" [Wise], Nov. 6, 1858, Reverdy Johnson Papers, LC.
43. Ward H. Lamon, *The Life of Abraham Lincoln, from His Birth to His Inauguration as President* (Boston: James R. Osgood and Company, 1872), p. 394; Wilson, *Rise and Fall,* 2: 567.
44. Hertz, p. 114; Lamon, p. 394; Newton, p. 180; Horace White, *The Life of Lyman Trumball* (Boston: Houghton Miflin Company, 1913), p. 87; David Donald, *Lincoln's Herndon* (New York: Alfred A. Knopf, 1948), pp. 112–13; *Congressional Globe*, 36th Cong., 1st sess., 1860, Appendix, pp. 157–64; George F. Milton, *The Eve of Conflict: Stephen A. Douglas and the Needless War* (Boston: Houghton Mifflin Company, 1934), p. 298.
45. Wilson, *Rise and Fall*, 2: 567–69; E. L. Baker to Trumball, May 1, 1858, Trumball Papers; *Congressional Globe*, 36th Cong., 1st sess., 1860, Appendix, pp. 157–64; John G. Nicolay and John Hay, *Abraham Lincoln, Complete Works,* 2 vols. (New York: Century Company, 1894), 1: 592.

46. *New York Post,* Mar. 24, 1858; *Congressional Globe,* 35th Cong., 1st sess., 1858, pp. 1299, 1325–26, 1406–9, 1411, 1487, 1512–13, 1512–16; *National Era,* Apr. 15, 1858; *New York Times,* May 1, 1858.
47. *Congressional Globe,* 35th Cong., 1st sess., 1858, pp. 1966, 2209; *National Era,* May 27, 1858; *Liberator,* May 21, 1858, one article quoting from *Boston Post*; May 28, 1858; Wilson, *Rise and Fall,* 2: 624–27.
48. *Congressional Globe,* 35th Cong., 1st sess., 1858, pp.1535, 1643–44, 1647; *National Era,* Apr. 22, 1858; Mann, *Life of Wilson,* p. 77; Lawrence to Wilson, Apr. 28, 1858, Lawrence Papers.
49. *Congressional Globe,* 35th Cong., 1st sess., 1857–1858, pp. 85–87, 2794, 2804, 2889 2894.
50. Ibid., 1858, pp. 2020, 2070–72, 2082–83, 2238–39; *National Era,* May 20, 1858; Mann, *Life of Wilson,* p. 77.
51. *Congressional Globe,* 35th Cong., 1st sess., 1858, pp. 2239–41, 2406; *National Era,* June 3, 1858.
52. Wilson, *Rise and Fall,* 2: 539–40, 590–91; Franklin B. Sanborn, ed., *The Life and Letters of John Brown, Liberator of Kansas and Martyr of Virginia* (Boston: Roberts Brothers, 1891), pp. 458–60; *Report of the Select Committee of the Senate Appointed to Inquire into the Late Invasion and Seizure of the Public Property at Harper's Ferry,* hereafter referred to as *Mason Report* (Washington, 1860), pp. 3, 8–10, 100–1, 140, 177, 253.
53. Wilson, *Rise and Fall,* 2: 591–92; Sanborn, p. 462; Frank P. Stearns, *Life and Public Services of George Luther Stearns* (Philadelphia: J. B. Lippincott Co., 1907), pp. 167–70; O. G. Villard, *John Brown, 1800–1859* (New York: Alfred A. Knopf, 1910), pp. 341–42; Howe to Wilson, Jan. 23, 1860, and copy of letter, Howe to Wilson, May 15, 1858, Howe Papers, MHS; *Mason Report,* pp. 15–16, 100–1, 141–45, 157–77, 232; Rossbach, pp. 163–64.
54. Wilson, *Rise and Fall,* 2: 591–92; Sanford, pp. 461–65; Stearns, *Life of Stearns,* pp. 169–70; *Mason Report,* pp. 14–16, 100–2, 157–77; Villard, pp. 339–42; Rossbach, pp. 162–74.
55. *Congressional Globe,* 35th Cong, 1st sess., 1858, pp. 2451–52, 2530–31, 3051–61; Wilson to Parker, June 5, 1858, Parker Papers; *Liberator,* July 2, 1858; Wilson, *Rise and Fall,* 2: 615–18; *New York Post,* June 8, 1858; June 17, 1858.
56. *New York Post,* June 2, 1858; *New York Times,* June 1, 1858; June 9, 1858; Seward, 2: 346–47; *Congressional Globe,* 35th Cong., 1st sess., 1858, p. 2013; Wilson to Parker, May 31, 1858, Parker Papers.
57. *Congressional Globe,* 35th Cong., 1st sess., 1858, pp. 2900–2; *Connecticut Courant,* June 19, 1858; *New York Tribune,* June 11–14, 1858; Nason and Russell, pp. 247–48; Wilson to Gwin, June 11, 1858, Autograph File, Beinecke Library, Yale; Seward, 2: 346–47; *Springfield Republican,* July 3, 1858; July 10, 1858.
58. Nason and Russell, pp. 248–49; *Boston Transcript,* June 14, 1858; *New York Tribune,* June 14, 1858; *New York Post,* June 12, 1858; *New York Times,* June 23, 1858.
59. Sumner to Howe [Mar. 1858], Howe Papers, Houghton; Eliot to Sumner, Feb. 19, 1858, Pierce to Sumner, Feb. 25, 1858, and Stone to Sumner, Mar. 12, 1858, Sumner Papers; Pearson, 1: 72–73, 79–82; Weiss, 2: 221–22; diary, Mar. 10 and 19, 1858, Adams Papers; Wilson, *Rise and Fall,* 2: 444; *Northampton Courier,* Mar. 23, 1858; Apr. 6, 1858; May 25, 1858.

60. *New York Tribune*, Mar. 10, 1860; Baum, p. 103; Stone to Sumner, Mar. 12, 1858 and Mar. 2 and Aug. 15, 1859, Sumner Papers; Robinson, "*Warrington*," pp. 425–26; Hesseltine, pp. 20–23.
61. *Springfield Republican*, May 8, 1858; June 24, 1858; *Congressional Globe*, 35th Cong., 1st sess., 1858, pp. 1858–1914, 1927–43; *New York Times*, May 8, 1858; *Northampton Courier*, June 22, 1858; diary, June 25, 1858, Adams Papers; *New York Tribune*, July 20, 1858; *New York Times*, July 16, 1858.
62. *Liberator*, Aug. 13, 1858, quoting from *Boston Courier*; *Springfield Republican*, July 31, 1858; Aug. 11, 1858; Sept. 4, 1858; Howe to Sumner, July 28, 1858, Howe Papers, Houghton.
63. Boston Trancript, July 24, 1858; *New York Tribune*, July 20, 1858; Sept. 10, 1858; *New York Times*, July 29, 1858; *Northampton Courier*, Sept. 7, 1858; Sept. 14, 1858; *Springfield Republican*, Sept. 8, 1858; Sept. 15, 1858.
64. Pike, pp. 424–26; Wilson to Giddings, Sept. 15, 1858, Giddings Papers; *Kennebec Journal*, Sept. 17, 1858; *New York Post*, Sept. 5, 1858; *Tribune Almanac*, 1859, pp. 44, 59; Rheta Childe Dorr, *Susan B. Anthony, the Woman Who Changed the Mind of a Nation* (New York: Frederick A. Stokes Company, 1928), p. 123; *National Era*, Oct. 21, 1858; *Boston Transcript*, Oct. 14, 1858; Wilson to Carey, Oct. 18, 1858, Henry C. Carey Papers in the Edward Carey Gardiner Collection, HSPa.
65. Wilson to Morgan, Sept. 20, 1858, Morgan Papers; *New York Tribune*, Sept. 28, 1858; *New York Post*, Sept. 28, 1858; *New York Times*, Sept. 28, 1858; *Tribune Almanac*, 1859, p. 45.
66. *Springfield Republican*, Oct. 16, 1858; *Boston Transcript*, Oct. 14, 1858; *New York Times*, Oct. 22, 1858.
67. Diary, Jan. 13, 1858, Sept., *passim*, Oct. 2 and 7, 1858, Adams Papers; Pierce to Sumner, Oct. 10, 1858, Sumner Papers; Adams, *Adams*, p. 105; *Boston Atlas*, Oct. 19, 1858; Duberman, *Adams*, p. 211; *Boston Traveller*, Oct. 28, 1858, and Extra.
68. Diary, Oct. 21 and 26, 1858, and B. Wood to Adams, Oct. 19, 1858, and F. A. Hobart to Adams, Oct. 21, 1858, Adams Papers; *New York Times*, Oct. 22, 1858; Oct. 28, 1858; Nov. 2, 1858; *Springfield Republican*, Oct. 23, 1858; Nov. 1, 1858; *Boston Transcript*, Oct. 23, 1858; Oct. 28–30, 1858; Nov. 3, 1858.
69. *Tribune Almanac*, 1859, pp. 44, 54–61; *New York Times*, Nov. 4, 1858; *New York Post*, Nov. 4, 1858.
70. *Boston Transcript*, Nov. 3, 1858; Winthrop, pp. 202–5.
71. Diary, Nov. 11, 1858; *Liberator*, Nov. 19, 1858.
72. E. L. Pierce to Chase, Nov. 5, 1858, Chase Papers, LC; Pierce to Sumner, Nov. 30, 1858, Sumner Papers; N. B. Judd to Trumball, Dec. 26, 1858, and Herndon to Trumball, Jan. 21, 1859, Trumball Papers.
73. Wilson to Giddings, Sept. 15, 1858, Giddings Papers; Giddings to his son, Dec. 3, 1858, Giddings-Julian Papers; *Liberator*, Dec. 10, 1858; diary, Dec. 1 and 2, 1858, Adams Papers; Wilson to Lawrence, Nov. and Nov. 26, 1858, Lawrence Papers; Pierce to Chase, Dec. 2, 1858, Chase Papers, LC; Pierce to Sumner, Nov. 30, 1858, and Wilson to George Sumner, Dec. 19, 1858, Sumner Papers.

Chapter 16

1. *Congressional Directory,* 35th Cong., 2d sess., 1859, pp. 54, 60; *New York Post,* Dec. 10, 1858; Dec. 11, 1858; *New York Times*, Dec. 10, 1858.
2. *Congressional Globe,* 34th Cong., 3d sess., 1857, p. 807; idem, 35th Cong., 1st sess., 1857, p. 62 and 1858, Appendix, pp. 374–77; idem, 35th Cong., 2d sess., 1858, pp. 6, 45; *National Era*, Feb. 26, 1857; May 28, 1858; Dec. 16, 1858; Dec. 30, 1858.
3. *Congressional Globe*, 35th Cong., 2d sess., 1858–59, pp. 49–56, 72, 139–45, 156, 304–10; *National Era*, Dec. 23, 1858; Feb. 10, 1859; *New York Post,* Dec. 20, 1858; Dec. 21, 1858; Jan. 13, 1859.
4. *Springfield Republican*, Jan. 14, 1859; *New York Tribune,* Jan. 12, 1859; Jan. 13, 1859; Jan. 28, 1859; *New York Times*, Jan. 14, 1859; *New York Post,* Jan. 13, 1859; *Congressional Globe*, 35th Cong., 2d sess., 1859, pp. 373–81, 442, 557–58, 607, 626–34; *National Era,* Jan. 20, 1859; Jan. 27, 1859; Feb. 3, 1859; *Boston Transcript*, Jan. 28, 1859.
5. *Congressional Globe,* 35th Cong., 2d sess., 1859, pp. 94–95, 187, 713, 734, 784, 857; *New York Tribune*, Feb. 11, 1859; *New York Times,* Mar. 1, 1859.
6. Stone to Sumner, May 21, 1858, Howe to Sumner, July 27, 1858, and A. B. Johnson to Sumner, Oct. 15, 1858, Sumner Papers; *New York Times*, Sept. 24, 1858.
7. State Finance Committee to "Dear Sir," Sept. 21, 1858, Adams Papers; Pickard, 2: 378–79; *Boston Transcript*, Nov. 3, 1858; *New York Tribune,* Nov. 5, 1858.
8. *Boston Transcript*, Jan. 11, 1858; Jan. 12, 1858; *Springfield Republican*, Jan. 12, 1858; Jan. 15, 1858; *New York Tribune,* Jan. 19, 1859; *Boston Journal*, Jan. 13, 1859; *Boston Atlas and Bee*, Jan. 13, 1859; Banks to Wilson, Jan. 13, 1859, Wilson Papers, LC; *Congressional Globe,* 35th Cong, 2d sess., 1859, p. 400.
9. Wilson to his wife, Jan. 13, 1859, Wilson Papers, South Natick Museum.
10. *New York Post*, Jan. 20, 1859; *New York Tribune,* Jan. 20, 1859; Feb. 24, 1859.
11. *New York Post*, Mar. 5, 1859; *National Era*, Feb. 17, 1859; Mar. 3, 1859; *Congressional Globe,* 35th Cong, 2d sess., 1859, pp. 993–94, 1467–73, 1499–1505.
12. *Springfield Republican*, Feb. 8, 1859; Mar. 19, 1859; Mar. 24, 1859; Apr. 6, 1859; *Congressional Globe*, 35th Cong, special sess., 1859, pp. 1685–92; *Tribune Almanac,* 1860, pp. 47, 63; *New Hampshire Patriot*, Mar. 9, 1859; Mar. 16, 1859; Wilson to Hawley, Jan. 31, 1859, Hawley Papers; *Connecticut Courant*, Mar. 19, 1859; Mar. 26, 1859; Apr. 6, 1859; Pierce to Sumner [Apr. 1859], Sumner Papers; Carl Schurz, *Speeches, Correspondence and Political Papers,* ed. Frederic Bancroft, 6 vols. (New York: Negro Universities Press, 1969), 1: 46.
13. Diary, May 9, 1859, Adams Papers; Pierce to Sumner [Apr. 1859] and May 31, 1859, and Bird to Sumner, Apr. 17, 1859, Sumner Papers; Mann, *Life of Wilson*, pp. 56–57; Pierce to Chase, Apr. 5 and 28, 1859, Chase Papers, LC; Schurz, *Speeches,* 1: 41–72; idem, *Reminiscences*, pp. 116–18; idem, *Autobiography* (New York: Charles Scribner's Sons, c. 1961), pp. 145–46; Claude M. Fuess, *Carl Schurz, Reformer, 1829–1906* (New York: Dodd, Mead & Company, 1932), pp. 63–64; *Liberator,* Apr. 22, 1859; *Springfield Republican,* Apr. 22, 1859; *New York Tribune*, Apr. 25, 1859; Apr. 30, 1859.
14. Schurz, *Speeches*, 1: 72–75; Pierce to Chase, Apr. 28, 1859, Chase Papers, LC; *Springfield Republican,* Apr. 21, 1859; Apr. 22, 1859; Apr. 27, 1859; Mann, *Life of Wilson*, pp. 57–58.

15. *Springfield Republican*, Apr. 27, 1859; *New York Post*, Apr. 28, 1859; *New York Tribune*, May 2, 1859; *National Era*, May 12, 1859; Pierce to Chase, Apr. 28, 1859, Chase Papers, LC.
16. Mann, *Life of Wilson*, pp. 58–59; *Boston Transcript*, May 4, 1859; *New York Tribune*, May 26, 1859; *National Era*, May 26, 1859; *Springfield Republican*, May 26, 1859; Pierce to Sumner, May 31, 1859, and J. D. Baldwin to Sumner, June 27, 1859, Sumner Papers; Pierce to Chase, Apr. 5, 1859, Chase Papers, LC.
17. *Boston Transcript*, May 4, 1859; June 14, 1859; July 5, 1859; diary, May 10, 1859, Everett Papers; *Liberator*, June 3, 1859; Oct. 7, 1859; Nason and Russell, pp. 255–67; diary, June 6, 1859, Adams Papers; *Natick Observer*, July 9, 1859.
18. *Springfield Republican*, Aug. 2, 1859; Aug. 12, 1859; Sept. 19, 1859; *Liberator*, Aug. 19, 1859; Aug. 26, 1859; *Boston Transcript*, Sept 9, 1859; *Natick Observer*, Aug. 20, 1859; Sept 17, 1859; Oct. 1, 1859; Oct. 8, 1859.
19. Wilson to Chase, May 18, 1859, Pierce to Chase, May 30, 1859, and Chase to Wilson, June 3, 1859, Chase Papers, LC; Foner, *Free Soil*, p. 210; Wilson to Claflin, Feb. 1, 1858, Claflin Papers.
20. Wilson to Schouler, Feb. 19, 1858, Schouler Papers; Lawrence to Wilson, Nov. 23, 1858, and Wilson to Lawrence, Nov. 25, 1858, Lawrence Papers; Wilson to Stansbury, Jan. 21, 1859, Wilson Papers, LC; Pierce to Sumner, May 31 and July 12, 1859, Sumner Papers; Pierce to Chase, May 30, and Sept. 21, 1859, Chase Papers, LC; *New York Tribune*, Oct. 27, 1859; Wilson to Carter, Dec 10 [1859], Carter Papers.
21. Don W. Wilson, *Governor Charles Robinson of Kansas* (Lawrence: University Press of Kansas, 1975), p. 69; Wilson to D. Robner, Sept. 10, 1859, Republican Party, Minnesota State Central Committee Papers, Minnesota Historical Society, St. Paul.
22. *Springfield Republican*, Sept. 21, 1859; Sept. 23, 1859; Oct. 5, 1859; Stone to Sumner, Aug. 15, 1859, Sumner Papers; Pierce to Chase, Sept. 21, 1859, Chase Papers, LC.
23. Wilson to Robner, Sept. 10, 1859, Republican Party, Minnesota Central Committee Papers; *Tribune Almanac*, 1860, pp. 47, 50, 60; *New York Post*, Oct. 13, 1859; Wilson to Chase, Oct. 14, 1859, Chase Papers, HSPa.
24. Rossbach, pp. 187–88; Stearns, *Life of Stearns*, pp. 171, 179; Sanborn to Henry Richards, May 15, 1908, Higginson Papers; *Mason Report*, pp. 22.
25. *New York Tribune*, May 26, 1859; Garrison, *Garrison*, 3: 487; Rossbach, p. 204; Stearns, *Life of Stearns*, pp. 171, 179–81; *Mason Report*, pp. 3, 16, 144–45, 238; Wilson, *Rise and Fall*, 2: 593; *Natick Bulletin*, Nov. 20, 1885.
26. *Boston Transcript*, Oct. 19, 1859; *Springfield Republican*, Oct. 19, 1859; Betty L. Mitchell, "Massachusetts Reacts to John Brown's Raid," *Civil War History* 19 (Mar. 1973): 65–69.
27. *New York Times*, Nov. 29, 1875; Eli Thayer, *A History of the Kansas Crusade* (New York: Harper & Brothers, 1889), p. 194; Garrison, *Garrison*, 3: 488–90; Mitchell, pp. 72–75; Lawrence, pp. 131–38; Stearns, *Life of Stearns*, p. 171.
28. *New York Times*, Oct. 26, 1859; *Liberator*, Nov. 4, 1859; *New York Post*, Oct. 26, 1859; Oct. 27, 1859; *New York Tribune*, Oct. 24, 1859; Oct. 27, 1859.
29. *Albany Journal*, Oct. 27, 1859; Oct. 31, 1859; *New York Tribune*, Nov. 1, 1859; Nov. 7, 1859; *Springfield Republican*, Nov. 1, 1859; (Watertown) *New York Reformer*, Nov. 3, 1859.
30. *New York Tribune*, Nov. 7, 1859; (Trenton, New Jersey) *Daily True American*, Nov. 3, 1859; *Tribune Almanac*, 1860, p. 48.

31. *Tribune Almanac,* 1860, pp. 47, 51, 59, 62; *Springfield Republican*, Nov. 9, 1859; *Natick Observer,* Nov. 12, 1859.
32. *Natick Observer,* Nov. 24, 1859; Dec. 10, 1859; Nason and Russell, pp. 267–69; Henry C. Wright, *No Rights, No Duties, or Slaveholders, as Such, Owe No Duties* (Boston: Henry C. Wright, 1860), pp. 31–33.
33. *Boston Transcript*, Nov. 31, 1859; Harriet Wilson to Mrs. Claflin, Feb. 5, 1860, Claflin Papers; Pierce, 3: 600–1; Mrs. Roger A. Pryor, *Reminiscences of Peace and War,* rev. ed. (New York: Macmillan Company, 1905), p. 82; Adams to Charles Francis Adams Jr., Apr. 1, 1860, Adams Papers; *Congressional Directory*, 36th Cong., 1st sess., 1859–60, 2d reg. ed., p. 64; Poore, 2: 23.
34. *Boston Transcript,* Nov. 28, 1859; *Congressional Directory*, 36th Cong., 1st sess., 1859–60, 2d reg. ed., p. ii; *Congressional Globe,* 36th Cong, 1st sess., 1859, p. 198.
35. *New York Post*, Dec. 5–7, 1859; diary, Dec. 3, 1859, Adams Papers; Hugh C. Bailey, *Hinton Rowan Helper, Abolitionist-Racist* (University, Alabama: University of Alabama Press, 1965), p. 44; *Congressional Globe*, 35th Cong., 1st sess., 1858, pp. 1459 and Appendix, p. 172; idem, 36th Cong., 1st sess., 1859, pp. 147–48.
36. Adams to Henry Adams, Jan. 16, 1860, Adams Papers; Forney, 1: 342; *Boston Transcript*, Feb. 2, 1860.
37. *Congressional Globe*, 36th Cong., 1st sess., 1859, pp. 11–12; *National Era*, Nov. 10, 1859; Dec. 15, 1859; Dec. 22, 1859; Mann, *Life of Wilson*, pp. 78–79; Wilson, *Rise and Fall*, 2: 601–2.
38. Henry C. Wright, *The Natick Resolution, or Resistance to Slaveholders. The Right and Duty of Southern Slaves and Northern Freemen* (Boston: Henry C. Wright, 1859), pp. 3–16.
39. *Congressional Globe,* 36th Cong., 1st sess., p. 12; *National Era*, Dec. 15, 1859; Nason and Russell, pp. 268–69; Wright, *No Rights*, p. 31.
40. *Congressional Globe,* 36th Cong., 1st sess., 1859, pp. 63–65; Wright, *Natick Resolution,* pp. 17–23; idem, *No Rights*, p. 23; Nason and Russell, pp. 269.
41. Mitchell, p. 75; C. Vann Woodward, *The Burden of Southern History,* rev. ed. (Baton Rouge: Louisiana State University Press, 1968), pp. 45–46; Donald, *Sumner*, p. 350; Thayer, p. 194; newspaper clipping of letter of D. McBridge to Doolittle, Dec. 31, 1859, James R. Doolittle Papers, Historical Society of Wisconsin, Madison; Wright, *Natick Resolution*, pp. 25–32.
42. *Natick Observer*, Dec. 10, 1859; *Springfield Republican,* Dec. 9, 1859; Mitchell, p. 78.
43. *Liberator*, Jan. 13, 1860, quoting from *New York Herald*; Wright, *No Rights*, pp. 20–21, 31–32; *Springfield Republican*, Jan. 9, 1860; Jan. 13, 1860; *Natick Observer*, Mar. 17, 1860.
44. Garrison, *Garrison,* 3: 482–84.
45. Clarke to Wilson, Jan. 27, 1860, and Wilson to Clarke, Jan. 29, 1860, Miscellaneous Papers, Houghton; Davis, "Liberty before Union," p. 83.
46. *Congressional Globe*, 36th Cong, 1st sess., 1859–60, pp. 98–107, 152, 257, 296–480; 494–99, 517–22; Charles H. Ambler, ed., "Correspondence of Robert M. T. Hunter, 1826—1876," in the *Annual Report of the American Historical Association, 1916,* 2 vols. (Washington: American Historical Association, 1918), 2: 278; Garrison, *Garrison*, 3: 494–95; *National Era*, Dec. 22, 1859; *Springfield Republican,* Dec. 21, 1859; *Natick Observer*, Dec. 24, 1859; Wilson to Clarke, June 29, 1860, James Freeman Clarke Papers, Houghton.

47. *New York Tribune,* Jan. 17, 1860; Jan. 18, 1860.
48. *Congressional Globe,* 36th Cong., 1st sess., 1860, pp. 568–72; *National Era,* Feb. 9, 1860; Wilson, *Rise and Fall,* 2: 660; *Liberator,* Feb. 3, 1860; *Springfield Republican,* Jan. 26, 1860.
49. *Congressional Globe*, 36th Cong., 1st sess., 1860, pp. 572–77; *National Era*, Feb. 9, 1860; Feb. 16, 1860; Wilson, *Rise and Fall,* 2: 660; *New York Times*, Jan. 26, 1860; *New York Tribune,* Jan. 26, 1860; *Springfield Republican*, Jan. 28, 1860; Mann, *Life of Wilson,* p. 79.
50. *Congressional Globe*, 36th Cong., 1st sess., 1860, pp. 592–98; Mann, *Life of Wilson,* pp. 79–80.
51. *New York Tribune,* Jan. 26, 1860; Jan. 27, 1860; Jan. 30, 1860; Feb. 6, 1860; *Springfield Republican,* Jan. 26, 1860; Jan. 27, 1860; Feb. 3, 1860; Wilson, *Rise and Fall,* 2: 652–53; C. D. Cleveland to Sumner, Jan. 29, 1860, Sumner Papers; R. A. Chapman to Dawes, Jan. 27, 1860, Dawes Papers; *Natick Observer*, Feb. 4, 1860.
52. Wilson to Lawrence, Dec. 19, 1859, Lawrence Papers; Wilson to Higginson, Dec. 24, 1859, and Sanborn to Higginson, Dec. 20 and 25, 1859, and Jan. 2, 1860, John Brown–Thomas Wentworth Higginson Papers, BPL; Sumner to Howe, Dec. 8, 1859, Howe Papers, Houghton; Rossbach, pp. 240–47; Richards, p. 445; Pickard, *Whittier Letters,* 3: 6.
53. *Mason Report*, pp. 30–32, 140–45.
54. Ibid., pp. 30–31, 100–1; *Springfield Republican,* Feb. 4, 1860; Richard Hinton, *John Brown and His Men* (New York: Funk & Wagnalls Company, 1894), pp. 135–37; *Natick Observer,* Jan. 28, 1860; *New York Times*, Feb. 11, 1860; *Congressional Globe*, 36th Cong., 1st sess., 1860, pp. 778–79, 848–50.
55. Harriet Wilson to Mrs. Claflin, Feb. 5, 1860, Claflin Papers; *Natick Observer,* Feb. 11, 1860; Mar. 3, 1860; *Boston Transcript*, Feb. 13, 1860; *Boston Advertiser*, Feb. 13, 1860; Wilson to Lawrence, Dec. 8, 1858, Mar. 17 and Apr. 7 and 12, 1860, Lawrence Papers; diary, *passim* Dec. 1859, Dec. 17, 1859, and Jan. 20, 21, 25 and 26, 1860, Adams Papers.
56. Diary, *passim*, Dec. 1860, and Everett to Hillard, Nov. 29, 1859, Everett Papers; Davis, "Liberty before Union," pp. 70–80, 102; O'Connor, pp. 137–41; Mrs. Chapman Coleman, ed., *The Life of John J. Crittenden,* 2 vols. (Philadelphia: J. B. Lippincott & Co, 1871), 2: 183–84; Hooper to Lawrence, Jan. 29, 1860, Lawrence Papers.
57. Davis, "Liberty before Union," pp. 92–102; diary, Dec. 3 and 17, 1859, Adams Papers; Coleman, pp. 182–85; Samuel Griswold Goodrich to Wilson, Jan. 31 [1860], Claflin Papers; Wilson to Chase, Feb. 5, 1860, Chase Papers, HSPa.
58. *New York Tribune,* Feb. 20, 1860; Griswold to Wilson, Jan. 31 [1860], Claflin Papers; George G. Fogg to Morgan, Jan. 28, 1860, Wilson to Morgan, Feb. 22, 1860, and Gideon Welles to Morgan, Feb. 25, 1860, Morgan Papers; Stone to Chase, Mar. 23, 1860, Chase Papers, LC.
59. D. L. Child to Wilson, Mar. 13, 1860, and Wilson to Child, Mar. 15, 1860, Anti-Slavery Manuscripts, BPL.
60. *Tribune Almanac,* 1861, pp. 39–40; *Springfield Republican*, Mar. 3, 1860; Mar. 23, 1860; Mar. 24, 1860; Mar. 27, 1860; Mar. 28, 1860; *New York Tribune,* Mar. 23, 1860; Mar. 26, 1860; Mar. 28, 1860; *Boston Transcript,* Apr. 3, 1860; *New York Times*, Mar. 28, 1860; Mar. 29, 1860; *Connecticut Courant*, Mar. 24, 1860; Mar. 31, 1860; Welles to Morgan, Mar. 14, 1860, Morgan Papers.

61. *Tribune Almanac,* 1861, pp. 39–40; *New York Times*, Apr. 6, 1860; Apr. 9, 1860; *Boston Transcript*, Apr. 3, 1860; Apri.6, 1860; *Springfield Republican*, Apr. 3, 1860; Apr. 4, 1860.
62. *Boston Advertiser*, June 13, 1860; Wilson, *Rise and Fall*, 2: 661–63; *Boston Transcript*, Feb. 13, 1860; Feb. 27, 1860; *Congressional Globe*, 36th Cong., 1st sess., 1860, pp. 2320–21, 2341–53.
63. Wilson, *Rise and Fall*, 2: 663–65.
64. Pierce, 3: 610–11; Wilson, *Rise and Fall*, 2: 627–29; Grimke, p. 315; diary, June 4, 1860, Adams Papers; *Springfield Republican*, June 6, 1860; *New York Tribune*, June 5, 1860.
65. Pierce, 3: 611–12; diary, June 9 and 10, 1860, Adams Papers; *Natick Citizen*, Mar. 21, 1879; *Liberator*, June 15, 1860; *New York Times*, June 10, 1860; *Springfield Republican*, June 6, 1860; June 12, 1860; Grimke, p. 317; *Congressional Globe*, 36th Cong., 1st sess., 1860, pp. 2590–2604; Wilson, *Rise and Fall*, 2: 631.
66. *Congressional Globe*, 36th Cong., 1st sess., 1860, pp. 357, 658, 1467, 1676–79; Wilson, *Rise and Fall*, 2: 579–80.
67. *Congressional Globe*, 36th Cong, 1st sess., 1860, pp. 1636–37.
68. Ibid., pp. 1684–88; *Springfield Republican*, Apr. 16, 1860; Apr. 20, 1860; *New York Tribune*, Apr. 13, 1860; Apr. 14, 1860; Wilson, *Rise and Fall*, 2: 581–82.
69. *Boston Transcript*, June 14, 1860; *New York Tribune*, June 18, 1860; Nason and Russell, p. 270.
70. Wilson, *Rise and Fall*, 2: 618–20; *Springfield Republican*, Mar. 5, 1860; *New York Times*, Mar. 2, 1860; Mar. 14, 1860; Mar. 21, 1860; *Congressional Globe*, 36th Cong., 1st sess., 1860, pp. 1118, 1245; *Boston Transcript*, Mar. 21, 1860; *Liberator*, Apr. 20, 1860.
71. *Congressional Globe*, 36th Cong., 1st sess., 1860, pp. 2207–11, 2269, 3067–68, 3099–110; *New York Times*, May 22, 1860; May 23, 1860; Wilson, *Rise and Fall*, 2: 620–23; *Boston Transcript*, June 6, 1860.
72. *Congressional Globe*, 36th Cong., 1st sess., 1860, pp. 1747–48, 1769, 2991–92; *Boston Transcript*, Apr. 20, 1860; May 4, 1860; *Springfield Republican*, Apr. 24, 1860; Apr. 28, 1860; Wilson to Hamilton Wilson, May 2, 1860, Wilson Papers, South Natick Museum.
73. *Congressional Globe*, 36th Cong., 1st sess., 1860, pp. 1508, 1991–2011, 2042–43, 3159, 3263–64; 3274; *New York Tribune*, May 10, 1860; May 11, 1860; June 23, 1860.
74. *National Era*, Mar. 22, 1860; *Congressional Globe*, 36th Cong., 1st sess., 1860, p. 1000, 1142–46, 3279; *New York Tribune*, June 27, 1860.
75. *New York Times*, late Feb. and Mar., 1860, *passim*; Crawford, *History of Natick*, p. 45; Faler, pp. 450–69; Dawley, p. 145; Foner, *Free Soil*, pp. 11–31; James L. Huston, "Facing an Angry Labor: the American Public Interprets the Shoemakers' Strike of 1860," *Civil War History* 28 (Sept. 1982): 200–6; Philip S. Foner, *History of the Labor Movement in the United States*, 3 vols. (New York: International Publishers, 1947), 1: 282–96.

Chapter 17

1. Wilson, *Rise and Fall*, 2: 689–90, 696–97.

2. Ibid., 690; *New York Tribune*, Apr. 14, 1860; Wilson to Carey, Apr. 16, 1860, Carey Papers; *New York Times*, May 5, 1860.
3. *New York Times*, Dec. 1, 1858; R. Gerald McMurty, ed., "Presidential Candidates of 1860," *Lincoln Lore*, 1518 (Aug. 1964): 1–3.
4. Wilson, *Rise and Fall*, 2: 694–95.
5. Ibid., 690–93; Kleeberg, pp. 62–64, 78; Johnson, *First Three Conventions*, pp. 83, 101, 105; Eldridge G. Keith, *A Paper on the Republican National Convention of 1860* (Urbana: University of Illinois, 1904), pp. 4, 12–13; Paul Kleppner, *The Third Electoral System, 1853–1892* (Chapel Hill: University of North Carolina Press, 1979), pp. 72–73; Emerson D. Fite, *The Presidential Campaign of 1860* (Port Washington: Kennikat Press, 1967), p. 122; Ashmun to Wilson, Apr. 22, 1860, Wilson Papers, LC; *Boston Transcript*, May 15, 1860; May 17, 1860.
6. *New York Tribune*, May 19, 1860; May 21, 1860; May 29, 1860; Wilson, *Rise and Fall*, 2: 694–95; Sumner to Seward, May 20, 1860, Seward Papers; diary, May 18, 1860, Adams Papers; Wilson to Stansbury, May 21, 1860, Wilson Papers, LC; *Boston Advertiser*, May 25, 1860; Seward, 2: 454–56.
7. *Liberator*, July 13, 1860.
8. Ibid; *National Anti-Slavery Standard*, July 14, 1860; July 21, 1860.
9. *Liberator*, July 13, 1860; July 20, 1860; *National Anti-Slavery Standard*, July 14, 1860; *Natick Observer*, July 14, 1860.
10. *Boston Advertiser*, July 12, 1860; *Springfield Republican*, July 12, 1860; July 14, 1860; July 21, 1860; Johannes, *Letters of Douglas*, pp. 497–98; Wilson to Israel Washburn Jr., Autograph File, Beinecke Library, Yale; Wilson, *Rise and Fall*, 2: 698–99.
11. *Boston Transcript*, July 18, 1860; July 19, 1860; July 24, 1860; Lawrence, p. 154; *New York Tribune*, July 25, 1860; July 27, 1860; *Natick Observer*, July 21, 1860; July 28, 1860.
12. *Springfield Republican*, Aug. 1, 1860; *Albany Journal*, July 30, 1860; Aug 1, 1860; Aug 3, 1860; Aug 4, 1860; *Albany Atlas and Argus*, Aug 3, 1860; Aug. 6, 1860 *New York Times*, Aug. 1, 1860; Aug. 6, 1860; *New York Tribune*, Aug. 10, 1860; Wilson to Lincoln, Aug. 25, 1860, R. T. Lincoln Papers.
13. Boston Transcript, Aug. 13, 1860; Aug. 14, 1860; Aug. 17, 1860; diary, Aug. 13, 1860, Adams Papers; Seward, 2: 459–60; *New York Tribune*, Aug. 17, 1860; Aug. 18, 1860; *Springfield Republican*, Aug. 18, 1860; *Kennebec Journal*, Aug. 17 to Sept. 7, 1860; Wilson to Lincoln, Aug. 25, 1860, R. T. Lincoln Papers.
14. *New York Tribune*, Aug. 27, 1860; *Tribune Almanac*, 1861, p. 39; *Boston Transcript*, Sept. 11, 1860; *Springfield Republican*, Sept. 8, 1860; Sept. 11, 1860; *Kennebec Journal*, Sept. 14, 1860.
15. Wilson to Lincoln, Aug. 25, 1860, R. T. Lincoln Papers; Roy P. Basle, ed. *The Collected Works of Abraham Lincoln*, 8 vols. (New Brunswick: Rutgers University Press, 1953), 4: 109.
16. Davis, "Liberty before Union," pp. 111–13; *Springfield Republican*, Aug. 24, 1860; Aug. 25, 1860; Aug. 27, 1860; Aug. 29, 1860; Aug. 30, 1860; *Boston Transcript*, Aug. 24, 1860; Aug. 29, 1860; diary, Aug. 20 and 30 and Sept. 1, 1860, Adams Papers; *Bird, a Biographical Sketch*, p. 49; Pearson, 1: 68, 92; *New York Tribune*, Aug. 27, 1860.
17. *Springfield Republican*, Sept. 5, 1860; *Boston Advertiser*, Sept. 7, 1860; Sept. 11, 1860; Sept. 12, 1860; *Boston Transcript*, Sept. 11, 1860; Sept. 12, 1860.

18. Henry Wilson, *The Position of John Bell and His Supporters* (Boston: Boston Bee Printing Company, 1860); *Springfield Republican*, Sept. 15, 1869; Sept. 18–20, 1860; Sept. 26, 1860; *Boston Advertiser*, Sept. 20, 1860; *Natick Observer*, Sept. 29, 1860.
19. Reinhart H. Luthin, *The First Lincoln Campaign* (Cambridge: Harvard University Press, 1944), pp. 168–71; *passim*, Aug.–Oct., 1860, Trumball papers; Wilmer C. Harris, *Public Life of Zarachiah Chandler, 1851–1875* (Lansing: Michigan Historical Collections, 1917), pp. 48–49; diary, Sept. 3 and 4, 1860, Adams Papers; Weed to Morgan, Sept. 26, 1860, Morgan Papers; Pierce, 3: 614.
20. Charles M. Knapp, *New Jersey Politics during the Period of the Civil War and Reconstruction* (Geneva, N. Y.: W. F. Humphrey, 1924), pp. 1–17; *New York Tribune*, Sept. 18, 1860; Sept. 21, 1860; *Newark Daily Advertiser*, Sept. 25, 1860; Sept. 28, 1860; Sept. 29, 1860; *New York Herald*, Oct. 3, 1860; Harriet Wilson to "Dear Sister," Oct. 7, 1860, Wilson Papers, South Natick Museum.
21. Diary, Oct. 12 and 13 and Nov. 8, 1860, Everett Papers; *New York Herald*, Oct. 11, 1860; Oct. 12, 1860; *Springfield Republican*, Oct. 13, 1860; Oct. 18, 1860; *Tribune Almanac*, 1861, pp. 47–48, 59–60, 62–63; *Boston Transcript*, Sept. 25, 1860; Oct. 10, 1860; *New York Times*, Oct. 9, 1860; *New York Tribune*, Oct. 17, 1860.
22. Pierce, 3: 614, 619; *Springfield Republican*, Oct. 13, 1860; *Natick Observer*, Oct. 13, 1860; diary, Oct. 16, 1860, Adams Papers; *Boston Transcript*, Oct. 16–19, 1860; Oct. 22, 1860.
23. *Springfield Republican*, Oct. 19, 1860; Oct. 20, 1860; Oct. 25, 1860; Oct. 30, 1860; *New York Tribune*, Oct. 26, 1860; Wilson to Sumner, Oct. 24, 1860, Sumner Papers; diary, Oct. 30, 1860, Adams Papers.
24. *Boston Transcript*, Oct. 31, 1860; Nov. 2, 1860; *Natick Observer*, Nov. 3, 1860; *Springfield Republican*, Nov. 6, 1860; Nov. 7, 1860; Stearns, *Life of Stearns*, p. 233; *Boston Advertiser*, Nov. 6, 1860; Peterson, p. 37; Burnham, pp. 191, 513; Congressional Quarterly Service, *Politics in America*, 3d ed. (Washington: Congressional Quarterly, 1969), p. 123.
25. *Boston Transcript*, Nov. 8, 1860; Wilson, *Rise and Fall*, 2: 699–700.
26. *Boston Advertiser*, Nov. 10, 1860; *Liberator*, Nov. 23, 1860; *Boston Courier*, Nov. 10, 1860; *New York Tribune*, Nov. 12, 1860; diary, Nov. 13, 1860, Adams Papers; *New York Times*, Nov. 12, 1860; Nov. 13, 1860; Merriam, 1: 274; Trumball to Wade, Nov. 9, 1860, Wade Papers; Howard K. Beale, ed., *Diary of Gideon Welles*, 3 vols. (New York: W. W. Norton, 1960), 1: 11; Seward to Fish, Dec. 11, 1860, Fish Papers.
27. Wilson, *Rise and Fall*, 2: 704; *Boston Transcript*, Nov. 24, 1860; Nov. 27, 1860; *New York Tribune*, Dec. 4, 1860.
28. Davis, "Liberty before Union," pp. 121–28; *Boston Advertiser*, Dec. 5, 1860; *Boston Transcript*, Dec. 4, 1860; Garrison, *Garrison*, 4: 1–8; Smalley, pp. 74–75, 84–86, 93–94; Pearson, 1: 133.
29. *Natick Observer*, Dec. 1, 1860; Dec. 15, 1860; *Congressional Directory*, 36th Cong., 2d sess, 1861, pp. 64–68; Seward, 2: 478–79; Pierce, 4: 4–9; Patrick M. Sowle, "The Conciliatory Republicans during the Winter of Secession" (Ph.D. diss., Duke University, 1963), pp. 15–23, 34–38; *Boston Advertiser*, Dec. 3, 1860; *New York Herald*, Dec. 4, 1860; Dec. 5, 1860.
30. *Congressional Globe*, 36th Cong, 2d sess., 1860, pp. 1, 3–5, 9–11; *New York Times*, Dec. 4, 1860; Dec. 5, 1860; *Boston Advertiser*, Dec. 7, 1860; *Boston Transcript*, Dec. 5, 1860; *Springfield Republican*, Dec. 6, 1860; diary, Dec. 5, 1860, Adams Papers; Wilson, *Rise and Fall*, 3: 15–21.

31. *Congressional Globe*, 36th Cong., 2d sess., 1860, pp. 24–35, 47–59; *Springfield Republican*, Dec. 15, 1860; Dec. 22, 1860; *New York Times*, Dec. 11, 1860; Dec. 18, 1860; Pearson, 1: 132–33; David M. Potter, *Lincoln and His Party in the Secession Crisis* (New Haven: Yale University Press, 1942), pp. 89–111; O. S. Ferry to Hawley, Dec. 11, 1860, Hawley Papers; Sowle, pp. 46–51; *Boston Advertiser*, Dec. 10, 1860; Merriam, 1: 174.
32. Pierce, 4: 12–13; Wilson to Chase, Dec. 15, 1860, Chase Papers, HSPa; Anderson, pp. 301–2, 307; Sowle, pp. 52–85; Potter, pp. 52–54; Davis, "Liberty before Union," pp. 130–31.
33. Wilson, *Rise and Fall*, 3: 60–71.
34. Sowle, pp. 151–56; Potter, pp. 156–61; Newton, pp. 280–81.
35. Henry Wilson, *Letter of Senator Wilson to Hon. Caleb Cushing* (Washington: National Republican Office, 1860); *Boston Transcript*, Dec. 17, 1860; *Springfield Republican*, Dec. 17, 1860; *Natick Observer*, Dec. 22, 1860.
36. Andrew to Sumner, Dec. 5, 1860, Sumner Papers; Morgan to Washburn, Dec. 12, 1860, Israel Washburn Papers; *Boston Advertiser*, Dec. 24, 1860; diary, Dec. 22 and 25, 1860, Adams Papers; *Boston Transcript*, Dec. 24, 1860; William B. Hesseltine, *Lincoln and the War Governors* (New York: Alfred A. Knopf, 1948), p. 110; Pearson, 1: 132–36; Joseph Schafer, ed., *Intimate Letters of Carl Schurz, 1841–1869* (New York: DaCapo Press, 1970), p. 238; Dawes to J. D. Colt, Dec. 23, 1860, Dawes Papers; *Natick Observer*, Jan. 5, 1861; *New York Times*, Dec. 31, 1860.
37. Curtis, 1: 329–35; Pearson, 1: 134, 137, 139; *New York Tribune*, Jan. 3, 1861; Alley to F. W. Bird, Jan. 1, 1861, Charles S. Bird Papers, Houghton; *New York Tribune*, Jan. 15, 1861; diary, Jan. 3, 1861, Adams Papers; Adams to Andrew, undated [probably Jan. 4, 1861] and Schouler to Andrew, Jan. 8, 1861, John A. Andrew Papers, MHS.
38. Wilson, *Rise and Fall*, 3: 96–102.
39. Sowle, pp. 107–47, 195–216; Potter, pp. 92–101; diary, Dec 16 and 27, 1860, and Jan. 3, 1861, and Dana to Adams, Dec. 20, 1860, Adams to Dana, Dec. 23, 1860, Adams to Horace Gray Jr., Dec. 30, 1860, Adams to Charles Francis Adams Jr., Dec. 30, 1860, and Henry B. Adams to Charles Francis Adams Jr., Dec. 22 and 26, 1860, Adams Papers; Pierce, 4: 9–12; *Boston Advertiser*, Jan. 1, 1861.
40. Potter, p. 60; Wilson, *Rise and Fall*, 3: 71, 73; *Congressional Globe*, 36th Cong, 2d sess., 1860–1861, pp. 185–205, 210–11, 239; Sowle, pp. 181–93, 211–13; *New York Tribune*, Jan. 4, 1861.
41. *Natick Observer*, Jan. 10, 1861.
42. Sowle, pp. 28–29; Wilson to Chase, Dec. 15, 1860, Chase Papers, HSPa; Dixon to Mark Howard [Dec. 21, 1860], James Dixon Papers, Connecticut Historical Society, Hartford; Duberman, *Adams*, p. 256; diary, Jan. 3, 1861, and Mar. 11, 1874, and Henry Adams to C. F. Adams Jr., Jan. 2, 1861, Adams Papers; Donald, *Sumner*, p. 378; telegram from Wilson to Lincoln, Jan. 4, 1861, Leonard Swett to Lincoln, Jan. 5, 1861, and Wilson to Lincoln, Jan. 5, 1861, R. T. Lincoln Papers.
43. Diary, Jan. 14, 1861, and *passim*, later Dec. 1860 and Jan. 1861 and Adams to Henry Adams, Jan. 15, 1861, Adams Papers; Dixon to Mark Howard, Jan. 2, 1861, Dixon Papers; Wilson, *Rise and Fall*, 3: 37–38; Potter, pp. 297–99; *Springfield Republican*, Jan. 12, 1861; *New York Tribune*, Jan. 17, 1861.
44. Adams to Andrew, Jan. 4, 1861, and Adams to Palfrey, Jan. 5, 1861, Adams Papers; Wilson, *Rise and Fall*, 3: 161–72; Sumner to Bird, Jan. 9, 1864, Charles Bird Papers; Seward to Wilson, May 28, 1870, Seward Papers; Marcus Benjamin, ed., *Washington*

during War Time (Washington: Grand Army of the Republic Committee on Literature for the Encampment, n.d.), pp. 16–18, 101.

45. Harriet Wilson to Mrs. Claflin, Jan. 14, 1861, Claflin Papers.
46. Diary, Jan. 3, 1861, Adams Papers; Adams to Andrew, Jan. 4, 1861, Wilson to Andrew, Jan. 16, 1861, and Sumner to Andrew, Jan. 23 and 24, 1861, Andrew Papers; *The War of the Rebellion; a Compilation of the Official Records of the Union and Confederate Armies,* 130 vols. (Washington: Government Printing Office, 1880–1901), ser. 3, 1: 37.
47. *Congressional Globe*, 36th Cong., 2d sess., 1861, pp. 250–59, 290, 426, 521, 542–43; *New York Times,* Jan. 10, 1861; Jan. 31, 1861.
48. *Congressional Globe*, 36th Cong., 2d sess., 1861, pp. 328–32, 341–44, 360–61, 379–89; Wilson, *Rise and Fall,* 3: 48–59; Henry Adams to C. F. Adams Jr., Jan. 17, 1861, Adams Papers; Sumner to Chase, Jan. 19, 1861, Chase Papers, LC; *National Anti-Slavery Standard,* Jan. 19, 1861; Trefouse, *Radical Republicans*, pp. 152–53; *New York Tribune,* Jan. 14, 1861; Sowle, p. 287.
49. Samuel S. Cox, *Eight Years in Congress, from 1857–1865* (New York: D. Appleton & Company, 1865), p. 28; *Congressional Globe*, 36th Cong., 2d sess., 1861, pp. 409, 443, 505–8, 521, 542–43; Colfax to Carter, Jan. 27, 1861, Carter Papers.
50. *Congressional Globe*, 36th Cong, 2d sess., 1861, pp. 444–47, 465, 484–89.
51. Ibid., pp. 484–87, 501–3, 536; Wilson, *Rise and Fall,* 3: 147–59; Nason and Russell, p. 288; *Natick Citizen,* Mar. 21, 1879; *New York Tribune*, Jan. 24, 1861; Jan. 29, 1861; Cowdin, p. 11.
52. *New York Times*, Jan. 16, 1861.
53. Sowle, pp. 310–13, 324, 362–65; Potter, pp. 116–26; Winthrop, pp. 212–15; Pierce, 4: 17–19; diary, Jan. 31, 1861 and letters, *passim*, early Feb., 1861, especially Henry Adams to C. F. Adams Jr., Feb. 5, 1861, Adams Papers.
54. *New York Times*, Jan. 25, 1861; Jan. 26, 1851; *New York Tribune*, Jan. 28, 1861; Jan. 29, 1861; Garrison, *Garrison,* 4: 1–8.
55. Pierce, 4: 13–14; diary, Jan. 23, 28, and 29 and Feb. 2 and 10, 1861, and Henry Adams to C. F. Adams Jr., Jan. 17 and Feb. 5 and 8, 1861, and Adams to Dana, Feb. 9, 1861, Adams Papers; John Bingham to Giddings, Feb. 1, 1861, Giddings Papers; Colfax to Carter, Jan. 27, 1861, Carter Papers; *Boston Transcript,* Jan. 25, 1861.
56. Wilson to Lincoln, Jan. 19, 1861, R. T. Lincoln Papers; Donald, *Sumner,* p. 382.
57. Seward to Adams, Feb. 4, 1861, and diary, Feb. 5, 1861, Adams Papers; Sumner to Andrew, Jan. 28, 1861, and Harrison Ritchie to Andrew, Feb. 6 and 8, 1861, Andrew Papers; Wilson to Seward, May 23, 1870 and Seward to Wilson, May 28, 1870, Seward Papers; *Springfield Republican,* Feb. 13, 1861; Henry Wilson, "Edwin M. Stanton," *Atlantic Monthly* 25 (Feb. 1870): 237–38; idem., "Jeremiah S. Black and Edwin M. Stanton," *Atlantic Monthly* 26 (Oct. 1870): 464–68.
58. *Boston Advertiser*, Feb. 16, 1861; *Natick Observer*, Feb. 23, 1861; *Congressional Globe,* 36th Cong., 2d sess., 1861, pp. 813–14, 991–93, 1026, 1065; *New York Tribune*, Feb. 21, 1861; Feb. 26–28, 1861; *New York Times*, Feb. 14, 1861.
59. *Congressional Globe*, 36th Cong., 2d sess., 1861, pp. 1088–94; Sowle, pp. 392–94.
60. *Boston Transcript, passim*, Feb. 12–23, 1861; *New York Times, passim*, Feb. 12–25, 1861; Sowle, p. 294–97, 371, 397–404; Giddings to Grotius R. Giddings, Feb. 5, 1861, Giddings Papers; Daniel W. Crofts, "Secession Winter: William Henry Seward and the Decision for War," *Civil War History* 65 (July 1984): 235–55; diary, Feb. 19, 1861, Adams Papers; Taylor, p. 451.

61. Robinson, *"Warrington,"* pp. 93–94; *Boston Advertiser*, Jan. 30, 1861; Feb. 1, 1861; *Springfield Republican*, Feb. 2, 1861; Feb. 7, 1861; *Boston Transcript*, Jan. 31, 1861; diary, Jan. 28 and Feb. 2, 1861, and Henry Adams to C. F. Adams Jr., Feb. 5, 1861, and Adams to C. F. Adams Jr., Feb. 10, 1861, Adams Papers; Pearson, 1: 156–57; Alley to Claflin, Jan. 28, 1861, Claflin Papers; Wilson to Andrew, Jan. 29, 1861, Andrew Papers; Davis, "Liberty before Union," pp. 210–12, 219–20.
62. Wilson, *Rise and Fall*, 3: 83–87.
63. *Congressional Globe*, 36th Cong., 2d sess., 1861, pp. 1088–94; Nason and Russell, pp. 289–96; *Natick Observer*, Feb. 23, 1861; *New York Tribune*, Feb. 22, 1861; *Liberator*, Mar. 22, 1861; Wilson, *Rise and Fall*, 3: 78–80.
64. *Congressional Globe*, 36th Cong., 2d sess., 1861, pp. 1088–94; Wilson, *Rise and Fall*, 3: 78–80; Nason and Russell, pp. 197–98; *New York Tribune*, Feb. 22, 1861; Feb. 23, 1861; *Liberator*, Mar. 15, 1861; Mann, *Life of Wilson*, pp. 86–89.
65. *New York Tribune*, Feb. 22, 1861; *Natick Observer*, Mar. 2, 1861; Whittier to Wilson, Feb. 23, 1861, John Greenleaf Whittier Papers, Essex Institute, Salem, Massachusetts; Nason and Russell, pp. 299–303; *Liberator*, Mar. 22, 1861; Garrison to Wilson, Feb. 26, 1861, Miscellaneous Papers, Houghton.
66. *New York Times*, Feb. 27–Mar. 1, 1861; *New York Tribune*, Feb. 27, 1861; Mar. 1, 1861.
67. *Congressional Globe*, 36th Cong, 2d sess., 1861, pp. 1271–74, 1280–85, 1303–18, 1342–63; Wilson, *Rise and Fall*, 3: 94–95; *New York Times*, Feb. 28–Mar. 2, 1861; *Springfield Republican*, Mar. 2, 1861; Mar. 6, 1861; *Boston Advertiser*, Mar. 6, 1861; Mar. 8, 1861; Sowle, pp. 434–43.
68. *Springfield Republican*, Mar. 9, 1861; *Baltimore Sun*, Mar. 5, 1861; *Congressional Globe*, 36th Cong., 2d sess., 1861, pp. 1402–3; Pierce, 4: 20; Wilson, *Rise and Fall*, 3: 42, 81–82; Phelps, pp. 365–66
69. *New York Tribune*, Mar. 5, 1861; *Springfield Republican*, Mar. 9, 1861; *Congressional Globe*, 37th Congress, Special Senate sess., 1861, pp. 1146, 1434, 1461; *Natick Observer*, Mar. 16, 1861.
70. *Boston Transcript*, Mar. 6, 1861; *Congressional Globe*, 37th Cong., Special Senate sess., 1861, pp. 1461–62; Robert W. Johannsen, "The Douglas Democrats and the Crisis of Disunion," *Civil War History* 9 (Sept. 1963): 242; *Boston Journal*, Mar. 21, 1861; Pierce, 4: 25.
71. George H. Mayer, *The Republican Party, 1854–1946* (New York: Oxford University Press, 1967), pp. 91–92; Carl R. Fish, "Lincoln and the Patronage," *American Historical Review* 8 (Oct. 1902): 53–59; *New York Times*, Mar. 7, 1861; Mar. 8, 1861; Mar. 13, 1861; Mar. 30, 1861; Apr. 5, 1861; *Boston Advertiser*, Apr. 1, 1861; *Springfield Republican*, Mar. 13–16, 1861; Mar. 22, 1861; Apr. 6, 1861; *Boston Transcript*, Mar. 14, 1861; Mar. 15, 1861; Mar. 30, 1861; Apr. 8–13, 1861; Sumner to Bird, Mar. 10, 1861, Bird Papers; Andrew to Sumner, Mar. 11, 1861, and Alley to Sumner, Mar. 13 and 15, 1861, Sumner Papers; Gattel, *Palfrey*, pp. 236–41; Pierce, 4: 32–33; diary, Mar. 28 and Apr. 3, 1861, Adams Papers; *New York Tribune*, Apr. 12, 1861; Apr. 13, 1861.
72. Fish, pp. 60–61; *Boston Transcript*, Mar. 21, 1861; Mar. 23, 1861; Sumner to Seward, Mar. 18, 1861, Seward Papers; Andrew to Wilson, Mar. 11, 1861, and Wilson to Andrew, Mar. 14, 1861, Andrew Papers.
73. *Tribune Almanac*, 1861, p. 56; *Springfield Republican*, Apr. 4, 1861; Apr. 6, 1861; *Boston Advertiser*, Apr. 3, 1861; *New York Tribune*, Apr. 4, 1861.

74. Wilson, *Rise and Fall*, 3: 200–11; Potter, pp. 323–74.
75. Ibid., 212.

BIBLIOGRAPHY

Manuscripts Cited

Adams Family Papers, Massachusetts Historical Society
John A. Andrew Papers, Massachusetts Historical Society
Anti-Slavery Manuscripts, Boston Public Library
Autograph File, Beinecke Library, Yale University
George Bancroft Papers, Massachusetts Historical Society
Nathaniel Banks Papers, Library of Congress
Charles S. Bird Papers, Houghton Library, Harvard University
Francis W. Bird Papers, Houghton Library, Harvard University
Samuel Bowles Papers, Yale University
George N. Briggs Papers, American Antiquarian Society
John Brown–Thomas Wentworth Higginson Papers, Boston Public Library
Burlingame Family Papers, Library of Congress
Benjamin F. Butler Papers, Library of Congress
Lewis D. Campbell Papers, Ohio Historical Society
Henry C. Carey Papers, Edward Carey Gardiner Collection, Historical Society of Pennsylvania
Robert Carter Papers, Houghton Library, Harvard University
Cartland Family Papers, Massachusetts Historical Society
Chamberlain Papers, Boston Public Library
Clipping Booklet, Morse Institute, Natick, Massachusetts
Salmon P. Chase Papers, Historical Society of Pennsylvania
Salmon P. Chase Papers, Library of Congress
Lydia Maria Child--John Greenleaf Whittier Papers, Library of Congress
Lydia Maria Child Papers, Anti-Slavery Collection, Cornell University
William Claflin Papers, Rutherford B. Hayes Library, Fremont, Ohio
James Freeman Clarke Papers, Houghton Library, Harvard University
Schuyler Colfax Papers, Library of Congress
Richard H. Dana Jr. Papers, Massachusetts Historical Society

John W. Davis Papers, American Antiquarian Society
Henry L. Dawes Papers, Library of Congress
James Dixon Papers, Connecticut Historical Society
James R. Doolittle Papers, Historical Society of Wisconsin
Edward Everett Papers, Massachusetts Historical Society
William P. Fessenden Papers, Library of Congress
Hamilton Fish Papers, Library of Congress
C. E. French Papers, Massachusetts Historical Society
William Lloyd Garrison Papers, Boston Public Library
William Lloyd Garrison Papers, Smith College Library
Joshua Giddings Papers, Ohio Historical Society
Joshua Giddings–George W. Julian Papers, Library of Congress
Simon Gratz Autograph Collection, Historical Society of Pennsylvania
John P. Hale Papers, New Hampshire Historical Society
Nathan Hale Jr. Papers, Smith College Library
Joseph R. Hawley Papers, Library of Congress
Thomas Wentworth Higginson Papers, Houghton Library, Harvard University
George Frisbie Hoar Papers, Massachusetts Historical Society
Howe Family Papers, Houghton Library, Harvard University
Samuel Gridley Howe Papers, Massachusetts Historical Society
Charles Hudson Papers, American Antiquarian Society
Samuel Hunt Papers, John Hay Library, Brown University
Reverdy Johnson Papers, Library of Congress
Amos A. Lawrence Papers, Massachusetts Historical Society
Joshua Leavitt Papers, Library of Congress
Robert Todd Lincoln Papers, Library of Congress
Horace Mann Papers, Massachusetts Historical Society
Miscellaneous Collection, Boston Public Library
Miscellaneous Papers, Houghton Library, Harvard University
Edwin D. Morgan Papers, New York State Library, Albany
George R. Morton Miscellaneous Papers, Rutherford B. Hayes Library
Marcus Morton Papers, Massachusetts Historical Society
Norcross Family Collection, Massachusetts Historical Society
John Gorham Palfrey Papers, Houghton Library, Harvard University
Theodore Parker Papers, Massachusetts Historical Society
Edward L. Pierce Papers, Houghton Library, Harvard University
Republican Party, Minnesota State Central Committee Papers, Minnesota Historical Society
Charles Robinson Papers, University of Kansas
Charles Robinson Papers, Kansas State Historical Society
William S. Robinson Papers, Boston Public Library
William Schouler Papers, Massachusetts Historical Society

William H. Seward Papers, University of Rochester
Gerrit Smith Papers, Syracuse University
Charles Sumner Papers, Houghton Library, Harvard University
Eli Thayer Papers, John Hay Library, Brown University
Lyman Trumball Papers, Library of Congress
Benjamin Wade Papers, Library of Congress
Emory Washburne Papers, Massachusetts Historical Society
Israel Washburn Jr. Papers, Library of Congress
Daniel Webster Papers, Dartmouth College
Gideon Welles Papers, Library of Congress
John G. Whittier Papers, Essex Institute, Salem, Massachusetts
Whittier-Pickard Papers, Houghton Library, Harvard University
Henry Wilson Papers, Library of Congress
Henry Wilson Papers, John Hay Library, Brown University
Henry Wilson Papers, New York Public Library
Henry Wilson Papers, South Natick Museum
Robert Winthrop Papers, Massachusetts Historical Society

Government Documents

Alleged Assault upon Senator Sumner, House Report, No. 182, 34th Congress, 1st session

Congressional Directory, 1855–1861

Congressional Globe, 1855–1861

Congressional Record, 1875

Laws of the State of New-Hampshire; Passed June Session, 1833

Laws of New Hampshire, vol.10, Second Constitutional Period, 1829–1835

Legislative Documents of the Massachusetts Senate (1840–1857), manuscript collection, Massachusetts State Library Archives

Massachusetts General Court, House, journal, 1841, 1842, 1846, 1850 manuscript, Massachusetts State Library Archives

Massachusetts General Court, House, *Documents printed by Order of the House of Representatives*, Massachusetts State Library Archives, 1841, 1842, 1846, 1850

Massachusetts, General Court, Senate, journal, 1844, 1845, 1851, 1852 manuscript, Massachusetts State Library Archives

New Hampshire, House of Representatives, journal, 1833

Official Report of the Debates and Proceedings in the State Convention Assembled May 4, 1853, to Revise and Amend the Constitution of the Commonwealth of Massachusetts 3 vols., Boston, Massachusetts

Report of the Select Committee of the Senate Appointed to Inquire into the Late Invasion and Seizure of the Public Property at Harper's Ferry [Mason Committee] Washington: 36th Congress, 1860

Newspapers

Albany Argus
Albany Journal
(Augusta, Maine) *Kennebec Journal*
(Baltimore) *Sun*
Boston Advertiser
Boston Atlas
Boston Bee
Boston Chronicle
Boston Commonwealth, 1851–1854
Boston Commonwealth, 1862–1875
Boston Courier
(Boston) *The Emancipator*
(Boston) *Daily Emancipator and Republican*
(Boston) *Free State Rally and Texas Chain-Breaker*
Boston Journal
(Boston) *The Liberator*
(Boston) *The Pilot*
Boston Post
(Boston) *Semi-Weekly Emancipator and Republican*
Boston Telegraph
Boston Transcript
Boston Traveller
Boston Whig
Cincinnati Gazette
(Columbus) *Ohio State Journal*
(Concord, New Hampshire) *Herald of Freedom*
(Concord) *New Hampshire Patriot*
Dedham Gazette
(Hartford) *Connecticut Courant*
Indianapolis Journal
(Jackson, Michigan) *American Citizen*
Lowell Courier
Natick Bulletin
Natick Citizen
Natick Observer
New York Herald

(New York) *The Independent*
(New York) *National Anti-Slavery Standard*
New York Post
New York Times
New York Tribune
New York Weekly Tribune
Newark Daily Advertiser
Northampton Courier
Philadelphia Press
Springfield Republican
(Trenton, New Jersey) *True American*
(Washington) *National Era*
(Washington) *National Intelligencer*
(Washington) *Union*
(Watertown) *New York Reformer*
Worcester Spy

Contemporary Magazines

Atlantic Monthly
(Brownson's) *Quarterly Review*

Works by Wilson

The Central American Question. Washington: Buell & Blanchard, 1856.

Defence of the Republican Party. Washington: Buell & Blanchard, 1857.

"Edwin M. Stanton," *Atlantic Monthly* 25 (Feb. 1870): 234–46.

A History of the Rise and Fall of the Slave Power in America. 3 vols. Boston: Houghton Mifflin Company, 1872–1877.

"Jeremiah S. Black and Edwin M. Stanton," *Atlantic Monthly* 26 (Oct. 1870): 463–75.

Letter of Senator Wilson to Hon. Caleb Cushing. Washington: National Republican Office, 1860.

The New Constitution. Boston: White & Potter, 1853.

Personalities and Aggressions of Mr. Butler. Washington: Buell & Blanchard, 1856.

The Position of John Bell and His Supporters. Boston: Bee Printing Company, 1860.

Speech at the First New England Temperance Convention, Boston, October 3rd, 4th, 1866. Boston: S.M. Usher, 1866.

Speech on Prohibition, Tremont Temple, April 15, 1867. n. p.New York : *American* Tract Society, 1867.

Stand By the Republican Colors! Washington: 1872.

State of Affairs in Kansas. Washington: Republican Association of the District of Columbia, 1856.

Unpublished Theses and Dissertations

Anderson, Godfrey T. "The Slavery Issue as a Factor in Massachusetts Politics from the Compromise of 1850 to the Outbreak of the Civil War." Ph.D. dissertation, University of Chicago, 1944.

Bean, William G. "The Transformation of Parties in Massachusetts, with Special Reference to the Antecedents of Republicanism, 1848–1860." Ph.D. dissertation, Harvard University, 1922.

Brown, Thomas H. "George Sewell Boutwell: Public Servant (1818–1905). "Ph.D. dissertation, New York University, 1979.

Davis, Stuart J. "Liberty Before Union: Massachusetts and the Coming of the Civil War." Ph.D. dissertation, University of Massachusetts, 1975.

Hodgson, Michael Catherine. "Caleb Cushing, Attorney General of the United States." Ph.D. dissertation, Catholic University of America, 1955.

Kenney, Jean C. "An Analysis of Political Alignments in Massachusetts as Revealed in the Constitutional Convention of 1853." M.A. thesis, Smith College, 1951.

Loubert, J. Daniel. "The Orientation of Henry Wilson, 1812–1856." Ph.D. dissertation, Boston University, 1952.

Mulkern, John R. "The Know-Nothing Party in Massachusetts." Ph.D. dissertation, Boston University, 1963.

Rice, Arthur H. "Henry B. Stanton as a Political Abolitionist." Ed.D. dissertation, Columbia University, 1968.

Sowle, Patrick M. "The Conciliatory Republicans during the Winter of Secession." Ph.D. dissertation, Duke University, 1963.

Books and Pamphlets

Abbott, Richard H. *Cobbler in Congress*. Lexington: University of Kentucky Press, 1972.

Adams, Charles Francis, Jr. *Charles Francis Adams*. Boston: Houghton Mifflin and Company, 1900.

Adams, Charles Francis, Jr. *Richard Henry Dana, Jr., a Biography*. 2 vols. Boston: Houghton Mifflin and Company, 1890.

Adams, Henry. *The Education of Henry Adams: an Autobiography*. Boston: Houghton Mifflin Company, 1918.

Albree, John, ed. *Whittier Correspondence from the Oak Knoll Collections, 1830–1892*. Salem, Mass.: Essex Book and Printing Club, 1911.

Ambler, Charles H., ed. "Correspondence of Robert M. T. Hunter, 1826–1876," *Annual Report of the American Historical Association.* vol.2. Washington: Government Printing Office, 1918.

American Anti-Slavery Society. *Annual Reports.* 1834–1841, 1854–1861. New York: American Anti-Slavery Society, 1834–1841, 1854–1861

American Anti-Slavery Society. *Proceedings of the American Anti-Slavery Society at Its Third Decade.* New York: American Anti-Slavery Society, 1864.

Ames, Blanche Butler. *Chronicles from the Nineteenth Century: Family Letters of Blanche Butler and Adelbert Ames.* 2 vols. Clinton, Mass.: Colonial Press, 1937.

Anbinder, Tyler. *Nativism and Slavery.* New York: Oxford University Press, 1992.

Austin, George L. *The History of Massachusetts from the Landing of the Pilgrims to the Present Time.* Boston: B. B. Russell, 1876.

Bacon, Oliver N. *A History of Natick.* Boston: Damrell & Moore, Printers, 1856.

Bailey, Hugh C. *Hinton Rowan Helper: Abolitionist-Racist.* University: University of Alabama Press, 1965.

Baldwin, Thomas W., comp. *Vital Records of Natick, Massachusetts to 1850.* Boston: F. H. Gilson & Co., 1910.

Bartlett, Irving H. *Daniel Webster.* New York: W. W. Norton & Company, 1978.

Bartlett, Irving H. *Wendell Phillips, Brahmin Radical.* Boston: Beacon Press, 1961.

Bartlett, Ruhl J. *John C. Fremont and the Republican Party.* New York: DeCapo Press, 1970.

Basler, Roy P., ed. *The Collected Works of Abraham Lincoln.* 8 vols. New Brunswick: Rutgers University Press, 1953.

Baum, Dale. *The Civil War Party System: The Case of Massachusetts, 1848–1876.* Chapel Hill: University of North Carolina Press, 1984.

Beale, Howard K., ed. *Diary of Gideon Welles.* 3 vols. New York: W. W. Norton, 1960.

Benjamin, Marcus, ed. *Washington during War Time.* Washington: Grand Army of the Republic Committee on Literature for the Encampment, n.d.

Bigelow, John. *Retrospections of an Active Life.* 5 vols. New York: The Baker & Taylor Co., 1909–1913.

Billington, Ray A. *The Protestant Crusade, 1830–1860.* New York: Rinehart Company, 1952.

Bird, Francis William, a Biographical Sketch. [By his children] Boston: privately printed, 1897.

Bishop, Frank M. *300th Anniversary of the First Congregational Church, Natick, Massachusetts.* Boston: Lincoln & Smith, 1951.

Blaine, James G. *Twenty Years of Congress.* 2 vols. Norwich, Conn.: Henry Hill Publishing Company, 1884–1886.

Bloun, Francis X. *The Boston Region, 1810–1850.* Ann Arbor: UMI Research Press, 1978.

Blue, Frederick J. *The Free Soilers: Third Party Politics, 1848–1854*. Urbana: University of Illinois Press, 1973.

Boutwell, George H. *Reminiscences of Sixty Years in Public Affairs*. 2 vols. New York: McClure, Phillips, 1902.

Brauer, Kinley J. *Cotton versus Conscience: Massachusetts Whig Politics and Southwestern Expansion, 1843–1848*. Lexington: University of Kentucky Press, 1967.

Brigham, Johnson. *James Harlan*. Iowa City: State Historical Society of Iowa, 1913.

Brock, William R. *Parties and Political Conscience American Dilemmas, 1840–1860*. Millwood, N.Y.: KTO Press, 1979.

Brockett, L. P. *Men of Our Day*. Philadelphia: Zeisler, McCurdy & Co., 1868.

Brooks, Noah. *Washington, D.C. in Lincoln's Time*. New York: Collier Books, 1962.

Buckingham, Joseph T. *Personal Memoirs and Recollections of Editorial Life*. 2 vols. Boston: Ticknor, Reed, and Fields, 1852.

Buel, J. W. *Heroes of the Plains*. St. Louis: Historical Publishing Company, 1884.

Burnham, W. Dean. *Presidential Ballots, 1836–1892*. Baltimore: Johns Hopkins Press, 1955.

Butler, Benjamin P. *Butler's Book: Autobiography and Personal Reminiscences*. Boston: A. M. Thayer & Co., 1892.

Child, David L. *An Appeal from David L. Child, Editor of the Anti-Slavery Standard, to the Abolitionists*. Albany: Albany Evening Journal, 1844.

Claflin, Mary B. *Under the Elms*. Boston: Thomas Y. Crowell, 1895.

Clark, George F. *History of Temperance Reform in Massachusetts, 1813–1883*. Boston: Clarke & Carruth, 1888.

Coleman, Mrs. Chapman, ed. *The Life of John J. Crittenden*. 2 vols. Philadelphia: J. B. Lippincott & Co., 1871.

Congdon, Charles T. *Reminiscences of a Journalist*. Boston: James R. Osgood and Company, 1880.

Congressional Quarterly Series. *Politics in America*. 3d ed. Washington: Congressional Quarterly, 1969.

Conklin, Edward P. *Middlesex County and Its People*. 5 vols. New York: Lewis Historical Publishing Company, 1927.

Corning, Charles R. *Amos Tuck*. Exeter, N.H.: The News Letter Press, 1902.

Cowdin, Elliott C. *A Tribute to the Memory of Henry Wilson*. New York: Union League Club of New York, 1875.

Cox, Samuel S. *Eight Years in Congress, from 1857–1865*. New York: D. Appleton & Company, 1865.

Crandall, Andrew W. *The Early History of the Republican Party, 1854–1856*. Boston: R. G. Badger, 1928.

Crawford, Michael. *History of Natick, Massachusetts, 1650–1976*. Natick: Natick Historical Commission, 1976.

Curtis, Benjamin R., Jr., ed. *A Memoir of Robert Benjamin Curtis*. 2 vols. Boston: Little, Brown and Company, 1879.

Curtis, Francis. *The Republican Party*. 2 vols. New York: G. P. Putnam's Sons, 1904.

Darling, Arthur B. *Political Changes in Massachusetts, 1824–1848*. New Haven: Yale University Press, 1925.

Dawley, Alan. *Class and Community: The Industrial Revolution in Lynn*. Cambridge: Harvard University Press, 1976.

Desmond, Humphrey J. *The Know-Nothing Party*. Washington: The New Century Press, 1904.

Donald, David. *Charles Sumner and the Coming of the Civil War*. New York: Alfred A. Knopf, 1960.

Donald, David. *Lincoln's Herndon*. New York: Alfred A. Knopf, 1948.

Dorr, Rheta C. *Susan B. Anthony, the Woman Who Changed the Mind of a Nation*. New York: Frederick A. Stokes Company, 1928.

Douglass, Frederick. *Life and Times of Frederick Douglass*. New York: Pathway Press, 1941.

Duberman, Martin B. *Charles Francis Adams, 1807–1886*. Boston: Houghton Mifflin Company, 1961.

Dwight, Timothy. *Travels in New-England and New-York*. 4 vols. New Haven: T. Dwight, 1821–1822.

Dyer, Oliver. *Great Senators of the United States Forty Years Ago*. New York: Robert Bonner's Sons, 1889.

Dyer, Oliver. *Phonographic Report of the Proceedings of the National Free Soil Convention*, 1848. Buffalo: G. H. Derby & Company, 1848.

Edelstein, Tilden G. *Strange Enthusiasm: A Life of Thomas Wentworth Higginson*. New Haven: Yale University Press, 1968.

Fairbank, Calvin. *Rev. Calvin Fairbank during Slavery Times*. New York: Negro Universities Press, 1969.

Faler, Paul G. *Mechanics and Manufacturers in the Early Industrial Revolution: Lynn, Massachusetts, 1780–1860*. Albany: State University Press, 1981.

Farmer, John, and Jacob B. Moore. *A Gazetteer of the State of New Hampshire*. Concord: Jacob B. Moore, 1823.

Fehrenbacher, Don E. *Prelude to Greatness: Lincoln in the 1850s*. Stanford: Stanford University Press, 1962.

First Congregational Church, Natick, Mass. *The Confession of Faith, with an Historical Sketch and List of Members*. Boston: Congregational House, 1877.

Fite, Emerson D. *The Presidential Campaign of 1860*. Port Washington, N.Y.: Kennikat Press, 1967.

Flower, Frank A. *History of the Republican Party*. Springfield: Union Publishing Company, 1884.

Fogg, Alonzo J. *The Statistics and Gazetteer of New Hampshire*. Concord: D. L. Guernsey, 1874.

Foner, Eric. *Free Soil, Free Labor, Free Men*. New York: Oxford University Press, 1970.

Foner, Philip S. *History of the Labor Movement in the United States*. 3 vols. New York: International Publishers, 1947.

Formisano, Ronald P. *The Transformation of Political Culture: Masssachusetts Politics, 1790s–1840s*. New York: Oxford University Press, 1983.

Forney, John W. *Anecdotes of Public Men*. 2 vols. New York: DaCapo Press, 1970.

Friedman, Lawrence J. *Gregarious Saints*. Cambridge: Cambridge University Press, 1982.

Fuess, Claude M. *Carl Schurz, Reformer, 1829–1906*. New York: Dodd, Mead & Company, 1932.

Fuess, Claude M. *Daniel Webster*. 2 vols. Hamden, Conn.: Archon Books, 1963.

Fuess, Claude M. *The Life of Caleb Cushing*. 2 vols. Hamden, Conn.: Archon Books, 1965.

Gardiner, Oliver C. *The Great Issue*. Westport, Conn.: Negro Universities Press, 1970.

Garrison, W. P., and Francis J. Garrison. *William Lloyd Garrison*. 4 vols. New York: Century Company, 1885–1889.

Gatell, Frank O. *John Gorham Palfrey and the New England Conscience*. Cambridge: Harvard University Press, 1963.

Gienapp, William E. *The Origins of the Republican Party, 1852–1856*. New York: Oxford University Press, 1987.

Gobright, Lawrence A. *Recollections of Men and Things at Washington*. Philadelphia: Claxton, Remsen & Haffelfinger, 1869.

Gould, Levi S. *Ancient Middlesex*. Somerville, Mass.: Somerville Journal Print, 1905.

Grimke, Archibald H. *The Life of Charles Sumner*. New York: Funk & Wagnalls Company, 1892.

Grinnell, Josiah B. *Men and Events of Forty Years*. Boston: D. Lothrop Company, 1891.

Groneman, Carol, and Mary Beth Norton, eds. *"To Toil the Live-Long Day": America's Women at Work, 1780–1980*. Ithaca: Cornell University Press, 1987.

Gunderson, Robert G. *The Log Cabin Campaign*. Louisville: University of Kentucky Press, 1957.

Hallett, Benjamin F. *Mr. Hallett's Reply to Mr. Wilson's "Personal Explanation."* n.p., 1856.

Hallett, Benjamin F. *A Question of Veracity Evaded by Senator Wilson and Again Settled Against Him*. n.p., 1856.

Hambleton, James F. *A Biographical Sketch of Henry A. Wise*. Richmond: J. W. Randolph, 1856.

Hamilton, Holman. *Zachary Taylor, Soldier in the White House*. Indianapolis: The Bobbs-Merrill Company, 1951.

Hamlin, Charles E. *The Life and Times of Hannibal Hamlin*. Cambridge: Riverside Press, 1899.

Hampel, Robert L. *Temperance and Prohibition in Massachusetts, 1813–1852*. Ann Arbor: UMI Research Press, 1982.

Handlin, Oscar. *Boston's Immigrants, 1790–1865*. Cambridge: Harvard University Press, 1941.

Handlin, Oscar, and Mary Flug Handlin. *Commonwealth, a Study of the Role of Government in the American Economy*. Rev. ed. Cambridge: Harvard University Press, 1969.

Harrington, Fred H. *Fighting Politician, Major General N. P. Banks*. Philadelphia: University of Pennsylvania Press, 1948.

Harris, Wilmer C. *Public Life of Zachariah Chandler, 1851–1875*. Lansing: Michigan Historical Collections, 1917.

Harrold, Stanley C., Jr. *Gamaliel Bailey and Anti-Slavery Union*. Kent: Kent State University Press, 1986.

Hart, Albert B., ed. *Commonwealth History of Massachusetts*. 5 vols. New York: Russell & Russell, 1966.

Haynes, George H. *Charles Sumner*. Philadelphia: George W. Jacobs & Company, 1909.

Hazard, Blanche Evans. *The Organization of the Boot and Shoe Industry in Massachusetts before 1875*. Cambridge: Harvard University Press, 1921.

Headley, P. C. *Massachusetts in the Rebellion*. Boston: Walker, Fuller and Co., 1866.

Henry Wilson, 18th Vice President of the United States. Farmington, N.H.: Farmington-New Durham Historical Society, 1954.

Herndon, William H., and Jesse W. Weik. *Herndon's Life of Lincoln*. Cleveland: The World Publishing Company, 1965.

Hersh, Blanche Gassman. *The Slavery of Sex: Feminist-Abolitionists in America*. Urbana: University of Illinois Press, 1978.

Hertz, Emmanuel. *The Hidden Lincoln*. New York: Blue Ribbon Books, 1940.

Hesseltine, William B. *Lincoln and the War Governors*. New York: Alfred A. Knopf, 1948.

Hill, Alonzo. *Memorial of the Hon. Charles Allen*. Cambridge: John Wilson and Son, 1870.

Hill, Hamilton A. *Memoir of Abbott Lawrence*. Boston: Wilson and Son, 1883.

Hinton, Richard. *John Brown and His Men.* New York: Funk & Wagnalls Company, 1894.

Hoar, George F. *Autobiography of Seventy Years*. 2 vols. New York: C. Scribner's Sons, 1903.

Hollister, Ovando J. *The Life of Schuyler Colfax*. New York: Funk & Wagnalls, 1886.

Hooker, Richard. *The Story of an Independent Newspaper*. New York: The Macmillan Company, 1924.

Howe, Julia Ward. *Reminiscences, 1819–1899*. New York: Negro Universities Press, 1969.

Hurd, D. Hamilton, comp. *History of Middlesex County*. 3 vols. Philadelphia: J. W. Lewis & Co., 1890.

Hurd, Duane H., ed. *History of Rockingham and Strafford Counties, New Hampshire* Philadelphia: J. W. Lewis & Co., 1882.

Huston, James L. *The Panic of l857 and the Coming of the Civil War*. Baton Rouge: Louisiana State University Press, 1987.

Isely, Jeter A. *Horace Greeley and the Republican Party, 1853–1861*. New York: *Octagon Books, 1965.*

Jaher, Frederic C. *The Urban Establishment*. Urbana: University of Illinois Press, 1982.

Johannsen, Robert W. *Stephen A. Douglas*. New York: Oxford University Press, 1973.

Johannsen, Robert W., ed. *The Letters of Stephen A. Douglas*. Urbana: University of Illinois Press, 1961.

Johnson, Allen, and Dumas Malone, eds. *Dictionary of American Biography*. 21 vols. New York: Charles Scribner's Sons, 1937–1944.

Johnson, Charles W., ed. *Proceedings of the First Three Republican National Conventions of 1856, 1860, and 1864*. Minneapolis: Charles W. Johnson, 1893.

Johnson, Oliver. *William Lloyd Garrison and His Times*. Boston: B. B. Russell & Co., 1879.

Julian, George W. *Political Recollections, 1840 to 1872*. New York: Negro Universities Press, 1976.

Kaestle, Carl F. *Pillars of the Republic*. New York: Hill and Wang, 1983.

Keith, Elbridge G. *A Paper on the Republican National Convention of 1860*. Urbana: University of Illinois Press, 1904.

Kleeberg, Gordon S. P. *The Formation of the Republican Party as a National Political Organization*. New York: Moods Publishing Company, 1911.

Kleppner, Paul. *The Third Electoral System, 1853–1892*. Chapel Hill: University of North Carolina Press, 1979.

Knapp, Charles M. *New Jersey Politics during the Period of the Civil War and Reconstruction*. Geneva, N.Y: W. F. Humphrey, 1924.

Kossuth in New England. Boston: John P. Jewett & Co., 1852.

Lamon, Ward H. *The Life of Abraham Lincoln.* Boston: James R. Osgood and Company, 1872.

Lawrence, William. *The Life of Amos A. Lawrence.* Boston: Houghton Mifflin Co., 1888.

Letters of William Lloyd Garrison, Wendell Phillips, and James G. Blaine. Concord: n.p., 1872.

Luthin, Reinhart H. *The First Lincoln Campaign.* Cambridge: Harvard University Press, 1944.

Mann, Jonathan B. *The Life of Henry Wilson.* Boston: James R. Osgood and Company, 1872.

Manning, Jacob M. *Sermons and Addresses.* Boston: Houghton Mifflin Company, 1889.

Massachusetts Anti-Slavery Society. *Annual Reports.* New York: Negro Universities Press, 1969.

Mayer, George H. *The Republican Party, 1854-1866.* New York: Oxford University Press, 1967.

Mayfield, John. *Rehearsal for Republicanism.* Port Washington, N.Y.: Continental Publishing Company, 1873.

McCabe, James. *Behind the Scenes in Washington.* New York: Continental Publishing Company, 1873.

McClure, Alexander K. *Recollections of Half a Century. Salem, Mass.*: Salem Press Company, 1902.

McIntyre, J. W., ed. *Writings and Speeches of Daniel Webster.* 18 vols. Boston: Little, Brown and Company, 1903.

McKay, Ernest. *Henry Wilson, Practical Radical.* Port Washington, N.Y.: Kennikat Press, 1971.

Melbourne, Percival G., ed. *Memoirs of a Senate Page, 1855–1859.* New York: Broadway Publishing Company, 1909.

Melder, Keith E. *The Beginnings of Sisterhood.* New York: Schocken Books, 1977.

Meltser, Milton, and Patricia G. Holland, eds. *Lydia Maria Child: Selected Letters, 1817–1880.* Amherst: University of Massachusetts Press, 1982.

Memorial Addresses of the Life and Character of Henry Wilson. Washington: Government Printing Office, 1876.

Merriam, George S. *The Life and Times of Samuel Bowles.* 2 vols. New York: The Century Company, 1885.

Merrill, Walter M., and Louis Ruchames, eds. *The Letters of William Lloyd Garrison.* 4 vols. Cambridge: Harvard University Press, 1970–1975.

Milton, George F. *The Eve of Conflict.* Boston: Houghton Mifflin Company, 1934.

Moore, E. D. *On Living Peaceably with All Men.* Boston: David H. Ela, 1842.

Mordell, Albert. *Quaker Militant: John Greenleaf Whittier*. Boston: Houghton Mifflin Company, 1933.

Morrow, Josiah, ed. *Life and Speeches of Thomas Corwin*. Cincinnati: W. H. Anderson & Co., 1896.

Morse, John T., Jr. *Memoir of Colonel Henry Lee*. Boston: Little, Brown and Company, 1905.

Munroe, James P. *A Life of Francis Amasa Walker*. New York: Henry Holt and Company, 1923.

Nason, Elias, and Thomas Russell. *The Life and Public Services of Henry Wilson*. Boston: B. R. Russell, 1876.

Nevins, Allan. *The Emergence of Lincoln*. 2 vols. New York: Charles Scribner's Sons, 1950.

Nevins, Allan. *Fremont, Pathmarker of the West*. New ed. New York: Longmans, Green and Co., 1955.

Nevins, Allan. *Ordeal of the Union*. 2 vols. New York: Charles Scribner's Sons, 1947.

New England Temperance Convention. *Proceedings of the First Convention . . ., Held . . . 1866*. Boston: J. M. Usher, 1866.

Newton, Joseph F. *Lincoln and Herndon*. Cedar Rapids, Iowa: The Torch Press, 1910.

Nicolay, John G., and John Hay. *Abraham Lincoln, Complete Works*. 12 vols. New York: The Century Press, 1894.

Norton, Sara, and M. A. DeWolfe Howe. *Letters of Charles Eliot Norton*. 2 vols. Boston: Houghton Mifflin Company, 1913.

Nye, Russel B. *William Lloyd Garrison and the Humanitarian Reformers*. Boston: Little, Brown and Company, 1955.

Oates, Stephen B. *To Purge This Land*. New York: Harper & Row, Publishers, 1970.

O'Connor, Thomas H. *Lords of the Loom*. New York: Charles Scribner's Sons, 1968.

Overdyke, William D. *The Know-Nothing Party in the South*. Baton Rouge: Louisiana State University Press, 1950.

Pearson, Henry G. *The Life of John A. Andrew*. 2 vols. Boston: Houghton Mifflin and Company, 1904.

Pessen, Edward. *Riches, Class, and Power before the Civil War*. Lexington, Mass.: D. C. Heath and Company, 1973.

Peterson, Svend. *A Statistical History of the American Presidential Elections*. New York: Frederick Ungar Publishing Company, 1963.

Phelps, Charles S. *Life and Public Services of Ulysses S. Grant*. Boston: Lee Shepard and Dillingham, 1872.

Pickard, John B. *John Greenleaf Whittier*. 3 vols. Cambridge: Belknap Press of Harvard University Press, 1975.

Pickard, Samuel T. *Life and Letters of John Greenleaf Whittier*. 2 vols. Boston: Houghton Mifflin and Company, 1899.

Pierce, Edward L. *Memoirs and Letters of Charles Sumner*. 4 vols. Boston: Roberts Brothers, 1877–1893.

Pike, James S. *First Blows of the Civil War*. New York: The American News Company, 1879.

Poore, Ben: Perley. *Reminiscences of Sixty Years in the National Metropolis*. 2 vols. Philadelphia: Hubbard Brothers Publishing, 1886.

Potter, David M. *Lincoln and His Party in the Secession Crisis*. New Haven: Yale University Press, 1942.

Potter, David M., and Don E. Fehrenbacher. *The Impending Crisis, 1848–1861*. New York: Harper & Row Publishers, 1976.

Pryor, Mrs. Roger A. *Reminiscences of Peace and War*. Rev. ed. New York: The Macmillan Company, 1905.

Rantoul, Robert. *Memoirs, Speeches and Writings*. Boston: John P. Jewett and Company, 1854.

Rayback, Joseph G. *Free Soil, the Election of l848*. Lexington: University of Kentucky Press, 1970.

Reunion of the Free Soilers of 1848. Boston: Albert J. Wright, 1877.

Richards, Laura E., ed. *Letters and Journals of Samuel Gridley Howe*. Boston: Dana Estes & Company, 1909.

Riddleberger, Patrick W. *George Washington Julian, Radical Republican*. Indianapolis: Indiana Historical Bureau, 1966.

Ridley, Joseph P. *Ridley's Directory of Natick*. Worcester, Mass.: Edward R. Fiske & Co., 1873.

Robinson, Mrs. William S. *"Warrington" Pen Portraits*. Boston: Lee and Shepard, 1877.

Rossbach, Jeffrey. *Ambivalent Conspirators*. Philadelphia: University of Pennsylvania Press, 1982.

Rothman, David J. *Politics and Power: the United States Senate*. Cambridge: Harvard University Press, 1966.

Sanborn, Franklin B., ed. *The Life and Letters of John Brown*. Boston: Roberts Brothers, 1891.

Scales, John. *History of Strafford County, New Hampshire*. Chicago: Richmond-Arnold Publishing Co., 1914.

Schafer, Joseph, ed. *Intimate Letters of Carl Schurz, 1841–1869*. New York: DaCapo Press, 1970.

Schurz, Carl. *Autobiography*. New York: Charles Scribner's Sons, 1961.

Schurz, Carl. *Charles Sumner, an Essay*. Urbana: University of Illinois Press, 1951.

Schurz, Carl. *Reminiscences*. 3 vols. New York: The McClure Company, 1907–1908.

Schurz, Carl. *Speeches, Correspondence and Political Papers*. 6 vols. New York: Negro Universities Press, 1969.

Schwartz, Harold. *Samuel Gridley Howe, Social Reformer*. Cambridge: Harvard University Press, 1956.

Scisco, Louis D. *Political Nativism in New York State* in Columbia University Studies in History, Economics and Public Law. New York: Columbia University Press, 1901.

Severance, Frank H., ed. *The Millard Fillmore Papers* in Publications of the Buffalo Historical Society, vols. 10 and 11. Buffalo: Buffalo Historical Society, 1907.

Seward, Frederick W. *Seward at Washington*. 3 vols. New York: Derby and Miller, 1891.

Sewell, Harriet W., ed. *Letters of Lydia Maria Child*. 4th ed. Boston: Houghton, Mifflin and Company, 1884.

Sewell, Richard H. *Ballots for Freedom*. New York: Oxford University Press, 1976.

Sewell, Richard H. *John P. Hale and the Politics of Abolition*. Cambridge: Harvard University Press, 1965.

Shapiro, Samuel. *Richard Henry Dana, Jr., 1815–1882*. East Lansing: Michigan State University Press, 1961.

Shenton, James P. *Robert John Walker, a Politician from Jackson to Lincoln*. New York: Columbia University Press, 1961.

Shotwell, Walter G. *The Life of Charles Sumner*. New York: Thomas Y. Crowell & Company, Publishers, 1910.

Smalley, George W. *Anglo-American Memories*. London: Duckworth & Co., 1911.

Smith, William E. *The Francis Preston Blair Family in Politics*. 2 vols. New York: The Macmillan Company, 1933.

Spencer, Donald S. *Louis Kossuth and Young America*. Columbia: University of Missouri Press, 1977.

Stanton, Henry B. *Random Recollections*. New York: Harper & Brothers, 1887.

Stearns, Frank P. *Cambridge Sketches*. Philadelphia: J. B. Lippincott Co., 1905.

Stearns, Frank P. *Life and Public Services of George Luther Stearns*. Philadelphia: J. B. Lippincott Co., 1907.

Storey, Moorfield. *Charles Sumner*. Boston: Houghton Mifflin and Company, 1900.

Storey, Moorfield, and Edward W. Emerson. *Ebenezer Rockwood Hoar*. Boston: Houghton Mifflin Company, 1911.

Story, Ronald. *The Forging of an Aristocracy*. Middletown, Conn.: Wesleyan University Press, 1980.

Stowe, Harriet Beecher. *Men of our Times*. Hartford, Conn.: Hartford Publishing Co., 1868.

Sumner, Charles. *The Works of Charles Sumner*. 15 vols. Boston: Lee and Shepard, 1870–1883.

Taylor, Clare. *British and American Abolitionists*. Edinburgh: Edinburgh University Press, 1974.

Thayer, Eli. *History of the Kansas Crusade*. New York: Harper & Brothers, 1889.

Thomas, Benjamin P. *Abraham Lincoln*. New York: Alfred A. Knopf, 1952.

Thornborough, Emma Lou. *Indiana in the Civil War Era, 1850–1880*. Indianapolis: Indiana Historical Bureau n.p., 1965.

Trefousse, Hans L. *Ben Butler*. New York: Twayne Publishers, 1957.

Trefousse, Hans L. *The Radical Republicans*. New York: Alfred A. Knopf, 1969.

Tribune Almanac for the Years 1838 to 1880, Inclusive. 3 vols. New York: New York Tribune, 1881.

van Deusen, Glyndon. *William Henry Seward*. New York: Oxford University Press, 1967.

Villard, O. G. *John Brown, 1800–1859*. New York: Alfred A. Knopf, 1943.

The War of the Rebellion: a Compilation of the Official Records of the Union and Confederate Armies. 130 vols. Washington: Government Printing Office, 1880–1901.

Weisenberger, Francis P. *The Life of John McLean*. Columbus: Ohio University Press, 1937.

Weiss, John. *Life and Correspondence of Theodore Parker*. 2 vols. New York: D. Appleton & Company, 1864.

White, Horace. *The Life of Lyman Trumball*. Boston: Houghton Mifflin Company, 1913.

Willey, Austin. The *History of the Antislavery Cause in State and Nation*. New York: Negro Universities Press, 1969.

Williams, Charles R., ed. *Diary and Letters of Rutherford B. Hayes*. 5 vols. Columbus: Ohio State Archaeological and Historical Society, 1922–1926.

Wilson, Don W. *Governor Charles Robinson of Kansas*. Lawrence: University Press of Kansas, 1975.

Wilson, James G., and John Fiske, eds. *Appleton's Cyclopaedia*. New York: D. Appleton and Company, 1889.

Wiltse, Charles, ed. *The Papers of Daniel Webster*. 6 vols. Hanover, N.H.: University Press of New England, 1974.

Winslow, Hubbard. *The Young Man's Aid to Knowledge, Virtue, and Happiness*. Boston: D. K. Hitchcock, 1837.

Winthrop, Robert C., Jr. *A Memoir of Robert C. Winthrop*. Boston: Little, Brown and Company, 1897.

Woodward, C. Vann. *The Burden of Southern History*. Rev ed. Baton Rouge: Louisiana State University Press, 1968.

Wright, Charles. *Our Political Practice*. Boston: Alfred Mudge & Son, Printers, 1864–1865.

Wright, Henry C. *The Natick Resolution*. Boston: the author, 1859.
Wright, Henry C. *No Rights, No Duties*. Boston: the author, 1860.

Periodicals

Appleton, Nathan. "Memoir of Abbott Lawrence," *Collections of the Massachusetts Historical Society* 4 (1858): 495–507.

Bacon, Harriet F. "Personal Recollections of Natick," *Historical Collections of the Historical Natural History and Library Society* 1 (1909): 34–42.

Bacon, John W. "Natick Public Libraries and Their Origin," *Historical Collections of the Historical Natural History and Library Society* 2 (1910): 42–43.

Bean, William G. "An Aspect of Know-Nothingism—the Immigrant and Slavery," *South Atlantic Quarterly* 23 (Oct. 1924): 319–34.

Bean, William G. "Puritan Versus Celt, 1850–1860," *New England Quarterly* 7 (Mar. 1934): 70–89.

Brunet, Michel. "The Secret Ballot Issue in Massachusetts Politics from 1851 to 1854," *New England Quarterly* 25 (Sept. 1952): 354–62.

Carmen, Harry J., and Richard H. Luthin. "Some Aspects of the Know Nothing Movement Reconsidered," *South Atlantic Quarterly* 39 (Apr. 1940): 213–34.

Child, Lucie M. "West Central Street: Its Trees and Residences," *Historical Collections of the Historical Natural History and Library Society* 2 (1910): 36–37.

Crofts, Daniel W. "Secession Winter: William H. Seward and the Decision for War," *New York History* 65 (July 1984): 229–56.

Cross, Ira. "Origin, Principles, and History of the American Party," *Iowa Journal of History and Politics* 6 (1906): 526–53.

Davis, Horace B. "The Occupations of Massachusetts Legislators, 1790–1950," *New England Quarterly* 24 (Mar. 1951): 89–107.

Duberman, Martin. "Some Notes on the Beginnings of the Republican Party in Massachusetts," *New England Quarterly* 34 (Sept. 1961): 364–70.

Edmands, Thomas F. "The Massachusetts Militia," *New England Magazine* 11 (Feb. 1895): 770–84.

"First Congregational Church Records, Rochester, N.H. Marriages by Rev. Joseph Haven." *New Hampshire Genealogical Record* 5 (Oct. 1908): 145–52.

Fish, Carl R. "Lincoln and the Patronage," *American Historical Review* 8 (Oct. 1902): 53–69.

Foner, Eric. "Politics and Prejudice: the Free Soil Party and the Negro, 1849–1852," *Journal of Negro History* 50 (1965): 239–56.

Gatell, Frank O. "Conscience and Judgement; the Bolt of Massachusetts Conscience Whigs," *The Historian* 21 (Nov. 1958): 18–45.

Gatell, Frank O. "Palfrey's Vote, the Conscience Whigs, and the Election of Speaker Winthrop," *New England Quarterly* 21 (June 1958): 218–31.

Graebner, Norman. "Thomas Corwin and the Election of 1848," *Journal of Southern History* 17 (May 1951): 162–79.

Greenwood, Grace. "An American Salon," *Cosmopolitan* 8 (1890): 437–47.

Harrington, Fred H. "The First Northern Victory," *Journal of Southern History* 5 (May 1939): 186–205.

Harrington, Fred H. "Fremont and the North-Americans," *American Historical Review* 44 (July 1939): 842–48.

Haynes, George H. "The Causes of Know-Nothing Success in Massachusetts," *American Historical Review* 3 (Oct. 1897): 67–82.

Haynes, George H. "A Chapter from the Local History of Know Nothingism," *New England Magazine* 15 (Sept. 1896): 82–96.

Haynes, George H. "A Know Nothing Legislature," *American Historical Association Annual Report* 1896, 1: 177–87.

Hoar, George F. "Charles Allen of Worcester," *Proceedings of the American Antiquarian Society*, new ser., 14 (Oct. 1901): 327–80.

Hofstadter, Richard. "The Tariff Issue on the Eve of the Civil War," *American Historical Review* 44 (Oct. 1938): 50–55.

Huston, James L. "Facing an Angry Labor: the American Public Interprets the Shoemakers' Strike of 1860," *Civil War History* 28 (Sept. 1982): 197–212.

Johannsen, Robert W. "The Douglas Democrats and the Crisis of Disunion," *Civil War History* 9 (Sept. 1963): 229–47.

Johnson, Reinhard O. "The Liberty Party in Massachusetts, 1840–1848," *Civil War History* 28 (Sept. 1982): 237–65.

Julian, George W. "The First Republican National Convention," *American Historical Review* 4 (1899): 312–22.

Mann, Jonathan B. "Henry Wilson's Boyhood," *Historical Collections of the Historical Natural History and Library Society* (1910): 27–35.

Marshall, Schuyler C. "The Free Democratic Convention of 1852," *Pennsylvania History* 22 (Jan. 1955): 146–67.

McNurty, R. Gerald, ed. "Presidential Candidates of 1860," *Lincoln Lore* 1518 (Aug. 1964): 1-3.

Mitchell, Betty L. "Massachusetts Reacts to John Brown's Raid," *Civil War History* 19 (Mar. 1973): 65–79.

Myers, John L. "The Beginning of Antislavery Agencies in New Hampshire, 1832–1835," *Historical New Hampshire* 25 (Fall 1970): 3–25.

Myers, John L. "The Major Effort of Antislavery Agents in New Hampshire, 1835–1837," *Historical New Hampshire* 26 (Fall 1971): 3–27.

Nason, Elias. "Biographical Sketch of Henry Wilson, Late Vice-President of the United States," *New England Historical and Genealogical Register* 32 (July 1878): 261–68.

Nichols, Roy. "Some Problems of the First Republican Presidential Campaign," *American Historical Review* 28 (Apr. 1923): 492–96.

Rawley, James A. "Financing the Fremont Campaign," *Pennsylvania Magazine of Biography and History* 75 (Jan. 1951): 25–35.

Ruchames, Louis. "Race, Marriage, and Abolition in Massachusetts," *Journal of Negro History* 40 (1955): 250–74.

Schouler, James. "The Massachusetts Convention of 1853," *Proceedings of the Massachusetts Historical Society,* 2d ser., 18 (1903–1904): 30–48.

Schouler, James. "The Whig Party in Massachusetts." *Proceedings of the Massachusetts Historical Society* 50 (Nov. 1916): 39–53.

Shapiro, Samuel. "The Conservative Dilemma: the Massachusetts Constitutional Convention of 1853," *New England Quarterly* 33 (June 1960) 207–24.

Siebert, Wilbur H. "The Underground Railroad in Massachusetts," *Proceedings of the American Antiquarian Society*, new ser., 45 (1935): 25–100.

Stegmaier, Mark J. "Intensifying the Sectional Conflict: William Seward versus James Hammond in the Lecompton Debate of 1858," *Civil War History* 31 (Sept. 1985): 197–221.

Stewart, James B. "The Aims and Impact of Garrisonian Abolitionism, 1840–1860," *Civil War History* 40 (Sept. 1969): 197–209.

Sweeney, Kevin. "Rum, Romanism, Representation, and Reform: Coalition Politics in Massachusetts, 1847–1853," *Civil War History* 22 (June 1976): 116–37.

Travis, Alonzo. "Felchville: Its Past, Present and Future," *Historical Collections of the Historical Natural History and Library Society* 2 (1910): 86–91.

Welter, Barbara. "The Cult of True Womanhood," *American Quarterly* 18 (Summer, 1966): 151–74.

Index

A

Adams, Charles Francis, 47, 65, 79, 156, 182, 311, 351, 395, 413
and coalition, 106, 108, 111, 130, 136, 139, 173, 175, 240
and Compromise of 1850, 121, 127, 134
and constitutional convention, 205–6, 213, 219, 223–24, 219, 226–29
and election of 1844, 56–57
and election of 1848, 85, 87, 91
and election of 1852, 185–87, 189–91, 193–94, 196, 201–2
and election of 1860, 421, 424, 427, 429
Free Soiler, 98, 103, 105–6, 109–10, 135, 137–38, 140, 142, 166–68, 174
and Kansas–Nebraska, 235, 358, 360
and Know Nothings, 250–51, 256, 294, 340
and newspapers, 75–76, 100–1, 124, 145, 257
and Republican party, 244–45, 261, 265, 297–302, 328, 342, 364, 384, 388
and separation from Whig party, 76–78, 82–84, 87, 93, 96
opinions of Wilson, 81, 115, 128, 173–74, 193, 206–7, 244, 253, 271, 299
relations with Wilson, 30, 46, 64, 86, 167, 173–74, 304, 359, 385, 387, 410
and secession crisis, 430–31, 433–36, 438–40, 444
and Senate election, 1851, 147–48, 154
Young Whigs, 52–54, 58–63, 66–69, 71, 74
Adams, John, 401
Adams, John Quincy, 22, 31, 35, 64, 76, 78, 86, 307
and the presidency, 32, 33, 37
and Texas, 52, 55, 68–69
Adams, S.P., 142, 144
Aiken, William, 310
Aldrich, P.M., 299
Allen, Charles, 52, 75, 350, 359, 393, 440
and breakup of Whig party, 77–78, 83, 201
and constitutional convention, 206, 208, 214, 216, 226
congressman and nominee, 100, 105, 108, 160, 165, 192, 276
and election of 1848, 87–90, 92–93, 97, 188
Free Soiler, 95–96, 106, 111, 113, 166, 168, 189, 193–94
and Kansas–Nebraska, 235, 240
and Know Nothings, 256, 261–62
and Republican party, 245, 297–300, 304, 307
Alley, John, 183, 323–24, 360, 397, 429, 433
and coalition, 108, 136, 146, 148, 150, 155, 160, 202

and constitutional convention, 205–6, 213–14
Free Soiler, 98, 110, 137–38, 144, 186, 189, 196, 220
and newspapers, 101, 145, 187
and Republican party, 261, 348, 365, 385–86, 444
Alvord, Daniel, 87, 98, 100, 110, 138, 168, 220, 340, 365
American Anti-Slavery Society, 18, 21, 43, 281, 350, 352, 406
American and Foreign Anti-Slavery Society, 43, 350
Anderson, Robert, 433, 445
Andrew, John, 78, 99, 137, 242, 246, 341, 410, 429, 441
and governorship, 96, 366, 385, 425, 432–34, 436, 439, 444
Anthony, Henry, 137, 270
Anthony, Susan B., 386
Appleton, Nathan, 34, 51, 58, 64, 68, 76, 77, 78, 96, 143, 345, 410
Ashmun, George, 87, 89–90, 126, 188, 280, 334, 421
Aspinwall, William, 245
Atchinson, David, 321, 325, 347
Avery, Samuel, 21

B

Bacon, Austin, 17
Bacon, John, 16, 242
Bacon, Oliver, 17
Bailey, Gamaliel, 91, 108, 134, 185, 227, 265, 267, 275, 294, 312, 382, 397
Bailey, Margaret, 276
Baker, E.C., 288, 301, 304, 346
Baker, Edward, 435
Bancroft, George, 33, 41, 57, 105, 156, 158
Banks, Nathaniel, 38, 46, 180, 351–52, 366 396–97
and ceremonial occasions, 169, 181, 197, 423–24
and coalition, 130, 138–139, 149–50, 167, 176, 185, 222
congressman, 202, 264, 310–11, 317, 326, 334, 346
and constitutional convention, 203, 206–7, 216
governor, 252, 363, 365, 367, 384, 386, 388, 395, 401, 406, 410
and Know Nothings, 250–51, 253, 262–63, 267
and Republican party, 301, 305–7, 312, 320, 330, 340–42, 379
and secession crisis, 425, 430, 432
and temperance, 118, 177
and Wilson, 127, 271, 329, 398, 411, 420
Barber, E.D., 190
Barker, James, 248, 288–89, 291
Bartlett, E.B., 288
Bates, Edward, 411, 420
Bates, Isaac, 59, 62
Bayard, James, 442
Beach, Edward, 299, 306, 366, 387
Bear, John, 38
Beecher, Henry Ward, 282
Beecher, Lyman, 177
Bell, James, 269
Bell, John, 238, 276, 314, 373–74, 411, 420, 425–26, 428
Bell, Joseph, 59, 63, 65, 188
Bell, Luther, 206
Benjamin, Judah, 383, 434, 441
Benton, Thomas Hart, 37, 175, 189, 312, 339, 348, 401
Bigelow, John, 130
Bigler, William, 257, 335, 374, 380, 382, 391, 416, 427
Bingham, John, 89, 322
Bingham, Kinsley, 413, 430
Bird, Francis, 179, 194, 239–40, 351–52, 359–60, 440
Conscience Whig, 78, 87, 93
and constitutional convention, 206, 215–16, 222
Free Soiler, 108, 135, 138, 168, 183, 185, 189, 220
and Kansas–Nebraska, 237, 240, 360
and Know Nothings, 251, 256, 268
and newspapers, 137, 145–46, 173

Republican 242, 244–45, 265, 337, 340–41, 363–66, 385, 425
Bird Club, 137, 385
Birney, James, 35, 44, 56–57, 104, 304
Birney, William, 307
Bishop, H.W., 200, 221, 223, 228, 262
Black, Jeremiah, 433
Blair, Francis, 105, 312, 316, 339, 343, 402
Blair, Frank Jr., 360
Bliss, George, 298
Bolles, John, 106, 171, 194, 196
Boot and shoe industry, 10–13, 25–28, 231
Borden, Nathaniel, 62, 160
Boston Whig, 75–76, 82, 91, 100
Boutwell, George, 118, 127, 222, 250, 324, 394, 397, 427, 440
  and coalition, 138, 146, 148, 166–68, 174, 176
  and constitutional convention, 206, 210–17
  Democratic party leader, 38, 66, 143
  governor, 110, 131, 150, 169, 175, 180–1, 182, 183, 197
  opinions of Wilson, 41, 216, 271–72
  and Republican party, 298–99, 306–7, 363, 384
  and Senate election, 1851, 148–49, 151, 154, 161–62
  in state legislature, 117, 122, 128–29
Bowen, Francis, 159, 213
Bowles, Samuel, 247, 287–90, 297–98, 302, 304–5, 307, 338, 340–41, 343, 365
Bradford, Samuel, 143
Breckenridge, John, 275, 329, 419, 423, 428, 431, 437
Brenton, Samuel, 346
Bright, Jesse, 427
Briggs, Asa, 403
Briggs, George, 67, 125, 147, 151, 176, 177, 410
  and constitutional convention, 206–7, 209, 214
  governor, acts of, 58, 63, 72, 76, 81, 114, 133
  and elections, 51, 57, 71, 77, 78, 84, 104, 113, 143, 167, 174
Brinkerhoff, Jacob, 295
Broderick, David, 371, 373–74, 378, 394
Brodhead, Richard, 278
Brooks, Noah, 273
Brooks, Preston, 322–28, 331, 334, 341, 343, 349, 353, 384
Brown, Albert, 347, 349, 351, 370, 373, 391, 394, 403
Brown, John, 137, 325, 358, 382–83, 385, 393, 399–406, 409, 429
Brown, John Jr., 410
Brown, Simeon, 260, 264
Browne, A.G., 236, 241, 389
Brownson, Orestes, 227, 250
Bryant, Nahum, 260, 267
Buchanan, James, 330, 348, 374, 381, 384, 386, 393, 416
  candidate for president, 186, 329, 338–345
  and Kansas, 356–57, 361, 369, 371–72, 376, 391
  and secession crisis, 430, 433, 436
  Wilson's views of, 36, 352, 359, 378, 401
Buckingham, Joseph, 78, 83, 96
  Free Soiler, 100, 129, 135, 139, 157, 163–64, 168
Buckingham, William, 396–97, 412
Buffington, Edward, 287, 299, 310, 322, 326, 346, 385, 388, 444
Bullock, Alexander, 240, 365
Burlingame, Anson, 88, 157, 180, 197, 272, 322, 344, 364, 385, 429
  campaign speaker, 168, 222, 281, 339,342, 366–67, 423, 425
  and constitutional convention, 205–6, 214
  Free Soiler, 92–93, 110, 136, 138–39, 160, 165–66, 168, 172
  and Kansas, 240, 372, 377
  and Know Nothings, 251, 256,

263, 268, 288, 388
and newspapers, 101, 145
nominee for office, 96, 171, 196, 345, 387, 428, 444
opinions of others, 183, 194
and Republican party, 245, 306, 310
and Washington violence, 333–35, 340, 349, 413
Burritt, Elihu, 38
Burns, Anthony, case of, 241–42, 244, 250
Butler, Andrew, 318, 321–22, 326, 331–32
Butler, Benjamin, 38, 138, 160
and constitutional convention, 206, 208, 210–11, 213, 216, 227
candidate for governor, 198, 397, 401, 410
Butler, Benjamin F., 187

C

Calhoun, John C., 36, 54–55, 57, 120, 130, 237
Calhoun, John, 356, 368, 373, 376
Cameron, Simon, 273, 343, 351, 353, 355, 373, 376–77, 398, 411
Campbell, John, 90
Campbell, Lewis, 295, 310, 324, 335
Carter, Robert 187, 193, 205, 218–20, 225, 246, 265, 298, 301, 437
Cass, Lewis, 151, 180, 256, 338, 356–57, 433
presidential candidate, 87, 91, 97, 104, 110, 185–86, 199, 319
senator, 311, 318, 321, 349
Chaffee, Calvin, 324, 345
Chandler, Zachariah, 47, 355, 443
Channing, William, 66–68
Chase, Salmon, 109, 180, 256, 350–51, 385
Free Soiler, 85, 91, 98, 109, 175, 186–91
governor, 294–95, 304–5, 366, 406
Ohio senator, 106, 183, 202, 233, 273–74, 277–79
and Republican party, 243, 312, 320, 329, 372, 398, 411, 420–21, 435
Chestnut, James, 408, 413
Child David, 57, 98, 179, 280, 412
Child, Linus, 52, 58, 61–63, 66, 77, 175, 238, 307
Child, Lydia Maria, 17–18, 327, 349, 353, 442
Childs, N.R., 172
Choate, Rufus, 57–59, 62, 89, 143, 188, 206, 208, 212, 216, 220
Claflin, William, 96, 261, 327, 348, 425, 429, 433
close associate of Wilson, 137, 168, 187, 220, 324, 360, 386, 397
Clark, Daniel, 430
Clark, J.B., 402
Clarke, James Freeman, 406, 431
Clay, Clement, 320, 394, 407
Clay, Henry, 37, 39, 107, 201, 237, 358, 401
and election of 1844, 50–51, 55–57, 76
and election of 1848, 79, 86, 88–90, 103
Clayton, John, 79, 86, 179, 264, 274, 311, 314
Clifford, John, 59, 63, 192, 199–201, 203, 208, 219, 221–22, 410, 432
Clingman, Thomas, 391, 407–8, 413, 430, 442
Coalition, see Free Soil, coalition
Cobb, Howell, 113
Cobden, Richard, 397
Cochrane, John, 400
Colbath, Abigail Witham, 2–4, 232
Colbath, Albert, 4
Colbath, Charles, 4, 18
Colbath, Freeman, 131
Colbath, George, 4, 30, 80
Colbath, James, 2
Colbath, John, 4, 8, 80
Colbath, Hannah Rollins, 2
Colbath, Olive Leighton, 2
Colbath, Samuel, 4, 8, 80

Colbath, Winthrop, 2, 4, 32, 232, 398, 410
Colfax, Schuyler, 287, 322, 326, 345, 377, 437
Collamer, Jacob, 317, 320, 348, 374, 409, 431
Comins, Lucius, 246, 263–64, 299, 380
Commonwealth, 146, 172–173, 187, 219, 257
Compromise of 1850, 119–133, 138, 142–43, 150, 167, 175, 186–87, 190, 192
Conkling, Roscoe, 423
Constitutional convention, 179–80, 203–20, 223–28
Conway, M.F., 358, 367
Conway, Moncure, 276
Coolidge, Timothy, 29
Coolidge, William, 13–16, 36
Coolidge, William Jr. 29
Corwin, Thomas, 38, 79, 81–82, 85–86, 97, 132, 183. 276, 401, 434
Covode, John, 377, 423
Cox, Samuel, 437
Cragin, Aaron, 271, 273
Crittenden, John, 79, 132, 276, 371, 373–74, 384, 411
    and secession, 430, 434, 437, 441–42
Curtis, Benjamin, 143, 152, 432
Curtis, George, 223
Curtis, Robert, 162–63
Cushing, Caleb, 163, 240, 348, 365, 386, 394–95, 429
    appointments to office, 175–76, 182–83
    candidate for governor, 83–84, 104, 113
    opponent of coalition, 138, 167, 186, 225–28
    and Senate election, 1851, 147, 149, 151–52, 154–55
    Wilson, opinions of, 426–27, 432

D

Damrell, William, 100–1, 124, 145, 263, 271, 342, 385
Dana, Charles, 334
Dana, Richard, 52, 102, 121, 132, 183, 235, 434, 440
    and coalition, 136, 139–40, 148–49
    and constitutional convention, 206, 211, 213–15, 218, 224, 226
    Free Soiler, 98–99, 108, 121, 141, 168, 191, 193, 222–23, 256
    opinions of Wilson, 3, 115, 134, 166, 196, 205, 268, 271
    and Republican party, 297–302, 304, 307
Davis, Charles, 366
Davis, Henry Winter, 434
Davis, John, 35, 51, 96, 203
    as senator, 33, 44, 60, 71, 79, 92, 124–25, 132–33, 183
Davis, Jefferson, 328, 370, 373, 384, 386, 392, 394, 408, 412, 414, 421, 423, 430, 433, 436
Davis, Timothy, 296, 342, 385
Dawes, Henry, 129, 137, 206, 270–71, 298, 342, 345, 351, 425
Dayton, William, 330, 333, 411, 444
Delano, Charles, 434, 444
Denver, J.W., 371
Devens, R.M., 186–87
Devereaux, George, 195, 266, 365
DeWitt, Alexander, 196, 202, 206, 234, 262–63, 296, 342, 353, 385
Dexter, Franklin, 298
Dix, John, 186
Dixon, James, 376, 435
Donaldson, J.B., 347
Doolittle, James, 351, 355, 405, 407, 432
Douglas, Stephen, 180, 275, 329
    candidate for president, 186, 419–24
    chairman, Territory Committee, 69, 279, 416
    Democratic leader, 239, 269, 278, 310, 378–80, 389
    and Kansas, 233–38, 252, 318, 333, 356–57, 368–74, 391
    opinions of Wilson, 271, 312, 443

Senate activities, 132, 321, 326, 383, 412–13, 434, 439, 441
Douglass, Frederick, 99, 141, 179, 281, 350
Douglass, H. Ford, 421–22
Dow, Neal, 177, 201, 367
Durkee, Charles, 269, 276
Dwight, William, 83

E

Earle, James, 110, 138, 185
Eastman, Anstress, 4–6, 14
Eastman, Nehemiah, 4–6
Edwards, Francis, 346
Elder, David, 168
Election of 1840, 37–39
Election of 1844, 51, 55–57
Election of 1848, 77–79, 81–85, 87–92
Election of 1852, 185–203
Election of 1856, 312–13, 316–17, 319–20, 328–30, 332–46
Elections of 1857–59, 363–67, 384–88, 400–2
Election of 1860, 398, 410–12, 416, 419–29
Elgin, James, Lord, 169
Eliot, Samuel, 133, 206, 238, 242, 302, 306–7, 364
Ely, Alfred, 266–67, 288, 291, 296, 303
Emancipator and Republican, 100–2, 106, 123–24, 132, 137, 145–46
Emerson, Ralph Waldo, 66, 156, 165, 281
English, William, 377
Evans, Josiah, 383–84
Everett, Edward, 15, 48, 151, 166, 197, 206, 394, 420, 423, 426–27
conservative Whig, 58, 125, 161, 223, 263, 324, 410
governor, 33, 35, 50, 51
opinions of Wilson, 3, 218, 280–81, 293, 306
senator, 203, 233, 236, 238, 240, 244, 273, 282, 323

F

Faulkner, Charles, 407
Felch, Asa, 12, 26–27
Fessenden, William, 105, 275, 278, 345, 348, 376, 398, 400, 411, 443
Field, David Dudley, 86
Fillmore, Millard, 236
president, 132, 134, 169, 180, 261, 313
as candidate, 90, 185–86, 290, 320, 326, 343–44, 364
Fitch, Graham, 374, 384, 408
Fitzpatrick, John, 250
Fogg, George 190, 317, 426, 439
Foot, Asahel, 60
Foot, Solomon, 402
Forbes, Hugh, 382, 409
Forney, John, 270–71, 274, 338, 353, 369, 377, 403, 426
Foster, Abby Kelly, 242, 422
Foster, John, 284, 287–90, 293, 296, 298–99, 301–3, 305–8
Foster, Lafayette, 239, 376
Foster, Stephen, 422
Fowler, Orin, 133, 140–41, 143, 165
Free Soil:
in 1848 campaign, 91, 95–99, 102–5
and coalitions, 106–13, 134–44, 165, 167, 171–75
Fremont, John:
and campaign of 1856, 329–30, 333, 338, 341–43, 345, 364, 387
and Wilson's opinions of, 272, 312, 319, 342, 352, 365
French, John, 21–22
French, Rodney, 168, 189, 193, 196
Fuller, Joseph, 36

G

Galloway, Joseph, 90
Gardner, Henry, 256, 266, 269, 283, 317, 324, 344, 384, 410, 432
and election of 1854, 260, 262–65
and election of 1855, 293–95,

300–6
and election of 1856, 333, 338–41, 345, 364, 385, 393
and elections of 1857 and 1858, 363, 366–67, 387–88
Know Nothing National Council, 287–88, 290, 312–13
Garrison, William Lloyd, 35, 76, 157, 184, 400, 431
abolitionist and editor, 21–22, 43, 44, 57, 153, 348, 350, 353, 407
attitude toward Wilson, 72, 122, 268, 271, 406, 422, 442
and Texas and Free Soil, 61, 66–68, 99, 105
Geary, John, 335, 347, 356–57
Giddings, Joshua, 184, 256, 326, 333, 350–53, 389, 410
congressman, 69, 84, 125, 200, 276
Free Soiler, 85, 87–88, 90, 95, 98
in New England, 76, 79, 96, 173, 307
and Republican party, 329, 338, 440, 442
Gillette, Francis, 239
Gooch, Daniel, 137, 429
Goodrich, John, 165, 177, 440
and Republican party, 245, 298, 301, 303, 306–7, 312, 364–65, 393, 444
Gourgas, Francis, 215
Grant, Ulysses, 350
Greeley, Horace, 2, 86, 105, 309, 320, 350
political stance, 34, 105, 310, 333, 343, 371, 379, 411, 431, 442
opinions of Wilson, 279, 312, 315, 318
Green, James, 377–78, 383, 394, 416, 437, 439
Greene, Nathaniel, 138
Griffin, Matthew, 13–14
Grimes, James, 257, 275, 414
Griswold, Whitney, 115, 206, 211, 213, 411
and coalition, 138, 148, 153, 158, 172, 183
Grow, Galusha, 354, 377
Gwin, William, 370, 380, 394

H

Hale, Charles, 385
Hale, John, 312, 339, 346, 350–52, 382
Free Soiler, 87, 91, 96–99, 188, 190–92, 196, 199–200, 256
in Massachusetts, 77, 165–166, 207, 254, 300
Free Soil senator, 106, 135, 183, 202, 233, 269, 276
Republican senator, 314–15, 321, 353–54, 369, 374, 376, 383, 430, 443
Hale, Nathan, 206
Hall, Robert, 263, 267, 299
Hallett, Benjamin, 110, 143, 156, 160, 306, 319
and constitutional convention, 206–7, 210–12, 214–16, 223, 225
Democratic leader, 33, 35, 279, 387
opposes coalition, 138, 147–48, 154, 167, 191–92
Ham, Benjamin, 39
Hamilton, Alexander, 401
Hamlin, Hannibal, 239, 340, 367, 370, 374, 381, 419, 424, 435
Hammond, James, 28, 374–75, 383, 403, 408, 416
Hanscom, S.P., 317
Harlan, James, 269, 318, 373, 415
Harper's Ferry attack, 399–406
Harvard College, 117, 158–60, 163, 166, 176, 213, 283, 423
Harrison, William Henry, 37, 39
Hawley, Joseph, 137
Hayden, William, 107
Hayes, Martin, 12–13, 131
Hayes, Rutherford, 125
Haynes, Israel, 160
Hazewell, Charles 110, 171, 225
Helper, Hinton, 375, 402–3
Henry, Patrick, 408

Henshaw, David, 33, 35, 71, 143, 150
Herndon, William, 376, 378–79, 389, 431, 440
Herring, Charles, 35–36
Herring, George, 16, 39, 45, 131
Higginson, Thomas, 157, 241, 287, 348, 351–53, 382
Hildreth, Richard, 187
Hillard, George:
  Conservative Whig, 60, 120, 122–24, 128, 197, 206, 213, 226
  cooperating with Wilson, 61, 68, 77, 238, 324
Hoar, E.R., 38, 52, 102, 128, 255–56, 431
  Conscience Whig, 52, 66–67, 73, 78, 87–88, 91
  Free Soiler, 96–97, 102, 121, 127, 133, 135, 226
  and Republican party, 301–2, 364, 440
Hoar, George, 127, 172, 245, 254–55, 271, 274
Hoar, Samuel, 52, 58, 115–18, 136, 139, 245, 251, 297–98, 360
Hooper, Samuel, 208, 411
Hopkins, Erastus, 91, 121–22, 128, 168, 172, 176, 188, 191, 340, 364–5
Holt, Joseph, 433, 444
Houston, Sam, 238, 312, 340
Howard, William, 317, 423, 436
Howe, Amasa, 29
Howe, Estus, 101, 110–11, 189
Howe, Mary, 29, 131, 153
Howe, Samuel Gridley, 78, 178, 182, 205–6, 263, 302, 400, 409, 430
  Free Soiler, 129, 235–36
  and newspapers, 145–46, 173, 187
  Republican, 265, 358, 366, 393
Hudson, Charles, 54, 56, 77, 100, 306
Hughes, John, 249
Hunt, Samuel, 28, 31, 39, 45, 56, 66, 80, 232
Hunter, Robert, 354, 394–95, 407
Huntington, Elisha, 66
Hyatt, Thaddeus, 410

I

Iverson, Alfred, 392, 404–5, 414, 430

J

Jackson, Andrew, 13, 32–33, 36–37, 39, 41, 56, 175, 212, 369, 408
Jackson, Francis, 129
Jackson, William, 44, 66, 86
  Free Soiler, 98, 110–11, 136, 138, 168, 189
  and newspapers, 76, 124, 146
Jay, John, 401
Jefferson, Thomas, 401
Jewell, Harvey, 137
Jewett, John, 146
Johnson, Andrew, 380–83
Johnson, Herschel, 424, 426
Johnson, Reverdy, 378
Johnson, William, 289
Jones, George, 335
Jones, James, 279
Judd, N.B., 389
Julian, George, 141, 190, 256, 276, 350

K

Kansas–Nebraska Act:
  and Pierce, 233–241, 297, 313–20, 325, 331, 333–36, 347–49
  and Buchanan, 356–61, 367–78, 380, 394, 398–99, 413, 437
Kasson, John, 96
Keitt, Lawrence, 322, 324, 377
Kellogg, William, 379, 386
Kelsey, William, 346
Keyes, Edward, 86, 169, 256
  and coalition, 108, 146, 151, 160, 168
  Conscience Whig, 81, 83, 87–88, 91–92
  and constitutional convention, 205–6, 209, 216
  Free Soiler, 110, 135–36, 142, 144, 187–88, 194, 220
  and Republican party, 244–45, 265, 298
  in state legislature, 143, 157, 164,

180, 183–84
Kimball, Moses, 265, 297, 299, 302, 423, 429
King, Preston, 134, 184, 276, 308, 346
Republican, 243, 300, 312, 355, 376, 413
Kossuth, Louis, 159, 180–83, 185, 188, 207
Knapp, Chauncey, 98, 100, 149, 263, 310
Knight, William, 5–6
Know Nothing movement:
formation and initial split, 247–51, 253–68, 282–94
weakening of party, 301–7, 312–13, 320, 329, 333, 339–41, 364–67
Know Somethings, 287, 290–91, 293, 297–98, 300
Kriesman, Herman, 307

L

Lamon, Ward, 379
Lane, Jim, 317–18, 369
Lane, Joseph, 326, 424
Lawrence, Abbott, 151, 206, 268, 271, 347
and annexation of Texas, 44, 54, 58, 68–69
and election of 1848, 86, 88, 90, 106
relations with Webster, 51–52, 59–60, 64, 81, 83, 126, 197
leader of Conservative Whigs, 34, 51, 59, 77, 221, 223, 238
Lawrence, Amos, 125, 240, 324, 347–48, 358, 360, 381, 400, 409–10, 423
Lawrence, Samuel, 226
Leavitt, Joshua, 61, 95, 99, 110, 148, 227, 276
Lecompte, Samuel, 325, 347
Legro, William, 13
LeMoyne, Julius, 190
Lewis, Samuel, 190
Lincoln, Abraham, 2, 351, 372, 379–80
candidate for national office, 330, 411, 419, 421–28
president–elect, 430–32, 440, 442–45
Whig, 38, 105, 250, 256, 269, 337
Lincoln, Ezra, 292
Lincoln, Levi, 35, 44, 47, 51, 60, 92, 410
Lincoln, Soloman, 86
Lord, Otis, 206
Loring, Edward, 241–42, 263, 283, 363, 384
Lovejoy, Owen, 402, 413
Lowndes, William, 237
Lunt, Charles, 107
Lunt, George, 90, 425
Lyman family, 34
Lyman, Joseph, 146, 173
Lynn, Mass., shoemaking in, 10–12, 25–27

M

Madison, James, 408
Mann, Horace, 47–48, 74, 92, 156, 205, 220, 397
congressman, 86–87, 133, 143, 165, 194, 276
and Free Soil, 97, 100, 102, 104, 126, 140–41, 168, 172, 192–93, 200–1
Mann, Jonathan, 13–14, 17, 36, 39, 404
Marcy, William, 186
Marsh, Thomas, 360
Martin, Luther, 408
Mason, George, 441
Mason, James, 125, 321, 323, 356, 394, 403, 407, 409–10, 414–15, 442
Mason Committee, 403, 409–10
Massachusetts Anti-Slavery Society, 37, 45, 61–62, 71–72, 121, 178, 202, 293, 421, 438
Massachusetts Emigrant Aid Company, 240, 297, 315, 317, 334, 348
Massachusetts government, reform, 157–58, 163, 178–79, 208–18, 282–83

Massachusetts legislature, description, 40,148–49
Matthew, Father, 177
May, Samuel J., 61, 99
Maynard, S.A., 110
McClure, Alexander, 269–70, 272–73
McLean, John, 55, 79, 85–86, 97, 175, 185, 276, 320, 329–30
"Melina", 30, 410, 435, 439, 443
Mexico and war, 74–76, 80–81
Military Affairs Committee, 1, 28, 273,355, 369, 391, 402, 437, 443
Militia, state, 46–47, 52, 64, 117–18, 131, 169, 179, 183, 211, 436
Mills, John, 99, 104, 147, 154, 160
Monroe, James, 237
Montgomery, William, 377, 433
Moore, Erasmus, 15, 18, 80, 397–98
Morey, George 147, 174, 245, 251
Morgan, Edwin, 333, 339, 342–43, 360, 386, 406, 411, 426
Morrill, Anson, 257, 300
Morrill, Justin, 271, 273, 275
Morris, Thomas, 20
Morris, Gouverneur, 401
Morse, Edwin, 17
Morse, Isaac, 13
Morton, Marcus, 105, 151, 154–56, 410
  candidate for governor, 33, 35, 51, 143
  and constitutional convention, 206, 209, 211, 214, 216–17
  faction leader, 71, 97, 109, 147, 200
Morton, Marcus Jr., 96, 99–100, 104, 136, 211, 213, 245
Morton, Nathaniel, 97, 109
Motley, John, 444
Munroe, Lucius, 29
Munroe, Mary Ann, 29

N

Nason, Elias, 232
Natick, Mass., 8–10, 12, 25, 30, 80, 169, 232, 355, 401
Natick Debating Society, 15–18, 30
New England Anti-Slavery Society, 18, 21, 179, 263
Nichols, Curtis, 100
Norton, Charles, 268

O

Oliver, Mordecai, 317
Orr, James, 310, 324, 373

P

Pangborn, E.Z., 272, 379, 388
Palfrey, John, 132, 139, 156–57, 203, 235–57, 256, 276, 311, 351, 444
  and coalition, 108, 130, 133–34, 136–37, 140, 143, 176, 201
  and Compromise of 1850, 121, 124, 127
  Conscience Whig, 52, 61, 67–69, 71, 77–79, 83–84, 93, 103
  and constitutional convention, 205, 219, 223–24, 226–29
  and Free Soil, 135, 142, 168, 174, 187–88, 193, 201
  and newspapers, 75, 76, 101, 124, 145–48, 173
  nominee for Congress, 78–79, 100, 103, 108, 111, 113, 115, 139–40, 160–61, 165–66
  and Wilson, 111, 134, 271, 206
  and Republican party, 244, 253, 265, 302, 364
Palmer, Joseph, 312
Panic of 1819, 7
Panic of 1837, 21, 25–26, 33, 35, 37, 42
Park, John, 38, 121, 142, 165, 168, 185
Parker, Theodore, 129, 141, 227, 241, 245, 283, 351–52, 382, 385
  opinions of Wilson, 268, 274, 328, 383
Payne, Abraham, 98
Pennington, William, 403
Perkin, E.O., 358
Phelps, Charles, 367, 385, 433, 444
Phillips, Stephen, 157, 205, 235, 240, 253, 356, 393
  coalition, role towards 106–8,

111, 136, 173
and election of 1848, 85, 87–88, 91–93, 102–4
and newspapers, 75, 101, 108, 124
Free Soiler, 95, 97–98, 108, 121, 166, 188, 189–91, 193, 223, 262
governor nominee, 96, 113, 135–36, 138, 143, 168, 174
and Republican party, 245, 252, 265, 268, 297, 300–2
and Senate election, 1851, 147–48, 150, 152, 154–55
and Texas, 44, 61–63, 67–69
Young Whigs, 52, 60, 66, 71, 74, 77–78, 83
Phillips, Wendell, 44, 71, 72, 137, 241, 268, 429
cooperation with Free Soilers, 68, 129, 141, 184, 350
and Wilson, 23, 72, 242, 287, 323, 439, 406
Pierce, Edward, 88, 137, 265, 278, 350, 364, 395–96, 402, 413, 425
Pierce, Franklin, 114, 275, 348, 431
candidate for president, 184, 186–87, 189, 197, 199–200, 329
president, 239, 249, 401, 297, 313–14, 318, 330–31, 347, 371
Pierce, Henry, 137, 366
Pierpont, John, 177, 245, 358, 431
Pillsbury, Parker, 132, 157, 280–81, 352, 422
Polk, James 55–56, 67, 74–75, 369, 430
Polk, Joseph, 414
Pomeroy, Samuel, 315, 317
Powell, Lazarus, 430
Pryor, Mrs. Roger, 402
Pugh, George, 348, 353, 373, 394

Q

Quincy, Edmund, 44, 61, 153, 242
Quincy, Josiah, 345, 363

R

Raleigh letter, 55–56
Rantoul, Robert Jr., 138, 148–49, 152, 161, 165–66, 182, 184, 191–92, 206, 276
Raynor, Kenneth, 264, 288
Read, John, 398, 411, 420
Reaf, Richard, 409
Redmond, Charles, 141, 157
Redpath, James, 410
Reeder, Andrew, 297, 313, 317, 343, 346
Republican party, creation of, 243–47, 252–53, 261, 292–308
Rice, Alexander, 346, 387, 427–29, 434, 444
Richardson, N.A., 38
Richardson, William, 310
Ritchie, Harrison, 439
Robinson, Charles, 314, 317, 325, 334, 343, 347–48, 358–59, 361, 369, 398
Robinson, Frederick, 152, 161, 167
Robinson, James, 196
Robinson, William, 38, 65, 103, 137, 341, 366
and constitutional convention, 207, 223, 226, 228
editor, 40, 91, 96, 100–1
opinions of Wilson, 41, 102, 203, 205–6, 254–55, 271, 385
and secession crisis, 425, 435, 440
Rockwell, Julius, 69, 244, 251, 267, 301–3, 305–7, 332, 363
Rugg, Henry, 289
Russell, Charles, 245
Russell, Lord John, 311
Russell, Thomas, 142, 144, 160–61, 164, 172, 177, 328, 367, 387

S

Saltonstall, Leverett, 34, 51, 59
Sanborn, Franklin, 137, 382, 409, 440
Santa Anna, Antonio de, 49
Schouler, William, 46, 84, 174, 436
and constitutional convention, 206, 210, 216, 227

editor, 40, 43, 126, 262
in legislature, 115–117, 122–23, 128, 169, 176
and Wilson, 40, 43, 131, 254
Schurz, Carl, 270–71, 395–96
Scott, Winfield, 80, 88–89, 185–88, 197, 199–201, 203, 411, 420, 436, 444
Secession, 433, 437–39
Sedgwick, Charles, 34, 100
Senate election, 1851, 146–56, 160–63
Seward, William, 276, 309, 351, 383, 402, 424, 429–30, 432
and John Brown, 382, 399
political stance, 34, 103, 130, 134, 180, 182, 315
and presidency, 320, 339
remains a Whig, 250, 256 269
and Republican party, 295, 372, 376
in secession crisis, 436–37, 439–40, 442, 444–45
in Senate, 183, 278, 314–15, 318, 321–23, 334, 349, 369, 373–74
and Wilson, 79, 86, 243, 329, 398, 411, 420–21, 432
Sewell, Samuel, 57, 61, 67, 129, 171, 173, 240
Seymour, Horatio, 431
Shadrach, 156
Shannon, Wilson, 313–14, 317, 334, 347
Shaw, Lemuel, 166
Sherman, John, 317, 402, 431
Simmons, James, 340, 355
Sims, Thomas, 156–57, 160
Slack, Charles, 165, 251, 265–67, 291, 293, 297, 303
Slade, William, 70
Slidell, John, 326, 348, 383, 395
Smith, Gerrit, 99, 190, 196, 200, 325, 347–48, 382, 400, 442
Smith, Horace, 144
Smith, Lucius, 101, 145
Smith, Persifer, 347, 357
Spooner, R.C., 75, 77
Spooner, William, 110, 124, 185, 220, 265, 347
Stansbury, E.L., 161, 166
Stanton, Edwin, 433
Stanton, F.P., 357, 367, 369, 371, 378
Stanton, Henry, 44, 61, 68–69, 106, 110, 134, 186, 340, 342, 426
Stearns, George, 137, 256, 360, 382–83, 399–400, 409, 412
Stephens, Alexander, 131, 286
Stetson, Caleb, 61, 66,100
Stevens, Thaddeus, 2, 125, 276
Stevenson, J.H., 422
Stevenson, J. Thomas 56, 59, 206, 425
Stone, James, 137, 177, 250, 256, 293
Free Soiler, 111, 183, 185, 187, 220
Republican, 265–67, 297, 328, 366
Stone, T.P.D., 20
Storrs, George, 22
Stowe, Calvin, 169
Stowe, Harriet Beecher, 276
Stuart, Charles, 371, 378, 391, 393–94
Sumner–Brooks affair, 321–24, 326–28, 331–35
Sumner, Charles, 180–82, 276, 281–82, 350–52, 384, 405, 421, 423, 440, 444
and constitutional convention, 202, 205–6, 208, 226
and Compromise of 1850, 121, 132, 160
and coalition, 113, 140, 144, 165, 172
on division within Whig party, 77–78, 81, 83–84
and election of 1848, 87–88, 96, 100, 102, 105
and election of 1852, 185, 191–92, 201
elections for state Senate, 133, 313
and Free Soil, 85, 91–93, 96, 106, 108–9, 135–36, 138, 165, 197, 222
illness after attack, 323, 327, 331, 339, 344, 349, 354, 367, 369–70, 402
and Kansas, 234–35, 237–38, 318,

413
and newspapers, 75–76, 108, 111, 124
and Republican party, 256, 294, 301, 306–7, 312, 340–41, 372, 387, 425
and secession crisis, 430, 432, 436–37, 439, 442–43
Senate elections, 142, 146–47, 150–56, 160–62, 174, 268
senator, 33, 176, 183–84, 194, 232–33, 278, 307, 315, 349, 354
See Sumner–Brooks affair
Sumner–Wilson compared, 41, 47, 127
and Wilson, 273–74, 179, 202, 280, 316, 349, 383–84, 393
Young Whigs, 52, 67–68, 71, 74, 353
Sumner, Increase, 261, 297, 299
Suttle, Charles, 241
Swan, Caleb, 110, 136, 138, 168, 220, 297, 342, 366, 386
Swift, John, 188, 191, 222–23, 241–42, 264, 298, 303, 367, 385

T

Tappan, Lewis, 191, 276
Taylor, Zachary, 74, 79–82, 86–90, 95, 103, 119, 122, 130–32, 134
Temperance, 31–32, 107, 118, 177–78, 201, 233, 253, 261–62, 367
Texas, 20, 23, 49
annexation, 55, 57, 62, 64
Massachusetts opposition to annexation, 44, 50, 53–55, 58–69
Thayer, Alexander, 15–16, 18
Thayer, Eli, 240, 260, 342, 380, 405, 427–28
Thompson, George, 18, 22, 153, 166
Thompson, Benjamin, 130, 140
Toombs, 281, 326, 333, 348, 354, 372, 391, 410, 415
Toucey, Isaac, 278
Trafton, Mark, 263, 301, 342
Train, Charles, 38, 87, 385, 423, 434
Trumball, Lyman, 239, 269, 327, 339, 345, 351, 380, 404, 407
and 1858 senatorship, 372, 376, 378
and secession crisis, 429, 431–32, 442–43
Tuck, Amos, 84, 350, 444
Tyler, John, 37, 39, 43, 50, 54, 57, 62

U

Upshur, Abel, 54

V

Vaughan, John, 90
Van Buren, John, 134, 186
Van Buren, Martin, 57, 239
and presidential campaign of 1848, 85, 91, 95–100, 103, 104, 135, 192
as president, 33, 35, 37, 49, 51, 56

W

Wade, Benjamin, 105, 243, 256, 276, 300, 351
and Kansas, 315, 318, 321, 326–27
in Senate, 47, 183, 200, 278, 348, 377, 393, 416, 443
Walcott, Edward, 10–12, 14, 26–27, 39, 66, 80, 87, 91, 355
Walcott, John, 27
Wales, E.L., 223
Walker, Amasa, 129, 157, 177, 298
and constitutional convention, 206, 208, 211, 213
Free Soiler, 104, 106–7, 148, 154, 168, 185, 189, 193–94, 220, 254
Free Soil speaker, 95, 98, 161, 187–88, 191, 242, 245
and Wilson, 37, 280, 291, 396, 442
Walker, Robert, 36, 55, 338, 357–61, 367–69, 371–72, 378
Walley, Samuel, 140, 166, 299, 306, 333

Washburn, Emory, 177, 221, 223, 244, 252, 262, 424, 432
Washburn, Henry, 303
Washburn, Israel Jr., 243
Washburne, C.C., 333
Washburne, Elihu, 275
Webb, Seth Jr., 100 183, 241
    Free Soiler, 121, 137, 142, 144, 185, 223
    and Republican party, 245–46, 303, 306, 338–39
Washington, D.C., in 1850s, 274–76, 309–10
Webster, Daniel, 105, 197, 282
    candidate for presidential nomination, 83, 86–92, 168, 175, 185–86, 192
    division among state Whigs, 51–52, 64, 77, 81, 83–84
    and election of 1848, 97, 99, 103
    and Mexican War, 76–77, 79
    role after Compromise, 134–35, 138, 139, 142–44, 166
    role in country, 33, 35, 50, 180
    and Senate election 1851, 148, 151
    and Texas, 44, 50–51, 54, 56–60, 69
    and Wilson, 15, 129, 132, 141, 164, 166, 188, 201
Webster, Fletcher, 88, 91, 97
Weed, Thurlow, 34, 86, 243, 269, 343, 351, 426, 430
Welles, Gideon, 239, 312, 316, 351, 376, 429, 435, 439, 444
Wentworth, Tappan 202
Whitehouse, George, 5, 32
Whitney, David, 25
White, George, 193
White, W.A., 124, 142, 144
Whitfield, John, 317, 346
Whittier, John Greenleaf, 48, 66, 105, 135, 146, 150–51, 276, 345, 409, 430
    opinions abut Wilson, 7, 268, 393, 441
Washington mission, 31, 68–69, 244
Wigfall, Louis, 430, 441
Wight, William, 17
Wilder, Marshall, 260, 265
Wilkinson, Morton, 402
Willey, Austin, 190
Williams, G.F., 173, 185
Williams, J.M.S., 137
Wilmot, David, 76, 80, 187, 276, 330, 366
Wilson, Harriet, 79, 310, 324, 326, 328, 435–36, 439, 443
    activities with Henry, 29–30, 131, 153, 232, 355, 370, 402, 429–30
    and her health, 80, 391, 398, 410, 416
Wilson, Henry,
    and abolitionists, 18, 22–23, 43–45, 65, 67, 71–73, 122, 129, 153, 349–353, 406, 421–22
    antislavery, becomes, 17–18, 20–23, 32
    and black rights, 52, 179, 209, 288, 380, 414
    campaigns of 1840–1844, 38–40, 42, 46, 56
    campaigns of 1845–48, 66–67, 71, 77–79, 82–84, 95–102, 105–6
    campaigns of 1849–51, 108–113, 135–43, 168–69, 172–75
    campaign of 1852, 186–98
    campaign of 1856, 312, 330–31
    campaigns of 1857–1859, 363–67, 384–88, 398–400
    campaign of 1860, 398, 400, 411–12, 416, 420–29
    and ceremonial activities, 169, 397, 423, 427
    Congregational pastors, relations with, 15, 28–29, 31, 41, 56, 232, 397–98
    and constitutional convention, 203–21, 223–28
    and District of Columbia, Senate, 311, 391, 414
    and economic policies, 42, 278, 331, 354–55, 381, 392

as editor-publisher, see *Emancipator and Republican*
and education, 4, 6, 20–21, 47, 271, 391–93, 414
family, 2–4, 232
and foreign affairs, 311–12, 383, 395, 415
governor nominee, 219–20, 222–23, 228, 252–54
hardworking nature of, 6, 13, 19–20, 26, 195, 272
see Harvard College
health, 19–20, 271–72, 281, 310, 400
state House, service in, 40, 42–43, 71–74, 114–17, 120–24, 128–29
housing in Natick, 13–14, 26, 30, 231–32
Indians, attitude towards, 179, 416–17
as Know Nothing, 247, 251, 253–69, 277–78, 280–81, 284–92, 295–96, 303–7
and labor, 28, 42, 116, 375–76, 417
life in New Hampshire, 4–8, 14, 20–23
and Lincoln–Douglas race, 378–80, 389
militia, 46, 131, 169, 183, 219, 397, 436
money, availability, 6–7, 21, 269–70, 394, 410
moral positions, 19, 47, 117, 270–71, 416
name changed, 7–8
as a nationalist, 18, 183, 188, 279
Natick, goes to, 8–9, 12, 14
as owner in boot and shoe industry, 26–28, 41, 79–80, 100, 102, 145, 149, 231, 269
personal characteristics, 269–73
personal controversies, 123–24, 195, 384, 404–6
physical appearance, 13–14, 80, 269
politics, initial interest in, 13–14, 32, 42
and religion, 14–15, 30–31, 270, 394
state Senate, service in, 45–48, 52–53, 62, 64, 146–49, 176, 182–83
senator, elections to, 265–69, 393–94
social connections, 14, 16, 27–29, 80
speaking ability, 38, 41, 273
temperance, 31–32, 118, 153, 177–78, 367
Texas annexation, opposition to, 53–55, 62–63, 65–70
and the West, Senate, 183, 279, 353–54, 380–82
Wilson, Henry Hamilton, 30, 79, 131, 153, 324, 402, 416
Winthrop, Robert, 132, 143, 151, 238, 206, 324, 365
aristocrat, 34, 88, 176, 197, 356
candidate for governor, 166–8, 173–74, 147, 203
congressman, 33, 51, 84, 113, 124–25, 132, 133, 141, 156, 172
relations with Wilson, 55, 292, 359, 388
leader of conservative Whigs, 76–78, 84, 89, 292
and Texas, 54, 58, 62–65
Wise, Henry, 277, 286, 315, 348, 373, 403–5
Wood, Fernando, 431
Woodman, George, 340
Wright, Charles, 3, 281
Wright, Elizur, 43, 67, 107, 113, 146, 156, 173, 298, 440
Wright, E.M., 267, 299
Wright, Henry, 242, 401, 403–6
Wright, Silas, 82

Y

Yancey, William, 427
Young Man's Aid, 18–19
Young Whigs, 52, 59–66, 68–69, 71, 74